Marine Mammal Conservation
and the Law of the Sea

Marine Mammal Conservation and the Law of the Sea

CAMERON S. G. JEFFERIES

PREFACE BY JOHN NORTON MOORE

Oxford University Press is a department of the University of Oxford. It furthers the University's objective of excellence in research, scholarship, and education by publishing worldwide. Oxford is a registered trademark of Oxford University Press in the UK and certain other countries.

Published in the United States of America by Oxford University Press
198 Madison Avenue, New York, NY 10016, United States of America.

© Oxford University Press 2016

All rights reserved. No part of this publication may be reproduced, stored in a retrieval system, or transmitted, in any form or by any means, without the prior permission in writing of Oxford University Press, or as expressly permitted by law, by license, or under terms agreed with the appropriate reproduction rights organization. Inquiries concerning reproduction outside the scope of the above should be sent to the Rights Department, Oxford University Press, at the address above.

You must not circulate this work in any other form
and you must impose this same condition on any acquirer.

Library of Congress Cataloging-in-Publication Data

Names: Jefferies, Cameron S. G., author.
Title: Marine mammal conservation and the law of the sea / Cameron S. G. Jefferies ; preface by John Norton Moore.
Description: New York : Oxford University Press, 2016. | Based on author's thesis (doctoral - University of Virginia, 2014). | Includes bibliographical references and index.
Identifiers: LCCN 2016013031 | ISBN 9780190493141 (hardback)
Subjects: LCSH: Marine mammals—Law and legislation. | Marine animals—Conservation—Law and legislation. | Wildlife conservation (International law) | Law of the sea. | BISAC: LAW / International.
Classification: LCC K3525 .J44 2016 | DDC 346.04/69595—dc23 LC record available at http://lccn.loc.gov/2016013031

---

9 8 7 6 5 4 3 2 1

Printed by Edwards Brothers Malloy, United States of America

Note to Readers
This publication is designed to provide accurate and authoritative information in regard to the subject matter covered. It is based upon sources believed to be accurate and reliable and is intended to be current as of the time it was written. It is sold with the understanding that the publisher is not engaged in rendering legal, accounting, or other professional services. If legal advice or other expert assistance is required, the services of a competent professional person should be sought. Also, to confirm that the information has not been affected or changed by recent developments, traditional legal research techniques should be used, including checking primary sources where appropriate.

(Based on the Declaration of Principles jointly adopted by a Committee of the American Bar Association and a Committee of Publishers and Associations.)

You may order this or any other Oxford University Press publication
by visiting the Oxford University Press website at www.oup.com.

Inspired by my family, the Southern J-Pod, and the tide pools of Mayne Island.

Dedicated to Finlay and Lennon and the hope for a world with room for all of us.

Spes et Fides

"Sea-change, a change wrought by the sea . . . an alteration or metamorphosis, a radical change."[1]

---

1. J.A. SIMPSON & E.S.C. WEINER, THE OXFORD ENGLISH DICTIONARY VOLUME XIV 780 (2d ed. 1989).

CONTENTS

Preface by John Norton Moore xi
Acknowledgments xiii
Abbreviations xv

1. Introduction 1
    I. Unfinished Business 1
    II. Conservation, Sustainability, and Other Key Terms 2
    III. Foundational Works 7
    IV. The Global Ocean 9
    V. Marine Mammals 10
        1. Scientific Classification, Description, and Distribution 10
        2. A Brief History of Human-Marine Mammal Interaction 12
            (i) Utilitarian Relationship 12
                (a) Cetaceans 12
                (b) Pinnipeds 15
            (ii) Cultural Relationship 16
        3. Current Conservation Status of Marine Mammals 17
    VI. Conclusion 19
    Notes 19

2. The Current Marine Mammal Regulatory Landscape 33
    I. Resource Type and Economic Considerations 33
    II. Legal Foundation of International Ocean Governance 35
        1. The United Nations Convention on the Law of the Sea 36
        2. Species and Area Based Approaches to Marine Mammal Management 38
            (i) Fur Seals and Pinniped Regulation 39
            (ii) The Great Whales and "Sustainable" Whaling 41
        3. Other Relevant Treaties and Organizations 50
        4. National Regulation 57
            (i) The United States, New Zealand, and Australia 58
            (ii) Nations That Take Marine Mammals 61
                (a) Great Whale Take 61
                (b) Small Cetacean Take 62
                (c) Pinniped Take 62
    III. Conclusion 63
    Notes 63

3. Goals for the Rational Conservation of Marine Mammals and Emerging Ethical Considerations 89
   I. Rational Decision-Making Model 89
      1. Problem Identification and Goal Setting 90
      2. Identification of Past Trends 90
      3. Assessment and Analysis of Alternatives, Decision-Making, and Recommendations 90
   II. Goals for This Work 91
      1. Promote the Rule of Law in the Oceans 91
      2. Expand Species Coverage 91
      3. Expand Issue Coverage 91
      4. Respect Competing Ocean Uses 91
      5. Promote Cooperation and Enhance Global Participation 92
      6. Incorporate Current Principles of International Law 92
      7. Utilizing Science-Based Decision-Making and Conservation Tools That Enable Holistic Management 92
      8. Promote Regional Implementation 92
      9. Build on the Existing Foundation 93
      10. Propose a Rational Arrangement 93
   III. Ethical Considerations 93
      1. Scientific Advances 95
         (i) The Cetacean Brain 96
         (ii) Behavior and Culture 97
      2. Marine Mammal Killing Methods 99
      3. Aboriginal Subsistence Whaling 104
      4. Features of a New Response 107
   IV. Conclusion 107
   Notes 108

4. Modern Threats to Marine Mammals 119
   I. Current Threats to Marine Mammals 120
      1. Global Climate Change 120
         (i) The Problem 120
         (ii) The Current Response 123
      2. By-Catch 125
         (i) The Problem 125
         (ii) The Current Response 126
      3. Ship-Strikes 127
         (i) The Problem 127
         (ii) The Current Response 128
      4. Environmental Pollution 130
         (i) The Problem 130
            (a) Traditional Pollution Problems 131
            (b) Emerging Concerns 132
         (ii) The Current Response 132
      5. Ecotourism (Marine Mammal Tourism) 137
         (i) The Problem 137
         (ii) The Current Response 138

II. Features of a New Response 140
  III. Conclusion 141
  Notes 141

5. The Case for an Implementing Agreement Pursuant to Articles 65 and 120 of UNCLOS and the Creation of an International Marine Mammal Commission 159
  I. Legally Justified Options for International Marine Mammal Conservation 160
    1. Status Quo 160
    2. An Improved ICRW/IWC 160
    3. The "Soft" Law Approach 164
    4. Proliferation of Bilateral and/or Regional Agreements 165
    5. Reliance on National Regulation 167
    6. A New International Regime 167
  II. UNCLOS Implementing Agreements 171
  III. The History and Interpretation of Articles 65 and 120 of UNCLOS 176
    1. The Drafting History of Articles 65 and 120 177
    2. Competing Interpretations of Articles 65 and 120 181
    3. Pertinent Characteristics of Articles 65 and 120 181
    4. Contemporaneous and Emerging State/International Organization Interpretations 184
    5. Academic Interpretations 188
    6. Preferred Interpretation(s) 191
  IV. Treaty Termination and International Organization Succession 193
    1. Treaty Termination 193
    2. Dissolution and Succession of International Organizations 195
  V. Jurisdictional Limits 197
  VI. Conclusion 199
  Notes 199

6. The Proposal: Part I—The Framework for a New Approach 213
  I. Introduction 213
  II. Constructing the Framework for a UN Marine Mammals Agreement 215
    1. Introductory Matters 215
      (i) Purpose and Objective 215
      (ii) Key Terms 216
      (iii) Scope of the New Regime 218
      (iv) The Best Available Scientific Information, Evidence, and Knowledge Standard 221
      (v) Encouraging Developing State Participation 223
      (vi) Developing and Transferring Marine Mammal Related Technologies 223
      (vii) Reservations, Declarations, and Relation to Existing Agreements 224
      (viii) Amending Annex I of UNCLOS 225
    2. Institutional Structure of the Proposed Regime 226
      (i) The International Marine Mammal Commission (IMMC) 226
      (ii) The IMMC's Subsidiary Structures 229

(iii) Transparency in Decision-Making 234
(iv) Regional Marine Mammal Organizations 235
3. Compliance, Enforcement, and Dispute Resolution 236
    (i) The Non-participant State Problem 236
    (ii) Compliance and Enforcement 238
    (iii) Dispute Resolution 241
4. Political Obstacles 245
III. Conclusion 251
Notes 251

7. The Proposal: Part II—The Secretariat, Regionalism, and Marine Protected Areas 269
  I. Introduction 269
  II. Institutional Structure and the Secretariat 270
      1. The Commission and Regional Organizations/Arrangements 270
      2. The Secretariat 270
  III. Regionalism 275
      1. What Is Regionalism? 275
      2. Benefits and Drawbacks of Regionalism 277
      3. Case Study 279
      4. Regionalism as Contemplated in the Proposed Agreement 282
      5. Conclusion 284
  IV. Marine Protected Areas 284
      1. MPAs Described 285
      2. Relevance of Emerging Science 288
      3. How MPAs Are Currently Utilized by the International Community 290
          (i) The ICRW/IWC 290
          (ii) Other International/Regional Arrangements 291
          (iii) Innovative Work 292
          (iv) Prospects Moving Forward 293
  V. Conclusion 295
  Notes 295

8. Concluding Thoughts 307
   Notes 312

Appendices
   Appendix 1: Extant and Recently Extinct Marine Mammal Species 315
   Appendix 2: Ocean Zones 323
   Appendix 3: Draft Agreement for the Implementation of the Provisions of the United Nations Convention on the Law of the Sea of 10 December 1982 Relating to the Conservation and Sustainable Management of Marine Mammals (Short form: UN Marine Mammals Agreement) 325
   Appendix 4: Structure of Proposed International Regime for the Conservation of Marine Mammals 373
Index 375

PREFACE

One of the most important remaining issues in achieving rational and sustainable oceans management is the protection of marine mammals. This book by Professor Cameron Jefferies is by far the most knowledgeable and forward-looking book to address this issue. It superbly develops the complex range of issues in rational management of marine mammals, the multiple threats affecting marine mammals, and the goals for a comprehensive conservation and sustainable management agreement. Of particular note, Professor Jefferies presents a detailed draft treaty for comprehensive management that, among other provisions, would create a new international management authority for marine mammals. This is an extremely thoughtful and detailed treaty proposal that deserves serious attention from foreign offices.

As Professor Jefferies details, issues concerning marine mammals, particularly whaling, were initially regarded as such a treaty killer that they were not initially addressed in the negotiations leading to the United Nations Convention on the Law of the Sea (UNCLOS). Rather, early on cetaceans were rather absurdly added to a list of highly migratory species of fish appearing as Annex I to the Convention. Subsequently, the United States, concerned that the optimum utilization provisions of the Convention might undermine its national law supporting protection rather than exploitation of marine mammals in the new 200-nautical-mile exclusive economic zone, introduced a provision that became Article 65 in the Single Negotiating Text to remove marine mammals from this full utilization obligation. There the issue stood until, following my return to the University of Virginia from chairing the National Security Council Interagency Task Force on the Law of the Sea (LOS), which formulated United States LOS positions, I sought to put together a coalition of states that would add a second sentence to Article 65 to support greater conservation, management, and study of cetaceans. Thanks to the superb work of a then NOAA scientist Barbara S. Moore, the then senator from Connecticut Lowell Weicker Jr., and the Connecticut Cetacean Society, among others, this led to the United States becoming more proactive on the issue and the near consensus addition in the negotiations of the now second sentence in Article 65 of UNCLOS. Strangely, though this provision to recognize the unique nature of cetaceans was successfully added to UNCLOS, the negotiators failed to remove cetaceans from the Annex I list of fish species, where it had never belonged. To this day, this widespread nongovernmental effort to protect cetaceans through addition of a specific article in a treaty then under negotiation stands as a testament to individual and NGO activism. As Margaret Mead noted: "Never ask whether individuals can change the world, it is the only thing that ever has." But, if the world will now take notice, Professor Jefferies has shown the way to rational management of marine mammals. This is not just theoretical academic work; *this is the real thing* from a brilliant and extremely knowledgeable expert on marine mammals.

The United Nations Convention on the Law of the Sea is one of the most important and successful multinational conventions in history. As Cameron fully understands, UNCLOS today provides the basic governing structure in the world's oceans. As such, he correctly drafts his proposed treaty as an agreement implementing the relevant articles of UNCLOS. In this, he is on solid ground following the earlier Part XI, deep seabed mining, and Fish Stocks, implementing agreements adopted by the States Parties to UNCLOS. His draft treaty is extremely sophisticated both in dealing with the myriad of problems besetting marine mammals and in incorporating the best of existing international law, and current agreements, to address these problems. Appropriately, for treaty parties his draft treaty would finally remove cetaceans from the Annex I list of Highly Migratory Species, a list relevant for fishery management but not for marine mammals. It would create a new International Marine Mammal Commission. It would recognize the importance of integration with regional arrangements, under the framework of a global approach, so important, among other issues, for the protection of cetaceans at risk in tuna purse seining. It also contains a thoughtful provision on indigenous and cultural/artisanal take, one of the many ongoing issues in rational marine mammal management. Further, it understands the crucial role of uncorrupted science in effective marine mammal management, and it develops an effective enforcement arrangement.

This book is not just an outstanding read because of the proposed treaty. It is also thoughtful and complete in analyzing the current marine mammal regulatory landscape, in exploring the goals for rational marine mammal management, in discussing ethical issues in the ongoing debates about marine mammals, and in examining the full-range of contemporary threats to marine mammals, from climate change to ecotourism itself. As befitting a professor at the prestigious University of Alberta Faculty of Law, as well as a holder of a Virginia SJD (the highest degree awarded by law schools), Cameron writes superbly. This book is not only an important read in oceans law, but an enjoyable one as well.

Deep differences remain today in national positions on marine mammals, particularly with respect to the permissibility of commercial whaling. Whatever their position, nations on all sides of these issues should take a careful look at what Professor Jefferies has proposed. If anything holds promise for bringing the disputants more closely together, it is this outstanding work by Professor Jefferies.

John Norton Moore[1]
Charlottesville, Virginia
January 12, 2016

---

1. Walter L. Brown Professor of Law at the University of Virginia School of Law and former United States Ambassador for the Law of the Sea Negotiations.

ACKNOWLEDGMENTS

I would like to extend my sincerest thanks to John Norton Moore for his significant mentorship and guidance. Thanks to Myron Nordquist, Paul Stephan, and Dr. Susan Lieberman for serving on my S.J.D. Supervisory Committee. I would also like to thank Mer McLernon, Julie Garmel, and Polly Lawson for their support and assistance. To my colleagues at the University of Alberta and especially David Percy, Joanna Harrington, John Law, Ubaka Ogbogu, Eric Adams, Elaine Hughes, Linda Reif, Peter Sankoff, Phil Bryden, and Paul Paton: thanks very much for your encouragement and feedback throughout. Thanks to Blake Ratcliff, Alden Domizio, and Oxford University Press for taking this work on.

I would like to thank award-winning Australian marine photographer Darren Jew for granting permission to use his photograph of a southern humpback whale off the Vava'u group of islands in the south pacific Kingdom of Tonga for the cover. Every southern winter, wildlife enthusiasts from around the glove travel to the remote island nation for the once in a lifetime experience of being in the water with humpback whales. Darren has been guiding in-water tours with humpbacks since 2001. He believes that well-managed encounters in appropriate locations play a significant and quantifiable role in the economy of developing nations and offer people memorable experiences that result in a unique connection between people, the ocean, and its inhabitants. Tonga has developed a regulated whale swimming industry over the last 20 years.

To Scott Jefferies, Mary Jefferies, and Sarah Jefferies: thanks for introducing me to the ocean and all its wonder. Also, thanks for reading the many drafts produced along the way.

Finally, and most important, thanks to Megs for all of her support and patience.

ABBREVIATIONS

ABNJ	Areas Beyond National Jurisdiction
ACCOBAMS	Agreement on the Conservation of Cetaceans of the Black Sea, Mediterranean Sea and Contiguous Atlantic Area
ASCOBANS	Agreement on the Conservation of Small Cetaceans of the Baltic, North East Atlantic, Irish and North Seas
CBD	Convention on Biological Diversity
CITES	Convention on International Trade in Endangered Species of Wild Fauna and Flora
CMS	Convention on Migratory Species
EEZ	Exclusive Economic Zone
EBM	Ecosystem-Based Management
FAO	Food and Agricultural Organization of the United Nations
ICJ	International Court of Justice
ICRW	International Convention for the Regulation of Whaling
ITLOS	International Tribunal for the Law of the Sea
IUCN	International Union for the Conservation of Nature
IWC	International Whaling Commission
MPA	Marine Protected Area
NAMMCO	North Atlantic Marine Mammal Commission
RFMO	Regional Fisheries Management Organization
RMP	Revised Management Procedure
UNCLOS	United Nations Convention on the Law of the Sea
UNEP	United Nations Environment Programme
UNGA	United Nations General Assembly

1

Introduction

"Walruses, seals, dolphins, sea lions, manatees, sea otters, whales, and polar bears—all are marine mammals, some of the most cherished and yet most exploited creatures on earth."[1]

I. UNFINISHED BUSINESS

Articles 65 and 120 of the United Nations Convention on the Law of the Sea (UNCLOS) create the possibility for the negotiation and implementation of a new international framework for the conservation and sustainable management of marine mammals, applicable to both maritime zones of national jurisdiction and those areas beyond national jurisdiction.[2]

To date, the potential for these Articles to facilitate rational marine mammal conservation has been insufficiently elucidated. Existing literature assessing international marine mammal conservation recognizes the potential for a new approach, but has not proposed a holistic response that incorporates both modern conservation ecology and science and recent successes in international governance, cooperation, and dispute resolution. Further, it is time to seriously consider the creation of an international commission that moves beyond the international management of a limited number of cetacean species. Although most marine mammal species are not being exploited at historical levels, many are still being hunted commercially, recreationally, and for subsistence purposes. More importantly, emerging anthropogenic threats to marine mammals, ethical considerations, and the current fragmented approach to marine mammal conservation makes improving this regime more pertinent and urgent than ever.

This book explores the complicated relationship between humans and marine mammals and the struggles associated with achieving effective management. After discussing the many dimensions of international marine mammal conservation and management, I propose the negotiation of a new multilateral convention that supersedes and replaces existing mechanisms and creates an International Marine Mammal Commission with regulatory jurisdiction over every marine mammal species (to the maximum extent permitted by Articles 65 and 120). Further, this proposed approach to marine mammal conservation will incorporate the success of regional implementation, facilitate the creation of a coordinated network of marine protected areas, require an observer scheme, and expressly provide recourse to established dispute resolution mechanisms.

This work is cognizant of the many political and legal hurdles that make the negotiation and implementation of a new multilateral agreement covering all marine mammal species an extremely daunting and highly ambitious task. I have opted to advance a proposal that covers all marine mammal species given that they all generally share similar life-history characteristics and are susceptible to the same anthropogenic forces.[3] The proposal also advances a comprehensive regime that addresses the lethal utilization (i.e., take/taking) and by-catch as well as other conservation concerns, such as marine pollution, the impacts of climate change, habitat degradation, and ship-strikes. As a practical limitation, the majority of this analysis is focused on the multifaceted regulatory aspects of lethal utilization.

II. CONSERVATION, SUSTAINABILITY, AND OTHER KEY TERMS

Both conservation and sustainability figure prominently in this work; indeed, these are both related management principles that tend to defy succinct summation. Considering "conservation" first, it is difficult to find a satisfactory working definition as employed by international governance regimes generally, or in relation to marine mammals specifically. There is considerable debate regarding the desired result of the international regulation of marine mammals—should marine mammals be managed for utilization like other living marine resources (what I term the "indefinite use approach" to conservation) or should they be conserved for the sake of preservation (what I term the "preservation approach" to conservation)? Common to both perspectives is the notion of conservation and the recognition that regulation is necessary to achieve either goal. It is important to understand how the term "conservation" is currently employed before indicating the definition that is preferred in this work.

Wildlife law and international environmental law both speak generally of the conservation of wildlife and of resources.[4] Still, "[w]hile conservation could be deemed a core legal principle of international environmental law, states have been reluctant to adopt it in any binding generalized form...."[5] Pertinent statements indicating the breadth and scope of conservation can be found in various international instruments, including:

(1) The International Union for the Conservation of Nature (IUCN) World Conservation Strategy,[6] which defines "conservation" in section 1.4 as: "the management of human use of the biosphere so that it may yield the greatest sustainable benefit to present generations while maintaining its potential to meet the needs and aspirations of future generations." Further, section 1.7 indicates that conservation is the positive duty: (a) "to maintain essential ecological processes and life-support systems"; (b) "to preserve genetic diversity"; and (c) "to ensure the sustainable utilization of species and ecosystems."[7]

(2) The IUCN World Charter for Nature (as adopted by United Nations General Assembly Resolution[8]), which provides that "conservation" includes the following principles:
   1. Nature shall be respected and its essential processes shall not be impaired.
   2. The genetic viability on the earth shall not be compromised; the population levels of all life forms, wild and domesticated, must be at least sufficient for their survival, and to this end necessary habitats shall be safeguarded.
   3. All areas of the earth, both land and sea, shall be subject to these principles of conservation; special protection shall be given to unique areas, to representative samples of all the different types of ecosystems and to the habitats of rare or endangered species.
   4. Ecosystems and organisms, as well as the land, marine and atmospheric resources that are utilized by man, shall be managed to achieve and maintain optimum sustainable productivity, but not in such a way as to endanger the integrity of those other ecosystems species with which they coexist.
   5. Nature shall be secured against degradation caused by warfare or other hostile activities.[9]
(3) The Convention on Biological Diversity (CBD),[10] which does not directly define "conservation," but rather contemplates "in-situ conservation" as "the conservation of ecosystems and natural habitats and the maintenance and recovery of viable populations of species in their natural surroundings and, in the case of domesticated or cultivated species, in the surroundings where they have developed their distinctive properties."[11]
(4) The Convention on Migratory Species (CMS),[12] in Article I, defines "conservation status of a migratory species" as "the sum of the influences acting on the migratory species that may affect its long-term distribution and abundance," proceeding to articulate that the status can only be designated as "favourable" if:
   (1) population dynamics data indicate that the migratory species is maintaining itself on a long-term basis as a viable component of its ecosystems;
   (2) the range of the migratory species is neither currently being reduced, nor is likely to be reduced, on a long-term basis;
   (3) there is, and will be in the foreseeable future sufficient habitat to maintain the population of the migratory species on a long-term basis; and
   (4) the distribution and abundance of the migratory species approach historic coverage and levels to the extent that potentially suitable ecosystems exist and to the extent consistent with wise wildlife management.[13]
(5) The Convention for the Conservation of Antarctic Marine Living Resources[14] indicates in Article II that "conservation" includes the principle of "rational use," and then provides the following principles of conservation:
   a) prevention of decrease in the size of any harvested population to levels below those which ensure its stable recruitment. For this

purpose its size should not be allowed to fall below a level close to that which ensures the greatest net annual increment;
b) maintenance of the ecological relationships between harvested, dependent and related populations of Antarctic marine living resources and the restoration of depleted populations to the levels defined in sub-paragraph (a) above; and
c) prevention of changes or minimization of the risk of changes in the marine ecosystem which are not potentially reversible over two or three decades, taking into account the state of available knowledge of the direct and indirect impact of harvesting, the effect of the introduction of alien species, the effects of associated activities on the marine ecosystem and of the effects of environmental changes, with the aim of making possible the sustained conservation of Antarctic marine living resources.[15]

(6) The Southern African Development Community Protocol on Wildlife Conservation and Law Enforcement, which defines "conservation" in Article I as "the protection, maintenance, rehabilitation, restoration and enhancement of wildlife to ensure the sustainability of such use;"[16] and

(7) Finally, the United States Marine Mammal Protection Act defines "conservation" and "management" as follows:

> The terms "conservation" and "management" means the collection and application of biological information for the purposes of increasing and maintaining the number of animals within species and populations of marine mammals at their optimum sustainable population. Such terms include the entire scope of activities that constitute a modern scientific resource program, including, but not limited to, research, census, law enforcement, and habitat acquisition and improvement. Also included within these terms, when and where appropriate, is the periodic or total protection of species or populations as well as regulated taking.[17]

Conservation, as a scientific endeavor, encompasses species, species' habitat and ecosystems, genetic variation, and the impact of human use on species and their habitat/ecosystem.[18] For the purposes of this book, "conservation" is best understood as an umbrella term that recognizes management as a necessary tool toward accomplishing the various legitimate goals of conservation, be it conservation to achieve indefinite use or conservation for the purposes of protection. This management requirement will be referred to as "sustainable management" throughout the remainder of this work, and will be considered in conjunction with the following working definition of "conservation" that is tailored for the purposes of the global governance of marine mammals:

i. The maintenance of a status[19] for stable or increasing marine mammal species/population(s) that, at a minimum, ensures the necessary composition, genetic variability, and ecosystem integrity[20] required for the long-term viability of the marine mammal species/population(s).[21]

ii. The recovery or rehabilitation of diminished marine mammal species/population(s) to a status that, minimally, ensures the necessary

composition, genetic variability, and ecosystem integrity required for the long-term viability of the marine mammal species/population(s).[22]
iii. The statuses referred to in subsections (i) and (ii) shall be informed by the best available science, including due consideration of the Red List of Threatened Species as maintained by the International Union for the Conservation of Nature.
iv. The status referred to in subsection (i) for stable or increasing populations does not preclude the rational take of marine mammals, when and where appropriate, so long as this take does not compromise the status identified therein.[23] Populations covered by subsection (ii) shall not be taken until such time as their recovery/rehabilitation is complete.
v. Conservation shall be achieved through sustainable management and threat mitigation.[24]

Given that the term "sustainable management" will also be used throughout this work, and that it is considered a necessary aspect of conservation, it is important to also consider what is meant by "sustainability." Just as the international community strives for a definition of conservation, defining "sustainability" is estimated to remain "a major preoccupation of international law, lawmakers, and institutions throughout the 21st century."[25] Sustainability represents an important principle of international governance that emerged through international soft law in the late 1980s and early 1990s,[26] and it is often considered in the context of "sustainable development," as contemplated in the Rio Declaration on Environment and Development,[27] or as "development that meets the needs of the present without compromising the ability of future generations to meet their own needs."[28] What is certain is that the notion of sustainability links the environment to both social factors (including economic considerations) and cultural factors.[29]

One explanation for why this concept defies succinct definition or concrete normative rule-generating force is that it remains a "framework" term, connected to other important principles such as: (1) the paramountcy of human needs; (2) integration of the environment and development; (3) intergenerational and intragenerational equity; (4) state sovereignty; (5) resource conservation; (6) the precautionary principle; (7) the concept that polluters should be responsible for the costs of their actions; (8) the concept that environmental impact assessments should be required; (9) the concept that international cooperation is necessary; (10) the concept that public participation in governance should be increased; and (11) the concept that achieving these goals requires enhanced regulatory control at all levels of governance.[30]

This work seeks to implement many of the principles indicated above, and acknowledges the interconnectedness of sustainability and conservation. Still, it is my position that the legal principle of sustainability, in this context, must embody longevity and the coexistence between humans and marine mammals, and although it does not preclude the lethal use or take of marine mammals by nations who can sufficiently justify such a take in the face of scientific uncertainty, it does not require a take from those nations who prefer to benefit from marine mammals through non-lethal uses either. Therefore, and as indicated previously, sustainability is employed as the guiding principle of marine mammal management in this book, referred to as "sustainable management," and shall be defined for the purposes of this work as follows:

   i. Management that seeks to achieve long-term human-marine mammal coexistence and encompasses the entire scope of regulatory activities necessary to conduct a modern management program, including, but not limited to research and study, the promulgation of regulations, and the production of best-practice standards and guidelines.[31]
   ii. Management that is guided by ecosystem-based management, intragenerational and intergenerational equity, the integration of the environment and development, and precaution in light of scientific uncertainty. It requires compliance, enforcement, and international and regional cooperation.[32] It does not preclude rational take of marine mammals, when and where appropriate and consistent with sound conservation science, nor the periodic or total protection of species or populations or an otherwise regulated taking.[33]

In sum, "conservation" is an umbrella concept that utilizes "sustainable management" to achieve the desired result. "Sustainable management," in turn, is best understood as embodying the full suite of subsidiary principles identified above, as necessary to achieve long-term coexistence between humans and marine mammals. There are a few other relevant terms that will assist the reader.

   i. "Ecosystem-based management" is holistic, integrated management that recognizes the uncertainty and natural variability of ecosystems but seeks to maintain ecosystem structure, function, and constituent parts.[34]
   ii. "Marine mammal" includes those species belonging to Order Cetacea, Order Sirenia, Order Pinnipedia, and the members of Order Carnivora that have adapted to the marine environment.[35]
   iii. "Marine Protected Area" means a discrete area of the ocean, established by law, designated to enhance the long-term conservation and/or sustainable management of the marine mammals therein.[36]
   iv. "Population" means a group of marine mammals of the same species or subspecies/stock in a common spatial arrangement that interbreed when mature.[37]
   v. "Precautionary decision-making" means decision-making that accords with the precautionary principle: "where there are threats of serious or irreversible damage, lack of full scientific certainty shall not be used as a reason for postponing cost-effective measures to prevent environmental degradation."[38]
   vi. "Take" means to intentionally hunt, capture, or kill, or attempt to hunt, capture, or kill any marine mammal, and to incidentally capture or kill as by-catch.[39] Take, which I will also refer to as lethal utilization, is to be distinguished from indirect take (meaning by-catch) and other sources of mortality such as habitat degradation, environmental pollution, and the consequences of climate change.
   vii. "Vessel" means any ship or craft, or any structure capable of navigation,[40] that is used for the purpose of taking, treating, transporting, scouting, locating, towing, or otherwise engaging marine mammals.[41]

III. FOUNDATIONAL WORKS

Marine mammals have long captured our attention. The relationship between humans and marine mammals is both cultural and utilitarian and dates back millennia. As an academic pursuit, this relationship is richly interdisciplinary, bridging sociological, anthropological, political, ethical, and legal disciplines.[42] Our relationship with marine mammals, and our understanding of the significance and intricacies of this relationship, continues to change, and the status quo is in need of reform. It is no surprise, then, that modern legal scholarship contains a considerable body of work directed at marine mammal conservation.

The successes, failures, and mechanics of existing international, regional, and national marine mammal regulatory regimes have been well-studied and described in the literature. Indeed, leading environmental and international law scholars such as Patricia Birnie,[43] Alexander Gillespie,[44] William Burke,[45] William Burns,[46] and Robert Friedhiem[47] have written extensively about marine mammal conservation and management issues (and cetacean conservation, in particular) in both a descriptive and prescriptive manner. Currently, authors[48] have focused their commentary on recent developments and attempts by the International Whaling Commission (IWC) to seek compromise in light of efforts to normalize or modernize the International Convention for the Regulation of Whaling (ICRW)[49] as well as on the recent *Whaling in the Antarctic (Australia v. Japan: New Zealand Intervening)* decision from the International Court of Justice (ICJ).[50] This work builds on the contribution made by these authors and aims to use the foundation that they have created to conceptualize a new multilateral convention in the form of a new implementing agreement to UNCLOS that establishes an International Marine Mammal Commission.

Pre–World War II scholarly works on marine mammal conservation and management focused mainly on efforts to gain international cooperation among whaling countries,[51] with some discussion of the international dispute over fur seal conservation in the Bering Sea.[52] Legal commentary on whaling became more frequent through the 1970s as the environmental movement became active and flaws in the regime established by the ICRW, as implemented by the International Whaling Commission, became apparent.[53] Scholarship on marine mammal conservation and management became even more abundant in the 1980s[54] as the negotiations for the United Nations Convention on the Law of the Sea concluded and the treaty opened for signature (in 1982), and with the introduction of the moratorium on commercial whaling by the IWC in 1982 (which became effective in 1986).[55] This wellspring of ideas regarding marine mammal conservation and management has persisted since the mid-1980s and, largely as a result of the work of nongovernmental organizations, has become increasingly critical of the existing international approach, especially as our understanding of, and relationship with, the ocean and its inhabitants matures.

A number of significant scientific advances have influenced legal thinking about the conservation and management of living marine resources—especially relating to our understanding of the impact of human interaction with the oceans. Legal literature currently accounts for our understanding that, in addition to direct lethal utilization (including over-exploitation), by-catch in fishing gear, marine pollution (be it physical, noise, chemical, or biological),[56] climate change,[57] navigation and vessel speed,[58] and even ecotourism[59] also seriously threaten marine mammal conservation efforts. It is critical that such threats are accounted for in a robust, comprehensive conservation and management scheme. Further, science demonstrates that ecosystem-based management[60] rather than species-specific regulation likely has the greatest chance of long-term success, and that ecosystem-based management can partially be achieved through a carefully constructed network of marine protected areas.[61]

Scientific investigation into cetacean brain structure and social behavior has led scholars to question the appropriateness of any continued consumptive use of this subset of marine mammals. The seminal legal ethics piece on the issue, titled *Whales: Their Emerging Right to Life*, written by Anthony D'Amato and Sudhir K. Chopra, was published in 1991.[62] Since publication, debate about the morality of consumptive (and certain non-consumptive uses of cetaceans, such as captivity in aquariums and zoos)[63] has persisted,[64] and so has the scientific discussion of cetacean intelligence and social structure.[65] Despite all of the advances described above, it is my contention that a new, holistic approach to marine mammal conservation is required as the current fragmented regional and international framework covers only certain species to the exclusion of others and is too focused on direct take to adequately address significant emerging concerns.[66]

This book is not the first to recognize the many shortfalls of the existing approach to the international conservation and management of marine mammals, including the lack of compliance and enforceability,[67] varied interpretation of contentious provisions,[68] and emergence of competing regimes.[69] Nor is it the first to suggest that Articles 65 and 120 of UNCLOS are capable of supporting the creation of a new international organization that supersedes the existing approach to species-specific conservation efforts.[70] Beyond the descriptive portions of this analysis, which focuses on the current approach to marine mammal conservation, this work presents a novel prescriptive dimension that contributes to marine mammal conservation and management by:

(1) Proposing the negotiation of a new multilateral treaty that supersedes and/or coordinates existing efforts to the extent possible;
(2) Describing the form, function, and substance of a new multilateral convention, applicable to all marine mammal species;
(3) Proposing the creation of the International Marine Mammal Commission to administer and implement the new multilateral convention;
(4) Incorporating the benefits of regional cooperation, enforcement, and implementation[71] into marine mammal conservation and sustainable management in a manner that accords with existing regional initiatives;
(5) Accounting for marine protected areas (MPAs) to implement ecosystem-based management, as established in existing literature,[72] intergovernmental policy, and other relevant sources to argue in favor of the creation of a global network of MPAs to help conserve marine mammal species throughout their range; and
(6) Proposing workable mechanisms for enforcement, compliance, transparency, and dispute resolution that have proved manageable in other international and regional fora.

In sum, I advance a rational approach to international marine mammal conservation and management in a manner that, to date, has merely been suggested. With these goals in mind, it is appropriate to provide the background information on the oceans that is necessary to understand the scope and purpose of this work.

IV. THE GLOBAL OCEAN

The importance of the global ocean cannot be overstated. Today, the ocean covers nearly three-quarters of the Earth's surface (139 million square miles) and represents the "cornerstone of our life-support system."[73] The ocean produces approximately 50 percent of the oxygen we breathe, absorbs 25–30 percent of the carbon from anthropogenic emission sources, and has buffered 80 percent of the heat added to the climate system since the Industrial Revolution.[74]

Although humans have used the ocean for millennia, the advances of the last few centuries have enabled its full and efficient exploitation for: (1) transportation, (2) national and international security, (3) recreating, (4) extracting nonliving resources (including oil and gas and mining), (5) producing renewable energy, (6) farming living resources, and (7) extracting living resources.[75] However, this full and efficient utilization is unsustainable, as population growth, economic development, and technological advances have forced us to recognize that the ocean is not an "inexhaustible resource."[76]

The expansive ocean continues to represent an alien environment as foreign to us, in many ways, as outer space.[77] A recently completed Census of Marine Life, compiled over the course of one decade by 2,700 scientists from 80 nations, concludes that there are some 250,000 known species of plants and animals in the ocean and that approximately 750,000 species of marine life have yet to be classified.[78] Persistent knowledge gaps can be attributed to the fact that up to 95 percent of the ocean has yet to be explored or scientifically surveyed, and that life can occur in some of the most inhospitable environments (including hypoxic environments and in temperatures approaching 400 degrees Celsius in deep sea hydrothermal vents).[79]

There is considerable work needed to improve our management of ocean life. Efforts are needed to enhance: (1) our baseline knowledge, (2) our understanding of how species react and respond to changes in their environment both temporally and spatially, (3) our understanding of patterns in ecosystem services and ecosystem functioning, (4) our understanding of how human activity is influencing marine life, and (5) our understanding of "what is needed to achieve sustainability in terms of management and recovery strategies and how these differ for different species and ecosystems."[80]

Beyond increasing our understanding of the basic chemical, physical, and biological processes of the ocean, the reality is that "[t]he ocean faces a multitude of interconnected threats that is unprecedented in modern history."[81] Its expansiveness and remoteness are also, in part, responsible for its "chronic neglect."[82] Unfortunately, the wide spectrum of ecological services provided by the ocean are now being "seriously degraded" by anthropogenic activities.[83]

The difficulty in addressing modern threats to the ocean is, to a great degree, a product of the fact that present threats are much more complex than the traditional problem of over-exploitation of living resources (the overfishing paradigm).[84]

Rather, "[t]he very chemical, thermodynamic and biological foundations of the ocean are being jeopardized by human activity."[85] Today's critical threats to ocean services include: (1) ocean acidification, (2) ocean warming, (3) ocean hypoxia, (4) sea level rise, (5) pollution, and (6) the overuse of marine resources.[86] Further, although some of these threats are well-understood (such as the over-exploitation of fisheries), our comprehension of others (for example, acidification, hypoxia, and sea level rise) is just starting to crystallize, while others are not well understood at all (the most critical knowledge gap being the consequence of the cumulative interaction of all of these threats).[87] Further, the loss of marine life ("defaunation") is increasing in pace and severity as part of the Anthropocene;[88] however, "there is still time and there exists mechanisms to avert the kinds of defaunation disasters observed on land."[89] Inevitably, the key is "managing human actions within the marine environment."[90]

This book focuses on the state of the intriguing and complicated relationship between marine mammals and humans. I will, by necessity, engage in an interdisciplinary discussion of marine mammals, as developing a rational legal framework requires an understanding of science, culture, ethics, and history.[91] The goal is to gather, assess, and critique current legal and scientific resources applicable to marine mammals and to propose a framework that builds on the existing foundation of international law to govern future interaction (both direct and indirect) between humans and marine mammals at both the international and regional level of ocean governance.

V. MARINE MAMMALS

1. Scientific Classification, Description, and Distribution

All marine mammals belong to the Kingdom Animalia, Phylum Chordata (animals with notochords), Subphylum Vertebrata (animals with vertebrates), Class Mammalia. There are 132 extant marine mammal species, and four species that have become extinct since the mid-eighteenth century as a direct, or indirect, result of human activity (the sea mink, Japanese sea lion, Steller's sea cow, and Caribbean monk seal).[92] Of the 132 extant species, it is possible that one (Omura's whale) is actually a genetically distinct species whereas another (the Yangtze River dolphin) recently became extinct.[93]

There is considerable variation among extant marine mammal species, but as mammals they share certain characteristics. Specifically, all marine mammals are warm-blooded, breathe air using lungs, have hair/fur, give birth to live young, and nurse their young with mother's milk produced in mammary glands.[94] In addition to these characteristic traits, marine mammals have adapted to living in an aquatic environment by developing hydrodynamic bodies to ease movement, fatty storage deposits called blubber to stay warm, efficient oxygen storage in body tissues (compared to terrestrial mammals) to maximize the time spent under water between surface breathing, and an ability to shunt blood to vital organs during deep dives.[95] As mammals, these species are also generally long-lived, have late onset of sexual maturity, and have low reproductive rates.[96] As William T. Burke notes, "[t]hese reproductive characteristics [which are particularly pronounced in the case of cetaceans] are in complete contrast to those of marine fish, which produce enormous numbers of offspring."[97] These life-history characteristics have considerable significance for conservation as they help explain why species have become depleted (and in the case of whaling why whalers switch from one species to the next), and also why it takes an extremely long time for many marine mammal species to return to stable population levels once depleted.

Of the five groups of mammals classified as marine, three groups independently developed the above-described adaptations.[98] These groups are: (1) Order Cetacea (known colloquially as the cetaceans, this grouping contains 88 species of whale, dolphin, and porpoise); (2) Order Sirenia (known colloquially as the sirenians, this grouping includes one species of dugong and three species of manatee); and (3) Order Pinnipedia (known colloquially as the pinnipeds, this group includes 35 species of seal, sea lion, and walrus).[99] Further, there are members of two terrestrial mammal groups (which both fall within Order Carnivora) that have adapted to a lifestyle that depends heavily on the marine environment for feeding and/or breeding and are classified as marine mammals, including: (1) six otter species, and (2) the polar bear.[100]

In terms of species distribution, marine mammals are generally found throughout the world's oceans in "almost all the different marine environments."[101] There are a variety of factors that influence marine mammal distribution, including life-strategy (i.e., breeding habitat, feeding style, food preference, and migration patterns) and anthropogenic pressures (i.e., adaptation to altered abundance of food sources and prevailing ecosystem conditions).[102]

Just as there are methods of scientifically classifying marine mammals, there are also a variety of ways to categorize their distribution. The most common method is by marine ecosystem type. Specifically, marine mammals can demonstrate a preference for coastal/littoral waters ("estuarine or near shore waters"), neritic waters ("waters on the continental shelf"), or oceanic waters ("waters beyond the continental slope, in the open seas or oceans").[103] Although it is difficult to identify species as being solely coastal, neritic, or oceanic, as most species will spend some time in more than one ocean zone, it is possible to provide a few basic examples.[104] Species commonly found in the coastal zone include the sea otter (*Enhydra lutris*), dugongs (*Dugong dugong*), and the bottlenose dolphin (*Tursiops truncatus*).[105] Species commonly found in the neritic zone include the California sea lion (*Zalophus californicus*) and the gray whale (*Eschrichtus robustus*).[106] Finally, species found primarily in the oceanic zone include the sperm whale (*Physeter macrocephalus*) and beaked whales, such as Hector's beaked whale (*Mesoplodon hectori*).[107]

A second method of classifying marine mammal distribution is by geographic range, as "characterized by latitudinal bands and average water temperatures."[108] Utilizing this scheme, marine mammals can have "tropical and/or subtropical, temperate, Antarctic, or Arctic distributions."[109] Although it is rare, some marine mammal species can be completely restricted to one geographic stratum, such as the polar bear (*Ursus maritimus*) and the narwhal (*Monodon monoceros*) in the Arctic.[110] Most species are found within multiple strata, especially if they are migratory. For example, orca (*Orcinus orca*) can be found in the Arctic, around the equator in the tropical band, and in the Antarctic.[111]

Another distinction of note that will become important in later discussions regarding the ICRW is the somewhat artificial distinction between what are colloquially known as "great whales" and other species of cetacean.[112] Today, we understand the term "great whale" to encompass those whales of great size (between 8 and 30 meters), including "the gray, humpback, right, blue, sperm, bowhead, fin, sei, Minke, pygmy right, and Byrde's whale."[113] As I will discuss in detail later, this distinction within Order Cetacea has led to considerable debate about which species can be regulated under the current international regime.

A final distinguishing feature between the various groupings of marine mammal species is the extent to which they utilize, or are dependent upon, the marine environment. Although cetaceans spend their entire lives in the ocean, this is not the case for the other groups of marine mammal species. Pinnipeds spend most of their lives in the oceans, but they return to land (or ice) for a variety of reasons, including breeding, mating, and raising young.[114] Sirenians are solely aquatic, whereas the polar bear utilizes sea ice for hunting, breeding, and denning with young, and sea otters live primarily in near-coastal waters, only occasionally coming to shore.[115]

The remainder of this introduction to marine mammals focuses on the historical relationship between humans and marine mammals and discusses discernible trends in the current conservation status of marine mammals. This survey helps illuminate why it is necessary to develop a new international approach to marine mammal management.

2. A Brief History of Human-Marine Mammal Interaction

Humans have utilized each group of marine mammals described above.[116] The human-marine mammal relationship can, at the highest level, be divided into two main categories: (1) utilitarian, and (2) cultural. It is important to understand both aspects to fully appreciate the current relationship between marine mammals and humans, which in turn informs the political, economic, ethical, and legal considerations of a rational approach to marine mammal conservation in the twenty-first century. Although I acknowledge that all marine mammals have been subject to utilitarian and cultural uses, the following analysis focuses on cetaceans and pinnipeds, as they represent the most useful case study and are broadly representative of the issues at hand.

(i) Utilitarian Relationship

(a) Cetaceans

The benefits of utilizing marine mammals are well understood—they are a source of animal protein and fat; they have tough, waterproof hides and fur; and their bones and sinuous tissue can be used for sewing or toolmaking.[117] These benefits would have been recognized by early humans who first scavenged from marine mammal carcasses washed up on shores, which motivated the development of "ingenious methods of capturing pinnipeds, sirenians, and cetaceans."[118]

Evidence of human use of marine mammals can be traced back to the late Pleistocene Epoch (c. 18,000 years ago)[119] if not earlier,[120] and it is understood that "cetacean and pinnipeds have formed a focus for human hunting and scavenging strategies for a very long time."[121] Archaeological discoveries suggest the following timeline for marine mammal use by humans: (1) cave drawings and engravings of seals from the Cosquer Cave in southern France indicate that the Solutrean people were scavenging (but not actively hunting for marine mammals) approximately 18,000 years ago;[122] (2) isotope analysis of 12,000-year-old human remains at Kendrick's Cave in Wales, United Kingdom, provides the "first direct evidence of the significant consumption of marine foods, and particularly marine mammals, by late Paleolithic [Old Stone Age] modern humans";[123] (3) a study of mammalian remains at Duncan's Point Cave, located at the south-central portion of the Sonoma County Coast in California, accords with other evidence found along the coast of California and Oregon suggesting that approximately 8,600 years ago humans were actively taking pinnipeds and sea otters (but still only scavenging for cetaceans);[124] and (4) recently discovered petroglyphs at the Bangu-dae archaeological site in South Korea depict humans hunting both pinnipeds and cetaceans (a number of identifiable species) from boats up to 8,000 years ago.[125]

It is important to note that marine mammal exploitation by humans is common across coastal cultures. As these archaeological examples demonstrate, the historical use of marine mammals occurred in what is modern day South Korea, southern France, and the Pacific coast of North America. Although the following list does not purport to be exhaustive, it is noted that marine mammals have also been a historically significant resource in the Arctic, the Faroe Islands (under Danish sovereignty), Greenland, Australia, New Zealand, Iceland, Norway, Indonesia, Russia, the Philippines, the Caribbean, and Japan.[126]

A second common theme is that human exploitation did not emerge as an issue of pressing concern for the continued existence of some species until the last few centuries with the advent of significant population growth, technological advances, and international trade and colonialism. These advances were coupled with a significant shift in the justification for marine mammal utilization—what was once "hunting as a means of survival" became "hunting for profit."[127]

Some species of marine mammal have been particularly susceptible to human exploitation. For example, Steller's sea cow (*Hydrodamalis gigas*), a slow moving, docile dugong that inhabited waters around Bering Island, located off the Kamchatka Peninsula, was first discovered by Europeans by Captain Bering in 1741.[128] After a few decades of intensive hunting, the last sea cow was killed only 27 years later in 1768.[129] Another example is the Caribbean monk seal (*Monachus tropicalis*), which was subject to an intensive directed hunt and killed opportunistically by whalers and other fishermen through the seventeenth and eighteenth centuries.[130] Caribbean monk seal populations were never able to recover, and the last confirmed sighting of the Caribbean monk seal occurred in 1952.[131] Fortunately, other marine mammal species have not been as susceptible to extinction, but there are many instances of population collapses and near extinctions. Although overexploitation has been a problem for many species of marine mammals in recent history, it has been of particular concern for fur seals, sea otters, and cetaceans from the eighteenth century to the present day.[132]

Cetacean exploitation is described in *Lyster's International Wildlife Law* (2nd ed.) as follows—"[t]he history of man's depletion of one species of great whale after another is perhaps the most infamous example of human mismanagement of the Earth's natural resources."[133] The emergence of commercial whaling has been linked to the Basque peoples who lived around the Bay of Biscay (the large coastal indentation of the Atlantic Ocean in what is modern day southwest France and northwest Spain), where they began to hunt the right whale using small boats and harpoons.[134] Basque whaling began as a "local concern," but by the twelfth and thirteenth centuries, the European markets emerged for the trading in whale products (including "oil, meat and later baleen").[135] By the early sixteenth century, the market for whale product had grown but the abundance of right whales in the Bay Biscay had dramatically decreased.[136] To satisfy this demand, Basque whalers ventured to Canada's eastern coast to hunt the abundant right and bowhead whale populations as they passed through the Strait of Belle Island, which separates Newfoundland from continental Canada.[137] At the end of the sixteenth century, bowhead and right whales were no longer abundant in the Strait of Belle Island, and Basque "whaling supremacy" gave way to the emergence of other whaling nations.[138]

As Adrienne Ruffle wrote in 2002, "[f]or centuries, whales provided valuable natural resources in the form of food and fuel to the world's population, and the whaling industry contributed substantially to the economic wealth of countries such as Norway, England, the Netherlands, the U.S. [United States], Japan and Russia."[139] The Dutch and the English emerged as the next two whaling powers, each initially seeking to control the hunt of the bowhead whales in the near-shore waters surrounding Greenland.[140] The Dutch became the most successful whaling nation in this region, but the British, French, Danes, and Germans also took advantage of initially plentiful stocks.[141] This boom was also short-lived, as it took approximately only one century to over-exploit the waters around Greenland, prompting these nations to shift their focus to the bowhead whales inhabiting the off-shore waters of the Arctic Ocean.[142] As bowhead whales became less abundant, whalers had to venture into more dangerous and remote waters where the economic and human costs associated with pursuing the hunt eventually outweighed its benefits.[143] By the end of the 1700s, the balance of power in the whaling industry had shifted once more as "American whaling would soon dominate the world."[144]

According to local legend, the Nantucket, New England, whaling industry began in earnest in 1712 when a whaling ship operating in near-coastal waters (as was common at this time), captained by Christopher Hussey, was blown out to sea.[145] As chance would have it, Captain Hussey found himself surrounded by sperm whales, one of which he captured and brought back to port after the storm had passed.[146] The sperm whale then became the target of the American whaling industry, which lasted for most of the eighteenth century and eventually reached from the northern waters of Davis Strait and Baffin Bay to the Falkland Islands/Malvinas off of South America and across the Atlantic to the west coast of Africa,[147] and was powered by a fleet of 600 whaling ships.[148] By the middle of the nineteenth century, whaling was coming to its conclusion in New England, as many whaling ships were burned by Confederate troops during the American Civil War (1861–1865), and the whale stocks were too diminished to justify the expenditure required to reform the fleet.[149] Also, by this point the American whaling industry had already, at least partially, shifted to the West Coast and the Pacific Ocean. Between 1846 and 1859, 14,500 right whales were killed in the Pacific Northwest.[150] With the discovery of gray whale breeding grounds off of Baja, California, there was only another 45 years of utilization before this stock also collapsed.[151]

The Industrial Revolution had a considerable impact on the modernization of whaling, and in many ways the technological advances that led to modern whaling facilitated access to the Southern Ocean surrounding Antarctica, a region previously unexploited. As described by Sarah Lazarus:

> Whaling technology remained largely unchanged for over 800 years. Whaling ships navigated the oceans under sail. On finding whales they dispatched small wooden boats that were also driven by the wind, if weather conditions were obliging, or by muscle power. When the crew reached their quarry they secured it with hand-thrown harpoons and stabbed it to death with long lances. The whalers were enormously successful in their pursuit of certain species but with their homespun equipment there remained a number of whales that they simply could not catch and kill.[152]

Major advances included the advent of steam-powered ships and, most significant, the invention of the "Greener Gun" (invented by English gunsmith William Greener), which was mounted on the bow of the whaling ship and subsequently adapted into a shoulder-mounted harpoon gun capable of firing "bomb lances" that exploded after impact.[153]

All the technological advances seemed to come together for the first voyage of the *Spes et Fides* ("Hope and Faith") in 1868, captained by Norwegian whaler Svend Foyn.[154] Specifically, the *Spes et Fides* was designed to function as both a "whaleship" and a "catcher boat" in "one sleek, speedy, highly maneuverable steam-powered vessel."[155] Additionally, the *Spes et Fides* was equipped with a cannon (as opposed to a harpoon gun) that fired a grenade-tipped harpoon up to 130 feet.[156] The *Spes et Fides* also had a steam-powered winch that reduced the number of struck whales that sunk before they could be secured.[157] The *Spes et Fides* demonstrated to the world that every large whale species, including roqual whales ("blue, fin, sei, Bryde's, minke and humpback whales") that were too fast to be caught using traditional whaling vessels, could now be killed.[158] And, after over-exploiting stocks in the Atlantic and Pacific Oceans, the Norwegian whaling fleet began to exploit the abundant whales of the previously inaccessible Southern Ocean.[159] In the 80 years after the start of Antarctic whaling in 1904, over 2 million whales were killed.[160]

This brief history of whaling has focused on the major advances and general trends in whaling. Before I move on to a similarly brief history of pinniped exploitation, it is worth noting that the Japanese, Russians, Spanish, Canadians, and several South American countries were also partaking in whaling during this period, and that subsistence hunting for all variety of cetacean continues.

(b) Pinnipeds

The archaeological evidence proving the utilitarian use of marine mammals by prehistoric man and early modern humans is as relevant to the history of pinniped use as it is to cetacean use (see description above). Seals have been exploited by man for approximately 30,000 years,[161] and "[h]istorically documented, industrial-scale exploitation of seals and sea lions by humans has driven many such species to the brink of extinction within decades of first cropping."[162] For example, even before seals were hunted commercially in New Zealand for their pelts, certain species had experienced localized extinctions,[163] and a similar fate befell a species in California prior to the arrival of Europeans.[164] This susceptibility to over-exploitation is likely a consequence of their biological characteristics, including life history, and the fact that seals must come to land to breed and molt, making both adults and juveniles vulnerable to terrestrial predation in a way that other sea mammals are not.

Pinnipeds are valuable for their oil, skins, ivory (from walruses), meat, and blubber.[165] They have been hunted throughout their global range for many millennia,[166] but commercially have been taken on an industrial scale for only approximately the last 250 years.[167] Like whales, the uses to which pinniped parts could be put evolved over time as well. For example, Steller sea lion whiskers were commonly used in China to clean opium pipes, and the genitals of mature males were powdered and consumed as an apparent aphrodisiac.[168] Just as the systematic over-exploitation of cetaceans was facilitated by technological advances, pinnipeds also became the victims of advances in hunting techniques and tools. Early pinniped hunting was conducted on land or sea ice by clubbing at close proximity. This technique gave way to the more effective harpoon gun, which was quickly replaced by the firearm.[169] The harpoon and firearm facilitated a pelagic hunt for pinnipeds, but they also promoted a wasteful hunt, as pinnipeds shot while in the water would often sink before they could be captured, a phenomenon called "sinking loss."[170]

The commercial take of pinnipeds has decreased considerably since the 1960s, although some still occurs. The continued take of fur seals (Harp seals) in Atlantic Canada in recent years has produced "a hotbed of debate in the international arena"[171] as the European Union has had a domestic ban on importing and marketing seal products since 2009, the legality of which was upheld in the face of a challenge by Norway and Canada at the World Trade Organization.[172] Some 30 other countries have also banned the sale of seal products.[173]

As important as it is to understand the utilitarian use of marine mammals, it is also critical to understand the culturally significant role that marine mammals have played throughout history. Both utilitarian and cultural aspects of human-marine mammal interaction inform our current relationship with marine mammals and will be critical in defining a rational approach to marine mammal conservation in the twenty-first century.

(ii) Cultural Relationship

The history of over-exploitation of marine mammals exists in uncomfortable juxtaposition with the cultural significance that humans have long afforded marine mammals. As Kubasek et al. proffer, "[w]alruses, seals, dolphins, sea lions, manatees, sea otters, whales, and polar bears—all are marine mammals, some of the most cherished and yet most exploited creatures on earth."[174]

Marine mammals have figured prominently throughout history in legends, folklore, and myths, which collectively "form the basis of many religious beliefs, value systems, and the way in which we perceive our place in the world and our interaction with other animals."[175] For example, dolphins appear in both the Greek and Roman mythology (c. 3,000–1,500 years ago), and Norwegian cave art (c. 9,000 years ago).[176] Traditional Maori folklore (New Zealand) suggests that their forefathers arrived on the shores of New Zealand on the backs of whales, and orca represent the protector for the Haida Aboriginal group of the North Pacific.[177] Pinnipeds also

Introduction

appeared in Greek, Norwegian, Western European, and Arctic Eskimo mythology and legend.[178]

The cultural significance of marine mammals decreased during the eighteenth and nineteenth centuries in the face of exploitation and commoditization. Arguably, attitudes have shifted again and "[r]ecent conservationist demands for sea mammal protection should be seen as a rebirth of affection for these singular creatures."[179] Marine mammals (especially whales) served as symbolic species during the modern environmental movement[180] and, more recently, Hollywood movies have helped propagate their "charismatic megafauna" persona. The shift that has occurred since the mid-twentieth century is so dramatic that a discussion of culture as it relates to marine mammals is, today, more likely to concern our perception of unique cultural interaction between marine mammals and the existence of mammalian social structure than the role that marine mammals occupy in folklore, legend, and myth.[181] The intricacies of this emerging ethical discussion of marine mammal intelligence and culture will figure prominently in Chapter 3.

3. Current Conservation Status of Marine Mammals

An essential assumption to the analysis contained in this book is that marine mammals are in fact in need of a different conservation approach, and that reconsidering the existing international and regional regime is in fact justified. The following discussion serves to discover trends in the status of marine mammals and to detail the data that will be used throughout the remainder of this work.

The IUCN, "[f]ounded in 1948 as the world's first global environmental organization," is currently "the largest professional global conservation network" and a "leading authority on the environment and sustainable development."[182] The IUCN has significant membership, including more than 200 governments and over 900 nongovernmental organizations.[183] In addition to organizational support, the IUCN utilizes the knowledge of nearly 11,000 scientists and experts that participate on a voluntary basis.[184] The IUCN advertises itself as "[a] neutral forum for governments, NGOs, scientists, business and local communities to find pragmatic solutions to conservation and development challenges," and it has "Official Observer Status at the United Nations General Assembly."[185] The IUCN is committed to contributing to national and regional conservation efforts around the world, and it utilizes its extensive membership to advocate for conservation at the international level of governance.[186] Perhaps the most influential initiative that the IUCN maintains on an ongoing basis is the IUCN Red List of Threatened Species (the "IUCN Red List").

The IUCN Red List purports to be "the most comprehensive information source on the status of wild species and their links to livelihoods" and strives "to convey the urgency and scale of conservation problems to the public and policy makers, and to motivate the global community to work together to reduce species extinctions."[187] Launched in 1963, the IUCN Red List is utilized by educational groups, government agencies, agencies involved in wildlife and natural resource planning, and nongovernmental organizations.[188] The IUCN Red List improved the objectivity and scientific robustness of their assessment procedure over a four-year consultation process in the early 1990s carried out within the IUCN Species Survival Commission (which is currently "a science-based network of more than 7,500 volunteer experts from almost every country of the world").[189] The result of this negotiation was the "precise and quantitative Red List Categories and Criteria" as adopted in 1994, and these criteria have been updated periodically since then.[190] As a result of its improved robustness, the IUCN Red List has been utilized by the United Nations as the source of extinction monitoring.[191] The IUCN Red List categorizes species as: Extinct (EX), Extinct in the Wild (EW), Critically Endangered (CR), Endangered (EN), Vulnerable (VU), Near Threatened (NT), Least Concern (LC), Data Deficient (DD), or Not Evaluated (NE).[192]

The summary of IUCN marine mammal species listings presented in Appendix I of this book indicates the following trends for different marine mammal groups. For Order Cetacea: (1) 22 species are listed as Least Concern (LC) (18 with an unknown population trend, two with a stable population trend, and two with an increasing population); (2) five species are listed as Near Threatened (NT) (two with a decreasing population trend, and three with an unknown population trend); (3) six species are listed as Vulnerable (VU) (five with decreasing populations and one with an unknown population); (4) seven species are listed as Endangered (EN) (one with an increasing population, one with a decreasing population, and five with an unknown population status); (5) there are two Critically Endangered (CR) species (one which is possibly extinct, and one with a decreasing population trend); (6) there are 45 species that are Data Deficient (DD) (all 45 have an unknown population trend, with one possibly being extinct); and (7) one that is not listed. Regarding species within Order Pinnipedia: (1) 19 species are LC (nine with an increasing population trend, four with a stable population trend, and six with an unknown population trend); (2) three species are VU (each with a decreasing population trend); (3) four species are EN (all with decreasing population trends); (4) one species is CR (with a decreasing population trend); (5) three species are DD (with unknown population trends); and (6) two species are Extinct (EX). For marine otters and polar bears (Order Carnivora): (1) two species are categorized as LC (both with stable population trends); (2) one is NT (with a decreasing population trend); (3) one is VU (with a decreasing population trend); (4) three species are categorized as EN (each with decreasing population trends); and (5) one is EX. Within Order Sirenia: (1) four species are VU (two with decreasing population trends and two with unknown population trends); and (2) one species is EX.

These data reveal three salient trends that serve to justify a new, rational, and robust approach to the international governance of marine mammals. First, each grouping of marine mammals contains species within the risk categories (namely Vulnerable, Endangered, and Critically Endangered). This suggests that the current framework for marine mammal management is inadequately addressing current threats. Second, there are 48 species of marine mammals that the IUCN simply do not know enough about to make an informed risk classification (these are the species categorized as DD). In addition, there are 81 species where scientists are unable to classify their population trend, and 23 other species whose population is decreasing, which serves to further justify the creation of a rational, robust, and effective management regime that accounts for existing knowledge gaps and areas of scientific uncertainty. The third trend is the abundance of species that are categorized as LC. Indeed, many species of cetacean and pinniped have rebounded to the point that a limited and closely monitored hunt may be possible within a sustainable management approach.

Any regime that is created must acknowledge that such a hunt may be possible, even for some species that have been historically mismanaged and over-exploited. The main barrier to reinstituting this sort of hunt may be the "powerful charisma of marine mammals" and a strong lobby (especially in North America, Europe, and South America) that advances a strong conservation and preservation approach that also seeks to provide some (or all) marine mammals with a right to life.[193] The emerging debate surrounding the ethical considerations of hunting marine mammals will be addressed in Chapter 3. Suffice it to say, there are a variety of perspectives on marine mammal conservation, but regardless of which perspective one subscribes to, this review emphasizes the importance of accounting for the actual status of each extant marine mammal species as we consider appropriate conservation strategies.

VI. CONCLUSION

Despite sharing certain basic mammalian characteristics, extant marine mammal species vary considerably in their life history, diet, size, distribution (both geographic and within different ocean zones), reliance on the ocean environment, and conservation status. Irrespective of these differences, I conclude that trends in marine mammal management justify seeking alternatives to the status quo. What was initially a problem of over-exploitation is now a multifaceted dilemma that calls into question many of our basic uses of the ocean. I have also introduced the existing gap in current literature that this work intends to fill and the contribution I hope to make toward achieving the rational conservation and management of marine mammals.

Having described the problem and historic trends, I will now turn to an overview of the prevailing approach to marine mammal conservation, as it exists at the international, regional, and national levels of governance, in an attempt to demonstrate why effective conservation is simply not feasible within the current fragmented approach.

NOTES

1. Nancy Kubasek et al., *Protecting Marine Mammals: Time for a New Approach*, 13 UCLA J. ENVTL. L. & POL'Y 1, 1 (1994–1995) ["Kubasek"].
2. 10 Dec. 1982, 21 I.L.M. 1261, 1833 U.N.T.S. 3 ["UNCLOS"]. Note that throughout this work I often refer to the new international regime proposed herein as a conservation regime; however, conservation is not well defined at the international level of governance, nor does it preclude sustainable management in this context—ideas that are discussed in some detail in Part II of this chapter.
3. Note that because the majority of existing literature focuses on cetaceans (whales, dolphins, and porpoises) and pinnipeds (seals, sea lions, and walruses), these marine mammals will figure prominently throughout this work.
4. *See* MICHAEL BOWMAN ET AL., LYSTER'S INTERNATIONAL WILDLIFE LAW 59 (2d ed. 2010) ["LYSTER'S INTERNATIONAL WILDLIFE LAW"]; *See* PATRICIA BIRNIE, ALAN BOYLE & CATHERINE REDGWELL, INTERNATIONAL LAW & THE ENVIRONMENT 655–657 (3d ed. 2009).

5. *See* Ved P. Nanda & George (Rock) Pring, International Environmental Law and Policy for the 21st Century 36 (2d ed. 2013) ["Nanda & Pring"].
6. International Union for the Conservation of Nature, *World Conservation Strategy* (1980).
7. *Id.*
8. G.A. Res. 37/7, U.N. Doc. A/RES/37/7, at Annex (Oct. 28, 1982) ["G.A. Res. 37/7"].
9. G.A. Res. 37/7, *supra* note 8.
10. 5 June 1992, 31 I.L.M. 818, 1760 U.N.T.S. 79.
11. *Id.* at art. 2.
12. 23 June 1979, 1651 U.N.T.S. 333 ["CMS"].
13. *Id.*
14. 20 May 1980, 33 U.S.T. 3476, 1329 U.N.T.S. 48 ["CCAMLR"].
15. *Id.* at art II.
16. 14 Aug. 1999, http://www.pmg.org.za/docs/2003/appendices/030625wildlifeprotocol.htm.
17. 16 U.S.C. § 1632 (2007) ["MMPA"].
18. Richard A. Primack, Essentials of Conservation Biology 5–6 (3d ed. 2002) ["Primack"].
19. *See* CMS, *supra* note 12, at art. I(1)(c) (defining the term "conservation status").
20. *See* The International Union for the Conservation of Nature, *World Conservation Strategy*, 1(4)–1(7) (1980), http://data.iucn.org/dbtw-wpd/edocs/WCS-004.pdf (defining "conservation" and recognizing that for the purposes of conserving living resources one must consider ecosystem processes, genetic diversity, and sustainable utilization); Primack, *supra* note 18, at 6 (describing the scope of conservation biology noting its focus on biodiversity, human impact on species, genetic variation, and ecosystems).
21. *See* MMPA, *supra* note 17, at § 1362(2) (recognizing the goal of increasing or maintaining populations without necessarily precluding take).
22. *See* CCAMLR, *supra* note 14, at art. II(3)(a) (indicating the need to maintain certain population levels).
23. *Id.* at art II(2) (indicating that conservation "includes rational use").
24. *See* Lyster's International Wildlife Law, *supra* note 4, at 59–60 (discussing the interaction between conservation and sustainable use).
25. Nanda & Pring, *supra* note 5, at 26.
26. *Id.* at 26–27.
27. United Nations Conference on Environment and Development, Rio de Janiero, Braz., June 3–14, 1992, *Rio Declaration on Environment and Development*, U.N. Doc. A/CONF.151/26/Rev.1 (Vol. 1), Annex I (Aug. 12, 1992) ["Rio Declaration"]; *see generally* United Nations Conference on Environment and Development, Rio de Janiero, Braz., June 3–14, 1992, *Agenda 21*, U.N. Doc A/CONF.151/26 (Aug. 12, 1992) ["Agenda 21"].
28. U.N. Commission on Environment and Development, *Our Common Future*, ¶ 27, U.N. Doc. A/42/427, Annex (1987).
29. Nanda & Pring, *supra* note 5, at 25–30.
30. *See id.* at 29 (summarizing the principles that inform sustainable development in the Rio Declaration and Agenda 21).
31. *Id.* § 1362(2).
32. Nanda & Pring, *supra* note 5, at 29 (summarizing the principles that inform sustainable development at international law).

33. MMPA, *supra* note 17, § 1362(2).
34. *See* Duncan E. J. Currie, *Ecosystem-Based Management in Multilateral Environmental Agreements: Progress towards Adopting the Ecosystem Approach in the International Management of Living Marine Resources*, WWF International 3–4 (2007); *see* ERICH HOYT, MARINE PROTECTED AREAS FOR WHALES, DOLPHINS, AND PORPOISES: A WORLD HANDBOOK FOR CETACEAN HABITAT CONSERVATION AND PLANNING 9–10 (2d ed. 2011) ["HOYT"].
35. MMPA, *supra* note 17, § 1362(1)(6).
36. *See* MARINE PROTECTED AREAS: A MULTIDISCIPLINARY APPROACH 2 (Joachim Claudet ed., 2011).
37. MMPA, *supra* note 17, § 1362(11).
38. Rio Declaration, *supra* note 27, at Principle 15.
39. MMPA, *supra* note 17, § 1362(13).
40. International Convention on Salvage, 28 April, 1989, 1953 U.N.T.S. 153, art. 1(b).
41. Dec. 2, 1946, 62 Stat. 1716, 161 U.N.T.S. 74, at arts. II(1) & (3) ["ICRW"].
42. *See* Cinnamon Piñon Carlarne, *Saving the Whales in the New Millennium: International Institutions, Recent Development and the Future of International Whaling Policies*, 24 VA. ENVTL. L.J. 1, 2 (2005–2006) ["Carlarne"] (noting that it the whaling conversation inevitably engages science, politics, and philosophy).
43. Patricia Birnie, *The International Organization of Whales*, 13 DENV. J. INT'L L. & POL'Y 309 (1983–1984); PATRICIA W. BIRNIE, INTERNATIONAL REGULATION OF WHALING: FROM CONSERVATION OF WHALING TO CONSERVATION OF WHALES AND REGULATION OF WHALE-WATCHING VOL. I (1985); Patricia Birnie, *The Role of Law in Protecting Marine Mammals*, 15(3) AMBIO 137 (1986); Patricia Birnie, *International Legal Issues in the Management and Protection of the Whale: A Review of Four Decades of Experience*, 29 NAT. RES. J. 903 (1989); Patricia Birnie, *Are Twentieth-Century Marine Conservation Conventions Adaptable to Twenty-First Century Goals and Principles?: Part I*, 12(3) INT'L J. MARINE & COASTAL L. 307 (1997); Patricia Birnie, *Are Twentieth-Century Marine Conservation Conventions Adaptable to Twenty-First Century Goals and Principles?: Part II*, 12(4) INT'L J. MARINE & COASTAL L. 488 (1997); Patricia Birnie, *Marine Mammals: Exploiting the Ambiguities of Article 65 of the Convention on the Law of the Sea and Related Provisions: Practice under the International Convention for the Regulation of Whaling*, in THE LAW OF THE SEA: PROGRESS AND PROSPECTS 261, 261 (David Freestone, Richard Barnes & David M. Ong eds., 2006).
44. Alexander Gillespie, *The Ethical Question in the Whaling Debate*, 9 GEO. INT'L. ENVTL. L. REV. 355 (1996–1997); Alexander Gillespie, *Whale-Watching and the Precautionary Principle: The Difficulties of the New Zealand Domestic Response in the Whaling Debate*, 17 N. Z. UNI. L. REV. 254 (1997); Alexander Gillespie, *Whaling under a Scientific Auspice: The Ethics of Scientific Research Whaling*, 3(1) J. INT'L WILDLIFE L. & P. 1 (2000) ["Gillespie, *Whaling under a Scientific Auspice*"]; Alexander Gillespie, *Aboriginal Subsistence Whaling: A Critique of the Inter-relationship between International Law and the International Whaling Commission*, 12 COLO. J. INT'L ENVTL. L. & POL'Y 77 (2001); Alexander Gillespie, *Small Cetaceans, International Law and the International Whaling Commission*, 2 MELB. J. INT'L L. 257 (2001) ["Gillespie, *Small Cetaceans*"]; Alexander Gillespie, *Environmental Threats to Cetaceans and the Limits of Existing Management*

Structures, 6 N. Z. J. OF ENVTL. L. 97 (2002) ["Gillespie, *Environmental Threats*"]; ALEXANDER GILLESPIE, WHALING DIPLOMACY (2005) ["WHALING DIPLOMACY"].

45. WILLIAM T. BURKE, THE NEW INTERNATIONAL LAW OF FISHERIES: UNCLOS 1982 AND BEYOND (1994) ["BURKE, UNCLOS 1982 AND BEYOND"]; William T. Burke, *A New Whaling Agreement and International Law*, in TOWARD A SUSTAINABLE WHALING REGIME 51 (Robert L. Friedheim ed., 2001).

46. William C. Burns, *The International Whaling Commission and Future of Cetaceans: Problems and Prospects*, 8 COLO. J. INT'L ENVTL. L. & POL'Y 31 (1997); William C. Burns, *The Forty-Ninth Meeting of the International Whaling Commission: Charting the Future of Cetaceans in the Twenty-First Century*, 9 COLO. J. INT'L ENVTL. L. & POL'Y 67 (1998); William C.G. Burns, *The Agreement on the Conservation of Cetaceans of the Black Sea, Mediterranean Sea and Contiguous Atlantic Area (ACCOBAMS): A Regional Response to the Threats Facing Cetaceans*, 1(1) J. INT'L WILDLIFE L. & P. 113 (1998) ["Burns, *ACCOBAMS*"]; William G.C. Burns, *From the Harpoon to the Heat: Climate Change and the International Whaling Commission in the 21st Century*, 13(2) GEO. INT. ENVTL. REV. 335 (2006) ["Burns, *From the Harpoon to the Heat*"].

47. Robert L. Friedheim, *Introduction: The IWC as a Contested Regime*, in TOWARD A SUSTAINABLE WHALING REGIME 3 (Robert L. Friedheim ed., 2001); Robert L. Friedheim, *Negotiating in the IWC Environment*, in TOWARD A SUSTAINABLE WHALING REGIME 200 (Robert L. Friedheim ed., 2001); Robert L. Friedheim, *Fixing the Whaling Regime: A Proposal*, in TOWARD A SUSTAINABLE WHALING REGIME 311 (Robert L. Friedheim ed., 2001).

48. *See* Jennifer L. Bailey, *Whale Watching, the Buenos Aires Group and the Politics of the International Whaling Commission*, 36(2) MAR. POL. 489 (2012); *see* Dan Goodman, *The "Future of the IWC": Why the Initiative to Save the IWC Failed*, 14(1) J. INT'L. WILDLIFE. L & POL'Y 63 (2011); *See generally* Mike Iliff, *Normalization of the International Whaling Commission*, 32(2) MAR. POL. 333 (2008); Mike Iliff, *The International Whaling Regime Post 2007*, 32(3) MAR. POL. 522 (2008); Mike Iliff, *Modernization of the International Convention for the Regulation of Whaling*, 32(3) MAR. POL. 402 (2008); Mike Iliff, *Compromise in the IWC: Is It Possible or Desirable?*, 32(6) MAR. POL. 997 (2008); Mike Iliff, *The Hogarth Initiative on the Future of the International Whaling Commission*, 34(3) MAR. POL. 360 (2010); Mike Iliff, *Contemporary Initiatives on the Future of the International Whaling Commission*, 34(3) MAR. POL. 461 (2010).

49. ICRW, *supra* note 41.

50. *See* Michael Heazle, *"See You in Court!": Whaling as a Two Level Game in Australian Politics and Foreign Policy*, 38 MAR. POL. 330 (2013); *see* Jeffrey J. Smith, *Evolving to Conservation?: The International Court's Decision in the Australia/Japan Whaling Decision*, 45 OCEAN DEV. & INT'L L. 301 (2014); Anastasia Telesetsky, Donald K Anton & Timo Koivurova. *ICJ's Decision in Australia v. Japan: Giving Up the Spear or Refining the Scientific Design?*, 45 OCEAN DEV. & INT'L L. 328 (2014), William de la Mare, Nick Gales & Marc Mangel, *Applying Scientific Principles in International Law on Whaling*, 345 SCI. 1125 (2014); Phillip J. Clapham, *Japan's Whaling following the International Court of Justice Ruling: Brave New World—or Business as Usual?*, 51 MAR. POL. 238 (2015); Anastasia Telesetsky & Seokwoo Lee, *After* Whaling in the Antarctic: *Amending Article VIII to Fix a Broken Treaty Regime*, 30 INT'L J. MARINE & COASTAL L. 700 (2015); Whaling in the Antarctic (Australia v. Japan: New Zealand Intervening), Judgment, [2014] ICJ Rep 226.

51. *See* Walter A. Foote, *World Cooperation in the Whaling Industry*, 2 Cum. Dig. Int'l L. & Rel. 27 (1931–1932); Larry L. Leonard, *Recent Negotiations toward the International Regulation of Whaling*, 35(1) Am. J. Int'l L. 90 (1941).

52. *See* Henry Flanders, *The Behring Sea Controversy*, 40 Am. L. Reg. 590 (1892); Russell Duane, *Decision of the Behring Sea Arbitrators*, 41 Am. L. Reg. 901 (1893); Theodore S. Woolsey, *Bering Sea Award*, 3 Yale L.J. 45 (1893–1894).

53. *See* Carl Q. Christol, John R. Schmidhauser & George O. Rotten, *Law and the Whale: Current Developments in the International Whaling Controversy*, 8(1) Case W. Res. J. Int'l L. 149 (1976); Lawrence A. Friedman, *Legal Aspects of the International Whaling Controversy*, 8 NYU J. Int'l L. & Pol'y 211 (1975–1976).

54. James A. R. Nafziger, *Global Conservation and Management of Marine Mammals*, 17 San Diego L. Rev. 591 (1979–1980); Joseph P. Rosati, *Enforcement Questions for the International Whaling Commission: Are Exclusive Economic Zones the Solution?* (1984) 14 Cali. W. Int'l L.J. 144; John Warren Kindt & Charles J. Wintheiser, *The Conservation and Protection of Marine Mammals*, 7 U. Haw. L. Rev. 301 (1985); Kimberly S. Davis, *International Management of Cetaceans under the New Law of the Sea Convention*, 3 B. U. Int'l L. J. 477 (1985) ["Davis"].

55. Gare Smith, *International Whaling Commission: An Analysis of the Past and Reflections on the Future*, 16(4) Nat. Resources Law. 543 (1984); Marlise Flis, *International Whale Conservation: Moby Dick's Last Hurrah*, 3 Hofstra Envtl. L. Dig. 30 (1986).

56. *See* Gillespie, *Environmental Threats*, *supra* note 44; Karen S. Scott, *International Regulation of Undersea Noise*, 53 Int'l & Comp L.Q. 287 (2004); E.C.M. Parson et al., *Navy Sonar and Cetaceans: Just How Much Does the Gun Need to Smoke before We Act?*, 56(7) Mar. Poll. Bull. 1248 (2008); Karen N. Scott, *Sound and Cetaceans: A Regional Response to Regulating Acoustic Marine Pollution*, 10(2) J. Int'l Wildlife L. & P. 175 (2007); Randall S. Abate, *NEPA, National Security, and Ocean Noise: The Past, Present, and Future of Regulating the Impact of Navy Sonar on Marine Mammals*, 13(4) J. Int'l Wildlife L. & P. 326 (2010).

57. Burns, *From the Harpoon to the Heat*, *supra* note 46; Hjalmar Vilhjalmmson, *Impact of Changes in Natural Conditions on Ocean Resources*, *in* Law, Science & Ocean Management 225 (Myron H. Nordquist et al. eds., 2007).

58. Tamara Nicole Norris, *Lethal Speed: An Analysis of the Proposed Rule to Implement Vessel Speed Restrictions and Its Impact on the Declining Right Whale Population as well as the Shipping and Whale-Watching Industries*, 13 Ocean & Coastal L.J. 339 (2007–2008); Angelina S.M. Vanderlaan & Christopher T. Taggart, *Vessel Collisions with Whales: The Probability of Lethal Injury Based on Vessel Speed*, 23 Marine Mammal Sci. 144 (2004).

59. A.M. Cisneros-Montemayor et al., *The Global Potential for Whale Watching*, 34 Mar. Pol'y 1273 (2010); J.E.S. Higham & D. Lusseau, *Urgent Need for Empirical Research into Whaling and Whale Watching*, 21(2) Conserv. Biol. 554 (2007).

60. Hoyt, *supra* note 34, at 2 (considering ecosystem-based management as "a regime that recognizes that ecosystems are dynamic and inherently uncertain, yet seeks to manage these human interactions within ecosystems in order to protect and maintain ecological integrity and to minimize adverse impacts").

61. *Id.*; Randall S. Abate, *Marine Protected Areas as a Mechanism to Promote Marine Mammal Conservation: International and Comparative Law Lessons for the United States*, 88 Or. L. Rev. 255 (2009) ["Abate, *Marine Protected Areas*"].

62. Anthony D'Amato & Sudhir K. Chopra, *Whales: Their Emerging Right to Life*, 85 AM. J. INT'L L. 21 (1991) (note that this was not the first discussion of the ethical consideration of whaling and whale conservation, *see* Luis Kutner, *The Genocide of Whales: A Crime against Humanity*, 10(3) LAWYER OF THE AMERICAS 784 (1978)).

63. *See* Sue J. Fisher & Randall R. Reeves, *The Global Trade in Live Cetaceans: Implications for Conservation*, 8(4) J. INT'L WILDLIFE L. & P. 315 (2007); Stuart R. Harrop, *From Cartel to Conservation and on to Compassion: Animal Welfare and the International Whaling Commission*, 6(1–2) J. INT'L WILDLIFE L. & P. 79 (2010) (note that the morality discussion is not limited to cetaceans, although this is where the majority of the legal literature has been produced. The other major area of concern is the continued hunt of seals; *see* Peter L. Fitzgerald, *"Morality" May Not Be Enough to Justify the EU Seal Products Ban: Animal Welfare Meets International Trade Law*, 14 J. INT'L WILDLIFE L. & P. 85 (2011)).

64. Sarah Suhre, *Misguided Morality: The Repercussions of the International Whaling Commission's Shift from a Policy of Regulation to One of Preservation*, 12 GEO. INT'L ENVTL. LAW REV. 305 (1999).

65. Lori Marino, Daniel W. McShea & Mark D. Uhen, *Origin and Evolution of Large Brains in Toothed Whales*, 281 ANAT. REC. 1247 (2004); Hal Whitehead et al., *Culture and Conservation of Non-humans with Reference to Whales and Dolphins: Review and New Directions*, 120 BIOL. CON. 427 (2004); Kevin N. Laland & Vincent M. Janik, *The Animal Cultures Debate*, 21(10) TRENDS ECOL. EVO. 542 (2006); Mark Peter Simmonds, *Into the Brains of Whales*, 100 APPL. ANIM. BEHAV. SCI. 103 (2006); Lori Marino et al., *Cetaceans Have Complex Brains for Complex Cognition*, 5(5) PLOS BIOL. 0966 (2007); and Hal Whitehead & David Lusseau, *Animal Social Networks as Substrate for Behavioural Diversity*, 294 J. THEOR. BIOL. 19 (2012).

66. *E.g.*, Cynthia E. Carlson, *The International Regulation of Small Cetaceans*, 21(3) SAN DIEGO L. REV. 578 (1984); Rachelle Adam, *The Japanese Dolphin Hunts: The Quest of International Legal Protection for Small Cetaceans*, 14 ANIMAL L. 133 (2008); Gillespie, *Small Cetaceans*, *supra* note 44 (these works support the position that the International Convention for the Regulation of Whaling likely does not cover small cetacean species, and because of this the International Whaling Commission has not taken action to regulate their direct hunt. Further, there is no international convention that globally manages pinnipeds (seals and sea lions) or sirenians (dugongs and manatees)).

67. *See* Joseph P. Rosati, *Enforcement Questions of the International Whaling Commission: Are Exclusive Zones the Solution?*, 14 CAL. W. INT'L L. J. 114 (1984); WHALING DIPLOMACY, *supra* note 44, at 357–77; Andrew Hutchison, *Baleen out the IWC: Is International Litigation an Effective Strategy for Halting the Japanese Scientific Whaling Program?*, 3 MqJICEL 1 (2006).

68. *E.g.*, Gillespie, *Whaling Under a Scientific Auspice*, *supra* note 44; Brian Trevor Hodges, *The Cracking Façade of the International Whaling Commission as an Institution of International Law: Norwegian Small-Type Whaling and the Aboriginal Subsistence Exemption*, 15 J. ENVTL. L. & LITIG. 295 (2000); Howard S. Schiffman, *Scientific Research Whaling in International Law: Objectives and Objections*, 8 ISLA J. INT'L & COMP. L. 473 (2001–2001); Yui Nishi, *Dolphins, Whales, and the Future of the International Whaling Commission*, 33 HASTINGS INT'L & COMP. L. REV. 285 (2010) (these articles discuss the contentious topics

such as scientific whaling in the Southern Ocean, small cetacean hunts, and Aboriginal subsistence whaling).
69. *See* Brettny Hardy, *Regional Approach to Whaling: How the North Atlantic Marine Mammal Commission Is Shifting the Tides for Whale Management*, 17 DUKE J. COMP. & INT'L L. 169 (2006).
70. *See* Steven Freeland & Julie Drysdale, *Co-operation or Chaos?—Article 65 of United Nations Convention on the Law of the Sea and the Future of the International Whaling Commission*, 2 MACQUARIE J. INT'L & COMP. ENVTL. L. 1, 4 (2005) (suggesting that UNCLOS establishes the possibility that other organizations can have a role in the conservation of cetaceans); *see also* Davis, *supra* note 54, at 512–13 (discussing the negotiating history of Article 65 and the possibility of a successor organization); *see also* Ted L. McDorman, *Canada and Whaling: An Analysis of Article 65 of the Law of the Sea Convention*, 29 OCEAN DEV. & INT'L L. 179, 184–85 (1998) (summarizing the various positions that have been advanced in the literature for, and against, various international organizations qualifying as regulatory bodies pursuant to Article 65 of UNCLOS).
71. *See* Burns, *ACCOBAMS*, *supra* note 46.
72. HOYT, *supra* note 34; Abate, *Marine Protected Areas*, *supra* note 61.
73. Stockholm Environment Institute, *Valuing the Ocean: Draft Executive Summary* 3 (2012), http://www.sei-international.org/mediamanager/documents/Publications/SEI-Preview-ValuingTheOcean-DraftExecutiveSummary.pdf ["Stockholm Environment Institute"].
74. *Id.* at 3.
75. *Id.*; *see also* Paul Holthus, *The Future of Sustainable Ocean Resource Use*, 51(8) SEA TECH. 7, 7 (2010).
76. Eric A. Posner & Alan O. Sykes, *Economic Foundations of the Law of the Sea*, 104 AM. J. INT'L L. 569, 569 (2010).
77. *See* Press Release, Census of Marine Life, First Census Shows Life in Planet Ocean Is Richer, More Connected, More Impacted than Expected (Oct. 4, 2010) (*available at* http://www.coml.org/pressreleases/census2010/PDF/Census-2010_News_Release-9-23-2010.pdf) ["Census of Marine Life"].
78. *Id.*
79. Ocean Biogeographic Information System, *Marine Biology: State of Knowledge*, OBIS (June 25, 2012, 3:21 AM), http://www.iobis.org/node/404 ["OBIS"].
80. *Id.*
81. Stockholm Environment Institute, *supra* note 73, at 1.
82. *Id.* at 2.
83. *Id.*
84. *Id.* at 3.
85. *Id.*
86. *Id.*
87. *Id.*
88. The Anthropocene is described as "the current epoch in which humans and our societies have become a global geophysical force," and began in the 1800s with the onset of rapid fossil fuel-based industrialization. Will Steffen, Paul J. Crutzen & John R. Mitchell, *The Anthropocene: Are Humans Now Overwhelming the Great Forces of Nature*, 36 AMBIO 614, 614 (2007).
89. Douglas J. McCauley et al., *Marine Defaunation: Animal Loss in the Global Ocean*, 347 SCI. 1255641-1, 1255641-5 (2015).

90. GRID-Arendal, *Why Value the Oceans? A Discussion Paper*, 1 (2012), http://www.grida.no/publications/teeb/.
91. Carlarne, *supra* note 42, at 2.
92. Appendix 1 provides a list of extant and recently extinct species of marine mammal as well as their current conservation status as summarized from the International Union for the Conservation of Nature ("IUCN").
93. *See* Samuel T. Turvey et al., *First Human-Caused Extinction of a Cetacean Species?*, 3 BIOL. LETT. 537 (2007) (these authors note that in light of an extensive visual and acoustic search for the Yangtze River Dolphin that located no individuals, "[w]e are forced to conclude that the baiji is now likely to be extinct, probably due to unsustainable by-catch in local fisheries").
94. The Marine Mammal Center, *Introduction to Marine Mammals*, http://www.marinemammalcenter.org/education/marine-mammal-information/ (last visited Feb. 12, 2016).
95. *Id.*
96. BURKE, UNCLOS 1982 AND BEYOND, *supra* note 45, at 257; *see* Ana D. Davidson et al., *Drivers and Hotspots of Extinction Risk in Marine Mammals*, 109 PNAS 3395, 3395 (2012) (noting that the natural histories of marine mammals are "not well documented," and that taken together, certain biological criteria—"adult body mass, geographic range size, life-history traits, social group size, trophic group, habitat, foraging location, taxonomic order, diet breadth, and migratory behavior"—can help us understand extinction pressures and risks. At 3396-3397 the authors discuss how low rates of reproduction, large body size, long reproductive cycles make it difficult for many marine mammal species to recover from over-exploitation and make them susceptible to other environmental threats).
97. BURKE, UNCLOS 1982 AND BEYOND, *supra* note 45, at 257.
98. Dale W. Rice, *Classification (Overall)*, in ENCYCLOPEDIA OF MARINE MAMMALS 234, 234–37 (William F. Perrin et al. eds., 2d ed. 2009) ["Rice"].
99. *Id.*
100. *Id.* at 237.
101. Jaume Forcada, *Distribution*, in ENCYCLOPEDIA OF MARINE MAMMALS 316, 316–21 (William F. Perrin et al. eds., 2d ed. 2009) ["Forcada"].
102. *Id.*
103. *Id.*
104. *Id.*
105. *Id.*
106. *Id.*
107. *Id.*
108. *Id.*
109. *Id.*
110. *Id.*
111. *Id.* (this distribution scheme is particularly relevant later in this book during the discussion of regional implementation of global standards. There are certain geographic zones that are "hotspots" for marine mammal life, including both polar regions).
112. ICRW, *supra* note 41 (note that the Annex on Nomenclature was attached as an Appendix to the ICRW during negotiation; it describes certain species that the parties to the 1946 meeting had in mind as they negotiated the text).

113. Vicki Osis et al., *The Great Whales: A Curriculum for Grades 6–9*, OREGON STATE UNIVERSITY MARINE MAMMAL INSTITUTE 5 (2008), http://mmi.oregonstate.edu/sites/default/files/Great_Whales_6-30-08.pdf.
114. Forcada, *supra* note 101, at 317.
115. *Id.* at 317–18.
116. Randall R. Reeves, *Hunting of Marine Mammals*, in ENCYCLOPEDIA OF MARINE MAMMALS 585, 585–88 (William F. Perrin et al. eds., 2d ed. 2009) ["Reeves"].
117. *Id.* at 585.
118. *Id.*
119. Lawrence Guy Straus, *Solutrean Settlement of North America? A Review of Reality*, 65(2) AM. ANTIQ. 219, 219 (2000) ["Straus"].
120. John Harwood, *Approaches to Management*, in MARINE MAMMAL ECOLOGY AND CONSERVATION: A HANDBOOK OF TECHNIQUES 325, 328 (Ian L. Boyd et al. eds., 2010) ["Harwood"] (discussing evidence and literature suggesting that seals may have been utilized up to 30,000 years ago).
121. Jacqui Mulville, *A Whale of a Problem? The Use of Zooarchaeological Evidence in Modern Whaling*, in THE EXPLOITATION AND CULTURAL IMPORTANCE OF SEA MAMMALS 154, 154 (Gregory G. Monks ed., 2005) ["Mulville"] (also, at 160, Mulville notes that "[a]lthough there is plentiful evidence for cetacean bone on archaeological sites. . . . there remains an ongoing debate on the purpose, frequency, and nature of such procurement").
122. Straus, *supra* note 119, at 222–23.
123. M. P. Richards et al., *Isotope Evidence for the Intensive Use of Marine Foods by Late Upper Palaeolithic Humans*, 49 J. HUM. EVOL. 390, 393 (2005).
124. Thomas A. Wake & Dwight D. Simons, *Trans-Holocene Subsistence Strategies and Topographic Change on the Northern California Coast: The Fauna from Duncan's Point Cave*, 22(2) J. CALIF. GT. BASIN ANTHRO. 295, 306 (2000) (noting that the disproportionate representation of juvenile pinniped remains at this site suggests that humans first starting hunting marine mammals at rookeries and haul-out sites. Indeed, this has led some anthropologists to suggest that this hunting strategy might have been an early example of marine mammal overexploitation, which in turn promoted the innovations necessary to hunt marine mammals in different ways).
125. Sang-Mog Lee & Daniel Robineau, *The Cetaceans of the Neolithic Rock Carvings of Bangu-dae (South Korea) and the Beginnings of Whaling in the North-West Pacific*, 108 L'ANTHROPOLOGIC 137, 137–38 (2004); *see also* BBC News, *Rock Art Hints at Whaling Origins: Stone Age People May Have Started Hunting Whales as Early as 6,000 BC, New Evidence from South Korea Suggests*, BBC NEWS (APR. 20, 2004, 10:33 AM), http://news.bbc.co.uk/2/hi/science/nature/3638853.stm.
126. *See generally* KATHY HAPPYNOOK, WHALING AROUND THE WORLD (2004); *see also* Reeves, *supra* note 116; *see also* Mulville, *supra* note 121, at 156–60.
127. Reeves, *supra* note 116, at 587.
128. Sirenian International, *Steller's Sea Cow* (Hydrodamalis gigas), Feb. 9 2005, http://www.sirenian.org/stellers.html.
129. *Id.*
130. The Monachus Guardian, *Monk Seal Fact Files: Caribbean Monk Seal*, MONACHUS-GUARDIAN.ORG, http://www.monachus-guardian.org/factfiles/carib01.htm (last visited Feb. 12, 2016).
131. *Id.*

132. Harwood, *supra* note 120, at 328–32 (another pertinent example of near extinction is the sea otter (*Enhyda lutris*). The sea otter historically ranged from "the northern Japanese archipelago, through the Aleutian Islands, and along the Pacific Coast of North America south to Baja California," in near coastal waters (*see generally* James A. Estes, *Sea Otter Predation and Community Organization in the Western Aleutian islands, Alaska*, 59(4) Ecology 822 (1978)), and in numbers between 150,000 and 300,000 (The IUCN Redlist of Threatened Species, *Enhydra lutris*, http://www.iucnredlist.org/apps/redlist/details/7750/0) (last visited Feb. 12, 2016). Local Aleut hunters began to hunt sea otters in the Bering Sea region approximately 2,500 years ago, but it was the arrival of Europeans in the region that led to rapid population collapse (*see* Jeremy B.C. Jackson, *Historical Overfishing and the Recent Collapse of Coastal Ecosystems*, 293 Sci. 629, 631 (2001)). Hunted extensively for their pelts between 1741 and 1911, sea otters became locally extinct in much of their historical range (reduced to just 2,000 total individuals (K.W. Kenyon, *The Sea Otter in the Eastern Pacific Ocean*, 68(1) N. Am. Fauna 352 (1969)), surviving only in "remnant populations in Alaska and the coast of central California" (Estes at 822). Although populations have rebounded in certain areas, there are still considerable threats to sea otter existence and the populations are now declining once again (The IUCN Redlist of Threatened Species, *Enhydra lutris*, http://www.iucnredlist.org/apps/redlist/details/7750/0) (last visited Feb. 12, 2016)).
133. Lyster's International Wildlife Law, *supra* note 4, at 150.
134. Sarah Lazarus, Troubled Waters: The Changing Fortunes of Whales and Dolphins 24 (2008) ["Lazarus"].
135. *Id.* at 24–26 (describing baleen—also known as "whalebone"—as "the plates that hang from the roof of the mouth of mysticete whales" and noting that "baleen is made of keratin—the same substance found in fingernails, hair, hooves, horns, and claws. It became indispensable because of two important properties: it is tough yet flexible, and when immersed in hot water it becomes pliant and can be molded. These qualities made it an excellent material for manufacturing a vast assortment of goods including fishing rods, whip handles, sweeps' brushes, chair seats, shoehorns and umbrella spokes. Whalebone also became a fashion essential used to make corsets, bustles, bodices, collars, ruffs and hoop skirts, and to stiffen the curls in elaborate wigs").
136. *Id.*
137. *Id.* at 26–27.
138. *Id.* at 27–28.
139. Adrienne M. Ruffle, *Resurrecting the International Whaling Commission: Suggestions to Strengthen the Conservation Effort*, 27 Brook. J. Int'l L. 639, 640 (2001–2002).
140. Lazarus, *supra* note 134, at 28–29 (noting that the competition was so fierce that these nations "interspersed their whaling with warfare," and eventually peace negotiations were required to settle differences. Also, note that whaling around Greenland utilized land spotters and chasing ships, and the whales were still being captured using handheld harpoons. Finally, the whaling industry had other local impacts as well, such as the influx of people in the town of Spitsbergen where whalers essentially set up shop. With the decline of near-shore whaling, the people also left).
141. *Id.* at 29–30.

142. *Id.* at 31.
143. *Id.* at 32.
144. *Id.; see* BURKE, UNCLOS 1982 AND BEYOND, *supra* note 45, at 257 (correctly noting that marine mammals are susceptible to over-exploitation because of their biological characteristics. Whales, in particular, are long-lived, do not start to reproduce until later in life, and generally have few offspring; together, these characteristics make them vulnerable to hunting pressure and also make it difficult for depleted species/populations to recover).
145. *Id.* at 32.
146. LAZARUS, *supra* note 134, at 32.
147. *Id.* at 33.
148. WHALING DIPLOMACY, *supra* note 44, at 3.
149. LAZARUS, *supra* note 134, at 45.
150. ANDREW DARBY, HARPOON: INTO THE HEART OF WHALING 23 (2008).
151. WHALING DIPLOMACY, *supra* note 44, at 4.
152. LAZARUS, *supra* note 134, at 49.
153. *Id.* at 50–51.
154. *Id.* at 61.
155. *Id.* at 62 (previously, whaleships, which had already been converted to steam power, would initially find and strike the whales, but small man-powered catching ships were used to pursue and kill the wounded whale).
156. *Id.*
157. *Id.* at 63.
158. LAZARUS, *supra* note 134, at 61.
159. *Id.* at 63.
160. *Id.* at 78.
161. Harwood, *supra* note 120, at 328.
162. D. Gifford-Gonzalez et al., *Archeofaunal Insights on Pinniped-Human Interactions in the Northeastern Pacific, in* THE EXPLOITATION AND CULTURAL IMPORTANCE OF SEA MAMMALS 19, 19 (Gregory G. Monks ed., 2005) ["Gifford-Gonzalez"].
163. Ian Smith, *Retreat and Resilience: Fur Seals and Human Settlement in New Zealand, in* THE EXPLOITATION AND CULTURAL IMPORTANCE OF SEA MAMMALS 6, 16 (Gregory G. Monks ed., 2005).
164. Gifford-Gonzalez, *supra* note 162, at 34.
165. Reeves, *supra* note 116, at 586–87.
166. *See generally* THE EXPLOITATION AND CULTURAL SIGNIFICANCE OF MARINE MAMMALS (Gregory G. Monks ed., 2005) (within which various articles detail the use of pinnipeds in New Zealand and Australia, Northeastern Pacific, Northwestern Canada, the Arctic, and Southern Europe, and in the Baltic Sea).
167. Harwood, *supra* note 120, at 332.
168. MARIANNE RIEDMAN, THE PINNIPEDS: SEALS, SEA LION AND WALRUSES xxii (1990) ["RIEDMAN"].
169. Reeves, *supra* note 116, at 586.
170. *Id.*
171. Courtney Pope, *For the Sake of the Seals*, 9 ASPER REV. INT'L. BUS. & TRADE L. 225, 225 (2009).
172. Panel Report, *European Communities—Measures Prohibiting the Importation and Marketing of Seal Products*, WT/DS40/R/DS401/R and ADD1 (Nov. 25, 2013); Appellate Body Report, *European Communities—Measures Prohibiting*

the *Importation and Marketing of Seal Products*, WT/DS400/AB/R and WT/DS401/AB4 (May 22, 2014) (Canada and Norway asserted that the ban was discriminatory and the EU defended its policy, which only allowed a limited Indigenous exception, on the basis that animal welfare concerns about the seal hunt justified the ban on the basis of public morality. The Panel and Appellate Body agreed, limiting their criticism to the scope of the policy's Indigenous exception).

173. *See* Katie Sykes, Joanna Langille & Robert Howse, *Whales and Seals and Bears, Oh My! The Evolution of Global Animal Law and Canada's Ambiguous Stance*, *in* CANADIAN PERSPECTIVES ON ANIMALS AND THE LAW 209, 220–21 (Peter Sankoff, Vaughan Black & Katie Sykes eds., 2015) (note that the interaction between international trade law and marine mammal conservation is a contentious, live issue also relevant to the discussion of cetacean conservation, but it is beyond the scope of the issues discussed in this work).

174. Kubasek, *supra* note 1.

175. Rochelle Constantine, *Folklore and Legends, in* ENCYCLOPEDIA OF MARINE MAMMALS 447, 447–48 (William F. Perrin et al. eds., 2d ed. 2009) ["Constantine"].

176. *Id.*

177. *Id.*

178. RIEDMAN, *supra* note 168, at xxi.

179. Peter M. Dobra, *Cetaceans: A Litany of Cain*, 7(1) B.C. ENVTL. AFF. L. REV. 165, 165 (1978).

180. *See, e.g.,* Arne Kalland, *Whale Totemization: Whale Symbolism and the Anti-whaling Campaign*, 46(2) ARCTIC 124 (1993) (discussing the role that the whale played in Greenpeace and World Wildlife Fund campaigns and the impact that this had on their conservation and on public opinion); *see also* Kieran Mulvaney, *The International Whaling Commission and the Role of Non-governmental Organizations*, 9 GEO INT'L ENVTL. L. REV. 347, 350–51 (1996–1997) (noting that many nongovernmental organizations were actively involved in a global movement to "Save the Whales" in the 1970s, which had the goal of ending commercial whale hunting and moving society toward whale protection).

181. *See* Constantine, *supra* note 175.

182. The International Union for the Conservation of Nature, *About IUCN*, IUCN, www.iucn.org/about/ (last visited Nov. 26, 2015).

183. *Id.*

184. *Id.*

185. *Id.*

186. *Id.*

187. International Union for the Conservation of Nature, *IUCN—The IUCN Red List*, IUCN www.iucn.org/about/work/programmes/species/our_work/the_iucn_red_list/ (last visited Oct. 31, 2015) ["Red List"].

188. *Id.*

189. International Union for the Conservation of Nature, *IUCN—Species Survival Commission*, http://www.iucn.org/about/work/programmes/species/who_we_are/about_the_species_survival_commission_/ (last visited Nov. 26, 2015).

190. Red List, *supra* note 187.

191. *See* United Nations, *The Millennium Development Goals Report 2011*, 51 (2011) (note that the IUCN Red List has also been incorporated as one of the indicators of the Aichi Biodiversity Targets produced through the Convention on

	Biological Diversity; *see* Convention on Biological Diversity, *Aichi Biodiversity Targets*, CBD (2012), http://www.cbd.int/sp/targets).
192.	International Union for the Conservation of Nature, *2001 IUCN Red List Categories and Criteria version 3.1 Second Edition*, http://www.iucnredlist.org/technical-documents/categories-and-criteria/2001-categories-criteria#categories at 14–15 (last visited Feb. 12, 2016).
193.	*See* Erik Jaap Molenaar, *Marine Mammals: The Role of Ethics and Ecosystem Considerations*, 6(2) J. INT'L WILDLIFE L. & POL'Y 31, 33 (2003).

2

The Current Marine Mammal Regulatory Landscape

"Law is an important factor in the conservation of marine mammals whether operating at the national, regional or international level."[1]

Patricia Birnie observed in 1979, after The Quissac Workshop on the Legal Aspects of Conservation of Marine Mammals (organized by the United Nations Environment Programme), that the experts in attendance "emphasized the need for finding mechanisms and other means for interrelating the now numerous ad hoc treaties, secretariats and international organizations concerned with various aspects of the conservation of marine mammals."[2] This chapter demonstrates that the current approach to international marine mammal conservation remains as fragmented and ad hoc as it was in 1979, and also that its rigidity renders it unable to respond to emerging threats or to adequately incorporate modern principles and norms of international governance. From this necessary overview of the current approach to marine mammal conservation, as it exists at the international and regional levels of governance (with mention of national efforts, as appropriate), the foundation for a rational international approach to marine mammal conservation will begin to emerge. Therefore, the purpose of this chapter is to provide an understanding of both the basis for the regulation of marine mammals and the current regulatory efforts, and to: (1) identify gaps in coverage (in terms of both species and area), (2) determine what has and has not worked well in the past, and (3) justify the new international regime that forms this book's central proposal.

I. RESOURCE TYPE AND ECONOMIC CONSIDERATIONS

Before embarking on a discussion of the current regulatory framework for the conservation of marine mammals, it is necessary to define the nature of this resource type and to indicate why regulation is justified.

According to the economic theory of international law, international regulation is necessary to "ameliorate international externalities."[3] International externalities exist in the ocean and are most pronounced when dealing with "common pool resources," which are those resources that are not subject to exclusive jurisdiction by one party (i.e., a state).[4] This is not a major problem for certain services that the ocean provides (such as non-consumption and nondestructive ocean science and exploration, recreational uses, or shipping) as these are "flow resources" that are not diminished by the previous user and are available to be used again directly after.[5] The common pool problem is of considerable concern regarding stock resources (where the "total physical quantity does not increase significantly over time," constituting "an economically significant reservoir with insignificant additions but with possible leakages").[6] Nonrenewable stock resources will eventually be depleted if extraction persists, and the time horizon for ultimate depletion is dependent on the size of the stock resource and the extraction rate (which, in turn, is dependent on consumer demand and extraction cost).[7] Although renewable stock resources (such as marine mammals) may be utilized in perpetuity, so long as the extraction rate does not exceed biological replacement, over-exploitation (and ultimate extinction) can occur if the rate of extraction (once again driven by consumer demand and extraction costs) is too high.[8]

These resources, which are also described as "common-property," may be held in common as they exist beyond national jurisdiction, but once captured by a user of the pool that portion of the resource becomes "exclusive property."[9] This renders common pool resources, such as oil deposits and high seas living resources, susceptible to over-exploitation because "multiple enterprises compete for the . . . resources from a common pool"[10] and states may act in a "rivalrous" manner, in which they act to secure their portion even in the face of diminishing quantity or quality of the resource.[11] In sum, economic theory suggests (and history has proven) that "rational private actors pursue their own economic interests without regard to the interests of other actors,"[12] which inevitably results in common pool resource depletion.

One possible resource management solution for resources that are either wholly situated within one sovereign's territory or that exist as a common pool resource not requiring legal regulation is voluntary cooperation.[13] Voluntary cooperation relies on all users agreeing to manage their behavior in a way that maintains the economic viability of the common pool resource. Unfortunately, voluntary cooperation is susceptible to abuse and to the free-rider problem wherein some actors choose not to comply with voluntary arrangements yet benefit from the voluntary action taken by the other users.[14] For resources located wholly within the territorial jurisdiction of one state, and in the absence of a voluntary agreement, it makes sense for the government to assert control over the resource.[15] The government may choose to exercise its property rights in a number of different ways. The two key methods of control include: (1) restrictions placed on the rate of consumption (i.e., temporal or spatial access restrictions applicable to all potential users), and (2) auctioning of rights (i.e., right to utilize a certain portion of the resource, or a complete auction whereby the entire stock is sold to private users with or without restrictions placed on future use).[16]

For living marine resources that reside (or at a minimum spend a certain amount of time) beyond areas of national jurisdiction, it is not possible for one government to claim control of the entire stock of that resource. Therefore, international cooperation is required to manage these common pool resources.[17] International cooperation is also required for living resources that migrate through more than one area of national jurisdiction, because each nation is incented to maximize the economic benefit of the resource while it is in that nation's jurisdiction.[18] International regulation is also susceptible to the free-rider problem because nations that choose to participate in international efforts to manage common pool resources, and expend resources in so doing, can have their efforts undermined by nations that pledge commitment but subsequently deviate from the prescription, or alternatively by those nations that opt to not participate in the first place.[19] If properly constructed and implemented, "international cooperation can enable nations to share the costs of regulation appropriately, or can create an international regulatory authority, to abate the free rider problem."[20] The difficulty in gaining international cooperation rests with the fact that states must perceive that it is more beneficial to act cooperatively rather than independently.[21] With these considerations in mind, I will now provide a brief overview of the legal foundation for cooperation and governance at the international level.

II. LEGAL FOUNDATION OF INTERNATIONAL OCEAN GOVERNANCE

In 1609, Hugo Grotius wrote his treatise titled *Mare Liberum* ("*The Free Sea*").[22] The legal analysis within *Mare Liberum* "advances and envisages an equal right of the Dutch to navigation and trade in the East Indies," which was, at the time, considered by the Portuguese to be an "exclusive prerogative and acknowledged monopoly."[23] The principle of res communis (the "common property") advanced by Grotius with respect to navigation, and use of the ocean generally, became (and remained) the prevailing view of and justification for freedom of navigation and use of ocean resources until the end of the nineteenth century.[24]

The nineteenth and twentieth centuries also witnessed the development and application of new technologies for the exploitation of living marine resources, resulting in new forms of conflict and cooperation.[25] Specifically, this led to two types of attempts to regulate high seas fishing: "(1) multilateral regulatory regimes established by high seas fishing states; [and] (2) unilateral measures by coastal states in areas adjacent to their territorial sea."[26] This period also witnessed confirmation of the principle of flag state jurisdictional exclusivity: "In virtue of the principle of the freedom of the seas, that is to say, the absence of any territorial sovereignty upon the high seas, no State may exercise any kind of jurisdiction over foreign vessels upon them."[27] As the twentieth century progressed, the commonly held perception that ocean resources were finite eroded and effort was taken to elucidate the emerging principles of cooperation and conservation by the International Law Commission and at the first two law of the sea conferences.[28] Ultimately, as a culmination of this effort and to help ensure that all states are able to enjoy the ocean for its many uses, the United Nations Convention on the Law of the Sea (UNCLOS) qualified traditional high seas freedoms in Article 87(2), declaring that "freedoms shall be exercised by all States with due regard for the interests of other States in their exercise of the freedom of the high seas."[29]

International law itself also evolved quite significantly since Grotius penned *Mare Liberum*, and it is currently recognized as a complex interaction between sources of law and various actors. For example, Article 38 of the Statute of the International

Court of Justice, which lists the sources that the International Court of Justice will apply when considering a dispute, provides a positivist foundation[30] for the existence and importance of international law:

Article 38
1. The Court, whose function is to decide in accordance with international law such disputes as are submitted to it, shall apply:
    a. international conventions, whether general or particular, establishing rules expressly recognized by the contesting states;
    b. international custom, as evidence of a general practice accepted as law;
    c. the general principles of law recognized by civilized nations;
    d. subject to the provisions of Article 59, judicial decisions and the teachings of the most highly qualified publicists of the various nations, as subsidiary means for the determination of rules of law.[31]

Further, the players in international law have also expanded beyond the traditional Westphalian model, which recognized states as the only legitimate actors, [32] to also include a number of cooperative international organizations (including intergovernmental organizations such as the United Nations, treaty-specific organizations, and nongovernmental organizations such as Greenpeace and the World Wildlife Fund), and even multinational corporations to a limited extent. Although these new actors play an important role in the lawmaking process, it is important to understand that they do not possess the legal rights and obligations of states. Each of the sources of law and each type of international actor indicated above factors into current international ocean governance and the management of marine mammals. The following description of oceans law governance will establish the foundation upon which the legal analysis contained in the remainder of this book is constructed.

1. The United Nations Convention on the Law of the Sea

International public law "respecting the oceans arises chiefly from international treaties and customary international law."[33] UNCLOS is the primary convention pertaining to international ocean governance, and is oft referred to as the "Constitution of the Oceans."[34] Negotiated in three distinct conferences over 24 years,[35] UNCLOS opened for signature on December 10, 1982, and came into force on November 14, 1994, one year after ratification by the sixtieth state.[36] Despite the fact that UNCLOS did not take effect until after other efforts to manage certain marine mammal species had occurred, it is important to begin this discussion of ocean governance with UNCLOS for two reasons: (1) UNCLOS codifies a number of customary rules and concepts that must be understood prior to discussing species-specific management, and (2) UNCLOS provides the framework within which this work proposes the negotiation of a new multilateral convention and creation of an International Marine Mammal Commission.

UNCLOS is unique, and significant, for many reasons. Procedurally, the negotiations at UNCLOS III were important because they proceeded by way of consensus regime-building[37] and the use of the "Gentlemen's Agreement,"[38] both of which were fairly novel for their time and proved to be effective at securing the cooperation between seemingly disparate groups of self-motivated participants.[39] Substantively, UNCLOS is important as it establishes, and describes, the following maritime zones: (1) a Territorial Sea that may not exceed 12 nautical miles (Art. 3); (2) a Contiguous Zone that may not exceed 24 nautical miles (Art. 33); (3) an Exclusive Economic Zone that may not exceed 200 nautical miles (Art. 57); (4) the Continental Shelf that, at a minimum, extends 200 nautical miles and potentially much farther (Art. 76); (5) the High Seas (Part VIII); and (6) "The Area" (otherwise known as the Deep Sea Bed, Part XI). In addition to describing and defining these maritime zones, UNCLOS also details the baselines from which each zone is measured.[40] Additionally, UNCLOS provides a comprehensive regime for maintaining freedom of navigation through the Territorial Sea (Part II, Section 3), through straits (Part III), and through archipelagic states (Art. 52). Further, UNCLOS provides for "Protection and Preservation of the Marine Environment" (Part XII), "Marine Scientific Research" (Part XIII), "Dispute Settlement" (Part XV), the management of nonliving marine resources, and the "Conservation and Management of the Living Resources of the High Seas (Part VII, Section 2), which forms the substance of this work.

One of the goals of the parties negotiating at UNCLOS III was to create a convention capable of "stand[ing] the test of time."[41] Toward this end, some of the principles embodied by UNCLOS are customary in nature,[42] other principles are detailed and provide substantive rights or obligations, whereas a third group serve as umbrella or framework provisions (these articles could also be referred to as placeholders) capable of being implemented at a later date.

Although some jurisdiction over sovereign rights within national exclusive economic zones has been passed by states to regional organizations, generally, the conservation of living marine resources within a nation's exclusive economic zone is a matter of national jurisdiction, whereby the coastal state is free to set the "allowable catch of the living resources in its exclusive economic zone," (Article 61(1)) as guided by the "best scientific evidence" (Article 61(2) and the goal of "maximum sustainable yield, as qualified by relevant environmental and economic factors" (Article. 61(3)). Further, this promotion of "optimum utilization" of living marine resources (Article 62(1)) contemplates access being granted to foreign fishing fleets if the coastal state cannot take the entire "allowable catch" itself (Article 62(2)). UNCLOS provides modified management objectives for straddling stocks ("[s]tocks occurring within the exclusive economic zones of two or more coastal States or both within the exclusive economic zone and in an area beyond and adjacent to it") in Article 63, for "Highly migratory species" in Article 64, "Anadromous stocks" (fish that breed and mature in freshwater and spend their adult life in the ocean) in Article 66, "Catadromous stocks" (fish that breed and mature in the ocean but spend their adult life in freshwater) in Article 67, "Sedentary species" in Article 68. Of particular interest is Article 65 regarding "Marine mammals":

> Nothing in this Part restricts the right of a coastal State or the competence of an international organization, as appropriate to prohibit, limit or regulate the exploitation of marine mammals more strictly than provided for in this Part. States shall cooperate with a view to the conservation of marine mammals and in the case of cetaceans shall in particular work through the appropriate international organizations for their conservation, management and study.[43]

Article 87 ("Freedom of the high seas") qualifies this traditional freedom with reference to the conditions established elsewhere in UNCLOS, by the operation of international law, and with reference to due regard to other states' rights and interests. The conservation and management of living marine resources on the high seas is addressed separately in Article 116 ("Right to fish on the high seas"), which provides that:

> All States have the right for their nationals to engage in fishing on the high seas subject to:
> (a) their treaty obligations;
> (b) the rights and duties, as well as the interests of coastal States provided for, *inter alia*, in article 63, paragraph 2, and articles 64 to 67; and
> (c) the provisions of this section.[44]

Further, Article 120 ("Marine mammals") in Section 2 ("Conservation and Management of the Living Resources of the High Seas") provides that:

> Article 65 also applies to the conservation and management of marine mammals in the high seas.[45]

The implementation of a framework provision is not without precedent. For example, the general obligations to cooperate ("either directly through appropriate subregional or regional organizations") and coordinate to ensure the conservation of straddling stocks provided in Article 63 of UNCLOS, and to cooperate ("directly or through appropriate international organizations") for the conservation of highly migratory species provided in Article 64 of UNCLOS, were found to be too general to ensure effective conservation.[46] At the request of the 1992 United Nations Conference on Environment and Development, the United Nations General Assembly convened, by Resolution 47/192, the United Nations Conference on Straddling Fish Stocks and Highly Migratory Species, which ultimately produced a new multilateral convention titled Agreement for the Implementation of the Provisions of the United Nations Law of the Sea of 10 December 1982 relating to the Conservation and Management of Straddling Fish Stocks and Highly Migratory Fish Stocks ("UN Fish Stocks Agreement").[47] Although it is beyond the scope of this section to detail the negotiation or key provisions of the UN Fish Stocks Agreement, suffice it to say it breathes life into the general provisions contained in Articles 63 and 64 of UNCLOS. The overarching purpose of this book is to similarly propose the form and substance of a new multilateral convention that implements Articles 65 and 120 in a meaningful manner. Before proceeding with a discussion of this proposal, it is necessary to consider the other components of the prevailing regime for marine mammal conservation.

2. Species and Area Based Approaches to Marine Mammal Management

As posited by William T. Burke in 1994, "[h]istorically, international regulatory attention has focused on several species of marine mammals."[48] Given the history of exploitation of pinnipeds and cetaceans described above, it should come as no surprise that early international conservation and management efforts focused on these commercially significant species. This section will briefly describe the regulation of sealing and whaling, past and present.

(1) Fur Seals and Pinniped Regulation

There is no "comprehensive global convention" for pinniped management.[49] Nonetheless, history has provided instances where, out of necessity, international cooperation has emerged. For instance, the necessity to regulate the pelagic hunt of the northern fur seal (*Callorhinus ursinus*) produced one of the first conservation treaties and an early, somewhat successful, arbitrated resolution to a conservation dispute.[50]

Prior to 1878, most of the take of northern fur seals in the Bering Sea by Russia, the United States, Japan, and the United Kingdom (through Canada) occurred on land (more precisely on islands) where seals would haul up to breed.[51] The largest population of fur seals inhabited the Pribilof Islands, which were purchased by the United States in 1867.[52] Shortly after purchasing these islands, the United States Congress prohibited pelagic sealing in the territorial sea surrounding Pribilof Island and set limits on the hunting that could occur on land.[53] These efforts did not stabilize the seal population and, in response to continued pelagic sealing, the United States asserted prescriptive and enforcement jurisdiction over an area of the Bering Sea that was outside of the ordinary three-mile territorial sea. In 1886 the United States seized three Canadian pelagic sealing vessels.[54]

The United Kingdom and the United States agreed to submit this issue to international arbitration in 1892, asking the arbiters to decide, inter alia: "Has the United States any right, and if so, what right of protection or property in the fur-seals frequenting the islands of the United States in Behring [sic] Sea when such seals are found outside the ordinary three-mile limit?"[55] Later that year the tribunal issued a ruling in favor of the United Kingdom, as well as a potentially workable solution. The tribunal's award made no distinction between fish and marine mammals for the purposes of high seas utilization[56] and found against the United States in all matters, conclusively stating that they "decide and determine that the United States has not any right of protection or property in the fur-seals frequenting the islands of the United States in [the] Bering Sea, when such seals are found outside the ordinary three-mile limit."[57] This landmark proclamation cemented the freedom of high seas for the take of living marine resources and the inability of a state to unilaterally regulate marine mammal (or fish) take outside of the territorial sea. The stage was set for future fisheries jurisdiction disputes.[58] Still, at the request of the United Kingdom and the United States, the tribunal proposed a conservation regime for both parties, which included "prohibited areas, closed seasons, limitations of the type of vessels, licensing, catch records, exchange of data, and other measures" to ensure stock sustainability.[59] Although a treaty was concluded to formalize this agreement, and a similar treaty was signed with Russia, the decrease in the northern fur seal population did not stop; a comprehensive mechanism was needed.

In 1911, Russia, the United States, the United Kingdom, and Japan signed the Convention for the Preservation and Protection of Fur Seals (the "Fur Seal Convention").[60] The Fur Seal Convention prohibited pelagic sealing (save a scientific exemption), gave the United States the exclusive right to regulate sealing in the Pribilof Islands, and established a compensation mechanism whereby the

United States would provide the other nations with a percentage of their catch or a monetary sum in the event that all sealing was prohibited.[61] Japan exited the treaty in 1941, but the 1957 Interim Convention on Conservation of North Pacific Fur Seals essentially picked up where this treaty left off and strengthened the regime by establishing a North Pacific Fur Seal Commission, which had the ability to pursue research and set catch limits.[62] This regime functioned until 1984 when it lapsed because the United States prohibited all commercial fur seal hunting. At that point legal authority to manage fur seals reverted to the state level.[63] Although the treaty regime described above has dominated much of the pinniped management discussion, there are three other treaty regimes of note.[64]

The first is the Convention in Conservation of Antarctic Seals (1972) ("Antarctic Seal Convention"), which is part of the Antarctic Treaty System (the ATS, being "the whole complex of arrangements made for the purpose of coordinating relations among states with respect to Antarctica").[65] The ATS applies to the ocean, ice shelves, and islands located south of 60°, and preserves the continent for "peaceful purposes."[66] The ATS includes a number of binding instruments, namely: the Antarctic Treaty, a Protocol on Environmental Protection to the Antarctic Treaty, Recommendations as adopted by the parties to the Antarctic Treaty, the Antarctic Seal Convention, and the Conservation of Antarctic Marine Living Resources.[67]

Over-exploitation of fur seals in South Georgia and the South Shetland Islands of the South Atlantic occurred by the 1820s.[68] The next century featured various management proposals, including the adoption of the Antarctic Treaty, and in 1964 an expedition was sent to assess the potential for a crabeater seal hunt.[69] Recognizing that existing measures did not prohibit a pelagic seal hunt, the states parties to the Antarctic Treaty initiated discussions on seal conservation. The Antarctic Seal Convention, which entered into force in 1972, is applicable to all seals in the Southern Ocean (the ocean located south of 60° and the continent of Antarctica).[70] The Antarctic Seal Convention has served as a conservation regime as no commercial hunt has occurred in the Southern Ocean since it came into force.[71] There are certain noteworthy features of this treaty, namely: (1) the Scientific Committee on Antarctic Research, an independent observer to the ATS, provides research recommendations to the parties and will report if the hunt is having a "significantly harmful effect" on seal populations (Article 5(4)(b)); (2) Annex I provides for sealing zones (Article 4), seal reserves (Article 5), and sealing seasons (Article 3); (3) reporting of a seal take is required in Article 5(7); and (4) this regime makes allowance for "special permits" issued for science, providing sustenance for man/dog, and for the take of specimens for educational purposes (Article 4). In addition to this comprehensive arrangement for the Southern Ocean, there are a number of other area-specific agreements, two of which are discussed here and one that is described in the section titled "Other Relevant Treaties and Organizations."

Seal management has also been an issue of concern for certain nations that utilize pinnipeds in the same region. The first is management of North East Atlantic seals, as coordinated by Russia and Norway through the Joint Norwegian-Russian Fisheries Commission.[72] This arrangement covers portions of the Barents Sea/White Sea and part of the Greenland Sea, and currently manages hooded seals and harp seals.[73] The Working Group on Seals assesses catch data and scientific information, and recommends future catches.[74] The most recent report by the Working Group on Seals notes that "[f]rom a scientific point of view there is no doubt that harp and hooded seal stocks in the North Atlantic are well managed and sustainably harvested with acceptable hunting methods."[75] Still, although Norway continues to allow a commercial hunt in this region, Russia has recently ceased all sealing activity and did not catch a single seal in 2011.[76]

The second bilateral agreement, the North West Atlantic Seals Agreement 1971 between Canada and Norway, strives for "the best possible protection of the seal stocks in this area and a rational utilization of these resources."[77] The treaty mainly concerns the harp seal, but has the potential to be expanded by the Commission to cover the bearded seal, hooded seal, and walrus (Article II). Most of the area covered by this treaty is now within Canada's Exclusive Economic Zone (EEZ), but cooperation is still necessary because Norway engages in pelagic sealing and the harp seal is highly migratory.[78] The majority of the sealing in this region now occurs within Canada's EEZ and, consequently, is managed by the Government of Canada.[79]

(ii) The Great Whales and "Sustainable" Whaling

Unlike pinniped regulation, there is, at least in theory, an international convention and international commission for the management of cetaceans. The International Convention for the Regulation of Whaling (ICRW), and the International Whaling Commission (IWC), which the ICRW establishes, has served as the world's primary international regime for the management of whales since it was signed into force in 1946.[80] Still, this was not the first attempt to regulate the lethal utilization of whales in the twentieth century.

As the world became aware of the problems associated with persistent overexploitation of whales post–World War I, the League of Nations attempted, through studies, to advance a framework for the regulation of global whale populations, without any success.[81] In 1931, the League of Nation's Convention for the Regulation of Whaling was opened for signature, and it came into force in 1935.[82] It purported to regulate the hunt for baleen whales in all waters including high seas and waters under national jurisdiction, restricted what whales could be caught, and mandated vessel licensing and catch statistic reporting.[83] This effort failed a few years after being instituted, but it "signaled the beginning of a new era in whaling."[84]

The next effort, the International Agreement for the Regulation of Whaling, was concluded in 1937 between nine European whaling nations.[85] It also purported to regulate whaling in all waters where factory ships and catcher vessels could whale, and expanded its scope to include both baleen and toothed whales.[86] Regulation took the form of catch restrictions, temporal limits to the pelagic whaling season, closure of certain areas of the ocean to factory ships, enforcement by flag states, and catch reporting.[87] This treaty was amended by protocol in 1938, 1944, and 1945, with the most significant amendments coming in 1944 with the decision to limit the hunt in the Southern Ocean and to institute the Blue Whale Unit (BWU) as the overarching criteria for setting catch limits.[88] The advent of World War II signaled further change to the whaling industry as many whaling fleets were significantly reduced by enemy ships; however, the end of the war also offered another opportunity to create a workable framework to regulate whaling.[89]

The United States called for the 1946 conference in Washington, DC, that produced the ICRW, which opened for signature on December 2 of that year.[90] The preamble of the ICRW reads:

> Considering that the history of whaling has seen over-fishing of one area after another and of one species of whale after another to such a degree that it is essential to protect all species of whales from further over-fishing.
> Desiring to establish a system of <u>international regulation for the whale fisheries to ensure proper and effective conservation and development of whale stocks</u> on the basis of the principles embodied in the provisions of the International Agreement for the Regulation of Whaling, signed in London on 8th June, 1937, and the protocols to that Agreement signed in London on 24th June, 1938, and 26th November, 1945.[91] [emphasis added]

In addition to observing that the 15 original parties to the ICRW recognized the history of over-exploitation, it is important to note from the outset that the ICRW was designed "to ensure proper and effective conservation and development of whale stocks and thus make possible the orderly development of the whaling industry"—meaning continued sustainable lethal utilization in what was essentially a club for whaling nations.[92] In order to achieve this aim, the ICRW has a number of important features:

(1) Scope of Coverage: The ICRW "applies to factory ships, land stations, and whale catchers under the jurisdiction of the Contracting Governments [nations that have ratified the treaty] and to the waters in which whaling is prosecuted by such factory ships, land stations, and whale catchers." Further, although the preamble references "all species of whales," there is considerable debate as to which cetacean species are covered by the ICRW. One interpretation holds that only the cetacean species included in the Annex on Nomenclature of Whales, which was attached to the final negotiating text in 1946, are within the ICRW's regulatory jurisdiction.[93] The alternative interpretation holds that the ICRW's regulatory jurisdiction is not limited to the Great Whale species.[94]

(2) The Schedule: Article I contemplates a Schedule, which forms part of the treaty. The Schedule (as described in Article V and amended by the ICRW Protocol) contains the action-oriented provisions meant to achieve "conservation and utilization of whale resources," through: "(a) protected and unprotected species; (b) open and closed seasons; (c) open and closed waters, including the designation of sanctuary areas; (d) size limits for each species; (e) time, methods, and intensity of whaling (including the maximum catch of whales to be taken in any one season); (f) types and specifications of gear and apparatus and appliances which may be used; (g) methods of measurement; (h) catch returns and other statistical and biological records; and (i) methods of inspection."[95]

(3) The International Whaling Commission (IWC): Article III of the ICRW creates the IWC as the mechanism to implement the ICRW. The Commission is comprised of one member from each "Contracting Government" to the ICRW, and each member has one vote (Article

III(1)). There are currently 89 member nations.[96] The Commission, which meets biennially, is tasked with implementing and revising the Schedule (Article V(1)), the latter being achieved only if there is a three-quarters majority vote (Article III(2)). Further, any such amendment is to be undertaken to "provide for the conservation, development, and optimum utilization of the whale resources," based on "scientific findings," and considering the interests of the whaling industry and whale consumers (Article V(2)). Article V(3) provides a mechanism by which governments can opt out of any such amendments. The IWC is also authorized to establish committees "as it considers desirable to perform such functions as it may authorize" (Article III(4)). Currently, the six committees are: (1) The Scientific Committee, (2) The Conservation Committee, (3) The Finance and Administration Committee, (4) The Aboriginal Subsistence Whaling Sub-Committee, (5) The Infractions Sub-Committee, and (6) The Working Group on Whale Killing Methods and Associated Welfare Issues.[97] The IWC also "co-ordinates and funds conservation work" and undertakes "extensive study and research on cetacean populations."[98] Finally, the IWC is empowered by Article VI of the ICRW to "make recommendations" to "any or all Contracting Governments on any matters which relate to whales or whaling and to the objectives and purposes of this Convention."[99]

(4) Enforcement: The ICRW clearly leaves enforcement of the action-oriented provisions of the regime (most notably, the Schedule) to Contracting Governments as a matter of national and flag state jurisdiction. Article IX(1) states that "[e]ach Contracting Government shall take appropriate measures to ensure the application of the provisions of this Convention and the punishment of infractions against the said provisions in operations carried out by persons or by vessels under its jurisdiction." Further, Article IX(2) directs that "[p]rosecution for infraction" shall be undertaken by the national government that has jurisdiction over the matter. In sum, the ICRW does not create an international enforcement mechanism or provide recourse to any international dispute resolution body.

(5) Commercial Moratorium: The commercial moratorium that took effect in 1986 can be found in paragraph 10(e) of the Schedule to the ICRW, which provides that "catch limits for the killing for commercial purposes of whales from all stocks for the 1986 coastal and 1985/86 pelagic seasons and thereafter shall be zero."[100]

(6) Scientific Whaling: Article VIII provides that "any Contracting Government may grant to any of its nationals a special permit authorizing that national to kill, take and treat whales for the purposes of scientific research," subject only to the obligation to report the issuance of such permits to the IWC. This provision has been subject to considerable scrutiny in the past 25 years, for reasons addressed in the following summary of IWC activity.

The history of the IWC can be broken into two distinct phases: (1) 1946–1981, characterized by a failure of the market-based approach and continued over-exploitation; and (2) 1981–present day, characterized by a moratorium on commercial whaling and emergence of the use of the scientific whaling loophole by two countries.[101] Each phase deserves some elaboration.

According to Sydney Holt, "[i]t is widely known that the International Whaling Commission ... presided during the first 20 years of its existence over the depletion of nearly all the world's populations, ... [a]nd the whaling industry, instead of enjoying an orderly development, experienced a disorderly, though long-drawn out, collapse."[102] The earliest years of IWC management were a complete failure, and the utilization of the BWU to set an overall catch quota led to competition between whaling fleets and continued over-exploitation, especially in the Antarctic.[103] In 1961 the IWC coordinated a scientific stock assessment using independent experts and their own Scientific Committee; this undertaking produced negotiated reductions in catch quotas that were phased in between 1965 and 1968.[104] Then, 1972 witnessed two important developments. First, the IWC did away with the much-maligned BWU in favor of species-specific catch limits. Second, an International Observer Scheme was implemented whereby the IWC appointed observers stationed within whaling operations who reported back on compliance matters. The IWC then instituted a "formal management procedure" in 1974 "designed to regulate the catches from each stock on an individual basis," founded on the fisheries principle of Maximum Sustainable Yield (MSY), which accounts for the biological criteria of each stock to set catch quotas at "a harvest that can be taken for an indefinite time without further depleting the stock."[105] The Scientific Committee sought to categorize each stock based on its relationship to MSY, and to then set catch quotas that would allow each stock to approach MSY.[106] Although attractive in design, this management procedure became unwieldy in application and led to disagreement and uncertainty, paving the way for the second phase of regulation—the moratorium.[107]

A moratorium on commercial whaling was first proposed by the United Nations Conference on the Human Environment, held in Stockholm, Sweden, in 1972 in the form of a 10-year ban explained in Recommendation 33 of the Action Plan that was considered by the IWC in 1973.[108] A moratorium became a topic of discussion for the IWC throughout the 1970s, which coincided with the emergence of the environmental movement, vocal environmental nongovernmental organizations, and, by the end of the 1970s, states who openly supported a moratorium.[109] In addition, IWC membership increased during this period as environmental organizations and powerful nations in the developed world helped transform the membership from one predominated by whaling nations into one concerned with conservation.[110] The IWC continued to struggle to implement the MSY principle in relation to most whale stocks, and in 1972 the United Nations Conference on the Human Environment unsuccessfully lobbied the IWC in favor of a moratorium.[111] Then, in 1982, the IWC voted 25 to 7 (with 5 states abstaining) in favor of instituting a moratorium on commercial whaling by 1986 through amendment to paragraph 10 of the Schedule.[112] As stated in the Chairman's Report of the 34th Meeting:

> Notwithstanding the other provisions of paragraph 10 [of the Schedule, which provides for stock classification around the principle of MSY], catch limits for the killing for commercial purposes of whales from all stocks for the 1986 coastal and the 1985/86 pelagic seasons and thereafter shall be zero. This provision will be kept under review, based upon the best scientific advice, and by 1990 at the

latest the Commission will undertake a comprehensive assessment of the effects of this decision on whale stocks and consider modification of this provisions and the establishment of other catch limits.[113]

Japan, the Soviet Union, Peru, and Norway formally objected to the moratorium as soon as it was passed, and, in accordance with Article V(3), this had the effect of exempting them from the amendment. Canada also acted in response to the proposed moratorium by withdrawing its membership in protest, effective June 30, 1982.[114] The IWC did reconsider the moratorium in 1990 as Japan, Norway, and Iceland opposed it, asserting that it was not scientifically supported.[115] Although Peru, the Soviet Union, and Japan eventually accepted the moratorium because of political pressure from the United States,[116] Norway announced that it would resume a limited commercial hunt for minke whales in 1992, and Iceland resumed commercial whaling in 2006, both of which continue today.[117] Although Japan maintains that it has not resumed commercial whaling, it has consistently utilized the scientific whaling clause found in Article VIII of the ICRW to pursue lethal scientific research.[118] The Japanese take approximately 1,000 great whales per year[119] and this whale meat enters the Japanese market as a consumer product.[120] This controversial so-called "special permit"/"scientific permit" exemption was recently litigated before the International Court of Justice in *Whaling in the Antarctic (Australia v. Japan: New Zealand Intervening)*, the implications of which I discuss below.[121]

The next stage in moving from lethal utilization to conservation came in the form of the creation of whale sanctuaries. The first whale sanctuary, the Indian Ocean Sanctuary, was proposed by Seychelles and established by a three-quarter majority vote of the IWC in 1979 as a mechanism to conserve whales in the area; no whaling of any sort was to be conducted within the sanctuary for a 10-year period.[122] The second sanctuary, the Southern Ocean Whale Sanctuary, was initially proposed by France in 1992 and voted into force in 1994.[123] According to author Judith Berger-Eforo, this "completed the transformation of the IWC from an international organization established to set quotas for commercial whaling, to an environmental watchdog group."[124] This sanctuary protects a significant proportion of the summer feeding grounds of the world's Southern hemisphere whale populations.[125] There have been numerous attempts to establish a new South Atlantic Sanctuary. The most recent attempt to secure a Whale Sanctuary in the South Atlantic at the 65th meeting of the IWC in 2014 failed to obtain the necessary three-quarters majority to pass.[126]

Despite sanctuary designation, Japan has consistently taken whales in the waters of the Southern Ocean Whale Sanctuary pursuant to the above-mentioned Article VIII "special permit[s],"[127] much to the IWC's chagrin.[128] The Japanese scientific take in the Southern Ocean Sanctuary was first conducted pursuant to the Japanese Whale Research Program under Special Permit in the Antarctic (JARPA), which occurred from 1987 to 2005.[129] Currently, JARPA is in its second phase, called JARPA II, which commenced in 2005–2006 and envisions a full complement of licenses to take 850 minke whales (with a 10 percent allowance adjustment), 50 fin whales, and 50 humpback whales.[130] Both programs have been implemented by the Japanese Institute of Cetacean Research, which contracts with Kyodo Senpaku for the actual whaling operations.[131] JARPA II is also the primary reason that the Australian government initiated proceedings against the Japanese government at the International Court of Justice (ICJ) (with New Zealand intervening).[132] On May 31, 2010, Australia announced in *Whaling in the Antarctic* its legal challenge to Japan's continued take of whales under the auspices of scientific whaling.[133] Australia asserted that "Japan's continued pursuit of a large-scale program of whaling under the Second Phase of its Japanese Whale Research Program under Special Permit in the Antarctic ("JARPA II") [is] in breach of obligations assumed by Japan under the International Convention for the Regulation of Whaling ("ICRW"), as well as its other international obligations for the preservation of marine mammals and the marine environment."[134] Both nations had filed declarations recognizing the compulsory jurisdiction to the ICJ pursuant to Article 36(2) of the Statute of the International Court of Justice, and the Court was unanimous in its determination that it had jurisdiction to hear the matter despite Japan's assertion that the wording of Australia's declaration excludes matters pertaining to contested exclusive economic zones.[135] The Court, by a vote of 12 to 4, concluded that the permits issued pursuant to JARPA II did not "fall within the provisions of Article VIII" and, as a result of this determination, held that JARPA II violated the ICRW Schedule's prohibition on commercial whaling, obligations with respect to taking and treating fin whales, and obligation to not take fin whales in the Southern Ocean Sanctuary.[136] The broader implications of *Whaling in the Antarctic* are explored in Chapter 6.[137]

In many respects it appears that the commercial moratorium is "de facto a permanent ban on commercial whaling," despite purporting to be a temporary and scientifically robust placeholder as a robust regime for determining catch limits as crafted by the IWC.[138] This first step to implementing this new, robust management plan, titled the "Revised Management Scheme" or "RMS" was the completion of the Comprehensive Assessment of all whale stocks by the Scientific Committee, as contemplated at the time the moratorium took effect.[139] This assessment took eight years, and resulted in the completion of the Revised Management Procedure (RMP), "a scientifically robust method of setting safe catch limits for certain stocks (groups of whales of the same species living in a particular area) where numbers are plentiful," providing a "method for calculating sustainable removal levels."[140] The RMP was adopted by resolution in 1994 (Commission Resolution 1994-5), but the IWC also recognized at this time that the catch limits set by the RMP could not be permitted until the other details of the RMS, including a new observer scheme, catch reporting method, and enforcement procedure, were incorporated into the Schedule.[141] The IWC has been working toward the creation and implementation of an RMS since the RMS Working Group was struck in 1994, but there has been little success.[142] Indeed, the IWC acknowledges that an impasse was encountered in 2006, and that no progress has been made since this time.[143] The IWC's 2011 Annual Report provides the following update:

> At its 2006 annual meeting, the commission accepted that an impasse had been reached at commission level on RMS discussions. There have been no specific discussions on the RMS in Plenary since then although the RMS was included as part of the discussions on the "Future of the IWC" held between 2007 and 2010 . . .[144]

The IWC, as it exists today, differs significantly from the earlier organizations concerned with the orderly development and sustainability of commercial whaling. In recognition of this transformation, the Japanese delegation at the 58th Annual Meeting proposed a resolution, now known as the St. Kitts and Nevis Declaration.[145] This declaration, adopted by a narrow majority vote as Resolution 2006-1, calls for the normalization of the IWC by returning to an implementation of the principles that the ICRW originally espoused.[146] Further, the declaration boldly predicts that the "IWC can be saved from collapse only by implementing conservation and management measures which will allow controlled and sustainable whaling which would not mean a return to historic over-exploitation and that continuing failure to do so serves neither the interests of whale conservation nor management."[147]

Challenging the efficacy of the ICRW/IWC regime is not a recent phenomenon. For example, Marlise Flis observed in 1986 that "[t]he inability to enforce its own provisions, coupled with political and economic pressure has reduced the IWC's effectiveness."[148] A common recognition that the prevailing regime is flawed and imperfect has prompted academic commentary offering perspectives on the issues at hand and the action that is needed.[149] Why is this now the right time to consider fundamental reform of the status quo?

The answer to this question, in my estimation, is twofold. First, it is appropriate to start considering all available options in light of the modern threats to marine mammals, as explored in Chapter 4. Second, the recognition that the ICRW/IWC regime is flawed and imperiled is not limited to academic discussion, as it has been considered by the IWC itself. The remainder of this discussion illuminates the idea that the IWC recognizes its institutional limitations, and highlights the recent events that serve to justify the contents of my proposal.

In 2007, the IWC embarked on an evaluative process called "The Future of the IWC."[150] This process was, in large part, triggered by the adoption of the St. Kitts and Nevis Declaration, adopted at the conclusion of the 58th Annual Meeting of the IWC.[151] The St. Kitts and Nevis Declaration states:

> commitment to normalising the functions of the IWC based on the terms of the ICRW and other relevant international law, respect for cultural diversity and traditions of coastal peoples and the fundamental principles of sustainable use of resources, and the need for science-based policy and rulemaking that are accepted as the world standard for the management of marine resources.[152]

This declaration introduced the notion of normalization to IWC discourse and "reaffirmed the commitment of the IWC to the original ideas of the [ICRW]."[153] Practically, this resolution entrenched the divide between the pro-whaling contingent of nations who oppose the commercial moratorium and support a return of a commercial hunt and the anti-whaling contingent of nations who oppose special permit whaling and promote the continuation of the moratorium.[154] The significance of this division cannot be ignored because it embodies the divergent positions regarding whaling "as a tradition to be preserved, abomination to be outlawed, or environmental challenge to be managed."[155] As noted by Dan Goodman, who is affiliated with the Institute of Cetacean Research in Tokyo, Japan, "[t]he dysfunctional nature of the IWC has become institutionalized as a result of the deep and seemingly irreconcilable philosophical and political divisions among the IWC member countries that support science-based management of whaling activities and those opposed to any harvesting of whales, except for what is called 'aboriginal/subsistence' whaling."[156] This work is alive to the consequences of intense anti-whaling or pro-whaling lobbying from governments and/or ENGOs (environmental nongovernmental organizations), and also the reality that the goal of achieving rational conservation may very well be frustrated by unreasonable positions on both ends of the spectrum. Still, this potential barrier should not dissuade consideration of every available option to achieve effective, rational conservation with the hope that "[w]hales and people can continue to co-inhabit the globe" for a very long time.[157]

The Future of the IWC project was driven by the Hogarth Initiative, named after the then-chairman of the IWC, Dr. Bill Hogarth,[158] and was conducted by a Small Working Group and a support group of 12 representative states.[159] It officially spanned the period between the 59th Annual Meeting (2007) and the 62nd Annual Meeting (2010),[160] and, in essence, sought to address how the IWC could "remain relevant" as the international organization charged with the conservation of the world's cetaceans.[161] This initiative engaged small working groups and inter-sessional meetings in the hope that the fissure between pro-whaling and anti-whaling nations could be bridged.[162] Unofficial side discussions also occurred throughout this process, including the Normalization of the International Whaling Commission (IWC) conference held in Tokyo, in February, 2007,[163] and the Pew Commission on Whale Conservation in the 21st Century conference, organized by the Pew Environment Group and held in Lisbon, Spain, in February 2009.[164] Another example of related side discussions is the so-called "Safety Net Initiative" that envisioned a new international organization to manage the use of plentiful species and ensure the recovery of depleted species; however, this proposal never came to fruition.[165] When the official Future of the IWC process came to an end in 2010, the Commission introduced the *Proposed Consensus Decision to Improve the Conservation of Whales*.[166] This proposal contained the following vision statement:

> The International Whaling Commission will work cooperatively to improve the conservation and management of whale populations and stocks on a scientific basis and through agreed policy measures. By improving our knowledge of whales, their environment, and the multiple threats that can affect their welfare, the Commission will strive to ensure that whale populations are healthy and resilient components of the marine environment.[167]

This document also acknowledged the fractured nature of the IWC,[168] that "the *status quo* is not an option for an effective multilateral organization,"[169] and provided a number of important components, including recommendations to:

- retain the moratorium on commercial whaling;
- suspend immediately for the 10-year period unilaterally-determined whaling under special permit, objections, and reservations;
- bring all whaling authorized by member governments under the control of the IWC;
- limit whaling to those members who currently take whales;
- ensure that no new non-indigenous whaling takes place on whale species or populations not currently hunted;

- establish caps for the next ten years that are significantly less than current catches and within sustainable levels, determined using the best available scientific advice;
- introduce modern, effective IWC monitoring, control and surveillance measures for non-indigenous whaling operations;
- create a South Atlantic Sanctuary; [*sic*]
- recognize the non-lethal value and uses of whales, such as whalewatching, as a management option for coastal States and address related scientific, conservation and management issues of such uses;
- provide a mechanism for enterprise and capacity building for developing countries;
- focus on the recovery of depleted whale stocks and take actions on key conservation issues, including bycatch, climate change and other environmental threats;
- set a decisive direction to the future work of the IWC including measures to reform the governance of the Commission; and
- establish a timetable and mechanism for addressing the fundamental differences of view amongst member governments in order to provide for the effective functioning of the Commission over the longer term.[170]

Despite prompting considerable discussion, the IWC did not adopt the proposed consensus agreement at the end of the 62nd Annual Meeting.[171] Unfortunately, this process failed to create traction or resolve the major divisive issues, including the continuation of the moratorium, whaling pursuant to nationally issued special permits, or compromise on the RMS.[172] This most recent failure to reach compromise is not altogether surprising as there is been a history of failed attempts.[173]

Normalization of the IWC has failed, and the lack of consensus among IWC member nations renders amendment of the antiquated ICRW highly unlikely.[174] Modernizing the current regime by utilizing "contemporary principles ... from other conventions whose aims are to ensure the conservation of marine biodiversity and promote healthy ecosystems" is a valid objective,[175] but the possibility of the emergence of a new international organization remains. For example, one of the recommendations from the working group associated with the Safety Net Initiative suggested that:

> an alternative to the current ICRW and IWC is required and that appropriate text should be developed to incorporate the following considerations: A convention type agreement, legally binding and restricted in membership that is global in scope, covers all cetaceans, and has a commission that makes regulations covering waters beyond national jurisdiction, provides recommendations related to cetacean use within economic exclusion zones (EEZs) at the request of the coastal State, and administers a benefit sharing program to assist research in developing countries.[176]

The failure of the Future of the IWC initiative to make meaningful progress, coupled with our continually expanding appreciation for the threats and challenges that face marine mammal conservation, renders the present an appropriate time to fully consider the substance and form of an alternative to the ICRW/IWC regime.

2014–2015 witnessed considerable international discussion surrounding the future of whaling. In addition to the ICJ decision, and the continuation of the IWC despite the failure of the Future of the IWC process to accomplish meaningful substantive change, whaling and the exploits of the Sea Shepherd Conservation Society have recently come before the American courts.[177] As it stands, Japan has announced its resumption of special permit whaling in the Southern Ocean Whale Sanctuary and has maintained its North Pacific JARPN II program under the auspices of the controversial scientific whaling exemption, Norway and Iceland continue their commercial hunt, South Korea recently indicated (then quickly withdrew) its intention to resume scientific whaling, and the potentially artificial distinction between Indigenous whaling and small-type coastal whaling remains while the IWC continues to focus its efforts on a wide variety of whale conservation issues including vessel strikes, small cetacean hunts, animal welfare concerns, whale entanglement in nets, whale watching, environmental pollution, and climate change.[178] It should come as no surprise, given this radical transformation and deviation from its original purpose, that other international fora for cetacean conservation have emerged since the implementation of the commercial moratorium. Indeed, this work is premised on my opinion that the IWC is no longer the most appropriate organization to lead the international conservation of cetaceans. With this in mind, it is appropriate to also consider the other international and regional organizations engaged with marine mammal management.

3. Other Relevant Treaties and Organizations

The first treaty that requires consideration is the Convention on Biological Diversity (CBD), which opened for signature in Rio de Janeiro during the 1992 United Nations Conference on Environment and Development.[179] The CBD's prime significance is that it was "the first international treaty to explicitly address all aspects of biodiversity," from conservation to sustainable use.[180] With respect to its role in the conservation and sustainable management of living marine resources, the CBD clearly establishes in Article 22 that it serves to regulate marine living resources only insofar as it does not conflict "with the rights and obligations of States under the law of the sea."[181] As a framework convention, the CBD operates to "fill the 'biodiversity' gaps in existing regulation" at both the national and international scale.[182] Regarding marine mammals specifically, the CBD "supplements the ad hoc approach to 'rational' or 'wise use' of common property or shard resources" in a few ways.[183]

First, although the CBD promotes both in situ (in nature) and *ex situ* (outside of natural habitats) conservation, in situ conservation is clearly prioritized over *ex situ* efforts. Article 8 identifies 13 in situ obligations that, inter alia, require states parties to establish protected areas, promote ecosystem protection, restore degraded habitat, control and/or prevent alien invasive species, respect and promote Indigenous knowledge, and legislate to protect threatened species.[184] These obligations are to be implemented "as far as possible and as appropriate."[185] Further, Article 7 supports in situ conservation by requiring states to identify and monitor important components of biological diversity.[186] Second, the CBD endorses the ecosystem approach, which the Conference of the Parties adopted as the preferred mechanism for implementation of the Convention's objectives.[187] Third, Article 14 speaks to the importance of using environmental impact assessments to minimize, as far as possible, the impact of actions or development on biological resources/diversity.[188] CDB implementation and the work of the Conference of the Parties (COP), more generally, is supported by the Subsidiary Body on Scientific, Technical and Technological Advice (SBSTTA).[189] The SBSTTA's work program continues to address "integrated marine and coastal area management; marine and coastal protected areas; sustainable use of marine and coastal living resources; mariculture; and alien species."[190]

The next treaty of import is the Convention on International Trade in Endangered Species of Wild Fauna and Flora (CITES).[191] Concluded on March 3, 1973, CITES recognizes the "ever-growing value of wild fauna and flora from aesthetic, scientific, cultural, recreational and economic points of view" and "that international co-operation is essential for the protection of certain species of wild fauna and flora against over-exploitation through international trade."[192] Although some have suggested that CITES "offers rather little protection of marine mammals,"[193] others note that "CITES is arguably the most successful of all international treaties concerned with the conservation of wildlife."[194]

CITES operates through an administrative permitting system whereby a plant or animal species listed on one of three appendices becomes subject to differing trade restrictions. A key feature of CITES is that it covers live and dead specimens, as well as "any readily recognizable part or derivative thereof."[195] Specifically, species listed on Appendix I (being "all species threatened with extinction which are or may be affected by trade")[196] are protected against trade by the strict permitting system described in Article III of CITES. Trade in species listed on Appendix II (being "all species which although not necessarily now threatened with extinction may become so unless trade in specimens of such species is subject to strict regulation in order to avoid utilization incompatible with their survival")[197] is limited to a level that "will not be detrimental to their survival," as permitted by Article IV. Finally, Appendix III allows individual nations to limit trade in certain species not listed on the other appendices and facilitates the cooperation of other states. CITES currently has 181 member nations[198] and lists approximately 931 species on Appendix I, 34,419 on Appendix II, and 147 species on Appendix III.[199]

In terms of marine mammals currently listed on the appendices, the most controversial listings, by far, relate to the great whales. Every whale species regulated by the IWC is listed on Appendix I of CITES, except for the common minke whale (*Balaenoptera acutorostrata*), which is listed on Appendix II.[200] These listings, made between 1975 and 1986,[201] were instituted to help maximize the effectiveness of the IWC moratorium on the commercial whale hunt.[202] This commitment was reaffirmed by the Conference of the Parties at COP-12, when the parties recommended by resolution that "the parties agree not to issue any import or export permit, or certificate for introduction from the sea, under this Convention for primarily commercial purposes for any specimen of a species or stock protected from commercial whaling by the International Convention for the Regulation of Whaling."[203] Japan sought review of the listing of the species covered by the IWC, on the basis that such listings were concluded without the scientific rigor that is currently employed to complete an Appendix I listing.[204] This request was ultimately unsuccessful, and the Conference of the Parties confirmed at COP-15 in 2010 that "[n]o periodic review of any great whale, including the fin whale, should occur while the moratorium by the

International Whaling Commission is in place."[205] The IWC, in Resolution 2007-4, officially acknowledges its cooperation with CITES, appreciates that "CITES recognizes the IWC's Scientific Committee as the universally recognized international organization with international expertise to review and evaluate the status of the world's whale stocks," and requests that ICRW Contracting Governments take no action to have the great whale species down-listed from Appendix I of CITES.[206] Also of note is that CITES lacks any enforcement mechanism or dispute resolution procedure independent of national enforcement.[207]

Including the great whale species listed above, there are currently 30 species of cetacean listed on Appendix I, 75 on Appendix II, and two on Appendix III. Regarding the pinnipeds, five species are listed on Appendix I, nine on Appendix II, and one on Appendix III. Three species of sirenian are listed on Appendix I, and two are listed on Appendix II. Six species of sea-frequenting otters are listed on Appendix I, four on Appendix II, and one on Appendix III. The polar bear is listed on Appendix II.[208] Despite the fact that controversy persists about the listing of cetaceans on the appendices to CITES and the overall effectiveness of the regime, CITES is a well-established regime that plays an important role in marine mammal conservation. However, its existence does not negate the necessity for, or preclude the creation of, an International Marine Mammal Commission as I propose here.

The second treaty of note is the Convention on the Conservation of Migratory Species of Wild Animals (CMS).[209] Just as the world responded to the pressures of international trade with CITES, CMS responded to the challenges of protecting species that migrate through various jurisdictions.[210] CMS has its origins in Recommendation 32 of the Action Plan produced at the 1972 Stockholm Conference on the Human Environment, which provided that "governments give attention to the need to enact international conventions and treaties to protect species inhabiting international waters or those which migrate from one country to another," specifically recommending a "broadly-based convention."[211] Germany took the lead in organizing the negotiation and drafting of the CMS, which opened for signature on June 23, 1979 and came into force on November 1, 1983.[212] The CMS currently has 116 states parties.[213]

The CMS is similar to CITES insofar as it utilizes appendices for affording protection to "Migratory Species"[214] within their "Range"[215] by "Range State[s],"[216] but as noted in *Lyster's International Wildlife Law* (2d ed.), the "system is . . . quite different from that adopted by CITES."[217] The treaty regime features the Conference of the Parties (which meets every three years) as the decision-making body capable of listing and delisting species, a Secretariat, a Standing Committee, Scientific Committee, and various working groups.[218] The CMS is implemented in two ways:

(1) Article III provides that "Endangered Migratory Species" ("endangered" meaning "in danger of extinction throughout all or a significant portion of its range") are to be listed on Appendix I, which then affords them a variety of protections, including Range State cooperation to effect habitat conservation and restoration (Article III(4)(a)), minimization of barriers to migration (Article III(4)(b)), and minimization of "factors" that do, or are likely to, endanger a species' conservation status (Article III(4)(c)). There is also a general prohibition on "taking" (defined as "taking,

hunting, fishing, capturing, harassing, deliberate killing, or attempting to engage in any such conduct") Appendix I species, subject to limited exceptions (Article III(5));

(2) Appendix II species are not covered by the same sort of restrictions applicable to Appendix I species. Rather, Article II(3)(c) provides that Range States for Appendix II species "shall endeavour to conclude Agreements covering the conservation and management of migratory species." Article IV(1) indicates that to be listed on Appendix II, and therefore suitable for such an agreement, migratory species simply have to "have an unfavourable conservation status and which require international agreements for their conservation and management, as well as those which have a conservation status which would significantly benefit from the international cooperation that could be achieved by an international agreement." Article V offers detailed guidelines for the form of such agreements, covering everything from descriptive elements (species and range covered) to dispute resolution, implementation, and monitoring. Finally, Article IV(4) provides that states parties to the CMS are encouraged to also conclude agreements for "any population or geographically separate part of the population" of a species that crosses jurisdictional lines.

Currently, there are 15 species of Cetacea, two species of Sirenia, two otter species, and one species of Pinnipedia listed on Appendix 1 of CMS, and as such the Range States for these species are obligated to protect them by taking the actions described above.[219] The majority of the conservation efforts applicable to marine mammals have occurred through formal agreements established to protect Appendix II species. It is of note that Appendix II lists many of the so-called small cetacean species that the IWC does not assert direct regulatory control over,[220] and the IWC cooperates with the CMS in terms of small cetacean conservation.[221] The following three agreements warrant further description:

(1) Agreement on the Conservation of Small Cetaceans of the Baltic, North East Atlantic, Irish and North Seas (ASCOBANS)[222]—ASCOBANS opened for signature in March 1992, and came into effect on March 29, 1994.[223] ASCOBANS was established mainly in response to diminishing common bottlenose dolphin populations in the region, but covers all small cetaceans in the Baltic Sea, North Sea, English Channel, Irish Sea, and a portion of the North East Atlantic.[224] The Conservation and Management Plan attached to ASCOBANS provides for habitat protection, by-catch reduction, and fishing gear restriction, pollution controls, and coordinated research;[225] indeed, ASCOBANS "is the first regional agreement that aims to provide comprehensive protection for small cetaceans from fisheries, pollution, and other threats."[226]
(2) Agreement on the Conservation of Cetaceans of the Black Sea, Mediterranean Sea and Contiguous Atlantic Area (ACCOBAMS)[227]—ACCOBAMS was concluded in November 1996, and came into force on June 1, 2001.[228] It covers the Black Sea, Mediterranean Sea, and

the "Contiguous area of the Atlantic Ocean west of Gibraltar."[229] ACCOBAMS, although being quite similar to ASCOBANS in that it utilizes a Conservation Plan, differs because it applies to both large and small cetaceans, and focuses on establishing protected areas and reducing the deliberate take of cetaceans.[230]

(3) Agreement on the Conservation of Seals in the Wadden Sea ("Wadden Sea Agreement")[231]—The Wadden Sea Agreement among Denmark, Germany, and The Netherlands came into force October 1, 1991.[232] This regional agreement focuses on the harbor seal and was initially contemplated to help recovery after phocine distemper devastated the population.[233] This agreement contemplates the creation of a Conservation and Management Plan (Article IV), coordinated research and monitoring (Article V), a general take prohibition (Article VI), habitat protection (Article VII), and pollution control (Article VIII). The Wadden Sea Agreement was initially quite successful, but a second outbreak of phocine distemper in 2002 has again reduced the harbor seal population.[234]

The CMS regime has also been responsible for the production of a number of memoranda of understanding for other marine mammals. Although the term "Memorandum of Understanding" (MoU) can refer to a variety of different international arrangements, in the context of the CMS they are "informal arrangements" that are not legally binding.[235] Rather, these MoUs leave the primary responsibility to protect the migratory species in question with each individual Range State and simply represent statements produced "in a spirit of mutual understanding and cooperation" that will facilitate future action to conserve the species (and/or the species' habitat) "individually or collectively."[236] MoUs may not have the same legal force as formal CMS agreements, but if they result in the production of legally binding Action Plans (which many of them contemplate) then they can be useful mechanisms.[237] To date, the CMS regime has produced the following MoUs addressing marine mammals: Memorandum of Understanding for the Conservation of Cetaceans and Their Habitats in the Pacific Islands Region, The Memorandum of Understanding on the Conservation and Management of Dugongs (*Dugong dugong*) and Their Habitats throughout Their Range, Memorandum of Understanding concerning Conservation Measures for the Eastern Atlantic Populations of the Mediterranean Monk Seal (*Monachus monachus*), and the Memorandum of Understanding concerning the Conservation of Manatee and Small Cetaceans of Western Africa and Macaronesia.[238] The CMS regime is notable in its reliance on regional agreement (both formal and informal) and regional implementation. The remainder of this section will detail other important regional arrangements.

The North Atlantic Marine Mammal Commission (NAMMCO) exists pursuant to the NAMMCO Agreement on Research, Conservation and Management of Marine Mammals in the North Atlantic, among Norway, Greenland, Iceland, and the Faroe Islands, that came into force on July 8, 1992.[239] NAMMCO began as a potential rival, or even successor organization to the IWC. It was created by pro-whaling states concerned by the IWC's reluctance to reinstitute a minke hunt that was supported by science.[240] NAMMCO purports to be an "international body for cooperation on the conservation, management and study of marine mammals in the North Atlantic."[241] In practice, NAMMCO is a regional organization that provides a forum for dialogue, cooperation, and consultation in pursuit of rational conservation and management, founded on the observation that it is easier to achieve, and maintain, cooperation at the regional level of governance.[242] It operates using a Plenary Council, Management Committees, a Scientific Committee, and a Secretariat.[243]

When NAMMCO was created, it was initially viewed as a potential replacement for the IWC; indeed, other IWC nations interested in continuing to hunt whales for commercial purposes threatened to pull out of the IWC to create similar regional agreements.[244] Still, NAMMCO has been able to coexist with the IWC rather than challenge its validity for a number of reasons. First, NAMMCO was not created to manage large whales and as such is not, strictly speaking, an alternative to the IWC.[245] Second, NAMMCO produces recommendations rather than binding resolutions or regulations that its member nations would otherwise be obliged to follow.[246] Third, NAMMCO, as a regional organization, is limited in its geographical jurisdiction and does not have jurisdictional capacity beyond the North Atlantic Ocean. Fourth, the "focus of [NAMMCO's] ... efforts for the last fifteen years [has been on] establishing a valid scientific base to describe marine mammal communities in the North Atlantic in order to become a credible research body."[247] NAMMCO has even succeeded at monitoring marine mammal hunting and at initiating ecosystem-based management.[248] NAMMCO's main advantage compared to the IWC regime, in my opinion, is that it has demonstrated a workable, regionally implemented alternative that brings together "nations with common interests," that "act as neighbors to each other, respecting NAMMCO recommendations."[249] Regionalism is a theme that I will return to in Chapters 6 and 7 when I propose an alternative structure for the international governance of marine mammals.

The next relevant international regime is The Global Plan of Action for the Conservation and Utilisation of Marine Mammals (MMAP), created through the joint effort of the United Nations Environment Programme (UNEP) and the United Nations Food and Agriculture Organization (FAO) between 1978 and 1983.[250] The United Nations recognized that it was desirable to build off existing national, regional, and international efforts to conserve marine mammals to create "a global programme,"[251] capable of responding to "growing international concerns about the status and need for conservation of marine mammal populations worldwide."[252] The goal of the MMAP was to "generate a consensus among governments on which to base their policies for marine mammal conservation."[253] The MMAP covers all marine mammal species and is constructed around the goals of "policy formulation, regulatory and protective measures, improvement of scientific knowledge, improvement of law and its application and enhancement of public understanding."[254] Many influential international organizations have signed the Memorandum of Understanding on Co-operation while nongovernmental agencies and intergovernmental agencies have both participated through the Planning and Co-ordinating Committee of the MMAP.[255]

The MMAP has "significantly contributed to the enhancement of technical and institutional capacities required for conservation and management of marine mammals in several developing regions of the world, such as Latin America and the

Caribbean, East and West Africa, and South East-Asia."[256] Further, the MMAP has coordinated action with CITES, CMS, and the Convention on Biological Diversity.[257] Still, it appears that the MMAP has been found wanting on multiple occasions. An early review completed in 1988 by the UNEP Regional Seas Programme indicated that the MMAP itself was inadequate, and there was little evidence to suggest that "the Plan [MMAP] has, in any significant way, contributed to inspire and mobilize those groups that have an interest in marine mammals."[258] UNEP initiated consultation on revision of the MMAP in 2000 at the 3rd Global Meeting of Regional Seas Conventions and Action Plans, intending to "retool this plan to increase its relevance and usefulness," but to date no formal changes have been made.[259] This leads to the need to discuss the roles that both the UNEP Regional Seas Programme and Regional Fisheries Management Organizations perform.

First, the UNEP Regional Seas Programme promotes sustainable ocean management by focusing on preventing ocean degradation and on preserving the coastal environment.[260] Aided by the UNEP Regional Seas Branch, Regional Seas programs are "prescriptions for sound environmental management to be coordinated and implemented by countries sharing a common body of water."[261] There are currently 13 Regional Seas programs that, taken together, engage 143 countries.[262] Each Regional Sea program is implemented through a legally binding regional convention, known as an Action Plan, which strives for a measure of uniformity but also enables regional modification.[263] Once completed, implementation of these various Action Plans is assisted by Regional Coordination Units and Regional Activity Centers.[264] It is of particular interest to this discussion that "UNEP has worked to build technical and institutional capacity in marine mammal conservation and management in several Regional Seas programmes," and that marine mammal conservation has been expressly incorporated into the Action Plans and/or Action Plan Protocols for the Mediterranean, South-East Pacific, Wider Caribbean, and East Africa.[265]

Second, there are Regional Fishery Bodies (RFBs). A RFB is "a group of States or organizations that are parties to an international fishery arrangement—work together towards the conservation and management of fish stocks."[266] The subset of RFBs that are of particular interest are Regional Fisheries Management Organizations (RFMOs), which are "international organizations dedicated to the sustainable management of fishery resources in international waters, such as tuna. The statutes and operational modes of each RFMO are adapted to its specific geographical circumstance and priorities."[267] The approximately 17 existing RFMOs that cover 91 percent of the world's oceans[268] are generally comprised of both coastal states and other nations that carry out distant water fishing in that area of the high seas.[269] Membership and participation in RFMOs is incentivized by the fact that coastal states and other interested states "share a practical and/or financial interest in managing and conserving fish stocks in a particular region."[270] Generally, there are two types of RFMOs: (1) those that manage tuna and swordfish (highly migratory species), and (2) those that manage pelagic fish and fish that live close to the ocean floor.[271] Each RFMO has a commission that serves as the "forum for nations to cooperate to ensure . . . long-term sustainable management."[272]

RFMOs have been bolstered by international agreements such as the UN Fish Stocks Agreement and the voluntary FAO Code of Conduct for Responsible

Fisheries.²⁷³ Together, these agreements empower RFMOs to "cooperate to establish catch limits, area closures, gear restrictions, and compliance and enforcement mechanisms; combat illegal fishing; minimize impacts on threatened species such as sea turtles, seabirds, and sharks; and oversee a program of scientific research."²⁷⁴ Of particular interest is the enforcement regime provided in the UN Fish Stocks Agreement, which retains the primacy of flag state jurisdiction but supplements it with enforcement by other RFMO member nations against non-flag state vessels and through port state measures.²⁷⁵

Certain RFMOs have also turned their attention to the problem of marine mammal by-catch. The leading example concerns the practice of purse-seine netting and dolphin by-catch in the Pacific tuna industry. The Inter-American Tropical Tuna Commission (IATTC), an RMFO, works (through the International Dolphin Conservation Program (IDCP))²⁷⁶ toward achieving zero by-catch for dolphins by procedure, gear restrictions, and observation/monitoring.²⁷⁷ This serves as a model for future RFMO participation toward achieving comprehensive marine mammal conservation and management that will be explored in greater detail in Chapters 6 and 7.

Despite presenting a promising model for regional implementation of international goals and standards, the following statement from the Pew Charitable Trusts provides a succinct summary of perceived RFMO shortfalls:

> Although these bodies play an important role in facilitating cooperation among fishing countries, they have historically failed to prevent overfishing and maintain healthy fish stocks. Many RFMOs were established at a time when ocean resources were believed to be almost inexhaustible and most were not designed to limit fishing effectively or to manage its impact on the broader marine ecosystem. Furthermore, members of RFMOs often lack the political will or clear incentives to decrease the number of vessels authorized to fish in a particular area, or to base decisions on scientific advice. These narrow mandates and lack of resolve often hinder an RFMO from acting to protect sharks or other species in its convention area. Enforcement and compliance are also major issues, because it is often difficult to identify vessels, ports, authorities, and countries that flout RFMO decisions.²⁷⁸

I will return to these initiatives when discussing regional implementation of the international framework proposed in Chapter 7. The remainder of this chapter briefly describes the dissonance that exists at the level of national regulation of marine mammals.

4. National Regulation

This section does not purport to comprehensively describe national marine mammal conservation efforts in coastal nations throughout the world. Rather, it identifies an important bifurcation in existing domestic approaches: (1) nations that employ a preservation approach to conservation, favoring non-consumptive uses of marine mammals; and (2) nations that employ a sustainable management approach that favors consumptive uses.

(1) THE UNITED STATES, NEW ZEALAND, AND AUSTRALIA

Although many nations around the world—including the Member States of the European Union[279]—have developed robust strategies to conserve and protect marine mammals, this case study focuses on the approaches taken in the United States, New Zealand, and Australia as being generally representative of a strong domestic pro-preservation approach. Not surprisingly, all three nations no longer pursue a commercial take of cetaceans. New Zealand stopped commercial whaling in 1964,[280] the United States in 1971,[281] and Australia in 1978.[282] Since then, each nation has enacted domestic legislation that affords all marine mammal species with considerable protection. Further, each nation recognizes that the current threats to marine mammals are varied and complex, and require a comprehensive response.

In the United States, marine mammal management occurs primarily within the regime created in 1972 by the Marine Mammal Protection Act (MMPA),[283] "enacted in response to increasing concerns among scientists and the public that significant declines in some species of marine mammals were caused by human activities."[284] The MMPA was innovative in that it: (1) replaced previously disparate state-run initiatives;[285] (2) protected population "stocks" ("a group of marine mammals of the same species or smaller taxa in a common spatial arrangement that interbreed when mature");[286] (3) established a moratorium (Title 1 Sec. 101) for the "take" (defined as meaning "to harass, hunt, capture, or kill, or attempt to harass, hunt, capture, or kill any marine mammal"[287]) of marine mammals in United States' waters and marine mammal importation, subject to limited exception;[288] (4) placed the burden of demonstrating that "proposed taking of living marine resources would not adversely affect the resource or the ecosystem" on the user of the resource;[289] and (5) replaced "maximum sustainable yield" with the concept of "optimum sustainable populations," being "the number of animals which will result in the maximum productivity of the population or the species, keeping in mind the carrying capacity of the habitat and the health of the ecosystem of which they form a constituent element."[290]

The MMPA was also innovative in its creation of the Marine Mammal Commission (MMC). The MMC, established by Title II of the MMPA, exists as "an independent agency of the U.S. Government.... to provide independent oversight of the marine mammal conservation policies and programs being carried out by federal regulatory agencies";[291] it is comprised of "three members who are nominated by the President and confirmed by the Senate."[292] The MMC is tasked with seven duties: (1) to review the efforts of the United States "pursuant to existing laws and international conventions relating to marine mammals"; (2) to continually review marine mammal stocks, hunting methods, protection methods, and applications for a permitted exception to the moratorium; (3) to conduct, or facilitate, studies on marine mammal conservation; (4) to issue recommendations to the appropriate representatives of the federal government regarding marine mammal conservation; (5) to recommend appropriate policies given current international treaties, and "suggest appropriate international arrangements for the protection and conservation of marine mammals"; (6) to recommend listing marine mammals as endangered; and (7) to issue recommendations on any other "measures as it deems necessary or desirable to further the policies" of the MMPA.[293]

The final aspect of the domestic marine mammal conservation in the United States that warrants discussion at this point is the use of domestic American law and policy to effectuate international marine mammal conservation. Given that enforcement of the moratorium on taking marine mammals is limited in its application to the American fishing fleet and foreign vessels fishing within American waters (i.e., the 200 nautical mile EEZ limit), the United States has taken additional legislative action to protect marine mammals.[294] The most relevant legislation is the U.S. Pelly Amendment,[295] which, in part, contains a series of punitive provisions designed to bring foreign fishermen into compliance with domestic American conservation measures.[296] The U.S. Pelly Amendment provides:

(a) Certification to President.
   (1) When the Secretary of Commerce determines that nationals of a foreign country, directly or indirectly, are conducting fishing operations in a manner or under circumstances which diminish the effectiveness of an international fishery conservation program, the Secretary of Commerce shall certify such fact to the President.
   (2) When the Secretary of Commerce or the Secretary of the Interior finds that nationals of a foreign country, directly or indirectly, are engaging in trade or taking which diminishes the effectiveness of any international program for endangered or threatened species, the Secretary making such finding shall certify such fact to the President.[297]

Based on the diminishing effectiveness test, section 4 provides that the "President may direct the Secretary of the Treasury to prohibit the bringing or the importation into the United States of any products from the offending country for any duration as the President determines appropriate" (as conducted in accordance with the World Trade Organization and other multilateral trade agreements), which has led to complex international litigation challenging the legality of its trade restrictions[298] and the section has also played a role in the whaling controversy and Japan's scientific whaling in the 1980s.[299] In the context of marine mammal conservation, the U.S. Pelly Amendment was most recently utilized in July 2011 when U.S. Department of Commerce Secretary, Gary Locke, certified Iceland for violating the IWC's international ban on commercial whaling. President Obama declined the opportunity to impose sanctions, opting instead to send an envoy to Iceland to monitor whaling and try to negotiate cessation.[300] The U.S. Pelly Amendment remains a somewhat controversial, yet successful, domestic tool for enforcing international conservation generally and marine mammal conservation specifically.

Pursuant to section 3A of New Zealand's Marine Mammals Protection Act 1978 (MMPA 1978), the "Department of Conservation shall administer and manage marine mammals and marine mammal sanctuaries."[301] Section 4 provides the general prohibition (subject to receiving a permit) on "taking or holding" marine mammals, and in this context "take" is defined as to mean "to take, catch, kill, injure, attract, poison, tranquillise, herd, harass, disturb, or possess," or "to brand, tag, mark," or "to flense, render down, or separate any part from a carcass," or to attempt to do any of the above.[302] In addition to this "take" prohibition, section 22 of the MMPA 1978 also provides for the designation of marine mammal sanctuaries, which can have activity restrictions, or other restrictions, as specified by the Minister of the Department of Conservation (section 22(3)).[303]

In addition to the MMPA 1978, the Department of Conservation's actions to conserve marine mammals are also directed by the Department of Conservation Marine Mammal Action Plan 2005–2010 ("Action Plan 2005-2010"), which indicates that the Department of Conservation will act "firstly to protect species, and secondly to manage human interactions and use."[304] The Action Plan 2005–2010 also provides detailed guidance organized species-by-species, replete with objectives, priorities, and action statements.[305] It is also worth noting that New Zealand has developed regulations to address the negative consequences of ecotourism in its Marine Mammals Protection Regulations 1992,[306] which "establish a public procedure for applying for permits to conduct passengers to view marine mammals and prescribe appropriate behaviour for all boats (and aircraft) in their vicinity."[307] New Zealand has also tackled whale-stranding events with an organized policy and has sought to reduce marine mammal by-catch from fisheries through "fishing prohibitions and restrictions" crafted in conjunction with the Ministry of Fisheries, which "effect set netting, trawling, and drift netting" and both commercial and recreational fishing.[308] Australia is similarly situated geographically and in terms of marine mammal abundance. The Australians have also emerged as leaders in marine mammal preservationist conservation.

Australia protects its marine mammal species (cetaceans, pinnipeds, and sirenians) through the Environment Protection and Biodiversity Conservation Act 1999 (EPBCA).[309] Regarding cetaceans, the Australian federal government asserts that it is "a world leader"[310] in this regard, and the main tool for conservation is the Australian Whale Sanctuary (the "Australian Sanctuary") established pursuant to section 225(2) of the EPBCA, which covers "all Commonwealth waters from the three nautical mile state waters limit out to the boundary of the Exclusive Economic Zone."[311] Sections 229–230 of the EPBCA provide that it is an offense to "kill, injure or interfere with a cetacean" within the Australian Sanctuary.[312] Further, all state and territorial governments have committed to afford cetaceans with the same level of protection for cetaceans within their state/territorial water.[313] The Australian government has also produced recovery plans for the five threatened whale species that inhabit Australian waters.[314]

Australia's EPBCA also addresses sirenians and pinnipeds. Specifically, every species of seal, sea lion, and dugong found in Australian waters is a "listed marine species" pursuant to section 248 of the EPBCA, which means that it is an "offence to kill, injure, take, trade, keep or move" any of these species without a permit (section 254).[315] A notable exception to this is that dugongs "may be legally hunted by Aboriginal and Torres Strait Islander people under section 211 of the *Native Title Act 1993* for personal, domestic or non-commercial communal needs," in recognition of the important role that they have traditionally played.[316] Three seal species receive extra protection as they are listed as having a vulnerable threatened status under section 178 of the EPBCA, meaning "any action that has, will have or is likely to have a significant impact on a threatened species must be referred to the Department of the Environment for assessment before the action goes ahead."[317] Finally, a recovery plan has been produced for three vulnerable seal species.[318] The government of Australia demonstrated its commitment to continued marine mammal conservation in December 2008 with the announcement of the International

Whaling and the Marine Mammal Conservation Initiatives Program, which provides "funding of more than $32 million over six-years for a comprehensive package of non-lethal whale research and other marine mammal conservation initiatives."[319]

(ii) Nations That Take Marine Mammals

A number of nations actively hunt marine mammals, and this is reflected in their policies (both domestic and international) and their regulatory framework.[320] These nations have a number of shared characteristics that may help explain their continuing marine mammal take, including a history of whaling, local consumption of marine mammal tissue, and trading practices that include marine mammal parts.[321] This section focuses on the major marine mammal hunts that continue for key species that retain commercial value. It is important to acknowledge that other marine mammals, including the sea otter, polar bear, and sirenian species, are also hunted in different regions of the world.

The marine mammal hunts that are currently being conducted by these nations fall into distinct categories: (1) a great whale take, (2) a small cetacean take, and (3) a pinniped take. I will now briefly address each category and the contribution made by each nation.

(a) Great Whale Take

Only a handful of nations currently take great whale species. Norway utilized the opt-out/objection provisions of the ICRW when the commercial moratorium on whaling came into effect, and continues to hunt up to 700 minke whales annually.[322] Similarly, Iceland pursues a commercial take for great whales, including the endangered fin whale, having utilized the opt-out/objection provision of the ICRW, and exports much of its national take to Japan.[323] Japan attracts the most attention for their continued whale hunt, owing to the number of whales they take, the scientific whaling justification advanced for the take, the location of the take, and the fact that they have become the target of the Sea Shepherd Conservation Society, a controversial environmental organization founded by Paul Watson.[324] Japan hunts minke whales in the Southern Whale Sanctuary and sei whales, sperm whales, and Bryde's whales in the North Atlantic.[325] At the 65th Annual Meeting of the IWC, Japan unsuccessfully proposed an amendment to the Schedule to allow small-type coastal whaling from the West Pacific minke whale stock in the Okhotsk Sea.[326] Japan has repeatedly sought the introduction of a small-type coastal whaling allowance since the commercial moratorium and has framed it as an attempt to relieve the burden on those coastal communities that are most significantly impacted by the IWC's commercial moratorium.[327]

Other nations have Aboriginal groups that continue to hunt great whale species. This hunt can take two forms. First, nations that belong to the IWC can submit "need statements" to the IWC Commission detailing "the cultural and nutritional requirements of the native communities for whaling," and the Commission can in turn set "strike and catch limits" (and other regulatory controls) to different nations based on the advice of the standing group of the Scientific Committee that addresses Aboriginal subsistence whaling.[328] Currently, "aboriginal subsistence whaling is permitted for Denmark (Greenland, fin and minke whales), the Russian Federation (Siberia, gray and bowhead whales), St. Vincent and The Grenadines

(Bequia, humpback whales) and the USA (Alaska, bowhead whales; Washington State, gray whales)."[329] The second form of Aboriginal take is that which occurs outside of the sanctioned IWC process. For example, Canada left the IWC in response to the commercial moratorium and its potential impact on Aboriginal subsistence whaling, and since 1982 has domestically regulated the hunt by its Inuit peoples (northern Aboriginal peoples) for bowhead whales, narwhal whales, and beluga whales (the latter two species do not qualify as great whale species) through cooperation and agreement between the Inuit and the government of Canada, Department of Fisheries and Oceans.[330] In addition to the continued take of great whale species, smaller whales, porpoises, and dolphins are also subject to direct hunts.

(b) Small Cetacean Take

A number of coastal nations are also engaged in the take of small cetaceans (whales other than the great whales, dolphins, and porpoises). Inhabitants of the Faroe Islands trace their consumption of whale meat back to the Vikings.[331] The Faroe Islands have traditionally hunted pilot whales using an activity called "grindadráp" or the "grind," whereby the whales are corralled into shallow inlets and fishermen proceed to stab the animals in the back of the neck until they are dead.[332] There were 14 grinds in 2010, which, in total, killed 1,107 whales.[333] Similar drives are organized for Risso's dolphins.[334]

Japan also has an extensive sanctioned small cetacean hunt, which kills an estimated 20,000 dolphins, porpoises, and whales (most notably the Dall's porpoise and Baird's beaked whale).[335] The traditional methods used to kill small cetaceans involve bow-mounted harpoons, handheld harpoon hunts, and drive hunts (similar to the Faroese grinds).[336]

Greenland's national small cetacean hunt uses a partial quota system, administered by the government of Greenland, Department of Fisheries, Hunting and Agriculture.[337] In 2011, Greenland set the quota for narwhal whales at 380 and the quota for beluga whales at 310,[338] while the hunt for harbor porpoise, white-sided/white-beaked dolphin, pilot whales, killer whales, and bottlenose dolphin proceeded without a quota.[339] Many of the nations that continue to hunt cetaceans also take pinnipeds, as described below.

(c) Pinniped Take

Seal hunts attract the attention of the media and environmental organizations, mainly because of the killing methods associated with such hunts. The take with the most notoriety is the Canadian hunt for the harp seal, hooded seal, and gray seal. The Canadian seal hunt is regulated by the government of Canada, Department of Fisheries and Oceans through an Integrated Fisheries Management Plan that seeks stakeholder input (which is important given the fact that the seal hunt has an important economic role for many communities) and strives for sustainability through application of the precautionary approach and Total Allowable Catch (TAC) limits.[340] The TAC for harp seals was 400,000 in 2011, up from 330,000 in 2010 and 280,000 in 2009.[341] The TAC for hooded seals has remained at 8,200 per year since 2007, while the TAC for grey seals was set at 60,000 in 2011, up from 50,000 in 2009 and 2010, and up from the 12,000 from 2007 and 2008.[342]

Commercial sealing is also pursued by Norway, which occurs in both Norwegian waters and within Iceland's EEZ.[343] In 2010, Norway killed 4,783 harp seals and 178 hooded seals.[344] Greenland also engages in a pinniped hunt for seals and walruses, with quotas only for walrus. In 2011, the walrus quota was set at 130, and the most recent catch data for seals indicates that 65,669 ringed seals, 1,986 hooded seals, 73,345 harp seals, 33 harbor seals, and 1,258 bearded seals were taken in 2009.[345] Sweden[346] and Finland[347] also maintain a hunt for grey seals and Baltic ringed seals. Iceland's take of seals is considerably less than these other nations as only 121 grey seals, 64 harbor seals, and 12 harp seals were hunted in 2010.[348] Finally, Namibia is the only nation in the southern hemisphere to sanction a seal hunt, and the government of Namibia has indicated, in response to criticisms levied by environmental groups, that the hunt is a necessary cull to reduce the impact that the burgeoning seal population is having on the coastal ecosystem; however, contradictory evidence suggests that the hunt is continued for economic profit.[349] This hunt of cape fur seals permits the taking of 80,000 seal pups and 6,000 bull seals.[350] Taken together, the statistics presented in this section demonstrate that marine mammal hunting is still significant in many regions of the world.

III. CONCLUSION

This chapter has demonstrated that regulatory efforts to effectuate marine mammal conservation are justified and necessary. Further, the assessment contained within indicates that marine mammal conservation is occurring at the international, regional, and national levels of governance. This fragmented response has created gaps in species coverage and habitat protection and has produced inconsistent conservation and management.

The sources of international law that govern marine mammals are both customary and codified as treaty law. UNCLOS includes framework provisions that contemplate heightened marine mammal conservation, and implementation of these provisions has the potential to remedy the deficiencies of the status quo. In Chapter 3, I establish the framework that guides the remainder of this analysis and consider the goals and objective of this work in some detail.

NOTES

1. Patricia Birnie, *The Role of Law in Protecting Marine Mammals*, 15(3) AMBIO 137, 137 (1986) ["Birnie, *The Role of Law*"].
2. Patricia Birnie, *Conservation of Marine Mammals—Law and Enforcement*, MAR. POL'Y 255, 257 (1980).
3. Eric A. Posner & Alan O. Sykes, *Economic Foundations of the Law of the Sea*, 104 AM. J. INT'L L. 569, 570 (2010) ("[f]or example, consider a firm that is conducting an activity that generates pollution, and assume that the pollution flows across the border to another nation. Because the harm occurs abroad, the government of the nation where the firm is located may have no incentive to take measures to control the pollution, even if such measures would be worth their costs from a global perspective") ["Posner & Sykes"].
4. *Id*. at 570–71 (note that this issue was brought to the forefront of the understanding of resource conservation at the end of the 1960s by Garrett Hardin (*Tragedy*

of the Commons, 162(3859) Sci. 1243 (1968) where he outlines this theory); *see also* Peter Stoett, The International Politics of Whaling 47–48 (1997) (asserting that "It is a popular error to consider the near-extinction of the great whales as a true 'tragedy of the commons.' No doubt, whales are part of what the sovereignty-dominated world political system has seen fit to declare is the commons. But the basic idea behind the tragedy of the commons is that, in order to pursue what on an individual level is self-interest, economic actors, such as medieval farmers or contemporary fishers, would allow their livestock to graze as much fallow common land or take as much common fish as possible. The tale of whaling may more properly be viewed as one of barely mitigated greed on the part of several actors [and] more a race for survival among whaling operations").

5. *See* James J. Sullivan & H. Fernando Arias, *Concepts and Principles for Environmental Economics*, 2 Envtl. Aff. 597, 606–07 (1972–1973) ["Sullivan & Arias"]; *see also* S.V. Ciriacy-Wantrup, Resource Conservation: Economics and Policies 38 (1952).
6. Sullivan & Arias, *supra* note 5, at 605.
7. John Warren Kindt & Charles J. Wintheiser, *The Conservation and Protection of Marine Mammals*, 7 U. Haw. L. Rev. 301, 304–05 (1985) ["Kindt & Wintheiser"].
8. *Id.* at 304–05.
9. Patricia Birnie, Alan Boyle & Catherine Redgwell, International Law & the Environment 194–95 (3d ed. 2009).
10. Posner & Sykes, *supra* note 3, at 571.
11. *Id.* at 573 (note that these authors correctly observe that the ocean also serves as a global commons in the way that states utilize it as a communal dumping ground for land-based sources of pollution and vessel-based sources of pollution. This commons problem is analogous to the climate change dilemma where the world's atmosphere is the global commons that is being polluted by each nation, without any direct ownership).
12. *Id.* at 574.
13. *Id.*; *see generally* Elinor Ostrom, Governing the Commons: The Evolution of Institutions for Collective Action (1990) (which assesses, in detail, the theoretical frameworks associated with commons governance).
14. This free-rider problem is quite pronounced in the climate change context (*see* Voluntary Approaches in Climate Policy 78–81 (Andrea Baranzini & Philippe Thalman eds., 2004)).
15. Posner & Sykes, *supra* note 3, at 574.
16. *Id.*
17. *Id.* at 575.
18. *Id.*
19. *Id.*
20. *Id.*
21. *Id.*
22. *See* Hugo Grotius: Mare Liberum 1609–2009 (Robert Feenstra ed., 2009) (which contains a reproduction of the original text—in Latin—from the first edition, and also an English translation).
23. *Id.* at x.
24. R.R. Churchill & A. Lowe, The Law of the Sea 2 (3d ed. 1999) ["Churchill & Lowe"].

25. Yoshinobu Takei, Filling Regulatory Gaps in High Seas Fisheries: Discrete High Seas Fish Stocks, Deep-Sea Fisheries and Vulnerable Marine Ecosystems 14 (2013) ["Takei"].
26. *Id.* (early multilateral attempts include the Convention Between Her Majesty, The German Emperor, King Of Prussia, The King Of The Belgians, The King Of Denmark, The President Of The French Republic, And The King Of The Netherlands, For Regulating The Police Of The North Sea Fisheries, The Hague, May 6, 1882).
27. The Case of the S.S. "Lotus", 1927 P.C.I.J. (ser. A) No. 10, at 25 (Sept. 7).
28. See Takei, *supra* note 25, at 16–27 (tracing these historical developments).
29. 10 Dec. 1982, 21 I.L.M. 1261, 1833 U.N.T.S. ["UNCLOS"].
30. Churchill & Lowe, *supra* note 24, at 5.
31. Statute of the International Court of Justice art. 38, 59 Stat. 1031, 39 AJIL Supp. 215 (1945) ["Statute of the ICJ"] (note that in addition to these sources, "soft law" has emerged as an area of significance, and "may be loosely defined as declared norms of conduct understood as legally nonbinding by those accepting the norms" (Jeffrey L. Dunoff, Steven R. Ratner & David Wippman, International Law: Norms, Actors, Process 36 (3d ed. 2010).
32. *See* Friedrich Kratochwil, *Legal Theory and International Law*, in Routledge Handbook of International Law 59–60 (David Armstrong ed., 2009) (indicating the theoretical equality of states under the Westphalian approach to international law).
33. Ted L. McDorman et al., International Oceans Law: Materials and Commentaries 11 (2005).
34. *See* Tommy T.B. Koh, *A Constitution for the Oceans* (adapted from remarks made between Dec. 6 and 11, 1982), http://www.un.org/Depts/los/convention_agreements/texts/koh_english.pdf (last visited Feb. 16, 2016) ["*A Constitution for the Oceans*"].
35. The Fist United Nations Conference on the Law of the Sea (UNCLOS I) took place between February 24 and April 29, 1958, and produced the four 1958 Geneva Conventions. The Second United Nations Conference on the Law of the Sea (UNCLOS II) convened between March 17 and April 26, 1960, and did not produce any negotiated agreements. The Third United Nations Conference on the Law of the Sea (UNCLOS III) was negotiated over nine years (1973–1982), by 160 nations, and the resulting negotiated treaty opened for signature on December 10, 1982 (*see* UNEP Shelf Programme, *Background to UNCLOS*, UNEP, http://www.continentalshelf.org/about/1143.aspx) (last visited Feb. 16, 2016).
36. *Id.*
37. *See* Barry Buzan, *Negotiating by Consensus: Developments in Technique at the United Nations Conference on the Law of the Sea*, 75(2) Am. J. Int'l L. 324, 324–26 (1981) (note that at 326, Buzan provides the following definition of consensus: "some form of decision making by consent that does not involve recourse to voting").
38. Tommy Koh, *Lecture for the UN Library: The Negotiating Process of UNCLOS III*, at 1, http://legal.un.org/avl/pdf/ls/Koh_T_outline_2.pdf.
39. *Id.* at 2 (here, Koh lists different groupings of states that were motivated by different ocean interests (i.e., archipelagic states, states with ocean straits, states with broad continental shelves, the developed states, and developing states)).
40. UNCLOS, *supra* note 29, at arts. 5 & 7.

41. *A Constitution for the Oceans, supra* note 34.
42. There are a number of customary legal principles contained in UNCLOS, with some commentators going so far as to assert that "most of its provisions are considered rules of customary law" (Daniela Diz Pereira Pinto, Fisheries Management in Areas beyond National Jurisdiction 196 (2013)). The most widely accepted customary principles are found in the Articles of Part XII ("Protection and Preservation of the Marine Environment"), which includes the Article 192 ("General Obligation") that: "States have the obligation to protect and preserve the marine environment" (*see* Philippe Sands & Jacqueline Peel, Principles of International Environmental Law 349–50 (2012)).
43. UNCLOS, *supra* note 29, at art. 65.
44. *Id.* at art. 116.
45. *Id.* at art. 120.
46. United Nations Briefing, *DOALOS/UNITAR Briefing on Developments in Ocean Affairs and the Law of the Sea 20 Years after the Conclusion of the United Nations Convention on the Law of the Sea, Wednesday, 25 and Thursday, 26 September 2002 United Nations Headquarters, New York, Conference Room 5*, http://www.un.org/Depts/los/convention_agreements/convention_20years/1995FishStockAgreement_ATahindro.pdf.
47. *Id.*; Dec. 4, 1995, 34 I.L.M. 1542, 2167 U.N.T.S. 3 ["UN Fish Stocks Agreement"]. Further, work is ongoing to negotiate a new implementing agreement to address the conservation and sustainable management of biodiversity in areas beyond national jurisdiction. *See* Division for Ocean Affairs and the Law of the Sea, Ad Hoc *Open-Ended Informal Working Group to Study Issues Relating to the Conservation and Sustainable Use of Marine Biological Diversity beyond Areas of National Jurisdiction*, (Mar. 13, 2015) http://www.un.org/depts/los/biodiversityworkinggroup/biodiversityworkinggroup.htm.
48. William T. Burke, The New International Law of Fisheries: UNCLOS 1982 and Beyond 257 (1994).
49. Birnie, *The Role of Law, supra* note 1, at 140 (this statement remains true today).
50. Michael Bowman et al., Lyster's International Wildlife Law 4 (2d ed. 2010) ["Lyster's International Wildlife Law"].
51. Kindt & Wintheiser, *supra* note 7, at 317.
52. *Id.*
53. *Id.* at 317–18.
54. *Id.*; *see also* H.W. Blodgett, *The Fur Seal Arbitration*, 3 N.W. L.R. 73, 81 (1895) (note that the American court system upheld the validity of these vessel seizures, based on the principle of "*mare clausum*" or "closed sea" over which the United States had authority).
55. Award between the United States and the United Kingdom relating to the rights of jurisdiction of United States in the Bering's sea and the preservation of fur seals, 267 Rep, Int'l. Arb. Awards (Aug. 15, 1893); Fur Seal Arbitration (U.S. v. Gr. Brit.), *reprinted in* 9 Fur Seal Arbitration: Proceedings of the Tribunal of Arbitration 263, 269 (1895) ["Fur Seal Arbitration"].
56. Simone Borg, Conservation on the High Seas: Harmonizing International Regimes for the Sustainable Use of Living Resources 143 (2012).
57. *Id.* at 269.
58. Other notable international disputes that contributed to the development of the regulation of high seas fisheries resources include: the Anglo Norwegian

Fisheries Jurisdiction Case (United Kingdom v. Norway), 1951 I.C.J. Rep. 116 (Dec. 18) (wherein the U.K. unsuccessfully challenged a Norwegian declaration that established an exclusive fisheries zone using baselines that accounted for Norway's deeply indented coastline); the Fisheries Jurisdiction Case (United Kingdom of Great Britain and Northern Ireland v. Iceland), 1974 I.C.J. Rep. 3 (July 25) (wherein the U.K. challenged Iceland's unilateral extension of its exclusive fisheries zone from 12 nm to 51 nm. The Court determined that Iceland could not exclude the U.K. from its expanded zone in light of an earlier agreement, but also that good faith negotiations had to occur between the states to equitably distribute fishery rights beyond the 12 nm zone, taking into account Iceland's particular reliance on these fishery resources); Fisheries Jurisdiction Case (Spain v. Canada), 1998 I.C.J. Rep. 432 (Dec. 4) (wherein Spain challenged Canada's enforcement of coastal fisheries law against Spanish flagged ships beyond its EEZ. The Court dismissed the case on jurisdictional grounds owing to its interpretation of the reservations in Canada's declaration of compulsory jurisdiction).

59. FRANCISCO ORREGO VICUNA, THE CHANGING INTERNATIONAL LAW OF HIGH SEAS FISHERIES 14–15 (1999); *see also* Fur Seal Arbitration, *supra* note 55, at 270–72; *see also* YOSHIFUMI TANAKA, THE INTERNATIONAL LAW OF THE SEA 226 (2012) (suggesting that this arbitral decision is an early example of the effort to "reconcile the interest of the distant-water fishing States and the need for conservation of marine species," and is also evidence of "the difficulty of the conservation of marine species migrating between marine spaces under and beyond national jurisdiction").

60. 7 July 1911, 37 Stat. 1542, T.S. No. 564.

61. 9 Feb. 1957, 8 U.S.T. 2283, 314 U.N.T.S. 105; *see also* Kindt & Wintheiser, *supra* note 7, at 318.

62. Kindt & Wintheiser, *supra* note 7, at 318–19 (a 1976 Protocol also enabled scientific research into the interaction between marine mammals and other marine life, and to set humane killing methods).

63. Marine Mammal Commission, *Annual Report to Congress: 1997*, at 65, (1998), http://mmc.gov/reports/annual/pdf/1997annualreport.pdf.

64. Note that there is also the bilateral agreement between Canada and Norway regarding the hooded seal, bearded seal, and walrus (Agreement between the Government of Canada and the Government of Norway on Sealing and the Conservation of the Seal Stocks in the Northwest Atlantic, July 15, 1971, C.T.S. 49).

65. 1 June 1972, 29 U.S.T. 441, 11 I.L.M. 251; U.S. Department of State, *Handbook of the Antarctic Treaty System Chapter II: The Antarctic Treaty System: Introduction*, 1, (2002), http://www.state.gov/documents/organization/15272.pdf.

66. 1959 Antarctic Treaty, art. 1, 1 Dec. 1959, 12 U.S.T. 794, 402 U.N.T.S. 71; Scientific Committee on Antarctic Research, *The Antarctic Treaty System: An Introduction*, (2016), http://www.scar.org/treaty/ ["Antarctic Treaty"].

67. *Id.* (the Antarctic Treaty, which entered into force in 1961, was initially signed and ratified by 12 nations (Argentina, Australia, Belgium, Britain, Chile, France, Japan, New Zealand, Norway, South Africa, the United States, and the Soviet Union)); 20 May 1980, 33 U.S.T. 3476, 1329 U.N.T.S. 48.

68. U.S. Department of State, *Handbook of the Antarctic Treaty System Chapter IX: Conservation of Antarctic Seals: CCAS*, 326, (2002), http://www.state.gov/documents/organization/15280.pdf.

69. *Id.*

70. *Id.*
71. *Id.*
72. Joint Norwegian-Russian Fisheries Commission, *Home*, http://www.jointfish.com/eng (last visited Feb. 16, 2016); *see also* Birnie, *The Role of Law, supra* note 1, at 140 (describing the precursors to this arrangement).
73. *See* Joint Norwegian-Russian Fisheries Commission, *Report of the Working Group on Seals*, (Oct., 2011), http://www.regjeringen.no/upload/FKD/Vedlegg/Kvoteavtaler/2012/Russland/NORRUS2011Appendix8.pdf ["*Report of the Working Group on Seals*"]; *see also* The Norwegian Ministry of Fisheries and Coastal Affairs, *Sealing*, (Mar. 19, 2013), http://www.fisheries.no/ecosystems-and-stocks/marine_stocks/mammals/seals/sealing/.
74. *Report of the Working Group on Seals, supra* note 73.
75. *Id.* at section 5.1.
76. *Id.*
77. Agreement between the Government of Canada and the Government of Norway on Sealing and the Conservation of the Seal Stocks in the Northwest Atlantic, preamble, July 15, 1971, C.T.S. 49.
78. Birnie, *The Role of Law, supra* note 1, at 140.
79. *Id.*
80. 2 Dec. 1946, 62 Stat. 1716, 161 U.N.T.S. 74 ["ICRW"]; *see* Kurkpatrick Dorsey, Whales & Nations: Environmental Diplomacy on the High Seas (2013) (providing a comprehensive historical analysis of the progression of whaling through the nineteenth and twentieth centuries).
81. *See* Cinnamon Carlarne, *Saving the Whales in the New Millennium: International Institutions, Recent Development and the Future of International Whaling Policies*, 24 Va. Envtl. L.J. 1, 4 (2005–2006) ["Carlarne"].
82. R. Gambell, *International Management of Whales and Whaling: An Historical Review of the Regulation of Commercial and Aboriginal Subsistence Whaling*, 48(2) Arctic 97, 98 (1993) ["Gambell"]; 23 Sept. 1931, U.S.T.S. 880, 349 L.N.T.S. 3586 ["1931 ICRW"]
83. Gambell, *supra* note 82.
84. *See* Carlarne, *supra* note 81, at 4; International Agreement for the Regulation of Whaling, June 8, 1937, 190 L.N.T.S. 79.
85. Carlarne, *supra* note 81, at 4.
86. Gambell, *supra* note 82, at 98.
87. *Id.*
88. *Id.* (note, the BWU was established by the whaling industry in the 1930s as a measure of the relative quantities of oil that a whale carcass produced. One blue whale produced as much as two fin whales, two-and-a-half humpback whales, and six sei whales. This controversial management unit would carry over into the ICRW).
89. *Id.* at 99.
90. Carlarne, *supra* note 81, at 5.
91. ICRW, *supra* note 80, at preamble.
92. *Id.* at preamble; *see* Lyster's International Wildlife Law, *supra* note 50, at 152 (discussing the objectives of the ICRW contained within the preamble, noting that "[t]he Convention clearly aims to achieve a situation where stocks have recovered sufficiently to be able to sustain controlled exploitation"); *see* Gerry Nagtzaam, The Making of International Environmental Treaties: Neoliberal and

CONSTRUCTIVIST ANALYSES OF NORMATIVE EVOLUTION 172 (2009) (identifying the IWC in its early days as "a whalers' club").

93. Alexander Gillespie, *Small Cetaceans, International Law and the International Whaling Commission*, 2 MELB. J. INT'L L. 257, 258 (2001) ["Gillespie, *Small Cetaceans*"] (discussing this controversy); *International Agreement for the Regulation of Whaling: The International Whaling Conference*, Wash., D.C., Nov. 20–Dec. 2, 1946, Final Act, Annex (available at 1 PATRICIA W. BIRNIE, INTERNATIONAL REGULATION OF WHALING: FROM CONSERVATION OF WHALING TO CONSERVATION OF WHALES AND REGULATION OF WHALE-WATCHING 701 (1985) (note that the Annex of Nomenclature of Whales includes the following species: bowhead whale, North Atlantic right whale, North Pacific right whale, southern right whale, pygmy right whale, humpback whale, blue whale, fin whale, sei whale, Bryde's whale, common minke whale, gray whale, sperm whale, and the Antarctic and Arctic bottlenose dolphin. With the exception of the bottlenose dolphin, the list is consistent with the traditional notion of the Great Whale species (*see generally* Gillespie, *supra* at 260)).

94. Gillespie, *supra* note 93; *see* Cynthia E. Carlson, *The International Regulation of Small Cetaceans*, 21(3) 21 SAN DIEGO L. REV. 578, 607–12 (1984) (describing how certain nations—the United States and Great Britain among them—supported IWC regulation of small cetaceans whereas other nations—Canada, Mexico, Brazil, and Japan among them—did not support this form of regulation); *see* William C. Burns, *The International Whaling Commission and the Regulation of the Consumptive and Non-consumptive Uses of Small Cetaceans: The Critical Agenda for the 1990s*, 13 WIS. INT'L L.J. 105, 129 (1994–1995) (noting that other nations that opposed IWC regulation of small cetaceans include Denmark, South Korea, Spain, Chile, and China).

95. ICRW, *supra* note 80, at art. V.

96. International Whaling Commission, *Membership and Contracting Governments*, IWC (2015), https://iwc.int/members.

97. International Whaling Commission, *Commission Sub-groups*, IWC (2015), https://iwc.int/commission-sub-groups.

98. International Whaling Commission, *History and Purpose*, IWC (2015), https://iwc.int/history-and-purpose.

99. ICRW, *supra* note 80.

100. *Id.* at 5 of the Schedule (as amended by the Commission at the 65th Annual Meeting, Portorož, Slovenia, September 2014) (noting that this moratorium was objected to in accordance with the ICRW by the "Governments of Japan, Norway, Peru and the Union of Soviet Socialist Republics," but Peru withdrew this objection in 1983, and Japan withdrew its objection in phases through 1987 and 1988. Norway and the Russian Federation have not withdrawn their objection. Further, when Iceland opted to rejoin the IWC in 2002, it reserved application of paragraph 10(e), which led to formal objections from a number of states. Also, note that paragraph 10(d) contains a prohibition on using factory ships and whale catchers to take regulated whales, save minke whales).

101. *See* Adrienne M. Ruffle, *Resurrecting the International Whaling Commission: Suggestions to Strengthen the Conservation Effort*, 27 BROOK. J. INT'L L. 639, 647–49 (2001–2002) (proposing this theoretical division for the functioning of the IWC).

102. *See* Carlarne, *supra* note 81, at 4 (citing SYDNEY HOYT, EARTH'S THREATENED RESOURCES 144 (1986)).

103. Gambell, *supra* note 82, at 99.
104. *Id.*
105. *Id.* at 100.
106. *Id.*
107. *Id.*
108. Rep. of the U.N. Conference on the Human Environment, June 5–16, 1972, A/CONF.48/14/REV. 1, 12 (1972) (providing in Recommendation 33 that *"It is recommended* that Governments agree to strengthen the International Whaling Commission, to increase international research efforts, and as a matter of urgency to call for an international agreement, under the auspices of the International Whaling Commission and involving all Governments concerned, for a 10-year moratorium on commercial whaling"); A.W. Harris, *The Best Scientific Evidence Available: The Whaling Moratorium and Divergent Interpretations of Science*, WM. & MARY ENV. L. & P. REV. 375, 377 (2005) ["Harris"].
109. Harris, *supra* note 108, at 377–78; *e.g.*, Kimberly S. Davis, *International Management of Cetaceans under the New Law of the Sea Convention*, 3 B.U. INT'L L.J. 477, 485 (1985) (noting that by 1977, less than half of the states at the IWC maintained a commercial whaling industry).
110. Robert L. Friedheim, *Introduction: The IWC as a Contested Regime, in* TOWARD A SUSTAINABLE WHALING REGIME 3, 5 (Robert L. Friedheim ed., 2001) [Friedheim, *Introduction*]; *see also* Harris, *supra* note 108, at 379.
111. Gambell, *supra* note 82, at 100.
112. International Whaling Commission, *Chairman's Report of the Thirty-Fourth Annual Meeting*, Brighton, U.K., July 19–24, 1982, at 3 ["*Chairman's Report of the Thirty-Fourth Annual Meeting*"].
113. *Id.* at 3 (note that the moratorium did make allowances for continued Aboriginal subsistence whaling).
114. *Status of the International Convention for the Regulation of Whaling*, 8, http://archive.iwcoffice.org/_documents/commission/convention_status.pdf; Ted L. McDorman, *Canada and Whaling: An Analysis of Article 65 of the Law of the Sea Convention*, 29 OCEAN DEV. & INT'L L. 179, 180 (1998); Gary D. Libecap, *Save the Whales*, DEFINING IDEAS (June 13, 2012), http://www.hoover.org/publications/defining-ideas/article/119886.
115. Joanna Matanich, *A Treaty Comes of Age for the Ancient Ones: Implications of the Law of the Sea for the Regulation of Whaling*, 8 INT'L LEGAL PERSP. 37, 46 (1996).
116. Ronald B. Mitchell, *International Regulation of Whaling: Case Study* (June 28, 1995), http://pages.uoregon.edu/rmitchel/cases/whale.shtml.
117. The Norwegian Ministry of Fisheries and Coastal Affairs, *Norwegian Whaling—Based on a Balanced Ecosystem* (Mar. 19, 2013), http://www.fisheries.no/ecosystems-and-stocks/marine_stocks/mammals/whales/whaling/; Icelandic Fisheries, *Overview of Iceland's Whaling Position*, http://www.fisheries.is/management/government-policy/whaling/.
118. *See* Japanese Whaling Association, *Questions and Answers*, http://www.whaling.jp/english/qa.html; *see* Nicholas J. Gales, *Japan's Whaling Plan under Scrutiny*, 435 NATURE 883 (June 16, 2005).
119. BBC News Asia, *Japan Ends Whaling Season Short of Quota*, BBC (Mar. 9, 2012, 6:23 AM), http://www.bbc.co.uk/news/world-asia-17312460 (note that in addition to the take of great whale species, Japan also conducts extensive

coastal operations for small cetaceans; *see* Randall S. Well, *Letter to Japanese Government regarding Dolphin and Small Whale Hunt*, SOCIETY FOR MARINE MAMMOLOGY (May 29, 2012, 2:13 PM), http://www.marinemammalscience.org/index.php?option=com_content&view=article&id=655&Itemid=183).

120. Junko Sakuma, *Whale Meat Doesn't Sell: The ICR Reports Miserable Result of Auction*, IKAN: IRUKA & KUJIRA (DOLPHIN & WHALE) ACTION NETWORK (May 22, 2012, 15:07), http://www.guardian.co.uk/environment/2012/jun/14/japan-appetite-whale-meat-wanes (noting that approximately three-quarters of the whale meat from JARPA II's 2011 expedition that entered the auction market did not sell).

121. Whaling in the Antarctic (Australia v. Japan: New Zealand Intervening), Judgment, [2014] ICJ Rep 226 ["Whaling in the Antarctic"].

122. *See* Government of Australia, *International Whaling Commission*, http://www.environment.gov.au/marine/marine-species/cetaceans/international/iwc (last visited Mar. 26, 2016) (indicating that the Indian Ocean Sanctuary was initially set to last for 10 years, and was upheld upon review in 1992 and 2002) ["*Australia: Whale Sanctuaries*"].

123. *Id.* at 2.

124. Judith Berger-Eforo, *Sanctuary for the Whales: Will This Be the Demise of the International Whaling Commission or a Viable Strategy for the Twenty-First Century?*, 8 PACE INT'L L. REV 439, 439 (1996).

125. *Australia: Whale Sanctuaries, supra* note 122, at 2.

126. International Whaling Commission, *The South Atlantic: A Sanctuary for Whales*, IWC/65/08 (Sept. 2014) (note that this proposal was submitted by Argentina, Brazil, and South Africa, and was motivated, in large part, by the fact that whale-watching contributes to the local economies of these states).

127. ICRW, *supra* note 80, at art. VIII (which provides that "[n]otwithstanding anything contained in this Convention any Contracting Government may grant to any of its nationals a special permit authorizing that national to kill, take and treat whales for purposes of scientific research subject to such restrictions as to number and subject to such other conditions as the Contracting Government thinks fit. . . . "); *see also* Maya Park, *Japanese Scientific Whaling in Antarctica: Is Australia Attempting the Impossible?*, 9 NZJPIL 193, 193 (2011) (stating that "[s]o-called scientific whaling has been criticized by non-governmental organisations (NGOs) and anti-whaling States as a loophole or a way of circumventing the moratorium on commercial whaling adopted by the IWC").

128. *See* International Whaling Commission, *IWC Resolution 1987-1: Resolution on Scientific Research Programmes*, (1987), https://archive.iwc.int/pages/search.php?search=%21collection72&k= (attempting to establish criteria for the national issuance of scientific whaling permits); *see* International Whaling Commission, *IWC Resolution 1996-7: Resolution on Special Permit Catches by Japan*, (1996), https://archive.iwc.int/pages/search.php?search=%21collection72&k= (requesting that Japan refrain from issuing special permits); *see* International Whaling Commission, *IWC Resolution 2001-7:Resolution on Southern Hemisphere Minke Whales and Special Permit Whaling*, (2001), https://archive.iwc.int/pages/search.php?search=%21collection72&k= (recommending that Japan cease JARPA until further information from the Scientific Committee is known); *see* International Whaling Commission, *IWC Resolution 2003-3: Resolution on Southern Hemisphere Minke Whales and Special Permit Whaling*, (2003),

https://archive.iwc.int/pages/search.php?search=%21collection72&k= (recommending that JARPA be limited to non-lethal research and that any such program not continue until the Scientific Committee has completed a review).

129. *See* Whaling in the Antarctic, *supra* note 121, at paras. 101–108 (providing a description of JARPA). It is also of note that Japan also pursues a similar, albeit smaller, research program in the North Pacific—the Japanese Whale Research Program under Special Permit in the North Pacific (JARPN). Similar to JARPA, JARPN has also had two implementation phases: JARPN I (1994–1999), and JARPN II (since 2000). This scientific whaling was not challenged by Australia and receives less attention than JARPA II, perhaps because there is not a North Pacific sanctuary.

130. Donald R. Rothwell, Australia v. Japan: *JARPA II Whaling Case before the International Court of Justice* 3 (July 2, 2010), http://www.haguejusticeportal.net/Docs/Commentaries%20PDF/Portal%20HJJ_Rothwell_Aust_Japan_EN.pdf (noting that Japan's controversial decision to hunt humpbacks never occurred, because of a request from the United States). The IWC has expressed its concern about the necessity of the research being conducted and the status of the whales being taken by JARPA II (*see* International Whaling Commission, *Resolution 2005-1; Resolution on JARPA II*, (2005), https://iwc.int/resolutions).

131. *See* The Institute of Cetacean Research, http://www.icrwhale.org/sitemap.html (last visited Dec. 2, 2015).

132. Whaling in the Antarctic, *supra* note 121.

133. *See* Press Release, International Court of Justice, Australia Institutes Proceedings against Japan for Alleged Breach of Obligations concerning Whaling, I.C.J. Press Release No. 2010/16 (June 1, 2010) (noting that Australia asserts that "The present Application concerns Japan's continued pursuit of a large-scale program of whaling under the Second Phase of its Japanese Whale Research Program under Special Permit in the Antarctic ('JARPA II'), in breach of obligations assumed by Japan under the International Convention for the Regulation of Whaling ('ICRW'), as well as its other international obligations for the preservation of marine mammals and the marine environment"; *see* Whaling in the Antarctic (Australia v. Japan), Application Instituting Proceedings, ¶ 40 (May 31, 2010), *available at* http://www.icj-cij.org/docket/files/148/15951.pdf ["Application"] (Australia is seeking declaration that Japan cease JARPA II, revoke existing national permits, and provide assurances that JARPA II (or any successor program) will accord with international legal obligations. It also annexes an Aide Memoire and Joint Demarche from December 21, 2007, signed by 30 states and the European Commission denouncing JARPA II); *see* Press Release, International Court of Justice, The Court Authorizes New Zealand to Intervene in Proceedings, I.C.J. Press Release No. 2013/2 (Feb. 13, 2013) (noting New Zealand's success in securing intervener status).

134. Application, *id.* at ¶ 1; *see* Whaling in the Antarctic (Australia v. Japan), Memorial of Australia, ¶ 7.1–7.12 (May 9, 2011), http://www.icj-cij.org/docket/index.php?p1=3&p2=1&case=148&code=aj&p3=1 ["Memorial"] (where Australia sets out in its remedy section that it seeks a declaration that Japan has violated its obligations under the ICRW to set a zero-catch quota for commercial take, to refrain from killing whales by factory ship (save minke whales), to refrain from the commercial take of fin whales in the Southern Ocean Sanctuary, and to order that Japan has a duty to stop special permit whaling pursuant to JARPA II and to refrain from initiating a similar program in the future).

135. *See* Whaling in the Antarctic (Australia v. Japan), Counter Memorial of Japan, ¶ 1.28, (Mar. 9, 2012), http://www.icj-cij.org/docket/index.php?p1=3&p2=1&case=148&code=aj&p3=1 ["Counter Memorial"] (where Japan details its opinion on jurisdiction); Whaling in the Antarctic, *supra* note 121, at paras. 30–41 (the jurisdiction dispute focused on the fact that Australia's optional declaration excluded "any dispute concerning or relating to the delimitation of maritime zones.... or arising out of, concerning, or relating to the exploitation of any disputed area of or adjacent to any such maritime zone pending its delimitation" (para. 31). Japan asserted that the presence of a contested Australian EEZ off of Antarctica triggered Austrlia's exclusion. The Court determined that to qualify for exclusion there had to be "[t]he existence of a dispute concerning maritime delimitation between the Parties," of which there was none (para. 37)).

136. *See* Whaling in the Antarctic, *supra* note 121, at para. 247.

137. *See* Jeffrey J. Smith, *Evolving to Conservation?: The International Court's Decision in the Australia/Japan Whaling Case*, 45 OCEAN DEV. & INT'L L. 301 (2014); Anastasia Telesetsky, Donald K. Anton & Timo Koivurova, *ICJ's Decision in Australia v. Japan: Giving up the Spear or Refining the Scientific Design?*, 45 OCEAN DEV. & INT'L L. 328 (2014); Phillip J. Clapham, *Japan's Whaling following the International Court of Justice Ruling: Brave New World—Or Business as Usual?*, 51 MAR. POL. 238 (2015); William de la Mare, Nick Gales & Marc Mangel, *Applying Scientific Principles in International Law on Whaling*, 345 SCI. 1125 (2015).

138. *See* Friedheim, *Introduction*, *supra* note 110, at 5.

139. *See* International Whaling Commission, *The Revised Management Procedure*, IWC, https://iwc.int/rmp (last visited Dec. 1, 2015) (providing a detailed discussion of the scientific analysis and modeling used to generate the catch limits permitted in the RMP) ["*Revised Management Procedure*"]; *see also* Gambell, *supra* note 79, at 101.

140. *Revised Management Procedure*, *supra* note 139; *see also* International Whaling Commission, *The Revised Management Procedure (RMP) for Baleen Whales*, IWC, https://iwc.int/rmpbw (last visited Dec. 1, 2015) (providing in section 3.6 titled "Adjusting for Other Sources of Human-Caused Mortality" that: "Catch limits calculated under the Revised Management Procedure shall be adjusted downwards to account for human-induced mortalities due to sources other than commercial catches. Each such adjustment shall be based on an estimate provided by the Scientific Committee of the size of adjustment required to ensure that total removals over time from each population and area do not exceed the limits set by the Revised Management Procedure. Total removals include commercial catches and other human-induced mortalities caused by Indigenous subsistence whaling, whaling under Special Permit for scientific research, whaling outside the IWC, bycatches and ship strikes to the extent that these are known or can be reasonably estimated.)"

141. *Revised Management Procedure*, *supra* note 133.

142. *Id.*

143. *Id.*

144. International Whaling Commission, *Annual Report of the International Whaling Commission 2011*, IWC 22 (2011), http://iwc.int/cache/downloads/cvhyx3ats48ck4oooo0ckwcsw/AnnualReport2011.pdf.

145. International Whaling Commission, *Resolution 2006-1: St. Kitts and Nevis Declaration*, http://archive.iwcoffice.org/meetings/resolutions/resolution2006.

htm ["*St. Kitts and Nevis Declaration*"]; M.J. Bowman, *"Normalizing" the International Convention for the Regulation of Whaling*, 29 MICH. J.I.L. 293, 294 (2008) ["Bowman"].
146. *St. Kitts and Nevis Declaration, supra* note 145 (wherein the parties "DECLARE our commitment to normalize the functions of the IWC based on the terms of the ICRW and other relevant international law, respect for cultural diversity and traditions of coastal peoples and the fundamental principles of sustainable use of resources, and the need for science-based policy and rulemaking that are accepted as the world standard for the management of marine resources").
147. *Id.*
148. Marlise Flis, *International Whale Conservation: Moby Dick's Last Hurrah*, 3 HOFSTRA ENVTL. L. DIG. 30, 31 (1986).
149. *E.g., see* Friedheim, *Introduction, supra* note 110, at 28–29 (noting that although the authors in this collection agree that the IWC's movement toward a preservationist regime is problematic, the commentary contained within does present varied opinion on a variety of issues, and that "[w]hile we agree that there are problems, we do not necessarily agree as to the severity of the problems, and we disagree on what, if anything, should be done").
150. International Whaling Commission, *Future of the IWC*, IWC (2015), https://iwc.int/future.
151. *St. Kitts and Nevis Declaration, supra* note 145; *see* Mike Iliff, *Normalization of the International Whaling Commission*, 32(2) MAR. POL. 333, 333 (2008) (noting that Japan and other pro-whaling nations supported the St. Kitts and Nevis Declaration).
152. *St. Kitts and Nevis Declaration, supra* note 145.
153. Iliff, *Normalization, supra* note 151.
154. Secretariat of the Pew Whales Commission, *Turning the Page: Bringing Whale Conservation into the 21st Century* 4–5, (2009) ["*Turning the Page*"] (which provides the following summary of the politically charged divide between pro-whaling and anti-whaling nations): "There is a significant group of countries, currently holding a majority of the votes at the IWC, who supports the continuation of the moratorium on commercial whaling as a necessary and legitimate decision under international law, entirely compatible with the principle of science-based policy and rule-making. This group of countries believes that conservation and management of whales must take account of all uses, including non-lethal uses (such as whale watching) which may be fundamentally compromised by lethal ones. It must also take account of all potential impacts on whale populations, not just directed kills. According to this school of thought, the potential impacts of climate change, changes in marine ecosystems due to overfishing, noise pollution and ship strikes due to the increase of commercial, military and recreational maritime activities, fishing gear entanglement, the concentration of persistent organic pollutants, and heavy metals in the food chain, and other such threats compound the impacts from hunting.

. . .

Opposed to this view, the group of countries opposing the continuation of the moratorium on commercial whaling (currently in the minority within the IWC) argues that the moratorium by definition was meant to be a temporary measure and that whaling should be allowed to resume because certain whale populations are showing signs of recovery, and others according to them are not endangered. They also say that commercial whaling and whale watching are not mutually exclusive.

155. Peter Bridgewater, *Whaling or Wailing*, 55(178) INT'L SOC. SCI. J. 555, 555 (2004) ["Bridgewater"].
156. Dan Goodman, *The "Future of the IWC": Why the Initiative to Save the IWC Failed*, 14(1) J. INT'L. WILDLIFE. L & POL'Y 63, 64 (2011); *see also* JUN MORIKAWA, WHALING IN JAPAN: POWER, POLITICS AND DIPLOMACY 1 (2009) (noting that "the Japanese government has allowed the issue [whaling] to take on a magnitude and significance far beyond its actual importance and, in the process, has made the continuation of whaling a national goal and a matter of national pride").
157. Bridgewater, *supra* note 155, at 559.
158. Mike Iliff, *The Hogarth Initiative on the Future of the International Whaling Commission*, 34(3) MAR. POL. 360, 360 (2010) ["Iliff, *The Hogarth Initiative*"].
159. *See* International Whaling Commission, *Proposed Consensus Decision to Improve the Conservation of Whales from the Chair and Vice-Chair of the Commission*, IWC/62/7rev, 1 (May 28, 2010), http://opc.ca.gov/webmaster/ftp/pdf/agenda_items/20100616/IWC%20Proposal%20(2).pdf ["*Proposed Consensus Decision*"].
160. International Whaling Commission, *Future of the IWC*, IWC (2015), http://www.iwcoffice.org/future ["*Future of the IWC*"].
161. Iliff, *The Hogarth Initiative, supra* note 158, at 360.
162. Mike Iliff, *Contemporary Initiatives on the Future of the International Whaling Commission*, 34(3) MAR. POL. 461, 461 (2010) ["Iliff, *Contemporary Initiatives*"] (commenting on the Australian contribution to this process (Government of Australia, *Whale Conservation and Management: A Future for the IWC* (2008) http://155.187.3.82/coasts/publications/pubs/iwc-future-paper.pdf, which, in large part, responds to the IWC's failure to address emerging threats to cetaceans. Iliff notes at 461 that the Australians suggested to "begin to address these issues by developing internationally-agreed, cooperative conservation management plans, taking into account all whale-related issues and threats and launching regional, non-lethal, collaborative research programs to improve management outcomes for cetaceans"; *see also Turning the Page, supra* note 154).
163. *Turning the Page, supra* note 154, at 2. This report also notes at 2–3 that at this conference the Japanese Fisheries Agency provided the following list for why the IWC is "dysfunctional":

- Its alleged disregard for international law (ICRW and treaty interpretation);
- Its alleged disregard for the principle of science-based policy and rule-making;
- Its alleged exclusion of whales from the principle of sustainable use of resources;
- Its alleged disrespect of cultural diversity related to food and ethics;
- Its alleged increasing emotionalism concerning whales;
- Its alleged institutionalized combative/confrontational discourse that discourages co-operation;
- Its alleged lack of good faith negotiations; and
- Its alleged pressure on scientists which results in a lack of consensus scientific advice from the Scientific Committee.

164. International Institute for Sustainable Development, *News: Pew Commission on Whale Conservation Holds Third Meeting*, IISD, http://water-l.iisd.org/news/pew-commission-on-whale-conservation-holds-third-meeting/ (last visited Dec. 2, 2015).
165. Iliff, *Contemporary Initiatives, supra* note 162, at 462–63.
166. *Proposed Consensus Decision, supra* note 159.
167. *Id.* at 4.
168. *Id.* (stating that "[t]he prevalent atmosphere of confrontation and mistrust among member governments has led to little progress being made on key practical matters of conservation and management since the early 1990s despite advances at a scientific level. This has created concerns among some members over the possible collapse of the IWC").
169. *Id.*
170. *Id.* at 5.
171. *Future of the IWC, supra* note 160.
172. Iliff, *Contemporary Initiatives, supra* note 162, at 361.
173. *E.g.*, Iliff, *The Hogarth Initiative, supra* note 158, at 360 (noting that previous efforts to increase cooperation at the IWC, including the so-called Irish Proposal of 1997 that put forth a compromise between the pro-whaling and anti-whaling factions of the IWC and the 1996 Chair's Proposal for a Way Forward on the RMS. Both failed to reduce tensions at the IWC); *see also* Mike Iliff, *Compromise in the IWC: Is It Possible or Desirable?*, 32(6) MAR. POL. 997, 997 (2008) (noting that the assumption is that without compromise the IWC will eventually collapse, and that compromise has been historically difficult to achieve).
174. Iliff, *Normalization, supra* note 153, at 337; *see also* Bowman, *supra* note 145 (which provides a detailed response to the St. Kitts and Nevis Declaration and assesses various possibilities for normalizing or modernizing the ICRW, suggesting at 485 that "[a]lthough the potential for normalization and modernization of the ICRW through the mechanisms of (i) a flexible and progressive approach to the interpretation of its terms generally, and (ii) further amendment of the Schedule, has shown to be considerable, it is not patently unlimited." This work acknowledges that purposive treaty interpretation and a return to first principles may serve to bolster the efficacy of the current regime, but focuses instead on the form and content of a comprehensive response to the current regime).
175. *See Turning the Page, supra* note 154, at 7–8, noting that modernization of the IWC could utilize the following listed principles:

- Application of the precautionary principle;
- Application of an integrated, ecosystem-based approach to biodiversity conservation (as opposed to a narrower ecosystem-based management to fisheries or an even narrower species-based approach);
- Establishment of a body to review compliance with new powers of enforcement, including a dispute settlement mechanism in line with modern international environmental law;
- Avoidance of reservations to new rules and provisions and elimination of the privilege to "opt out" from any such rules and provisions when adhering to the regime (in line with UNCLOS and the majority of modern MEAs [multilateral environmental agreements]);

- Recognition and regulation of non-lethal use of cetaceans as a legitimate and optimum use of the whale resources;
- Good faith negotiation on the future of the provision in ICRW Article VIII whereby restrictions to whaling may currently be undermined by the unilateral issuance of special permits.

Principles such as these help inform the goals established in this chapter. It is this author's contention that these objectives can be incorporated into a new multilateral convention for the conservation of marine mammals that creates a new commission to aid in the implementation of said objectives.

176. Iliff, *Contemporary Initiatives*, supra note 162, at 463.
177. See Donald Rothwell, *Japan, Australia, Sea Shepherd: A Whale of a Legal Web*, THE DRUM (Jan. 4, 2013), http://www.abc.net.au/unleashed/4452644.html (discussing the intricate legal issues that are set to play out in the foreseeable future); see also F.3d, 2013 WL 2278588, 13 Cal. Daily Op. Serv. 5242, 2013 Daily Journal D.A.R. 6656 (9th Cir. (Wash.) May 24, 2013) (NO. 12-35266) ["Institute of Cetacean Research"] (in which the Court of Appeals for the Ninth Circuit (Washington) overturned a district court ruling that denied the Institute of Cetacean Research's injunctive request and claim of piracy against the Sea Shepherd brought pursuant to the Alien Tort Statute); see also Anthony Bergin, *Southern Ocean Pirates: What's in a Name?*, ASPI: AUSTRALIAN STRATEGIC POLICY INSTITUTE (Mar. 21, 2013), http://www.aspistrategist.org.au/southern-ocean-pirates-whats-in-a-name/ (describing how the Sea Shepherd Conservation Society follows and obstructs the Japanese whaling activities pursuant to JARPA II each year). The discussion has now turned to competing opinions about piracy. The Court of Appeals decision of Institute of Cetacean Research, Kyoda Senpaku Kaisha Ltd, Tomoyuki Ogaya and Toshiyuki Miura v. Sea Shepherd Conservation Society and Paul Watson, No. 12-35266 D.C. No. 2:11-cv-02043-RAJ, authored by Chief Judge Kozinski, provided the following statement linking Sea Shepherd activity to piracy, at 2:

> You don't need a peg leg or an eye patch. When you ram ships; hurl glass containers of acid; drag metal-reinforced ropes in the water to damage propellers and rudders; launch smoke bombs and flares with hooks; and point high-powered lasers at other ships, you are, without a doubt, a pirate, no matter how high-minded you believe your purpose to be.

The Court of Appeal was satisfied that Sea Shepherd direct-intervention activity meets the definition of piracy in Article 101 of UNCLOS, which importantly requires "illegal acts of violence or detention, or any act of depredation, committed for private ends by the crew or the passengers of a private ship...." The Sea Shepherd Conservation Society has responded by initiating legal action of their own in the Netherlands (where the Sea Shepherd Conservation Society registers its vessels) against the crew of one of the Japanese factory ships for actions (ship ramming, water canon use, and explosions) that the conservation group alleges constitute piracy in their own right (see AFP, *Sea Shepherd Sues Whalers for Piracy in Dutch Court*, THE JAPAN TIMES (Mar. 22, 2013), http://www.japantimes.co.jp/news/2013/03/23/national/sea-shepherd-sues-whalers-for-piracy-in-dutch-court/#.Vl9I5HarSUk)).

178. International Whaling Commission, *Conservation and Management*, IWC (2015), http://iwc.int/conservation.
179. 5 June 1992, 31 I.L.M. 818, 1760 U.N.T.S. 79 ["CBD"].
180. Lyster's International Wildlife Law, *supra* note 50, at 593 (2d ed. 2010).
181. CBD, *supra* note 179.
182. Lyster's International Wildlife Law, *supra* note 50, at 594; CBD, *supra* note 179, at art. 4.
183. *Id.*
184. *Id.*at art. 8.
185. *Id.*
186. *Id.* at art. 7; Lyster's International Wildlife Law, *supra* note 50, at 604.
187. *See* COP VII of the Convention on Biological Diversity, *Decision V/10*, Annex A, at para. 1.
188. CBD, *supra* note 179, at art. 14.
189. *Id.* at art. 25.
190. Erika J. Techera, Marine Environmental Governance: From International Law to Local Practice 75 (2012).
191. Mar. 3, 1973, 27 U.S.T. 1087, 993 U.N.T.S. 243 ["CITES"] (additionally, it is worth noting that CITES is administered through a Secretariat, housed in Geneva, and by the United Nations Environment Program. Further, the Conference of the Parties is the action oriented body of the treaty).
192. *Id.* at preamble.
193. James A.R. Nafziger, *Global Conservation and Management of Marine Mammals*, 17 San Diego L. Rev. 591, 601–02 (1979–1980) (note that since Nafziger wrote this, the number of species of marine mammal covered by the Appendix system has increased).
194. Lyster's International Wildlife Law, *supra* note 50, at 484.
195. CITES, *supra* note 191, at art. I.
196. *Id.* at art. II.
197. *Id.*
198. Convention on International Trade in Endangered Species of Wild Fauna and Flora, *Member Countries*, http://www.cites.org/eng/disc/parties/index.php (last visited June 22, 2015).
199. Convention on International Trade in Endangered Species of Wild Fauna and Flora, *The CITES Species*, http://www.cites.org/eng/disc/species.php (last visited June 22, 2015).
200. Convention on International Trade in Endangered Species of Wild Fauna and Flora, *Interpretation and Implementation of the Convention: Species Trade and Conservation Issues, Cetaceans*, at 1, 14th Cop14 Doc. 51 (June 2007) ["*Interpretation and Implementation*"].
201. *Id.*
202. *See* International Whaling Commission, *Resolution to the CITES*, http://iwc.int/cache/downloads/2dgyfmncdbdwoso88ck444kg8/Resolution%201978%20sp.pdf (this Resolution, passed at a Special Meeting in December 1978, requested that the Conference of the Parties to CITES, at its second meeting, take all possible measures to support the IWC ban on commercial whaling for certain species and stocks of whales).
203. Convention on International Trade in Endangered Species of Wild Fauna and Flora, *Conservation of Cetaceans, Trade in Cetacean Specimens and the*

Relationship with the International Whaling Commission, Resolution Confc. 11.4 (Rev. Cop12), (2002), http://www.cites.org/eng/res/11/11-04.php ; *see also* LYSTER'S INTERNATIONAL WILDLIFE LAW, *supra* note 50, at 187 (describing unsuccessful attempts made by Norway and Japan to have the minke whale downlisted to Appendix II).

204. *Interpretation and Implementation, supra* note 200.
205. Convention on International Trade in Endangered Species of Wild Fauna and Flora, *Decisions of the Conference of the Parties to CITES in Effect after Its 15th Meeting*, at 21, (2010), http://www.cites.org/eng/dec/valid15/E15-Dec.pdf.
206. International Whaling Commission, *Resolution 2007-4: Resolution on CITES*, (June 3, 2007) http://iwc.int/cache/downloads/2yfkueebw9essk0o8gkkw8kog/Resolution%202007.pdf.
207. Carlarne, *supra* note 81, at 22.
208. Convention on International Trade in Endangered Species of Wild Fauna and Flora, *Appendices I, II and III*, http://www.cites.org/eng/app/2013/E-Appendices-2013-06-12.pdf (last visited Feb. 16, 2016) (these statistics represent my summary of the relevant data contained within this document).
209. 23 June 1979, 1651 U.N.T.S. 333, art. I(1)(c) ["CMS"].
210. Richard Caddell, *International Law and the Protection of Migratory Wildlife: An Appraisal of Twenty-Five Years of the Bonn Convention* (2005) 16 COLO. J. INT'L ENVTL L. & POL'Y 113, 113–14 (2005) ["Caddell"]. For example, species can experience a variety of threats along their migratory routes, and unless they receive adequate protection at every stage of this migration, their existence can be threatened (*see* LYSTER'S INTERNATIONAL WILDLIFE LAW, *supra* note 50, at 535).
211. United Nations Environment Programme, *United Nations Conference on the Human Environment: Action Plan*, Recommendation 33, http://www.unep.org/Documents.Multilingual/Default.Print.asp?DocumentID=97&ArticleID=1506&l=en (last visited Feb. 16, 2016).
212. Caddell, *supra* note 210, at 114.
213. Convention on the Conservation of Migratory Species of Wild Animals, *Parties to the Convention on the Conservation of Migratory Species as at 1 April 2013* (Apr. 1, 2013), http://www.cms.int/en/document/list-cms-parties-0.
214. CMS, *supra* note 209, at art. I (which defines "Migratory Species" as "the entire population or any geographically separate part of the population of any species or lower taxon of wild animals, a significant proportion of whose members cyclically and predictably cross one or more national jurisdictional boundaries").
215. *Id.* at art. I (which defines "Range" as "all the areas of land or water that a migratory species inhabits, stays in temporarily, crosses or overflies at any time on its normal migration route").
216. *Id.* (where "Range State" is defined "in relation to a particular migratory species" to mean "any State . . . that exercises jurisdiction over any part of the range of that migratory species, or a State, flag vessels of which are engaged outside national jurisdictional limits in taking that migratory species").
217. LYSTER'S INTERNATIONAL WILDLIFE LAW, *supra* note 50, at 537.
218. Convention on Migratory Species, *Organizational Structure of CMS*, CMS http://www.cms.int/en/about/organizational-structure (last visited June 12, 2015).
219. Convention on the Conservation of Migratory Species of Wild Animals (CMS), *Appendices I and II of the Convention on the Conservation of Migratory Species of Wild Animals (CMS) (as amended by the Conference of the Parties in 1985,*

1988, 1991, 1994, 1997, 1999, 2002, 2005, 2008 and 2011)—*Effective: 23rd February 2012*), http://www.cms.int/documents/appendix/appendices_e.pdf (a review of this document indicates that the following marine mammal species on Appendix I include: fin whale; blue whale; sei whale; humpback whale; bowhead whale; sperm whale, North Atlantic right whale, North Pacific right whale, southern right whale, common bottlenose dolphin, short beaked common dolphin (Mediterranean), Atlantic humpback dolphin, La Plata dolphin, Irrawaddy dolphin, South Asian river dolphin, Mediterranean monk seal, marine otter, southern river otter, West Indian manatee, and the West African manatee).

220. *Id.* (note that Appendix II is more extensive as it lists 44 cetacean species, four sirenian species, and three pinniped species).

221. *See* International Whaling Commission, *Small Cetaceans*, IWC (2015), http://iwc.int/smallcetacean. It has oft been suggested, by scholars and the IWC Sub-Committee on Small Cetaceans, that "an international body is needed to manage all stocks of cetaceans not on the IWC schedule" (Hugo Nijkamp & Andre Nollkaemper, *The Protection of Small Cetaceans in the Face of Uncertainty: An Analysis of the ASCOBANS Agreement*, 9 Geo. Int'l Envtl. L. Rev. 281, 286–87 (1996–1997) ["Nijkamp & Nollkaemper"]). Indeed, Nijkamp and Nollkaemper suggest at 287 that "[a]s the IWC itself has proven unable or unwilling to take on this role [of small cetacean conservation], states could use the Bonn Convention [CMS] to fill a gap in the international legal protection of small cetaceans."

222. 17 Mar. 1992, 1772 U.N.T.S. 217 ["ASCOBANS"].

223. *See* Lyster's International Wildlife Law, *supra* note 50, at 190.

224. *Id.* at 191 (note that the area covered by ASCOBANS was expanded recently to better complement and coordinate with another regional agreement).

225. *See* Convention on Migratory Species, *ASCOBANS: Conservation and Management Plan*, CMS, http://www.cms.int/species/ascobans/ (last visited Dec. 2, 2015).

226. Lyster's International Wildlife Law, *supra* note 50, at 191–92; *see also* Nijkamp & Nollkaemper, *supra* note 221, at 281.

227. 24 Nov. 1996, 2183 U.N.T.S. 303 ["ACCOBAMS"].

228. Lyster's International Wildlife Law, *supra* note 50, at 194.

229. *Id.*

230. *Id.* at 194–95.

231. Agreement on the Conservation of Seals in the Wadden Sea (1990), http://www.cms.int/species/wadden_seals/sea_text.htm.

232. Lyster's International Wildlife Law, *supra* note 50, at 561.

233. *Id.*

234. Maarten Bakker, *Distemper Kills Thousands of European Seals*, ENS (Sept. 17, 2002), http://www.ens-newswire.com/ens/sep2002/2002-09-17-02.html.

235. Lyster's International Wildlife Law, *supra* note 50, at 562.

236. Memorandum of Understanding concerning Measures for the Eastern Atlantic Populations of the Mediterranean Monk Seal 3 (2007).

237. *E.g., see id.* at Section 3 detailing the purpose of the annexed Action Plan.

238. CMS, Memorandum of Understanding for the Conservation of Cetaceans and Their Habitats in the Pacific Islands Region (Sept. 15, 2006), http://www.cms.int/species/pacific_cet/pacific_cet_bkrd.htm; CMS, The Memorandum of Understanding on the Conservation and Management of Dugongs (*Dugong dugong*) and Their Habitats throughout Their Range (Oct. 31, 2007),

http://www.cms.int/species/dugong/; CMS, The Memorandum of Understanding concerning the Conservation of Manatee and Small Cetaceans of Western Africa and Macaronesia (Oct. 3, 2008), http://www.cms.int/species/waam/.

239. Agreement on Research, Conservation and Management of Marine Mammals in the North Atlantic. Apr. 9, 2012 ["NAMMCO Agreement"].
240. Brettny Hardy, *Regional Approach to Whaling: How the North Atlantic Marine Mammal Commission Is Shifting the Tides for Whale Management*, 17 DUKE J. COMP. & INT'L L. 169, 179 (2006) ["Hardy"].
241. The North Atlantic Marine Mammal Commission, *Welcome to the North Atlantic Marine Mammal Commission*, http://www.nammco.no/ (last visited Dec. 4, 2015).
242. *Id.; see also* NAMMCO Agreement, *supra* note 239, at preamble; *see also* Hardy, *supra* note 240, at 180.
243. Hardy, *supra* note 240, at 184.
244. *Id.* at 171 (citing William C. Burns, *The International Whaling Commission and Future of Cetaceans: Problems and Prospects*, 8 COLO. J. INT'L ENVTL L. & POL'Y 31, 51–52 (1997)).
245. *Id.* at 189 (note that Iceland initially withdrew from the IWC when NAMMCO was created, but ultimately rejoined the IWC in 2002 while simultaneously objecting to the moratorium).
246. *Id.* at 188.
247. *Id.* at 190.
248. *Id.* at 194.
249. *Id.* at 192; *see generally* Nigel Bankes, *The Conservation and Utilization of Marine Mammals in the Arctic Region*, *in* THE LAW OF THE SEA AND THE POLAR REGIONS: INTERACTIONS BETWEEN GLOBAL AND REGIONAL REGIMES 293, 296–321 (Erik J. Molenaar, Alex H. Oude Elferink & Donald R. Rothwell eds., 2013) (examining the Arctic region and the interaction of various international, regional, and bilateral agreements that coexist in this region).
250. FAO/UNEP, The Global Plan of Action for the Conservation and Utilisation of Marine Mammals, *UNEP Regional Seas Reports and Studies No. 55* (1985), http://www.unep.org/regionalseas/publications/reports/RSRS/pdfs/rsrs055.pdf.
251. UNED Regional Seas, *Marine Mammal Action Plan*, http://www.unep.ch/regionalseas/main/hmarmams.html (last visited Dec. 3, 2015) ["*Marine Mammal Action Plan*"].
252. *Id.*
253. *Id.*
254. *Id.*
255. *See* United Nations Environment Programme: Regional Seas, *UNEP's Marine Mammal Action Plan*, http://www.unep.ch/regionalseas/home/mmapover.htm (last visited Dec. 3, 2015) (noting that this Memorandum of Understanding on Co-operation has been signed by the FAO, World Wide Fund for Nature (WWF), Greenpeace International, IUCN, the International Fund for Animal Welfare, the Intergovernmental Oceanographic Commission (IOC/UNESCO), and the Inter-American Tropical Tuna Commission (IATTC)) ["*UNEP's Marine Mammal Action Plan*"].
256. *Marine Mammal Action Plan, supra* note 251.
257. *Id.*

258. United Nations Environment Programme, Marine Mammals Plan of Action: evaluation of its development and achievements, UNEP Regional Seas Reports No. 102, 8 (1988).
259. *UNEP's Marine Mammal Action Plan, supra* note 255.
260. UNEP Regional Seas Programme, *About*, http://www.unep.org/regionalseas/about/default.asp (last visited Dec. 3, 2015) ["Regional Seas Programme"].
261. *Id.*
262. *Id.* (noting that these regional programs are the "Black Sea, Wider Caribbean, East Asian Seas, Eastern Africa, South Asian Seas, ROPME Sea Area, Mediterranean, North-East Pacific, Northwest Pacific, Red Sea and Gulf of Aden, South-East Pacific, Pacific, and Western Africa").
263. *Id.*
264. Regional Seas Programme, *supra* note 260.
265. UNEP Regional Seas, *About UNEP and Marine Mammals*, http://www.unep.org/regionalseas/marinemammals/about/default.asp (last visited Dec. 3, 2015) ["*About UNEP and Marine Mammals*"].
266. Food and Agriculture Organization of the United Nations, *Regional Fishery Bodies*, http://www.fao.org/fishery/rfb/en (last visited Dec. 3, 2015).
267. European Union, *Regional Fisheries Management Organization: Fact Sheet*, 1, http://ec.europa.eu/fisheries/documentation/publications/cfp_factsheets/rfmo_en.pdf (last visited June 12, 2015) ["*Fact Sheet*"].
268. The Pew Charitable Trusts: Environmental Initiatives, *Guide to Regional Fisheries Management Organizations* (Feb. 23, 2012), http://www.pewenvironment.org/news-room/other-resources/guide-to-regional-fisheries-management-organizations-rmfos-85899371954 ["*Guide to RFMOs*"].
269. *Fact Sheet, supra* note 267.
270. *Guide to RFMOs, supra* note 268.
271. *Fact Sheet, supra* note 267.
272. U.S. Department of State, *Regional Fisheries Management Organizations*, http://www.state.gov/e/oes/ocns/fish/regionalorganizations/ (last visited June 12, 2015) ["U.S. Department of State"].
273. UN Fish Stocks Agreement, *supra* note 47; Food and Agriculture Organization of the United Nations, *FAO Code of Conduct for Responsible Fisheries*, FAO Doc. 95/20/Rev/1 (1995) ["*FAO Responsible Fisheries*"].
274. U.S. Department of State, *supra* note 272.
275. *See* Rosemary Rayfuse, *To Our Children's Children's Children: From Promoting to Achieving Compliance in High Seas Fisheries*, 20 INT'L J. MARINE & COASTAL L. 509, 513–14 (2005).
276. Agreement on the International Dolphin Conservation Program, art. II(1), [1998] PITSE 4 (established this international effort).
277. Inter-American Tropical Tuna Commission, *Active IATTC and AIDCP Resolutions and Recommendations (*)*, http://www.iattc.org/ResolutionsActiveENG.htm (last visited June 12, 2015).
278. *Guide to RFMOs, supra* note 268.
279. *See* LYSTER'S INTERNATIONAL WILDLIFE LAW, *supra* note 50, at 188–89 (noting that "[t]he European Union has adopted a number of measures restricting the ability of any of its Member States to facilitate the future operation of a whaling industry, and also the ability of non-EU states to either engage in whaling operations within EU waters or to sell whale products within the EU,"

and summarizing the important EU mechanisms discussed below); *see also* Peter Davies, *Legality of Norwegian Commercial Whaling under the Whaling Convention and Its Compatibility with EC Law*, 43(2) I.C.L.Q. 270 (1994); *see also* Peter Davies, *Iceland and European Union Accession: The Whaling Issue*, 24(23) GEO. INT'L ENVTL. L. REV. 23 (2011). The major mechanisms used by the European Union to achieve conservation include: (1) the Habitats Directive (Council Directive 92/43, 1992 O.J. (L2067) 7) lists all cetacean species on Annex IV, which, pursuant to Article 12 require robust protections from member states such as the prohibition on "deliberate capture or killing," "deliberate disturbance," and "deterioration or destruction of breeding sites or resting places"; (2) the Whale Product Regulation (Council Regulation 348/81, art. 1, 1981 1981 O.J. (L39) 1 (EC)) that effectively prohibits future import of whale products; (3) domestic implementation of CITES (Council Regulation 338/97, 1997 O.J. (L61) 1); and (4) the promotion of a common international position on whaling that emphasizes habitat protection, implementation of global standards and regulations, small cetacean protections, and continued conservation work (*see* Europa, *Whaling*, http://europa.eu/legislation_summaries/maritime_affairs_and_fisheries/fisheries_resources_and_environment/l28198_en.htm (last visited Feb. 16, 2016).

280. New Zealand Government, *The Conservation of Whales in the 21st Century*, 15 (2004), http://www.doc.govt.nz/upload/documents/conservation/native-animals/marine-mammals/conservation-whales-c21.pdf; *Perano—the Last Whaling Station in New Zealand*, ENVIROHISTORY NZ (May 22, 2010 4:14 PM), http://envirohistorynz.com/2010/05/22/perano-the-last-whaling-station-in-new-zealand/.

281. *See* Gary Griggs, *California Whaling*, SANTA CRUZ SENTINEL (Sep. 24, 2011), http://seymourcenter.ucsc.edu/OOB/090_California%20Whaling.pdf; *see* Jeanne Yeomans, *Whaling Industry Doomed*, THE DAY (Nov. 17, 1971), http://news.google.com/newspapers?nid=1915&dat=19711117&id=2PcgAAAAIBAJ&sjid=lnMFAAAAIBAJ&pg=924,2942528 (the last commercial whaling station, the Richmond whaling station in San Francisco Bay, closed in 1971 when Secretary of Commerce Maurice Stans ordered an end to commercial whaling on March 1, 1971, after all large whale species had been placed on the endangered species list).

282. Australian Government: Department of Sustainability, Environment, Water, Population and Communities, *Whale Conservation*, http://www.environment.gov.au/marine/marine-species/cetaceans/whale-conservation (last visited Dec. 3, 2015) ["*Whale Conservation*"] (noting that "Australia has become a world leader in the protection and conservation of whales since the end of Australia's whaling industry in 1978").

283. 16 U.S.C. § 1632, at § 1361 (2007) ["MMPA"]; *see also* NOAA Fisheries Service, *Office of Protected Resources and the Marine Mammal Protection Act: MMPA Fact Sheet*, http://www.nmfs.noaa.gov/pr/pdfs/mmpa_factsheet.pdf (last visited Dec. 3, 2015) ["*MMPA Fact Sheet*"] (noting that Congress was motivated to enact the MMPA because of sustained commercial whaling and because of cetacean by-catch in the tuna fishery); *see also* Laura L. Lones, *The Marine Mammal Protection Act and International Protection of Cetaceans: A Unilateral Attempt to Effectuate Transnational Conservation*, 22(997) VAND. J. TRANSNAT'L L. 997, 998–98 (1989) (citing to Ken Schoolcraft, Jr., *Recent Developments, Congress*

Amends the Marine Mammal Protection Act, 62 Or. L. Rev. 257 (1983); David M. Levin, *Toward Effective Cetacean Protection*, 12 Nat. Res. L. 549, 562–64 (1979); J.E. Scarff, *The International Management of Whales, Dolphins, and Porpoises: An Interdisciplinary Assessment (Pt. 1)*, 6 Ecol. L.Q. 323, 379 (1976); and Kenneth Brower, *The Destruction of Dolphins*, The Atlantic, 35, 37 (July 1989) (where Brower provides an excellent account of the controversial tuna fishing technique called purse seining that was detrimentally impacting dolphin populations within, and outside of, American waters: "All this changed in the early 1960s, with the application of purse-seining techniques to tuna fishing. Since then any dolphins sighted in the ETP have been rounded up with 'seal bombs' (underwater explosives that originated in the days of the California sardine fishery, when they were used to discourage seals from raiding the nets) and speedboats and encircled by a mile-long fence of net, its upper edge buoyed by a line of floats—the 'corkline'—its lower edge hanging several hundred feet deep. Cables draw the bottom of the seine tight, trapping the dolphins and any tuna swimming underneath. Toward the end of each 'set' on dolphins the crew is supposed to follow a procedure called backdown, which is intended to allow the dolphins to escape over the corkline of the net, but often—in darkness or on high seas, from equipment failure, human error, or some unexpected panic by the dolphins—something goes wrong and dolphins die. As a rule only a handful drown, or dozens, but occasionally, in what are called disaster sets, hundreds die, even thousands. The 1960s were catastrophic for dolphins. By the end of the decade between a quarter and a half million dolphins were being killed annually in the ETP. Hardest hit were spotted dolphins, next spinner dolphins, and then common dolphins. Since 1960, according to the best available figures, six million dolphins have been killed by purse seiners in the ETP").

284. *MMPA Fact Sheet, supra* note 283.
285. *Id.*
286. MMPA, *supra* note 283, at § 1362; *MMPA Fact Sheet, supra* note 283.
287. MMPA, *supra* note 283, at § 1362(13).
288. *Id.* at § 1374 (which provides that waiver permits can be issued by the Secretary of Commerce for limited circumstances including public display, photography, and scientific research).
289. *MMPA Fact Sheet, supra* note 283.
290. MMPA, *supra* note 283, at § 1362(9); *MMPA Fact Sheet, supra* note 283.
291. Marine Mammal Commission, *About the Marine Mammal Commission*, http://mmc.gov/about/welcome.shtml (last visited June 12, 2015).
292. Marine Mammal Commission, *The Commission*, http://mmc.gov/commission/welcome.shtml (last visited June 12, 2015).
293. *See About the Marine Mammal Commission, supra* note 291.
294. *See generally* A.L. Pannel, *Exporting Conservation: Going Abroad with U.S. Marine Mammal Protection*, 14(2) Environs 30 (1991).
295. Pelly Amendment to the Fisherman's Protective Act of 1967, 22 U.S.C. Title 22 § 1978 (2006) (amending 22 U.S.C. § 1978 (1971)) ["Pelly Amendment"]; *see also* U.S. Fish & Wildlife Service: International Affairs, *Pelly Amendment*, https://www.fws.gov/international/laws-treaties-agreements/us-conservation-laws/pelly-amendment.html (last visited Feb. 16, 2016) (noting that the Pelly Amendment can be used to "embargo wildlife products" when a nation is

undermining the effectiveness of an international conservation regime that is in force for the United Sates and has particular relevance with respect to CITES); *see* Kaitlin M. Norjan, *Shark Laws with Teeth: How Deep Can U.S. Conservation Laws Cut into Global Trade Regulations?*, 19 ANIMAL L. 185, 197 (2012–2013) (noting that the expanded Pelly Amendment has also been utilized by the United States in the context of tiger, sea turtle, and tiger conservation); *see also* The Packwood-Magnuson Amendment to the Fishery Conservation and Management Act 16 U.S.C. Title 16 § 1821 (1982) (amending 16 U.S.C. § 1801) (which allows similar certification and reduction of foreign fishing quotas within the exclusive economic zone).

296. Andrew Nowell Porter, *Unraveling the Ocean from the Apex Down: The Role of the United States in Overcoming Obstacles to an International Shark Finning Moratorium*, 35 ENVIRONS ENVTL. L & POL'Y 231, 252 (2011–2012).

297. Pelly Amendment, *supra* note 295.

298. *Id.; see* Robert Howse, *The Appellate Body Rulings in the Shrimp/Turtle Case: A New Legal Baseline for the Trade and Environment Debate*, 27 COLUM. J. ENVTL. L. 491, 491 (2002) (noting that this is an issue of "whether trade restrictions to protect the environment are permissible under the law of the GATT/WTO [General Agreement on Tariffs and Trade/World Trade Organization] system." This sort of dispute has played out regarding fishing practices that protect dolphins and turtles from being captured in by-catch.

299. *See* Letter from Timothy J. Ragen, Exec. Dir., Marine Mammal Commission, to P. Michael Payne, Chief, Permits and Conservation Division, Office of Protected Resources, National Marine Fisheries Service (June 18, 2012) (*available at* http://www.mmc.gov/letters/pdf/2012/trumble_permit%20_061812.pdf) (discussing how the this certification process has been used three times in response to continued Japanese whaling); *see* Japanese Whaling Ass'n v. American Cetacean Society, 478 U.S. 221 (1986) (a dispute that was initiated by American conservation groups seeking a declaration that certification was mandatory for every violation of the quota system established by the IWC in its Schedule. They were unsuccessful in obtaining such an order as the majority of the Supreme Court of the United States concluded that the language does not require automatic certification based on every deviation from the quotas established in the Schedule); *see also* Melinda K. Blatt, Case Note, *Woe for the Whales: Japanese Whaling Association v. American Cetacean Society, 106 S. Ct. 2860 (1986)*, 55 U. CIN. L. REV. 1285 (1987) (providing a summary of the decision and an assessment of its impact).

300. Agence France-Presse, *Obama Waives Sanctions on Iceland Whaling*, THE RAW STORY (Sep. 15, 2011), http://www.rawstory.com/rs/2011/09/15/obama-waives-sanctions-on-iceland-whaling/.

301. Marine Mammal Protection Act 1978, section 3A (N.Z.) ["MMPA 1978"].

302. *Id.* at section 2(1).

303. *See* New Zealand Government: Department of Conservation, *Marine Mammal Conservation*, http://www.doc.govt.nz/about-us/our-role/managing-conservation/marine-mammal-conservation/ (last visited June 12, 2015) (indicating that to date there have been six marine mammal sanctuaries designations pursuant to the MMPA 1978); *see also* MMPA 1978 (which provides other conservation tools, including: section 3C ("Conservation Management Strategies"); section 3D ("Conservation Management Plans"); and section 3E ("Population Management Plans")).

304. Rob Suisted & Don Neale, *Department of Conservation Marine Mammal Action Plan 2005–2010*, at 5 (2004), http://www.doc.govt.nz/global/Conservation/The-marine-mammal-action-plan.pdf.
305. *Id.* at 18–85.
306. Marine Mammal Protection Regulations 1992, SR 1992/322 regs 18–20 (N.Z.).
307. New Zealand Government: Department of Conservation, *Marine Mammals: DOC's Role*, http://www.doc.govt.nz/conservation/native-animals/marine-mammals/docs-role/ (last visited Dec. 3, 2015).
308. *Id.*
309. *Environment Protection and Biodiversity Conservation Act 1999* (Cth) (Austl.) ["*EPBCA*"].
310. *Whale Conservation*, *supra* note 282.
311. *EPBCA*, *supra* note 309.
312. *Id.*
313. *Id.*
314. *Whale Conservation*, *supra* note 282.
315. *EPBCA*, *supra* note 309.
316. Government of Australia, *Dugongs* (Jan. 9, 2012), http://www.environment.gov.au/coasts/species/dugongs/; *id.* at section 8.
317. Government of Australia, *Seals and Sea Lions* (Dec. 4, 2015), http://www.environment.gov.au/marine/marine-species/seals-and-sea-lions ["*Seals and Sea Lions*"].
318. *Id.*
319. Government of Australia, *International Protection of Whales* (Dec. 4, 2015), http://www.environment.gov.au/marine/marine-species/cetaceans/international.
320. Note that some nations, such as Canada, appear to occupy a position between these two nation groupings. Marine mammals are hunted in Canada by northern Aboriginal peoples for subsistence purposes, and in Atlantic Canada mainly by way of the fur seal hunt.
321. *See generally* Randall R. Reeves, *Hunting of Marine Mammals*, in Encyclopedia of Marine Mammals 585, 585–88 (William F. Perrin et al. eds., 2d ed. 2009) (detailing the history of hunting cetaceans, pinnipeds, sirenians, sea otters, and polar bears); *see generally* Daniel Francis, A History of World Whaling (1990) (providing an account of whaling from the sixteenth century until the modern moratorium); *see generally* Arne Kalland & Frank Sejersen, *Marine Mammals and Northern Cultures* (2005) (providing an account of why marine mammals have been particularly important for Northern cultures).
322. New Zealand Government, *The Conservation of Whales in the 21st Century— Whaling outside the Moratorium*, http://www.doc.govt.nz/publications/conservation/native-animals/marine-mammals/conservation-of-whales-in-the-21st-century/conserving-whales-a-challenge-for-the-21st-century/whaling-outside-the-moratorium/ (last visited June 12, 2015) ["*The Conservation of Whales in the 21st Century*"].
323. John Vidal, *Iceland Resumes Fin Whale Hunting after Two-Year Break*, The Guardian (June 19, 2013), http://www.theguardian.com/environment/2013/jun/19/iceland-fin-whale-hunting-greenpeace. http://www.nrdc.org/wildlife/whaling.asp; *see* Alexander Gillespie & Al Matthews, *Iceland's Reservation at*

the *International Whaling Commission*, 14 Eur. J. Int'l L. 977 (2003) (discussing Iceland's reservation to the moratorium).

324. *See* Sea Shepherd, *Sea Shepherd*, http://www.seashepherd.org (last visited June 12, 2015).

325. New Zealand Government, *The Conservation of Whales in the 21st Century*, 15 (2004), http://www.doc.govt.nz/upload/documents/conservation/native-animals/marine-mammals/conservation-whales-c21.pdf; *see also* Humane Society International, *Japan's Whaling Season End as Another IWC Meeting Approaches* (Apr. 5, 2012), http://www.hsi.org/news/news/2012/04/whaling_season_ends_IWC_approaches_040512.html.

326. *Japan's Proposal and Its Background for Schedule Amendment to Permit the Catching of Minke Whales from the Okhotsk Sea-West Pacific Stock by Small-Type Coastal Whaling Vessels*, IWC/65/9 (2014).

327. *Id.* (note that this unsuccessful proposal sought permission to take 17 minke whales per annum from 2014 to 2018).

328. International Whaling Commission, *Aboriginal Subsistence Whaling*, IWC (2015), https://iwc.int/aboriginal (note that strikes/catch limits can carry forward for years that the Aboriginal community does not fill its quota).

329. *Id.*

330. *See* Anthony Speca, *Speca: In the Belly of the Whaling Commission*, Northern Public Affairs (June 18, 2012), http://www.northernpublicaffairs.ca/index/in-the-belly-of-the-whaling-commission/; *see* Fisheries and Oceans Canada, *Under Water World: Beluga* (Apr. 22, 2013), http://www.dfo-mpo.gc.ca/Science/publications/uww-msm/articles/beluga-eng.htm; *see* Fisheries and Oceans Canada, *Under Water World: Narwhal* (Apr. 22, 2013), http://www.dfo-mpo.gc.ca/Science/publications/uww-msm/articles/narwhal-narval-eng.htm.

331. *Grindadráp Photos: Faroe Islands' Pilot Whale Slaughter*, News (June 7, 2010), at 3, http://www.3news.co.nz/Grindadrap-photos-Faroe-Islands-pilot-whale-slaughter/tabid/1160/articleID/256999/Default.aspx.

332. *Id.*

333. North Atlantic Marine Mammal Commission, *NAMMCO Annual Report 2011*, 439 (2012), http://www.nammco.no/webcronize/images/Nammco/976.pdf ["NAMMCO Annual Report 2011"].

334. Animal Welfare Institute, *Small Cetacean Hunts in the Faroe Islands*, http://awionline.org/content/small-cetacean-hunts-faroe-islands (last visited Dec. 3, 2015).

335. Animal Welfare Institute, *Small Cetacean Hunts*, https://awionline.org/content/small-cetacean-hunts (last visited June 12, 2015) ["*Small Cetacean Hunts*"].

336. *Id.*; *see also* Rachelle Adam, *The Japanese Dolphin Hunts: The Quest of International Legal Protection for Small Cetaceans*, 14 Animal L. 133, 148–55 (2008) (highlighting the sustainability concerns associated with the Japanese hunts); *see also* Government of the United Kingdom: Department for Environment, Food & Rural Affairs, *Protecting Whales: A Global Responsibility*, https://www.gov.uk/government/uploads/system/uploads/attachment_data/file/183344/protecting-whales__1_.pdf (last visited Feb. 16, 2016) (questioning the sustainability of the Japanese porpoise drive).

337. NAMMCO Annual Report 2011, *supra* note 333, at 453.

338. *Id.* at 455.

339. *Id.* at 454.

340. Fisheries and Oceans Canada, *Managing Canada's Commercial Seal Harvest* (Feb. 2, 2012), http://www.dfo-mpo.gc.ca/fm-gp/seal-phoque/facts-faits/facts-faitsd-eng.htm.
341. Fisheries and Oceans Canada, *Sealing in Canada—Frequently Asked Questions* (Mar. 21, 2013), http://www.dfo-mpo.gc.ca/fm-gp/seal-phoque/faq-eng.htm.
342. *Id.*
343. NAMMCO Annual Report 2011, *supra* note 333, at 485.
344. *Id.*
345. *Id.* at 453–54.
346. *National Management Plan for the Grey Seal Stock in the Baltic Sea: The Grey Seal* (Halichoerus grypus), https://www.havochvatten.se/download/18.576c1ba d139e467697d80006088/1348912841150/Förvaltningsplan_gråsäl_120924.pdf (last visited Mar. 30, 2016).
347. Finnish Game and Fisheries Research Institute, *Seals*, http://www.rktl.fi/english/game/seals/ (last visited Dec. 3, 2015).
348. NAMMCO Annual Report 2011, *supra* note 333, at 485.
349. BBC News Africa, *Namibia's Controversial Annual Seal Hunt Set to Begin*, BBC (Jul. 14, 2012, 23:50 ET), http://www.bbc.co.uk/news/world-africa-18845596; Felix Njini, *Seal Cull in Namibia to Be Record Low as Pups Evade Clubs*, Bloomberg (Nov. 13, 2014, 07:27 MST), http://www.bloomberg.com/news/articles/2014-11-12/seal-cull-in-namibia-to-be-record-low-as-pups-evade-clubs.
350. *Id.*

3

Goals for the Rational Conservation of Marine Mammals and Emerging Ethical Considerations

> "Changes in the current arrangements are inevitable. Most knowledgeable observers agree that the whaling regime cannot be saved simply by standing loyally by and hoping that the current conflicts will resolve themselves with the passage of time. This observation need not lead to conclusions of gloom and doom. Periods of crisis give rise to rare opportunities to reconstitute or reconstruct management systems as well as to the danger of complete collapse leaving a management vacuum."[1]

This chapter identifies the theoretical framework that informs my remaining analysis. In addition to establishing the basic decision-making model I employ, this chapter also fulfills a fundamental aspect of the rational decision-making process, namely goal setting. Without carefully constructed goals, it is not possible to fully apply the rational decision-making process. After establishing these goals, the remainder of the chapter engages in a discussion of the ethical considerations that inform the relationship between man and marine mammal, and considers how ethics influence conservation and management decisions. Scientific advances that inform our understanding of animal ethics and animal welfare must be considered and weighed against the utilitarian dimension of the human-marine mammal relationship moving forward. Although the ethical justifications fall short of requiring a permanent zero-catch quota for cetaceans (or other marine mammals more generally), they do warrant a reconsideration of killing methods and efforts needed to standardize and implement best practices.

I. RATIONAL DECISION-MAKING MODEL

In advancing effective implementation of Articles 65 and 120 of the United Nations Convention on the Law of the Sea (UNCLOS),[2] and rational conservation of marine mammals generally, it is essential that sound evidence (be it scientific or otherwise) is assessed and the resulting legal recommendations be both feasible and pragmatic.[3] As such, the logic and argumentation employed in this work utilizes a modified version of the "rational-comprehensive decision-making model,"[4] which accords with the following framework:

1. Problem Identification and Goal Setting

The problematic regulatory relationship between humans and marine mammals is no longer just concerned with over-exploitation; rather, marine mammals are susceptible to a whole host of issues, including by-catch, climate change, marine pollution (i.e., chemical pollution, biological pollution, and noise pollution), vessel-strikes, and other non-consumptive disturbances (i.e., whale watching/tourism and other forms of ecotourism).

2. Identification of Past Trends

This book builds upon the foundation established by international law and existing scholarship. Having already introduced the brief history of marine mammal over-exploitation and the prevailing fragmented legal framework in Chapters 1 and 2, in Chapter 4 I will identify the emerging trends in marine mammal management (both issues and current anthropogenic threats) before proceeding to provide, and add to, the legal analysis surrounding Articles 65 and 120 of UNCLOS in Chapter 5.

3. Assessment and Analysis of Alternatives, Decision-Making, and Recommendations

Chapters 5 to 7 move into prescriptive analysis and assessment. Chapter 5 assesses mechanisms to improve the existing fragmented approach to marine mammal management and proposes the creation of an International Marine Mammal Commission pursuant to a new multilateral treaty—by way of implementing an agreement pursuant to UNCLOS—that supersedes and replaces the International Convention for the Regulation of Whaling (ICRW)[5] and coexists with other existing efforts to manage marine mammals. This chapter also addresses the practical considerations (financial, political, and geographical) associated with decision-making, international cooperation, and the process of crafting and implementing a new international treaty and creating the International Marine Mammal Commission within our resource-restricted world.

Chapters 6 and 7 explore critical aspects of a new international treaty for the international conservation and sustainable management of marine mammals. They examine how this proposed agreement will strive to address the current threats to marine mammals identified in Chapter 4, and also how regional coordination is facilitated using framework provisions and minimum conservation requirements that will be implemented regionally. I explore international enforcement and compliance, transparency, and dispute resolution in an attempt to remedy these oft-encountered barriers to effective international governance. I also examine the role of a bolstered treaty Secretariat to help implement and coordinate the goals of the new agreement with existing regimes, the use of regionalism, and the use of a robust, internationally coordinated network of marine protected areas to help achieve ecosystem-based conservation.

II. GOALS FOR THIS WORK

1. Promote the Rule of Law in the Oceans

As my proposal contemplates an implementation agreement pursuant to UNCLOS, it is critical that it seeks to add to the success and legacy of UNCLOS by promoting the rule of law in the ocean[6] and by enhancing the efficacy of sustainable living marine resource management. To be successful, rational marine mammal conservation must be guided by clearly defined legal principles that create certainty of expectation for member states, account for enforcement, provide for monitoring and compliance, and enable recourse to dispute resolution processes.

2. Expand Species Coverage

At a minimum, any alternative to the current ICRW/IWC regime must expand jurisdiction to all cetacean species; however, the proposal in this work suggests expanding species coverage even further. In addition to sharing similar biological characteristics and life histories, the survey of current threats contained in Chapter 4 indicates that marine mammals face similar conservation and management concerns and, as such, my proposal contemplates the creation of an implementing agreement that features a commission with jurisdiction over all marine mammal species, so far as this is possible given the maritime zones established by UNCLOS. I recognize that this is an ambitious proposal. Nevertheless, it is the logical starting point for any comprehensive alternative.

3. Expand Issue Coverage

It is also critical to expand the scope of issues covered by the convention and commission that replaces and supersedes the ICRW/IWC. This new regime should endeavor to either make regulations or recommendations, or otherwise be engaged with the following issues: direct lethal utilization/take, climate change, by-catch, ship-strikes, environmental pollution (broadly defined), and marine mammal tourism. So far as any of the above listed issues are covered by an existing international scheme, the new commission should formalize its cooperation with other international organizations, its lobbying efforts with different regimes, and/or its information dissemination processes to ensure that marine mammals are afforded an appropriate level of consideration within existing issue-specific regimes. The new implementing agreement should also be drafted with the flexibility needed to respond to new issues as they emerge.

4. Respect Competing Ocean Uses

The overarching purpose of this book is to enhance marine mammal conservation and management. As such, it is essential throughout to recognize and account for various competing interests in the ocean. For example, rational decision-making precludes advancing marine mammal conservation to the exclusion or undue detriment of commercial shipping and/or military objectives, which both represent critical uses of the ocean. Therefore, this work strives to accommodate both commercial and military considerations by advancing a measured proposal.

5. Promote Cooperation and Enhance Global Participation

UNCLOS generally, and especially in negotiations at the Third United Nations Conference on the Law of the Sea, is notable for the consensus negotiating process employed as well as the comprehensive negotiating texts that embodied compromise and fostered cooperation between groups of nations with seemingly disparate interests.[7] UNCLOS currently has 167 states parties.[8] Additionally, the implementing agreement relating to migratory fish stocks and straddling fish stocks has 82 ratified member nations.[9] My proposal recognizes the importance of advancing a compromise that bridges the gap between pro-utilization and pro-preservation states in a manner that promotes a sustainable future for the world's marine mammals.

6. Incorporate Current Principles of International Law

International governance and leading principles in the area of international law relating to environmental law and wildlife conservation and/or management have advanced significantly since the ICRW was finalized in 1946. Indeed, the IWC has been hindered, in part, by the ambiguity and antiquity of its enabling convention, which has enabled disparate interpretation of key provisions. This proposal is founded on particular principles of international environmental governance, including: sustainability, the precautionary principle, ecosystem-based management (the ecosystem approach), and intergenerational equity.

7. Utilizing Science-Based Decision-Making and Conservation Tools That Enable Holistic Management

Implementing the principles identified above, in this context, requires constructing a proposal that is flexible enough to account for our evolving relationship with marine mammals. It is critical that the decision-making process employed by the new commission be predicated on sound peer-reviewed science. Further, the holistic approach to marine mammal conservation necessary to address the various threats to marine mammals requires the use of innovative conservation tools, such as marine protected areas (MPAs).

8. Promote Regional Implementation

Regionalism enables cooperation and coordination at a level of governance that functionally allows a response to both regional and local concerns. The success of the UNEP Regional Seas Programme and regional agreements for cetacean conservation, such as the Agreement on the Conservation of Small Cetaceans of the Baltic,

North East Atlantic, Irish and North Seas[10] (ASCOBANS) and the Agreement on the Conservation of Cetaceans of the Black Sea, Mediterranean Sea and contiguous Atlantic Area[11] (ACCOBAMS), justify regional implementation. The case for regional implementation is also bolstered by the success of Regional Fisheries Management Organizations pursuant to the Agreement for the Implementation of the Provisions of the United Nations Convention on the Law of the Sea of 10 December 1982 Relating to the Conservation and Management of Straddling Fish Stocks and Highly Migratory Fish Stocks (the "UN Fish Stocks Agreement").[12] The purpose of promoting regional implementation is to help implement international regulation and decision-making rather than replace it. Regional implementation of global standards and regulations has the potential to enhance enforcement, monitoring, compliance, operational efficiency, and operational flexibility to the changing environment.

9. Build on the Existing Foundation

My proposal is a comprehensive alternative to the current approach to marine mammal conservation at the international level of governance. Regulatory succession must be alive and responsive to current trends and conditions; indeed, change for the sake of change is not sufficient justification for regulatory reform. This work seeks to build on the current foundation of marine mammal conservation by utilizing what has been successful, internationally, regionally, and nationally, and then acting to address shortfalls. Ultimately, the goal is a normatively sound proposal that acknowledges the practicalities and multifactorial realities of marine mammal conservation.

10. Propose a Rational Arrangement

In 2001, ocean policy expert Robert L. Friedheim crafted a proposal to fix the international whaling regime that he "designed to get peoples, governments and their delegates, and representatives from nongovernmental organizations (NGOs) thinking about how to negotiate a more satisfactory outcome than the present stalemate."[13] Then, in 2008, Professor Michael Bowman offered a detailed assessment of various possibilities for normalizing or modernizing the ICRW, emphasizing purposive treaty interpretation and a return to first principles to secure effectivity.[14]

This current work is both theoretical and practical. Although it is important to frame the proposal developed in this work within a robust theoretical framework, it is equally important to ground the proposal with reference to political and practical realities, with the appreciation that rational conservation and management requires compromise. One cannot ignore that whaling, and marine mammal conservation generally, is contentious, acrimonious, emotional, and politically driven. Therefore, enhancing marine mammal conservation and management remains an academic exercise with real-world consequences.

III. ETHICAL CONSIDERATIONS

Marc Bekoff, Professor Emeritus of ecology and evolutionary biology at the University of Colorado, posits that "[o]ur relationship with other animals is a complex, ambiguous, challenging, and frustrating affair, and we must continually reassess how we should interact with other non-humans."[15] This analysis of the ethical considerations that inform human-marine mammal interaction proceeds by describing emerging ethical considerations and then assessing how they should inform the new multilateral regime I propose.

Many perceive marine mammals, and cetaceans in particular, as being unique. Perhaps it is that because we imagine marine mammals to possess a sort of alien intelligence, or because we tend to anthropomorphize their actions and/or behaviors in accordance with their status as "charismatic megafauna," or because we associate marine mammals as guides to, or touchstones from, the unknown ocean environment.[16]

Alternatively, the shift from viewing marine mammals as a living natural resource to marine mammals as objects of preservation may simply have been driven by incredibly successful storytelling and lobbying by a transformed IWC membership base that no longer values whaling.[17] This perspective is informed by the fact that opposition to whaling has morphed over the decades from the "ecological argument that whales are endangered" to the ethical argument that cetaceans are somehow unique and should not be killed.[18] Environmental organizations have also utilized and propagated human sympathies for marine mammals and have transformed them into symbols for environmental action.[19] Whaling nations (namely Iceland, Norway, and Japan) urge sustainable use of whales and point to what they perceive as a fundamentally hypocritical Western perspective that whales deserve special protection but other animals, such as cows or pigs, do not.[20]

The scope of the ethical discussion surrounding marine mammals is difficult to reduce to a single issue. At one level we are asked to consider whether it is more appropriate to approach marine mammal conservation from the perspective of animal welfare (which does not oppose some utilitarian use so long as activities are conducted in an appropriately humane manner) or from the perspective of animal rights (which asserts that we do not have dominion over other living things, and as such they should be free from human interference or molestation).[21] At the second level we must consider whether this ethical discussion extends to all marine mammals or only cetaceans. A third order consideration is if this discussion is limited to direct lethal utilization and whether it should be expanded to include other issues such as the consequences of keeping marine mammals in captivity (at zoos or theme parks), the use of marine mammals in aquatic petting/feeding experiences, the impact of ecotourism, or the ethics associated with lethal or nonlethal research programs.[22] Finally, it is necessary to consider the tension between asserted cultural rights (such as Aboriginal whaling) and similar assertions from other pro-whaling nations.

It is beyond the scope of this work to engage in a comprehensive exploration of each level of discussion, or to advance the philosophical debate on this issue. Rather, the purpose here is to survey the contents of the existing ethical discussion and peer-reviewed literature to assess whether there exists an ethical justification for maintenance of a permanent moratorium and zero-catch quota. If the answer to the above question is no, then the discussion must focus on how to account for significant marine mammal characteristics, and our appreciation for them, in a rational manner.

1. Scientific Advances

Legal literature regarding marine mammal conservation and the ethical issues surrounding marine mammal utilization often relies on science to justify its suggestions and/or conclusions. This area of study is necessarily interdisciplinary as it is critical to base conservation decisions on the best available science.[23] A leading example of this intersection is the 1991 article titled "Whales: Their Emerging Right to Life" by Anthony D'Amato and Sudhir Chopra.[24] Here, the authors assert that whales "are sentient, they are intelligent, they have their own community, and they can suffer,"[25] noting that scientific literature suggests that whales may have "higher than human intelligence,"[26] have a brain that "in some instances is six times bigger than the human brain" with a more complex neocortex,[27] and be capable of complex intraspecific communication and some interspecific communication.[28] D'Amato and Chopra rely on limited research to propose and justify the transition toward international preservation of cetaceans and to promote progression toward an expanding conception of rights entitlement for whales that provides a right to life that is morally and legally justified as "the consequence of an emerging humanist right in international law."[29] We cannot simply accept the argument advanced by D'Amato and Chopra because it relies on scant scientific literature that, in some instances, borders on popular literature.[30]

Still, the idea that whales deserve a right to life persists and has even entered public discourse.[31] In May, 2010, The Helsinki Group (which was created from a conference on cetacean rights) produced a document titled "Declaration of Rights for Cetaceans: Whales and Dolphins" (the "Declaration") that provides the following principles:

1. Every individual cetacean has the right to life;
2. No cetacean should be held in captivity or servitude; be subject to cruel treatment; or be removed from their natural environment;
3. All cetaceans have the right to freedom of movement and residence within their natural environment;
4. No cetacean is the property of any State, corporation, human group or individual;
5. Cetaceans have the right to the protection of their natural environment;
6. Cetaceans have the right not to be subject to the disruption of their cultures;
7. The rights, freedoms and norms set forth in this Declaration should be protected under international and domestic law;
8. Cetaceans are entitled to an international order in which these rights, freedoms and norms can be fully realized;
9. No State, corporation, human group or individual should engage in any activity that undermines these rights, freedoms and norms; and
10. Nothing in this Declaration shall prevent a State from enacting stricter provisions for the protection of cetacean rights.[32]

It is worth noting that The Helsinki Group consists of professors, researchers, and members of nongovernmental organizations dedicated to cetacean conservation.[33] The Helsinki Group initiative received considerable media exposure in the summer of 2012 as the Declaration was discussed at the 2012 annual meeting of the American Association for the Advancement of Science (AAAS).[34] Here, a symposium on the Declaration emphasized that "a variety of scientific studies have found that whales and dolphins are capable of advanced cognitive abilities (such as problem-solving, artificial 'language' comprehension, and complex social behaviour), indicating that these cetaceans are far more intellectually and emotionally sophisticated than previously thought."[35] Further, the symposium addressed the observation that "while marine scientists have been uncovering greater intellectual and emotional sophistication in cetaceans, some countries have continued to support the killing of dolphins and to press for the resumption of commercial whaling."[36] The end goal of this movement appears to be recognition for cetaceans as nonhuman legal persons, deserving of the benefits of legal protection.[37] The remainder of this section will address some of the emerging scientific observations, leading into a discussion of the killing methods currently used during marine mammal hunting and the tension that persists regarding Aboriginal subsistence whaling.

Current scientific consideration of the uniqueness of cetaceans far surpasses what D'Amato and Chopra had at their disposal and can be distilled to two broad areas: (1) study of the cetacean brain, and (2) study of cetacean cognition and behavior (including cetacean culture). Each is deserving of attention.

(1) The Cetacean Brain

Over time,[38] cetaceans deviated from their terrestrial mammalian counterparts some 50–60 million years ago[39] and from primates approximately 92 million years ago.[40] Since this divergence, cetaceans have adapted to aquatic life and have "evolved large brains and an expanded neocortex [the portion of the mammalian brain associated with higher function, such as the sense perception and conscious reasoning] with a high degree of gyrification compared to ungulates."[41] As noted by M.P. Simmonds, "[t]he size and complexity of the brain has long been used as a basic indicator of intelligence."[42] Cetaceans are the only mammalian group, other than primates, that exhibit this degree of encephalization (exaggerated brain size compared to body mass),[43] and this feature, coupled with the comparative complexity of the structural organization of cetacean brains,[44] forms the foundation of a number of competing hypotheses regarding the significance of these features.[45] It is notable that the dolphin family generally exhibits the highest encephalization of all cetaceans.[46] The importance of these observations is succinctly summarized by Bearzi and Stanford in *A Bigger, Better Brain*:

> Of all the species on our planet, only a handful has possessed a high degree of intellect: apes, and humans (including many extinct forms of both), dolphins, whales, and some others, such as elephants. The brains of an ape and a dolphin differ in their external morphology and neuroanatomical organization, in particular their cortical cytoarchitecture, which in dolphins has less cellular differentiation. Despite these differences, primate (including human) and dolphin brains share important similarities. For one, the brains of dolphins and apes increased in size and complexity over their evolutionary history. Both possess a high encephalization quotient (EQ) due to their unusually large brain-to-body-size ratios. EQ is the ratio of an animal's actual brain size to its expected brain

size based on measurements of other animals its size. In both dolphins and apes, the neocortex is also more elaborately developed compared to that of other animals. Also distinctive is the neocortical gyrification, or folding of the cerebral cortex—which in dolphins surpasses that of any primate—and the presence of spindle-shaped neurons, which have been linked in people to social fluency and the ability to sense what others think. Only recently were those neurons found in bottlenose dolphins.[47]

The last two sentences of the above quotation highlight an issue that currently attracts considerable attention. The spindle cells referred to are called von Economo neurons, and they are found in humans and other primates, elephants, and cetaceans.[48] These cells are associated with social interaction and emotional response, and in humans are believed to be responsible for "our social organisation, empathy, speech, intuition about the feelings of others, and rapid 'gut' reactions."[49]

Anatomical studies first identified von Economo neurons in large cetacean species, such as the humpback whale, and in odontocete species with the largest brains, such as orca and sperm whale.[50] A subsequent study indicates that von Economo cells are also found, in a similar distribution, in smaller odontocetes such as the bottlenose dolphin, Risso's dolphin, and the beluga whale.[51] Interestingly, von Economo neurons have also been reported in the Atlantic walrus and the Florida manatee, which are obviously not cetaceans, in different quantities and distributions.[52] These recent observations suggest to some that the presence of this sort of neuron in large mammals "represents a common evolutionary trait among large mammals contributing to specialized neuronal networks in a taxon-specific manner, dependent upon their cortical distribution."[53] However, it is also possible that this type of neuron is "a phylogenetically ancient neuron type rather than an emergent specialized neuron."[54]

It is clear that the cetacean brain, and perhaps the brain of certain other marine mammals, is unique in structure and organization. Still, it is apparent that more research is required to determine the consequence of such developments. Before assessing the relevance of these discoveries, I first turn to a survey of advances in our understanding of marine mammal cognition and behavior.

(ii) Behavior and Culture

Although anatomical and neurological studies help us understand what makes marine mammals unique, they do not tell the entire story. To complete this assessment, it is necessary to consider work that investigates other important aspects of marine mammals, namely behavior and culture.

Dolphin behavior has been extensively studied. In a recent book titled *In Defense of Dolphins: The New Moral Frontier*, philosopher Thomas White (one of the founding signatories of The Helsinki Group) surveys scientific studies and other observations in search of answers to the following questions: "What kind of beings are dolphins? What does the answer to this question say about the ethical character of human/dolphin interaction?"[55] In addition to an examination of anatomy and physiology, White also surveys the capacity of dolphins to feel and think,[56] problem solve and comprehend language,[57] and exhibit social intelligence.[58] White's findings are summarized below.

With respect to conscious thought and the capacity to feel, White concludes that "[t]he dolphin brain appears to support a consciousness" that allows these animals to: "be aware of themselves and others"; "experience at least basic emotions"; "engage in some degree of abstract, conceptual thought"; and "choose their action."[59] Regarding problem-solving and language comprehension, White's survey suggests that "[d]olphins appear to be able to solve complex problems by thinking about them, to think creatively and abstractly, and to understand an artificial language."[60] Finally, White concludes that dolphins utilize their "cognitive and affective capacities" for survival in a manner that exhibits social organization through cooperation, relationship formation, and complex communication.[61]

A similar survey of literature, with reference to conservation considerations, was completed by Mark Simmonds.[62] This analysis considers studies that suggest intelligent behavior (i.e., imitation, behavioral modification, and the capacity to play)[63] and the ability to utilize their environment to their benefit (such as bubble manipulation from their breathing[64] and the use of sea sponges to protect their beaks while searching for food).[65] It also considers studies that indicate self-awareness in bottlenose dolphins,[66] and emotions such as parental grief and love.[67] Simmonds also emphasizes the importance of group living[68] and the emerging idea that cetaceans demonstrate social culture.[69] Given the considerable attention that has been paid to the notion of cetacean culture, this emerging area is worthy of independent consideration.

Culture, in the context of cetacean interaction, has been described as "information or behavior—shared by a population or subpopulation—which is acquired from conspecifics through some form of social learning."[70] Another definition considers animal culture "as all group typical behavior patterns, shared by members of animal communities, that are to some degree reliant on socially learned and transmitted information."[71] The importance of culture in this context is that it "is one of the attributes of cetaceans that most sets them apart from the majority of other nonhuman species and is likely underpinned by advanced social learning."[72] It is posited that culture can exist between individuals of the same generation (called horizontal culture) or that it can exist between generations (known as vertical culture).[73] One of the oft-cited examples of cetacean culture is the social structure of orca pods, which "consist of a highly stable, hierarchical set of relationships based on the *matriline*, that is, the family group consisting of a mother and her offspring," which comes to have unique communication and association patterns.[74] Commentators suggest that evidence of culture (both horizontal and vertical) can also be found in the bottlenose dolphin (i.e., social learning capability), baleen whales (i.e., learned mating songs), the curious behavior of some smaller toothed whale species,[75] and matrilineal social structure in sperm whales.[76] It has even been suggested that synchronized breathing patterns observed in pilot whales is a tool to strengthen social bonds, perhaps preferentially demonstrated during times of stress.[77]

The practical significance of cultural structures for nonhuman animals is that they can influence evolution and selection pressures by allowing "organisms to become partially disconnected from their environments," which can ultimately result in different physical characteristics, and can even result in the mass adoption of non-beneficial behavior.[78] In terms of consequences for the conservation or management of marine species, biologist Hal Whitehead suggests that "[s]ocial learning and culture may be important factors in translocation success, and should sometimes be considered when delineating population units for conservation and management. We should aim to protect cultural as well as genetic diversity."[79] Still, the discussion of cetacean culture has not been free from controversy or debate.

A number of objections have been raised in response to the assertion that cetaceans utilize culture, and a review of existing literature suggests that further research is needed. Some writers have challenged the assertion that "intraspecific behavioural variation" is a result of cultural influence rather than of environmental pressure or genetics.[80] Ruling out competing explanations for unique behavior is a fundamental hurdle, as is our ability to correctly interpret different behaviors.[81] Based on these limitations, some have concluded that future research should focus on the extent to which behavior is socially learned, or cultural, versus the extent to which it is the product of ecological pressures or genetics.[82] It is important to consider the implications that these unique marine mammal characteristics have for conservation.

The preceding discussion has surveyed the current scientific justification for reconsidering our interaction with marine mammals, and this survey reflects the reality that most literature on this issue is focused on cetaceans. Recent advances do, in my opinion, suggest that cetaceans are unique mammals that have complex brains that feature intriguing spindle cells, demonstrate intelligent behavior, exhibit emotional reactions, and might have a form of social culture that influences intraspecific interactions. However, I am of the opinion that the current discussion of ethics falls short of justifying a perpetual zero-catch quota, largely because of the potential ramifications of leading with such a position.

The overarching goal of this work is to promote rational decision-making regarding international cetacean conservation. Advancing this goal necessitates being alive to nonstarter issues that could ruin multinational negotiations that aim to produce an alternative to the current ICRW/IWC regime by negotiating an agreement to implement Articles 65 and 120 of UNCLOS. I suggest that leading with a proposal similar to the Cetacean Declaration of Rights qualifies as such a nonstarter issue. Even though the current regime has had a commercial moratorium in place for over two decades and has halted large-scale commercial whaling, the reality is that cetaceans are still hunted. Whaling for large species persists pursuant to special permit scientific whaling and the Aboriginal subsistence exemption, and has arguably become more prevalent for smaller species. The most appropriate mechanism for addressing our evolving understanding of cetaceans, and all marine mammals for that matter, is to ensure that all of our interactions are guided by the best available science and appropriate welfare considerations. The following section considers current killing methods used in marine mammal hunts, and then the discussion turns to the tension that exists with respect to Aboriginal subsistence whaling.

2. Marine Mammal Killing Methods

The above discussion investigated the claim that cetaceans are unique animals. The purpose of this section is to consider our ability to account for the potential intelligence, social nature, and emotional capacity of cetaceans, and to ask whether, or how, these considerations extend to all marine mammals. I previously concluded that our current understanding of the cetacean brain and cetacean behavior does not yet warrant a perpetual zero-catch quota. This conclusion is bolstered by the observation that advancing such a position within the context of proposed treaty negotiations likely represents a nonstarter issue capable of collapsing negotiations aimed at creating a new international regime that addresses marine mammal conservation and sustainable management. A second difficulty with advancing this position is that it does not accord with our perspective on killing other species, whether they are domestic livestock or other wildlife species.[83]

The alternative advanced in this work attempts to reach an understanding of the interests of the pro-whaling contingent, the anti-whaling contingent, Indigenous whalers, and others who have historically been involved in whaling. To accomplish this, I propose a regime that addresses marine mammal conservation holistically, meaning it will cover both direct and indirect threats to marine mammals in a manner consistent with our scientific understanding and ethical appreciation for them to the maximum extent practicable. Further, this work focuses on enhancing the efficacy of marine mammal killing methods by recognizing that "[t]he objective must be that if any animals are to be killed, they should be killed humanely, whoever does it."[84]

A variety of methods are currently used to kill marine mammals. The methods employed vary based on a number of factors, including geographical location, type of species, type of boat used, and type of hunt (i.e., commercial or Aboriginal and/or coastal or open-water).[85] The humaneness of marine mammal hunting is an issue considered by both the IWC (through its Working Group on Whale Killing Methods)[86] and NAMMCO (through its Committee on Hunting Methods).[87] This discussion of the relative humaneness of killing methods draws from work conducted by each organization, and generally has two major components: (1) what criteria determine or establish death, and (2) what killing mechanisms/methods are currently employed.

The IWC has worked to improve the "humaneness of whaling operations since 1959."[88] In 1980, the IWC adopted "time to death" (TTD) criteria (the "IWC Criteria") for whales, being "the time taken for the mouth to slacken, the flipper to slacken and all movements to cease."[89] Establishing a TTD is an important exercise because, according to NAMMCO, it "gives an indication of whether or not a killing method is acceptable from an animal welfare point of view."[90] That such criteria exist for whales is remarkable in and of itself; Arctic veterinarian S.K. Knudsen noted in 2005 that "[t]he only other species in which official criteria of death have been formulated is humans."[91] NAMMCO recognizes that our understanding of death criteria has been and is currently evolving.[92] Further, NAMMCO cites Knudsen's work in reviewing death criteria to note that an animal that is unconscious and rendered insensitive may fail to meet the IWC criteria due to involuntary reflexive motions, leading to an overestimation of the TTD.[93] NAMMCO also notes that there are no death criteria for seals[94] and a review of NAMMCO's assessment of killing methods for small cetaceans raises questions about the applicability of the IWC Criteria to small cetaceans.[95] This review suggests that the IWC Criteria do not necessarily reflect the best available scientific evidence. Moving forward it is important to consider the suitability of alternative criteria, such as an "irreversible loss of consciousness"[96] and/or irreversible damage to the cortex and deeper regions of the brain,[97] and whether there is scientific justification for amendment

Goals for Rational Marine Mammal Conservation

to existing criteria. It is now necessary to consider the methods employed during hunting, and whether best practices align with current marine mammal hunting techniques (with particular attention paid to Aboriginal methodology).

Much of the available information on marine mammal hunting, TTD, and killing methods is the result of national self-reporting to organizations such as the IWC and NAMMCO. Indeed, the IWC has encouraged such reporting by resolution (Resolution 1999-1 and 2001-2) whereas NAMMCO utilizes voluntary self-reporting.[98] With respect to the killing methods themselves, "neural disruption" is the preferred mechanism for killing marine mammals[99] and there are a variety of ways that this can be achieved. At this point it is useful to consider common killing methods for marine mammals:[100]

(1) Large Cetaceans—According to the IWC Chairman's Report to the Commission on the Workshop on Whale Killing Methods and Associated Welfare Issues of 2003, "the use of appropriately powerful penthrite grenades, fired from improved delivery systems represents the current state of 'best practice' for a primary killing method,"[101] and is much more efficient at killing whales than the cold harpoon method (being a harpoon without any attached explosive device).[102] Penthrite, an explosive developed around World War I and commonly used for demolition,[103] is particularly effective as it combines mechanical destruction and bleeding with a shockwave that can also kill the targeted whale.[104] Norway first demonstrated its use in 1983, and reported that the rate of instant kills increased from 2.7 percent to 45 percent.[105] The Chairman's Report also comments that the rifles represent the preferred secondary killing tool, and that testing of different caliber guns and ammunition type is improving this approach.[106] NAMMCO's data reflects a similar trend, noting that harpoon guns loaded with penthrite grenades now represent the norm as the primary killing tool for the Norwegian minke whale hunt, the Greenland minke and fin whale hunt, the Japanese minke hunt (coastal and offshore), and the Japanese hunt for the sperm whale, fin whale, sei whale, and Bryde's whale.[107] Finally, Iceland has also used a harpoon loaded with a penthrite grenade as the primary killing method for their fin whale hunt.[108] Still, not all large whales are being killed according to this best practice. For example, the United States reported that in 2011, 20 whales were killed using a less effective black powder grenade, 7 were killed using the penthrite grenade, and 12 were taken using a combination of both.[109] Although the percentage of bowhead whales being killed by penthrite is increasing (up from only two in 2010),[110] there is still work to be done to ensure that the most effective tool is being universally used.

(2) Small Cetaceans—There is less uniformity in the methods employed to kill small cetaceans. Techniques used by hunters located on land, ice, or in boats include: (1) harpoons (either thrown by hand or fired by gun); (2) exploding grenade (generally only employed for the largest species of this category); (3) personal firearms (of various caliber and ammunition type); (4) lances, spears, and knives; and (5) nets.[111] Generally, the technique employed varies by tradition, environmental

condition, weapon availability, and economic situation.[112] For example, harpoons and/or rifles represent the primary killing method employed in Greenland in their hunt of the harbor porpoise, narwhal, beluga, white-sided dolphin, white-beaked dolphin, orca, and long-finned pilot whale, and in Canada where northern Aboriginal peoples hunt beluga and narwhal.[113] In contrast, the drive hunts in the Faroe Islands and in Japan utilize more traditional tools such as an iron-tipped (or ball-pointed) hook and stabbing knife/spinal lance (Faroe Islands) or a thrown lance/spinal lance (Japan).[114] NAMMCO suggests that advances in methodology have been made that have enhanced the efficacy and humaneness of both drive hunts.[115] Finally, a small percentage of narwhal whales are taken in Greenland through net hunting, which is the most controversial hunting method as it likely causes unnecessary stress.[116]

(3) Seals—Seals, throughout the world are killed on land, on ice, or in the water using "firearms, hakapik [a club with an iron pick and hammer mounted on one end], clubs, nets and traps."[117] The general goal in hunting seals is to "achieve instant or rapid insensibility to avoid unnecessary pain and reduce the risk of losing the animal [by sinking]."[118] This can be accomplished through mechanical stunning (meaning a hand-propelled blow to the cranial region) or through the use of a firearm (for which no international standard exists).[119] Animals will often be bled after they are caught to ensure that they are dead.[120] Nets and traps are also employed in areas where other hunting methods are not practical, but they also represent a less efficient method of hunting.[121] Finally, it should be noted that both Canada and Norway have established domestic processes and regulations for their large scale seal hunts.[122] Although similar information has not been produced for other marine mammals, seals represent a useful analog, and it can reasonably be inferred that firearms (supplemented by nets and traps) represent the primary killing techniques for sea lions, walruses, and otters.

The summary provided above suggests that hunting marine mammals poses different considerations than hunting terrestrial mammals or killing farmed animals.[123] For example, hunters have to contend with prey that can dive for considerable periods of time, that may sink when struck, and that often have to be hunted over considerable distances, making it impossible to employ techniques akin to the captive bolt that is used in slaughterhouses. What, then, is the standard that should be promoted? NAMMCO proposes that "the ideal weapon from an animal welfare point of view should render the animal instantly and irreversibly unconscious and insensible to pain, until death."[124] For large whales, this means utilization of the most efficient penthrite grenade system that is available. For small cetaceans, this means the use of an exploding harpoon (where appropriate) as supplemented by the use of the most appropriate rifle (defined by caliber and ammunition type). For seals (and other similarly situated marine mammals), this means use of the most appropriate rifle (defined by caliber and ammunition type), supplemented by application of appropriate manual force and/or bleeding of the animal. A new international commission should seek to regulate the killing methods to the maximum extent practicable. Where culture and/or tradition favor the use of other killing methods within areas of national jurisdiction (such as the small cetacean drives and organized seal hunts), the international organization could contribute by recommending improved techniques as they become available. Finally, an appropriate standard should also be developed for marine mammals that are either fatally wounded through ship-strikes or entanglement or stranded without the possibility of recovering.[125]

The final consideration that should be emphasized is the role that education plays in ensuring humane hunting. Even if a best standard can be developed for hunting different categories of marine mammal, killing effectiveness and efficiency is still limited by the competence of the individuals engaged in the hunt. In addition to reducing animal suffering, proper training enhances hunter safety and public perception. For these reasons, the role of education is recognized and lauded by both the IWC and NAMMCO. Specifically, the IWC Working Group on Whale Killing Methods and Associated Welfare Issues provided the following statement in their Report to the 64th Annual Meeting regarding Norway's efforts to educate and train hunters on effective whale killing:

> Norway has also played a major role in assisting other countries with training and improved technology. In accord with the IWC Action Plan, Dr. Egil Øen of Norway has worked co-operatively with hunters, scientists, authorities, and whale hunters' organizations in Norway, Canada (Nunavut and Nunavik), Greenland, Iceland, Japan, The Russian Federation (Chukotka) and the USA (Alaska). Norwegian scientists have also participated in and chaired expert group meetings in NAMMCO on whale killing data assessment and lectured in local workshops and training sessions for hunters.[126]

As suggested above, NAMMCO has taken a more proactive approach to training and information dissemination. For example, with respect to killing large whales, the NAMMCO Committee on Hunting Methods has summarized the different training programs employed by relevant nations, and concludes as follows:

> ... whaling takes place in many different regions/countries and that it therefore may be difficult to make a requirement for standardized training programmes. However the importance of training and education in order to secure efficient killing both from an economical and animal welfare point of view and also with respect to hunter safety was highly emphasized. The EG [Expert Group] acknowledged the importance of regular training and exchange of information in order to achieve more efficient hunts and to improve animal welfare. It was regarded as essential to combine theoretical education with physical meetings in order to exchange information and experiences. The processes of sampling and recording of data should also be included in the training programmes.[127]

This Expert Group that assessed large-whale killing methods also "recommended that NAMMCO develop a standard handbook for hunters giving relevant information *inter alia* on weapons, killing techniques and animal welfare."[128] With respect to small cetaceans, the Committee on Hunting Methods provides anatomical renderings depicting the impact of different wounds,[129] and also visual depictions of preferred target zones for various small cetaceans that are hunted by rifle.[130] This effort represents the sort of information that could inform international training and education efforts. Finally, the NAMMCO Committee on Hunting Methods also addresses education with respect to seal hunting, concluding that it is critically important in the areas of "animal behavior, anatomy, physiology, ballistics, ethics, legislation, handling of carcass etc.," a list that may very well reflect the proper content of any educational program aimed at enhancing the efficiency and humaneness of any marine mammal hunt.[131] Before addressing how these considerations can be accommodated by a new treaty, it is necessary to assess the meaning and content of Aboriginal whaling.

3. Aboriginal Subsistence Whaling

A distinction between commercial whaling operations and Aboriginal[132] whaling existed before the current ICRW/ICW regime was negotiated. For example, Article 3 of the 1931 Convention for the Regulation of Whaling, negotiated under the auspices of the League of Nations, provided that:

> The present Convention does not apply to aborigines dwelling on the coasts of the territories of the High Contracting Parties provided that:
> (1) They use only canoes, pirogues or other exclusively native craft propelled by oars or sails;
> (2) They do not carry firearms;
> (3) They are not in the employment of persons other than aborigines;
> (4) They are not under contract to deliver the products of their whaling to any third person.[133]

Currently, and as characterized by the IWC in 1981, Aboriginal whaling means:

> Whaling for the purposes of local aboriginal consumption carried out by or on behalf of aboriginal, indigenous or native peoples who share strong community, familial, social and cultural ties related to a continuing traditional dependence on whaling and the use of whales.[134]

Further, the same report indicates that "[t]he definition of subsistence whaling does not prevent the use of modern technology, and there is good reason to recommend improvement in the weapons, powder and bombs currently employed to further reduce the struck but lost rate."[135] To take advantage of the Aboriginal subsistence whaling exemption, a contracting nation must apply to the IWC through a "need statement" that sets out the cultural and nutritional basis for the application.[136] This approach is summarized by the IWC as follows:

> It is the responsibility of national governments to provide the Commission with evidence of the cultural and subsistence needs of their people. The Scientific Committee provides scientific advice on safe catch limits for such stocks. Based on the information on need and scientific advice, the Commission then sets catch limits, recently in five-year blocks.[137]

Because the Aboriginal exemption catch limits referenced above require amendment to the Schedule to the ICRW, securing the requisite three-quarter-majority vote of the Commission can be difficult. If passed, the catch limits are set in five-year blocks and appear in the Schedule where other catch limits and catch restrictions are set. For example, Article 13 concerning baleen whales details how Aboriginal subsistence catch limits are determined in relation to the principle of maximum sustainable yield, while Article 13(a)(4) provides that Aboriginal hunters are limited in that "it is forbidden to strike, take or kill calves or any whale accompanied by a calf."[138] Currently, Aboriginal peoples within Danish territory (Greenlanders), the Russian Federation (Chukotka natives), St. Vincent and The Grenadines (Bequian whalers), and the United States of America (Makah Tribe and Alaskan Eskimos) are sanctioned by the IWC to conduct Aboriginal subsistence whaling.[139] These nations have agreed, and affirmed to the IWC, that:

(1) Subsistence hunting is for food to meet cultural and nutritional needs;
(2) The safety of his crew is a whaling captain's most important responsibility;
(3) With safety assured, achieving a humane death for the whale is the highest priority; and
(4) Efforts to modernize our whaling equipment and practices can only be made within the context of each communities' [sic] economic resources and the need to preserve the continuity of our hunting traditions.[140]

Importantly, Article 13 of the Schedule notes that "[a]ll Aboriginal whaling shall be conducted under national legislation that accords with this paragraph [which outlines pertinent restrictions]."[141]

Our present understanding of Aboriginal (or Indigenous) whaling is considerably different than it was in the first half of the twentieth century, but many challenges remain. Although it is beyond the scope of this work to describe and/or address each issue in detail, an understanding of the relevant considerations is necessary as it informs the creation of a new regime. One persistent problem is that many Aboriginal groups have historically relied quite heavily on the spoils of whaling (for both subsistence and cultural purposes) and the collapse of whale populations, as a result of twentieth-century commercial whaling operations and not Aboriginal whaling, has resulted in "the destruction of vast numbers of traditional local or even national cultures, both of indigenous people and, indeed, of many cultural and ethnic subgroups within the dominant modern peoples."[142] This is an especially relevant consideration when determining whether Aboriginal peoples should be allowed to continue to hunt endangered species when they did not significantly contribute to the species becoming endangered.[143] Similarly, the European Union has enacted a ban on the importation and exportation of products made from seals,[144] which affects Aboriginal communities that profit from large-scale seal hunts.[145] Reconciling the future of Aboriginal whaling in the context of over-exploited stocks and endangered species has proved difficult.

A second issue is that Aboriginal whaling occurs in areas of the world outside the auspices of the IWC. For example, Canada's Inuit population conducts whaling and has in the past taken bowhead whales without the IWC's permission.[146] Another example is whaling in the Azores region of Portugal, which is justified on a subsistence basis and occurs without the IWC's permission.[147] Further, many coastal Aboriginal communities utilize small cetaceans, such as the narwhal and beluga, which are outside the jurisdiction of the IWC to regulate.

Further problems have arisen because the IWC does not define the term "Aboriginal," or "Aboriginal subsistence," resulting in ambiguities as to which groups qualify for this exemption.[148] This is not a unique problem in international law as "Indigenous" remains a term that has "eluded definition at the international level."[149] For example, Japan has applied to the IWC for the Aboriginal subsistence for coastal whaling of minke whales, citing centuries of cultural practice.[150] Norway also allows coastal whaling of minke whales that is not sanctioned by the IWC, and has voiced the concern that the IWC is a politically motivated body that lacks authority to make cultural determinations.[151] It is also possible to question whether the IWC has adequately captured our current understanding of Indigenous, either in its application of the "needs statement" or in its broader goals. Specifically, it is open to discussion whether this treatment accords with the United Nations Declaration of Rights of Indigenous Peoples[152] or the Convention on Biological Diversity, which emphasized the connection between Indigenous communities and biological resources (in its Preamble), the need for "respect, preservation, and maintenance of indigenous and local communities" (Article 8(j)), and recognized that the conservation of biological diversity can be enhanced by understanding and applying Aboriginal knowledge (Article 10).[153]

Finally, recent experiences indicate that training, education, technology transfer, and monetary contribution can be employed to standardize indigenous killing methods. The 2012 IWC Report of the Working Group on Whale Killing Methods and Associated Welfare Issues provides the following salient example describing a weapons-enhancement project undertaken by the Alaska Eskimo Whaling Commission[154] and assisted by Norwegian training and a financial contribution from the United States government and the North Slope Borough municipal district of Alaska:

> Mr George Noongwook, Chairman of the Alaska Eskimo Whaling Commission (AEWC), said that the eleven whaling villages represented by the AEWC in 2011 struck 51 bowhead whales and landed 38, for an efficiency rate of 75%. He reviewed the conditions in the spring and fall hunts, noting that the ice conditions in the 2011 spring hunt were very poor.
>
> Mr Noongwook then reviewed the weapons improvement program undertaken by the AEWC, and explained that the use of the new penthrite projectiles is continuing to expand, with only three of the eleven villages still needing to be trained in their use. *The hunters are pleased with the new grenade and are especially grateful for Dr Egil Øen's collaboration and work on development and training of the new weapons. He also stated that in the spring hunt in 2012, the use of penthrite increased. In closing, Mr Noongwook noted that the penthrite projectiles are very expensive to buy and ship, and thanked the North Slope Borough and the US Government for their continued financial support of the weapons improvement programme.* [emphasis added]
>
> ...
>
> The Working Group thanked the USA for this information and the presentation. Norway, Australia, UK and Mexico in particular commended the USA

and the AEWC for the great progress made. *Norway stressed the importance of human safety and of respecting local traditions and culture when assisting with the development of new weapons to improve the TTD for subsistence whaling. Local knowledge plays an extremely important role in both weapon improvements and training. He welcomed the news that two new villages were now using penthrite weapons, noting that full scale uptake of the penthrite weapon will bring even more improvements to TTD for the hunts and reduce struck-lost rates.*[155] [emphasis added]

In sum, these persistent issues could effectively be addressed in a properly crafted international treaty regime that responds to our current understanding of what it means to be Indigenous and our current appreciation for the ethical considerations that should guide our interaction with marine mammals.

4. Features of a New Response

With this assessment complete, it is necessary to consider how our understanding of the ethical considerations that inform our relationship with marine mammals should be addressed in a new multilateral treaty for the conservation and sustainable management of marine mammals that establishes an International Marine Mammal Commission. Recall that the position advanced in this book is that our present scientific understanding of marine mammals (and cetaceans in particular) justifies a reconsideration of our relationship and utilization, but does not justify a perpetual zero-catch quota. The observations highlighted below connect the ethics discussion to the killing methods discussion contained in this chapter by promoting the objective that "if any animals are to be killed, they should be killed humanely, whoever does it."[156]

First, it is apparent that maximizing animal welfare requires continued emphasis on humane killing methods. This can be accomplished, in part, through the creation of species-specific best-practice guidelines, formalized education and information dissemination, and technology transfer and investment. Second, it is important to continue the trend that is emerging at the IWC where nations are discussing the most humane and ethical way to kill a cetacean beyond directed hunts, such as entanglement and stranding situations. Third, with respect to Aboriginal subsistence whaling, it is important that a new convention: (1) defines "Indigenous/Aboriginal subsistence whaling" in a manner that expands and clarifies current reliance on cultural significance and nutritional need, (2) distinguishes "Indigenous/Aboriginal subsistence whaling" from whaling that is historically significant to a population, and (3) promotes the use of the same humane killing methods identified above by Indigenous hunters through education, information dissemination, technology transfer, and monetary investment. These observations inform the detailed proposal for a new multilateral convention provided in Chapters 6 and 7.

IV. CONCLUSION

This chapter has demonstrated that it is an appropriate time to consider an alternative to the ICRW/IWC. The failure of the IWC initiative, titled the Future of the IWC, justifies consideration of a new international regulatory response to marine mammal conservation.

Goal setting is a critical aspect of rational decision-making. The objectives I have identified establish the basis for the legal analysis and proposal that follow. Further, although animal welfare concerns must figure prominently in any new approach to marine mammal conservation and sustainable management, they do not justify a perpetual zero-catch quota; indeed, advancing the position that no future take is allowed likely represents a nonstarter position that would scuttle future negotiations. Before embarking on the legal analysis related to the creation of a new multilateral convention and commission, and the substance of said new regime, it is necessary to consider the impact of current threats to marine mammals that justify moving beyond simply regulating direct lethal utilization.

NOTES

1. Oran R. Young et al., *Subsistence, Sustainability, and Sea Mammals: Reconstructing the International Whaling Regime*, 23 OCEAN COAST. MANAGE. 117, 119 (1994).
2. 10 Dec. 1982, 21 I.L.M. 1261, 1833 U.N.T.S. 3.
3. ITZHAK GILOBA, RATIONAL CHOICE 5–9 (2010) (noting at page 5 that rational choice asks that we recognize "the dichotomy between feasibility and desirability," and the necessity of addressing uncertainty and operating assumptions).
4. *See* Keith Bartholomew, *Land Use-Transportation Scenario Planning: Promise and Reality*, 34 TRANSP. 397, 408 (2007); *see generally* Herbert A. Simon, *A Behavioral Model of Rational Choice*, 69(2) Q. J. ECON. 99 (1958).
5. 2 Dec. 1946, 62 Stat. 1716, 161 U.N.T.S. 74 ["ICRW"].
6. John H. McNeill, *The Strategic Significance of the Law of the Sea Convention (1994–1995)* 7 GEO. INT'L ENVTL. L. REV. 703, 703 (1994–1995).
7. Hugo Caminos & Michael R. Molitor, *Progressive Development of International Law and the Package Deal*, 79 AM. J. INT'L L. 871, 873 (1985).
8. United Nations Division for Ocean Affairs and Law of the Sea, *Chronological Lists of Ratifications of, Accessions and Successions to the Convention and the Related Agreements as at 20 September 2013*, http://www.un.org/Depts/los/reference_files/chronological_lists_of_ratifications.htm ["*Chronological Lists of Ratifications*"].
9. *Id.*
10. 17 Mar. 1992, 1772 U.N.T.S. 217.
11. 24 Nov. 1996, 2183 U.N.T.S. 303.
12. 4 Dec. 1995, 34 I.L.M. 1542, 2167 U.N.T.S. 3.
13. Robert L. Friedheim, *Fixing the Whaling Regime: A Proposal*, in TOWARD A SUSTAINABLE WHALING REGIME 311, 314 (Robert L. Friedheim ed., 2001).
14. M.J. Bowman, *"Normalizing" the International Convention for the Regulation of Whaling*, 29 MICHIGAN J.I.L. 293, 485 (2008).
15. Mark Bekoff, *Ethics and Marine Mammals*, in ENCYCLOPEDIA OF MARINE MAMMALS 396, 396 (William F. Perrin et al. eds., 2d ed. 2009) ["Bekoff"].
16. *See* Robert L. Friedheim, *Introduction: The IWC as a Contested Regime*, in TOWARD A SUSTAINABLE WHALING REGIME 3, 25–26 (Robert L. Friedheim ed., 2001) (discussing the role that media has played in shaping our appreciation for certain animals, such as whales and elephants).
17. *See* Sarah Shure, *Misguided Morality: The Repercussions of the International Whaling Commission's Shift from a Policy of Regulation to One of Preservation*, 12

18. Arne Kalland, *Whale Totemization: Whale Symbolism and the Anti-whaling Campaign*, 46(2) ARCTIC 124, 124 (1993) (note that some commentators have even gone so far as to assert that the continued hunting of whales is a genocide, *e.g.*, Luis Kutner, *The Genocide of Whales: A Crime against Humanity*, 10(3) LAWYER OF THE AMERICAS 784 (1978)).
19. Kalland, *supra* note 18, at 125; *see also* International Fund for Animal Welfare, *Our Work: Saving Seals*, http://www.ifaw.org/canada/our-work/saving-seals(last visited Feb. 16, 2016); The Humane Society of the United States, *Seal Hunt*, http://www.humanesociety.org/issues/seal_hunt/ (last visited Feb. 16, 2016); Greenpeace International, *Whaling*, http://www.greenpeace.org/international/en/campaigns/oceans/whaling/?accept=a1942c8f82a8aa089d7f467351a602a2 (last visited Feb. 16, 2016); Sea Shepherd Conservation Society, *Defending Whales*, http://www.seashepherd.org/whales/ (last visited Feb. 16, 2016).
20. Terry McCarthy, *Japan Says Whales Not Sacred Cows*, THE INDEPENDENT (May 11, 1993), http://www.independent.co.uk/news/world/japan-says-whales-not-sacred-cows-2322188.html; *see also* Anne M. Creason, *Culture Clash: The Influence of Indigenous Cultures on the International Whaling Regime*, 35 CAL. W. INT'L L.J. 83, 96 (2004-2005) (indicating that whales have traditionally been viewed as "big fish, and therefore, an exploitable natural resource" in Japan); *see also* ALEXANDER GILLESPIE, WHALING DIPLOMACY 432-35 (2005) ["GILLEPSIE, WHALING DIPLOMACY"] (discussing vote-buying—through foreign aid or otherwise—at the IWC as a reason that other nations are pro-whaling even though they do not carry out significant whaling operations).
21. Bekoff, *supra* note 15, at 398-99.
22. *Id.* at 399-400.
23. Mark Peter Simmonds, *Into the Brains of whales*, 100 APPL. ANIM. BEHAV. SCI. 103 (2006) ["Simmonds"] (suggesting that any discussion of cetacean intelligence must be based on science, as unsupported assertions of intelligence weaken the efficacy of scientifically based observations and lend credibility to those skeptical of cetacean social behavior or complex cognition).
24. Anthony D'Amato & Sudhir K. Chopra, *Whales: Their Emerging Right to Life* (1991) AM. J. INT'L L. 21 (1991).
25. *Id.* at 21.
26. *Id.*
27. *Id.* (citing to Burnell, *The Evolution of Cetacean Intelligence*, *in* MIND IN THE WATERS 52 (J. McIntyre ed., 1974) and JOHN C. LILLY, THE MIND OF THE DOLPHIN: A NONHUMAN INTELLIGENCE 63 (1967)).
28. *Id.* (citing to JOHN C. LILLY, MAN AND DOLPHIN (1961)).
29. *Id.* at 41 and 48.
30. *E.g., see id.* at 21 (citing to D. DAY, THE WHALE WAR 152 (1987)).
31. *See* Jeff Warren, *Whale Rising*, READER'S Digest, July 2012 (note that this is the title story for this edition, which states on the cover: "Whales are people too. The science proves it. Get ready for a new world order"); *see also* Joshua Foer, *It's Time for a Conversation: Breaking the Communication Barrier between Dolphins and Humans*, May 2015 (this is the feature article for this edition).

32. The Helsinki Group, *Declaration of Rights for Cetaceans: Whales and Dolphins*, http://www.cetaceanrights.org/ (last visited Aug. 15, 2013).
33. *See* The Helsinki Group, *Declaration of Rights for Cetaceans: Whales and Dolphins*, 2–4 (2010), http://www.cetaceanrights.org/pdf_bin/helsinki-group.pdf.
34. *See Dolphins Deserve Same Rights as Humans, Say Scientists*, BBC WORLD NEWS (Feb. 21, 2012, 10:54 AM), http://www.bbc.co.uk/news/world-17116882; *see also Whales Are People, Too: A Declaration of the Rights of Cetaceans*, THE ECONOMIST (Feb. 25, 2012), http://www.economist.com/node/21548150.
35. *Declaration of Rights for Cetaceans: Ethical and Policy Implications of Intelligence*, AAAS, http://aaas.confex.com/aaas/2012/webprogram/Session4617.html (last visited Aug. 15, 2013).
36. *Id.*
37. *See* Brandon Keim, *New Science Emboldens Long Shot Bid for Dolphin, Whale Rights*, WIRED (July 19, 2012, 6:30 AM), http://www.wired.com/wiredscience/2012/07/cetacean-rights/ (this idea has also been associated with the more polarized group People for the Ethical Treatment of Animals (PETA), which initiated a lawsuit in 2011 in United States federal court seeking constitutional rights for five orca dolphins who perform at marine parks; *see* David Crary & Julie Watson, *PETA Lawsuit Seeks to Expand Animal Rights*, ASSOCIATED PRESS (Oct. 25, 2011), http://news.yahoo.com/peta-lawsuit-seeks-expand-animal-rights-222219887.html. PETA, acting as next friends for the five orca, "brought action against the operator of sea aquarium, seeking declaratory and injunctive relief that whales were being held by operator in violation of slavery and involuntary servitude provisions of Thirteenth Amendment" (Tilikum *ex rel.* People for the Ethical Treatment of Animals, Inc. v. Sea World Parks & Entm't, Inc., 842 R. Supp 2d 1259 ((S.D. Cal. 2012) at background). Sea World argued that the plaintiffs lacked standing to bring the action, and the court agreed, noting that the Thirteenth Amendment only applies to humans. Accordingly, it held that "[b]ecause Plaintiffs are without standing to bring this action, no 'case' or 'controversy' exists and this court lacks subject matter jurisdiction" (at 6)); *see also* Government of India, Ministry of Environment and Forests, *Policy on Establishing Dolphinarariums—Regarding*, F. No. 20-1/2010-CZA(W) (May 17, 2013) (which provides that: "Whereas cetaceans in general are highly intelligent and sensitive, and various scientists who have researched dolphin behavior have suggested that the unusually high intelligence; as compared to other animals means that dolphin should be seen as "non-human persons" and as such should have their own specific rights and is morally unacceptable to keep them captive for entertainment purpose").
38. It is important to note that the cetacean brain is different than other marine mammal brains, and is the most studied and discussed of the marine mammals. *See generally*, Camilla Butti et al., *The Neocortex of Cetaceans: Cytoarchitecture and Comparison with Other Aquatic and Terrestrial Species*, 1225 ANN. N.Y. ACAD. SCI. 47 (2011) ["Butti"] (which compares the cetacean brain to other mammalian brains. At 51 these authors note that the sirenian brain lacks the complexity of the cetacean brain, and is also smaller. At 51–52 this article also notes that pinniped brains exhibit similarities to terrestrial carnivores in terms of brain complexity and size).
39. *See* P.D. Gingerich & M.D. Uhen, *Likelihood Estimation of the Time of Origin of Cetacean and the Time of Divergence of Cetacean and Artiodactyla*, 2 PALEO-ELECTRONICA 1, 11013 (1998), http://palaeo-electronica.org/1998_2/ging_uhen/issue2.htm.

40. *See* Simmonds, *supra* note 23, at 105.
41. Camilla Butti et al., *Total Number and Volume of Von Economo Neurons in the Cerebral Cortex of Cetaceans* (2009) 515 J. COMP. NEURO. 243, 243 ["Butti et al."].
42. Simmonds, *supra* note 23.
43. Lori Marino, Daniel W. McShea & Mark D. Uhen, *Origin and Evolution of Large Brains in Toothed Whales*, 281 ANAT. REC. 1247, 1247 (2004) ["Marino, McShea & Uhen"] (also at 1248 noting that the "Encephalization is typically expressed as an encephalization quotient (EQ). EQ is an index that quantifies how much larger or smaller a given animal's brain is relative to the expected brain size for an animal at that body size," citing to H.J. JERISON, EVOLUTION OF THE BRAIN AND INTELLIGENCE (1973)).
44. *See generally* L. Marino, *A Comparison of Encephalization between Odontocete Cetaceans and Anthropoid Primates* (1998) 51 BRAIN BEHAV. EVO. 230.
45. *See* Butti et al., *supra* note 41, at 244; *see also* P.R. Manger, *An Examination of Cetacean Brain Structure with a Novel Hypothesis Correlating Thermogenesis to the Evolution of a Big Brain* 81 BIOL. REV. 293 (2006) (suggesting that a complex brain organ is required to assist in heat regulation to account for heat loss to water); *see also* Lori Marino et al., *Cetaceans Have Complex Brains for Complex Cognition*, 5(5) PLOS BIOL. 0966 (2007) ["Marino et al."] (responding to the thermogenesis argument by suggesting that cetacean brain size and complexity is a result of their highly social existence and cognitive traits); *see also* Simmonds, *supra* note 23, at 105 (noting that cetaceans have high sensory demands owing to the fact that they utilize ambient sound and/or echolocation to navigate).
46. Marino et al., *supra* note. at 1254.
47. Maddalena Bearzi & Craig Stanford, *A Bigger, Better Brain*, 98(5) AM. SCI. 402, 402–03 (2010).
48. *See* Ingfei Chen, *Brain Cells for Socializing: Does an Obscure Nerve Cell Help Explain What Gorillas, Elephants, Whales—and People—Have in Common?*, SMITHSONIAN MAG. (June 2009), http://www.smithsonianmag.com/science-nature/The-Social-Brain.html.
49. Andy Coghlan, *Whales Boast the Cells That Make Us Human*, NEW SCIENTIST (Nov. 27, 2006), http://www.newscientist.com/article/dn10661-whales-boast-the-brain-cells-that-make-us-human.html (citing to Helen Phillips, *The Cell That Makes Us Human* (2004), 182(2452) NEW SCIENTIST 32).
50. *See* Pactrick R. Hof & Estel van der Gucht, *Structure of the Cerebral Cortex of the Humpback Whale, Megaptera novaeangliae (Cetacea, Mysticeti, Balaenopteridae)*, 290 ANAT. REC. 1, 27 (2007).
51. Butti et al., *supra* note 41, at 243.
52. Butti, *supra* note 38, at 54 (citing to C. Butti & P.R. Hof, *The Insular Cortex: A Comparative Perspective*, 9 DEV. PSYCHOBIOL. 477 (2010)).
53. *Id.* at 55.
54. Mary Ann Raghanti et al., *An Analysis of Von Economo Neurons in the Cerebral Cortex of Cetaceans, Artiodactyls, and Perissodactyls*, 792 BRAIN STRUC. FUNCT. (2014).
55. THOMAS WHITE, IN DEFENSE OF DOLPHINS: THE NEW MORAL FRONTIER ix (2007) ["WHITE"].
56. *Id.* at 46–80.
57. *Id.* at 81–116.
58. *Id.* at 117–54.

59. *Id.* at 80.
60. *Id.* at 81.
61. *Id.* at 154.
62. Simmonds, *supra* note 23.
63. *Id.* at 105–06 (citing to S. Norris, *Creatures of Culture? Making the Case for Cultural Systems in Whales and Dolphins*, 59 BioSci. 9 (2002) ["Norris"]; A. Whitten, *Imitation and Cultural Transmission in Apes and Cetaceans*, 24 Behav. Brain. Sci. 359 (2001); and Mercado et al., *Memory for Recent Actions in the Bottlenose Dolphin* (Tursiops truncatus*): Repetition of Arbitrary Behaviours Using an Abstract Rule*, 26(2) Anim. Learn. Behav. 210 (1998)).
64. Simmonds, *supra* note 23, at 106 (citing to R. Smolker et al., *Sponge-Carrying by Dolphins (Delphinidae,* Tursiops *sp.)—a Foraging Specialization Involving Tool Use*, 103 Ethology 454 (1997)).
65. *Id.* (citing to McCowan et al., *Bubble Ring Play of Bottlenose Dolphins (*Tursiops truncatus*): Implications for Cognition*, 114 J. Comp. Psychol. 98 (2000)).
66. *Id.* at 107 (citing to D Reiss and L Marino, *Mirror Self-Recognition in the Bottlenose Dolphin: A Case of Cognitive Convergence* (2001) 98 PNAS 5937 (2001)).
67. *Id.* at 107 (citing to N.A. Rose, *A Death in the Family*, in The Smile of the Dolphin (M. Berkoff ed., 2000); N.A. Rose, *Giving a Little Latitude*, in The Smile of the Dolphin (M. Berkoff ed., 2000).
68. Simmonds, *supra* note 23, at 109–11.
69. *Id.* at 111–12.
70. *See* L. Rendell & H. Whitehead, *Cetacean Culture: Still Afloat after The First Naval Engagement of the Culture Wars*, 24 Brain Sci. 360, 360 (2001).
71. Kevin N. Laland & Vincent M. Janik, *The Animal Cultures Debate*, 21(10) Trends Ecol. Evo. 542, 542 (2006) ["Laland & Janik"].
72. Marino et al., *supra* note 45, at 0970.
73. Hal Whitehead et al., *Culture and Conservation of Non-humans with Reference to Whales and Dolphins: Review and New Directions*, 120 Biol. Con. 427, 428 (2004) ["Whitehead et al."].
74. Norris, *supra* note 63, at 10.
75. Whitehead et al., *supra* note 73, at 429.
76. Norris, *supra* note 63, at 11.
77. Valerie Senigaglia & Hal Whitehead, *Synchronous Breathing by Pilot Whales*, 28(1) Mar. Mam. Sci. 213, 218 (2012).
78. Kevin N. Laland, *Animal Cultures*, 18(9) Cur. Biol. 366, 367 (2008).
79. Hal Whitehead, *Conserving and Managing Animals That Learn Socially and Share Cultures*, 38(3) Learn. Behav. 329, 329 (2010).
80. *See* Laland & Janik, *supra* note 71, at 543 (citing to P.J.O. Miller, *Cetacean Science Does Not Have to Be Pseudoscience*, 24 Behav. Brain Sci. 347 (2001) and V. M. Janik, *Is Cetacean Social Learning Unique?*, 24 Behav. Brain Sci. 337 (2001)).
81. Laland & Janik, *supra* note 71, at 543–44.
82. *Id.* at 545; Michael Krutzen, Carel van Schaik & Andrew Whiten, *The Animal Cultures Debate: Response to Laland and Janik*, 22(1) Trends Ecol. Evol. 6, 6 (2007).
83. Alexander Gillespie, *The Ethical Question in the Whaling Debate*, 9 Geo. Int'l. Envtl. L. Rev. 355, 364 (1996–1997) ["Gillespie, *The Ethical Question*"].
84. *Id.* at 366.

85. *See generally* NAMMCO, *Report of the NAMMCO Expert Group Meeting on Best Practices in the Hunting of Seals* (2009) ["NAMMCO Seal Report"]; NAMMCO, *Report of the NAMMCO Expert Group Meeting on Assessment of Whale Killing Data* (2012) ["NAMMCO Whale Killing Data"]; NAMMCO, *Report of the NAMMCO Expert Group Meeting to Assess Hunting Methods for Small Cetaceans* (2011) ["NAMMCO Hunting Small Cetaceans"].
86. International Whaling Commission, *Welfare Issues*, http://iwc.int/welfare (last visited Feb. 16, 2016) ["*Welfare Issues*"].
87. North Atlantic Marine Mammal Commission, *Committee on Hunting Methods*, http://www.nammco.no/about-nammco/committee-on-hunting-methods/ (last visited Feb. 16, 2016).
88. *Welfare Issues, supra* note 86.
89. *See* IWC, *Report of the Workshop on Human Killing Techniques for Whales*, IWC/ 30/15; *see also* S.K. Knudsen, *A Review of the Criteria Used to Assess Insensibility and Death in Hunted Whales Compared to Other Species*, 169(1) VET. J. 42, 42 (2005) ["Knudsen"].
90. NAMMCO Hunting Small Cetaceans, *supra* note 85, at 11.
91. Knudsen, *supra* note 89, at 42.
92. NAMMCO Whale Killing Data, *supra* note 85, at 7.
93. *Id.* at 7 (citing to Knudsen, *supra* note 89, at 51).
94. NAMMCO Seal Report, *supra* note 85, at 9.
95. NAMMCO Hunting Small Cetaceans, *supra* note 85, at 9–11.
96. *Id.* at 10.
97. NAMMCO Seal Report, *supra* note 85, at 16.
98. *E.g.*, International Whaling Commission, *Resolution 1991-1: Resolution Arising from the Workshop on Whale Killing Methods*, (1991), http://iwc.int/cache/downloads/88j2cltuk5sss00gcwgw4gcws/Resolution%201999.pdf (encouraging national reporting on the "number [of whales] killed by each method, the number killed instantaneously, times to death, number of whales targeted and missed, number of whales struck and lost, calibre of rifle where used, number of bullets used and methods to determine unconsciousness and/or time to death (TTD)"); *e.g.*, International Whaling Commission, *Resolution 2001-2: Resolution on Whale Killing Methods*, (2001), http://iwc.int/cache/downloads/50hhbtfffg4cokk8cwk-g8w8s4/Report%20of%20Working%20Group%20on%20Whale%20Killing%20Methods%20and%20Associated%20Welfare%20Issues%202011.pdf (which encourages reporting regarding "technical developments within whale killing technologies and to submit, to the extent possible, relevant information, including variance data on times to death" and "to provide relevant comparative data from killing of other large mammals"); *e.g.*, International Whaling Commission, *Annex E of the Annual Report of the International Whaling Commission 2003: Report of the Workshop on Whale Killing Methods and Associated Welfare Issues* 85 (2003), http://archive.iwcoffice.org/_documents/meetings/workshop2003.pdf (which contains a *Revised Action Plan on Whale Killing Methods* at Annex 4).
99. NAMMCO Hunting Small Cetaceans, *supra* note 85, at 13.
100. It should be noted that Norway has been responsible for much of the research regarding the humane killing of marine mammals. *See* Knudsen, *supra* note 89, at 48 (noting that "[s]ince 1981, Norway has been acting as a driving force in the efforts to improve the hunting techniques for whales when a research program was initiated to find better methods for killing minke whales").

101. J. Geraci & N. Gales, *Chairman's Report to the Commission on the Workshop on Whale Killing Methods and Associated Welfare Issues* (2003), http://iwc.int/welfare ["*Chairman's Report*"].
102. NAMMCO Whale Killing Data, *supra* note 85, at 9.
103. Rosanne Pagano, *Eskimos Try New Explosive for Hunting Whales*, MILWAUKEE J. SENTINEL (Nov. 27, 2005), http://news.google.com/newspapers?nid=1683&dat=20051127&id=TMcoAAAAIBAJ&sjid=PkUEAAAAIBAJ&pg=6810,4244938.
104. NAMMCO Whale Killing Data, *supra* note 85, at 10.
105. *Id.* at 9.
106. *Chairman's Report, supra* note 101.
107. NAMMCO Whale Killing Data, *supra* note 85, at 8–16.
108. *Id.*
109. International Whaling Commission, *Report of the Working Group on Whale Killing Methods and Associated Welfare Issues*, IWC/64/Rep. 6, 2 (June 25, 2012), http://iwc.int/cache/downloads/4hrf4z3yyzy8so0wggws0swwg/64-Rep6.pdf ["*Report on Whale Killing Methods*"].
110. *Id.*
111. NAMMCO Hunting Small Cetaceans, *supra* note 85, at 8.
112. *Id.* at 9.
113. *Id.* at 19–30.
114. NAMMCO Hunting Small Cetaceans, *supra* note 85, at 14–19.
115. *Id.*
116. *Id.* at 27.
117. NAMMCO Seal Report, *supra* note 85, at 9.
118. *Id.*
119. NAMMCO Seal Report, *supra* note 85, at 9–10 & 16.
120. *Id.* at 18.
121. *Id.* at 17–18.
122. *Id.* 18–19.
123. *Id.* at 13.
124. NAMMCO Hunting Small Cetaceans, *supra* note 85, at 7.
125. *Report on Whale Killing Methods, supra* note 109, at 2 (indicates that the IWC—and its Contracting Governments—are alive to these issues and are starting to conduct work to address them. For example, New Zealand indicated that "determining how best to euthanise whales was an important issue for many governments and encouraged others to report their experiences and data," whereas IWC Working Groups have considered how to best euthanize whales that are stranded or hopelessly entangled, and have concluded that further research and consideration is required, but that the following approach should be considered (at 4–5):

    (1) establish a dynamic entanglement response section on the IWC Website;
    (2) consider establishing an international entanglement database;
    (3) facilitate data exchange;
    (4) promote establishment of national entanglement response networks;
    (5) provide advice to member governments;
    (6) develop a proposal for an international workshop on entanglement prevention;
    (7) continue to promote an IWC-managed fund for entanglement response).

126. *Report on Whale Killing Methods, supra* note 109, at 4.
127. NAMMCO Whale Killing Data, *supra* note 85, at 21.
128. *Id.*
129. NAMMCO Hunting Small Cetaceans, *supra* note 85, at 12–13.
130. *Id.* at 19–21.
131. NAMMCO Seal Report, *supra* note 85, at 19 (also noting at 17 that to be efficient, killing using clubs requires an understanding of cranial anatomy for different species as preferred target zones exist).
132. Gillespie, Whaling Diplomacy, *supra* note 20, at 201 (noting that a traditional definition of Aboriginal is the "original inhabitants of a place, commonly before the arrival of 'others'," which is probably not as broad as our current understanding of the word "Indigenous," which is a more inclusive term. Although I use "Aboriginal" and "Indigenous" interchangeably in this section, "Indigenous" likely represents the more acceptable term and will be used during consideration of an improved definition of "Indigenous subsistence whaling" in Chapter 6).
133. 23 Sept. 1931, U.S.T.S. 880, 349 L.N.T.S. 3586; *e.g.*, R. Gambell, *International Management of Whales and Whaling: An Historical Review of the Regulation of Commercial and Aboriginal Subsistence Whaling*, 48(2) Arctic 97, 98, 101 (1993) (indicating that the first Schedule to the ICRW provided that "It is forbade to take or kill gray whales or right whales except when the meat and products of such whales are to be used exclusively for local consumption by the aborigines"); *e.g.*, Alexander Gillespie, *Aboriginal Subsistence Whaling: A Critique of the Inter-Relationship between International Law and the International Whaling Commission*, 12 Colo. J. Int'l Envtl. L. & Pol'y 77, 97 (2001) ["Gillespie, *Aboriginal Subsistence Whaling*"] (noting that pursuant to the Agreement on the Conservation of Polar Bears, Nov. 15, 1973, 27 U.S.T.S. 3918, 13 I.L.M. 13, Indigenous peoples are identified by the requirement that they hunt polar bears using "traditional methods." This requirement is found in Article III(d) of the Agreement on the Conservation of Polar Bears, which provides that:

   1. Subject to the provisions of Articles II and IV any Contracting Party may allow the taking of polar bears when such taking is carried out:
      a) for bona fide scientific purposes; or
      b) by that Party for conservation purposes; or c) to prevent serious disturbance of the management of other living resources, subject to forfeiture to that Party of the skins and other items of value resulting from such taking; or d) by local people using traditional methods in the exercise of their traditional rights and in accordance with the laws of that Party; or e) wherever polar bears have or might have been subject to taking by traditional means by its nationals.
      2. The skins and other items of value resulting from taking under sub-paragraph (b) and (c) of paragraph 1 of this Article shall not be available for commercial purposes.

134. *See* G.P. Donovan, *The International Whaling Commission and Aboriginal/Subsistence Whaling: April 1979 to July 1981*, Report of the International Whaling Commission: Special Issue 4 (1982), 81, 83, http://iwc.int/cache/downloads/eb18o2tayzkkg44c8cck0ocs0/RIWC-SI4-pp79-86a.pdf ["Donovan"].

135. *Id.* at 83.
136. *See* International Whaling Commission, *Aboriginal Subsistence Whaling*, IWC, https://iwc.int/aboriginal (last visited Dec. 11, 2015).
137. *Id.*
138. ICRW, *supra* note 5, at art. 13 of the Schedule (as amended by the Commission at the 64th Annual Meeting Panama City, Panama, July 2012).
139. *Aboriginal Subsistence Whaling, supra* note 136; *see* IWC Report of the Aboriginal Subsistence Whaling Sub-Committee, IWC/64/Rep3 Agenda Item 7, 13.
140. International Whaling Commission, *Report of the Aboriginal Subsistence Whaling Sub-Committee*, IWC/64/REP 3, Annex I (June 27, 2012), https://archive.iwc.int/pages/view.php?ref=3287&search=%21collection81&order_by=relevance&sort=DESC&offset=0&archive=0&k=&curpos=2&restypes= [*"Report of the Aboriginal Subsistence Whaling Committee"*].
141. ICRW, *supra* note 5, at art. 13 of the Schedule (as amended by the Commission at the 64th Annual Meeting Panama City, Panama, July 2012).
142. Harry N. Scheiber, *Historical Memory, Cultural Claims, and Environmental Ethics in the Jurisprudence of Whaling Regulation*, 38 OCEAN & COAST. MAN. 5, 35 (1998).
143. *See* Gillespie, *Aboriginal Subsistence Whaling, supra* note 133, at 138–39 (noting that "[t]here are currently no specific international laws stating that all such species [endangered species] *must* be preserved. Nevertheless, it is arguable that such a mandate is part of customary international environmental law. Within some of the treaties designating certain species as endangered and therefore protected, there are exceptions made to accommodate indigenous needs. However, the general rule is that such exceptions for indigenous peoples must not be detrimental to the survival of the population concerned").
144. Regulation (EC) No. 1007/2009, of the European Parliament and the Council of 16 September 2009 on trade in seal products, L 286/36.
145. Kalland *supra* note 18, at 3.
146. *See* Ted L. McDorman, *Canada and Whaling: An Analysis of Article 65 of the Law of the Sea Convention*, 29 OCEAN DEV. & INT'L L. 179, 179 (1998).
147. *See* Gillespie, *Aboriginal Subsistence Whaling, supra* note 133, at 78.
148. *See* Brian Trevor Hodges, *The Cracking Façade of the International Whaling Commission as an Institution of International Law: Norwegian Small-Type Whaling and the Aboriginal Subsistence Exemption*, 15 J. ENVTL. L. & LITIG. 295, 304 (2000) ["Hodges"]; Gillespie, *Aboriginal Subsistence Whaling, supra* note 133, at 96; GILLESPIE, WHALING DIPLOMACY, *supra* note 20, at 205–06 (noting that "it would be useful for the IWC to have a fixed definition of the term for the purposes of determining eligibility for ASW consideration. The signatories are working with a concept which has broad political implications and which is currently defined in several different and inconsistent ways. A single definition for the purposes of the treaty may permit justifiable distinctions to be drawn between the claims of competing groups with similar whaling traditions"; *see* Cinnamon Piñon Carlarne, *Saving the Whales in the New Millennium: International Institutions, Recent Development and the Future of International Whaling Policies*, 24 VA. ENVTL. L.J. 1, 11 (2005–2006) (asking "How are aboriginal and subsistence communities defined? What are the rights of aboriginal versus coastal communities? Must these communities show social, cultural or economic dependence on the whaling industry? How many and

what types of whales should these communities be allowed to harvest? What type of gear will the communities be allowed to use?").

149. Robert Howse & Joanna Langille, *Permitting Pluralism: The Seal Products Dispute and Why the WTO Should Accept Trade Restrictions Justified by Noninstrumental Moral Values*, 37 YALE J. INT'L L. 367, 402 (2012) (citing to Benedict Kingsbury, *"Indigenous Peoples" in International Law: A Constructivist Approach to the Asian Controversy*, 92 AM. J. INT'L L. 414 (1998)).

150. Gillespie, *Aboriginal Subsistence Whaling, supra* note 133, at 114.

151. *See* Hodges, *supra* note 148, at 314–315.

152. G.A. Res. 61/295, U.N. Doc. A/RES/61/295 (Sept. 13, 2007).

153. 5 June 1992, 31 I.L.M. 818, 1760 U.N.T.S. 79; *see* Gillespie, *Aboriginal Subsistence Whaling, supra* note 133, at 97; *see* MILTON M.R. FREEMAN ET AL., INUIT, WHALING, AND SUSTAINABILITY 104–05 (1998) (noting that Agenda 21 also calls on the international community to incorporate Aboriginal management practices as a mechanism to help achieve sustainable development).

154. ALASKA ESKIMO WHALING COMMISSION, http://www.aewc-alaska.com (last visited Feb. 16, 2016); *see also* Amber A. Lincoln, *Alaska Eskimo Whaling Commission, in* ENCYCLOPEDIA OF THE ARCTIC 28, 28–29 (2005) (noting that the AEWC was created to help justify an IWC-sanctioned Indigenous hunt for bowhead whales and today it "is recognized as a Alaska Inuit-run organization that manages Indigenous whaling and determines policy. . . . [and] works to preserve and protect bowhead whales and their habitat, as well as Inuit whaling and culture through a program of regulation, scientific research, and education").

155. *Report on Whale Killing Methods, supra* note 109, at 3.

156. Gillespie, *The Ethical Question, supra* note 83, at 366.

4

Modern Threats to Marine Mammals

> "[T]he world is not yet ready for comprehensive, ecological management of marine mammals."[1]

The United Nations Regional Seas Programme acknowledges that "[t]he marine mammals, among them whales, seals and dolphins, are threatened in many ways—by direct killing, accidental capture, and by our inadvertent destruction of their food and habitats. They are threatened all over the globe, with few places to hide."[2] Chapters 1 and 2 evince that international and national efforts to conserve marine mammals have, generally speaking, focused on regulating the direct lethal utilization of commercially important species. This chapter acknowledges that although the direct take of marine mammals remains a concern that must be addressed by any multilateral international convention and commission interested in marine mammal conservation, both the existence of multiple other threats and the evolving ethical relationship with marine mammals justify the creation of a new, comprehensive approach to marine mammal conservation and management. Specifically, the consequences of what I will refer to as the current threats, including climate change, by-catch, environmental pollution (be it chemical pollution, physical pollution, noise pollution, or other), ship-strikes, and ecotourism (be it whale watching, seal watching, or other forms of marine mammal tourism) are not adequately addressed by existing international marine mammal conservation efforts. The impact of these threats is exacerbated by persistent overarching concerns such as the alteration and loss of marine mammal habitat and the general degradation of the marine environment.

This chapter exemplifies the interaction among science, law, and the rational conservation and management of living marine resources. Specifically, the "[s]cientific challenges of great contemporary significance [that have emerged] as we grapple with oceans issues include understanding the linkages [between and within zonal management areas] to provide genuine ecosystem management and sustainable development, understanding discrete environmental problems such as the threat to coral reefs and declining fish stocks, and enhanced understanding for more effective utilization of ocean resources such as methane hydrates or new genetic resources."[3] It also adds to the list of challenges by addressing the scientific basis of our interaction with marine mammals. The analysis proceeds by describing the current understanding of modern threats to marine mammals and assessing how these issues inform the new multilateral regime I propose in this work.

I. CURRENT THREATS TO MARINE MAMMALS

When the International Convention for the Regulation of Whaling (ICRW) was negotiated, and the International Whaling Commission (IWC) subsequently created as the international organization responsible for the management of large cetaceans, the primary concern addressed by contracting nations was the systematic over-exploitation of whales that had characterized the history of whaling. This task was undertaken to "make possible the orderly development of the whaling industry."[4] Now, some 70 years removed from the negotiation of the ICRW/IWC regime, it should come as no surprise that the threats facing cetaceans, and marine mammals more generally, have changed.[5] As noted by Alexander Gillespie, cetaceans currently face "different threats, but just as deadly as the traditional forms of whaling that have commonly led to their over-exploitation."[6] Alison Reiser recognizes that the debate over whether to lift the moratorium on the commercial take of cetaceans that has occurred since it came into force in 1986, and has at times threatened to collapse the entire institution, has happened against a backdrop of considerable advancement in our "understanding of marine ecosystems and how human activities affect them."[7]

A literature review indicates that in addition to the overarching concerns of habitat loss and marine environment degradation, the most pressing specific threats to marine mammals include: (1) global climate change, (2) by-catch, (3) ship-strikes, (4) environmental pollution, and (5) ecotourism (marine mammal tourism).[8] Professor Gillespie acknowledges that these emerging threats affect more marine mammal species than just cetaceans.[9] This observation is particularly salient as the analysis contained in this chapter demonstrates that current threats are applicable to the majority of—if not all—marine mammal species, and that this commonality justifies a uniform legal response. The following section explores each specific threat identified above and the current international response, and concludes by noting the characteristics of a new international regime needed to effectively account for these current threats.

1. Global Climate Change

(I) THE PROBLEM

The Intergovernmental Panel on Climate Change (IPCC)[10] defines climate change as "any change in climate over time, whether due to natural variability or as a result of human activity."[11] Climate change is the subject of both domestic and international law and policy and, to date, the legal response to climate change (especially with respect to efforts aimed at mitigation through the reduction of carbon dioxide emissions) is notable for both its innovation and its failure. It is not within the scope of this work to provide a detailed discussion of mechanisms of climate change or a nuanced account of either the domestic or international response. Still, the following discussion is premised on the position that climate change is, at least partially, a consequence of anthropogenic action, most notably the addition of greenhouse gases to the Earth's atmosphere, and that climate change is presently occurring. Further, this work adopts the IPCC's position from the recently released Fifth Assessment Report, which predicts that surface warming, relative to 1986–2005 temperatures, will likely increase by 0.3–0.7 degrees Celsius by 2016–2035 and by 0.3–4.8 degrees Celsius by 2081–2100,[12] and that such warming will have measurable consequences (including sea level rise, ice melt, changes to air and ocean circulatory patterns, the water cycle, and the cryocycle).[13] These changes will have a perceptible impact on marine ecosystems.

The oceans are affected by climate change because "[o]cean climate is largely defined by its temperature, salinity, ocean circulation and the exchange of heat, water and gases (including carbon dioxide) with the atmosphere."[14] In short, changes to Earth's atmosphere and climate result in changes to the oceans' chemistry and life-sustaining properties, and these ocean-specific consequences are relevant to this assessment. First, it is estimated that alterations to global atmospheric circulation patterns will "inevitably affect the world ocean surface layers in the same directions, both due to simple heat exchange [between the atmosphere and the ocean] and different storm activity."[15] The consequences of warming may be most pronounced in the polar regions where alterations to physical processes "may upset the specific gravity balance of Arctic and Antarctic waters and reduce the flow of cold bottom water into deep ocean basins," disrupting ocean circulation.[16] Second, scientific predictions summarized by the IPCC indicate that oceans will likely experience increased incidence of acidification, reduced sea ice cover, higher sea levels, reduced ecosystem functioning, reduced productivity, and reduced biodiversity.[17]

In 2001, the IPCC identified marine mammals as "sensitive indicators of changes in ocean environments."[18] This classification is based on scientific observations that marine mammals will be significantly affected by changes to prey distribution, prey abundance, and sea ice reduction.[19] Our understanding of how marine mammals will be impacted and how they might respond to climate change is an area of current investigation and conjecture. One factor to be mindful of throughout this discussion is that although it is tempting to speak in generalities, there is considerable variation among marine mammal species. The impact that climate change will have on marine mammal species depends on the ecological scale of each species. Ecological scale is "determined by intrinsic life history characteristics and, for marine mammals, can extend from years to centuries in time and from tens to thousands of kilometers in space."[20]

One useful way to conceptualize how climate change impacts marine mammals is to consider its effects at different latitudinal regions.[21] This assessment approach makes it possible to differentiate between polar-regions, temperate-regions, and tropical-regions. At the poles, the disappearance of multi-year sea ice and glacial coverage impacts those species that utilize sea ice for hunting, breeding, rest, or reproduction (namely the polar bear, walrus species, and seal species).[22] Further, it is predicted that the loss of Arctic sea ice, which is occurring at a rate of 9 percent per year, "will precipitate complex and cascading interactions among physical and biological components of the Arctic ecosystem."[23] Still, reduced sea ice might not be detrimental for all marine mammals that utilize the Arctic, as migratory cetaceans that forage during periods of low sea ice will be able to arrive earlier and depart later.[24]

While Arctic sea ice is experiencing record levels of melt and retreat, reports suggest that sea ice coverage in Antarctica may actually be increasing.[25] Antarctic sea ice serves an important role in the development and survival of krill in the waters surrounding continental Antarctica. Krill, the small crustacean that forms the base of the Southern Ocean food web as prey for penguins, seals, and many migratory baleen whales, utilize sea ice for cover and feed on algae that form under the sea ice during the winter.[26] An increased abundance of krill will impact the population structure for many marine mammal species. By way of example, it has already been demonstrated that increased krill abundance is positively correlated with increased survivorship of seal pups.[27]

Marine mammals in temperate and tropical regions are likely to experience climate change quite differently than polar marine mammal species. The primary concern associated with climate change in these regions is ocean acidification[28] and coral bleaching,[29] although the ultimate consequences of both are still being investigated.[30] In addition to these alterations to the ocean environment, sea level rise and increased storm activity might reduce available habitat for marine mammal species that need to haul out of the ocean, and it might also increase mortality of young marine mammals.[31]

Other impacts of climate change are less latitude specific. For example, it is hypothesized that migratory marine mammals will have to alter the timing of migration patterns, which are "broad-scale annual migrations . . . between feeding and breeding areas [that have] evolved to maximize foraging, reproductive success, and off-spring survival."[32] Feeding is generally recognized as a concern because many marine mammal species rely on periods of excessive feeding followed by prolonged periods of minimal or no feeding.[33] Long-term data assessing the polar bear populations of Western Hudson Bay and Baffin Island (both in Canada) indicate that both body size and body condition of polar bears in this region are gradually diminishing.[34] A second general consequence of climate change is the impact of both disease and toxins because "[r]ates of pathogen development, disease transmission, and host susceptibility are all influenced by climate, with a greater incidence of disease anticipated with warming."[35] Finally, it is important to be cognizant of the indirect consequences of climate change. The major concern in this regard is the increased accessibility to the polar-regions as reduced seasonal ice cover and a general reduction in the integrity of multi-year ice enables increased commercial and recreational vessel traffic and new prospects for oil and gas development as well as commercial fishery operations.[36] Such developments expose a whole host of threats, including by-catch, ship-strikes, environmental pollution, and negative consequences of ecotourism.[37]

Some scientists suggest that marine mammal species may be well positioned to respond to the consequences of climate change given that they are warm-blooded and generally exhibit complex behavior and decision-making capability;[38] however, this does not change the reality that "available evidence suggests that many populations are highly vulnerable to the impacts of climate change."[39] It must also be acknowledged that our scientific understanding of many marine mammal species and their use of different habitat is still "at a fairly basic level,"[40] and that science has only recently moved from the realm of theoretical discussion to actual assessment and modeling of marine mammal redistribution in response to changing conditions. One such study from 2011 authored by Kristin Kaschner et al., titled *Current and Future Patterns of Global Marine Mammal Biodiversity*, assesses global hotspots of marine mammal biodiversity and concludes that there will be "some climate-change-driven range expansion or contraction," further predicting that "over the course of the next 40 years, negative effects such as net range contractions may be modest for most species, while a number of species might benefit from substantial increases in optimal habitat."[41] This article warns that the models employed fail to predict beyond the end of the first half of the twenty-first century, and that the more dramatic or severe climate change consequences are predicted to occur in the latter half of this century.[42]

In sum, existing scientific literature clearly demonstrates that climate change is a live issue for marine mammal conservation, and that "[i]t is increasingly clear that future conservation and management regimes for marine mammals need to take climate change into account."[43] What then is the current international response and, more important, what is the appropriate response?

(II) THE CURRENT RESPONSE

Global climate change is being addressed by law and policy in two main ways. The first response is characterized by international and domestic regulation seeking to reduce the severity of anthropogenic global climate change by mitigating greenhouse gas emissions. The international framework for reducing greenhouse gas emissions is embodied by the United Nations Framework Convention on Climate Change (UNFCCC).[44] The UNFCCC is a framework convention that relies on implementing protocols, such as the Kyoto Protocol, to set emission reduction targets and create innovative mechanisms for achieving reductions. Having concluded the Kyoto Protocol's first compliance period, UNFCCC parties agreed to extend the second compliance period to 2020 and in December, 2015, concluded negotiations on the Paris Agreement Under the United Nations Framework Convention on Climate Change at the 21st Conference of the Parties, which will open for signature in April, 2016 and bind the international community post-2020.[45] International efforts to curb greenhouse gas emissions have had limited success, but it is not within the scope of this work to assess the shortcomings of this international response.[46] Rather, this work is concerned with the second type of climate change response, namely adaptation.[47] Here, the international community must grapple with the consequences of climate change as they occur, and international organizations must consider and account for them as legal and policy decisions are made.

The IWC has publicly acknowledged the impact of climate change on cetaceans for some time. Specifically, in 1993 the IWC requested that the Scientific Committee establish a "special workshop" on climate change and the consequences for cetaceans.[48] This workshop occurred in 1996 and resulted in a report that acknowledged the difficulty of gathering reliable data about the consequences of climate change for cetaceans, but concluded that "the available evidence is sufficient to warrant some general concern for cetaceans."[49] The IWC Scientific Committee also created the Standing Working Group on Environmental Concerns (SWGEC) in 1997, which regularly considers climate change. Another workshop on climate change occurred in 2008, which resulted detailing the current understanding of how climate change is impacting cetaceans.[51] It is not evident that the IWC can contribute much more to the climate change discussion at this point.

Professor Gillespie suggests that the only option available to the IWC to address climate change is to "urge its member governments to join international efforts to reduce greenhouse gas emissions," and that "it is reflective of the unfortunate situation of the international community not adequately confronting the problem of climate change."[52] William Burns is similarly skeptical regarding the ability of the IWC to address climate change now that they acknowledge that it is happening. Specifically, he posits that the IWC likely lacks the resources necessary to conduct and report on climate change studies given the expense of both cetacean research (owing to the migratory and pelagic aspects of cetacean behavior) and climate change research (which utilizes predictive modeling).[53] Further, Burns questions whether the IWC is in a position to meaningfully address the results of any studies it produces.[54] Burns also questions whether the IWC can account for the consequences of climate change if the current moratorium on commercial whaling is lifted; specifically, he questions whether the proposed RMP, as the "mechanism for estimating the abundance of discrete species and sustainable catch limits," accounts for climate change impacts as even the most depleted species that are not being hunted will be detrimentally impacted by climate change.[55] In conclusion, Burns offers a perspective similar to that of Gillespie, suggesting that the IWC should focus on lobbying efforts, especially in relation to international treaty regimes operating in regions that are identified as being particularly susceptible to climate change.[56] He concludes that if the IWC fails to act in the face of climate change, its "ultimate legacy may be that it saved whales from extinction by commercial harvesting but failed them in their time of greatest need."[57]

Author Alison Reiser provides a slightly different perspective on how the consequences of climate change should be addressed by an international organization responsible for cetaceans. Specifically, she asserts that this novel problem "requires that we use our [ocean] governance institutions to reduce human-caused mortality from pollution, ship strikes, fishing-gear entanglement, and ocean noise, and the reduced health of individuals and populations that these conditions lead to."[58] In essence, this suggestion requires governance and regulatory bodies to incorporate international environmental law norms such as the precautionary principle[59] and ecosystem-based management[60] directly into their mandate.[61] These principles must be implemented in a substantive manner by being incorporated directly into the obligation-forming sections of the convention. Reiser suggests that the appropriate example that demonstrates how this can be accomplished is the Commission for the Conservation of Antarctic Marine Living Resources (CCAMLR), which was created in 1982 pursuant to the Convention on the Conservation of Antarctic Marine Living Resources[62] in response to increasing commercial pressure in the Antarctic krill industry and which directly implemented these governing principles.[63] Alternatively, the World Wildlife Fund suggests that the IWC can implement ecosystem-based management by focusing on "strengthen[ing] the resilience of species and ecosystems" by: (1) protecting "adequate and appropriate space," (2) acting to "[l]imit all non-climate related stresses," and (3) applying "[a]daptive management" (being the institutional flexibility and capability to respond to our changing understanding of climate change and its consequences).[64] Implementing these principles may very well require a paradigm shift in the way in which the IWC has historically operated, a shift that may be crucial for the long-term conservation and management of cetaceans and all marine mammals.

Existing literature makes a strong case that one of the most serious consequences of climate change is its interaction with other current threats, because the consequences of climate change are compounded by "bycatch, habitat degradation, overfishing of prey species and pollution."[65] With this interaction in mind, this discussion now turns to a description of these other threats.

2. By-Catch

(i) The Problem

The second threat to be considered is by-catch and incidental catch. Technically, by-catch encompasses two different situations. First, it refers to the unintended capture of species that are not the target of the fishing operation (which "are generally unwanted and discarded," also referred to as "incidental catches").[66] Second, it refers to instances where the captured species is not the target of the fishery but the unintended catch has commercial value and is kept rather than discarded.[67] Still, by-catch is commonly "used to describe any sort of unintended capture"[68] and is employed in its broader sense in this discussion. Semantics aside, a study on marine mammal by-catch published in 2006 offered the following assessment about its consequences: "[a]s we look to the future, fisheries bycatch poses the single greatest threat to many populations of marine mammals in the United States and elsewhere."[69] More recent studies have confirmed the significance of the by-catch threat.[70]

Although by-catch was once regarded as a benefit for fishermen who were able to capitalize on catching species that had some value in addition to that of their targeted catch, the rapid development of fishing technology and practices over the last few decades has escalated by-catch to a "critical issue for some marine mammal populations."[71] Further, our understanding of by-catch continues to progress, as evidenced by emerging scientific literature that recognizes by-catch as a multifaceted and complex issue. For example, in addition to the mortality associated with marine mammals dying from being entangled in fishing gear or being kept by fishermen, there is also concern surrounding "depredation," the situation whereby "marine mammals remove captured fish from nets or lines," which reduces targeted catches and fosters animosity toward marine mammals.[72] Although it is difficult to obtain accurate by-catch statistics because by-catch is not consistently reported, a study from 2006 utilized data from the United States in an attempt to extrapolate to a global by-catch estimate for marine mammals.[73] This study concluded that the total global annual by-catch mortality for marine mammals is in the hundreds of thousands,[74] and may be as high as 653,364 marine mammals (307,753 cetaceans and 345,611 pinnipeds).[75] This study cites gill-net fishing as the leading cause of mortality.[76]

This discussion of the consequences of by-catch is not merely academic, as evidenced by the recent extinction of the baiji (Yangtze River dolphin).[77] It is hypothesized that "the primary factor [resulting in the extinction of the baiji] was probably unsustainable by-catch in local fisheries," which utilize electric fishing, gill nets and other indiscriminate fishing practices.[78] Another marine mammal species seriously threatened by by-catch is the vaquita (a porpoise species inhabiting a portion of the Gulf of California).[79] Estimates suggest that fewer than 600 individuals remain and that annual mortality from gill-net by-catch may be as high as 40–80 individuals, with local efforts to reduce by-catch proving ineffective.[80] If by-catch mortality continues at this rate, the vaquita may well become the next marine mammal species to go extinct. Another pertinent example is net entanglement, which is one of the two main causes of North Atlantic right whale mortality and has played a considerable role in preventing the recovery of this species since the end of its commercial take.[81]

The other pertinent example is the curious interaction between dolphin and tuna that has been capitalized upon by fishermen. As described previously in Chapter 2, fishermen in the eastern tropical Pacific Ocean recognized that tuna schools follow dolphin schools and "that they could catch large tuna by herding dolphin schools with speedboats and then surrounding them with long, deep, purse seine nets," which were then closed at the top, catching both dolphin and tuna.[82] This fishing technique continued through the 1960s uncontested, with dolphin mortality estimated between 200,000 and 500,000 individuals.[83] This issue prompted considerable public concern, and the introduction of domestically labeled "dolphin safe"[84] tuna products and a fishing practice called the "backdown procedure" that allows a dolphin to escape once encircled by the seine net by submerging a portion of it.[85] Still, this "dolphin safe" response has been the subject of dispute between Mexico and the United States since 1991, and has been challenged twice through the General Agreement on Tariffs and Trade and most recently through the World Trade Organization.[86] Putting aside the issue of domestic labeling and trade restrictions, how is the by-catch problem being addressed at the international level of governance in relation to marine mammals?

(II) THE CURRENT RESPONSE

By-catch has been considered by the IWC since 2002; indeed, by-catch is one of the issues investigated on a regular basis by the Working Group on Estimation of Bycatch and Other Human-induced Mortality.[87] This group considers available evidence pertaining to ship-strike data and whale entanglement, among other concerns.[88] The reason for such considerations is that the IWC's RMP, as mentioned in the above discussion of climate change, indicates that if commercial whaling is to start again, "recommended catch limits must take into account estimates of mortality due to *inter alia* bycatch, ship strikes and other human factors...."[89] In addition to being an incomplete response to the by-catch problem as it relates to marine mammals generally (recall that the IWC only applies to certain large whale species), the IWC notes that this is not a complete response to by-catch even as it relates to species covered by the ICRW, as "such mortality can be of conservation and management importance to populations of large whales other than those to which the RMP might be applied."[90] If we consider the examples of the baiji and vaquita, it is apparent that by-catch will most profoundly impact species that are already depleted, and with respect to the IWC, it is those species that would not likely be hunted even if the RMP enters into force if the commercial moratorium is lifted. In terms of a response coordinated by the IWC, the Scientific Committee supports the establishment of a group that helps enable local responses to entanglement concerns and a database that centralizes entanglement data from around the world.[91]

Scientists echo the need for improved by-catch data.[92] They also point to the concern that marine mammal interaction with fishing gear is not a well understood phenomenon, and that the studies necessary to fully understand this interaction will take some time to complete.[93] In addition to a need for more complete data, they also point to a need to reduce by-catch in gill-net fisheries, noting that "[a]n ideal mitigation measure would reduce the effort or cost of dealing with bycatches, or increase the catch of target species, and thus improve the livelihood of a fisherman."[94] Just as the backdown procedure has proved useful in reducing dolphin by-catch, an option is to focus on technological advances that reduce marine mammal interaction with fishing gear. One such invention is the use of "pingers" that are attached to nets and emit "an intermittent, short, high-pitched noise that most fish cannot hear but that appears to repel or warn off marine mammals," which can reduce harbor porpoise and sea lion by-catch by up to 90 percent.[95] New Zealand, France, and the United Kingdom are also experimenting with "marine mammal escape devices" that route marine mammals through an escape hatch but do not otherwise impact fish catches.[96] Other ideas include international technology transfers to help implement mitigation techniques in developing countries, utilizing the United Nations Food and Agriculture Organization to test and evaluate mitigation measures, and perhaps even the creation of a "global marine mammal bycatch fund" to support innovation and enhanced mitigation.[97]

Some successful action has occurred at the regional level of governance through the Inter-American Tropical Tuna Commission (IATTC).[98] The IATTC, which is a Regional Fisheries Management Organization (RFMO), has a multilateral sister agreement titled the Agreement on the International Dolphin Conservation Program (AIDCP), which established an International Dolphin Conservation Program (IDCP) and exists as a functional international mechanism that seeks to "progressively reduce incidental dolphin mortalities in the tuna purse-seine fishery in the Agreement Area to levels approaching zero, through the setting of annual limits."[99] The AIDCP sets a maximum annual limit of dolphin mortality at 5,000,[100] and works to achieve its ultimate objective through a variety of mechanisms, including: (1) on-board observers (Article XIII), (2) compliance mechanisms (Article XVI), and the use of an International Review Panel (Article XII), which addresses dolphin-mortality certificate distribution and gear recommendations. There are a variety of other techniques utilized pursuant to the AIDCP that will be discussed in greater detail by way of a regionalism case study in Chapter 7.

All told, there is considerable work that has to be completed before we fully understand the by-catch problem. Similarly, there is definitely room for an improved response to this threat. What is certain is that the by-catch dilemma demonstrates the complexity of addressing current threats to marine mammals, an observation that is also apparent when considering the problem of other negative interactions between marine mammals and human uses of the ocean.

3. Ship-Strikes

(i) The Problem

The importance of ocean transport for the movement of goods and people cannot be understated. As noted by authors James Corbett and James Winebrake, "[w]ith respect to maritime shipping, the international movement of goods relies on a global freight transportation system that includes trans-oceanic, coastal, and inland waterway routes."[101] These authors characterize ocean transportation as a "cornerstone" of globalization.[102] In terms of capacity, as of the end of 2011, "today's world fleet of propelled sea-going merchant ships of no less than 100 GT [gross tonnage] comprises 104,304 ships of 1,043,081,509 million GT with an average age of 22 years; they are registered in over 150 nations and manned by 1.5 million seafarers of virtually every nationality. The world's cargo carrying fleet as of 2011 is 55,138 ships of 991,173,697 GT and 1,483,121,493 dwt [deadweight tonnage] and the average age is 19 years."[103] In addition to the movement of goods, the cruise ship industry is "the fastest growing travel sector in the world,"[104] with the Cruise Lines International Association (CLIA) indicating that annual average passenger growth has increased since 1980 at a rate of 7.5 percent per annum[105] with 25 new ships scheduled for introduction between 2012 and 2015.[106] In addition to the traditional pollution concerns associated with seafaring traffic, negative vessel-marine mammal interaction represents an emerging threat.

The impact of vessel collisions with marine mammals is difficult to accurately quantify because such collisions often go unreported, and scientists examining deceased marine mammals often have to speculate about a cause of death.[107] Still, the incidence of negative marine mammal-vessel interactions has increased in recent decades because of increasing vessel mass and vessel speed.[108] Although ship-strikes are a potential issue for all marine mammal species, this phenomenon has been best documented for the North Atlantic right whale and the Florida manatee. For example, it is hypothesized that North Atlantic right whale populations that were initially depleted by over-exploitation have failed to recover because of vessel strikes and fishing gear entanglement.[109] This critically endangered species might be particularly at risk of vessel strikes due to distinct foraging habits in certain waters that see individuals spend more time on the surface.[110] Similarly, the slow-moving manatee that spends considerable time in shallow waters and near the surface is particularly vulnerable to vessel collisions, and an estimated 90 percent of human-related mortality in Florida's waters is the result of vessel strikes.[111] Ship-strikes are now being recognized as a problem for other large and small cetacean species,[112] and are becoming of particular concern in the Arctic where vessel traffic is increasing (for both commercial and recreational purposes).[113]

In addition to enhancing ship-strike reporting, current scientific literature considers marine mammal migratory patterns and habitat use to suggest that what is required to effectively reduce marine mammal mortality is the development of vessel operating guidelines that establish speed restrictions and route alterations.[114] Scientists also consider as a mitigation strategy the use of sonic alarms to warn marine mammals of approaching vessels.[115] With this description of the problem and understanding of current science in mind, it is necessary to consider the current response.

(ii) The Current Response

The scientific observations highlighted above have not gone unnoticed by law and policymakers and academics. For example, Jeremy Firestone asserts that the "successful management of vessel strikes depends on the ability to understand the risk of an interaction between a vessel and a whale at a given point and time as well as the effects of that interaction."[116]

Existing management efforts at the domestic level targeting the ship-strike problem have utilized vessel speed and route restrictions, and have also recognized the important role that the International Maritime Organization (IMO) plays in addressing this issue. For example, because of its endangered status, the manatee is protected in the United States by both the Endangered Species Act[117] and the Marine Mammal Protection Act.[118] The U.S. Fish & Wildlife Service has assisted the State of Florida in creating manatee refuges and sanctuaries, and Florida has produced speed-zone boating restrictions for 13 counties critical for the manatee.[119] Working to educate about these restrictions and to enforce them remains an ongoing effort.[120] The manatee is not the only marine mammal that the United States has endeavored to protect from ship-strikes.

The North Atlantic right whale is also particularly vulnerable to ship-strikes, and similar mechanisms have been utilized for its protection. The National Marine Fisheries Service (NMFS) has produced, and revised, a Recovery Plan for the North Atlantic Right Whale (*Eubalaena glacialis*)[121] that seeks to respond to the current threats facing this species. NMFS has taken a variety of regulatory and non-regulatory steps to attempt to reduce ship-strikes. Although this discussion is focused primarily on the regulatory efforts, it is worth noting that NMFS has promoted education and outreach, produced ship speed advisories, recommended shipping routes, produced aerial surveys and reports on right whale movement, and promoted voluntary vessel speed reduction in certain designated management areas.[122] With respect to the regulatory response, NMFS promulgated the Right Whale Ship Strike Reduction Rule[123] requiring "[a]ll vessels greater than or equal to 65 ft (19.8 m) in overall length and subject to the jurisdiction of the United States and all vessels greater than or equal to 65 ft in overall length entering or departing a port or place subject to the jurisdiction of the United States"[124] to slow to 10 nautical miles per hour or less in designated Seasonal Management Areas (which cover feeding areas in the Northeast, migratory and calving grounds in the Mid-Atlantic, and calving and nursery grounds in the Southeast).[125] NOAA and the U.S. Coast Guard have implemented a Mandatory Ship Reporting System, endorsed by the IMO, that requires ships greater than 300 gross tons to report their presence in designated right whale habitat to a land-station, and in response they are informed about recent right whale sightings and precautionary measures they can employ.[126] Finally, NOAA has promulgated a rule that prohibits vessels from approaching within 500 yards of right whales,[127] and the State of Massachusetts has enacted a similar rule.[128] The United States' proposal to amend traffic and separation schemes to IMO to address similar concerns along America's West Coast has been approved.[129]

The IMO has helped to develop appropriate shipping routes and lanes to assist in the protection of the North Atlantic right whale, demonstrating how ship-strikes can effectively be addressed by the international community. The IMO, as the "United Nations specialized agency with responsibility for the safety and security of shipping and the prevention of marine pollution by ships,"[130] is responsible for establishing international ship routes pursuant to Chapter V of the International Convention for the Safety of Life at Sea.[131] For example, the IMO adopted the Bay of Fundy Traffic Separation Scheme ("Scheme") in 1982, which was implemented by

Transport Canada in 1983.[132] This Scheme was designed to help facilitate the movement of vessel traffic through a region used heavily for fishing, but failed to account for the feeding activities of North Atlantic right whales that occurred in the same area, resulting in a number of whale casualties.[133] Subsequently, stakeholder collaboration was initiated and "the collaborative effort between government agencies, the shipping and fishing industries, and the scientific community was rewarded by the adoption by the International Maritime Organization (IMO) of the amended traffic separation scheme."[134] This amended scheme has greatly reduced instances of whales being spotted within the designated shipping lanes, thereby averting possible negative vessel-whale interactions, and clearly demonstrates the role that the IMO can play in marine mammal conservation.[135]

A review of the effectiveness of IMO efforts to reduce large whale strikes published in 2012 indicates that three nations (Canada, Spain, and the United States) have approached the IMO a collective 10 times with submissions to reduce whale strikes.[136] This study concluded that well-constructed and documented national proposals submitted to the IMO were likely to be approved, and that nations should consider the domestic actions (i.e., regulatory requirements, monitoring, and enforcement) needed to create an effective traffic separation scheme.[137] Further, this assessment suggests that properly implemented schemes are generally successful at reducing whale strikes and that "[t]he relative success of IMO-adopted navigational measures speak to the influence and international reach of the IMO, and make it a powerful forum for coastal States to implement whale conservation measures and for addressing a range of marine environmental issues, especially where shipping has been identified as a threat to the ocean environment."[138] By way of update, since this review was completed, Panama[139] has presented a submission to the IMO (with the assistance of the IWC) to institute traffic separation schemes in the heavily used Panama Canal to effect whale conservation,[140] and the United States submitted a proposal to revise the Santa Barbara Channel traffic separation scheme to reduce whale collisions.[141]

As indicated above, the IWC has also taken an interest in ship-strikes as they impact cetaceans. Specifically, both the Scientific Committee and the Conservation Committee have been tasked with addressing the ship-strike concern.[142] Ship-strikes are relevant to the Scientific Committee because the RMP is to account for other mortality sources when assessing catch limits.[143] The IWC proffers that the Conservation Committee affords member states the opportunity to report on their national efforts to reduce ship-strikes and to coordinate support for national initiatives, such as the proposed Panama Canal traffic separation scheme.[144] These recent advances suggest that both the IMO and other international organizations dedicated to marine mammal conservation have an important role to play in assessing ship-strike mortality and facilitating an effective response, both nationally and internationally. This discussion will now turn to what is likely the most diffuse and difficult current threat to address—environmental pollution.

4. Environmental Pollution

(i) The Problem

Our understanding of environmental pollution is continually expanding. For example, even the very definition of pollution continues to evolve. A working definition of pollution is "the release of a potentially harmful chemical, physical, or biological agent to the environment as a result of human activity."[145] Article 1(4) of UNCLOS offers further guidance and defines "pollution of the marine environment" as "the introduction by man, directly or indirectly, of substances or energy into the marine environment, including estuaries, which results or is likely to result in such deleterious effects as harm to living resources and marine life, hazards to human health, hindrance to marine activities, including fishing and other legitimate uses of the sea, impairment of quality of sea water and reduction of amenities."[146] A recent study that reviews the marine mammal listing on the IUCN Red List and compares the listing to the various threats facing marine mammals concludes that pollution represents the "most pervasive" threat.[147] The following summary of the impact of pollution on marine mammal species reflects our changing understanding of pollution and encompasses both traditional pollutants and emerging areas of concern, such as underwater noise pollution.

(a) Traditional Pollution Problems

The pollutants of primary concern are persistent organic pollutants (POPs). According to the United States Environmental Protection Agency, POPs are "toxic chemicals that adversely affect human health and the environment around the world."[148] POPs are robust pollutants, meaning they do not rapidly decay, and their impacts are not localized at their point of production because they can be transported considerable distances through atmospheric air and/or water.[149] The international community has identified 12 POPs, appropriately referred to as the "Dirty Dozen," as being notoriously harmful.[150] These chemicals traditionally enter the environment through their agricultural and industrial applications, or as a byproduct of industrial combustion.[151]

Marine mammals generally occupy top trophic positions in ocean food webs and have life-history characteristics that render them particularly susceptible to contamination by environmental pollutants.[152] As noted by G.J. Pierce et al., "[l]ong-lived apex predators are particularly at risk . . . due to bio-accumulation (increasing concentration with age in individuals) and biomagnifications (higher levels higher up the food chain, especially when moving from gill-breathing animals like fish and cephalopods to air-breathing animals like marine mammals)."[153] Mammals are also particularly susceptible because pollutants accumulate in fatty tissue, such as blubber,[154] and are passed through mother's milk ("lactational transfer"),[155] meaning toxins magnify in concentration from one generation to the next.[156] This food web analysis also has implications for human health, as those around the world who rely on marine mammals as a staple protein source may be exposed to unhealthy contaminate levels.[157] A striking example, and one that is still being investigated, is the so-called "stinky whale" phenomena.[158] Since 2007, Indigenous hunters off of Siberia have reported catching gray whales "that smell so foul even the dogs won't eat them," and that sicken anyone who eats them.[159] This phenomenon is not limited to gray whales as reports of foul smelling walruses, bearded seals, and ringed seals have also been made.[160] The cause has yet to be positively identified.

The consequences of marine mammal exposure to POPs are well documented, and include: (1) a reduction in the effectiveness of immune system functionality,[161] (2) increases in the instances of infection,[162] (3) reproductive failure,[163] and (4) liver, intestinal, and endocrine problems.[164] Taken together, these effects have the potential to negatively impact the overall health of marine mammal populations.[165]

Although POPs seemingly receive the most attention in existing literature, it is important to note that other types and sources of traditional pollution also pose a risk to marine mammals. Other pollutants of note include: (1) heavy metals,[166] (2) plastics,[167] (3) industrial runoff and sewage waste from coastal development,[168] (4) oil spills and vessel leaks,[169] and (5) harmful algal blooms.[170] In addition to these traditional forms of pollution, the scientific community is increasingly demonstrating concern about the consequences of increased acoustic pollution in the marine environment.

(b) Emerging Concerns

In March 2012, at the 16th meeting of the parties of the Convention on Biological Diversity, the Subsidiary Body on Scientific, Technical and Technological Advice released a document titled *Scientific Synthesis on the Impacts of Underwater Noise on Marine Biodiversity and Habitats*.[171] This document summarizes our current understanding of the impact that anthropogenic noise has on ocean ecosystems, finding that: (1) "[a]nthropogenic noise in the marine environment has increased markedly over the last 100 or so years as the human use of the oceans has grown and diversified,"[172] and (2) that "[e]ffective management of anthropogenic noise in the marine environment should be regarded as a high priority for action at the national and regional level."[173] The major sources of anthropogenic underwater noise are: (1) sea traffic vessel noise, (2) marine dredging activities, (3) oil and gas recovery, (4) seismic exploration and marine surveys, and (5) naval sonar (in particular "active sonar systems" such as "Low-Frequency Active (LFA) Sonar").[174] Further, these sources add to an already noisy underwater environment where undersea volcanoes, earthquakes, and surface lightning strikes create noise.[175]

Water is an excellent conductor of sound,[176] and marine mammals rely on sound for every major aspect of their lives, including "navigation, prey location and capture, predator avoidance, and communication (including during migration and reproduction)."[177] The first study hypothesizing the linkage between anthropogenic noise pollution and an impact on marine mammal populations was published in 1971.[178] Since then, the scientific community has confirmed both the important role of sound for marine mammals and that anthropogenic disruption can have significant consequences. For example, a review of the impact of anthropogenic noise pollution on marine mammals, published in 2007, categorizes impacts as either: (1) fatal, or (2) chronic.[179] The most acute form of direct mortality is cetacean-stranding events whereby whales beach themselves and die, whereas chronic impacts include "[i]ncreased stress levels, abandonment of important habitat, and 'masking' or the obscuring or interference of natural sounds."[180] Other authors describe the same impacts but categorize the consequences as behavioral or physical.[181] Regardless of how these impacts are categorized, it is apparent that they represent a conservation concern that needs to be addressed.

(ii) The Current Response

In 2002, author Alexander Gillespie opined, regarding cetacean conservation, that environmental threats are " . . . different threats, less visible, but just as deadly as the traditional forms of whaling that have commonly lead to their over-exploitation."[182] Consideration of the international response to these concerns needs to be both general and specific. Broad general obligations will be considered first.

UNCLOS sets forth a number of obligations relevant to this discussion.[183] Specifically, Article 192 provides that "States have the obligation to protect and preserve the marine environment," while Article 193 confirms that the sovereign right to develop natural resources is to be conducted "in accordance with their duty to protect and preserve the marine environment."[184] Article 194 is also of import, and reads as follows:

1. States shall take, individually or jointly as appropriate, all measures consistent with this Convention that are necessary to prevent, reduce and control pollution of the marine environment from any source, using for this purpose the best practicable means at their disposal and in accordance with their capabilities, and they shall endeavour to harmonize their policies in this connection.
2. States shall take all measures necessary to ensure that activities under their jurisdiction or control are so conducted as not to cause damage by pollution to other States and their environment, and that pollution arising from incidents or activities under their jurisdiction or control does not spread beyond the areas where they exercise sovereign rights in accordance with this Convention.
3. The measures taken pursuant to this Part shall deal with all sources of pollution of the marine environment. These measures shall include, *inter alia*, those designed to minimize to the fullest possible extent:
   (a) the release of toxic, harmful or noxious substances, especially those which are persistent, from land-based sources, from or through the atmosphere or by dumping;
   (b) pollution from vessels, in particular measures for preventing accidents and dealing with emergencies, ensuring the safety of operations at sea, preventing intentional and unintentional discharges, and regulating the design, construction, equipment, operation and manning of vessels;
   (c) pollution from installations and devices used in exploration or exploitation of the natural resources of the seabed and subsoil, in particular measures for preventing accidents and dealing with emergencies, ensuring the safety of operations at sea, and regulating the design, construction, equipment, operation and manning of such installations or devices;
   (d) pollution from other installations and devices operating in the marine environment, in particular measures for preventing accidents and dealing with emergencies, ensuring the safety of operations at sea, and regulating the design, construction, equipment, operation and manning of such installations or devices.
4. In taking measures to prevent, reduce or control pollution of the marine environment, States shall refrain from unjustifiable interference with activities carried out by other States in the exercise of their rights and in pursuance of their duties in conformity with this Convention.
5. The measures taken in accordance with this Part shall include those necessary to protect and preserve rare or fragile ecosystems as well as the habitat of depleted, threatened or endangered species and other forms of marine life.

Other relevant obligations detailed in UNCLOS include: (1) Article 207 ("Pollution from land-based sources"), which provides that states shall address this issue at the national level, and "harmonize" responses at the appropriate regional level; (2) Article 208 ("Pollution from seabed activities subject to national jurisdiction"), which provides that states shall address the pollution associated with the use of the seabed within national jurisdiction, and "harmonize" responses at the appropriate regional level; (3) Article 209 ("Pollution from activities in the Area"), which provides that pollution created from the use of the seabed in areas beyond national control shall be regulated by international rules and regulations; (4) Article 210 ("Pollution by dumping"), which requires states to regulate national dumping and cooperate toward creating international regulation; (5) Article 211 ("Pollution from vessels"), which provides that states shall address vessel pollution through appropriate international organizations; and (6) Article 212 ("Pollution from or through the atmosphere"), which provides that states will take action to address atmosphere-based pollution.

Taken together, these Articles seem to address many of the concerns identified previously, and Gillespie notes that these general obligations have been used to form regional agreements to address pollution[185] in conjunction with the UNEP Regional Seas Programme.[186] Beyond the general obligations contemplated in UNCLOS, it is also necessary to consider the response from the IWC and specific international regimes.

The IWC has been aware of the risk to cetaceans posed by environmental threats since the Scientific Committee noted as much in 1973.[187] The IWC subsequently created Appendix 10 (the Resolution on Preservation of the Habitat of Whales and the Marine Environment) in 1981, which indicated that "responsible member governments of the IWC should take every possible measure to ensure that degradation of the marine environment ..." that harms cetaceans, or those consuming cetaceans, is avoided.[188] The IWC continued to work on this issue through the 1980s and 1990s,[189] and then in 1998 the IWC formalized "Environmental Concerns" as a regular agenda item that the Scientific Committee addressed in a Working Group and reported on annually:

> ... the Scientific Committee would report annually on its progress in non-lethal research on environmental concerns, and Contracting Governments could report annually on national and regional efforts to monitor and address the impacts of environmental change on cetaceans and other marine animals.[190]

The Scientific Committee, in furtherance of this goal and in accordance with Resolution 2000-7,[191] promulgates State of the Cetacean Environment Reports (SOCERs).[192] SOCERs are produced annually for a predetermined region (i.e., Indian Ocean, Arctic Ocean, Black Sea and Mediterranean, etc.) as a "non-technical periodic summary of the positive and negative events, developments and conditions in the marine environment that are relevant to cetaceans."[193] These regional reports are combined every four to six years to create a global SOCER.[194] Despite the general obligations found in UNCLOS and IWC's initiatives, the following observation by Gillespie, made in 2002, holds true today:

> [d]espite these general international and regional approaches, the protection of the ocean in an international sense cannot be found in any single codified

document which addresses all problems. Rather, the protection of the marine environment, and the species therein, from pollution is found in a number of diverse areas and particular threats, which together, appear to represent an overall umbrella; however, this umbrella has many holes in it.[195]

There are various explanations for why no single, comprehensive, international response to marine pollution exists. First, our understanding of pollution is a dynamic issue that is evolving over time. Second, unless pollution impacts human use of the marine environment (e.g., marine animals become too toxic to consume or too scarce to observe) pollution is an externality that does not justify regulatory intervention. Third, restricting pollution impacts many important industrial pursuits (e.g., oil and gas development), recreational pursuits (e.g., cruise lines), and critical national interests (e.g., security). Fourth, the international community has responded on an ad hoc basis to many of the critical threats. The remainder of this section will briefly highlight the existing issue-specific international efforts relevant to marine mammal management.

The first international response of note is the Stockholm Convention on Persistent Organic Pollutants ("Stockholm Convention").[196] The Stockholm Convention was adopted on May 22, 2001, and opened for signature on May 23 of the same year;[197] it is administered by the UNEP.[198] The Stockholm Convention came into force on May 17, 2004, 19 days after the fiftieth state ratification was deposited (in accordance with Article 26(1)).[199] There are currently 152 signatories to the Stockholm Convention and 146 states parties.[200] The Stockholm Convention represents the international response to persistent organic pollutants, as described previously. This regime initially applied to the "dirty dozen" POPs, but has since been expanded through agreement at Conferences of the Parties to cover 22 chemicals.[201] The Stockholm Convention addresses POPs and other listed chemicals in a number of ways, including: (1) phasing out production, (2) restricting import and/or export of certain products, (3) banning or limiting use of certain products, and (4) requiring the production of national implementation plans.[202] This regime is coordinated with two other UNEP-implemented treaties, namely the Basel Convention on the Control of Transboundary Movements of Hazardous Wastes and Their Disposal and the Rotterdam Convention on the Prior Informed Consent Procedure for Certain Hazardous Chemicals and Pesticides in International Trade.[203] This regime has proved fairly effective[204] and represents one of many international responses to pollution.

The second international regime of note addresses the voluntary disposal of waste at sea, which is otherwise known as dumping. The Convention on the Prevention of Marine Pollution by Dumping of Wastes and Other Matter 1972 (the "London Convention") addressed this issue by seeking regulatory control of dumping.[205] Dumping represents one mechanism through which radioactive waste and heavy metals that impact marine mammals enter the marine environment.[206] The IMO, which implements this regime, indicates that because of it:

> The unregulated dumping and incineration activities that developed in the late 1960s and early 1970s have been halted. Parties to the Convention agreed to control dumping by implementing regulatory programmes to assess the need for, and the potential impact of, dumping. They eliminated dumping of certain

types of waste and, gradually, made this regime more restrictive by promoting sound waste management and pollution prevention. Prohibitions are in force for dumping of industrial and radioactive wastes, as well as for incineration at sea of industrial waste and sewage sludge.[207]

The London Convention, regarded as being quite successful at regulating dumping,[208] currently has 87 states parties,[209] and is recognized as customary international law.[210] The efficacy of this regime was boosted in 2006 when the Protocol to the Convention on the Prevention of Marine Pollution by Dumping of Wastes and Other Matter, 1972 ("London Convention Protocol") came into force.[211] The London Convention Protocol emphasizes both the precautionary principle and the polluter-pays principle, and strengthens the regime by restricting all dumping, save permitted dumping of those substances listed in Annex I of the Agreement.[212] This regime is also regarded as being generally successful,[213] but improvements are needed in the areas of technical cooperation, scientific evaluation, and improved compliance.[214]

The IMO is also responsible for implementation of the International Convention for the Prevention of Pollution from Ships (MARPOL),[215] which is the "main international convention covering prevention of pollution of the marine environment by ships from operational or accidental causes."[216] MARPOL and the Protocol of 1978 Relating to the International Convention for the Prevention of Pollution from Ships (which responded to oil tanker spills) entered into force on October 2, 1983, and amended the previous agreement.[217] The MARPOL regime currently has a number of annexes that detail regulatory control, including: (1) Annex I ("Regulations for the Prevention of Pollution by Oil"), which addresses oil from operational vessel sources and accidental sources; (2) Annex II ("Regulations for the Control of Pollution by Noxious Liquid Substances in Bulk"), which controls pollution associated with the mass transport of hazardous liquids; (3) Annex III ("Prevention of Pollution by Harmful Substances Carried by Sea in Packaged Form"), which standardizes packing and documentation for transporting hazardous goods; (4) Annex IV ("Prevention of Pollution by Sewage from Ships"), which limits sewage discharge in accordance with sewage treatment specifications and prescribed distances from land; (5) Annex V ("Prevention of Pollution by Garbage from Ships"), which limits garbage discharge and bans the addition of plastics to the ocean; and (6) Annex VI ("Prevention of Air Pollution from Ships"), which limits the emission of nitrogen oxide, sulfur oxide, particulate matter, and ozone- depleting substances from ship exhaust.[218] The MARPOL regime is also regarded as having been quite successful at achieving its goals.[219]

The final source of regulation that will be considered in this section is the prevailing approach to the regulation of noise pollution. Unlike the other regulatory approaches to pollution discussed above, there is "no multilateral convention on undersea noise which seeks to operationalize the obligations incurred under UNCLOS 1982."[220] Noise pollution has proved difficult to regulate internationally as it is different than other sources of pollution (i.e., "[u]nlike most other forms of pollution, noise does not damage the marine environment per se. Rather, its harm lies in the injury caused to marine life, particularly marine mammals, and the consequent damage caused to a marine ecosystem through the loss or displacement of a species"[221]). Further, noise pollution comes from a variety of sources (i.e., oil and gas, military, shipping, and recreational),[222] and its regulation is likely to engage issues of national security.[223] Still, the paucity of international regulation should not be construed as a lack of concern or absence of emerging efforts to regulate.

In 2007, author Karen Scott emphasized the emerging regional response to undersea noise regulation in *Sound and Cetaceans: A Regional Response to Regulating Acoustic Marine Pollution*.[224] Scott asserts that the noise pollution associated with offshore oil and gas, whale watching/tourism, coastal development, and renewable energy development are all well-suited for regional regulation, like any other pollution source, but that the issue of pollution associated with vessel construction standards must be addressed by the IMO.[225] Noise pollution can also be managed at the regional level through enhanced "general regulation of activities within the maritime environment," through the "designation of specially protected areas," and by affording "special protection of endemic vulnerable species."[226] The recent synthesis on undersea noise pollution commissioned by the Secretariat of the Convention on Biological Diversity also recognizes the work that has been completed at the regional level of governance and emphasizes the need for further national and regional regulation as well as mitigation efforts,[227] whereas an investigation into a mass stranding event of melon-headed whales in Madagascar facilitated by the IWC demonstrates the sort of collaborative effort required to understand and address this threat.[228]

It is clear that both the impacts of pollution on marine mammals and existing management approaches to pollution are varied and complex. As Gillespie asserts regarding the IWC's insufficient response to environmental issues, "[t]here is little more that the IWC can do in solving these problems, as the solutions which are intimately connected to a clean and healthy ocean can only be resolved in other international, regional and national forums which directly address the specific threats."[229] The proposal I advance in Chapters 6 and 7 supports this assertion and presents an option that institutionalizes the role that the competent international organization responsible for the conservation of marine mammals could occupy.

5. Ecotourism (Marine Mammal Tourism)

(i) The Problem

Marine mammal watching—what I refer to more broadly as marine mammal tourism—is defined in the UNEP *Report of the Regional Workshop on Marine Mammal Watching in the Wider Caribbean Region* as "tours by boat, air or from land, with some commercial aspect, to see and/or listen to [marine mammals]."[230] The dominant form of marine mammal tourism is whale watching/tourism, which has been credited with "the building of a constituency out of the general public that is interested in and sympathetic to marine mammals, the sea, and marine conservation."[231] It is important to keep in mind that, generally speaking, all marine mammal species are of interest to humans, who will pay to view them. For example, within the United States there are commercial operations that facilitate viewing of polar bears, whales, dolphins, porpoises, seals, sea lions, walruses, sea otters, and manatees; however, existing research predominately addresses whale watching/tourism, as this is the most developed marine mammal tourism industry.[232] The following assessment focuses on whale watching/tourism, with reference to other forms of marine mammal watching as applicable.

Whale watching, the organized "human activity of encountering cetaceans in their natural habitat," can be traced back to the 1940s and gray whale observation at the Scripps Institution of Oceanography.[233] Whale watching gradually developed into a commercial endeavor and also a vehicle for scientific observation and research.[234] An assessment of the global economics of whale watching published in 2009 (completed by Economists at Large as commissioned by the International Fund for Animal Welfare) indicates that in the 2008 calendar year, 13 million people from 119 countries went whale watching, producing US$2.1 billion in expenditures.[235] Further, this report suggests that over 13,200 individuals are employed worldwide by the 3,300 whale watching operators that offer commercial services.[236] Finally, whale watching is increasing at a rate of approximately 3.7 percent annually, with the highest instances of growth occurring in Asia, Europe, Central America, South America, Pacific Island nations, and the Caribbean.[237] Interestingly, whale watching/tourism has even emerged as an important economic activity in nations that continue to pursue commercial whaling, such as Japan and Norway.[238]

Recent studies assert that whale watching (and all marine mammal tourism by implication) has yet to reach its full potential. For example, a 2010 estimate indicates that an additional US$413 million, and 5,700 jobs, could be generated by starting whale watching operations in coastal countries where whale watching is not currently occurring.[239] Moreover, this study found that "[t]he number of total tourist arrivals, as well as the number of marine mammal species and their relative abundance within a country's EEZ were significantly . . . and positively correlated with the number of whale watchers,"[240] and that approximately 20 percent of total economic benefit associated with whale watching is generated in the developing world.[241] Marine mammal tourism also has the potential to educate participants on different conservation and management concerns; however, maximizing educational benefits requires a level of structure and organization that is not always present.[242]

It should come as no surprise that marine mammal tourism is not completely benign with respect to its potential impacts on targeted species. For example, author Erich Hoyt suggests that whale watching results in behavioral changes as whales respond to attention from boats by diving longer and/or actively avoiding certain areas, which in turn can disrupt reproduction, shift natural distribution patterns, and potentially even reduce survival rates.[243] A recent study assessing the impact of marine mammal tourism on the Indo-Pacific bottlenose dolphin in Port Stephens, New South Wales, Australia, provides evidence corroborating Hoyt's hypothesis as it concludes that "in the presence of dolphin-watching boats dolphins spent less time on critical activities, such as feeding, resting, and socialising."[244] A second potential problem is the interaction between whaling and whale watching. For example, Hoyt proffers that whaling potentially reduces the number of whales available for whale watching, negatively alters whale behavior, reduces the ability for whale watching to promote conservation, and impacts the broader tourism industry.[245] With this background in mind it is now appropriate to turn to a description of the prevailing marine mammal tourism management framework.

(ii) The Current Response

The current management response to marine mammal tourism, in the context of whales, is plagued with inconsistency and enforcement issues.[246] Hoyt suggests that there are "too many boats on the water in a limited area, too many close approaches and sometimes collisions with cetaceans, strain on the infrastructure of local communities from too many visitors, and a lack of guidelines and regulations and/or enforcement of them."[247] This statement should not be taken to mean that there is a dearth of guidance or whale watching standards. Author Carole Carlson maintains an "ongoing compendium of whalewatch guidelines and regulations [from] around the world."[248] This analysis represents a summary of "22 regulations, 15 codes of conduct, 9 guidelines for operators and 4 decrees," and recognizes that "19 non-governmental and one inter-governmental organization(s) have developed guidelines."[249] Still, this assessment does not purport to represent a statement of best practice, and it also does not discuss which guides have utilized scientific considerations in their creation or implementation.[250] As it can logically be assumed that most marine mammal tourism occurs within nation's EEZs (and indeed, likely within territorial seas), guidelines and practices will inevitably vary based on national capacity and priority. Nonetheless, there are a number of ways in which international organizations and treaty regimes can contribute to improved whale tourism practices, as the remainder of this section illustrates.

It is particularly relevant to highlight the contribution that the IWC has made to the regulation of whale watching. Since 1996, the IWC has taken it upon itself to monitor and advise on global whale watching/tourism.[251] Academic commentary is alive to the fact that there is a degree of tension associated with the coexistence of commercial whaling regulation and whale watching,[252] but also acknowledges that a pro-whaling position and use of whale watching do not necessarily have to be mutually exclusive.[253] Regardless of this unresolved tension, the IWC has taken the following action:

(1) Produced IWC whale watching guidelines,[254] which are structured around three main principles: (a) to manage the development of whale watching to minimize adverse impacts, (b) to design and implement whale watching delivery systems that minimize adverse impacts, and (c) to enable cetaceans to control the whale watching experience (i.e., duration and proximity).[255]
(2) Compiled and published existing regulations from around the world, which presents guidelines, regulations, and best practice standards from national jurisdictions around the world, including the standards recommended by ACCOBAMS.[256]
(3) Prepared a *Five Year Strategic Plan for Whalewatching: 2011–2016*, which also has the goal of sustainable whale watching and indicates various objectives and mechanisms that can be used to help promote coordination between the IWC and the local implementation of whale watching.[257]
(4) Is working to create a "Handbook for Whale Watching" to serve as a "web-based living and evolving tool. It will support whalewatching operators, national and regional regulators, and others involved in the sector."[258]

As this summary of IWC whale watching initiatives demonstrates, optimal whale watching/tourism can also be assessed through the sustainability lens. This sustainability goal has been addressed in the literature, and a succinct articulation has been provided by Emily Lambert et al. in a paper titled *Sustainable Whale-Watching Tourism and Climate Change: Towards a Framework of Resilience*, which notes the following two components of sustainable whale watching: (1) "reducing and managing negative interactions between whale-watching boats, cetaceans and their natural habitat," and (2) "achieving economic stability."[259] Although the IWC has taken the critical first steps toward promoting and advancing sustainable development, there is still work to be done. Moving forward, there is hope that some of the reforms I suggest below might actually be possible given that the Latin American and Caribbean State contingent at the IWC (the so-called "Buenos Aires Group") has prioritized whale watching in exercising their voting power.[260]

First, the IWC's guiding principles for whale watching could be much more detailed and explanatory, and a new international organization that covers all marine mammal species could promote guidelines with greater species coverage. These standards should also be accompanied by an educational component assisting implementation. Second, and more important, the international community could work to promote ecotourism and the conservation benefits of properly designed whale watching and marine mammal tourism generally. For example, A.M. Cisneros-Montemayor et al. posit that "[i]nsufficient guidance on adequate implementation, as well as a lack of foresight as to the potential benefits from it, seem to be the main reasons for these [developing coastal] countries not entering the whale watching market."[261] With this in mind, it is interesting to consider whether emerging principles such as common but differentiated responsibility, technology transfer, or foreign investment could play a role in enhancing the future of marine mammal tourism, and whether developed nations interested in promoting whale watching/tourism could assist via formalized knowledge and/or technology transfers to help developing nations establish the infrastructure required for viable marine mammal tourism.[262]

II. FEATURES OF A NEW RESPONSE

In light of this assessment, it is necessary to consider how current threats to marine mammals can be addressed in a new multilateral treaty for the conservation of marine mammals that establishes an International Marine Mammal Commission.

First, it is apparent that the focus of any multilateral treaty negotiated to effectuate marine mammal conservation and sustainable management, and the commission created pursuant to this treaty that is mandated with the responsibility of implementing the treaty, must expressly incorporate the precautionary principle, ecosystem-based management, and sustainability as guiding principles. Second, it is evident that this regime must complement rather than replace or disrupt the existing international and regional initiatives that are entrenched, functional, and successful at addressing current threats. The new regime should institutionalize and formalize cooperation and coordination between the new International Marine Mammal Commission and other institutions (save those which it replaces). It would not be practical, feasible, or necessary for this new commission to become the leading authority on climate change or navigation and shipping, especially as these issues may be outside the regulatory jurisdiction of the commission. Rather, the new commission should seek to maximize its lobbying and enhance its cooperation with other, more-appropriately situated international organizations. Third, the new international regime must build upon the foundation that the IWC has created as it has turned its attention toward current threats since the introduction of the commercial moratorium in 1986. Fourth, the convention and its associated institutions must be crafted broadly enough and with sufficient flexibility to accommodate and respond to our evolving scientific and technical understanding of these emerging threats. These observations inform the detailed proposal and draft Articles for a new multilateral convention, as provided in Chapters 6 and 7.

III. CONCLUSION

This chapter has investigated and assessed the scientific justification for a new international regime for the conservation of marine mammals. The present regime has been measured against a host of current threats to marine mammals, and the basis of our understanding of the ethical objectives that should guide our interaction with marine mammals, and has been found wanting.

Before proposing the contents of a new regime and describing how the new regime can rectify the shortcomings identified in this chapter and the fragmented regulatory approach to marine mammal conservation previously identified, it is necessary to establish the legal basis and jurisdictional and practical limits that inform the proposed response.

NOTES

1. James A R. Nafziger, *Global Conservation and Management of Marine Mammals*, 17 SAN DIEGO L. REV. 591, 614 (1979–1980).
2. UNEP Regional Seas, *Marine Mammal Action Plan*, http://www.unep.ch/regionalseas/main/hmarmams.html (last visited June 12, 2015).
3. John Norton Moore, *Setting the Scene: Introductory Remarks*, in LAW, SCIENCE & OCEAN MANAGEMENT 95, 96 (Myron H. Nordquist et al. eds., 2007).
4. 2 Dec. 1946, 62 Stat. 1716, 161 U.N.T.S. 74, at preamble.
5. For a recent scientific summary of the anthropogenic threats to marine mammals, see Marthán Bester, *Marine Mammals—Natural and Anthropogenic Influences*, in GLOBAL ENVIRONMENTAL CHANGE 167 (Bill Freeman ed., 2014).
6. Alexander Gillespie, *Environmental Threats to Cetaceans and the Limits of Existing Management Structures*, 6 N.Z. J. ENVTL. L. 97, 97 (2002) [Gillespie, *Environmental Threats*]; see generally ALEXANDER GILLESPIE, WHALING DIPLOMACY 45–105 (2005) (offering a similar review of modern threats to cetaceans) ["WHALING DIPLOMACY"].
7. Alison Reiser, *Whales, Whaling, and the Warming Oceans*, 36 ENVTL. AFF. 401, 402 (2009) ["Reiser"].
8. See Henry R. Huntington, *A Preliminary Assessment of Threats to Arctic Marine Mammals and Their Conservation in the Coming Decades*, 33 MAR. POL. 77, 77 (2009) (expanding the list of global threats to marine mammals identified as "disease, sound, contaminants, harmful algal blooms, direct fisheries, indirect fisheries impacts, habitat change, and environmental change" from REYNOLDS ET AL., MARINE MAMMAL RESEARCH: CONSERVATION BEYOND CRISIS (2005), by adding direct mortality associated with hunting and/or ship-strikes); see also Nigel Bankes, *The Conservation and Utilization of Marine Mammals in the*

Arctic Region, in THE LAW OF THE SEA AND THE POLAR REGIONS: INTERACTIONS BETWEEN GLOBAL AND REGIONAL REGIMES 293, 293–94 (Erik J. Molenaar, Alex H. Oude Elferink & Donald R. Rothwell eds., 2013) (noting that existing threats include: "human harvest, food availability, predation, entanglement and bycatch, climate change, ship strikes, pollution, habitat and feeding ground degradation, and marine noise").

9. Gillespie, *Environmental Threats, supra* note 6, at 97–98.
10. *See* International Panel on Climate Change, *Organization* http://www.ipcc.ch/organization/organization.shtml#.UHh7529kyW4 (last visited June 12, 2015) (noting that the IPCC was created in 1988 by the United Nations Environment Programme and the World Meteorological Organization (with the endorsement of the United Nations General Assembly) to synthesize the world's understanding of climate change, and to provide information on both the socio-economic and environmental consequences of climate change. The IPCC is both a scientific organization (responsible for assessing the current state of knowledge through the efforts of thousands of voluntary scientists) and an intergovernmental organization that encourages government participation (and currently has 195 government members). The IPCC produces a variety of documents that are reviewed and endorsed by member governments).
11. International Panel on Climate Change, *2007: Summary for Policymakers, in* CLIMATE CHANGE 2007: THE PHYSICAL SCIENCE BASIS. CONTRIBUTION OF WORKING GROUP I TO THE FOURTH ASSESSMENT REPORT OF THE INTERGOVERNMENTAL PANEL ON CLIMATE CHANGE 1, 2 (S. Solomon et al. eds., 2007) ["*2007 Summary for Policy Makers*"].
12. International Panel on Climate Change, *Summary for Policymakers, in* CLIMATE CHANGE 2013: THE PHYSICAL SCIENCE BASIS. CONTRIBUTION OF WORKING GROUP I TO THE FIFTH ASSESSMENT REPORT OF THE INTERGOVERNMENTAL PANEL ON CLIMATE CHANGE 15 (Thomas F. Stocker et al. eds., 2013).
13. *See id.* at 16–20; *see also 2007 Summary for Policymakers, supra* note 11, at 7–22 (for a detailed discussion of the potential consequences of climate change).
14. Peter G.H. Evans et al., *Climate Change and Marine Mammals*, 90(8) J. MAR. BIOL. ASSOC. U.K. 1483, 1483 (2010) ["Evans et al."].
15. Hjalmar Vilhjalmsson, *Impact of Changes in Natural Conditions on Ocean Resources, in* LAW, SCIENCE & OCEAN MANAGEMENT 225, 225 (Myron H. Nordquist et al. eds., 2007) ["Vilhjalmsson"].
16. *Id.* at 230–31.
17. A. Fishclin et al., *Ecosystems, Their Properties, Goods and Services, in* CLIMATE CHANGE 2007: IMPACT, ADAPTATION AND VULNERABILITY. CONTRIBUTION OF WORKING GROUP II TO THE FOURTH ASSESSMENT REPORT OF THE INTERGOVERNMENTAL PANEL ON CLIMATE CHANGE 212, 234–36 (M.L. Parry et al. eds., 2007); Sue E. Moore, *Climate Change, in* ENCYCLOPEDIA OF MARINE MAMMALS 238, 238 (William F. Perrin et al. eds., 2d ed. 2009) ["S. Moore"].
18. International Panel on Climate Change, *Working Group II: Impacts, Adaptation and Vulnerability—Chapter 6: Coastal Zones and Marine Ecosystems, Marine Mammals and Seabirds*, 6.3.7 (2007) http://www.ipcc.ch/ipccreports/tar/wg2/index.php?idp=291#637.
19. *Id.*
20. S. Moore, *supra* note 17, at 238–39 (which distinguishes impacts based on polar regions compared to temperate and/or tropical regions); *see also. e.g.,* Colin D.

Macleod, *Global Climate Change, Range Changes and Potential Implications for the Conservation of Marine Cetaceans: A Review and Synthesis*, 7 ENDANG. SPECIES RES. 125, 125–31 (2009) ["MacLeod"] (noting that cetacean distribution is mainly determined by water temperature, water depth, and prey abundance/distribution, and also predator avoidance and conditions required for reproduction. Further, he indicates that climate change will alter the ability for cetacean species to find their preferred habitat and may even result in species becoming isolated in particular geographical locations).

21. S. Moore, *supra* note 17, at 238–39.
22. *Id.; see also* W. Elliot & M. Simmonds, *Whales in Hot Water? The Impact of a Changing Climate on Whales, Dolphins and Porpoises: A Call for Action* 6–7 (2007), http://awsassets.wwf.org.au/downloads/sp141_g_whales_in_hot_water_1may07.pdf ["*Whales in Hot Water?*"] (noting that sea ice edge is a very important foraging spot for northern cetaceans, such as the beluga (who feed on Arctic cod congregated in this area of heightened biological productivity) and narwhal (who might use the sea ice to take refuge from predatory orca)).
23. S. Moore, *supra* note 17, at 239.
24. *Id.*
25. Daniel Stone, *Antarctic Sea Ice Hits Record High? Does That Mean Earth Isn't Warming Up?*, NAT'L GEOGRAPHIC NEWS (Oct. 13, 2012), http://news.nationalgeographic.com/news/2012/10/121013-antarctica-sea-ice-record-high-science-global-warming/.
26. *See* V. Loeb et al., *Effects of Sea-Ice Extent and Krill or Salp Dominance on the Antarctic Food Web*, 387 NATURE 897, 897–98 (1997); *see also Whales in Hot Water?*, *supra* note 22, at 9 (noting that "krill overwinter under the ice, and feed on algae found under the ice surface. Thus, the sea ice edge is the area of highest productivity in the Southern Ocean ecosystem and the main foraging site for many whale species").
27. S. Moore, *supra* note 17, at 239.
28. *See* Scott Doney, *The Dangers of Ocean Acidification*, 294(3) SCI. AM. 58, 59 (2006) (noting that CO_2 from fossil fuel emissions enters the ocean and reduces the pH of the ocean, which is naturally alkaline (basic), thereby reducing the capability of corals to grow. At 62, this article also notes that marine organisms that create calcium carbonate (for shells and other structural features) will also be limited in growth capability, and many of these tiny organisms form a critical component of the diet of certain marine mammals).
29. *See* Ove Hoegh-Guldberg, *Climate Change, Coral Bleaching and the Future of the World's Coral Reefs*, 50 MAR. FRESHWATER RES. 839, 843 (1999) (discussing increasing average water temperatures as one explanation for mass coral die-off, which results in coral bleaching (essentially the death of a portion, or entirety, of a reef). At 860 the article notes that the impact of coral bleaching events is predicted to be significant for marine mammals that utilize coral reefs as important habitat).
30. S. Moore, *supra* note 17, at 239.
31. *Id.* at 239–40.
32. *Id.* at 240 (also noting that more data are needed to determine the extent to which migratory pattern changes are already occurring).
33. *See* M.A. Castellini & L.D. Rea, *The Biochemistry of Natural Fasting at Its Limits*, 48(6) EXPERIENTIA 575, 580 (1992) (indicating periods of fasting for pinnipeds

34. S. Moore, *supra* note 17, at 240–41.
35. *Id.* at 241.
36. *Whales in Hot Water?*, *supra* note 22, at 7–8; *see also* Pete Evans, *Arctic Thaw Heats Up Northwest Passage Dreams*, CBC News (Sept. 13, 2012, 8:27 AM), http://www.cbc.ca/news/business/story/2012/09/11/f-franklin-northwest-passage-arctic.html (these issues are a common area of discussion and debate in Canada). Although the Northwest Passage has yet to fully open, the Northern Sea Route ("across the top of Russia") is now functioning (*see* Margaret Blunden, *Geopolitics and the Northern Sea Route*, 88 Intl. Aff. 115, 115 (2012); *see also* Northern Sea Route Information Office, "Northern Sea Route", http://www.arctic-lio.com/ (last visited June 15, 2015)).
37. *Whales in Hot Water?*, *supra* note 22, at 7.
38. Evans et al., *supra* note 14, at 1483.
39. Mark P. Simmonds & Stephen J. Isacc, *The Impacts of Climate Change on Marine Mammals: Early Signs of Significant Problems*, 41(1) Orxy 19, 25 (2007) ["Simmonds & Isacc"].
40. Evans et al., *supra* note 14, at 1485.
41. Kristin Kaschner et al., *Current and Future Patterns of Global Marine Mammal Biodiversity*, 6(5) PLoS ONE 1, 9 (2011).
42. *Id.*
43. Simmonds & Isacc, *supra* note 39, at 25.
44. 31 Dec. 1992, 1771 U.N.T.S. 107, 31 I.L.M. 849.
45. *Doha Outcome: Kyoto Protocol Lives, Global Climate Deal by 2015*, Envtl. News Servs. (Dec. 8, 2012), http://ens-newswire.com/2012/12/08/doha-outcome-kyoto-protocol-lives-global-climate-deal-by-2015/; UNFCCC, "COP21", http://www.cop21.gouv.fr/en (last visited Feb. 17, 2016); United Nations Framework Convention on Climate Change Twenty-first Conference of the Parties, Nov. 30–Dec. 11, 2015, *Adoption of the Paris Agreement*, U.N. Doc. FCCC/CP/2015/L.9 (Dec. 12, 2015).
46. *See* Peter Lawrence, Justice for Future Generations: Climate Change and International Law (2014); Sumudu Atuputta, *Climate Change: Disappearing States, Migration, and Challenges for International Law*, 4 Wash. J. Envtl. L. & Pol'y 1 (2014–2015); Jason Obold, Matthew Burns & Caroline Baker, *Impressions from Durban: COP-17 and Current Climate Change Policies* (2012) 23 Colo. J. Int'l Envtl L. & Poly 389.
47. *Whales in Hot Water?*, *supra* note 22, at 12.
48. International Whaling Commission, *Report of the Workshop on Climate Change and Cetaceans*, SC/61/Rep4, 2 (2009) ["*Climate Change and Cetaceans*"].
49. *Id.* at 1.
50. *Id.* at 2.
51. *Id.*
52. Whaling Diplomacy, *supra* note 6, at 69.
53. William G.C. Burns, *From the Harpoon to the Heat: Climate Change and the International Whaling Commission in the 21st Century*, 13(2) Geo. Int. Envtl. Rev. 335, 351 (2006).

54. *Id.*
55. *Id.* 352–53.
56. *Id.* at 354.
57. *Id.* at 359.
58. Reiser, *supra* note 7, at 409.
59. *See* United Nations Conference on Environment and Development, Rio de Janiero, Braz., June 3–14, 1992, *Rio Declaration on Environment and Development*, U.N. Doc. A/CONF.151/26/Rev.1 (Vol. 1), Annex I (Aug. 12, 1992) (the starting point for a discussion of the precautionary principle is Principle 15, which provides that: "In order to protect the environment, the precautionary approach shall be widely applied by States according to their capabilities. Where there are threats of serious or irreversible damage, lack of full scientific certainty shall not be used as a reason for postponing cost-effective measures to prevent environmental degradation).''
60. Duncan E.J. Currie, *Ecosystem-Based Management in Multilateral Environmental Agreements: Progress towards Adopting the Ecosystem Approach in the International Management of Living Marine Resources*, WWF International, 1–2 (2007) (which defines ecosystem-based management as a method that "emphasises a holistic, participatory and integrated approach and is contrasted with a more narrowly focused biological and usually single species-oriented approach. It aims to manage human interactions with ecosystems and all associated organisms, rather than only individual species. As the term ecosystem-based management shows, it is management based on the properties of the relevant ecosystem(s), rather than a single species. The focus of management is maintaining the natural structure and function of ecosystems, including the biodiversity and productivity of natural systems and identified important species"); *see* Deep Sea Conservation Coalition, *The Ecosystem Approach: Its Mandate and Implementation*, SOUTH PACIFIC RFMO (Aug. 28, 2007), http://www.southpacificrfmo.org/assets/4th-Meeting-September-2007-Noumea/SP-04-Inf-3%20DSCC%20ecosystem%20 approach%20brief.pdf; *see also* Reiser, *supra* note 7 (noting that ecosystem-based management is not foreign to the IWC as it was recognized in the St. Kitts and Nevis Declaration, IWC Resolution 2006-1, which proclaims that "the issue of management of whale stocks must be considered in a broader context of ecosystem management since eco-system management has now become an international standard").
61. Reiser, *supra* note 7, at 409.
62. 20 May 1980, 33 U.S.T. 3476, 1329 U.N.T.S. 48.
63. Commission for the Conservation of Antarctic Marine Living Resources, *About CCAMLR* (Apr. 23, 2015), http://www.ccamlr.org/en/organisation/about-ccamlr.
64. *Whales in Hot Water?, supra* note 22, at 12.
65. MacLeod, *supra* note 20, at 132.
66. Simon Northridge, *Bycatch, in* ENCYCLOPEDIA OF MARINE MAMMALS 167, 167 (William F. Perrin et al. eds., 2d ed. 2009) ["Northridge"].
67. *Id.; see also* Andrew Read, Phebe Drinker & Simon Northridge, *Bycatch of Marine Mammals in the U.S. and Global Fisheries*, 20(1) CON. BIOL. 163, 164 (2006) (noting that this circumstance is also called "nontarget catch") ["Read, Drinker & Northridge"].
68. Northridge, *supra* note 66.
69. Read, Drinker & Northridge, *supra* note 67, at 164.

70. Rebecca L. Lewison et al., *Global Patterns of Marine Mammal, Seabird, and Sea Turtle Bycatch Reveal Taxa Specific and Cumulative Megafauna Hotspots*, 1111 PNAS 5271; Randall R. Reeves, Kate McClellan & Timothy B. Werner, *Marine Mammal Bycatch in Gillnet and Entangling Net Fisheries, 1990–2011*, 20 ENDANG. SPECIES RES. 71 (2013).
71. Northridge, *supra* note 66, at 167.
72. Andrew J. Read, *The Looming Crisis: Interactions between Marine Mammals and Fisheries*, 89(3) J. MAMM. 541, 541 (2008) ["Read"].
73. Read, Drinker & Northridge, *supra* note 67, at 165.
74. *Id.* at 163.
75. *Id.* at 166 (also, at 168 the authors "acknowledge that the estimates we present here are crude and likely to be biased, but it is clear that the global bycatch of marine mammals is very large").
76. *Id.*
77. *See* Samuel T. Turvey et al., *First Human-Caused Extinction of a Cetacean Species?*, 3 BIOL. LETT. 537 (2007).
78. *Id.* at 537.
79. Northridge, *supra* note 66, at 168.
80. *Id.* at 168; *see also* Rojas-Bracho et al., *Conservation of the Vaquita Phocoena sinus*, 36 MAM. REV. 179 (2006).
81. Jeremy Firestone, *Policy Considerations and Measures to Reduce the Likelihood of Vessel Collisions with Great Whales*, 36 B.C. ENVTL. AFF. L. REV. 389, 389–90 (2009) ["Firestone"].
82. Northridge, *supra* note 66, at 167.
83. *Id.*
84. *Id.*
85. *Id.* at 169.
86. The most recent dispute is between Mexico and the United States in US–Tuna II (Mexico) (*see* United States–Measures concerning the Importation, Marketing and Sale of Tuna and Tuna Products, WT/D5381/R (World Trade Organization, Report of the Panel, Sept. 15, 2011); *see also* United States–Measures Concerning the Importation, Marketing and Sale of Tuna and Tuna Products, WT/D5381/AB1R (World Trade Organization, Report of the Appellate Body, May 16, 2012)). *See* World Trade Organization, *Dispute Settlement: D5381* (Aug. 8, 2013), http://www.wto.org/english/tratop_e/dispu_e/cases_e/ds381_e.htm (which provides a useful summary of the issues and outcomes. Specifically, Mexico challenged America's domestic regulations (Dolphin Protection Consumer Information Act, 16 U.S.C. § 1385, Dolphin-safe labeling standards, 50 C.F.R. § 216.91, and Dolphin-safe requirements for tuna harvested in the ETP by large purse-seine vessels, 50 C.F.R. §216.92), which together establish the "dolphin-safe" tuna product label system. Mexico contended "that the measures at issue, which establish the conditions for use of a 'dolphin-safe' label on tuna products and condition the access to the US Department of Commerce official dolphin-safe label upon bringing certain documentary evidence that varies depending on the area where tuna contained in the tuna product is harvested and the fishing method by which it is harvested are inconsistent, *inter alia*, with Articles I:1 and III:4 of the GATT 1994 [General Agreement on Tariffs and Trade 1994, 1867 U.N.T.S. 187, 33 I.L.M. 1153] and Article 2.1, 2.2 and 2.4 of the TBT Agreement [Agreement on Technical Barriers to Trade, 1868 U.N.T.S. 120]." The Panel concluded that the

American process did not discriminate against Mexico, that the restrictions were stricter than necessary to achieve their objective, and that the relevant international standard would not be sufficient for the United States to achieve its goals. The Appellate Body reversed the Panel's determination that the restrictions did not discriminate against Mexico, reversed the finding that the "dolphin safe" restrictions imposed by the United States were more restrictive than necessary, and did not agree that a relevant international standard was clearly identifiable); *see also* 50 C.F.R. § 216 (2013), which has been amended in accordance with the findings of the Appellate Body of the WTO in an attempt to both strengthen dolphin protection and conform with international trade law.

87. Scientific Committee of the International Whaling Commission, *Report of the Scientific Committee*, J. CETACEAN RES. MANAGE. 14 1, 13 (Suppl.) (2013) ["*Report of the Scientific Committee*"].
88. *Id.*
89. *Id.*
90. *Id.*
91. *Id.* at 14.
92. Read, *supra* note 72, at 545.
93. Northridge, *supra* note 66, at 169.
94. Read, *supra* note 72, at 546.
95. Northridge, *supra* note 66, at 169 (this summary notes that the use of pingers may not be benign as they may actually force marine mammals to avoid certain feeding areas, and can also be expensive and time-consuming to attach and maintain for fishermen, limiting their attractiveness).
96. Northridge, *supra* note 66, at 169.
97. Read, *supra* note 72, at 546.
98. The IATCC was initially established by the Convention for the Establishment of an Inter-American Tropical Tuna Commission, U.S.-C.R., May 31, 1949, 80 U.N.T.S. 3, 1 U.S.T. 230 ["Inter-American Tropical Tuna Commission"] which was amended and strengthened in 2003 by the Convention for the Strengthening of the Inter-American Tropical Tuna Commission, [2005] EUTSer 2, OJ L 15 ["Antigua Convention].
99. Agreement on the International Dolphin Conservation Program, art. II(1), [1998] PITSE 4 ["AIDCP"].
100. *Id.* at art. V.
101. James J. Corbett & James J. Winebrake, *The Role of International Policy in Mitigating Global Shipping Emissions*, 16 BROWN J. WORLD AFF. 143, 144 (2009–2010).
102. *Id.*
103. International Maritime Organization, *International Shipping Facts and Figures—Information Resources on Trade, Safety, Security, Environment*, MARITIME KNOWLEDGE CENTER 9 (Mar. 6, 2010), http://www.imo.org/KnowledgeCentre/ShipsAndShippingFactsAndFigures/TheRoleandImportanceofInternationalShipping/Documents/International%20Shipping%20-%20Facts%20 and%20Figures.pdf.
104. Karin Harris et al., *Spatial Pattern Analysis of Cruise Ship-Humpback Whale Interactions in and near Glacier Bay National Park, Alaska*, 49(1) ENVTL. MAN. 44, 44 (2012) ["Harris et al."].

105. Cruise Lines International association (CLIA), *2012 Industry Update* 4 (2012), http://www.cruising.org/sites/default/files/pressroom/2012CLIAIndustryUpdate.pdf.
106. *Id.* at 11.
107. Firestone, *supra* note 81, at 391.
108. Angelia S.M. Vanderlaan et al., *Probability and Mitigation of Vessel Encounters with North Atlantic Right Whales*, 6 ENDANG. SPECIES RES. 273, 274 (2009) ["Vanderlaan et al."].
109. Scott D. Kraus et al., *North Atlantic Right Whales in Crisis*, 309 SCI. 561, 561 (2005) ["Kraus et al."].
110. *See* Susan E. Parks et al., *Dangerous Dining: Surface Foraging of North Atlantic Right Whales Increases Risk of Vessel Collisions*, 8 BIOL. LETT. 57 ["Parks et al."].
111. Press Release, Center for Biological Diversity, Population Estimate Finds Too Many Manatees Suffer Death-by-Boat-Strike (June 15, 2009), (http://www.biologicaldiversity.org/news/press_releases/2009/manatee-06-15-2009.html).
112. International Whaling Commission, *Whales and Ship Strikes: A Problem for Both Whales and Vessels*, IWC (2013), https://iwc.int/ship-strikes ["IWC Ship Strikes"]; *see* Angelina S.M. Vanderlaan & Christopher T. Taggart, *Vessel Collisions with Whales: The Probability of Lethal Injury Based on Vessel Speed*, 23 MARINE MAMMAL SCI. 144, 145 (2004).
113. *See* Harris et al., *supra* note 104, at 44–45; *see also* Henry P. Huntington, *A Preliminary Assessment of Threats to Arctic Marine Mammals and Their Conservation in the Coming Decade*s, 33(1) MAR. POL. 77, 79–80 (2009).
114. *See generally* Parks et al., *supra* note 110; Harris et al., *supra* note 104; Kraus et al., *supra* note 109; Vanderlaan et al., *supra* note 108.
115. Phil McKenna, *Sonic Alarm Save Marine Mammals from Ship Strike*, NEW SCIENTIST (May 20, 2009), http://www.newscientist.com/article/dn17163-sonic-alarm-saves-marine-mammals-from-ship-strike.html.
116. Firestone, *supra* note 81, at 392.
117. Endangered Species Act of 1973 as amended, 16 U.S.C. §§ 1531–1544 (2000).
118. 16 U.S.C. § 1632(2) (2007).
119. David W. Laist & Cameron Shaw, *Preliminary Evidence That Boat Speed Restrictions Reduce Deaths of Florida Manatees*, 22(2) MAR. MAMM. SCI. 472, 472 (2006).
120. U.S. Fish & Wildlife Services: North Florida Ecological Services Office, *Florida Manatee Recovery Plan: Third Revision* 34 (Oct. 2001), http://www.fws.gov/northflorida/Manatee/Recovery%20Plan/2001_FWS_Florida_Manatee_Recovery_Plan.pdf.
121. National Marine Fisheries Service, *Recovery Plan for the North Atlantic Rights Whale* (Eubalaena glacialis*): Revision*, NOAA (May 26, 2005), http://www.nmfs.noaa.gov/pr/pdfs/recovery/whale_right_northatlantic.pdf.
122. National Oceanic and Atmospheric Administration: Office of Protected Resources, *North Atlantic Right Whales* (Eubalaena glacialis), NOAA (Aug. 27, 2013), http://www.nmfs.noaa.gov/pr/species/mammals/cetaceans/rightwhale_northatlantic.htm.
123. Speed Restrictions to Protect North Atlantic Right Whales, 50 C.F.R. § 224.105 (2011).
124. *Id.* at § 224.105(a).

125. National Oceanic and Atmospheric Administration: Fisheries Service, *Compliance Guide for Right Whale Ship Strike Reduction Rule* (50 C.F.R. § 224), at 2, http://www.nmfs.noaa.gov/pr/pdfs/shipstrike/compliance_guide.pdf.
126. National Oceanic and Atmospheric Administration: Office of Protected Resources, *Mandatory Ship Reporting System for North Atlantic Right Whales* (June 2, 2014), http://www.nmfs.noaa.gov/pr/shipstrike/msr.htm.
127. North Atlantic Right Whale Protection, 50 C.F.R. § 217 & 222 (1997); see National Oceanic and Atmospheric Administration: Northeast Regional Office, *North Atlantic Right Whales*, http://www.nero.noaa.gov/Protected/mmp/viewing/regs/ (last visited June 15, 2015).
128. Northern Right Whales, 322 C.M.R. 12.00 (1993).
129. Coast Guard District Eleven, *Changes to Offshore Traffic Separation Schemes off San Francisco Bay* (2013), http://www.uscg.mil/d11/vtssf/TSSflyer.pdf.
130. International Maritime Organization, *Introduction to IMO* (2013), http://www.imo.org/About/Pages/Default.aspx.
131. 1 Nov. 1974, 1184 U.N.T.S. 278, 32 U.S.T. 47; International Maritime Organization, *Ships' routeing* (2015), http://www.imo.org/en/OurWork/Safety/Navigation/Pages/ShipsRouteing.aspx.
132. Canadian Whale Institute, *Bay of Fundy Shipping Lanes*, http://www.rightwhale.ca/shippinglanes-routesnavigation_e.php (last visited June 15, 2015).
133. *Id.*
134. *Id.*
135. *Id.*
136. Gregory K. Silber et al., *The Role of the International Maritime Organization in Reducing Vessel Threat to Whales: Process, Options, Action and Effectiveness*, 36 Mar. Pol. 1221, 1221–33 (2012) ["Silber et al."].
137. *Id.* at 1231.
138. *Id.*
139. *See* Hector M. Guzman et al., *Potential Vessel Collisions with Southern Hemisphere Humpback Whales Wintering off Pacific Panama*, 29 Mar. Mamm. Sci. 629 (2013); *see also* Hector M. Guzman, *Population Size and Migratory Connectivity of Humpback Whales Wintering in Las Perlas Archipelago, Panama*, 31 Mar. Mamm. Sci. 90 (2015).
140. *See* International Whaling Commission, *Proposal of the Republic of Panama for the Establishment of Traffic Separation Schemes and Prevention of Vessel Collision with Whales*, IWC/64/CC23 Rev1 (June 26, 2012), http://iwc.int/cache/downloads/7331ybhucz8c8ok4gk4co8000/64-CC23%20Rev1.pdf.
141. Government of the United States, *United States Voluntary National Cetacean Conservation Report, 2012*, at 7 (2012), http://www.nmfs.noaa.gov/ia/species/marine_mammals/inter_whaling/2012_cetacean_conservation_report.pdf.
142. *See* IWC Ship Strikes, *supra* note 112; International Whaling Commission, *The Berlin Initiative on Strengthening the Conservation Agenda of the International Whaling Commission*, IWC/55/4 Rev (2003) (which cemented the IWC's conservation agenda, contemplated enhanced collaboration with other international regimes, and established the Conservation Committee).
143. International Whaling Commission, *Report of the Conservation Committee*, IWC/64/Rep 5 Rev, at 2 (June 26, 2012), https://archive.iwc.int/pages/view.php?ref=3289&search=%21collection81&order_by=relevance&sort=DESC&offset=0&archive=0&k=&curpos=4.

144. *Id.* at 4.
145. L.S. Weilgart, *The Impacts of Anthropogenic Ocean Noise on Cetaceans and Implications for Management*, 85 Can. J. Zool. 1091, 1092 (2007) ["Weilgart"].
146. 10 Dec. 1982, 21 I.L.M. 1261, 1833 U.N.T.S. 3, at art. 1(4) ["UNCLOS"].
147. Davidson et al., *supra* note 87, at 3395.
148. United States Environmental Protection Agency, *Persistent Organic Pollutants: A Global Issue, A Global Response*, US EPA, http://www.epa.gov/international/toxics/pop.html (last visited June 15, 2015).
149. *Id.*
150. *Id.* (noting that the "Dirty Dozen" includes the following chemicals: aldrin, chlordane, dichlorodiphenyl trichlorethane, dieldrin, heptachlor, hexachlorobenzene, mirex, toxaphene, polychlorinated biphenyls, polychlorinated dibenzo-p-dioxins, and polychlorinated dibenzofurans).
151. *Id.*
152. Chris Metcalfe, *Persistent Organic Pollutants in the Marine Food Chain*, United Nations University (Feb. 23, 2012), http://unu.edu/publications/articles/persistent-organic-pollutants-in-the-marine-food-chain.html ["Metcalfe"] (noting that the effect of this position in the food web means pollutants entering the ocean accumulate or magnify as they progress up the various levels in the food web, being found in greatest concentrations at the top).
153. G.J. Pierce et al., *Bioaccumulation of Persistent Organic Pollutants in Females Common Dolphins* (Delphinus delphis) *and Harbour Porpoises* (Phocoena phocoena) *from Western European Seas: Geographical Trends, Causal Factors and Effects on Reproduction and Mortality*, 153(2) Envtl. Poll. 401, 402 (2007) ["Pierce et al."].
154. *Id.*
155. Metcalfe, *supra* note 152.
156. *See* Shinsuke Tanabe, Hisato Iurata & Ryo Tatsukawa, *Global Contamination by Persistent Organochlorines and Their Ecotoxicological Impact on Marine Mammals* 154 Sci. Total Env't 163, 171 (1994).
157. Cameron Jefferies, *Assessing a Public Health Justification for Reducing Whale Consumption in Northern Canada*, 18(1) Health L. Rev. 12 (2009).
158. *See* Amitabh Avasthi, *Tainted Whales Must Stink or Swim*, 198(2655) New Scientist 41 2008 ["Avashti"].
159. *Id.* at 41.
160. *Id.*
161. Pierce et al., *supra* note 153; *see* R.L. De Swart, Impaired Immunity in Seals Exposed to Bioaccumulated Environmental Contaminants (1995) (Ph.D. dissertation, Erasmus Universiteit); *see* P.S. Ross, Seals, Pollution and Disease: Environmental Contaminant-Induced Immuno-suppression (1995) (Ph.D. dissertation, Universiteit Utrecht).
162. Pierce et al., *supra* note 153; *see generally* A.J. Hall et al., *The Risk of Infection from Polychlorinated Biphenyl Exposure in Harbor Porpoise* (Phocoena phocoena): *A Case-Control Approach*, 114(5) Envtl. Health Per. 704 (2006).
163. Pierce et al., *supra* note 153; *see generally* P.J.H. Reijnders, *Man-Induced Factors in Relation to Fertility Changes in Pinnipeds*, 11 Envtl. Conserv. 61 (1984); *see generally* P.J.H. Reijnders, *Reproductive Failure in Common Seals Feeding on Fish from Polluted Coastal Waters*, 324 Nature 456 (1986).

164. *See* Gillespie, *Environmental Threats, supra* note 6, at 102; *see generally* T. Colborn & M.J. Smolen, *Epidemiological Analysis of Persistent Organic Pollutants on Cetaceans*, 146 Rev. Envtl. Cont. & Tox. 91 (1996); *see generally* T. Troisi, *Toxic Effects of PCBs on Marine Mammals* (1996) 2 Soundings 1 (1996).
165. Pierce et al., *supra* note 153, at 1 (noting that the connections and impacts are still being studied and investigated, suggesting that further research is required).
166. Edward C.M. Parsons, An Introduction to Marine Mammal Biology and Conservation 239 (2012) ["Parsons"] (noting that heavy metals, such as lead and mercury, also accumulate in marine mammals with harmful consequences).
167. *Id.* at 241–42 (noting that plastics and other forms of solid waste that end up in the ocean and do not biodegrade are hazardous to marine mammals if consumed or if they entangle individuals).
168. *Id.* (noting that this can lead to disease outbreaks).
169. *Id.* at 242–43 (noting that oil spilled through tanker accidents or well-blowouts, such as the Deep Water Horizon incident, can be harmful and potentially fatal to marine mammals if they are in the area of the disaster or if they ingest prey species that have been affected).
170. Parsons, *supra* note 166, at 241 (noting that nutrient loading in the ocean can result in increased numbers of phytoplankton and/or algal blooms, which can produce toxins that are harmful to marine mammals).
171. Convention on Biological Diversity: Subsidiary Body on Scientific, Technical and Technological Advice, *Scientific Synthesis on the Impacts of Underwater Noise on Marine Biodiversity and Habitats*, UNEP/CBD/SBSTTA/16/INF/12 (12 March 2012) ["CBD Synthesis"].
172. *Id.* at 2.
173. *Id.* at 4.
174. Karen S. Scott, *International Regulation of Undersea Noise*, 53 Int'l & Comp L.Q. 287, 289 (2004) ["Scott, *International Regulation*"]; Weilgart, *supra* note 145, at 1094.
175. Weilgart, *supra* note 145, at 1093.
176. Scott, *International Regulation, supra* note 174, at 288.
177. Caroline R. Weir & Sarah J. Dolman, *Comparative Review of the Regional Marine Mammal Guidelines Implemented during Industrial Seismic Surveys, and Guidance towards a Worldwide Standard*, 10(1) J. Int'l Wildlife L. & Pol'y (2007).
178. R. Payne & D. Webb, *Orientation by Means of Long Range Acoustic Signaling in Baleen Whales*, 188(1) Ann. N Y. Acc. Sci. 110 (1971).
179. Weilgart, *supra* note 145, at 1092.
180. *Id.* (note that stranding events are quite highly publicized. They are also contentious as they are quite often linked to military operations and sonar in particular. *See, e.g.*, Joel R. Reynolds, *Submarines, Sonar and the Death of Whales: Enforcing the Delicate Balance of Environmental Compliance and National Security in Military Training*, 32(3) Wm. & Mary Envtl. L. & Pol'y Rev. 759 (2008)).
181. Scott, *International Regulation, supra* note 174, at 291.
182. Gillespie, *Environmental Threats, supra* note 6, at 97.
183. *Id.* at 105–06.
184. UNCLOS, *supra* note 146.

185. Gillespie, *Environmental Threats, supra* note 6, at 106–08 (noting, as examples, the Convention for the Protection of the Mediterranean Sea against Pollution, Feb. 16, 1976, 1102 U.N.T.S. 27 and framework regional treaties for Kuwait, South East Pacific, Red Sea and Gulf of Eden, South Pacific Region, Wider Caribbean Region, and Eastern African Region).
186. *Id.* at 106.
187. International Whaling Commission, 25th Annual Report 27 (1976); Gillespie, *Environmental Threats, supra* note 6, at 98.
188. International Whaling Commission, *Chairman's Report of the Thirty-Second Annual Meeting, Appendix 10: Resolution on Preservation of the Habitat of Whales and the Marine Environment*, Rep. Int. Whal. Comm. 32 (1980); Gillespie, *Environmental Threats, supra* note 6, at 99.
189. Gillespie, *Environmental Threats, id.* at 99–100.
190. International Whaling Commission, *Environmental Change* (2013), https://iwc.int/environment (note that the IWC indicates that environmental change, for the purposes of this endeavor, includes "pollution, cetacean diseases, anthropogenic sound, climate change and ecosystem modeling").
191. International Whaling Commission, *Resolution 2000-7: Resolution on Environmental Change and Cetaceans*, https://archive.iwc.int/pages/search.php?search=%21collection72&k= (last visited June 15, 2015).
192. International Whaling Commission, *SOCER—State of the Cetacean Environment Report*, http://iwc.int/socer (last visited June 15, 2015).
193. *Id.*
194. *Id.*
195. Gillespie, *Environmental Threats, supra* note 6, at 108.
196. 22 May 2001, 2256 U.N.T.S. 119, 40 I.L.M. 532.
197. Stockholm Convention on Persistent Organic Pollutants, *Stockholm Convention on Persistent Organic Pollutants*, http://www.pops.int/documents/signature/signstatus.htm (last visited June 15, 2015) ["Stockholm Convention"].
198. United Nations Environment Programme, *Stockholm Convention: About the Convention*, http://chm.pops.int/Convention/tabid/54/Default.aspx (last visited June 15, 2015).
199. Stockholm Convention, *supra* note 197.
200. *Id.*
201. Secretariat of the Stockholm Convention, *Success Stories: Stockholm Convention 2001-2011*, at 9 (2012) ["*Success Stories*"].
202. United Nations Environment Programme, *Ridding the World of POPS: A Guide to the Stockholm Convention on Persistent Organic Pollutants* 7 (2005), http://www.pops.int/documents/guidance/beg_guide.pdf.
203. *See* United Nations Environment Programme, *The Hazardous Chemicals and Wastes Conventions* 1 (2003), http://www.pops.int/documents/background/hcwc.pdf; Basel Convention on the Control of Transboundary Movements of Hazardous Wastes and Their Disposal, Mar. 2, 1989, 28 I.L.M. 657, 1673 U.N.T.S. 126; Rotterdam Convention on the Prior Informed Consent Procedure for Certain Hazardous Chemicals and Pesticides in International Trade, Sept. 10, 1998, 2244 U.N.T.S. 337, 38 I.L.M. 1.
204. *See generally Success Stories, supra* note 201.
205. 1972, 26 U.S.T. 2403, 1046 U.N.T.S. 120 ["London Convention"]; International Maritime Organization, *London Convention and Protocol: Their Role and*

Contribution to the Protection of the Marine Environment (2011) ["*London Convention and Protocol*"].
206. Gillespie, *Environmental Threats, supra* note 6, at 115–16.
207. *London Convention and Protocol, supra* note 205, at 2.
208. Gillespie, *Environmental Threats, supra* note 6, at 115.
209. International Maritime Organization, *Status of the London Convention and Protocol*, (Dec. 12, 2015), http://www.imo.org/en/OurWork/Environment/LCLP/Pages/default.aspx.
210. Gillespie, *Environmental Threats, supra* note 6, at 115.
211. 1972, Nov. 7, 1996, 36 I.L.M. 1.
212. London Convention, *supra* note 205, at Annex I (which provides that dumping, once approved, is permitted for:

   1. Dredged material
   2. Sewage sludge
   3. Fish waste, or material resulting from industrial fish processing operations
   4. Vessels and platforms or other man-made structures at sea
   5. Inert, inorganic geological material
   6. Organic material of natural origin
   7. Bulky items primarily comprising iron, steel, concrete and similar unharmful materials for which the concern is physical impact and limited to those circumstances, where such wastes are generated at locations, such as small islands with isolated communities, having no practicable access to disposal options other than dumping.
   8. CO_2 streams from CO_2 capture processes (added under the amendments adopted in 2006, which entered into force in 2007)).

213. Gillespie, *Environmental Threats, supra* note 6, at 115.
214. *London Convention and Protocol, supra* note 205, at 4.
215. 2 Nov. 1973, 12 I.L.M. 1319, 1340 U.N.T.S. 184.
216. International Maritime Organization, *International Convention for the Prevention of Pollution from Ships (MARPOL)*, http://www.imo.org/about/conventions/listof-conventions/pages/international-convention-for-the-prevention-of-pollution-from-ships-(marpol).aspx (last visited June 16, 2015) ["IMO MARPOL"].
217. 17 Feb. 1978, 1340 U.N.T.S. 61, 17 ILM 546.
218. IMO MARPOL, *supra* note 216.
219. Gillespie, *Environmental Threats, supra* note 6, at 112–13 (it must be noted that MARPOL is not the only international response to ocean pollution. Another notable example, which can be categorized as soft law, as discussed by Gillespie at 120, is the 1995 Global Programme of Action for the Protection of the Marine Environment from Land Based Activities ("GPA"). The GPA, as a component of the United Nations Environment Programme, provides a forum for nations to gather and to cooperate toward reducing land-based sources of pollution (*see* United Nations Environment Programme, *Global Programme of Action for the Protection of the Marine Environment from Land Based Activities*, http://www.gpa.unep.org (last visited June 16, 2015)). Interested nations met last in January 2012, with the goal of working toward a new implementation approach that will carry forward until 2016 (*see* United Nations Environment Programme, *Third*

Intergovernmental Review Meeting on the Implementation of the GPA, http://unep.org/gpa/resources/IGR3.asp)).
220. Scott, *International Regulation, supra* note 174, at 298.
221. Karen N. Scott, *Sound and Cetaceans: A Regional Response to Regulating Acoustic Marine Pollution*, 10(2) J. INT'L WILDLIFE L. & P. 175, 185 (2007) ["Scott, *Sound and Cetaceans*"].
222. *Id.* at 178–79.
223. *See generally* Randall S. Abate, *NEPA, National Security, and Ocean Noise: The Past, Present, and Future of Regulating the Impact of Navy Sonar on Marine Mammals*, 13(4) J. INT'L WILDLIFE L. & P. 326, 327 (2010) ["Abate"] (describing the interplay between naval sonar and environmental groups in the United States as a "common manifestation of the tensions between national security and environmental protection objectives." The article details the challenges that have been made in American courts to naval sonar testing using NEPA (National Environmental Policy Act), and questions whether a balance between naval necessity and environmental protection can be captured using NEPA).
224. Scott, *Sound and Cetaceans, supra* note 221, at 177.
225. *Id.* at 198; *contra* Caroline R. Weir & Sarah J. Domla, *Comparative Review of the Regional Marine Mammal Mitigation Guidelines Implemented during Industrial Seismic Surveys, and Guidance towards a Worldwide Standard*, 10(1) J. INT'L WILDLIFE L. & POL. 1, 19 (2007) (which advocates for the development of a minimum best practice guideline for mitigation and/or minimization of noise pollution during seismic exploration in light of global inconsistency (i.e., "[t]his lack of consistency needs to be addressed so that a minimum 'best practice' with a scientific basis offering adequate protection to all marine mammal species is adopted worldwide")).
226. Scott, *International Regulation, supra* note 174, at 310; *see also* Abate, *supra* note 223, at 354 (where he indicates that the goal of enhanced international marine mammal protection can be reached in three ways: "protect species, protect habitat, and promote regional and international cooperation on marine mammal conservation").
227. CBD Synthesis, *supra* note 171, at 4–5 (noting "[o]ver the last decade the issue of underwater noise and its effects on marine biodiversity have received increasing attention at the international level. The Convention on the Conservation of Migratory Species (CMS), the International Whaling Commission (IWC), the United Nations General Assembly (UNGA), the European Parliament and European Union, the International Union for Conservation of Nature (IUCN), the International Maritime Organization (IMO), the OSPAR Convention for the Protection of the Marine Environment of the North-East Atlantic, the Convention on the Protection of the Marine Environment of the Baltic Sea Area (HELCOM), the Agreement on the Conservation of Cetaceans in the Black Sea Mediterranean Sea and Contiguous Atlantic Area (ACCOBAMS) and the Agreement on the Conservation of Small Cetaceans of the Baltic, North East Atlantic, Irish and North Seas (ASCOBANS) have all considered the negative effects of anthropogenic underwater noise through the adoption of resolutions or recognition of the issue for the marine environment." This proceeds to note at 5–6 that "[a]lthough noise is a recognized form of pollution, sources of noise in the marine environment are not regulated at the international level. There has been progress made at the regional level (e.g., OSPAR, ASCOBANS,

228. *See* International Whaling Commission, *Independent Review of a 2008 Mass Stranding in Madagascar* (2013), http://iwc.int/2008-mass-stranding-in-madagascar (noting that "the IWC facilitated a review of the circumstances of the stranding in conjunction with the US Marine Mammal Commission, the US National Oceanic and Atmospheric Administration, the US Bureau of Ocean Energy Management, ExxonMobil Exploration and Production (Northern Madagascar) Ltd, the International Fund for Animal Welfare, the Wildlife Conservation Society and the Government of Madagascar. An independent scientific review panel (ISRP) of five experts was invited to conduct a formal examination of the available facts"); *see* B.L. SOUTHALL ET AL., FINAL REPORT OF THE INDEPENDENT SCIENTIFIC REVIEW PANEL INVESTIGATING POTENTIAL CONTRIBUTING FACTORS TO A 2008 MASS STRANDING OF MELON-HEADED WHALES (*PEPONOCEPHALA ELECTRA*) IN ANTSOHIHY, MADAGASCAR 4 (2013) (concluding that a "high frequency active mapping sonar" system was the primary cause for the stranding event).
229. Gillespie, *Environmental Threats, supra* note 6, at 105.
230. United Nations Environmental Programme, *Report of the Regional Workshop on Marine Mammal Watching in the Wider Caribbean Region* 1 (2011), http://www.cep.unep.org/meetings-events/7th-spaw-cop/IGM15_UNEP%28DEPI%29CAR%20WG.34INF.9_EN.pdf/view.
231. Erich Hoyt, *Whale Watching*, in ENCYCLOPEDIA OF MARINE MAMMALS 1223, 1227 (William F. Perrin et al. eds., 2d ed. 2009) ["Hoyt, *Whale Watching*"] (noting that whale watching can also serve an educational function); *see* Michael Luck, *Education on Marine Mammal Tours as Agent for Conservation—But Do Tourists Want to Be Educated?*, 46 OCEAN & COAST. MAN. 943 (2003) ["Luck"] (suggesting that tourists do in fact want to be educated during marine mammal watching tours).
232. *See, e.g.*, J.E.S. Higham & D. Lusseau, *Urgent Need for Empirical Research into Whaling and Whale Watching*, 21(2) CONSERV. BIOL. 554, 558 (2007) ["Higham & Lusseau"] (where these authors indicate that there is a need for more empirical evidence on whale watcher demographics, the "carrying-capacity" of whale watching, and the effects of whaling on whale watching).
233. Hoyt, *Whale Watching, supra* note 231, at 1223.
234. *Id.*
235. S. O'Connor et al., *Whale Watching Worldwide: Tourism Numbers, Expenditures and Expanding Economic Benefits* 23 (2009), http://41.215.122.106/dspace/bitstream/0/4304/1/whale%20watching%20worth%20billions.pdf ["O'Connor et al."].
236. *Id.*
237. *Id.*
238. Hoyt, *Whale Watching, supra* note 231, at 1225.
239. A.M. Cisneros-Montemayor et al., *The Global Potential for Whale Watching*, 34 MAR. POL'Y 1273, 1273 (2010) ["Cisneros-Montemayor et al."].
240. *Id.* at 1274.
241. *Id.* at 1275.
242. Luck, *supra* note 231, at 953.

243. Hoyt, *Whale Watching, supra* note 231, at 1226; *see generally* Erich Hoyt & Glen T. Hvenegaard, *A Review of Whale-Watching and Whaling with Applications for the Caribbean*, 30 COASTAL MAN. 381 (2002).
244. Andre Steckenreuter, Luciano Moller & Robert Harcourt, *How Does Australia's Largest Dolphin-Watching Industry Affect the Behaviour of a Small and Resident Population of Indo-Pacific Bottlenose Dolphins?*, 97 J. ENVTL. MAN. 14, 18 (2012) (this study tends to confirm the results in D. Lusseau & J.E.S. Higham, *Managing the Impacts of Dolphin-Based Tourism through the Definition of Critical Habitats: The Case of Bottlenose Dolphins* (Tursiops spp.) *in Doubtful Sound, New Zealand*, 25(6) TOURISM MGMT. 657 (2004) ["Lusseau & Higham"]; *see also* K.A. Stockin et al., *Tourism Affects the Behavioural Budget of the Common Dolphin* Delphinus sp. *in the Hauraki Gulf, New Zealand*, 355 MAR. ECOL. PROG. SER. 287 (2008)).
245. Hoyt, *Whale Watching, supra* note 231, at 1225.
246. *Id.*
247. *Id.*
248. *See* Carole Carlson, *An Analysis of Whalewatch Guidelines and Regulations around the World*, IWC SC/64/WW5 (2011), https://iwc.int/whalewatching.
249. *Id.* at 1 (note, this assessment provides a summary of many key aspects of whale watching, including: (1) "Permitting, Training and Reporting," (2) vessel operation when whales are in the vessel's vicinity, (3) "Recommended Caution Zone for Vessel Approach and Departure," (4) vessel speed and engine control, (5) time spent observing the whales, (6) the number of vessels allowed in the whales' vicinity, (5) approach distances (including approaches for mother and calf pairs), (6) recommended direction of approach, (7) permitted human-whale interactions, (8) distances between whales and aircraft, and (9) special codes for particular species).
250. *Id.*
251. International Whaling Commission, *Whale Watching* (2013), http://iwc.int/whalewatching ["IWC Whale Watching"]; *see also* International Whaling Commission, *General Principles for Whalewatching* (1996), http://iwc.int/wwguidelines#manage ["IWC Whale Watching Principles"].
252. Lusseau & Higham, *supra* note 244.
253. Cisneros-Montemayor et al., *supra* note 239, at 1277.
254. *IWC Whale Watching Principles, supra* note 251.
255. *Id.*
256. International Whaling Commission, *A Review of Whale Watch Guidelines and Regulations around the World: 2012 Version*, IWC, https://iwc.int/whalewatching document (last visited June 16, 2015).
257. International Whaling Commission, *Five Year Strategic Plan for Whalewatching*, IWC (2011), https://iwc.int/whalewatching (last visited June 16, 2015).
258. IWC Whale Watching, *supra* note 251.
259. Emily Lambert et al., *Sustainable Whale-Watching Tourism and Climate Change: Towards a Framework of Resilience*, 18(3) J. SUS. TOUR. 409, 415 (2010).
260. *See* Jennifer L. Bailey, *Whale Watching, the Buenos Aires Group and the Politics of the International Whaling Commission*, 36(2) MAR. POL. 489 (2012).
261. Cisneros-Montemayor et al., *supra* note 239, at 1276.
262. *Id.* at 1276–77 (recognizing at 1276 that basic whale watching can be "launched with little initial investment and can be carried out by local fishers who are

already familiar with the area," and that "[w]hile this study offers an estimate of potential revenue from whale watching, there is much less information regarding the possible costs (e.g., foregone fishing opportunities or foreign aid contingent on expressions of support for whaling) of marine mammal conservation, necessary for a full cost-benefit analysis to be undertaken. This is clearly an interesting future research project, particularly as the widespread development of whale watching industries may contribute to a shift of votes at the IWC, and a dissolution of the blocs that have made it largely dysfunctional").

5

The Case for an Implementing Agreement Pursuant to Articles 65 and 120 of UNCLOS and the Creation of an International Marine Mammal Commission

> "Explicitly agreed and effective arrangements are required for meaningful conservation and allocation. *Ad hoc* approaches among a group of individual states are not adequate."[1]

Chapter 4 introduced certain prevailing scientific considerations that should inform twenty-first century marine mammal conservation. This chapter builds on this scientific foundation, recognizing that the "[v]iews of scientists concerning the measures required have little effect unless developed into a regulatory framework prescribing what states should and should not do."[2] The major inquiry engaged in this chapter is whether marine mammal governance is properly situated at the global, regional, or coastal state level. I conclude that global governance of marine mammals should remain (or become) primary, with regional cooperation and coastal state regulatory consonance emerging as the necessary secondary mechanisms in pursuit of rational marine mammal management.[3] As the path toward any new international regime for the conservation of marine mammals will be fraught with obstacles, it is critical that the proposal for its negotiation is buttressed and justified by a strong legal case.

This analysis proceeds as follows: (1) the legal options available to remedy the shortcomings of the current international regime addressing marine mammal conservation are identified, and the election to proceed by way of an implementing agreement pursuant to the United Nations Convention on the Law of the Sea (UNCLOS)[4] is justified; (2) the option of proceeding by implementing agreement is discussed in greater detail, with reference to previous implementing agreements and proposed implementing agreements; (3) the negotiating history of Articles 65 and 120 of UNCLOS is explored, competing interpretations are identified and reconciled against the backdrop of the prevailing regime, and the preferred interpretation is articulated; and (4) the jurisdictional considerations that will inform the proposal contained in Chapters 6 and 7 are identified. This assessment concludes that the case for the creation of an implementing agreement pursuant to Articles 65 and 120 is strong, and that it is a logical mechanism by which marine mammal conservation can be effectuated moving forward in the twenty-first century.

I. LEGALLY JUSTIFIED OPTIONS FOR INTERNATIONAL MARINE MAMMAL CONSERVATION

Having established that the current approach to the international conservation of marine mammals is fragmented, inconsistent, and in need of reform, it is necessary for us to consider the options available to facilitate coherence, cooperation, and effective conservation. Each option, although theoretically available, must also be assessed considering practical considerations.

The proceeding assessment considers the following: (1) maintenance of the status quo, (2) amendment of the International Convention for the Regulation of Whaling (ICRW)[5] and/or amendment of the Schedule to the ICRW (retaining primacy of an international organization), (3) reliance on "soft law" to guide marine mammal conservation (produced at the international level), (4) the proliferation of bilateral and/or regional agreements (passing priority to regional and/or bilateral arrangements), (5) reliance on national conservation schemes, and (6) the creation of a new, negotiated international regime (both outside the UNCLOS regime and pursuant to the UNCLOS regime). This assessment proceeds with a brief discussion of each option before progressing to a detailed consideration of the preferred approach.

1. Status Quo

The first option is maintenance of the status quo. This default option does not require any alteration, amendment, or reform. My analysis in Chapters 2 to 4 has demonstrated that the status quo is far from ideal; indeed, the status quo is fragmented (in terms of inconsistent regional and coastal state regulation), insufficient (in terms of species coverage and threat coverage), and outdated (in terms of failing to incorporate modern conservation principles). Continuation of the status quo would feature the ICRW/IWC regime as the primary international organization concerned with large cetaceans, regional organizations addressing small cetaceans (and sometimes large whales or marine mammals generally) with varying goals, and different national regulatory responses. This is clearly an inadequate response and deviation from the status quo is justified.

2. An Improved ICRW/IWC

A second option is an improved ICRW/IWC regime. At first blush, this option has some appeal as the time, energy, and cost associated with fixing the current regime may be less than what is required to negotiate and implement a replacement. This option is also bolstered by the fact that three proposed renegotiations toward a new whaling convention have failed.[6] Still, this author is skeptical about the possibility of achieving the necessary alterations given the stalemate that has existed at the IWC since shortly after the commercial moratorium was introduced, and the failure of the IWC to gain meaningful traction through the "Future of the IWC" process. Nonetheless, it is important to recognize that in certain quarters this is the preferred option. This discussion will turn to a description of current proposals to remedy the shortcomings of the ICRW/IWC regime.

Although a number of authors have considered the possibility of altering the current ICRW/IWC regime to better account for cetacean conservation,[7] there are two particularly detailed proposals that contemplate enhancing the efficacy of the ICRW/IWC regime. The first is a proposal by Professor Robert Friedheim in *Towards a Sustainable Whaling Regime*.[8] Here, Friedheim asserts that "[t]he IWC needs not be thrown out like the baby with the bath water, and a new whaling regime or regimes need not be created. The IWC does not require extensive structural reform."[9] The core of Friedheim's proposal is founded on the Revised Management Procedure (RMP), accepted and endorsed by IWC Resolution in 1994, as a scientifically robust "mathematical algorithm that is used to estimate stock size and is adjusted so that the impact of any change, including human consumptive uses, can be estimated with reasonable certainty."[10] Full implementation of the RMP is contingent on development of the Revised Management Scheme (RMS) and its incorporation into the Schedule; Friedheim envisions an RMS that functions as follows:

> The "scheme" is the management program that should be in place before any resumption of whaling is authorized. It should (1) control entry into the "fishery" by authorizing *who* has the right to catch *what* and in what *numbers*, *where*, and *when*; (2) resolve whether the exploiter *pays* for an exclusive right to use a common pool resource owned by all peoples of the world; and (3) develop an implementation scheme that contains IWC plenary oversight, field inspection, market control, certification, verification (including third-party audits), and enforcement rules including sanctions for violations so that observers can ensure that cheating does not become a problem.[11]

Friedheim's proposal suggests striking an expert committee to propose an RMS as a "form of single negotiating text," which is then negotiated.[12] Ultimately, the proposal envisions an RMS that has the following features being implemented as an amendment to the Schedule: (1) an Implementation Subcommittee of the Technical Committee, which is subject to supervision by the plenary, will be created to supervise the implementation scheme in a transparent manner; (2) "field inspection corps" will be created to supervise whaling (this inspection corps should consist of nationals from both whaling and non-whaling nations, could incorporate NGO (nongovernmental organization) participation, and inspectors could accompany whalers at sea. Inspection would also occur at coastal landing sites, and monitoring should be assisted by modern technology such as satellite transponders); (3) only vessels that are currently in "good standing" with respect to compliance on a newly created Register of Whaling Vessels would be issued permits to whale; (4) third-party DNA testing audits of national markets selling whale products should be facilitated, and companies and markets that pass inspections could be awarded a "legally caught" identifier; and (5) punishment should remain with the nation that sponsors the whaler and/or whaling vessel, which could be incentivized by empowering the newly created Implementation Subcommittee with the ability to request quota reductions from the plenary for nations that fail to punish those who violate the new scheme.[13]

Friedheim's proposal also addresses three other problematic issues, namely coastal whaling, Aboriginal subsistence whaling, and whaling within the Southern Ocean Sanctuary. With respect to the IWC's jurisdiction to regulate small cetacean hunts and coastal whaling, he emphasizes the need to create a suitable regulatory scheme. With reference to Article 65 of UNCLOS, Friedheim characterizes the IWC's legal ability to regulate within the 200 nautical mile exclusive economic zone as "somewhat murky," but emphasizes that coastal states that engage in this sort of whaling should be incentivized to participate through subsidized management costs, as developing nations that engage in small-type coastal whaling will quickly develop efficient exploitation techniques.[14] This proposal recommends enhanced participation by coastal states through "a permissible whaling scheme for the EEZ," and facilitated regional coordination through regional organizations, which are in turn linked "into the arms of the IWC."[15]

Although Friedheim stops short of recommending a complete overhaul of the definition of Aboriginal whaling, he does recommend enhanced engagement of Aboriginal whalers and emphasizes an approach that also accommodates "other subsistence whalers and artisanal whalers."[16] Friedheim endorses an existing definition of "artisanal whalers" produced by social scientists, and summarizes it as follows: "[i]t would require that whaling be conducted by socially defined groups, that whaling involve practices that are socially reproducible over time, that permissible whaling practices be valued along a number of dimensions (not just economic), and that it be biologically sustainable."[17] Finally, his proposal seeks to limit the controversy over whale hunting within the Southern Ocean Sanctuary by accommodating Japan's desire to pursue commercial hunting in this region through the implementation of a limited minke whale take.[18] All told, Friedheim suggests that the success of this proposal hinges on the "willingness of reasonable people on both sides to accept the risk of resuming some whaling" so long as that risk is measured and not unreasonable; indeed, he suggests that this risk is necessary to advance appropriate ocean management.[19]

The second significant proposal of note comes from Professor Michael Bowman through a paper made available to the IWC as it embarked on the "Future of the IWC" process in 2007, wherein Bowman provides a detailed description of relevant norms and an application of such norms to the IWC. One portion of his assessment begins with the premise that "it is surely to be expected that a convention concluded as long ago as the ICRW might require some quite significant fine-tuning if it is to be capable of continuing to fulfill its functions into the new millennium," and that the treaty interpretation principles of good faith, interpretation "in light of other relevant rules of international law," and *ut res magis valeat quam pereat* (a rule of construction that treaty interpretation should enable ongoing treaty vitality) enable ICRW evolution.[20] Bowman identifies the following issues as requiring attention: "(i) the biological scope of the ICRW, in terms of species covered; (ii) aboriginal whaling; (iii) scientific whaling; (iv) the amendment procedures themselves, and specifically the power to exclude their effect by registering an objection; and (v) the current restriction of the substantive focus of the ICRW to direct exploitation."[21] The analysis summarized below purports to provide "progressive adaptation to change, and particularly changes mandated by the evolving dictates of the broader legal system."[22]

Professor Bowman provides two approaches to normalizing the ICRW/IWC: (1) through a flexible interpretation of the "open-textured expression" contained in the treaty, and (2) by recourse to amendment of the ICRW and/or the Schedule.[23] Regarding the first option, Bowman identifies four phrases within the ICRW that can be interpreted in a manner that responds to the changed circumstances while remaining faithful to the original objectives: (1) "the great natural resources represented by the whale stocks," (2) "whaling," (3) "orderly development of the whaling industry," and (4) "proper conservation of whale stocks" (with each phrase being found in the preamble to the ICRW). With respect to the first phrase, and particularly the term "resource," Bowman suggests it is possible to reconsider the utilitarian use of whales to now encompass their value with respect to the educational and recreational benefit associated with ecotourism, their genetic value, and their contribution to ocean ecosystems.[24] Similarly, the other three phrases can be reasonably interpreted to encompass the benefits of whale watching/tourism and the non-consumptive value of whales.[25]

The second option presented is to amend the ICRW itself or the Schedule. Bowman's assessment begins by examining three power-conferring sections of the ICRW, suggesting that they could be used to help normalize this regime without requiring amendment.[26] Specifically, Article IV(1) provides that the IWC can study and investigate whales and whaling (Article IV(1)(a)), assess statistics relating to whale stock trends and conditions (Article IV(1)(b)), and appraise, study, and disseminate information regarding how to maintain or increase whale stocks.[27] Article IV(2) indicates that the IWC "shall" independently or collaboratively publish reports on its activities.[28] Article III(4) provides the IWC with the discretion to establish committees to perform authorized functions.[29] In sum, Bowman suggests that the IWC could utilize these articles more fully in search of holistic whale management but that "such developments fall a long way short of establishing a comprehensive regime for cetaceans."[30]

Regarding the amendment itself, Bowman presents two options. The first is to amend the existing Schedule, and the second is to amend the ICRW itself. With respect to the Schedule, which "represents the principal mechanism both for the imposition of detailed substantive obligations on the Member States, and for the modification and refinement of these obligations over time," the pertinent considerations are located in Article V.[31] This assessment postulates that the main obstacle preventing RMP implementation, and perhaps even inclusion of the RMS in the Schedule, is that discussion, to date, has failed to adequately assess whether consumptive whaling can coexist with the modern use of whales, which features whale watching/tourism, and should also attempt to embrace the relevant principles associated with implementation of the Convention on Biological Diversity.[32] Besides questions related to whether the necessary amendments fit within the permissible amendment categories established in Article V(1), such amendments must also meet the "necessary" test set out in Article V(2)(a) whereby Schedule amendments "shall be such as are necessary to carry out the objectives and purposes of this Convention and to provide for the conservation, development, and optimum utilization of the whale resources."[33] Even if these obstacles can be overcome, Article III(2) establishes that a three-quarters majority vote of present voting members is required to implement Article V amendments, and Article V(3) establishes an opt-out/objection mechanism for dissident states.[34] Finally, fundamental alteration to the ICRW/IWC regime requires amendment of the ICRW itself.[35] As the ICRW does not contain an amending formula the presumption, as codified in Article 40 of the Vienna Convention on the Law of Treaties,[36] is that every Member State has to agree to the amendment for it to take effect. While this is not impossible, as evidenced by the Protocol agreed to by every Member State in 1956, it would be extremely difficult to achieve in the current climate as full member ratification would once again be required.

In conclusion, Bowman proffers that "'normalization' of the Whaling Convention in light of current economic, social, and cultural circumstances, evolving conservation policy and contemporary legal norms will require a great deal more than simply the abandonment of the moratorium on commercial whaling and the reestablishment of harvesting quotas," and that "the failure of the IWC to assume full responsibility for the regulation of all contemporary manifestations of cetacean exploitation appears to be the major cause of its current dysfunction, coupled with a tendency to pay insufficient regard to strictly legal, as opposed to purely political, considerations."[37]

The options presented by Friedheim and Bowman regarding ICRW/IWC reform have theoretical and/or practical benefits and drawbacks. In terms of benefits, an obvious advantage is that reforming an existing regime is potentially more efficient (both in terms of expended time and expended resources) than creating a new one. A second advantage is that, through time, the problems associated with the existing regime have crystallized and become readily apparent. Although this does not make crafting an appropriate solution any easier, it does assist in establishing goals for reform. Regarding disadvantages of attempting to reform the ICRW/IWC regime, the obvious one is that the pro-whaling bloc of nations (featuring Norway, Iceland, and Japan) is seemingly deadlocked and at odds with the anti-whaling bloc of nations (featuring the United States, Australia, New Zealand, European Union Member States, and South American States), and compromise remains elusive and highly politicized. A second notable disadvantage is that even if compromise can be reached on a few of the issues that have stalled the ICRW/IWC regime, rational conservation requires holistic management, which is not likely to be achieved through one or two alterations to the status quo. A third disadvantage is that continuation of the ICRW/IWC regime outside of the auspices of UNCLOS leaves little chance of fully reconciling the international approach to the regulation of marine mammals with Articles 65 and 120 of UNCLOS. A fourth disadvantage is that reform of the ICRW/IWC limits the potential to facilitate either regional coordination or new, strengthened relationships between international organizations. Finally, the potential for reform of the ICRW/IWC has been extensively investigated whereas the contents of a new international agreement have not. This assessment of available alternatives will now turn to the possibility of using a "soft" law approach to address the conservation of marine mammals.

3. The "Soft" Law Approach

A third option is the production of, and reliance on, "soft" law instruments related to global marine mammal conservation. This "soft" law category encompasses normative standards that are "characteristically expressed in written form" and presented as "declarations, resolutions, recommendations, charters, and codes of practice that are generated by the processes of international intercourse."[38] Soft law does not fit squarely into the international legal sources statement found in Article 38(1) of the Statute of the International Court of Justice,[39] and differs from formal legal sources in that it does not create legally enforceable obligations (save, arguably, the obligation to give "serious consideration to their implementation").[40] Nonetheless, soft law has a number of advantages. First, the creation of soft law can help bolster existing policy or practice in an area and "may lead eventually to the emergence of new customary law or the negotiation of new treaties."[41] Second, soft law enables norm articulation in areas where states are not yet willing to commit to legally binding obligations.[42] Third, treaties are difficult and expensive to negotiate and, even when negotiations are successful, often simply produce diluted compromises.[43] Further, and assuming that successful treaty negotiations occur, there is no guarantee that treaties will be sufficiently ratified and/or enter into force.[44] These perceived advantages make soft law particularly attractive as a mechanism for legal evolution in areas of international concern that are dynamic or expanding quickly.[45] Prominent soft law examples in the area of international environmental law include: (1) the 1992 Rio Declaration on Environment and Development, (2) Agenda 21, and (3) the FAO [Food and Agriculture Organization] Code of Conduct on Responsible Fisheries.[46]

Soft law is also relevant to marine mammal conservation. An example of its application is the Whale Watching Principles produced by the IWC.[47] Such guidelines do not create obligations, even for IWC member states, but at the same time they represent an effort to produce a best-practice standard, informed by science, for minimizing cetacean disruption from the disruption associated with whale watching/tourism activities. Still, this author is of the opinion that soft law represents one tool by which rational marine mammal conservation can be achieved rather than a complete solution in and of itself. Additionally, although recent history suggests that negotiating new treaties may have its own set of challenges,[48] the successful negotiation of UNCLOS and the 1995 UN Fish Stock Agreement evidences the fact that rational oceans law and policy can still successfully be negotiated in treaty form. Finally, replacing an existing treaty regime (albeit a flawed and outdated one) with soft law does not represent an ideal solution and it would fail to address outstanding compliance and dispute resolution problems. Therefore, the proposal contained in Chapters 6 and 7 will contemplate the use of soft law, utilized by a newly created International Marine Mammal Commission that exists pursuant to a negotiated implementation agreement within the auspices of UNCLOS.

4. Proliferation of Bilateral and/or Regional Agreements

A fourth option to consider is the proliferation of bilateral and/or regional agreements that pursue marine mammal conservation. It is important to consider the viability of this option for three reasons. First, regional cooperation has proved to be a fruitful level of governance for marine issues (i.e., UNEP's Regional Seas Programme) and is contemplated by UNCLOS insofar as "[t]he LOS Convention endorses the regional approach mainly with respect to the conservation and management of living resources [Part V], the protection and preservation of the marine environment [Part XII, Section 2], and the development and transfer of marine technology [Part XIV]."⁴⁹ Regional cooperation pursuant to the UN Fish Stocks Agreement has proved particularly useful in coordinating regional cooperation with respect to straddling and highly migratory fish stocks as Regional Fisheries Management Organizations (RFMOs) "are expected to comply with international law and to operate in accordance with internationally-agreed standards and protocols."⁵⁰

Second, regional arrangements for marine mammal conservation already exist and have largely been created in response to the perceived shortcomings of the ICRW/IWC. For example, NAMMCO, which manages the marine mammals of the North Atlantic, was "born out of dissatisfaction with the IWC's zero catch quota, lack of IWC competence to deal with small cetaceans, and the need for an organization to deal with other marine mammals such as seals."⁵¹ Other notable examples include ACCOBAMS and ASCOBANS, agreements negotiated pursuant to the CMS.⁵² These agreements fill one regulatory gap that exists under ICRW/IWC as they address the small cetacean conservation and embrace modern threats to cetaceans by addressing habitat protection and pollution.⁵³

Third, regional implementation represents a rational mechanism through which coordination, cooperation, and compliance can be facilitated and incentivized. As noted by Birnie et al., "[a]t one level, regional arrangements are simply a means of implementing policies which are necessary in the interests of a specific community of states and which can best be tackled on a regional basis."⁵⁴ Further, regionalism can be fostered using determinable geographical areas, shared historical experiences, "developed, socio-cultural, political, or economic linkages" that make certain areas of the world unique, and a sense of working to address issues that constitute "collective affairs," such as marine conservation.⁵⁵ Indeed, maximizing such similarities might lead to the conclusion that the most effective form of agreement is limited to those states "most immediately involved."⁵⁶ Finally, high seas fisheries enforcement and compliance has been advanced by RFMOs pursuant to the UN Fish Stock Agreement, which enables vessel boarding and inspection for compliance with RFMO regulations and to limit illegal, unreported fishing, and also vessel black listing that prevents noncompliant vessels from docking at RFMO state ports.⁵⁷ Taken together, the ability to foster cooperation among like-minded, similarly situated states and improved high-seas enforcement suggests that regional coordination has an important role to play in marine mammal conservation.

Although regional arrangements could, in theory, become so prevalent and linked that they ultimately constitute global marine mammal conservation, I suggest that the likelihood of this occurring is increased if regional cooperation is coordinated under the auspices of an international organization. Further, and as noted by Gillespie, "regional organizations need to be complementary to the primary international organization, namely the IWC, in this area," as it is important that the work of the international organization not be undermined.⁵⁸ Burke appears to support this assertion, noting that "[r]egional management is also not inconsistent with creating a global entity devoted to overall cognizance and action to be sure that regional measures in toto are adequate or need to be supplemented or complemented to ensure general effectiveness and to avoid gaps in coverage and reporting."⁵⁹ For these reasons, the proposal contained in Chapters 6 and 7 advances regional cooperation, but does so in a manner that recognizes its utility as a tool to implement regulations, standards, and best-practice guidelines that are promulgated by an international organization. Coastal states form the basic unit for international marine mammal conservation and management, and as such it is appropriate to now consider an alternative to the status quo whereby regulation is wholly left to coastal states.

5. Reliance on National Regulation

A fifth option is to decentralize the regulation of marine mammals by focusing on national regulation, largely to be promulgated by the world's coastal states. As explored in Chapter 2, existing national regulation lacks consistency and coherence. Some states prefer the "no take" approach whereby marine mammals are guarded against direct and indirect harm within zones of national jurisdiction, whereas other nations continue to take marine mammals extensively for both commercial and subsistence purposes.

In addition to a lack of consistency, the notion that the world's highly migratory or pelagic marine mammals species found on the high seas can be effectively regulated without the participation of international and/or regional organizations is deeply flawed. Nonetheless, coastal states do have the ability to regulate marine mammal uses within their internal waters, territorial waters, archipelagic waters, and EEZ, and they do have an important enforcement role to play with respect to the actions of their nationals and flag state vessels. Coastal states are also essential to the implementation of international regulations and best-practice guidelines, are necessary to sustain monitoring and compliance initiatives, can contribute as models through the development of novel and/or forward-looking conservation strategies, and remain the basic unit of regional and international cooperation and coordination. Further, nothing prevents states from either accepting or rejecting the competence of an international organization within zones of national jurisdiction.[60] Therefore, the proposal contained in Chapters 6 and 7 recognizes and incorporates the important role that coastal states play in effective marine mammal conservation, stressing that coastal state regulation alone cannot represent a viable solution to this problem. This discussion will now turn to consider the alternative to the status quo that forms the foundation of my proposal.

6. A New International Regime

The assessment of possible alternatives to the status quo provided above indicates that although regional organizations, soft law, and coastal regulation all have a role to play in the pursuit of rational and effective marine mammal conservation, the most appealing option remains international regulation by an international organization that is created pursuant to a new negotiated multilateral agreement. The previous assessment of the scope of the amendment and/or evolutionary process required to meaningfully address the shortcomings of the ICRW/IWC, the likelihood of said amendments and/or evolutionary process occurring, and the inability of the ICRW Contracting Governments to reach a compromise through the recent "Future of the IWC" process, tends to suggest that the practical benefits associated with pursuing amendment of the current regime rather than negotiating a new agreement (i.e., less money, less time, and existing goodwill) either do not exist in this instance, or do not outweigh the benefits associated with negotiating a new regime (as outlined below).

The possibility of a new whaling agreement was contemplated by Professor Burke in *Toward a Sustainable Whaling Regime*, where he suggests that the inability to revise the ICRW indicates that a new whaling agreement is the necessary solution.[61] Burke's assessment starts with the observation that according to custom, the take of living marine resources (including whales) on the high seas is permissible, and states are "obligated to prescribe conservation measures for these operations and to cooperate for this purpose."[62] In essence, this translates to a customary duty that requires states that harvest resources on the high seas to "take conservation measures."[63] This duty is also informed by the customary duties to contribute to fisheries research, to negotiate, and to cooperate.[64] Still, Burke acknowledges in another work that there is no customary law principle prohibiting marine mammal take,[65] which is still a valid statement today. Burke's assessment also emphasizes that a new whaling agreement must be clearly and unambiguously drafted, contemplate and enable peaceful dispute resolution, account for emerging governance principles, contain an enforcement regime (meaning "monitoring, surveillance, inspection, reporting, adjudication, trial, and penalty"), and be "guided by the best scientific evidence available."[66] This proposal stops short of providing a draft of what a new convention would look like; however, it does assert the position that a new agreement is an option worth pursuing. Burke's work generally supports the importance of the two additional questions that must be addressed before moving forward: first, what species should be covered by the new international agreement?; and second, should the new international agreement be a stand-alone international convention or should it be brought under the auspices of UNCLOS as an implementing agreement?

Regarding species coverage, there are three dominant forms that a new agreement could take. One option is to negotiate a more robust regime that covers only large cetacean species, akin to current species coverage at the IWC. This is not a favorable option for the simple reason that small cetaceans are subject to the same threats as large cetaceans, and that their exclusion from IWC regulatory competency is one of the most contentious issues currently facing the ICRW/IWC regime. The second option is to negotiate a new agreement that expressly applies to all cetacean species. This option is preferable to the first, and would address the concerns held by those commentators who rightly assert that governance reform is necessary to protect those cetacean species that are not covered by the ICRW/IWC.[67] The drawback of this option is that it does not account for other marine mammal species whose conservation could also benefit from international governance, be it in the form of regulatory control, catch quotas, or best-practice hunting guidelines. Accordingly, a third option is the negotiation of an international agreement that expands coverage to all marine mammal species. This option is bolstered by a number of observations: (1) the current threats that face cetaceans, as explored in Chapter 4, threaten all marine mammal species; (2) other marine mammal species could benefit from the promulgation of best-practice guidelines for hunting and marine mammal tourism; (3) the existing regulatory framework for the conservation and management of other marine mammals is as fragmented and in need of reform as it is for cetaceans; and (4) if the decision is made to negotiate a new international agreement pertinent to marine mammals, such negotiations should aim to be as robust and comprehensive as possible, with the hopes that such a regime will be able to respond to novel threats as they emerge in the future. For these reasons, the option favored for the purposes of this proposal is the negotiation of a new international agreement applicable to all marine mammal species, to the maximum extent practicable. The second consideration is whether this new agreement should be negotiated outside of the UNCLOS regime or brought within its auspices.

The ICRW/IWC is an example of an international regime that exists outside of the auspices of the United Nations (UN). This is not to say that it is not influenced by resolutions of the United Nations General Assembly (UNGA) or UNCLOS, simply that the ICRW is not a treaty that was negotiated under the aegis of the UN and that the IWC is not an organization that falls within the United Nations System of Organizations.[68] Perhaps this is not surprising given that the UN was founded in 1945, in the aftermath of World War II, "by 51 countries committed to maintaining international peace and security, developing friendly relations among nations and promoting social progress, better living standards and human rights."[69] The ICRW, on the other hand, was born out of a series of agreements and protocols that had been initiated at the international level in 1931 under the auspices of the League of Nations, culminating in a negotiating session in Washington, DC, in 1946.[70] Nonetheless, given that the preferred course of action endorsed here is the creation of a new international organization, it is necessary to consider whether the new regime that replaces and supersedes the ICRW/IWC will exist separate from the UN or should properly be brought within its auspices.

The argument in favor of bringing the new negotiated regime within the auspices of the UN is attractive for a number of reasons. First, the UN has developed a strong environmental presence (i.e., the United Nations Environment Programme),[71] has made considerable progress in the area of oceans law and policy (i.e., UNCLOS and the UN Regional Seas Programme), and has held a number of successful conferences producing meaningful international treaties (i.e., United Nations Framework Convention on Climate Change and the Convention on Biological Diversity). Second, UNCLOS has proven to be a dynamic treaty capable of evolution through implementing agreement, and is regarded by the UNGA as the "legal framework within which all activities in the oceans and seas must be carried out" and "of strategic importance as the basis for national, regional and global action and cooperation in the marine sector."[72] The importance of UNCLOS was also endorsed in chapter 17 of Agenda 21,[73] where it is noted in Article 17.1 that UNCLOS "sets forth the rights and obligations of States and provides the international basis upon which to pursue the protection and sustainable development of the marine and coastal environment and its resources."[74] Most recently, the UN adopted, by resolution, "The Future We Want" document produced at the United Nations Conference on Sustainable Development in June 2012.[75] This document also acknowledges the importance of UNCLOS and calls for "all its parties to fully implement their obligations under the Convention."[76] An assessment of implementing agreements pursuant to UNCLOS and the role this author envisions that such an implementing agreement could play in enhanced international marine mammal conservation can be found in Sections II and III of this chapter. Third, the United Nations emphasizes "good faith" as a guiding principle for state behavior. For example, Article 2(2) of the Charter of the United Nations provides that "All Members, in order to ensure to all of them the rights and benefits resulting from membership, shall fulfill in good faith the obligations assumed by them in accordance with the present Charter,"[77] and Principle 27 of the Rio Declaration on Environment and Development provides that "States and people shall cooperate in good faith and in a spirit of partnership in the fulfilment of the principles embodied in this Declaration and in the further development of international law in the field of sustainable development."[78] It is apparent to this author that the role of good faith in the process of negotiating a new international treaty cannot be underestimated given the contentious issues associated with marine mammal conservation and the polarization that has essentially blocked reformatory efforts to date. Fourth, bringing the regime within the auspices of the UN would enable any agency that it creates to seek advisory opinions from the ICJ. Accordingly, and for all these reasons, this analysis proceeds on the basis that it is preferable to bring this new regime within the ambit of the UN.

Having indicated that it is preferable to bring international marine mammal conservation within the auspices of the UN, and that UNCLOS provides the appropriate framework for implementation, it is also necessary to consider the possibility of creating a new international regime through the negotiation of an Annex to UNCLOS. There are currently nine Annexes to UNCLOS, covering a wide range of matters.[79] The most intriguing Annex for the purposes of this discussion is Annex II, titled "Commission on the Limits of the Continental Shelf," which creates the Commission on the Limits of the Continental Shelf (CLCS) that exists "to facilitate the implementation of the United Nations Convention on the Law of the Sea (the Convention) in respect of the outer limits of the Continental Shelf beyond 200 nautical miles (M) from the baselines from which the breadth of the territorial sea is measured."[80] The brief Annex that creates the CLCS identifies how it implements Article 76 of UNCLOS, establishes the CLCS's composition (Article 2), defines the process for states to follow in submitting their proposals (Article 4), describes the scientific and technical subcommissions (Article 5), and sets the process for subcommission recommendation to the CLCS (Article 6). The CLCS currently meets twice annually at the UN Headquarters in New York[81] and has established a Trust Fund to help developing nations assess possible extended continental shelf claims.[82] The theoretical benefits of proceeding in this manner as opposed to a new implementing agreement are twofold. First, negotiating a new Annex involves only states parties to UNCLOS, which is fewer than the total number of states that would be involved in the negotiation of an implementing agreement. Second, the CLCS suggests that complex issues can be addressed through a commission created pursuant to an Annex. Still, the complexity of marine mammal conservation warrants full consideration and negotiation, and this analysis will proceed on the basis that a comprehensive implementing agreement is preferable.

With this survey of available options now complete, the conclusion is that a new treaty regime that supersedes and replaces the ICRW/IWC, negotiated and implemented within the auspices of the UN, represents the preferred course of action. This analysis of the case for an implementing agreement pursuant to Articles 65 and 120 of UNCLOS and the creation of an International Marine Mammal Commission now shifts to consider the role of implementing agreements as a tool to implement UNCLOS.

II. UNCLOS IMPLEMENTING AGREEMENTS

As indicated previously, UNCLOS is regarded as a "Constitution for the Oceans."[83] When UNCLOS opened for signature on December 10, 1982, in Montego Bay, Jamaica, the treaty represented a package deal[84] that had been successfully and painstakingly negotiated through the use of working groups, a consensus mechanism,[85] and a "consolidating document."[86] UNCLOS, as a product of these negotiations, represents a comprehensive oceans law regime that:

> marked the culmination of work involving participation by more than 150 countries representing all regions of the world, all legal and political systems, all degrees of socio-economic development, countries with various dispositions regarding the kinds of minerals that can be found in the sea-bed, coastal States, States described as geographically disadvantaged with regard to ocean space, archipelagic States, island States, and landlocked States.[87]

Despite UNCLOS's utility, one must not forget that each article represents the product of intense negotiation and scrutiny, and that some Articles simply exist as placeholders requiring future negotiation;[88] indeed, there was "an understanding during the conference [UNCLOS III] that it would not be possible to resolve every law of the sea issue, and that some matters would need future resolution via additional agreements or protocols."[89] Further, and as the 1990s began, UNCLOS had not yet reached the requisite number of deposited ratifications as established in Article 308(1) to enter into force.[90]

This quickly changed after the negotiation of an implementing agreement titled "Agreement Relating to the Implementation of Part XI of the United Nations Convention on the Law of the Sea of 10 December 1982"[91] (the "1994 Implementing Agreement"), and UNCLOS entered into force on November 16, 1994.[92] A second implementing agreement was negotiated in 1995, titled the "Agreement for the Implementation of the Provisions of the United Nations Convention on the Law of the Sea of 10 December 1982 Relating to the Conservation and Management of Straddling Fish Stocks and Highly Migratory Fish Stocks" (the "UN Fish Stocks Agreement").[93] Finally, the international community is poised to start negotiating a new legally binding implementing agreement to address issues of biodiversity conservation and preservation in areas beyond national jurisdiction. To date, Greenpeace,[94] the IUCN,[95] and The Pew Environment Group[96] have each considered the role for this sort of implementing agreement.[97] In theory, implementing agreements "can be characterized as representing a deepening and facilitating of UNCLOS obligations."[98] The following will consider each use/proposed use of an implementing agreement in support of the conclusion that an implementing agreement is the appropriate mechanism to employ in pursuit of rational marine mammal conservation.

The 1994 Implementing Agreement relates to Part XI of UNCLOS, which is titled "The Area." The "Area" is also a term defined in Article 1 of Part I ("Introduction") of UNCLOS as "the seabed and ocean floor and subsoil thereof, beyond the limits of national jurisdiction." Part XI, as negotiated at UNCLOS, is notable as it provides for resource development in the Area (Section 3) and establishes an International Seabed Authority (Section 4) to administer and regulate resource development in the Area through an organ of the International Seabed Authority called the "Enterprise" (Article 170). Support from the American delegation for Part XI faded under the Reagan administration, especially in respect to technology transfer (Article 144) and consideration of resources in the Area being regarded as the "common heritage of mankind" (Article 136); indeed, America was one of four nations that voted against the final text of the convention at the eleventh negotiating session of UNCLOS III in April 1982.[99] Efforts to secure American ratification persist.[100]

After UNCLOS opened for signature, America's concern over Part XI spread as other Western states became skeptical about the new international authority that would administer the development of this common heritage resource.[101] This was particularly troubling as strong Western support was necessary to secure widespread implementation and regime effectiveness.[102] Some nations, including the United States and the United Kingdom, enacted legislation enabling the issuance of domestic licenses to pursue deep sea mining and international collaboration to avoid license overlap.[103] The stalemate was broken by the United Nations Secretary-General, who facilitated the negotiation of the necessary amendments to Part XI through a United Nations General Assembly Resolution, which "formally agreed upon an Agreement Relating to the Implementation of Part XI of the United Nations Convention on the Law of the Sea of 10 December 1982."[104] At its core, the 1994 Implementing Agreement:

> sought to address many of the key concerns which had been raised by the United States and others in the aftermath of UNCLOS III, dealing with issues such as the institutional costs for States Parties in giving effect to the Part XI arrangements, the operation of the Enterprise, decision-making procedures within the assembly of the International Seabed Authority, the transfer of technology, and the production and economic assistance policies of the Authority.[105]

Article 2(1) of the 1994 Implementing Agreement provides that it, and Part XI of UNCLOS, "shall be interpreted and applied together as a single instrument. In the event of any inconsistency between this Agreement and Part XI, the provisions of this Agreement shall prevail."[106] Further, Articles 4 and 5 establish the mechanisms through which states can bind themselves to the 1994 Implementing Agreement, which is especially relevant with respect to those states that had already deposited their UNCLOS ratification.[107] Shortly thereafter, UNCLOS received the necessary number of deposited ratifications and entered into force on November 16, 1994. As of the time of writing, 166 nations have ratified UNCLOS and 145 nations have ratified the 1994 Implementing Agreement.[108] The 1994 Implementing Agreement was quickly followed by another such agreement that addressed an issue that was not sufficiently resolved by UNCLOS III—the management and conservation of highly migratory species and straddling stock fish species.

Articles 63 ("Stocks occurring within the exclusive economic zones of two or more coastal States or both within the exclusive economic zone and in an area beyond and adjacent to it") and 64 ("Highly migratory species") embody the fundamental premise that managing living natural resources that are not wholly contained within the EEZ of one state requires cooperation and coordination. This basic problem can arise in a number of contexts, such as the shared/joint stock problem wherein "stocks migrate between EEZs of two or more States,"[109] or the straddling stock problem wherein "stocks of fish … migrate between, or occur in both, the EEZ of one or more States and the high seas."[110] Together, the management of these species is complicated by the reality that a management scheme introduced by one state can be frustrated by another state's inadequate management and that catches must be allocated between states (including nations that may be fishing the portion of the stock that is in the high seas).[111] These Articles read as follows:

Article 63
Stocks occurring within the exclusive economic zones of two or more coastal States or both within the exclusive economic zone and in an area beyond and adjacent to it
1. Where the same stock or stocks of associated species occur within the exclusive economic zones of two or more coastal States, these States shall seek, either directly or through appropriate subregional or regional organizations, to agree upon the measures necessary to coordinate and ensure the conservation and development of such stocks without prejudice to the other provisions of this Part.
2. Where the same stock or stocks of associated species occur both within the exclusive economic zone and in an area beyond and adjacent to the zone, the coastal State and the States fishing for such stocks in the adjacent area shall seek, either directly or through appropriate subregional or regional organizations, to agree upon the measures necessary for the conservation of these stocks in the adjacent area.

Article 64
Highly migratory species
1. The coastal State and other States whose nationals fish in the region for the highly migratory species listed in Annex I shall cooperate directly or through appropriate international organizations with a view to ensuring conservation and promoting the objective of optimum utilization of such species throughout the region, both within and beyond the exclusive economic zone. In regions for which no appropriate international organization exists, the coastal State and other States whose nationals harvest these species in the region shall cooperate to establish such an organization and participate in its work.
2. The provisions of paragraph 1 apply in addition to the other provisions of this Part.[112]

These articles, as stand-alone provisions, do contemplate cooperation through governance structures above the state level, and Article 63(1) suggests that "States concerned are required to negotiate arrangements for the management of shared stocks in good faith and in a meaningful way"; however, there is no obligation to conclude such agreements.[113] Further, Article 64 seeks cooperation but fails to provide any substantive guidance on how to achieve this goal.[114] Finally, Articles 118 and 119 echo the applicability of the same cooperation principles toward the management of fisheries on the high seas, but also fail to provide substantive guidance.[115]

With these framework provisions in mind and with UNCLOS not yet in force, the UN initiated negotiations in the early 1990s toward the completion of the 1995 Fish Stocks Agreement, which entered into force on December 11, 2001.[116] As of the time of writing, the UN Fish Stocks Agreement has 80 ratifications.[117] The 1995 Fish Stocks Agreement is important for a number of reasons, many of which will be considered in some detail in Chapters 6 and 7, as they help inform the proposed text of the new multilateral agreement for the conservation of marine mammals found therein. For the purposes of this discussion a list of the important contributions made by the UN Fish Stocks Agreement will suffice: (1) Article 6 ("Application of the precautionary approach") is important as it expressly provides that the precautionary approach will be employed by the international community as it seeks the conservation and management of straddling and highly migratory fish; (2) Part III, containing Articles 8 to 16, breathes life into the cooperation that was contemplated by Articles 63 and 64 of UNCLOS, and is especially noteworthy as it contemplates the use of RFMOs as a particularly useful medium for regional cooperation; (3) Part VI provides novel enforcement and compliance mechanisms to help achieve the goals of the agreement, at the flag state level, subregional/regional level, and international level. Part VI provides for boarding and inspection mechanisms (Article 22) and empowers port state action (Article 23); (4) Part VII differentiates between developing states and developed states and the work that can be done to empower developing states; (5) Part VIII emphasizes recourse to peaceful dispute resolution; (6) Article 31(2) in Part IX enables states parties to take action consistent with the Agreement to prevent non-states parties from undermining the effectiveness of the regime, rendering the enforcement and compliance regime applicable to non-states parties; and (7) Article 4 indicates that the 1995 Fish Stocks Agreement "shall be interpreted and applied in the context of and in a manner consistent with the Convention," which is different than the interpretation scheme provided for the 1994 Implementing Agreement.[118] In addition to the two existing implementing agreements, it is also necessary to consider if and/or how additional implementing agreements have been considered, as the existence of additional proposed implementing agreements bolsters the case for a new implementing agreement.

The third example involves ongoing efforts to conserve, protect, and sustainably use the biodiversity in areas beyond national jurisdiction (BBNJ). This is an extremely relevant example because the UN is actively working to address the conservation and sustainable use of marine biodiversity in these areas. In 2011, the UNGA provided the following request, by Resolution:

> the Secretary-General [is] to convene, in accordance with paragraph 73 of resolution 59/24 of 17 November 2004 and paragraphs 79 and 80 of resolution 60/30, with full conference services, a meeting of the Ad Hoc Open-ended Informal Working Group, to take place from 31 May to 3 June 2011, to provide recommendations to the General Assembly, and requests the Secretary-General to make every effort to meet the requirement for full conference services within existing resources.[119]

Since this request, the Ad Hoc group mentioned above has convened on a number of occasions,[120] most recently from January 20 to 23, 2015.[121] The participants in this most recent meeting—including 104 UN member states, two nonmember states, nine intergovernmental organizations, four specialized international agencies, and four UN affiliated funds/programs[122]—discharged their obligation and, by consensus, recommended to the UN that it "develop an international legally binding instrument under the Convention on the conservation and sustainable use of marine biological diversity of areas beyond national jurisdiction."[123] Further, the Group recommended that the resulting treaty holistically address "marine genetic resources, including questions on the sharing of benefits, measures such as area-based management tools, including marine protected areas, environmental impact assessments and capacity-building and the transfer of marine technology."[124] Although it might be some time yet before an intergovernmental negotiating conference is called, it is possible to look at some existing work produced by different nongovernmental organizations (NGOs) to consider the scope of this new implementing agreement.

In 2008, Greenpeace released a document titled "Suggested Draft High Seas Implementing Agreement for the Conservation and Management of the Marine Environment in Areas beyond National Jurisdiction," which contemplates "an implementing agreement [that] would be comprehensive and legally binding, and build upon the existing provisions of UNCLOS, providing a clear mandate to protect biodiversity on the high seas, based on the precautionary principle and ecosystem-based management."[125] Similarly, an IUCN proposal from 2008 titled "Elements of a Possible Implementation Agreement to UNCLOS for the Conservation and Sustainable Use of Marine Biodiversity in Areas beyond National Jurisdiction," emphasizes "protection and preservation of the marine environment," "equitable and efficient utilization of their resources," and "cooperation."[126] Specifically, the IUCN recommends "improving co-ordination between sectors, and clarifying responsibilities to 'protect and preserve' based on modern developments," and that "the application of cross-sectoral integrated management and co-operation to make operational an ecosystem-based approach in the ABJN, with a focus on conservation and sustainable use of natural resources, would be a significant step forward."[127] Finally, The Pew Environment Group's proposal contemplates the use of an implementing agreement that is able to incorporate many of the modern principles of international and regional governance, including: (1) "[a]rea based-management tools" such as marine protected areas; (2) environmental impact assessments and strategic environmental assessments; (3) maintenance of records detailing marine genetic resources and how such records should be shared; (4) technology transfer; and (5) capacity-building.[128] Each proposed agreement highlights the same potential benefits of an implementing agreement. They help advance the original goals of UNCLOS, promote the rule of law and oceans law and policy, incorporate modern principles and tools, and enable an international response to emerging problems. These proposals will be relied on further in Chapters 6 and 7, where annotated draft articles for the implementing agreement regarding Articles 65 and 120 of UNCLOS are provided.

Although "[t]he term implementing agreement is not found in the Law of the Sea Convention itself,"[129] it properly represents an "important tool"[130] for "developing the legal framework for the law of the sea."[131] The above examples demonstrate that implementing agreements can, and will continue, to be utilized to reach meaningful and effective compromise on lingering and/or novel problems. Accordingly, I maintain that an implementing agreement is the most appropriate course of action to pursue to effect marine mammal conservation pursuant to UNCLOS, so long as Articles 65 and 120 are sufficiently robust and can support this implementation. With this goal in mind, this analysis now shifts to a discussion of the history and interpretation of Articles 65 and 120.

III. THE HISTORY AND INTERPRETATION OF ARTICLES 65 AND 120 OF UNCLOS

Having surveyed the available options for reform, and having identified an implementing agreement pursuant to Articles 65 and 120 of UNCLOS as the most appropriate mechanism by which to proceed, it is now necessary to consider Articles 65 and 120 (collectively the "Articles") in greater detail. Specifically, this analysis examines both the drafting history of the Articles and the various interpretations that have been offered for them since UNCLOS opened for signature. In so doing, I demonstrate that they are capable of bearing the proposed implementing agreement.

Before proceeding to this analysis, it is important to hold in mind certain sections surrounding Articles 65 and 120. Specifically, Article 65 exists within Part V ("Exclusive Economic Zone") whereas Article 120 is found within Section 2 ("Conservation and Management of the Living Resources of the High Seas") of Part VII ("High Seas"). Dealing first with Part V, Article 56 establishes a state's sovereign rights within the exclusive economic zone (EEZ), and Article 57 establishes its breadth. Article 61 sets the basic conservation regime applicable to the living resources within the EEZ, which is notable for a number of reasons, including: (1) it vests authority to set the "allowable catch" for living resources within the EEZ with the coastal state (Article 61(1)); (2) it indicates that the coastal states "shall" ensure by proper conservation and management that species are not "endangered by over-exploitation," with reference to reliance on the "best scientific evidence available" (Article 61(2)); (3) it contemplates appropriate cooperation between coastal states and "competent international organizations, whether subregional, regional or global," to achieve proper conservation and management (Article 61(2)); and (4) it contemplates efforts to restore populations to levels that can sustain "maximum sustainable yield, as qualified by relevant environmental and economic factors" (Article 61(3)).[132] Article 62 builds off of Article 61 and, without prejudicing the maximum sustainable yield scheme from the Article, indicates that "optimum utilization"[133] shall be promoted for living resources within the EEZ and also establishes a scheme for distributing catch that the coastal state cannot utilize (Article 62(2)). It also contemplates a variety of regulatory mechanisms that a coastal state can use to ensure that foreign fishing vessels within its EEZ are compliant with catch allowances (Article 62(4)).

Articles 63 to 68 are particularly relevant for the purposes of this discussion because they address the different types of living marine resources that occur wholly (or at least partially) within state EEZs and that require distinct consideration. Article 63 pertains to straddling fish stocks, and Article 64 addresses highly migratory species. As I have previously noted, these sections can no longer be considered in isolation, as the UN Fish Stocks Agreement elucidates these obligations. Article 66 is applicable to anadromous species, namely those fish species that breed in freshwater but spend the majority of their adult lifecycle in saltwater (i.e.,

The Case for an Implementing Agreement 177

salmon). This Article vests the states bearing the rivers in which the anadromous species breed with primary regulatory responsibility and provides that, except in certain circumstances, anadromous species are only to be fished landward of the limits of the EEZs of said states. In a related fashion, Article 67 addresses catadromous species, namely those species that breed in saltwater but spend their adult lives in freshwater lakes or rivers (i.e., the American eel). This Article vests primary regulatory responsibility with the coastal states where these species spend the "greater part of their lifecycle" (Article 67(1)), and ensures that harvesting shall only occur in waters landward of the limits of the EEZ of said states. Finally, Article 68 indicates that Part V does not apply to sedentary species, being defined in Article 77 of Part VI ("Continental Shelf") as "organisms which, at the harvestable stage, either are immobile on or under the seabed or are unable to move except in constant physical contact with the seabed or the subsoil," and regulated by the same.

Article 120 is found in the living resources portion of Part VII, which addresses the high seas. Article 116 enshrines a general freedom of the fisheries on the high seas, but notes that this is subject to supervening treaty obligations, coastal state rights, duties, and interests as found in Articles 63(2) and 64 to 67 (as discussed above), and finally other restriction limits contemplated in Part VII. Article 117 creates the duty for states to cooperate with respect to the conservation of high seas resources, and Article 118 reinforces this duty to cooperate and specifically contemplates inter-state cooperation for states that are exploiting either the same resource or different resources that exist in the same area (which can be accomplished through regional or subregional fishery organizations). Article 119 indicates that high seas fishery quota setting should be guided by best available scientific evidence in pursuit of the modified maximum sustainable yield threshold. With this introduction complete, I now focus this analysis on Articles 65 and 120.

1. The Drafting History of Articles 65 and 120

This summary of the history of Articles 65 and 120 does not turn on a wholly novel assessment of the primary documentation used during negotiations, as the negotiating history for each UNCLOS section has been thoroughly investigated and memorialized through the efforts of the Center of Oceans Law and Policy at the University of Virginia, School of Law.[134] Further, Patricia Forkan, former Executive Vice President of the Humane Society of the United States, and long-time cetacean advocate on both the domestic and international scene, provided testimony on the legislative history and interpretation of Article 65 of UNCLOS to the Senate Foreign Relations Committee in October 2003, as part of the Hearings on the United Nations Convention on the Law of the Sea.[135] This section also includes information taken from a telephone interview[136] with Professor John Norton Moore, who is currently the Director of the Center for Oceans Law and Policy at the University of Virginia, School of Law, and was also the "ambassador and deputy representative to the president to the law of the sea conference" between 1973 and 1976.[137] These sources will be considered in concert as I highlight pertinent considerations from the history of these sections.

Conventional wisdom leading up to UNCLOS III held that engaging the whaling question in UNCLOS negotiations could seriously threaten the negotiations.[138] Still, the application of UNCLOS to the conservation of marine mammals was a live issue during UNCLOS III at the Second Committee[139] where it emerged in the context of promoting cooperation among concerned coastal states, international organizations, and other interested states, and also in the context of considering how conservation schemes for living resources could be effected through regional organizations.[140] It is also notable that at this time the IWC turned its attention to how it could be improved, the possibility of a commercial moratorium, and even renegotiation of the ICRW itself.[141] For example, when the IWC convened a Preparatory Meeting on the Revision of the International Convention for the Regulation of Whaling in 1978, both the United States and the environmental NGO community supported revisions that would have seen the creation of an International Cetacean Commission permanently focused on the protection of all cetaceans.[142] With this context in mind, I will now trace the evolution of the wording of what became Article 65.[143]

Many marine mammal species are regionally migratory, and many cetacean species are globally migratory, which supports the conclusion that a global organization is necessary.[144] It also supports the position that it is inappropriate to try to regulate marine mammals by listing them in Annex I of UNCLOS, as the approach had been until this time.[145] Still, it took some time before the final wording of Article 65 emerged. At the 2nd Session of UNCLOS III, the United States proposed a draft article applicable to marine mammals that, for the first time, contemplated addressing marine mammals as something distinct from other highly migratory species, as is currently addressed in Article 64.[146] This early manifestation provided:

> Notwithstanding the provisions of this chapter with respect to full utilization of living resources, nothing herein shall prevent a coastal State or international organization, as appropriate, from prohibiting the exploitation of marine mammals.[147]

This wording was considered further by the Informal Group of Juridical Experts (otherwise known as the Evenson Group), which proposed the following wording for an article addressing marine mammals in 1975:

> Nothing in this Convention shall restrict the right of a coastal State or international organization, as appropriate, to prohibit, regulate and limit the exploitation of marine mammals. States shall co-operate either directly or through appropriate international organizations with a view to the protection and management of marine mammals.[148]

The proposed amendment is significant because, in addition to the ability for coastal states or appropriate international organizations to prohibit exploitation and the ability to otherwise regulate their taking, it adds a second sentence that introduces an obligation to cooperate with respect to the "protection and management" of marine mammals.[149] Work occurred outside of the official American delegation by individuals interested in whale conservation (including Professor Moore and scientist Barbara Moore), who, with the support of NGOs such as the Connecticut Cetacean Society (later known as the Cetacean Society International),[150] drafted an Article that contained a second sentence reflecting the need for international cooperation and the presence of a global organization.[151] The next amended wording

The Case for an Implementing Agreement

came in 1976 at the 4th Session of UNCLOS III. This iteration reflected work that had been completed privately,[152] and provided as follows:

> Nothing in the present Convention restricts the right of a coastal State or international organization, as appropriate, to prohibit, regulate and limit the exploitation of marine mammals. States shall co-operate either directly or through appropriate international organizations with a view to the protection and management of marine mammals.[153]

This amendment simply removed the "shall" from the first sentence. Still, this wording tends to suggest that at this point the parties were working toward a provision that firmly distinguishes marine mammals from other highly migratory species.[154] This draft wording was again subjected to proposed amendment by Peru at the 7th Session in 1978, which ultimately led to the following proposed wording:

> Subject to the provisions of article 61, paragraph 2, and article 64, nothing in the present Convention restricts the right of a coastal State within its exclusive economic zone, or the competence of an international body with respect to measures to be applied also outside that zone, to regulate, limit, or prohibit the exploitation of marine mammals.
>
> States shall co-operate either directly or through appropriate international organizations with a view to the protection and management of marine mammals.[155]

Interestingly, Peru's amendments, had they been accepted, would have indicated that international cooperation for the purposes of marine mammal conservation can be achieved through international, regional, and even subregional organizations, and that it is also subject to the regime established for highly migratory species. This wording did not satisfy the United States, which proposed the following at the Resumed 7th Session:

> Nothing in the present Convention restricts the right of a coastal State or the competence of an international organization, as appropriate, to prohibit more strictly, regulate or limit the exploitation of marine mammals. States shall cooperate with a view to the conservation of marine mammals through an international organization for conservation and study of marine mammals.[156]

This wording did not gain the necessary traction to move the international community toward consensus, and in response the United States proposed the following wording at the Resumed 8th Session of UNCLOS III in 1978:

> Nothing in this Part restricts the right of a coastal State or the competence of an international organization, as appropriate, to prohibit, limit or regulate the exploitation of marine mammals more strictly than provided for in this Part. States shall co-operate with a view to the conservation of marine mammals and in the case of cetaceans shall work in particular through the appropriate international organizations for their conservation, management and study.[157]

It is worth noting that the reference to appropriate international organizations in the plurality is significant because this addition was initially suggested by Japan during a meeting of an informal working group, indicating that as the section purports to cover all cetaceans, by-catch should be left with regional fishery organizations.[158] This wording was included, word for word, in a working document of the Second Committee at the 9th Session of UNCLOS III and was adopted into the Informal Composite Negotiating Text (ICNT) on March 21, 1980.[159] It is also necessary to consider certain comments made at the time of its adoption. First, United States ambassador Elliot Richardson stated that:

> The text that was incorporated into the ICNT, Rev. 2 was the product of lengthy negotiations with approximately 25 States of all persuasions and geographical regions. It was supported (or not objected to) at an informal meeting of Committee II and in Plenary. In fact, several speakers represented States which were not part of the representative group. It was particularly gratifying that speakers included representatives of the major whaling nations as well as those States primarily interested in the protection and conservation of marine mammals.
>
> The new provision establishes a sound framework for the protection of whales and other marine mammals with critical emphasis on international cooperation. It exempts marine mammals from the optimum utilization requirements of other provisions of the ICNT Rev. 2 and permits States and competent international organizations to establish more stringent conservation regulations than otherwise mandated in ICNT, Rev. 2. Indeed, it explicitly permits States and international organizations to prohibit the taking of marine mammals. The text also preserves and enhances the role of the International Whaling Commission (or a successor organization). It recognizes the role of regional organizations in the protection of marine mammals, which are often taken incidental to fishing operations. In sum, the article is a basic and sound framework with which States and international organizations may pursue the future protection of these wonderful creatures for generations to come.[160]

Although pro-whaling nations such as Norway and Iceland supported Article 65 as it became part of the ICNT,[161] without comment, Japan offered the following statement from the floor:

> My delegation continues to consider that the concept of optimum utilization also applies to marine mammals. Consequently, there is no need to single out marine mammals in a special provision, or to focus on cetaceans in such a provision. As a practical matter, however, we can support this text on the understanding, with regard to the second sentence, that these activities do not necessarily need to be undertaken simultaneously with the first sentence, but on an individual (per species) basis when appropriate with consultations with other nations.[162]

Article 120 did not experience the same drafting evolution. This makes sense because the primary purpose of Article 120 is to extend application of the laboriously negotiated Article 65 to the high seas, thereby removing it from the default high seas regime for living marine resources found in Section 2 of Part VII. Having summarized the negotiating history of the UNCLOS provisions relating to marine mammals, it is now appropriate for us to turn to their subsequent interpretation and analysis for the purposes of establishing that they are capable of bearing implementation through subsequent agreement.

2. Competing Interpretations of Articles 65 and 120

It is necessary to briefly describe the appropriate principles of treaty interpretation before commencing this discussion of how Articles 65 and 120 of UNCLOS have been interpreted over time. Treaty interpretation is guided by the Vienna Convention on the Law of Treaties (VCLT), which also reflects customary international law in this regard.[163] Articles 31 and 32 are the treaty interpretation sections that require consideration. Article 31, titled "General Rule of Interpretation," states in the first subsection that "[a] treaty shall be interpreted in good faith in accordance with the ordinary meaning to be given to the terms of the treaty in their context and in the light of its object and purpose," whereas the second and third subsections provide an explanation regarding what documents, taken together, comprise the document that is being interpreted. Article 32, titled "Supplementary Means of Interpretation," provides that "[r]ecourse may be had to supplementary means of interpretation, including the preparatory work of the treaty and the circumstances of its conclusion, in order to confirm the meaning resulting from the application of article 31, or to determine the meaning when the interpretation according to article 31" is either "ambiguous or obscure" or leads to a "manifestly absurd or unreasonable" result. Taken together, these VCLT provisions direct the reader to look first to the contextualized ordinary meaning, with supplementary recourse to preparatory work in certain circumstances.

The remainder of this analysis will proceed by examining: (1) the characteristics of Articles 65 and 120 that invite treaty interpretation and supplemental implementation, (2) the contemporaneous and emergent interpretations ascribed to these sections by UNCLOS negotiating parties and international organizations, (3) the academic interpretations presented after UNCLOS opened for signature, and (4) the interpretation(s) that are preferred for the purposes of this work. It must be kept in mind throughout the remainder of this section that this chapter's purpose is to justify the use of an implementing agreement to give effect to the regime that is possible pursuant to Articles 65 and 120 rather than using these Articles to justify the creation of new regime external to UNCLOS.

3. Pertinent Characteristics of Articles 65 and 120

Practically, it is necessary to understand the scope of each clause. The first sentence of Article 65, as reproduced below, is a statement of jurisdictional competency[164] that contemplates coastal state and/or international organization's regulatory authority over marine mammals within the EEZ:

> Nothing in this Part restricts the right of a coastal State or the competence of an international organization, as appropriate, to prohibit, limit or regulate the exploitation of marine mammals more strictly than provided for in this Part.[165]

The second sentence is the cooperation clause,[166] linking states (not limited to coastal states) to international organizations (expressly stated in its plurality):

> States shall cooperate with a view to the conservation of marine mammals and in the case of cetaceans shall in particular work through the appropriate international organizations for their conservation, management and study.[167]

Article 120 essentially represents an extension of application as it renders Article 65 applicable to the high seas:

> Article 65 also applies to the conservation and management of marine mammals in the high seas.[168]

The second point of interest is the cumulative effect of these Articles. As explained by authors Freeland and Drysdale, Articles 65 and 120 work in concert to "create a specific management regime for marine mammals in the EEZ and high seas, and to allow for a different regime within the EEZ from that of 'optimum utilization.'"[169] Certain features of this management scheme are clearly identified in the first sentence of Article 65, through which a "coastal State is entitled to limit or prohibit the exploitation of such species rather than establishing an allowable catch and promoting the objective of optimum utilization," whereas international organizations are empowered to "limit or prohibit the exploitation of marine mammals, both within and beyond the EEZ."[170] Cooperation between states and international organizations with respect to marine mammals generally is not described in the second sentence of Article 65, but with respect to cetaceans, this sentence contemplates that states "shall work through" international organizations for "conservation, management and study." In sum, these Articles establish an "overall management framework" for marine mammal species.[171]

Even though it is clear that these Articles create a marine mammal conservation and management framework, a deeper reading exposes numerous ambiguities and uncertainties that have opened the door to competing state interpretations and scholarly debate. Author Kimberly Davis has appropriately identified that this management framework creates an "umbrella," which has facilitated competing interpretation,[172] whereas Professor Birnie notes that Article 65 is "one of the most opaque articles in the LOSC,"[173] which is reflective of the lengthy negotiation process.[174] Pertinent ambiguities and uncertainties include the following:

(1) The content of the duty to conserve marine mammals is not described;[175]
(2) These Articles do not indicate when a coastal state should have primary authority to act and when an international organization should have primary authority;[176]
(3) What conservation and management criteria should be used by coastal States and/or international organizations? There is no guidance on how to balance "scientific, ecological, cultural, aesthetic, and moral values";[177]
(4) The first sentence of Article 65 fails to provide guidance about when it is appropriate for an international organization to have competence to regulate marine mammals;[178]

(5) The second sentence of Article 65 does not provide guidance on what is required to meet the duty to cooperate with respect to the general conservation of marine mammals;[179]
(6) UNCLOS does not offer a definition for "appropriate international organizations" as used in Article 65 in the context of cetacean "conservation, management and study" in the second sentence of Article 65;[180]
(7) UNCLOS does not define the obligation to "work through" in relation to cetacean conservation in the second sentence of Article 65.[181] Specifically, it does not indicate when a state must work through an international organization, nor does it indicate how this obligation can be discharged once triggered.[182]

The final potential ambiguity that must be addressed before proceeding to an assessment of the competing interpretations of these Articles is the fact that certain cetaceans are listed on Annex I of UNCLOS.[183] Annex I lists the highly migratory species that, by virtue of said listing, are covered by the management regime created in Article 64. Annex I contains two categorical listings of note. First, the listings under the heading "Dolphin" provides "*Coryphaena hippurus; Coryphaena equiselis,*" both of which are not cetaceans. *Coryphaena hippurus* is a fish commonly known as the dolphin fish or mahi mahi[184] while *Coryphaena equiselis* is a fish also commonly called mahi mahi.[185] This misidentification imports ambiguity[186] and could be removed through amendment.

Second, the listings under the heading "Cetaceans" provides "Family *Physeteridae*; Family *Balaenopteridae*; Family *Balaenidae*; Family *Eschrichtiidae*; Family *Monodontidae*; Family *Ziphiidae*; Family *Delphinidae*." There are competing schools of thought regarding the consequences of certain cetaceans being listed on Annex I. The predominate position is that the inclusion of cetaceans represents a "technical error arising from the fact that at one time articles 64 and 65 were one article."[187] The remedial solution to this is the removal of the cetacean listings from Annex I by amendment.[188] The competing interpretation is that Article 65 does not create a management scheme for marine mammals that is distinct from the scheme found in Article 64 as they were initially conceived of as one article.[189] Davis argues in support of this position, asserting that "the better approach would be to read articles 64 and 65 together, treating article 65 as modifying the basic scheme set forth in article 64," and further, that this means that the only marine mammal species that would be protected by Article 65 are those listed in Annex I.[190] It also follows from this interpretation that marine mammal species not listed on Annex I will then fall within the default management scheme established in Articles 61 and 62.[191] The interpretation preferred in this work is that the inclusion of certain cetaceans on Annex I is a technical error and that this can be remedied by way of an amendment included in the implementing agreement that is being proposed, which will create an interpretation of Annex I that is binding upon ratifying nations.

Having identified the contentious phrases and terms within these Articles, this discussion turns to a consideration of the various interpretations that have been presented by states and international organizations, both during the negotiating process and afterward.

4. Contemporaneous and Emerging State/International Organization Interpretations

It is appropriate to begin this discussion with consideration of the interpretation that is favored by the United States, as the United States is responsible for the very existence of Articles 65 and 120. First, in a letter from Professor John Norton Moore to the Honorable Elliot Richardson (then head of the U.S. delegation to the third conference of the law of the sea), Professor Moore provided the following comment on the possibility of the IWC becoming an International Cetacean Commission:

> At the present time such an organization exists (the IWC) although the United States has sought to strengthen it as an International Cetacean Commission, aimed less at "whaling" and more at "cetacean protection". The recent moratorium within the IWC suggests that the organization can be strengthened substantially along these lines and that within the next few years the time may be right for favorable international consideration of efforts for a strengthened ICC.[192]

The position of the United States was also clarified by George Taft[193] at the last session of UNCLOS III in a statement from the Department of State:

> The appropriate/primary international organization referred to in Article 65 is the International Whaling Commission or a successor organization. Certain regional organizations, which are concerned with the regulation of fishing, may also appropriately play a role as cetaceans are occasionally taken as incidental catch to fishing activities. It is further understood that the minimum standards for the protection of cetaceans apply throughout the migratory range of such cetaceans whether within or beyond the exclusive economic zone.[194]

These statements tend to indicate that the United States viewed Article 65 as being *lex specialis* with respect to marine mammals and capable of trumping Articles 61 and 62.[195] Further, although these statements do not elucidate the content of the duty to cooperate with respect to marine mammals generally or cetaceans in particular, they do contemplate the IWC qualifying as the appropriate international organization, recognize the possibility that regional organizations can also play a role, and, perhaps most important for the purposes of this work, envisage the evolution of international marine mammal conservation and the possibility of an emergent successor international organization that will qualify as an "appropriate international organization."

In 1997, in response to Canada's decision to issue national licenses for an Aboriginal bowhead whale hunt without consulting the IWC, President Bill Clinton delivered a message to Congress regarding Canada's actions.[196] President Clinton provided the following comment on Article 65 of UNCLOS:

> International law, as reflected in the 1982 United Nations Convention on the Law of the Sea, obligates countries to work through the appropriate international organization for the conservation and management of whales.[197]

As the United States is not a state party to UNCLOS, this statement suggests that the United States believes that Article 65 represents customary international law.[198]

Indeed, there is likely a "high degree of acceptance that there is an international legal requirement for States to work through the appropriate international organizations in order to conserve, manage, and study whales."[199] Still, even if Article 65 represents custom and binds non-states parties, this position does not clarify the content of this duty, or how the obligation can be discharged, beyond indicating that management decisions should be made through international organizations rather than unilaterally and that the international regulatory process should be followed by states.[200] I will return to the academic commentary on this point later in this discussion.

The Canadian position is quite different than that presented above, and it is useful to consider it in terms of Canada's interpretation of the second sentence of Article 65. The following is an extract from the Statement by the delegation of Canada dated April 2, 1980, as presented at the 9th Session of UNCLOS III:

> The current United States proposal for a change to the existing text of article 65 of the revised negotiating text would require States to "work through the appropriate international organizations" for the conservation management and study of cetaceans. The Canadian delegation supports the text proposed by the United States as an improvement over the current text in providing a better basis for the conservation of marine mammals, and wishes to have recorded the following interpretation of the second sentence of the proposed text:
>
> (a) The obligation for any particular State is to "work through" an appropriate international organization. In other words there is no obligation on any State to "work through" more than one appropriate international organization;
>
> (b) The obligation to "work through" an appropriate international organization as regards individual stocks of cetaceans arises as regards any particular stock only when the status of the stock is such that the attention of the appropriate international organization is necessary to assist in the conservation, management and study of the stock;
>
> (c) the [sic] obligation to "work through the appropriate international organizations" can be fulfilled through consultation with the scientific bodies of such organizations in the process of development of measures in accordance with the development of sovereign rights and obligations of coastal States within their 200-mile zones.[201]

In short, this statement demonstrates that Canada's position is that there is more than one possible appropriate international organization, that states do not need to work through more than one, that the obligation is only triggered if international effort is required to help a particular cetacean stock, and that the duty of "work through" can be discharged through "consultation with the scientific bodies" in a manner that recognizes EEZ sovereign rights.[202]

The third country that requires consideration is Japan, a staunchly pro-whaling nation. Japan's perspective on marine mammal conservation and management pursuant to UNCLOS may not be surprising given its history of commercial hunting and its demonstrated political will to maintain whaling—which persists today.[203] During Second Committee deliberation on Article 65, Japan did not go so far as to indicate that an organization other than the IWC qualified as an appropriate international organization, but the Japanese delegation did make the following statement from the floor:

> My delegation continues to consider that the concept of optimum utilization also applies to marine mammals. Consequently, there is no need to single out marine mammals in a special provision, or to focus on cetaceans in such a provision. As a practical matter, however, we can support this text on the understanding, with regard to the second sentence, that these activities do not necessarily need to be undertaken simultaneously with the first sentence, but on an individual (per species) basis when appropriate with consultations with other nations.[204]

This statement evidences Japan's preference to bring marine mammals within an optimum utilization regime, as contemplated by Articles 61 and 62. Also, it indicates that Japan considers it appropriate to sever the first and second sentences of Article 65 such that, in operation, accepting the duty to cooperate through international organizations would not necessarily lead to the state's acceptance of the ability of said international organization to regulate marine mammals (as provided in the jurisdiction clause). It is worth noting that other pro-whaling nations such as Norway and Iceland did not provide similar floor statements during this process, opting to simply state their support for Article 65.[205]

Before moving on, we must also acknowledge the subsequent state practice of these pro-whaling nations. Specifically, Iceland withdrew from the IWC in 1992 to create NAMMCO, an action that Forkan suggests was taken to "unseat the IWC as the organization with jurisdiction over whale conservation and management."[206] Norway, Greenland, and the Faroe Islands were also involved in the creation of NAMMCO, which, despite becoming an effective organization in its own right, has not legitimately threatened to unseat the IWC.[207] As noted in the section above addressing the drafting history of Articles 65 and 120, Japan advocated in favor of pluralizing "international organization" to enable the by-catch problem to be addressed through regional fisheries organizations.[208] Further, Japan has contemplated the creation of a new international organization to rival the IWC, or alternatively its withdrawal from the IWC in favor of joining NAMMCO.[209] Despite this posturing, Japan has neither left the IWC nor has it joined NAMMCO, and the IWC persists, albeit precariously. This change in position is evidence of an interpretation of Article 65 that allows more than one international organization to manage marine mammals.

Interpretive guidance can also be had by looking at what the United Nations Division of Ocean Affairs and the Law of the Sea: Office of Legal Affairs ("UN Oceans Division"), in its capacity as UNCLOS Secretariat, has said on this issue.[210] The UN Oceans Division publishes Law of the Sea Bulletins, which consolidate ocean law updates and facilitate information exchange. Bulletin No. 31, published in 1996, contains a section describing what is meant by "[c]ompetent or relevant international organizations," as used in UNCLOS.[211] This umbrella phrase is meant to encompass the "[n]umerous provisions in the Convention [that] make reference to 'competent' or 'appropriate' international organizations ... [or that] refer just to 'international organizations' or 'specialized agencies' or more broadly to 'multilateral programmes' or 'international channels.'"[212] Here the UN Oceans Division provides a table highlighting their understanding of the international organizations that qualify for the purposes of each reference in UNCLOS.[213] Regarding

Article 65 and the "Duty of States to work through the *appropriate international organizations* for the conservation, management and study of cetaceans," the UN Oceans Division indicates that the FAO, IWC, and UNEP all qualify as appropriate.[214] With this interpretation in mind, it is also necessary to consider the guidance that has emerged pursuant to other UN initiatives.

This is an appropriate time to consider the contribution that Agenda 21[215] makes to this discussion. Agenda 21 is one of the outputs of the 1992 UN Conference on Environment and Development (UNCED), as convened by the UNGA.[216] Agenda 21 is a non-binding action plan that is state-oriented and covers a range of international environmental issues, including protection of the oceans.[217] Chapter 17 of Agenda 21—titled "Protection of the Oceans, All Kinds of Seas, Including Enclosed and Semi-Enclosed Seas, and Coastal Areas and the Protection, Rational Use and Development of Their Living Resources" ("Chapter 17")—promotes, among other goals: (1) integrated management and coastal protection, (2) marine protection, (3) "sustainable use and conservation of marine living resources of the high seas," (4) "sustainable use and conservation of marine living resources under national jurisdiction," and (5) the strengthening of cooperation and coordination at the international and regional level of governance.[218] Section 17.46 lists a series of objectives regarding the conservation and sustainable use of living marine resources found on the high seas, which includes developing said resources to meet human needs and facilitating utilization at the point of "maximum sustainable yield as qualified by relevant environmental and economic factors, taking into consideration relationships among species." These goals are qualified by section 17.47, which states:

> Nothing in paragraph 17.46 above restricts the right of a State or the competence of an international organization, as appropriate, to prohibit, limit or regulate the exploitation of marine mammals on the high seas more strictly than provided for in that paragraph. States shall cooperate with a view to the conservation of marine mammals and, in the case of cetaceans, shall in particular work through the appropriate international organizations for their conservation, management and study.

This section is a direct transcription of Article 65 of UNCLOS with the exception of the addition of "high seas" to the first paragraph. Chapter 17 also provides the following statement regarding international and regional cooperation and coordination in section 17.61:

> States recognize:
> (a) The responsibility of the International Whaling Commission for the conservation and management of whale stocks and the regulation of whaling pursuant to the 1946 International Convention for the Regulation of Whaling;
> (b) The work of the International Whaling Commission Scientific Committee in carrying out studies of large whales in particular, as well as of other cetaceans;
> (c) The work of other organizations, such as the Inter-American Tropical Tuna Commission and the Agreement on Small Cetaceans in the Baltic and North Sea under the Bonn Convention, in the conservation, management and study of cetaceans and other marine mammals.[219]

Chapter 17 then provides in section 17.62 that "States should cooperate for the conservation, management and study of cetaceans." Although these provisions are not binding, they do have interpretive value,[220] and taken together, they tend to provide weight to the argument that the IWC has a legitimate claim to being recognized as the primary international organization for whales.[221]

In sum, these Articles, and Article 65 in particular, became the subject of differing interpretation during drafting and at the time of agreement, and as exemplified by Chapter 17, have affected the subsequent development of international discussion. This interpretative divergence has opened the door to academic commentary, which also espouses a variety of positions regarding the appropriate scope and effect of Articles 65 and 120.

5. Academic Interpretations

Academic interpretation of these Articles has emerged in a variety of contexts. For example, scholarly interpretation has been undertaken during the course of assessing whether the IWC has the authority to regulate small cetaceans[222] during discussion of the state of global marine mammal conservation,[223] during the Future of the IWC process,[224] and in the course of considering the general impact of UNCLOS.[225] Professor Cinnamon Carlarne suggests that "UNCLOS's perplexing tenets reflect the growing polarization of opinions on the whaling issue. In fact, both proponents and opponents of whaling argue that UNCLOS supports their positions,"[226] and also that academic opinions relating to the proper interpretation of Articles 65 and 120 are as varied as state positions.[227] The following survey of competing academic interpretations seeks to further the appreciation of Articles 65 and 120 by identifying the most persuasive interpretation and assessing whether these Articles can support an implementing agreement that creates a new international marine mammal organization.

The first category of noteworthy academic interpretations are those that acknowledge the existing ambiguity and uncertainty found in these provisions and attempt to guide proper application or discuss the general impact of UNCLOS. For example, Professor Birnie states that "[i]t is not clear through which institutional mechanisms states must cooperate to conserve cetaceans or how many organizations are 'appropriate' for this purpose," and that the plurality simply reflects the by-catch issue.[228] In a recent work, authors Birnie, Boyle, and Redgwell assert that the effect of Article 65 is not limited to the EEZ, that optimum utilization of marine mammals is not required, and that reference to "organizations" provides states with the choice of which institution they prefer to "work through."[229] Further, it seems generally accepted that the optimum utilization scheme contemplated in Articles 61 and 62 is not applicable to marine mammals, but that the reference to "international organizations" might open the door to other organizations, such as NAMMCO, to assert their appropriateness.[230] Author Stefan Asmudsson, writing as the head of the International Affairs Office of the Ministry of Fisheries of Iceland, has also provided an opinion on the ability of international organizations to regulate whaling, stating that Article 65 does not justify the imposition of a whaling ban "on all coastal States without a valid scientific justification," and that "Article 65 . . . clearly keeps the door open for other organisations than the IWC to have competence regarding the management of whaling."[231]

William Burke addressed his perspective on the general impact of UNCLOS on marine mammal regulation in *The New International Law of Fisheries: UNCLOS 1982 and Beyond*.[232] Here, Burke contends that the regulatory competence provided in the first sentence of Article 65 is consistent with international law because a "coastal State remains free to exercise its sovereign rights by delegating authority to an international body to make decisions regarding marine mammals that might otherwise be within coastal jurisdiction,"[233] and that this regulatory competence is extended to the high seas through Article 120.[234] According to Burke, one possible interpretation of Article 65 is that states parties to UNCLOS that are not states parties to the ICRW are nevertheless obligated to follow the IWC's regulatory authority as representative of appropriate minimum conservation standards, unless these states can prove that the IWC's regulation is unnecessary.[235] Burke has some trouble accepting this interpretation as it implies that non-IWC states would be bound by IWC regulations that do not have to be followed by IWC states parties that have taken advantage of the available objection procedure.[236] An opposing interpretation, according to Burke, is that those negotiating and drafting Article 65 contemplated the ICRW/IWC only when crafting the obligation to "work through the appropriate international organizations," and that the plurality of "international organizations" simply contemplates the role that regional fishery organizations play in managing the by-catch issue.[237] Burke is not entirely persuaded by this later interpretation either, noting that "it seems anomalous to seek to restrict organizational co-operation to a single entity with a sustained record of ineffectiveness, due largely to the deficiencies of its own charter."[238] In subsequent writing, Burke reiterated that the language of Article 65 does not support the position that membership in a particular organization is required, and also that "work through" can be met through "attendance at annual meetings, collaboration in working out acceptable conservation measures, timely submission of information and data, recognition and acceptance of scientific findings, voluntary observance of prescribed conservation measures, coordination with enforcement schemes, and no doubt others."[239]

The contesting interpretations recognized by Professor Burke also emerge in the writings of Professor Ted McDorman, who has assessed Article 65 from the Canadian perspective and with the purpose of determining whether Article 65 creates a "'backdoor' entry for the IWC to regulate non-IWC members."[240] McDorman emphasizes that the first sentence of Article 65 is simply permissive, meaning "Article 65 does not impose on States a distinct regime for marine mammals, although coastal States may choose to implement one"; essentially international organizations become the appropriate mechanism through which marine mammal regulation occurs only when they are delegated regulatory authority by the coastal nations.[241] McDorman also contends that the second sentence of Article 65 falls short of expressly granting international organization authority over cetaceans within the EEZ.[242] Regarding the interaction between international organizations and coastal states contained in Article 65, McDorman argues that Article 65 strongly encourages coastal states to provide regulatory authority to an international organization, but falls short of requiring it.[243] In terms of the meaning of "appropriate international organizations," McDorman references the UN Oceans Division work provided in Law of the Sea Bulletin No. 31 to support the position that although the IWC likely currently occupies this role, it is not the only organization capable of doing so.[244] In light of the fact that Article 65 fails to provide interpretive criteria to aid in the determination of what makes an organization appropriate, McDorman suggests that in this absence, "[p]rovided that an international organization is engaged in constructive conservation, management, and study of cetaceans, that organization should be considered as potentially being an appropriate organization for the purposes of Article 65."[245] McDorman also turns his attention to the content of the duty to "work through" an appropriate organization, and suggests that this obligation to cooperate, as an action requiring good faith, can be met through membership in an organization, participation with the organization, or compliance with the organization's regulatory output (even if the state is not a member), but that requiring membership to meet this obligation is too onerous a burden.[246] He concludes that this duty to cooperate requires, at a minimum, "a positive contribution or sharing of experience, expertise, or information designed to positively assist the work of the international organization."[247] Further interpretive guidance exists in the context of the regulation of small cetaceans and in the context of proposals to improve the current regime.

A second category of interpretations emerges in the context of international regulation of small cetaceans and the need to regulate both large and small cetaceans at the international level. Professor Gillespie asserts that the IWC should assume primary responsibility for the regulation of small cetaceans (as complemented by regional efforts),[248] and that support for international regulation over small cetaceans can be found in Article 65 and Agenda 21 (which references the IWC, speaks also about "other cetaceans," and makes note of "other organizations").[249] Author Cynthia Carlson also favors a "comprehensive management system ... for all cetacean species,"[250] asserting that Articles 65 and 120 enable international organizations to "set minimum standards for the conservation and protection of marine mammals throughout their migratory ranges, both within and beyond the EEZ of a signatory state";[251] queries whether international organizations can permissibly regulate within EEZs without coastal state consent;[252] and posits that "neither article 65 nor any other 1982 Convention provision precludes a cooperative management scheme for cetaceans, small and large, by appropriate international and regional organizations, and coastal States."[253] A further but related circumstance in which academic interpretation of these Articles arises is in the context of improving the IWC and/or considering an alternative regime for the international conservation and management of marine mammals.

The main author of note who suggests that these Articles can be used to improve the efficacy of the ICRW/IWC is Kimberly Davis in her work titled *International Management of Cetaceans under the New Law of the Sea Convention.*[254] Here, Davis employs an interpretation of these Articles using Articles 31 and 32 of the VCLT in support of the position that these Articles present the opportunity to effectively enhance the existing regime.[255] Davis's application of the ordinary meaning approach first identifies the mandatory obligation to cooperate with respect to marine mammals and to "work through" the "appropriate international organizations."[256] The analysis then suggests that Article 65 "defers to the appropriate, existing organizations to impose uniform minimum conservation measures ... for individual species," and that the use of "the" in front of "appropriate international organizations" signifies that the IWC is the organization that is being contemplated.[257] This interpretation grapples with the content of the conservation standard contemplated in Article 65, suggesting that it is likely higher than the duty to simply avoid over-exploitation but not as high as a protectionist standard; however, it minimally creates "a duty to avoid the risk of extinction of cetacean species with a reasonable degree of scientific certainty."[258] With respect to the obligation to "work through" an international organization, Davis is satisfied that the content of this duty minimally requires membership and likely renders IWC regulations binding on UNCLOS states parties to the extent that they are necessary to achieve the conservation standard identified above.[259] In sum, Davis asserts that "[t]he proper interpretation of article 65, in light of the policies expressed by the Convention, and the only one which renders article 65 effective, is to place upon States which are party to the Convention and which would object to IWC regulation, the burden of showing that a regulation promulgated by the IWC is not necessary to meet the minimum conservation standard before the objection is allowed."[260]

Now having surveyed the various interpretations surrounding Articles 65 and 120 of UNCLOS, it is appropriate to focus on the relevance of these interpretations to the proposal being advanced.

6. Preferred Interpretation(s)

I share the opinion that Articles 65 and 120 represent "a measure of hope that whalers and protectionist states will find a way to compromise."[261] Taking into consideration the positions and interpretations presented above, and affording the ordinary meaning of the words primacy with consideration of supplementary material as appropriate, this author prefers the interpretation detailed below.

First, and at the highest level of consideration, Article 65 contemplates a framework conservation and management scheme that is separate and distinct from the default regulatory regime provided in Articles 61 and 62. This position is supported by the fact that the first sentence expressly states that "[n]othing in this Part" limits the ability of a coastal state or competent international organization to regulate, or indeed prohibit, marine mammal exploitation "more strictly than provided for in this Part." It logically follows that the principle of optimum utilization is not applicable to marine mammal management and conservation. Further, and still at the highest level of interpretation, Article 65 should properly be recognized as separate and distinct from Article 64, and it is not necessary to interpret the marine mammal provisions in light of the considerations owing to highly migratory species; indeed, this work has already indicated its support for removing cetaceans from Annex I of UNCLOS. The remainder of this interpretation will consider the relevant clause(s) of both Articles 65 and 120.

Regarding Article 65, the first task is to consider the jurisdictional clause. Having already established that marine mammals are exempt from the principle of optimum utilization, this clause acknowledges the capability of a coastal state to "prohibit, limit or regulate" marine mammal exploitation as desired. Still, it does not require coastal states to implement a certain regulatory standard; however, and when read in conjunction with the second clause, the argument can be made that coastal regulation should be undertaken in a manner that does not frustrate the duty to conserve marine mammals. With respect to the competence of an international organization to regulate marine mammals within the EEZ, I am persuaded that the inclusion of the words "as appropriate" reflects the position that coastal sovereign rights in the EEZ shall only be limited to the extent that the coastal state consents to the delegation of such authority, and that the most effective means of securing this consent is through a multilateral agreement that expressly confers an international organization with such regulatory authority. This author recognizes that this preferred interpretation is potentially problematic owing to the fact that states do currently recognize the competence of the IWC within their EEZs, and any movement away from this would be met with considerable opposition from conservationist nations owing to the possibility that withheld consent could expose many species to hunting. This discussion will now consider the cooperation/conservation clause of Article 65.

I acknowledge the ambiguity and uncertainty contained in the words "cooperate," "conservation," "work through," and "appropriate international organizations." Still, these words do not frustrate logical interpretation. The term "cooperate" should simply be understood as the promotion of coordinated effort toward rational conservation and management; indeed, it seems patently obvious in light of the modern threats identified in this work that ensuring the longevity of many marine mammal species is a task that requires international guidance and direction. The duty to cooperate is connected to "conservation," and should be understood both in light of this connection and the effect of the first sentence of Article 65. Specifically, conservation may indeed encapsulate a spectrum of interpretations ranging from limited exploitation to a commercial moratorium, and conservation will require regulation and direction. This conservation duty likely should be understood as something higher than simply an obligation to avoid over-exploitation, but at the same time it does not necessarily mandate a protectionist position that stops all utilitarian use of marine mammals. Conservation is not well defined in other international environmental treaties,[262] and this presents an opportunity to once again consider the content of conservation and to import into marine mammal maintenance the goals of ecosystem conservation and holistic management.

The content of the conservation duty is also connected to the obligation to "work through" international organizations for cetaceans. This author agrees that Article 65 should not be interpreted to bind non-IWC (or successor organization) members to the regulations that the organizations promulgate. Still, membership in the appropriate international organization should remain the goal to maximize the extent to which the international organization is able to gain jurisdictional competence and facilitate coordinated effort. Although voluntary adherence to international regulation should not be dissuaded, full membership and active dialogue in the regulatory process should be incentivized. With respect to "appropriate international organizations," a plain reading gives meaning to the plurality that was expressly negotiated, and also supports the position of the United States, and that of some academic commentators, that although the IWC currently qualifies as the most appropriately situated international organization to conserve, manage, and study cetaceans, this wording enables the emergence of a successor organization (as contemplated by the United States) that is able to accomplish the same goals. Further, although this section fails to define the criteria that make an international organization "appropriate," the argument can be made that a successor organization that addresses modern threats to cetaceans and is able to facilitate more effective cooperation is not only an appropriate international organization, it is the most appropriate forum. Finally, this author does not contest the role that other organizations, such as the FAO and UNEP (as identified by the UN Oceans Division) and/or regional fisheries organizations (as identified by Japan and in Chapter 17 of Agenda 21), can play in contributing to marine mammal conservation.

Article 120 simply represents the extension of applicability of Article 65 to the high seas. This extension imports the considerations provided in the analysis of Article 65 with the one important distinction being the fact that the appropriate international organization, as representative of collective state expression, is the prime source of regulation. In other words, the competence of an international organization is not subject to state consent on the high seas, and Article 120 should be read to reflect this.

What does this preferred interpretation mean for the feasibility of an implementing agreement? First, it is apparent that Articles 65 and 120 can support an implementing agreement that creates a new international commission that becomes the most appropriate international organization for the conservation of marine mammals in the twenty-first century. Second, even if Article 65 is now reflective of a principle of customary international law as asserted by the United States under the Clinton administration, the content of this duty remains uncertain and in need of elaboration. Moreover, the basic framework created by these Articles represents an opportunity for the international community to breathe life into these provisions in a manner that: (1) accords with basic principles of international law; (2) facilitates regional cooperation as necessary without compromising the primacy of international governance; (3) contemplates conservation as a holistic principle that engages marine mammals, their ecosystems, and our lethal and non-lethal uses of them; and (4) encourages the rule of law in EEZs and on the high seas. The essential task becomes the creation of a rational regime that maximizes the willingness of both pro-whaling and anti-whaling nations to join, and "work through," an international organization that strikes an appropriate compromise by focusing on commonalities rather than divergences. Having established that Articles 65 and 120 can, in fact, bear an implementing agreement that strives to replace the current ICRW/IWC regime, it is necessary for us to now consider treaty termination and the process of organization succession.

IV. TREATY TERMINATION AND INTERNATIONAL ORGANIZATION SUCCESSION

The final inquiry to be made prior to examining the content of the proposed implementing agreement and the functions of the new international commission is the legal basis for terminating the ICRW and the possibility of functional succession between international organizations, with the IWC being replaced by a new International Marine Mammal Commission. These are related but distinct questions that will be addressed in turn. This assessment considers treaty termination first and then proceeds to a discussion of the dissolution and succession of international organizations.

1. Treaty Termination

This analysis is interested in the termination of a multilateral treaty, being the instance where "the treaty ceases to exist for all States parties,"[263] and requires an analysis of two treaties, the first being the VCLT and the second the ICRW itself.

The VCLT, as a binding treaty in its own right and also, as generally reflective of customary international law, sets out a treaty termination regime in Section 3 ("Termination and Suspension of the Operation of Treaties") of Part V ("Invalidity, Termination and Suspension of the Operation of Treaties"), which starts with the acknowledgement in Article 54(a) that the termination of a treaty can occur in accordance with provisions contained in the treaty itself.[264] It follows from a state's ability to negotiate treaties that states are also able to contemplate, negotiate, and memorialize the "exit" provisions for the same regime.[265] For this reason it is necessary to consider the ICRW itself to determine whether it provides guidance or contemplates treaty termination among its Contracting Governments.

Article X of the ICRW provides the process for ratification and indicates where ratifications are to be deposited (Article X(3)) and how many ratifications are needed prior to the treaty entering into force (Article X(4)), but does not contemplate termination. Article XI is also relevant, as it provides the method by which a Contracting Government can withdraw from the Convention. The relevant portion of Article XI reads as follows:

> Any contracting Government may withdraw from this Convention on 30th June, of any year by giving notice on or before 1st January, of the same year to the depository Government, which upon receipt of such a notice shall at once communicate it to the other Contracting Governments. Any other Contracting Government may, in like manner, within one month of the receipt of a copy of such a notice from the depository Government give notice of withdrawal, so that the Convention shall cease to be in force on 30th June, of the same year with respect to the Government giving such notice of withdrawal.[266]

Although the above section guides Contracting Governments' ability to withdraw from the ICRW, the treaty is silent on how and/or when the entire treaty regime will/can come to an end. However, this does not mean that states are effectively stuck with this international regime as the VCLT provides other mechanisms through which treaty termination can be effected.

Regarding the VCLT, Article 54(b) provides that "[t]he termination of a treaty may take place ... at any time by consent of all the parties after consultation with the other contracting States." At its essence, this provision simply provides that all states parties can agree to no longer be bound by the treaty, or in other words can terminate the agreement. This unanimous consent to terminate is not dissimilar to what I previously indicated would be required to amend the ICRW, as evidenced by the one Protocol that was negotiated by all Contracting Governments in 1956. The VCLT also provides the following in Article 59:

Termination or suspension of the operation of a treaty implied by conclusion of a later treaty

1. A treaty shall be considered as terminated if all the parties to it conclude a later treaty relating to the same subject matter and:
    (*a*) it appears from the later treaty or is otherwise established that the parties intended that the matter should be governed by that treaty; or

(*b*) the provisions of the later treaty are so far incompatible with those of the earlier one that the two treaties are not capable of being applied at the same time.
2. The earlier treaty shall be considered as only suspended in operation if it appears from the later treaty or is otherwise established that such was the intention of the parties.[267]

In short, Article 59 contemplates the negotiation of a subsequent agreement, which either intends to replace the existing treaty or, in operation, as a result of incompatibility cannot exist simultaneously. Other mechanisms for treaty termination contemplated in the VCLT include: (1) reduction of the number of ratified nations below the minimum number required by the treaty (Article 55), (2) material breach (Article 60), (3) impossibility of performance (Article 61), and (4) emergence of a new preemptory norm of international law (Article 64). Indeed, one author has asserted that the argument could be made that treaty termination could be achieved through either the assertion of a fundamental change in circumstance (i.e., the world community is interested in the protection of whales rather than continued whaling) or a material breach of the treaty given the fact that it is no longer being used to regulate whaling.[268] Still, the above listed termination mechanisms are not relevant to the situation at hand, and in any event this author is of the opinion that Article 59 remains the most appropriate mechanism for termination, as the existence of a new agreement governing the same subject matter is a prerequisite for termination.

Despite the fact that the current ICRW/IWC regime is inadequate and ineffective in species coverage, issues coverage, and enforcement/compliance, it still represents an international regime that has considerable Contracting Government support, and through which biennial meetings continue to occur, resolutions are created, and relevant problems are discussed by states. In short, this flawed status quo is preferable to an international lacuna. Further, the new implementing agreement proposed in this work will have subject matter overlap, but will also embody subject matter expansion and evolution. Achieving the new treaty regime needed to implement an Article 59 termination of the ICRW requires successful negotiations leading to the conclusion of a new treaty by all parties to the current treaty. The successful negotiation, conclusion, and ratification of a new treaty regime represent a formidable task, but should not constitute the sort of obstacle that dissuades the necessary processes from commencing. Rather, a new treaty provides an opportunity to expressly state that, as between states parties, a new treaty regime replaces the ICRW. With this possibility in mind, I will now turn to a discussion of the successor international organization that this proposal suggests can replace the IWC.

2. Dissolution and Succession of International Organizations

As noted above, a related but distinct question is the ability to dissolve the IWC as an international organization and to then replace that organization with a new organization. One must remain cognizant of the practical realities of the theoretical proposal, and this is a particularly relevant consideration at this point in the discussion. The IWC is a fully functional international organization that has served as the operative organ of the ICRW since its inception, and it has a number of committees, subcommittees, working groups, and global partnerships, as well as employees, property, assets, and potential liabilities. Although practical matters should not deter the quest for a more effective commission that is alive and responsive to the modern threats facing marine mammals, they can also not be ignored.

Dissolution of an international organization can be understood as the "cessation of the existence of an organization."[269] Although it is true that the complete dissolution of an international organization may be rare, it is not impossible.[270] Dissolution is often a necessary precursor to international organization succession because a working regime may be frustrated by the existence of two competing organizations.[271] Another consideration surrounding the dissolution of international organizations is the identification of who, or what, assumes the functional responsibilities that rested with the dissolved international organization.[272] Robert Myers has identified five particular situations in which succession can occur: (1) the act of replacement whereby an existing organization is effectively replaced by another organization, (2) the act of absorption whereby an international organization that has a limited mandate is subsumed by a second international organization that has a wider mandate, (3) the act of merger between two (or more) international organizations, (4) the act of division whereby one international organization is divided or a subsidiary diverges from the parent organization, and (5) the act of functional transference whereby a limited number of tasks are granted to a different international organization.[273]

Beside these broad categorizations, only limited guidance regarding the rules governing dissolution and/or succession exists. As Ramses Wessel notes, "with regard to the legal basis for dissolution, the decision-making procedure, the form of a succession as well as the consequences, practice has not been able to contribute to the formation of customary rules which would apply in the absence of written rules."[274] Despite the absence of rules, it is understood that conventional succession involves the formation of a new international organization through the creation of a subsequent agreement,[275] and that succession can be facilitated if the membership remains the same.[276] The counterpoint to this is that both dissolution and succession can be rendered more difficult if the existing international organization has a well-developed and relatively independent existence from the agreement that created it.[277] It is prudent to consider these factors in light of the IWC.

The IWC exists pursuant to Article III of the ICRW. Article III contemplates: that it will be created by the Contracting Governments (Article III(1)); that it will be presided over by an elected Chairman and Vice-Chairman (Article III(2)); that it can create its own Rules of Procedure (Article III(2)); that it can select its own Secretary and staff (Article III(3)); that it can "set up, from among its own members and experts or advisers, such committees as it considers desirable to perform such functions as it may authorize" (Article III(4)); and that the IWC is responsible for convening meetings (Article III(8)). As well, and as previously discussed, the IWC is the decision-making body charged with making certain decisions via a simple majority, and decisions provided in Article V (including Schedule amendments) by three-fourths majority. The IWC has also come to coordinate and monetarily assist whale conservation efforts and help reduce other forms of mortality (i.e., ship-strikes and entanglement concerns) and indirect impacts associated with whale watching.[278] The IWC also has six subgroups, namely the Scientific Committee,

Conservation Committee, Finance and Administration Committee, Aboriginal Subsistence Whaling Sub-Committee, Infractions Sub-Committee, and the Working Group on Whale Killing Methods and Associated Welfare Issues.[279] Still, this proposal avoids the concern that dissolution will lead to a governance void, by recommending the creation of a succession commission that will build off the institutional lessons that the IWC has demonstrated, but also strives to craft it as an institution that is prepared to contribute toward addressing modern threats to all marine mammal species.

This section has demonstrated that it is possible to dismantle the current ICRW/IWC regime and replace it with an implementing agreement negotiated pursuant to UNCLOS that establishes a new international organization responsible for the global conservation of marine mammals. There are practical barriers to the creation of this regime, but these do not outweigh the potential benefits associated with a new, comprehensive response to marine mammal conservation.

V. JURISDICTIONAL LIMITS

The final criteria that must be contemplated before moving to the proposal are the jurisdictional limits that will inform the scope of the proposal. These limits should be understood in three ways. First, what limits inform the scope of species coverage advanced in the proposal. Second, what the zones of regulation in the ocean mean for the interaction between national and international regulation. Third, what the appropriate scope is for issue coverage.

Regarding species coverage, the first issue to consider is whether the new international treaty and international commission will purport to cover all marine mammal species or if it will be limited to cetaceans. The research surveyed indicates that considerable tension surrounds the fact that the ICRW/IWC does not currently regulate the take of small cetaceans. Therefore, it is imperative that the new regime addresses this obvious defect and extends the regulatory scope for contracting governments to all cetaceans. I argue that this does not constitute sufficient coverage of species. Rather, and recalling that Articles 65 and 120 require international cooperation for the conservation of all marine mammals, the proper application of ecosystem-based management and the precautionary principle necessitates the inclusion of all marine mammal species in this regulatory regime as far as the other two jurisdictional considerations allow. The review of current scientific literature found in Chapter 4 suggests that modern threats to marine mammals are not species-specific, and that comprehensive conservation and management should err on the side of overinclusion. The discussion of the ethics of continued marine mammal hunting found in Chapter 3 highlights the importance of education, training, technology transfer, and development of best-practice guidance. Taken together, the goal of broad species coverage does not mean all species must be approached in the same manner (i.e., that the commercial take of cetaceans should be regulated in the same manner as the commercial take of pinnipeds). Further, although it may be appropriate to provide for regulation of certain marine mammal species, such as highly migratory cetacean species, it is possible that considerable progress toward the proper conservation and/or humane treatment of others can occur through the development of best-practice guidelines or recommendations.

Regarding jurisdictional interaction between coastal states and international organizations, this work acknowledges the nine maritime zones that currently exist: (1) internal waters (Article 8), (2) the territorial seas (Article 2), (3) the contiguous zone (Article 33), (4) the continental shelf (Articles 76 and 77), (5) the exclusive fishing zone, (6) the EEZ (Articles 55 and 56), (7) archipelagic waters (Article 49), (8) the Area (Articles 133 and 134), and (9) the high seas (Articles 86 and 89).[280] The relevant maritime zones for this discussion include internal waters, the territorial sea, the exclusive economic zone, the archipelagic waters, and the high seas. Internal waters, the territorial sea, and archipelagic waters are the subject of full regulatory control for coastal states, subject to the right of innocent passage through the territorial sea (Article 17) and innocent passage or archipelagic sea lanes passage through archipelagic waters (Articles 52 and 53).[281] States also have sovereign rights in the EEZ and may exercise regulatory authority so long as they do not offend the applicable management scheme. Therefore, the principle guiding the division of regulatory authority in these zones is such that coastal state sovereignty shall be paramount unless the coastal state has consented to the exercise of authority by an international organization, which is appropriate because "a coastal State remains free to exercise its sovereign rights by delegation authority to an international body to make decisions regarding marine mammals that might otherwise be within coastal jurisdiction."[282] It is interesting to note that the ICRW indicates in Article I(2) that it applies to "all waters in which whaling is prosecuted by such factory ships, land stations and whale catchers."[283] Although Article 311(2) of UNCLOS indicates that it does not "alter the rights and obligations" arising from "other agreements compatible with this Convention," this compatibility is unsettled, and although it may be preferable to account for jurisdictional considerations in a manner consistent with UNCLOS moving forward, it should be noted that any derogation from the current jurisdiction afforded to the IWC by the ICRW is likely to be met with considerable opposition from those states primarily concerned with conservation.[284] With respect to the high seas, Article 65 provides international organizations with authority to take primary responsibility over marine mammal conservation, and membership in such an organization should be required for a nation to engage in activities that impact marine mammal conservation.

The third jurisdictional issue that must be addressed is that of issue scoping, namely the issues that will be covered by the proposed draft implementing agreement. This work has already presented the case for expanding issue coverage beyond direct exploitation and take, given the implications of other direct and indirect modern threats. Therefore, the proposal contained in the subsequent chapters seeks to address, in a holistic fashion, the entire spectrum of modern threats, to the maximum extent practicable and in a manner that incorporates the tools necessary to achieve ecosystem-based management. Further, the proposal attempts to remedy the shortfalls of the current ICRW/IWC regime by proposing an enforcement/compliance regime that utilizes vessel inspection, regional implementation as necessary, best-practice guidelines, and recommendations regarding issues that fall primarily within the jurisdiction of coastal states, and recourse to peaceful dispute resolution through recognized mechanisms. Taken together, these three jurisdictional considerations establish the boundaries and guiding principles for the regime proposed in this work.

VI. CONCLUSION

This chapter has presented the legal case in support of a new international law regime for the conservation of marine mammals by investigating and assessing various alternatives to the status quo, including the possibility of improving the ICRW/IWC, transitioning to a soft law approach, increasing reliance on bilateral and/or regional agreements, focusing on national regulation, or creating a new international regime that is either negotiated external to the UN or brought within the auspices of the UN as an implementing agreement pursuant to UNCLOS. Accordingly, this assessment identifies the negotiation of an implementing agreement pursuant to UNCLOS as the most attractive option. A survey of the drafting history of Articles 65 and 120 as well as an analysis of their interpretation by states and academics produces a preferred interpretation and the conclusion that these Articles can support implementation by way of a new agreement.

NOTES

1. William T. Burke, The New International Law of Fisheries: UNCLOS 1982 and Beyond, 267–77 (1994) ["Burke, UNCLOS 1982 and Beyond"].
2. Patricia Birnie, *The Role of Law in Protecting Marine Mammals*, 15(3) AMBIO 137, 137 (1986) ["Birnie, *The Role of Law*"].
3. I subscribe to the perspective of international law that recognizes it as a distinct legal system. Although reliant on national implementation, the process of which varies by source of law and by country, this work emphasizes the ability of international law to foster coherence and consistency across jurisdictions and to enhance legal order.
4. 10 Dec. 1982, 21 I.L.M. 1261, 1833 U.N.T.S. 3 ["UNCLOS"].
5. 2 Dec. 1946, 62 Stat. 1716, 161 U.N.T.S. 74 ["ICRW"].
6. *See* 1 Patricia W. Birnie, International Regulation of Whaling: From Conservation of Whaling to Conservation of Whales and Regulation of Whale-Watching 549–74 (1985) (detailing three attempts to change the whaling regime and the failure of each, concluding "that the present convention and the international rules concerning treaty interpretation already provide sufficient mechanisms for the changes required if the political will to use them exists or can be stimulated").
7. *See* Marie Clara Maffei, *The International Convention for the Regulation of Whaling* 305 (1997); *see also* Adrienne M. Ruffle, *Resurrecting the International Whaling Commission: Suggestions to Strengthen the Conservation Effort*, 27 Brook. J. Int'l L. 639, 640 (2001–2002); *see also* Steven Freeland & Julie Drysdale, *Co-operation or Chaos?—Article 65 of United Nations Convention on the Law of the Sea and the Future of the International Whaling Commission*, 2 Macquarie J. Int'l & Comp. Envtl. L. 1, 4 (2005) ["Freeland & Drysdale"]; Anastasia Telesetsky & Seokwoo Lee, *After* Whaling in the Antarctic: *Amending Article VIII to Fix a Broken Treaty Regime*, 30 Int'l J. Marine & Coastal L. 700 (2015).
8. Robert L. Friedheim, *Fixing the Whaling Regime: A Proposal*, in Toward a Sustainable Whaling Regime 311 (Robert L. Friedheim ed., 2001) ["Friedheim, *Fixing the Whaling Regime*"].
9. *Id.* at 314.
10. *Id.*

11. *Id.* at 316.
12. *Id.* at 322–23.
13. *Id.* at 320–23.
14. *Id.* at 324–25.
15. *Id.* at 326–27.
16. *Id.* at 325–26.
17. *Id.* at 326 (citing to Oran R. Young et al., *Subsistence, Sustainability, and Sea Mammals: Reconstructing the International Whaling Regime*, 23 OCEAN COAST. MANAGE. 117, 117–27 (1994)).
18. *Id.* at 329–30.
19. *Id.* at 331.
20. M.J. Bowman, *"Normalizing" the International Convention for the Regulation of Whaling*, 29 MICH. J.I.L. 293, 427 (2008) ["Bowman"].
21. *Id.* at 486.
22. *Id.* at 459.
23. *Id.*
24. *Id.* at 460–62.
25. *Id.* at 463–69.
26. *Id.* at 473.
27. *Id.*
28. *Id.*
29. *Id.*
30. *Id.* at 474.
31. *Id.*
32. *Id.* at 449–51 (providing a summary of the relevant provisions of the Convention on Biological Diversity, 5 June 1992, 31 I.L.M. 818, 1760 U.N.T.S. 79. These include: (1) an obligation for Contracting Parties to the CBD to cooperate for the sustainable use and conservation of biological resources in areas beyond national control (Art. 5); (2) to create management strategies for those species that have experienced over-exploitation (Art. 8(1)); and (3) an indication that it will take precedence when another regime seriously threatens biological diversity (Art. 22(1))).
33. *Id.* at 475–76.
34. *Id.* at 478.
35. *Id.* at 485.
36. 23 May 1969, 1155 U.N.T.S. 331, 8 ILM 679 ["Vienna Convention"].
37. Bowman, *supra* note 20, at 497.
38. *Id.* at 310–11.
39. *See* Statute of the International Court of Justice, 59 Stat. 1031, 39 AJIL Supp. 215 (1945); *see* PATRICIA BIRNIE, ALAN BOYLE & CATHERINE REDGWELL, INTERNATIONAL LAW & THE ENVIRONMENT 34 (3d ed. 2009) ["BIRNIE ET AL."] (providing an introduction to soft law).
40. Bowman, *supra* note 20, at 311.
41. BIRNIE ET AL., *supra* note 39, at 34.
42. *Id.*
43. C.M. Chinkin, *The Challenge of Soft Law: Development and Change in International Law*, 38(4) INT'L & COMP. L.Q. 850, 860 (1989).
44. *Id.*
45. BIRNIE ET AL., *supra* note 39, at 37.

46. *Id.* at 35; United Nations Conference on Environment and Development, Rio de Janiero, Braz., June 3–14, 1992, *Rio Declaration on Environment and Development*, U.N. Doc. A/CONF.151/26/Rev.1 (Vol. 1), Annex I (Aug. 12, 1992) ["Rio Declaration"]; *see* United Nations Conference on Environment and Development, Rio de Janeiro, Braz., June 3–14, 1992, *Agenda 21*, U.N. Doc A/CONF.151/26 (Aug. 12, 1992) ["Agenda 21"]; Food and Agriculture Organization of the United Nations, *FAO Code of Conduct for Responsible Fisheries*, FAO Doc. 95/20/Rev/1 (1995).

47. International Whaling Commission, *General Principles for Whalewatching* (1996), http://iwc.int/wwguidelines#manage.

48. *See* W. Michael Reisman, *The Democratization of Contemporary International Law-Making Processes and the Differentiation of Their Application*, in DEVELOPMENTS OF INTERNATIONAL LAW IN TREATY MAKING 15, 19 (Rüdiger Wolfrum & Volker Röben eds., 2005)(reflecting that "[i]n a bygone era, international law was defined . . . as law between states. As states were the only active 'subjects' of international law, a corollary of the definition was that only states made law, whether explicitly through agreements, or implicitly, through their cumulative behavior." This passage proceeds to note that there are currently a range of actors involved in international law and policy, including "national and international officials, the elites of non-governmental organizations running the gamut from those concerned with wealth through to those concerned with religious rectitude, transnational business entities, gangs and terrorists, and individuals"); *see also* Don K. Anton, *"Treaty Congestion" in Contemporary International Law*, in ROUTLEDGE HANDBOOK OF INTERNATIONAL ENVIRONMENTAL LAW ANU 651 (2013) (indicating at 652 that there was a rapid increase in international environmental treaties during the 1970s to 1990s, and at 653 that to a certain extent this progression has slowed since 2002. Still, the view taken in this work seems to be that treaty law still represents an effective mechanism through which norms can be created and enforced, and that recent experiences should not dissuade the contemplation of new treaty law in the area of international environmental law and oceans law).

49. *See* E. Franckx, *Regional Marine Environment Protection Regimes in the Context of UNCLOS*, 13 INT'L J. MARINE & COASTAL L. 307, 313 (1998).

50. *See* A. Willock & M. Lack, *Follow the Leader: Learning from Experiences and Best Practice in Regional Fisheries Management Organizations*, WWF INTERNATIONAL & TRAFFIC INTERNATIONAL 1 (2006).

51. David S. Caron, *The International Whaling Commission and the North Atlantic Marine Mammal Commission: The Institutional Risks of Coercion in Consensual Structures*, 89 AM. J. INT'L L. 154, 164 (1995) (paraphrasing the comments made at the inaugural NAMMCO meeting).

52. James A.R. Nafziger, *Global Conservation and Management of Marine Mammals*, 17 SAN DIEGO L. REV. 591, 597 (1979–1980) ["Nafziger"] (Nafziger notes that other regional agreements specifically addressing, or at least touching on marine mammals, include the Antarctic Treaty, the Convention for the Conservation of Antarctic Seals, and the Agreement on the Conservation of Polar Bears).

53. *See* Marji Prideaux, *Discussion of a Regional Agreement for Small Cetacean Conservation in the Indian Ocean*, 32 CAL. W. INT'L L.J. 211, 234–35 (2001–2002) (describing the development and functioning of these agreements) ["Prideaux"]; *see* Alexander Gillespie, *Small Cetaceans, International Law and the International Whaling Commission*, 2 MELB. J. INT'L L. 257, 289 (2001) ["Gillespie, *Small*

Cetaceans"] (noting that regional organizations have come to play an important role in protecting small cetaceans, and that both anti-whaling and pro-whaling nations tend to agree that they occupy this important function).

54. BIRNIE ET AL., *supra* note 39, at 392.
55. Prideaux, *supra* note 53, at 232.
56. Nafziger, *supra* note 52, at 596.
57. United Nations, *Resumed Review Conference on the Agreement Relating to the Conservation and Management of Straddling Fish Stocks and Highly Migratory Fish Stocks*, UNITED NATIONS DEPARTMENT OF PUBLIC INFORMATION 3 (May, 2010), http://www.un.org/Depts/los/convention_agreements/reviewconf/FishStocks_EN_F.pdf.
58. Gillespie, *Small Cetaceans, supra* note 53, at 303.
59. William T. Burke, *A New Whaling Agreement and International Law*, in TOWARD A SUSTAINABLE WHALING REGIME 51, 59 (Robert L. Friedheim ed., 2001) ["Burke, *A New Whaling Agreement*"].
60. Gillespie, *Small Cetaceans, supra* note 53, at 282.
61. Burke, *A New Whaling Agreement, supra* note 59, at 51.
62. *Id.* at 52.
63. BURKE, UNCLOS 1982 AND BEYOND, *supra* note 1, at 275 (noting that evidence for the duty to conserve marine living resources on the high seas can be found in many places, including: (1) the *Fisheries Jurisdiction Case (UK v. Iceland)*, 1974 ICJ Rep. 3, where the majority noted at paragraph 31 that "It is one of the advances in maritime international law, resulting from the intensification of fishing, that the former laissez-faire treatment of the living resources of the sea in the high seas has been replaced by a recognition of a duty to have due regard to the rights of other States and the needs of conservation for the benefit of all"; and (2) Article 117 of UNCLOS, which states that "All States have the duty to take, or to cooperate with other States in taking, such measures for their respective nationals as may be necessary for the conservation of the living resources of the high seas").
64. BURKE, UNCLOS 1982 AND BEYOND, *supra* note 1, at 277.
65. *Id.*
66. *Id.*
67. *See* Cynthia E. Carlson, *The International Regulation of Small Cetaceans*, 21(3) SAN DIEGO L. REV. 578, 618 (1984) ["Carlson"] (stating that "[t]hus, regardless of whale size or geographical location, the real issue is whether an effective international regime can be developed, agreed to, and implemented for the regulation of these 'other' cetaceans, or cetacean species currently without regulatory protection that might be in need of it."); *see* Patricia Birnie, *Small Cetaceans and the International Whaling Commission*, 10 GEO. INT'L ENVTL. L. REV. 1, 25 (1997–1998) ["Birnie, *Small Cetaceans*"] (stating that "[w]hile the IWC can study, advise and make recommendations, the IWC cannot control incidental catch and by-catch of small cetaceans. This is probably the greatest threat to their survival. Power to control this vests with the tuna and other fisheries commissions. Unfortunately the IWC does not have the power to regulate pollution and the great variety of other threats that degrade the habitat of small cetaceans . . ."); *see generally* Gillespie, *Small Cetaceans, supra* note 53.
68. *See* United Nations, *United Nations System Directory*, UNITED NATIONS SYSTEM, http://www.unsystem.org/ (last visited June 17, 2015) (which provides a representation of the United Nations system).

69. United Nations, *About the UN*, UNITED NATIONS, http://www.un.org/en/about-un/index.html (last visited June 17, 2015).
70. R. Gambell, *International Management of Whales and Whaling: An Historical Review of the Regulation of Commercial and Aboriginal Subsistence Whaling*, 48(2) ARCTIC 97, 98–99 (1993).
71. United Nations Environment Program, *About UNEP*, http://www.unep.org/Documents.Multilingual/Default.asp?DocumentID=43&ArticleID=3301&l=en (last visited June 17, 2015) (noting that UNEP "established in 1972, is the voice for the environment within the United Nations system. UNEP acts as a catalyst, advocate, educator and facilitator to promote the wise use and sustainable development of the global environment. To accomplish this, UNEP works with a wide range of partners, including United Nations entities, international organizations, national governments, non-governmental organizations, the private sector and civil society").
72. G.A. Res. 67/78, at 2, U.N. Doc. A/RES/67/78 (Apr. 18, 2013).
73. Agenda 21, *supra* note 46; *see* BIRNIE ET AL., *supra* note 39, at 52 (describing Agenda 21 as "a programme of action covering many issues, including climate change, deforestation, desertification and protection of the oceans. Although not legally binding it is potentially relevant to interpretation of treaties and other instruments adopted in accordance with its provisions").
74. Agenda 21, *supra* note 46, at art. 17.1.
75. G.A. Res. U.N. Doc. A/RES/66/288 (July 27, 2012).
76. *Id.* at para. 159.
77. U.N. Charter art. 2, para 2.
78. Rio Declaration, *supra* note 46.
79. *See* UNCLOS, *supra* note 4, at art. 1(4) (also, at Annexes (Annex I ("Highly Migratory Species"), Annex II (Commission on the Limits of the Continental Shelf), Annex III ("Basic Conditions of Prospecting, Exploration and Exploitation"), Annex IV ("Statute of the Enterprise"), Annex V ("Conciliation"), Annex VI ("Statute of the International Tribunal for the Law of the Sea"), Annex VII ("Arbitration"), Annex VIII ("Special Arbitration"), and Annex IX ("Participation by International Organizations")).
80. United Nations Division for Ocean Affairs and Law of the Sea, *Commission on the Limits of the Continental Shelf: Purpose, Functions and Sessions*, http://www.un.org/Depts/los/clcs_new/commission_purpose.htm#Purpose (last visited June 17, 2015).
81. *Id.*
82. United Nations Division for Ocean Affairs and Law of the Sea, *Trust Fund for the Purpose of Facilitating the Preparation of Submissions to the Commission on the Limits of the Continental Shelf for Developing States, in Particular the Least Developed Countries and Small Island Developing States, and Compliance with Article 76 of the United Nations Convention on the Law of the Sea* (Dec. 11, 2009), http://www.un.org/Depts/los/clcs_new/trust_fund_article76.htm.
83. *See* Tommy T.B. Koh, *A Constitution for the Oceans* (adapted from remarks made between Dec. 6 and 11, 1982), http://www.un.org/Depts/los/convention_agreements/texts/koh_english.pdf.
84. UNITED NATIONS CONVENTION ON THE LAW OF THE SEA: A COMMENTARY VOLUME I, 18 (Myron Nordquist ed., 1985) ["UNCLOS COMMENTARY VOL. I"] (noting that the Second Committee was tasked with the negotiation of issues of general applicability to the law of the sea, including the EEZ and territorial sea).

85. *Id.* at 20.
86. *Id.* at 21.
87. *Id.* at 17.
88. *See generally* UNCLOS COMMENTARY VOL. I, *supra* note 84; UNITED NATIONS CONVENTION ON THE LAW OF THE SEA: A COMMENTARY VOLUME II (Myron Nordquist ed., 1993) ["UNCLOS COMMENTARY VOL. II"]; *see generally* UNITED NATIONS CONVENTION ON THE LAW OF THE SEA: A COMMENTARY VOLUME III (Myron Nordquist ed., 1995); *see generally* UNITED NATIONS CONVENTION ON THE LAW OF THE SEA: A COMMENTARY VOLUME IV (Myron Nordquist ed., 1991); UNITED NATIONS CONVENTION ON THE LAW OF THE SEA: A COMMENTARY VOLUME V (Myron Nordquist ed., 1989).
89. *See* DONALD R. ROTHWELL & TIM STEPHENS, THE INTERNATIONAL LAW OF THE SEA 20 (2d ed. 2016) ["ROTHWELL & STEPHENS"].
90. *Id.* at 18.
91. 1836 U.N.T.S. 3, DOC. A/RES.48263, http://treaties.un.org/doc/Publication/UNTS/Volume%201836/volume-1836-I-31364-English.pdf ["1994 Implementing Agreement"].
92. *Id.* at 19.
93. 4 Dec. 1995, 34 I.L.M. 1542, 2167 U.N.T.S. 3 ["UN Fish Stocks Agreement"].
94. Greenpeace, *Suggested Draft High Seas Implementing Agreement for the Conservation and Management of the Marine Environment in Areas beyond National Jurisdiction*, GREENPEACE INTERNATIONAL (2011), http://www.greenpeace.org/international/Global/international/publications/oceans/2011/Greenpeace%20draft%20Implementing%20Agreement%2013Feb2008.pdf ["Greenpeace Suggested Draft"].
95. International Union for the Conservation of Nature, *IUCN Launches Four Online Papers to Inform International Discussions on Marine Biodiversity in ABNJ*, IUCN (Apr. 30, 2008), http://iucn.org/news_homepage/news_by_date/?870/IUCN-launches-four-online-papers-to-inform-international-discussions-on-marine-biodiversity-in-ABNJ (specifically, this webpage links to each online paper, and the one of most interest is Sharelle Hart, *IUCN Environmental Policy and Law Papers Online—Marine Series No. 4: Elements of a Possible Implementation Agreement to UNCLOS for the Conservation and Sustainable Use of Marine Biodiversity in Areas beyond National Jurisdiction* (2008), https://cmsdata.iucn.org/downloads/iucn_marine_paper_4.pdf ["Hart"]).
96. The Pew Environmental Group, *Potential Elements of an UNCLOS Implementing Agreement*, PEW CHARITABLE TRUSTS, http://www.pewtrusts.org/en/about/news-room/press-releases/2012/04/25/potential-elements-of-an-unclos-implementing-agreement (last visited June 18, 2015) ["Pew Proposal"].
97. *See generally* United Nations Divisions for Ocean Affairs and Law of the Sea, *Ad-hoc Open-Ended Working Group to Study Issues Relating to the Conservation and Sustainable Use of Marine Biological Diversity beyond Areas of National Jurisdiction*, DOLAS (Mar. 13, 2015), http://www.un.org/depts/los/biodiversityworkinggroup/biodiversityworkinggroup.htm (which provides information relating to the most current discussions at the United Nations relating to this issue); *see also* Group of 77 and China, *Submission by the Group of 77 and China for the Compilation Document of the United Nations Conference on Sustainable Development* (2012), RIO + 20 UNITED NATIONS CONFERENCE ON SUSTAINABLE DEVELOPMENT, http://www.uncsd2012.org/content/documents/399UNCSD%20

RIO-%20complete%20submission-final.pdf (wherein the Group of 77 and China also lend support to a new implementing agreement pursuant to UNCLOS).
98. Hart, *supra* note 95, at 9.
99. ROTHWELL & STEPHENS, *supra* note 89, at 14.
100. *See* Ernst Z. Bowers & Gregory B. Poling, *Advancing the National Interests of the United States: Ratification of the Law of the Sea*, CSIS: CENTER FOR STRATEGIC & INTERNATIONAL STUDIES (May 25, 2012), http://csis.org/publication/advancing-national-interests-united-states-ratification-law-sea.
101. ROTHWELL & STEPHENS, *supra* note 89, at 18.
102. *Id.*
103. *Id.* (citing to Deep Seabed Hard Mineral Resources Act 1980; Deep Sea Mining (Temporary Provisions) Act 1981; 1984 Provisional Understanding regarding Deep Seabed Matters between Belgium, France, the Federal Republic of Germany, Italy, Japan, the Netherlands, the United Kingdom, and the United States, *Basic Documents* No. 38).
104. *Id.; see* G.A. Res. 48/263, A/RES/48/263 (Aug. 17, 1994).
105. ROTHWELL & STEPHENS, *supra* note 89, at 18–19 (citing to the 1994 Implementing Agreement, *supra* note 91).
106. *Id.* at 18–19.
107. *Id.* at 19.
108. United Nations Division for Ocean Affairs and Law of the Sea, *Chronological Lists of Ratifications of, Accessions and Successions to the Convention and the Related Agreements as at 3 October 2014*, http://www.un.org/Depts/los/reference_files/chronological_lists_of_ratifications.htm ["*Chronological Lists of Ratifications*"].
109. R.R. CHURCHILL & A.V. LOWE, THE LAW OF THE SEA 294 (3d ed. 1999) ["CHURCHILL & LOWE"].
110. *Id.* at 305.
111. *Id.*
112. UNCLOS, *supra* note 4.
113. CHURCHILL & LOWE, *supra* note 109, at 294 (noting that this position is bolstered by international jurisprudence, such as *North Sea Continental Shelf*, [1969] *ICJ Rep.* 1, at 47 and *Fisheries Jurisdiction*, [1974] *ICJ Rep.* 3, at 32.)
114. *Id.* at 305.
115. ROTHWELL & STEPHENS, *supra* note 89, at 20.
116. *Id.* at 19–20.
117. *Chronological Lists of Ratifications*, *supra* note 108.
118. *See* ROTHWELL & STEPHENS, *supra* note 89, at 20; *see also* CHURCHILL & LOWE, *supra* note 109, at 308–10.
119. G.A. Res. 65/37, ¶ 163, U.N. Doc. A/RES/65/37 (Mar. 17, 2011).
120. *See* G.A. Res. 66/231, ¶¶ 166–167, U.N. Doc. A/RES/66/231 (Apr. 5, 2012).
121. United Nations Division for Ocean Affairs and Law of the Sea, Ad-hoc *Open Ended Informal Working Group to Study Issues Relating to the Conservation and Sustainable Use of Marine Biological Diversity beyond Areas of National Jurisdiction*, http://www.un.org/Depts/los/biodiversityworkinggroup/biodiversityworkinggroup.htm (last visited July 2, 2015).
122. United Nations Division for Ocean Affairs and Law of the Sea, Ad-hoc *Open Ended Informal Working Group to Study Issues Relating to the Conservation and Sustainable Use of Marine Biological Diversity beyond Areas of National*

123. *Letter Dated 13 February 2015 from the Co-Chairs of the Ad Hoc Open-Ended Informal Working Group to the President of the General Assembly*, Annex ¶ 1(e), U.N. Doc. A/60/706 (Feb. 13, 2015).
124. *Id.* ¶ 1(f).
125. *Greenpeace Suggested Draft*, *supra* note 94, at 2.
126. Hart, *supra* note 95, at 9.
127. *Id.*; *see also* IUCN World Conservation Congress [IUCN-WCC], *Implementing Conservation and Sustainable Management of Marine Biodiversity in Areas beyond National Jurisdiction* 3, IUCN WCC-2012-Res-074-EN (Sept. 5–15, 2012) (calling upon the international community to negotiate an implementing agreement pursuant to UNCLOS to address biodiversity beyond areas of national jurisdiction).
128. Pew Proposal, *supra* note 96, at 1.
129. JAMES HARRISON, MAKING THE LAW OF THE SEA: A STUDY IN THE DEVELOPMENT OF INTERNATIONAL LAW 113 (2011).
130. *Id.* at 114.
131. *Id.* at 113.
132. *See* European Commission, *Facts and Figures of the Common Fisheries Policy: Basic Statistical Data* 4 (2012), http://ec.europa.eu/fisheries/documentation/publications/pcp_en.pdf (defining "maximum sustainable yield" as the "optimal value of catches that can be taken each year without threatening the future reproductive capacity of a fish stock").
133. Note that optimum utilization differs from maximum sustainable yield in that the prescribed quota can be altered on the basis of relevant economic and environmental factors.
134. *See* UNCLOS COMMENTARY VOL. II, *supra* note 88, at xiii (which indicates that this effort intends to be a "comprehensive, objective multi-volume analysis of the development of the 1982 United Nations Convention on the Law of the Sea").
135. Patricia Forkan, *The Legislative History and Interpretation of Article 65 of the Law of the Sea Convention*, Testimony Submitted Oct. 14, 2003, http://www.hsi.org/assets/pdfs/HSUS_testimony_LOS.pdf ["Forkan"].
136. Telephone Interview with Professor John Norton Moore, Walter L. Brown Professor of Law and Director, Center for Oceans Law and Policy, University of Virginia, School of Law (June 10, 2013) ["Professor Moore Interview"].
137. UNIVERSITY OF VIRGINIA, SCHOOL OF LAW: FACULTY, http://www.law.virginia.edu/lawweb/Faculty.nsf/FHPbI/1192475(last visited Feb. 17, 2016).
138. Professor Moore Interview, *supra* note 136.
139. UNCLOS COMMENTARY VOL. I, *supra* note 84, at xxvi.
140. UNCLOS COMMENTARY VOL. II, *supra* note 88, at 660.
141. Forkan, *supra* note 135, at 2–3.
142. *Id.* at 3.
143. Professor Moore Interview, *supra* note 136 (describing the history of the negotiation of Article 64, which is also useful to consider for the purpose of this discussion. Moore indicates that it makes intellectual sense to manage highly migratory fish on a stock-by-stock basis throughout their range given the need to manage beyond areas of national jurisdiction. Politically, the negotiation of Article 64 was informed by the problem of creeping fishing jurisdiction claims

by certain South American countries, which would arrest and detain American fishermen and their vessels in areas that these nations claimed to have exclusive jurisdiction over. The American response was to allow the State Department to cease providing economic or military assistance to these nations. The president was able to utilize a national security exception to the imposition of such restrictions, which was often employed. Early efforts to resolve these tensions by the U.S. Department of State Fisheries Office included a proposed bilateral agreement between the United States and Ecuador, which eventually fell through. This issue was taken over by the U.S. Department of State Law of the Sea Office, which opted to pursue a comprehensive approach through the Law of the Sea negotiations that would provide for regional organizations, environmental standards, allocations based on a five-year moving average, and a regional approach to the tuna-dolphin problem. The United States led this negotiation, and it was working well and appeared to have a broad-base of support until the U.S. Department of State Fisheries Office was given control again, negotiations were dropped, and the composition of the American Law of the Sea delegation was significantly altered. As a result, Article 64 was produced, which required subsequent negotiation to be given effect).

144. *Id.*
145. *Id.*
146. *See* Kimberly S. Davis, *International Management of Cetaceans under the New Law of the Sea Convention*, 3 B.U. INT'L L.J. 477, 500 (1985) ["Davis"] (noting that marine mammals had previously been subsumed under the draft article addressing highly migratory species); *see* UNCLOS COMMENTARY VOL. II, *supra* note 88, at 600.
147. UNCLOS COMMENTARY VOL. II, *supra* note 88, at 660.
148. *Id.* at 661.
149. *Id.*
150. Robbins Barstow, *The U.S. and the Law of The Sea*, 13 (3) WHALES ALIVE! (2004), http://csiwhalesalive.org/newsletters/csi04303.html.
151. Professor Moore Interview, *supra* note 136.
152. *Id.*
153. UNCLOS COMMENTARY VOL. II, *supra* note 88, at 660.
154. *Id.*
155. *Id.* at 662.
156. *Id.* at 660.
157. *Id.* at 662.
158. Forkan, *supra* note 135, at 3.
159. *Id.* at 4.
160. *Id.* at 4–5 (citing to Letter from the Honorable Elliott L. Richardson, Ambassador at Large, and Special Representative of the President to the Law of the Sea Conference, U.S. Mission to the United Nations, to Patricia Forkan, Human Society International (Apr. 29, 1980)).
161. *Id.* at 5 (citing to Committee II of UNCLOS III, *Deliberations on Article 65 Amendment*, Floor Statements (Mar. 21, 1980)).
162. *Id.*
163. Case concerning Territorial Dispute (Libyan Arab Jamahiriya/Chad), 1994 I.C.J. 6, ¶ 41 (Feb. 3) (evidencing the fact that the ICJ believes that Articles 31 and 32 are customary international law); Vienna Convention, *supra* note 36.

164. See Ted L. McDorman, *Canada and Whaling: An Analysis of Article 65 of the Law of the Sea Convention*, 29 OCEAN DEV. & INT'L L. 179, 181 (1998) ["McDorman"].
165. UNCLOS, *supra* note 4, at art. 65.
166. McDorman, *supra* note 164, at 182.
167. UNCLOS, *supra* note 4, at art. 65.
168. *Id.* at art. 120.
169. Freeland & Drysdale, *supra* note 7, at 18.
170. CHURCHILL & LOWE, *supra* note 109, at 317.
171. Carlson, *supra* note 67, at 605.
172. Davis, *supra* note 145, at 505 (Davis also suggests at 508–09 that this framework language demonstrates a willingness to defer difficult decisions to a later time).
173. Patricia Birnie, *Marine Mammals: Exploiting the Ambiguities of Article 65 of the Convention on the Law of the Sea and Related Provisions: Practice under the International Convention for the Regulation of Whaling*, in THE LAW OF THE SEA: PROGRESS AND PROSPECTS 261, 261 (David Freestone, Richard Barnes & David M. Ong eds., 2006) ["Birnie, PROGRESS AND PROSPECTS"].
174. *Id.* at 269.
175. *See* Joanna Matanich, *A Treaty Comes of Age for the Ancient Ones: Implications of the Law of the Sea for the Regulation of Whaling*, 8 INT'L LEGAL PERSP. 37, 61 (1996) ["Matanich"]; *see also* Davis, *supra* note 146, at 515.
176. Nafziger, *supra* note 52, at 608.
177. *Id.*
178. *Id.*
179. *See* Birnie, PROGRESS AND PROSPECTS, *supra* note 173, at 273.
180. *See* Nafziger, *supra* note 52, at 608; *see* McDorman, *supra* note 164, at 182.
181. *See* Davis, *supra* note 146, at 515; *see* McDorman, *supra* note 164, at 164; *see* Carlson, *supra* note 67.
182. *See* McDorman, *supra* note 164, at 182; *see also* YOSHIFUMI TANAKA, THE INTERNATIONAL LAW OF THE SEA 229–30 (2012) ["TANAKA"] (summarizing the interpretive difficulties associated with the Articles).
183. UNCLOS, *supra* note 4, at Annex I.
184. The IUCN Red List of Threatened Species, *Coryphaena hippurus*, http://www.iucnredlist.org/details/154712/0 (last visited July 3, 2015).
185. The IUCN Red List of Threatened Species, *Coryphaena equiselis*, http://www.iucnredlist.org/details/170350/0 (last visited Jul. 3, 2015).
186. Birnie, PROGRESS AND PROSPECTS, *supra* note 169, at 263.
187. William T. Burke, *The Law of the Sea Convention Provisions on Conditions of Access to Fisheries Subject to National Jurisdiction*, 63 OR. L. REV. 73, 115 (1984) ["Burke, *Access to Fisheries*"]; *see also* Nafziger, *supra* note 52, at 610.
188. Barbara S. Pijanowski, *Comments on Fisheries and the Law of the Sea*, 11 MAR. TECH. SOC. J. 34, 35 (1977) (asserting, with reference to an earlier version of Article 64, that "[t]his article should remain unchanged, but the annex listing highly migratory species should be changed by deleting all references to cetaceans"); *see also* Nafziger, *supra* note 52, at 610 (recognizing that amendment is one option); *see contra* UNCLOS COMMENTARY VOL. II, *supra* note 88, at 664 (noting as a different position that Article 65 essentially overrides cetacean listings in Annex I such that they do not have any operative effect).
189. Davis, *supra* note 146, at 500.
190. *Id.*

191. *Id.*
192. Letter by John Norton Moore (Walter L. Brown Professor of Law and Director of the Center for Ocean Law and Policy, UVA) to the Honorable Elliot L. Richardson, August 15, 1979.
193. George Taft is an attorney with the U.S. Department of State and was the Director of the Office of the Law of the Sea Negotiations and a member of the U.S. Delegation to UNCLOS III.
194. Forkan, *supra* note 135, at 6 (citing to a statement prepared by George Taft et al. (State Department) for the last session of the Law of the Sea Conference, Aug. 22, 1980).
195. UNCLOS Commentary Vol. II, *supra* note 88, at 664.
196. William J. Clinton, *Message to the Congress on Canadian Whaling Activities: February 10, 1997*, The American Presidency Project, http://www.presidency.ucsb.edu/ws/?pid=53558 (last visited Feb. 17, 2016); *see also* Dan Goodman, *Land Claim Agreements and the Management of Whaling in the Canadian Arctic*, *in* The 11th International Abashiri Symposium 39, 39–47 ["Goodman, *Land Claims*"] (discussing the Canadian policy that was challenged by the United States, indicating that the co-management of marine mammals in Canada's north is necessary pursuant to constitutionally protected land claim agreements).
197. *Id.*
198. *See* McDorman, *supra* note 164, at 187; *see* Patricia Birnie, *Conservation of Marine Mammals—Law and Enforcement*, Mar. Pol'y 255, 256 (1980) (questioning whether/the extent to which Article 65 qualifies as customary international law).
199. McDorman, *supra* note 164, at 187.
200. *Id.* at 188.
201. *Id.* at 183 (reproducing the *Statement by the Delegation of Canada Dated 2 April 1980*, 13 Third United Nations Conference on the Law of the Sea: Official Records, UN Sales No. E.81.V.5, 104 (1991)).
202. Patricia Birnie, Alan Boyle & Catherine Redgwell, International Law & the Environment 724 (3d ed. 2009) ["Birnie et al."].
203. *See* Jun Morikawa, Whaling in Japan: Power, Politics and Diplomacy 119 (2009) (noting that certain "elite elements of the bureaucracy" in Japan have contributed to the maintenance of whaling).
204. Forkan, *supra* note 135, at 5 (citing to Committee II, Deliberations on Article 65 amendment, Floor statements, Mar. 21, 1980).
205. *Id.*
206. *Id.*
207. *Id.*; *see* Goodman, *Land Claims, supra* note 191, at 47 (indicating that Canada has observed and participated with NAMMCO and has also considered joining this organization).
208. Forkan, *id.* at 3.
209. *Id.* at 5.
210. Division for Ocean Affairs and Law of the Sea: Office of Legal Affairs, *Law of the Sea Bulletin No. 31*, 79 (1996).
211. *Id.*
212. *Id.*
213. *Id.* at 81–95.

214. *Id.* at 82.
215. Agenda 21, *supra* note 46.
216. BIRNIE ET AL., *supra* note 202, at 50.
217. *Id.* at 52.
218. Agenda 21, *supra* note 46, at 17.1.
219. *Id.*
220. BIRNIE ET AL., *supra* note 202, at 52.
221. Gillespie, *Small Cetaceans, supra* note 53, at 258.
222. *See* Carlson, *supra* note 67; *see* Gillespie, *Small Cetaceans, supra* note 53, at 283–84.
223. *See* Nafziger, *supra* note 52.
224. Freeland & Drysdale, *supra* note 7.
225. *See* Burke, *Access to Fisheries, supra* note 187; *see* BURKE, UNCLOS 1982 AND BEYOND, *supra* note 1, at 276–77; Davis, *supra* note 146.
226. Cinnamon Piñon Carlarne, *Saving the Whales in the New Millennium: International Institutions, Recent Development and the Future of International Whaling Policies*, 24 VA. ENVTL. L.J. 1, 30 (2005–2006).
227. *Id.* at 31 (stating that "currently, UNCLOS's intentions remain ambiguous, as neither legal experts nor UNCLOS parties can agree on an acceptable interpretation").
228. Birnie, *The Role of Law, supra* note 2, at 142.
229. BIRNIE ET AL., *supra* note 202, at 723–25.
230. MICHAEL BOWMAN ET AL., LYSTER'S INTERNATIONAL WILDLIFE LAW 184 (2d ed. 2010) ["LYSTER'S INTERNATIONAL WILDLIFE LAW"].
231. Stefan Asmundsson, *Whaling, in* LAW, SCIENCE & OCEAN MANAGEMENT 459, 466 (Myron H. Nordquist et al. eds., 2007).
232. BURKE, UNCLOS 1982 AND BEYOND, *supra* note 1.
233. *Id.* at 268.
234. *Id.* at 270.
235. *Id.* at 286.
236. *Id.* at 284–86; *see* McDorman, *supra* note 164, at 185.
237. BURKE, UNCLOS 1982 AND BEYOND, *supra* note 1, at 287 (citing to Davis, *supra* note 146, at 504–05).
238. *Id.* at 287.
239. Burke, *A New Whaling Agreement, supra* note 59, at 55.
240. *See* McDorman, *supra* note 164, at 181.
241. *Id.* at 182.
242. *Id.*
243. *Id.* at 184; *see also* DAVID J. ATTARD, THE EXCLUSIVE ECONOMIC ZONE IN INTERNATIONAL LAW, 189 (1987) (noting that states are "urged" to work through the appropriate organizations).
244. McDorman, *supra* note 164, at 185.
245. *Id.* at 186.
246. *Id.*
247. *Id.* at 187.
248. Gillespie, *Small Cetaceans, supra* note 53, at 303.
249. *Id.* at 284–85.
250. Carlson, *supra* note 67, at 618.
251. *Id.* at 606.

252. *Id.* at 600.
253. *Id.* at 606–07.
254. Davis, *supra* note 146 (note that Friedheim in *Fixing the Whaling Regime, supra* note 8, also considers Article 65 in his proposal to improve the ICRW/IWC, but here he focuses mainly on the jurisdictional aspects of Article 65, and at 324 states that "Article 65 of UNCLOS, the only provision to deal with whales, conveys responsibility for whales to international organizations (please note the plural), but it is remarkably silent about where the responsibilities of coastal States end and those of international organizations begin, implying possible overlapping jurisdiction in the EEZ").
255. Davis, *supra* note 146, at 490.
256. *Id.* at 503.
257. *Id.* at 512–13; *see also* Freeland & Drysdale, *supra* note 7, at 30 (for support of the position that the IWC represents the only current effective organization).
258. *Id.* at 514; *see also* Matanich, *supra* note 175, at 59 (where she questions the content of this conservation duty, asking whether the meaning of "conservation" is similar or dissimilar to "cessation of use," which is a protectionist standard, or "conservative use," which is perhaps in line with sustainable use).
259. *Id.* at 515; *see also* Matanich, *supra* note 175, at 57–58 (who shares the position that the duty to "work through" essentially "compels states to follow the IWC, as it is currently the only international regime for the management of whaling").
260. Davis, *supra* note 146, at 515.
261. Matanich, *supra* note 175, at 71.
262. *See* BIRNIE ET AL., *supra* note 202, at 655–57 (recall that the SADC Protocol on Wildlife Conservation and Law Enforcement defines conservation in Article 1 as "the protection, maintenance, rehabilitation restoration and enhancement of wildlife and includes the management of use of wildlife to ensure the sustainability of such use").
263. Lawrence R. Helfer, *Terminating Treaties, in* THE OXFORD GUIDE TO TREATIES 634, 634 (Duncan Hollis ed., 2012) ["Helfer"] (citing to M.E. VILLAGER, COMMENTARY ON THE 1969 VIENNA CONVENTION ON THE LAW OF TREATIES 694 (2009)).
264. MALCOLM N. SHAW, INTERNATIONAL LAW 685–90 (7th ed. 2014).
265. Helfer, *supra* note 263, at 634.
266. ICRW, *supra* note 5.
267. Vienna Convention, *supra* note 36.
268. Jon L. Jacobson, *Whales, the IWC, and the Rule of Law, in* TOWARDS A SUSTAINABLE WHALING REGIME 80, 83–85 (Robert L. Friedheim ed., 2001) (assessing replacement of the ICRW).
269. Ramses A. Wessel, *Dissolution and Succession: The Transmigration of the Soul of International Organizations, in* RESEARCH HANDBOOK ON THE LAW OF INTERNATIONAL ORGANIZATIONS 342, 344 (Jan Klabbers & Asa Wallendahl eds., 2011) ["Wessel"].
270. *Id.* at 343–44.
271. *Id.* at 350.
272. *Id.* at 344.
273. PATRICK R. MYERS, SUCCESSION BETWEEN INTERNATIONAL ORGANIZATIONS 15 (1993); *see also* Wessel, *supra* note 269, at 349.
274. Wessel, *id.* at 355.

275. *Id.* at 351.
276. *Id.* at 348.
277. *Id.* at 345.
278. International Whaling Commission, *History and Purpose*, IWC (2015), https://iwc.int/history-and-purpose.
279. International Whaling Commission, *Commission Sub-Groups*, IWC (2015), https://iwc.int/commission-sub-groups.
280. UNCLOS, *supra* note 4; *see* Birnie, *Small Cetaceans, supra* note 67, at 11 (note that the exclusive fishery zone is not recognized in UNCLOS but is recognized as the fishery zone beyond the territorial sea for nations that have not claimed a full EEZ).
281. Birnie, Small Cetaceans, *supra* note 67.
282. *See* BURKE, UNCLOS 1982 AND BEYOND, *supra* note 1, at 268.
283. ICRW, *supra* note 5; Birnie, *Small Cetaceans, supra* note 67, at 11; LYSTER'S INTERNATIONAL WILDLIFE LAW, *supra* note 230, at 155.
284. *Id.*

6

The Proposal

Part I—The Framework for a New Approach

"A governance framework for whales must enable and encourage participants and stakeholders to cooperate in a spirit of global partnership to conserve, protect and restore the health and integrity of the global whale populations as part of the overall goal of the sustainable development of the oceans and seas. It must integrate with other elements of international governance to that wider goal, implementing the ecosystem and precautionary approaches."[1]

I. INTRODUCTION

The next two chapters introduce and justify a new approach to international marine mammal conservation. This proposal is framed as a legally justifiable implementing agreement negotiated pursuant to the United Nations Convention on the Law of the Sea (UNCLOS).[2] As I have argued elsewhere in this book, a reasonable interpretation of Articles 65 and 120 of UNCLOS indicates that in addition to being able to support such implementation, these Articles require it to be fully realized. The International Convention for the Regulation of Whaling[3] (ICRW) and its associated International Whaling Commission (IWC) has become a stalled regime that should be replaced by a new comprehensive conservation strategy. This proposal is premised on the assertion that global governance should be expanded both in terms of species coverage and issue coverage, that global regulatory governance should be supplemented by soft law, that coastal state and flag state responsibility should be bolstered, that regional implementation of international standards is appropriate, and that compliance, enforcement, and peaceful dispute resolution must feature prominently. The preparatory work necessary to create such an implementing agreement could occur at a negotiating conference convened pursuant to a United Nations General Assembly Resolution.

Political and ideological agendas have the potential to scuttle the negotiation and/or implementation of this proposed approach, just as they have jeopardized international cetacean conservation by the IWC through the majority of its history. This does not negate the necessity, nor should it reduce the desire, to continue to work toward sustainable coexistence between humans and marine mammals; indeed, it makes the pursuit of rational marine mammal conservation that much more important. Those states that prefer conservation for the purposes of sustainable management and lethal use and those states that prefer conservation for habitat protection and species protection have one critical similarity—both desire the continued existence of marine mammals. Although there are only three countries that continue to hunt whales commercially, marine mammal hunting continues pursuant to controversial scientific permits, indigenous whaling occurs outside of the authority of the IWC, small cetaceans are taken in large numbers, and, although the lingering memory of the disastrous consequences of unregulated over-exploitation of large whale species haunts management practices, the modern threats of climate change, environmental pollution, by-catch, and ecotourism do not receive enough consideration.

It is ironic that the sustainability of our relationship with marine mammals may very well depend on allowing a limited commercial take, which remains the critical sticking point between the anti-whaling and pro-whaling blocks. The rational position is that a limited commercial take, continued Indigenous hunt, and recognized artisanal/cultural hunt, to the extent that is scientifically justified (in accordance with the precautionary principle), can coexist with coastal state and/or regional decisions to set and enforce commercial zero-catch quotas, ecosystem-based management, best practice guidelines for marine mammal tourism and humane killing, technology transfer and training, and international cooperation toward minimization of by-catch, ship-strike mortality, and climate-change reduced disruption/mortality.

One of the main reasons for the IWC's ineffectiveness is that it toils within the strictures of the outdated ICRW. Fortunately, there have been considerable oceans law developments since the ICRW that inform my proposal. In addition to UNCLOS, this proposal draws from the workings of the United Nations Agreement for the Implementation of the Provisions of the United Nations Convention on the Law of the Sea of 10 December 1982 Relating to the Conservation and Management of Straddling Fish Stocks and Highly Migratory Fish Stocks[4] ("UN Fish Stocks Agreement"), the Convention on Biological Diversity[5] (CBD), and various regional agreements (including the constituting agreement for the North Atlantic Marine Mammal Commission[6] (NAMMCO), the Agreement on the Conservation of Small Cetaceans of the Baltic and North Seas[7] (ASCOBANS), the Agreement on the Conservation of Cetaceans of the Black Sea, Mediterranean Sea and Contiguous Atlantic Area[8] (ACCOBAMS)), and various secondary sources. I employ these sources to aggregate and modify pertinent principles for application to marine mammal conservation and management.

In this chapter, I present the framework for a new implementing agreement, titled Draft Agreement for the Implementation of the Provisions of the United Nations Convention on the Law of the Sea of 10 December 1982 Relating to the Conservation and Sustainable Management of Marine Mammals ("UN Marine Mammals Agreement" or "Agreement"). This introduction is organized thematically, addressing: (1) introductory matters; (2) the institutional structure of the proposed regime; (3) enforcement, compliance, and dispute resolution mechanisms; and (4) political obstacles. It incorporates and defines key principles of international governance, frames the scope of regulation, promotes regional implementation and compliance, provides recourse to peaceful dispute resolution, facilitates institutional cooperation, and attempts to balance the pro- and anti-whaling positions that must be reconciled to sustain marine mammal populations through the twenty-first century and beyond. My intention is to be comprehensive, robust, and realistic.

Chapter 7 builds on this framework by considering the functionality of the proposed regime in greater detail. The bolstered use of a Secretariat, the promotion of regionalism, and the use of marine protected areas (MPAs) are three crucial aspects of the proposal that require further elaboration, which is accomplished here. Appendix 3 provides a complete draft agreement reflective of the remainder of Chapters 6 and 7.

II. CONSTRUCTING THE FRAMEWORK FOR A UN MARINE MAMMALS AGREEMENT

1. Introductory Matters

(i) PURPOSE AND OBJECTIVE

I am convinced that an agreement creating a comprehensive regime for the conservation and sustainable management of marine mammals is necessary and in the interest of humankind. To this end, I envision a UN Marine Mammals Agreement that recognizes, elucidates, and implements the potential for rational conservation and management embodied in Articles 65 and 120 of UNCLOS in pursuit of the long-term conservation and sustainable management of marine mammals.[9] Importantly, this Agreement should not "prejudice the rights, jurisdiction and duties of States" under UNCLOS and "shall be interpreted and applied in the context of and in a manner consistent with" the same.[10] It should be founded on the consensus that marine mammals have historically been subject to overexploitation, and resolve to enhance cooperation among states. The common interest goal reflected by this consensus is the maintenance of marine mammal species/populations for the benefit of present and future generations. Achieving it requires the international community to address and ultimately surmount the obstacles that have prevented the IWC from effectively and rationally conserving and sustainably managing cetaceans, namely, inadequate species and threat coverage, noting also that there are specific problems with the IWC's current approach to "scientific" whaling, Aboriginal whaling, and space-based management, and also the ICRW's reservation and amendment process.

A new approach must also recognize, at the outset, that: (1) specific financial, scientific, and technological assistance should be afforded to developing states to ensure their effective participation in sustainable marine mammal management; (2) science-based and ecosystem-based management are critical and integral to oceans governance, including marine mammal conservation; (3) more effective compliance, monitoring, and enforcement by flag states, port states, and coastal states is required; (4) the social, cultural, and economic significance of the consumptive and non-consumptive aspects of humankind's use of marine mammals is legitimate and must be respected; (5) achieving marine mammal conservation will contribute to the rule of international law and the maintenance of international peace and security; and (6) the general principles and rules of international law shall continue to govern those issues not covered by UNCLOS or this Agreement.

(II) KEY TERMS

It is also imperative that the UN Marine Mammal Agreement establishes workable definitions for the terms and principles it employs. This is an opportunity to ascribe meaning to broad principles, such as conservation and sustainability, within the context of marine mammal conservation, and to embody the logic behind proceeding in this manner. I provided some of these definitions in Chapter 1 of this work, but they warrant revisiting in the context of this proposal.

"*Conservation*"[11] means:

i. The maintenance of a status[12] for stable or increasing marine mammal species/population(s) that, at a minimum, ensures the necessary composition, genetic variability, and ecosystem integrity[13] required for the long-term viability of the marine mammal species/population(s).[14]
ii. The recovery or rehabilitation of diminished marine mammal species/population(s) to a status that, minimally, ensures the necessary composition, genetic variability, and ecosystem integrity required for the long-term viability of the marine mammal species/population(s).[15]
iii. The statuses referred to in subsections (i) and (ii) shall be informed by the best available science, including due consideration of the Red List of Threatened Species as maintained by the International Union for the Conservation of Nature.
iv. The status referred to in subsection (i) for stable or increasing populations does not preclude the rational take of marine mammals, when and where appropriate, so long as this take does not compromise the status identified therein.[16] Populations covered by subsection (ii) shall not be taken until such time as their recovery/rehabilitation is complete.
v. Conservation shall be achieved through sustainable management and threat mitigation.[17]

"*Conservation and sustainable management measures*" are measures to conserve and

sustainably manage one or more population or species of marine mammal, as established by the International Marine Mammal Commission and included as part of the Annex to the proposed Agreement, or otherwise, and adopted, applied and/or implemented consistently with the relevant rules of international law as reflected in UNCLOS and the proposed Agreement.[18]

"*Ecosystem-based management*" means holistic, integrated management that recognizes the

uncertainty and natural variability of ecosystems but seeks to maintain ecosystem structure, function, and constituent parts.[19]

"*Marine Protected Area*" means a discrete area of the ocean, established by law, designated to

enhance the long-term conservation and/or sustainable management of the marine mammals therein.[20]

"*Population*" means a group of marine mammals of the same species or subspecies/stock in a

common spatial arrangement, that interbreed when mature.[21]

"*Sustainable management*" means:

i. Management that seeks to achieve long-term human-marine mammal co-existence and encompasses the entire scope of regulatory activities necessary to conduct a modern management program, including, but not limited to, research and study, the promulgation of regulations, and the production of best-practice standards and guidelines.[22]
ii. Management that is guided by ecosystem-based management, intragenerational and intergenerational equity, the integration of the environment and development, and precaution in light of scientific uncertainty. It requires compliance, enforcement, and international and regional cooperation.[23] It does not preclude the rational take of marine mammals, when and where appropriate and consistent with sound conservation science, nor the periodic or total protection of species or populations or an otherwise regulated taking.[24]

These key definitions link the overarching idea of "conservation" with the technique of "sustainable management," as implemented through "conservation and sustainable management measures." This definition of "conservation" connects the scientific, legal, and practical considerations of marine mammal conservation through the identification of relevant "conservation statuses." Importantly, it directly acknowledges the possibility of rational take, acknowledging that the proposed UN Marine Mammal Agreement strives to be more than a preservationist regime.

"Sustainable management" is positioned to help guide the conservation objective. As defined here, it expressly contemplates management efforts beyond consumptive/direct use or take of marine mammals, in recognition of the fact that management must also account for indirect, current threats. It also expressly incorporates other important subsidiary objectives that are crucial to sustainability, such as ecosystem-based management, precaution, environmental equities, and the need for cooperation, monitoring, compliance, and enforcement.

Third, "conservation and sustainable management measures" are introduced as the legally binding measures that the International Marine Mammal Commission (IMMC), empowered as the new decision-making body by this Agreement, is competent to promulgate.

(iii) Scope of the New Regime

In turning to the scope of application for the proposed UN Marine Mammal Agreement it is important to recall the first sentence of Article 65 of UNCLOS, which reads: "Nothing in this Part restricts the right of a coastal State or the competence of an international organization, as appropriate, to prohibit, limit or regulate the exploitation of marine mammals more strictly than provided for in this Part [Exclusive Economic Zone "EEZ"]," and that Article 120 extends its operation to the high seas. As such, and with respect to states parties, this new Agreement should provide the IMMC that it creates with regulatory primacy over all marine mammal species on the high seas and with regulatory competence for the conservation and sustainable management of marine mammals within the EEZs of coastal states to the extent that the coastal state consents to the IMMC exerting regulatory governance over this maritime zone. This shall not prejudice the sovereign rights of coastal states for the purpose of prohibiting, limiting, or regulating marine mammal take within areas under national jurisdiction as provided for in UNCLOS.[25] Recalling the heightened obligation imposed upon states by the second clause of Article 65, as well as the broad scope of regulatory jurisdiction currently held by the IWC, it is appropriate for the Agreement to provide the IMMC with authority over the conservation and sustainable management of all cetaceans within the EEZ of ratified states parties. In short, this Agreement should maintain international primacy over cetaceans and enable consent-based regulation of other marine mammal species. This is still not as broadly worded as the jurisdiction provision in the ICRW,[26] which purports to apply "to all waters in which whaling is prosecuted by such factory ships, land stations, and whale catchers," but is an appropriate starting point in light of UNCLOS's zonal management scheme.

Another important introductory matter is the scope of the general principles set out in the Agreement. General principles present an opportunity to breathe life into the duty to cooperate with respect to the conservation of all marine mammals and the obligation to "work through the appropriate international organizations" to manage, study, and conserve cetaceans, as articulated in the second clause of Article 65 of UNCLOS. Specifically, and in addition to the base obligation for states parties to adopt, as appropriate, the conservation and sustainable management measures for marine mammals established by the IMMC to maintain or restore the species/population(s) to the appropriate conservation status, the proposed Agreement should also articulate that:

(1) Conservation and sustainable management measures shall be based upon the best available scientific information, evidence, and knowledge, shall account for the precautionary principle, and shall be designed to:
   i. withstand the pressures of any permitted and limited commercial take;
   ii. take into account the interests of Indigenous and Cultural/Artisanal takes as defined in this Agreement;
   iii. account for the impact of current and emerging direct and indirect threats to marine mammals, including, inter alia, the consequences of climate change, environmental degradation and environmental pollution (including noise pollution), by-catch, ship-strikes, and marine mammal tourism; and
   iv. account for the economic realities of developing states.

(2) Scientific research shall be promoted and scientific information, evidence, and knowledge shall be gathered and disseminated. Such research shall, in particular, assess the impact of any marine mammal take as well as the impact of other human activities. States parties shall work to minimize/mitigate, inter alia, the direct and/or indirect effects of climate change, by-catch, ship-strikes, habitat degradation, pollution (chemical, physical, and noise), ocean dumping, and marine mammal tourism upon marine mammal species/population(s). I offer more consideration of the role of science and the proposed scientific standard below.

(3) Conservation and sustainable management measures shall be implemented and enforced directly or through regional marine mammal organizations and/or arrangements, and effective monitoring, control, and surveillance shall be utilized.[27]

Simply requiring conservation and sustainable management measures to account for the precautionary principle insufficiently implements this important and ambiguous principle that, at its root requires caution "when information is uncertain, unreliable or inadequate" and eschews reliance on the "absence of adequate scientific information ... as a reason for postponing or failing to" establish, adopt, apply and/or implement said measures.[28] At the outset, I concede that further operationalization of the precautionary principle is a formidable task. As noted by Professor Jorge Viñuales:

> precaution is a multi-layered concept involving a broad consensual meaning and more specific controversial ones. It is hard to disagree with the adage that it is better to prevent the occurrence of disaster than to deal with it once it has occurred. But when one tries to move beyond this broad meaning to more operational characterizations of precaution, controversy becomes the rule.[29]

Fortunately, the proposed UN Marine Mammal Agreement can draw from Article 6 of the UN Fish Stocks Agreement, which offers a robust version of the precautionary approach to the conservation and management of living marine resources.[30] Application of the precautionary principle is necessarily premised on pursuit of the best available scientific information, evidence, and knowledge available—the frailties of which I will discuss in due course—and is forward-looking in that it contemplates revision and flexibility in light of changing conservation status for a species/population(s) or in light of a natural phenomenon or unexpected disaster that threatens a marine mammal species/population. Implementation efforts also demand consensus that every level of governance engaged in the new regime, be it states, the IMMC and/or any other regional organizations/arrangements, "shall apply the precautionary approach widely ... in order to protect living marine resources and preserve the marine environment."[31] So long as this consensus can be achieved, implementation can then focus on:

(1) enhancing decision-making by "obtaining and sharing the best available scientific information [evidence and knowledge] and implementing improved techniques for dealing with risk and uncertainty";[32]

(2) ensuring, on the basis of the best available scientific information, evidence, and knowledge that the appropriate conservation statuses are not compromised, and to determine the appropriate course of action if they are—connecting the precautionary principle to conservation status, as previously defined;[33]

(3) stipulating that "uncertainties relating to the size and productivity" marine mammal species/populations, "existing and predicted oceanic, environmental and socio-economic conditions," any approved commercial take, any approved Indigenous or cultural/artisanal subsistence take, and any other known direct or indirect human impacts are accounted for;[34]

(4) mandating the development of research programs and data collection mechanisms that investigate the impacts of human activity and environmental factors on marine mammal species/population(s), and adopting the necessary plans to ensure species and habitat conservation.[35] Further, and to ensure that existing conservation and sustainable management measures are functioning properly, monitoring should be enhanced for any marine mammal species/population(s) subject to an approved commercial take when its conservation status is of concern;

(5) making special provision for any marine mammal species/population previously subject to an IWC commercial moratorium, or any species/population subject to a proposed commercial take and/or Indigenous and/or cultural/artisanal subsistence take, by expeditiously developing cautious measures that will remain in force until the data is clear that said species may be taken;[36]

(6) providing that the IMMC shall produce emergency conservation and sustainable management measures in the event that a "natural phenomenon" negatively impacts the conservation status of a regulated marine mammal species. These measures need only be temporary and shall be based upon the best available scientific information, evidence, and knowledge;[37] and

(7) acknowledging, in accordance with Articles 65 and 120, that states, acting independently, through the IMMC or through regional organizations/arrangements, can prohibit the commercial take of marine mammals even when an assessment of a conservation status of marine mammal species/population(s) suggests that a regulated take will not compromise the conservation status. Marine mammals are not subject to the goal of optimum utilization, and application of the precautionary principle in this context should not be understood to require a take even if the conservation status suggests that one is supportable.[38]

Continuing with a discussion of the centrality of conservation and sustainability measures, we see that it is important that a new UN Marine Mammal Agreement promote measure compatibility to account for UNCLOS's zonal structure. In light of the desire to promote consistency and coherence, and recognizing the primacy of the IMMC to regulate on the high seas and its ability to regulate within areas of national jurisdiction with consent, it is crucial that states agree:

(1) to cooperate through the IMMC toward the timely promulgation and implementation of appropriate conservation and sustainable management measures;
(2) that consenting coastal states whose nationals take, or intend to take, marine mammals from marine mammal species/populations in areas of national jurisdiction shall seek, through the IMMC, to agree to the conservation and sustainable management measures necessary for the conservation of these species/populations;
(3) that the coastal states and states whose nationals take, or intend to take, marine mammals from species/populations in a defined region shall seek to adopt, apply, and/or implement the conservation and sustainability measures agreed to by the IMMC through the appropriate regional organization or arrangement;
(4) that in promulgating conservation and sustainable management measures, existing measures, the biological characteristics of marine mammals, ecosystem and environmental factors, and human take or other uses are accounted for. Although the new Agreement supersedes and replaces the ICRW, and being cognizant of functional regimes, especially at the regional level, that address marine mammals, including NAMMCO, ACCOBAMS, ASCOBANS, CCAMLR, it is imperative that any existing measures are accounted for during the production of new conservation and sustainable management measures. Similarly, pending the promulgation of new compatible conservation and sustainable management measures, the commercial moratorium on all cetacean species regulated by the IWC should continue until such a time as the IMMC agrees on the appropriate course of action. The controversial "Scientific Permit" exception to the commercial moratorium found in Article VIII of the ICRW commercial moratorium shall no longer be available for states parties; and
(5) that in the event that a state or states contest(s) adherence to the provisional arrangement described above, or assert(s) that the reasonable timeline for creating or implementing the appropriate new measures has lapsed, they have recourse to dispute resolution.[39]

(IV) THE BEST AVAILABLE SCIENTIFIC INFORMATION, EVIDENCE, AND KNOWLEDGE STANDARD

Professor Jasanoff, a leading expert on the intersection of science and the law, acknowledges that the legal community increasingly values scientific information as reliable evidence, and has explored the ways in which scientific experts offer critical insight into legal issues.[40] Science is capable of providing neutral and objective assessment, and is obviously preferable to value-based regulation.[41] The scientific method traditionally involved the following steps: (1) question development, (2) research and hypothesis articulation, (3) experimentation and investigation, (4) conclusion formulation, and (5) publication and communication of results.[42]

Through this method of incremental knowledge production, "[s]cience seeks truth and approaches it through a long process of experimentation; it is often most comfortable giving answers as ranges of probability rather than bottom line, linear causal relationships."[43] This sort of answer often does not satisfy those who lack scientific training who may overestimate science's ability to answer the big picture or "bottom line" questions that concern the public.[44]

As I have observed elsewhere,[45] both scientific evidence and scientific uncertainty have played an important role in the ICRW/IWC regime; indeed, they have "been used to justify both over-exploitation and preservation."[46] The decision-making standard that I propose for this new Agreement, and the one that is common in international environmental agreements, is the best available scientific information, evidence, and knowledge.[47] Simply asserting that the IMMC's management decisions shall be based on the best available scientific evidence standard does not immunize against the possibility that such information will be put to use to justify differing positions. Still, the role for science within international environmental lawmaking and law implementation is blatantly clear: the result of scientific method reveals environmental problems and provides remedies.[48] Additionally, science-based decision-making is preferable to other approaches to wildlife conservation and management, including value-based decision-making.[49]

Assuming that all parties accept science-based decision-making as the appropriate mechanism and some version of best available science as the correct standard, this regulatory approach has limitations. Consider the following: (1) "demand[ing] that regulators should use 'good science' as a basis for their standardizing decisions [does not clarify] . . . what counts as science (let alone good science) for policy purposes,"[50] and this is likely to be contested;[51] (2) to what extent should experts be empowered or entitled to contribute to regulatory decision-making, and how does one determine which experts are allowed to participate?; (3) "the use of science as the basis for policy making . . . is by no means a simple or straightforward means of establishing a consensus-based and, therefore, workable environmental management regime."[52] Regulatory science will inevitably conflict with powerful political or ethical regulatory objectives, and reconciliation is difficult.[53] As the scientific experts involved with Australia's ICJ petition in *Whaling in the Antarctic* noted after the conclusion of the case: "the misrepresentation of science to advance non-science agendas is a common feature in disputes involving economic, social, or political values."[54] The production of science and its results can be manipulated, even co-opted, by national political bodies, nongovernmental organizations or other lobby groups,[55] and political actors, and by the fact that the ultimate decision-making authority resides with the regime's lawmaking institution.[56]

Scientific uncertainty is another limitation associated with implementation of this standard. In the marine mammal conservation context, sources of uncertainty and error exist in "sampling and monitoring resources," a general "lack of knowledge of population dynamics," and the "seemingly unpredictable natural variability in population parameters," and also with "problems in [the] enforcement of [conservation] measures."[57] Fortunately, progress continues to be made in marine mammal science, and we now know more about global species distribution, critical habitat, and the impact of fisheries by-catch,[58] and application of the precautionary principle can aid in mitigating the consequences of uncertainty. Marine mammal scientists constitute a functional epistemic network[59] that focuses on recognized uncertainties.⁶⁰ The mere existence of this network does not mean that its product will be appropriately applied by international decision-makers and as such I will consider later in this chapter how scientific experts are embedded in the proposed regime when I describe the role of the IMMC's subsidiary scientific body.

(v) ENCOURAGING DEVELOPING STATE PARTICIPATION

International marine mammal conservation and management is not immune to the impacts of resource disparity and other developing/developed world inequities that complicate most international environmental problems. Developing states stand to gain environmentally and economically if they are able to effectively manage their marine mammal populations for the benefit of present and future generations. Accordingly this regime must assist developing states in realizing these benefits, recognizing that some permutation of common but differentiated responsibility is applicable to the long-term conservation of marine mammals.

The first step in addressing these discrepancies is recognizing that developing states need assistance. In "giving effect to the duty to cooperate in the establishment [and implementation] of conservation and [sustainable] management measures [for marine mammals], States shall take into account the special requirements of developing States," which include: "the vulnerability of developing States which are dependent on the exploitation of living marine resources; and the need to ensure that such measures do not result in transferring, directly or indirectly, a disproportionate burden of conservation action onto developing States."⁶¹ The goal of assistance is to enhance the ability for developing states to conserve and sustainably manage marine mammals and to facilitate their participation in the structures created by the regime.⁶² Particular forms of cooperation that can help close the gap include: technical and technological assistance, including technology transfer; financial assistance, including funding and development of observer programs; "human resources development [and] advisory and consultative assistance"; enhanced "collection, reporting, verification, exchange and analysis of scientific data and related information" techniques; improved local "monitoring, control, surveillance, compliance and enforcement, including training and capacity-building";⁶³ and assistance in implementing the Agreement and in meeting any costs associated with dispute resolution.⁶⁴

(vi) DEVELOPING AND TRANSFERRING MARINE MAMMAL RELATED TECHNOLOGIES

The need for technical and technological cooperation features in several international regimes, including UNCLOS, the CBD, and the World Trade Organization Agreement on Trade-Related Aspects of Intellectual Property Rights. Throughout this work, I have emphasized the importance of technological advances in reducing some of the direct and indirect harms associated with our use of the oceans generally, and marine mammals particularly. Examples include developments in killing methods and technologies, fishing gear advances and innovative by-catch avoidance techniques, noise pollution reduction technologies, and even advances in marine mammal tourism. The broad purpose of addressing technological cooperation and assistance in the new Agreement is to foster domestic innovation and then transference, as appropriate, of that innovation at the regional and international level, encouraging, as much as possible, uptake of these advances in the developing world in furtherance of the objectives described above.

The structures created by this Agreement provide a forum through which states can cooperate to "actively [promote] the development and transfer of technology relating to [marine mammals] on fair and reasonable terms and conditions"[65] and to incent "enterprises and institutions ... for the purposes of promoting and encouraging technology transfer to developing [states parties] in order to enable them to create a sound and viable technological base" for marine mammal conservation and management.[66] The goals of technological development and transference include the development of new knowledge and technologies related to marine mammals, the creation of the infrastructure needed to access and transfer such innovations, and the training of nationals in developing states to create the necessary human resources to administer new knowledge and technologies.[67] Achieving these goals requires the establishment of new programs for technology transfer, the promotion of conditions conducive to concluding "agreements, contracts and other similar arrangements," organizing "conferences, seminars and symposia on scientific and technological subjects," and promoting "the exchange of scientists and of technological and other experts" to help establish and maintain national observer programs and to implement other conservation and sustainable management objectives.[68] Finally, and upon request and with the goal of "accelerating the social and economic development of the developing States,"[69] states parties shall assist in promoting technological capabilities. This assistance shall extend to "the preparation of laws and regulations" that restrict the use and prevent the abuse of such technologies, and shall assist in domestic implementation of the technologies.[70]

(VII) Reservations, Declarations, and Relation to Existing Agreements

Building on the theme of consensus, and recognizing the problematic annex/objection process that is available to Contracting Governments to the ICRW/IWC, I propose as a starting point a prohibition on reservations or exceptions to the proposed Agreement.[71] I acknowledge that certain reservations may be appropriate, even reasonable, and that the benefit of allowing certain reservations is that the flexibility it imports might help facilitate the trade-offs necessary to achieve compromise. However, it makes sense to begin with the position that no reservations will be allowed, recognizing that this could be reconsidered during negotiations when the nature and consequence of such reservations could be ascertained and evaluated.

Excluding reservations does "not preclude a State or entity, when signing, ratifying or acceding" to the proposed Agreement "from making declarations or statements, however phrased or named, with a view, *inter alia*, to the harmonization of its laws and regulations with the provisions of this Agreement, provided that such declarations or statements do not purport to exclude or to modify the legal effect of the provisions of this Agreement in their application to that State or entity."[72]

The Agreement can also memorialize its relation to other international and regional treaties. First and foremost it should stipulate that it "shall prevail, as between States Parties, over the [ICRW of 2 December 1946]."[73] It can also stipulate that this "Agreement shall not alter the rights and obligations of States Parties which arise from other agreements compatible with this Agreement and which do not affect the enjoyment by other States parties of their rights or the performance of their obligations under this Agreement."[74] Those rights and obligations that, in their exercise, "would cause a serious damage or threat" to the conservation and sustainable management of marine mammals are incompatible with this Agreement.[75] Nothing in the above would prevent states parties from "modifying or suspending the operation of provisions of this [proposed] Agreement, applicable solely to the relations between them, provided that such agreements do not relate to a provision derogation from which is incompatible with the effective execution of the object and purpose of this Agreement, and provided further that such agreements shall not affect the application of the basic principles embodied herein, and that the provisions of such agreements do not affect the enjoyment by other States Parties of their rights or the performance of their obligations under this Agreement."[76]

(VIII) AMENDING ANNEX I OF UNCLOS

The final introductory matter that should be addressed by the new Agreement is the remedial action necessary to amend Annex I ("Highly Migratory Species") of UNCLOS to correct the inclusion of cetaceans and the reference to dolphin, both of which are properly recognized as drafting errors.

The preferred option to address this issue is through the amendment procedures contained in UNCLOS. Specifically, Article 312 provides an amending process that is available 10 years after the treaty has entered into force, which contemplates convening a conference and addressing the issue through consensus. Alternatively, Article 313 offers a simplified amendment process that does not require a conference. Outside of UNCLOS itself we can look to Article 41 of the Vienna Convention on the Law of Treaties, titled "Agreement to Modify Multilateral Treaties between Certain of the Parties Only."[77] As UNCLOS does not provide for this form of modification directly, rendering Article 41(a) inappropriate in the circumstances, one must consider whether it satisfies the test described in 41(b), which reads:

> (b) the modification in question is not prohibited by the treaty and:
> (i) does not affect the enjoyment by the other parties of their rights under the treaty or the performance of their obligations;
> (ii) does not relate to a provision, derogation from which is incompatible with the effective execution of the object and purpose of the treaty as a whole.[78]

The first prerequisite is satisfied as this sort of amendment is not expressly prohibited by UNCLOS, and similarly this amendment would not frustrate existing rights or effective execution of its object and purpose. Specifically, consider that the UN Fish Stocks Agreement addresses highly migratory species and offers evidence of state practice pertaining to the exercise of rights pursuant to Annex I. The state-coordinated regional action to conserve and manage highly migratory species to date suggests that this Annex has simply been interpreted to cover dolphin-fish rather than dolphin, and also that it has not prompted state action to regulate cetaceans as highly migratory fish stocks.[79] Consequently, neither obligations nor expectations are compromised as this modification, as between states parties, simply corrects and implements the existing state of understanding. The necessary amendment could be achieved through a simple provision in the new Agreement that states:

> As between those States which are States Parties to both this Agreement and the Convention, the Convention is modified as follows:
> a. Paragraph 15 of Annex I of the Convention is amended to read: "15. Common dolphinfish: *Coryphaena hippurus*; *Coryphaena equiselis*."
> b. Paragraph 17 of Annex I is deleted.

2. Institutional Structure of the Proposed Regime

As hinted above, this new regime utilizes a new infrastructure to achieve its objectives. In short and as I elaborate below, the proposed hierarchical structure engages states, the new IMMC (including its subordinate committees), and regional implementation/enforcement mechanisms. Appendix 4 visually represents this hierarchical structure.

(i) The International Marine Mammal Commission (IMMC)

The IMMC is the key intergovernmental organization created and empowered by the new Agreement and, as the Agreement's decision-making body, is the forum for the pursuit of the long-term conservation and sustainable management of marine mammals and effective implementation of the Agreement.[80] Similar to its predecessor, the IWC, the IMMC would be composed of one member appointed by each state party, who may be accompanied by his or her advisors;[81] the Commission should be free to invite outside experts to attend its meetings.[82]

In furtherance of UNCLOS's consensus model, the IMMC should also be encouraged to make decisions by consensus.[83] If consensus remains elusive, the default threshold for non-critical decisions made at its meetings should be set at a simple majority.[84] Critical decisions, including financial decisions, Agreement amendments, and the creation and amendment of any Annex[85] (which is where the Management Plan and other conservation and sustainable management measures would reside), shall require a two-thirds majority from voting members.[86] Each member shall have one vote.[87] Importantly, this consensus-based decision-making mechanism that defaults to a simple-majority requirement that is replaced by a two-thirds supermajority for critical decisions accords with the standards set in CBD, CITES, and ACCOBAMS, and attempts to alleviate some of the difficulties exemplified with the IWC's three-quarters supermajority requirement.[88]

As the decision-making organ, the IMMC sits atop the rest of the regime's structures. As such, it is responsible for establishing "from its own members and advisors"[89] the committees needed to achieve its objectives. I suggest that this includes a Scientific Committee, an Indigenous and Cultural/Artisanal Subsistence Take Committee, and other Sustainable Management Committees, as appropriate.[90] The IMMC shall also set "guidelines and objectives for the work"[91] of these Committees. Recognizing the importance of existing regional organizations that are interested in marine mammal conservation, the IMMC is tasked with approving the adequacy of existing or proposed regional marine mammal organizations/arrangements. Once approved, the regional organization/agreement is qualified to perform any regional organization/arrangement functions as the Agreement contemplates. This approval can be rescinded, if necessary.[92] Because of the transdisciplinary nature of its work, the IMMC's efforts shall be based upon the best available scientific information, evidence, and knowledge. Working independently or in conjunction with its committees or approved regional/international organizations/agencies, the IMCC shall: (1) investigate marine mammal conservation and sustainable management and species/population conservation statuses, (2) collect and assess statistical data regarding the "current condition and trend" of marine mammal species/populations and the direct and/or indirect impacts of human activity on said species/populations, and (3) "study, appraise, and disseminate information regarding methods of" conserving and sustainably managing marine mammal populations.[93] Together, these efforts should assist in the pursuit of the best available information and help avoid duplication of efforts.

The main function of the IMMC is the production of binding conservation and sustainable management measures. In following the format of the ICRW/IWC regime, which also accords with more recent international environmental treaty law, these measures should form part of an Annex to the Agreement. In updating and amending the scope of measures contemplated by Article V(1), I propose the following measures: (1) approval of a Management Plan, as recommended by the Scientific Committee. The Management Plan should function like the IWC's proposed RMP for baleen whales, which remains an appropriate analog to guide any commercial take given its precautionary considerations, area based management, and robust catch algorithm;[94] (2) approval of monitoring, reporting, and compliance requirements that accompany the adoption, application, and/or implementation of the Management Plan. Recognizing that monitoring and compliance is one of the contentious issues that has thwarted recent action by the IWC, it is important that states parties focus on producing appropriate and workable measures; (3) approval of total allowable commercial take limits for those species whose take is within the regulatory competence of the Commission, as set by the Scientific Committee through application of the Management Plan. Subsequent distribution of allowable commercial take quotas to regional marine mammal organizations/arrangements, upon the request of an approved regional marine mammal organization/arrangement; (4) approval of Indigenous and/or cultural/artisanal take as recommended by the Indigenous and Cultural/Artisanal Subsistence Take Committee in conjunction with the Scientific Committee; (5) approval of individual Marine Protected Areas, or a network of Marine Protected Areas, as recommended by the Scientific Committee. MPAs can play an important role in achieving holistic ecosystem-based management, and this is justification for including them as a tool within the host of available conservation and sustainable management measures. The application of MPAs would have to be reconciled with the existing sanctuary scheme and with areas of permissible marine mammal take generally. The form and functioning of MPAs require more attention than can be given here; therefore, MPAs will be investigated at greater length in Chapter 7; (6) designation of "protected and unprotected species," "open and closed" seasons for approved takes, "open and closed waters" in light of MPA designation; (6) approval of "gear and apparatus" type and specification used for marine mammal take, and size and sex restrictions for any approved take; (7) measures to combat illegal, unreported, and unregulated marine mammal take, to adequately and appropriately respond to and mitigate the problem of by-catch, and to adequately and appropriately respond to and mitigate the direct and/or indirect effects of climate change, ship-strikes, habitat degradation, pollution (chemical, physical, and noise), ocean dumping, and marine mammal tourism, as appropriate; and (8) approval of any other conservation and sustainable management measures the Commission deems necessary for marine mammals. This includes consideration of recommendations from the Scientific Committee, the Indigenous and Cultural/Artisanal Subsistence Take Committee, and/or other Sustainable Management Committees.[95] This catch-all imports the flexibility into conservation and sustainable management measures that is necessary to enable the Commission to adapt and evolve to emerging circumstances going forward.

There are other legitimate action-oriented mechanisms that involve important aspects of marine mammal conservation that are not covered by the scope of conservation and sustainable management regulation. One is to approve and disseminate best-practice standards and guidance documents, as produced by the Scientific Committee, Indigenous and Cultural/Artisanal Subsistence Take Committee, or other Sustainable Management Committees. This allows the IMMC (and relevant committees) to work in the areas of humane-killing, marine mammal tourism, and public/technical education, and to produce soft law guidance. Another is to make recommendations to states parties regarding marine mammal conservation and sustainable management, including model domestic legislation.[96] This empowers the IMMC to promote domestic coherence and to remain relevant to issues that are international in scope despite a primarily domestic nexus. Similarly, it allows the IMMC to "contact, through the Secretariat, the executive bodies of conventions dealing with matters covered" by the Agreement "with a view to establishing appropriate forms of cooperation with them."[97] Logistically, the IMMC shall administer the financial mechanism[98] established by the Agreement, promote the peaceful settlement of disputes, and strive for transparency by publishing reports and pertinent information related to marine mammal conservation and sustainable management.

The Agreement should require the IMMC to meet within the first year after it enters into force, and should prescribe a schedule that mandates ordinary meetings be held on a biennial basis with the possibility of extraordinary meetings being convened on an emergency basis "by the Secretariat on the written request of at least two-thirds of the members."[99] Because it is crucial that the new regime fosters cooperation while seeking to reduce redundancy in regional and international governance, and also that it ensures that relevant stakeholders have the ability to observe and participate in the IMMC's meetings, existing regimes and qualified organizations should be accounted for. With respect to existing regimes, their secretaries shall be entitled to send observers to both ordinary and extraordinary meetings.[100] Other bodies and nongovernmental organizations qualified in marine mammal conservation and sustainable management[101] will be able to apply to the Secretariat in advance of a meeting to be qualified as an observer,[102] in accordance with any rules of procedure established by the Secretariat.[103] Observer participation shall occur in accordance with the procedures established by the Secretariat, and such observers shall be entitled to active participation but not be eligible to vote.[104]

(ii) The IMMC's Subsidiary Structures

The IMMC is the focal point of the new regime but in and of itself it is insufficient to achieve the goals and objectives that I have proposed. Existing conservation regimes, including the ICRW/IWC, evince the importance of supporting subsidiary structures. Accordingly, and as briefly introduced above, the Agreement shall also create and empower committees and a robust secretariat to help achieve long-term conservation and sustainable management. This section introduces the functionality and utility of these subsidiary bodies.

The first committee that the Agreement tasks the IMMC with establishing is the Scientific Committee. It is my opinion that decision-making ought to utilize the best available information, evidence, and knowledge standard despite some of the difficulties associated with operationalizing this approach. As such, science occupies a central role in this regime. Science and scientific information is essential to promoting rational decision-making, implementing the precautionary principle, and sustainably managing any direct use/take that exists at the same time as current threats. Achieving science-based decision-making necessitates recourse to scientific experts, who should constitute the new Scientific Committee.

Analogous to the IWC's Scientific Committee, I envision an organ populated by scientific experts appointed by the states parties[105] that, subject to IMMC approval, can invite other experts to help conduct the Committee's business;[106] I also propose allowing observers to have full entitlement to active participation. In all instances, the Committee's work should be based upon the best available scientific information, evidence, and knowledge standard. Some of the tasks for this Scientific Committee are straightforward and align with existing efforts of analogous bodies. For example, it should be responsible for assessing the conservation status of those marine mammal species covered by the Agreement.[107] It should also be responsible for: (1) providing scientific advice in response to requests from the IMMC and the regime's other subsidiary bodies;[108] (2) designing, coordinating, and recommending to the IMMC a Management Plan for those species covered by the Agreement;[109] (3) proposing the total allowable take limits for marine mammal species regulated by the IMMC, pursuant to the Management Plan and in accordance with the Agreement's guiding principles;[110] (4) proposing, in conjunction with the Indigenous and Cultural/Artisanal Subsistence Take Committee (introduced below), recommended subsistence take limits; and (5) recommending to the IMMC protected and unprotected species as well as open and closed waters/seasons.[111]

Other tasks I contemplate for this Scientific Committee deviate somewhat from the status quo but are crucial to furthering the regime's objectives: (1) recommending to the IMMC the establishment of a network of MPA to achieve ecosystem-based management. This network can include areas of the high seas and areas within national jurisdiction (with coastal state consent), and shall be designed in cooperation with other international organizations and without prejudice to existing international agreements, as facilitated by the Secretariat. This tool replaces the existing whale sanctuary approach, and its potential benefits are explored more extensively in the next chapter; (2) working cooperatively with the IMMC to produce best-practice standards and guidelines for activities that directly or indirectly impact the sustainable management of marine mammals, including: marine mammal tourism and other forms of ecotourism, by-catch mitigation, mitigation of sound/noise in the marine environment, humane killing techniques and killing technologies and associated welfare issues, and education and training mechanisms for those who directly take or otherwise use marine mammals.[112] This builds off of the IWC's current approach to whale watching and NAMMCO's approach to animal welfare, and contemplates the use of soft law guidance for areas that are either not conducive to regulation or beyond the IMMC's core regulatory function.

The second subcommittee I propose is the Indigenous and Cultural/Artisanal Subsistence Take Committee. This is an incredibly important subcommittee that will contribute to the IMMC's difficult regulatory function of administering a subsistence harvest. The necessity of recognizing and allowing for subsistence use of marine mammals is obvious, but defining the scope of such provisions and crafting appropriate working definitions has historically been, and is still, a difficult task.

The Indigenous and Cultural/Artisanal Subsistence Take Committee that I propose is populated by experts appointed by states parties and, subject to IMMC approval, can invite other experts to participate in its work; observers shall be entitled to active participation.[113] As Professor Gillespie notes in his analysis of current subsistence whaling, "[t]he inability of the international environmental legal community to arrive at a singular definition of indigenous has been mirrored in the history of the IWC."[114] He further notes that "it would be very useful for the IWC signatories to adopt a suitable method by which indigenous peoples may be identified."[115] This new Agreement represents an opportunity to craft workable definitions that remedy this shortfall and advance our understanding of subsistence take:

> *"Indigenous"* is understood in this context as a generic, umbrella term that encompasses other, sometimes preferred, titles including, *inter alia*, tribe, ethnic group, band, first nations, and first people,[116] and includes, *inter alia*, those peoples for which "aboriginal subsistence whaling (ASW)" is currently authorized by the IWC.[117] It also includes those peoples that, despite not being recognized pursuant to the ASW exemption at the IWC, meet and/or sufficiently fulfill, *inter alia*, the following criteria:
>
>   i. they self-identify as ethnically distinct;
>   ii. they have historically experienced significant exploitation, disruption, or dislocation;
>   iii. they have a lengthy connection with the region in question; and
>   iv. they desire to retain a distinct identity.
>
> This inquiry can also be assisted by the following indicia:
>
>   i. they are not the dominant group in the particular State;
>   ii. they identify a strong cultural association with an identified location;
>   iii. they demonstrate historical continuity of occupation, likely by descent, with previous occupants of an identified location;
>   iv. they demonstrate sociocultural and/or socioeconomic differences from the surrounding population;
>   v. they demonstrate distinctive traits, like language, race, spiritual, or material culture; and
>   vi. they are perceived as Indigenous by the surrounding population and/or recognized as Indigenous in national/local laws, regulations, or administrative processes.[118]

"*Cultural*" means a marine mammal take that, despite not being conducted by peoples that

> qualify as Indigenous, is traditional in that it has a history of occurrence, transference of knowledge, occurs locally, represents a core aspect of community for the people concerned, and/or qualifies as an important food source.[119] The loss of a cultural subsistence take is likely to have a significant negative impact upon the peoples in question.[120]

"*Artisanal*" means local, family-oriented hunting, producing and consuming activities that are

> primarily based on traditional knowledge that demonstrate sustainability. Artisanal use does not preclude community-scale informal trading in marine mammal products.[121]

"*Subsistence*" means that the processes and procedures of marine mammal take, production, and

> distribution are locally organized (i.e., family- or kinship-centered), organized and/or structured in a manner that is separate and distinct from modern regulatory or market-based controls, and carried out primarily to satisfy nutritional demands. Subsistence take does not prevent limited, localized trade and/or monetized commerce and it does not require the application of traditional techniques/technology to qualify as such.[122]

With these terms in mind, the Indigenous and Cultural/Artisanal Subsistence Take Committee can then turn its attention to performing a number of important functions, including:

(1) reviewing applications from states parties made on behalf of groups within their territorial borders that identify as Indigenous, Cultural, or Artisanal and who seek approval of take-quota allocations on the basis of a proposed subsistence take.[123] This Committee should employ the following factors in determining whether an Indigenous, Cultural, or Artisanal application warrants take-quota allocation:
   i. the application supports a "socially defined group" that shares the necessary social arrangement to qualify for an Indigenous, Cultural, or Artisanal take as the maintenance of this social arrangement is significantly dependent upon a marine mammal take or the processing/consumption of marine mammal products. Non-economic benefits/purposes are required;
   ii. the application supports a geographically limited take that is associated with coastal and/or "shore-based communities." Marine mammal take beyond areas of national jurisdiction will not be permissible unless every other criteria identified in this paragraph is established;
   iii. the application supports "social reproducibility" in that the rules and knowledge directing the marine mammal take in question are passed inter-generationally within the same community/aggregation, usually in an oral manner and over an extended period of time;

iv. the application supports a take that is valued multidimensionally, be it historically, culturally, socially, economically, and nutritionally (as an important aspect of the preferred diet). Economic significance may be important but in isolation is insufficient to satisfy this criterion;

v. the application supports historical evidence of use of the species in question in an attempt to avoid unnecessary species shifting; and

vi. the application indicates that effective monitoring for sustainability of the take will occur and that the take will otherwise enable biological sustainability.[124]

(2) coordinating with the Scientific Committee to assess whether the marine mammal species/population in question can support a subsistence take.

(3) recommending catch-quota allocations for Indigenous, Cultural and/or Artisanal take to the IMMC.

(4) reviewing the appropriateness of other conservation and sustainable management measures as they relate to Indigenous, Cultural, and/or Artisanal take or other uses.

Two final points warrant consideration. First, the Indigenous and Cultural/Artisanal Subsistence Take Committee should be empowered to work with the Commission and other international organizations, where appropriate, to create a subsistence certification program, which enables trade in marine mammal products beyond the local level so long as such trade otherwise complies with international law.[125] It is foreseeable that such a trade in marine mammal products derived from a permitted subsistence take may arise, and that a product certification program is one approach to help verify the origin of such products. The functionality of such a certification or labeling regime is beyond the scope of this work, and represents an area for future investigation.

Second, Gillespie recognizes that despite the valid goal of facilitating an appropriate subsistence take, it is imperative that any such take not be allowed to threaten the extinction of any species.[126] Accordingly, the Agreement should stipulate that the Indigenous and Cultural/Artisanal Take Committee shall not recommend to the IMMC, and that the IMMC shall not approve catch-quota allocations for a subsistence take if the species is threatened with extinction, as determined by the Scientific Committee using best available scientific evidence and knowledge and IUCN Red List criteria. If uncertainty exists, no catch-quota allocations shall be given, in accordance with the precautionary principle.[127]

This expansion of subsistence to include an indigenous, cultural, and artisanal component is premised on Friedheim's assessment that "small-type coastal whaling," as carried out in certain communities around the world, is related to but distinct from the indigenous whaling that currently qualifies for the ASW exception.[128] For example, Japan has requested application of this exemption for certain coastal communities that take certain cetaceans, as has Greenland.[129] This marine mammal take is currently occurring and does not fit properly into the ASW category. Therefore, this new approach responds by accepting Friedheim's endorsement of the definitions related to cultural and artisanal take provided in existing scholarship and adapting them for use in this Agreement.[130]

Although the Scientific Committee and the Indigenous and Cultural/Artisanal Subsistence Take Committee are the two bodies I have focused on here, other committees are also likely needed to accomplish the goals established by this Agreement, as implemented by the IMMC. For example, recall the IWC's current subgroups: (1) the Scientific Committee, (2) the Conservation Committee, (3) the Finance and Administration Committee, (4) the Aboriginal Subsistence Whaling Sub-Committee, (5) the Infractions Sub-Committee, and (6) the Working Group on Whale Killing Methods and Associated Welfare Issues.[131] To that end, the new Agreement must contemplate other committees and set the parameters for their creation.

I propose that these new committees fall under the general heading of "Sustainable Management Committees" and that the IMMC be empowered to create such Sustainable Management Committees "from among its own members and advisors ... as it considers necessary to perform the functions it [authorizes]."[132] I envision Sustainable Management Committees performing the following functions in accordance with their respective mandates and expertise:

(1) recommending conservation and sustainable management measures to the IMMC;
(2) recommending best-practice guidelines or standards for the conservation and sustainable management of marine mammals to the IMMC;[133]
(3) working cooperatively with the Scientific Committee and/or Indigenous and Cultural/Artisanal Subsistence Take Committee to produce best-practice standards and guidelines for activities that directly and/or indirectly impact the conservation and sustainable management of marine mammals;[134] and
(4) recommending issues requiring further study or research to the IMMC.[135]

Revamped committees are not the only subsidiary bodies within the new regime positioned to play an important role. Secretariats are most often recognized for performing critical but seemingly mundane administrative functions such as arranging meetings and reporting on the functionality of the international regime that they help administer. Secretariats can also perform other functions, some of which may be critical to the success of this proposed regime; therefore, the development of a robust Secretariat is an appropriate institutional feature to consider for this proposed regime. Secretariats exist as the supportive body for a variety of international conventions, including United Nations Framework Convention on Climate Change (UNFCCC),[136] CITES,[137] and the Antarctic Treaty System.[138] Each secretariat varies in terms of function and institutional independence, and the particular analog that makes sense in this situation is the Secretariat of the Convention on Biological Diversity (SCBD).

The SCBD has been empowered by the Conference of the Parties (COP) to work toward "facilitating exchange of information, exploring harmonization or efficiencies of reporting requirements, [and] exploring the possibility of coordinating work programmes."[139] The SCBD has contributed to the CBD's goals through: (1) "knowledge-brokerage," being the act of gathering, synthesizing, and disseminating research and potential solutions; (2) "negotiation-facilitation," being issue-based formal and informal cooperation; and (3) "capacity-building," being general assistance in implementing the CBD through the production of best-practices, monitoring, technological development and distribution, and administrative support.[140] The SCBD has formalized cooperation with other relevant international organizations tasked with implementing or administering treaties through Memoranda of Understanding; indeed, such agreements are in place with CITES and the CMS.[141] Cooperation and collaboration can take many other informal forms as well, including presentations, discussions, and written reports.[142] Coordination and assistance is not limited to the international level of governance, as the SCBD can also contribute to implementation efforts at a national level.[143]

In the context of this proposed Agreement, cooperation and coordination with other international organizations are key elements of holistic conservation and management. Although this proposed Agreement legitimately provides the IMMC with the jurisdiction to promulgate regulatory conservation and sustainable management measures governing the take of marine mammals and other relevant issues, the survey of current threats contained in Chapter 4 indicates that other factors that the IMMC cannot directly regulate will figure prominently in the long-term conservation of marine mammals. For example, ship-strike mitigation and navigational issues more generally fall within the purview of the IMO; climate change science is being addressed by the IPCC, and its global regulatory issues occur through the UNFCCC; many migratory species are protected pursuant to CMS; Antarctic issues are addressed through the Antarctic Treaty System; and a host of regional arrangements are actively engaged in local management and conservation of marine mammals (including NAMMCO, ACCOBAMS, and ASCOBANS). One way to help ensure that the IMMC's marine mammal conservation perspective is being heard in these other fora is to task the Secretariat with attending the annual meetings of relevant international bodies and, when appropriate, empowering it to lobby for the adoption of regulatory mechanisms, standards, guidelines, or decisions that promote marine mammal conservation and sustainable management.[144] Another mechanism is "to coordinate with other relevant international bodies and, in particular, to enter into such administrative and contractual arrangements as may be required for the effective discharge of its functions."[145] This also works to account for the diversity of threats by empowering cooperation and coordination between this regime and existing efforts, formally and informally. More can be said about the Secretariat and, as such, I explore its functionality in greater detail in Chapter 7.

(III) Transparency in Decision-Making

Transparency in decision-making should be a goal of any international organization. Indeed, a common criticism of the IWC is that it lacks transparency.[146] As recently as at the 63rd Annual Meeting of the IWC, the United Kingdom proposed transparency reforms, stating:

> It is important that the IWC's business is seen to be conducted effectively, based on integrity and transparency. A widely perceived lack of transparency within the Commission can diminish the standing, authority and the effectiveness of the IWC, especially if the organisation is unable to point to specific rules and

measures that demonstrate that it is a credible organisation capable of operating effectively and at its full potential.[147]

In 2014, at its 65th Annual Meeting, the IWC affirmed "the important role of civil society in its proceedings and in ensuring" that it "remains an open, transparent and fully accountable organization," and to this end it adopted a number of amendments to its Rules of Procedure.[148] A new Agreement provides the opportunity to address transparency concerns by mandating that the IMMC "shall provide for transparency in its decision-making process and other activities," demanding the same from the regime's subsidiary bodies. This can be at least partially accomplished by a clause that stipulates that representatives from regional marine mammal organisations/arrangements, intergovernmental organizations, and NGOs concerned with marine mammal conservation and sustainable management "shall have timely access to the record and reports" of the IMMC and any subsidiary body, "subject to the procedural rules on access ... [which] shall not be unduly restrictive."[149]

(iv) Regional Marine Mammal Organizations

One of the main deviations from the status quo in this proposal is the creation and utilization of regional marine mammal organizations and/or arrangements. The impetus behind the promotion of regionalism will be one of the issues explored in greater detail in Chapter 7, but for the purposes of this discussion of institutional design it is important to understand the proposed role for regional organizations/arrangements in this new regime.

The IMMC remains the primary decision-making body in this arrangement, charged with, among other things, establishing conservation and sustainable management measures. Regional organizations/arrangements will complement IMMC activities by functioning to implement these measures in a manner that engages the appropriate management unit (whether that be the species as a whole or certain populations of said species) while working to promote participation by aligning similarly situated states.[150]

Regional arrangements provide another forum for coastal states and other states interested in marine mammal conservation and sustainable management to pursue cooperation and implementation of the Agreement, "taking into account the specific characteristics of the region" in question.[151] Based upon the regionalism model found in the UN Fish Stocks Agreement, this proposed Agreement will call for good faith regional consultations among states parties to establish "appropriate arrangements to ensure conservation and [sustainable] management" of marine mammals.[152] Once established, these regional organizations/arrangements will ideally have the competence to adopt, apply, or implement the IMMC's conservation and sustainable management measures, and states (coastal or otherwise) that take, or propose to take, marine mammals on the high seas "shall give further effect to their duty to cooperate by becoming members or participants" in the appropriate regional marine mammal organization/arrangement, or by otherwise agreeing to adopt the organization's measures. Membership should be open to all states that have a "real interest" in the marine mammal species/population(s) concerned.[153]

In essence, this proposal envisions regional organizations/arrangements operating as an intermediary between states and the IMMC in the following manner. Preexisting or newly created regional organizations/arrangements must seek approval from the IMMC to be recognized as an appropriate regional instrument. Then, approved organizations/arrangements can apply to the IMMC for the allocation of quotas to take species regulated by the IMMC. Only those states that are "members of such an organization or participants in such an arrangement, or which agree to apply the conservation and [sustainable] management measures established by such organization or arrangement, shall have access to the [take of the marine mammal species/population] to which those measures apply."[154]

As we turn now to the specific functions of regional cooperation, the proposed Agreement will contemplate that, through approved regional marine mammal organizations or arrangements, states shall:

(1) adopt, apply, and implement conservation and sustainable management measures;
(2) agree to participatory rights, including preferred take quotas, and apply to the IMMC for approval prior to allocating said rights;
(3) adopt, apply, and implement any of the best-practice standards or guidelines for the take or other use of marine mammals as produced by the IMMC;
(4) contribute to the work of the IMMC's Scientific Committee;
(5) adopt, apply, and implement "effective monitoring, control, surveillance and enforcement" mechanisms;
(6) "agree on means by which the interests of new members of the organization or new participants in the arrangement will be accommodated";[155]
(7) promote peaceful dispute settlement;
(8) "ensure the full cooperation of their relevant national agencies and industries in the" adoption, application, or implementation of the conservation and sustainable management measures produced by the IMMC; and
(9) report to the IMMC on an annual basis.[156]

Finally, transparency in decision-making is also important at the regional level of governance where implementation of conservation and sustainable management measures occurs, and should be subject to scrutiny from the IMMC and also externally, as appropriate.[157]

3. Compliance, Enforcement, and Dispute Resolution

(i) The Non-participant State Problem

To start, and to aid proper functionality and effectiveness, this new international regime must encourage widespread support and buy-in from a diverse group of states with seemingly divergent positions. Before introducing specific enforcement, compliance, and dispute resolution mechanisms, it is necessary to consider the status of those states that end up as nonmembers of the proposed IMMC and/or nonmembers to regional organizations/arrangements. It is imperative that the States that do agree to be bound by the proposed Agreement and the IMMC's conservation and sustainable management measures have confidence that their efforts will not be compromised by those free-riders that choose to not participate but still take regulated marine mammal species.[158] The Agreement should articulate that "States Parties shall take measures consistent with this Agreement and international law to deter the activities of vessels flying the flag of non-parties which undermine the effective implementation of this Agreement."[159] Additionally, the Agreement should make it clear that nonmembership in the new regime does not excuse UNCLOS signatories from cooperating with respect to marine mammal conservation and management, as outlined in Articles 65 and 120.[160] Second, any marine mammal take that occurs without permission of an approved regional organization/arrangement constitutes an unregulated take that is therefore illegal.

Empowering those states that are bound by new regulatory measures to take lawful action against states that act in a manner that undermines this Agreement's effectiveness necessitates enforcement mechanisms, as I outline in the next section. This proposal does not deviate from the primacy of flag state responsibility, but rather reinforces that states parties "shall take such measures as may be necessary to ensure that vessels flying its flag comply with [those international measures, as agreed to by the IMMC and adopted, applied and/or implemented regionally] and that such vessels do not engage in activity which undermines the effectiveness of such measures."[161] They shall also:

(1) "authorize the use of vessels flying its flag for [the take of marine mammals] on the high seas where it is able to exercise effectively its responsibilities";
(2) "control [flagged] ... vessels on the high seas by means of licenses, authorizations or permits, in accordance with any applicable procedures agreed" at the Commission or regionally;
(3) establish and maintain "a national record of vessels entitled to fly its flag and authorized to be used to take marine mammals on the high seas"[162] and enter the appropriate vessels in this record;[163]
(4) require vessel and gear identification and marking in accordance with international standards;[164]
(5) require recording and "timely reporting of vessel position, [take] of target and non-target species and other relevant data in accordance with standards for collection of such data" established or adopted at the Commission or regionally;[165]
(6) require verification of the take of "target and non-target species through such means as observer programmes, identification schemes, unloading reports, supervision of transshipment and monitoring of landed catches and market statistics through [DNA testing] or otherwise";[166]
(7) monitor and control vessels and their marine mammal take operations through measures such as: the "implementation of national inspection schemes and regional schemes for cooperation and enforcement" and "requirements for such vessels to permit access by duly authorized inspectors from other States"; "the implementation of national observer

programmes and regional observer programmes"; and "the development and implementation of vessel monitoring systems, including, [global positioning and] satellite transmitter systems, in accordance with any national programmes and those which have been agreed by the" IMMC or regionally;[167]

(8) regulate high seas transshipment to ensure that conservation and sustainable management measures are not undermined;[168] and

(9) regulate the take of marine mammals to achieve compliance with those measures agreed at the IMMC and adopted, applied, and/or implemented regionally.[169]

A first step in combatting unauthorized action by nonparticipant state flagged vessels is the creation of a vessel database, maintained by the IMMC, which assists in determining which vessels are participating in an unregulated or otherwise illegal marine mammal take. Precedent for this exists in the High Seas Vessels Authorization Record (HSVAR), which is maintained by the FAO and "contains distinctive and descriptive elements of high seas fishing vessels as well as information on registration and authorizations status, infringements etc."[170] On the basis of this information, participating states can then act against these vessels in accordance with the enforcement mechanisms provided for in the proposed Agreement, including vessel boarding and inspection and port state action (i.e., denial of entry, refusal to land or transshipment the catch, or inspection).

(ii) Compliance and Enforcement

Compliance and enforcement form a critical component of this new regime because "[r]egulation entails both the prescription of rules and standards and their enforcement."[171] From the outset, one must be mindful that "compliance" and "enforcement" are in fact two distinct concepts.[172] Compliance "may be defined as the conformance by a state with its international obligations," whereas enforcement requires "control and sanction," with control being "the processes of invoking compulsion in order to achieve the sought after compliance" and sanction being "the formal application of the law through judicial or other processes and includes actions taken to prosecute and punish non-compliance."[173] One unfortunate unifying feature of compliance and enforcement in the area of oceans law generally, and marine mammal conservation specifically, is that efforts have consistently proved inadequate.

Before commenting on how enforcement and compliance can be addressed in the new Agreement it is appropriate to recall the limited consideration given to these critical issues in Article IX of the ICRW, which reads:

1. Each Contracting Government shall take appropriate measures to ensure the application of the provisions of this Convention and the punishment of infractions against the said provisions in operations carried out by persons or by vessels under its jurisdiction.
2. No bonus or other remuneration calculated with relation to the results of their work shall be paid to the gunners and crews of whale catchers in respect of any whales the taking of which is forbidden by this Convention.

3. Prosecution for infractions against or contraventions of this Convention shall be instituted by the Government having jurisdiction over the offence.
4. Each Contracting Government shall transmit to the Commission full details of each infraction of the provisions of this Convention by persons or vessels under the jurisdiction of that Government as reported by its inspectors. This information shall include a statement of measures taken for dealing with the infraction and of penalties imposed.[174]

The simplicity and brevity of this provision is insufficient to address the issues associated with compliance and enforcement of any controversial take of mammals that, in many instances, occurs on the high seas beyond national jurisdiction.

Broadly stated, the proposed approach does not deviate from the primacy of flag state jurisdiction and national enforcement, but it does provide a detailed alternative to the present inadequacy that utilizes and modifies the innovative compliance and enforcement scheme contemplated by the UN Fish Stocks Agreement.[175] The UN Fish Stocks Agreement approach to compliance and enforcement emphasizes three key elements: (1) detailed flag state duties, (2) codified customary port state action, and (3) inspection and enforcement on the high seas.[176] Indeed, this Agreement does not propose the creation of a new international group to enforce established measures, but it does bolster existing roles and responsibilities and promotes regional enforcement in the hopes that similarly situated states are motivated to promote compliance and enforcement.

A logical starting place is the articulation of the duties owed by all states parties under the new Agreement. In ensuring compliance with the Agreement and the Annex's conservation and sustainable management measures, states parties shall "take legislative, administrative or policy measures, as appropriate, with the aim of ensuring compliance by their nationals, including, where appropriate, making contravention of duties imposed by this Agreement or undermining of conservation and [sustainable] management measures an offence under national legislation and taking all appropriate steps to discourage nationals from participating in activities in breach of this Agreement."[177] Further, states parties shall "ensure that sanctions applicable in respect of such contraventions shall be of sufficient gravity as to be effective in securing compliance with the requirements of this Agreement and to deprive offenders of the benefits accruing from their illegal activities."[178] These obligations call upon all states parties to achieve domestic implementation and secure national compliance. This is one way to work toward minimizing the problems associated with reflagging and flags of convenience and to inject a concrete compliance and enforcement objective into what can otherwise be a nebulous concept.

The remaining compliance and enforcement mechanisms must strike a compromise between flag state jurisdiction, port state jurisdiction, and permissible high seas action. Addressing flag state jurisdiction first, a new Agreement shall start with the base obligation of ensuring that vessels flying its flag comply with those conservation and sustainable management measures for marine mammals agreed at the IMMC and adopted, applied, and/or implemented regionally. In operationalizing this duty, flag states shall: (1) "enforce such measures irrespective of where violations occur"; (2) investigate any alleged violation "immediately and fully . . . which may include the inspection of the vessels concerned" and report on the result of the investigation to the IMMC, regional organization, or concerned state; (3) compel "any vessel flying its flag to give information to the investigating authority regarding vessel position, catches, gear, operations and related activities in the area of the alleged violation"; (4) refer any case supported by sufficient evidence "to its authorities with a view to instituting proceedings without delay in accordance with its laws and, where appropriate, detain the vessel concerned"; (5) and ensure that "a vessel [that] has been involved in the commission of a serious violation" of conservation and sustainable management measures does not engage in the take of marine mammals on the high seas until all sanctions imposed by its flag state have been complied with. Investigations and proceedings shall be undertaken expeditiously, and remedial action against vessel "masters and other officers" involved in said violations should be available.[179]

Flag states cannot be expected to go it alone, and the new Agreement should seek to complement their efforts with international cooperation, be it through the IMMC or regional organizations/arrangements, to achieve compliance and enforcement with respect to conservation and sustainable management measures. Such cooperation should encompass assistance and information-sharing for the purposes of national investigations, vessel identification, evidence sharing through the Secretariat, cooperation between coastal states and flag states for potential violations by vessels now on the high seas that occurred within areas of national jurisdiction, and finally recourse to regional deterrence and enforcement procedures so far as they exist.

Given the emphasis that this proposed regime places on regional cooperation and implementation, it should not be surprising that regional compliance and enforcement mechanisms should also feature prominently in this scheme. Specifically, the new Agreement should adopt the vessel inspection mechanism found in Article 21 of the UN Fish Stocks Agreement whereby inspectors from a state party belonging to a regional organization/arrangement can inspect other state party flagged vessels on an area of the high seas covered by the regional agreement, for the purpose of ensuring compliance with conservation and sustainable management measures, irrespective of their membership in that particular regional organization/arrangement. This boarding and inspection scheme would also contemplate: (1) the creation of boarding and inspecting procedures by the IMMC, to be regionally implemented; (2) inspection vessel identification requirements; (3) inspecting notification to the flag state following the discovery of evidence of the violation of conservation and sustainable measure; (4) complementary flag state or inspecting state enforcement action for violations;[180] (5) action to be taken against a flagless vessel reasonably suspected of taking marine mammals; and (6) liability arising from unwarranted inspection action. Similar to the approach used in the UN Fish Stocks Agreement, the IMMC may establish procedures for boarding and inspection that accord with a basic boarding and inspection scheme that obliges actors from both the flag state and inspecting state to behave in certain ways.[181]

Based on Article 23 of the UN Fish Stocks Agreement, which reflects customary international law, certain port state compliance and enforcement mechanisms should also be promoted.[182] Port state action is an important piece of the compliance and enforcement puzzle as port states have sovereign control over their ports and offshore terminals and, therefore, can exercise jurisdiction regarding access (subject to the caveat that access shall be allowed in instances of duress or emergency); and inspection of documentation, gear, apparatus, and any marine mammal take that is on-board; as well as other appropriate control measures. Further,

"States may adopt regulations empowering the relevant national authorities to prohibit landings and transshipments where it has been established that the catch has been taken in a manner that is contrary to [or undermines the effectiveness of] conservation and [sustainable] management measures" as established by the IMMC and adopted, applied, and/or implemented regionally.[183] The IMMC could further coherence and consistency by producing best-practice guidelines for port inspection or port control mechanisms that could be adopted/promoted by the regional organizations and arrangements.

Finally, the proposed Agreement should require states to cooperate through the IMMC and/or regional marine mammal organizations and arrangements to deter, reduce, and eliminate illegal, unreported, and unregulated (IUU) take of marine mammals in accordance with international law. IUU fishing is "a major threat to the sustainable management and conservation of world fisheries"[184] that many RFMOs struggle to address, and it can occur in the form of stateless vessels that are taking living marine resources or vessels flagged in states that are not party to the UN Fish Stocks Agreement.[185] IUU was addressed by the FAO in 2001 through the production of a voluntary agreement called the International Plan of Action to Prevent, Deter and Eliminate IUU Fishing (the IPOA-IUU).[186] The FAO indicates that the IPOA-IUU serves as a "'toolbox'—that is, a set of tools for use in dealing with IUU fishing in its many forms. Not all tools in the toolbox are appropriate for use in all situations. The choice of tools will depend on the particular circumstances in a fishery."[187]

The most relevant consideration here is how states can cooperate through the IMMC or regional organizations/arrangement to combat IUU as it relates to the take of marine mammals. First, states parties can seek to board and inspect vessels that they believe (or reasonably assume) to be engaged in a marine mammal take in an area covered by a regional organization or arrangement. For flagged vessels that are not party to the Agreement, boarding and inspection can occur so long as consent is obtained from the vessel.[188] With respect to stateless vessels, boarding and inspection can occur without consent, owing to its stateless status.[189] Second, port states (within or outside of the regulated area) can restrict access, landing, or transshipment of the vessels presumed to be engaged in IUU in accordance with their sovereignty (as discussed above).[190] Third, identification of vessels known or suspected to be engaging in IUU enables states to cooperate in the production of a vessel list (called "blacklists"), which are publicized and advertised in case such vessels are spotted elsewhere.[191] RFMOs have created "Non-Contracting Party Schemes" in regional agreements to address this issue in more detail and in accordance with particular concerns (an example being Chapter VIII of the Northwest Atlantic Fisheries Organization Conservation and Enforcement Measures).[192] The IMMC should consider the production of a similar system as a conservation and sustainable management measure, which could then be adopted, applied, and implemented by the appropriate regional organizations. The IMMC's Secretariat is well-positioned as the regime's organ capable of helping establish, maintain, and disseminate vessel lists.

(III) Dispute Resolution

The ICRW does not contemplate recourse to international dispute resolution. The absence of a dispute resolution mechanism recently came to the fore during the dispute between Australia and Japan (with New Zealand intervening in support of Australia) before the International Court of Justice (ICJ) regarding the interpretation of Article VIII of the ICRW, "special permit" scientific whaling, and Japan's JARPA II whaling program. Disputes can come before the ICJ in a few consent-based ways. First, a treaty can expressly provide recourse to the Court for states parties. Second, states can accept the ICJ's jurisdiction to adjudicate a particular issue by Special Agreement. Third, Article 36(2) of the Statute of the International Court of Justice provides that states "may at any time declare that they recognize as compulsory ipso facto and without special agreement, in relation to any other state accepting the same obligation, the jurisdiction of the Court in all legal disputes" involving treaty interpretation, questions of international law, the existence of a fact that proves a breach of an international obligation, or the type of reparation owed in light of a breached obligation.[193]

Australia utilized the Article 36(2) optional declaration mechanism as the basis for its challenge to JARPA II's scientific whaling as both Australia (on March 22, 2002) and Japan (on July 9, 2007) had registered optional declarations. Japan's optional declaration does not contain any reservations, but does stipulate reciprocity. Important for this dispute, Australia's declaration reserved against:

> any dispute concerning or relating to the delimitation of maritime zones, including the territorial sea, the exclusive economic zone and the continental shelf, or arising out of, or concerning, or relating to the exploitation of any disputed area of or adjacent to any such maritime zone pending its delimitation.[194]

Japan contested jurisdiction in written and oral argument, maintaining that the second clause of the reservation, "or relating to the exploitation of any disputed area of or adjacent to any such maritime zone pending its delimitation," is disjunctive of the first and applicable to both delimitation disputes and "other kinds of disputes involving the exploitation of maritime zones or adjacent areas pending delimitation."[195] Put another way, Japan asserted that JARPA II takes place in an area of the Southern Ocean in or around Australia's disputed EEZ appurtenant to its sovereignty claim to a part of continental Antarctica.[196] Australia's responded with an interpretation of "disputed area" that applies only to marine areas subject to overlapping claims—such as Australia's delimitations that were ongoing with New Zealand and Timor-Leste at the time the declaration was made—and of "exploitation" that covers those resources actually within a disputed area.[197] In seeking "the interpretation which is in harmony with a natural and reasonable way of reading the text, having due regard to the [declaring State's] intention,"[198] the ICJ favored Australia's interpretation of its reservation and unanimously dismissed Japan's objection.[199]

Any successor to the ICRW must facilitate access to dispute resolution. Although it might be impossible to avoid jurisdictional contests and other such preliminary matters, any complex regime that relies on modern principles and mechanisms of international law must contemplate a better route to consent-based dispute resolution than reliance on Special Agreement or fortuitous reciprocal optional declarations. The robust dispute resolution process in UNCLOS exists in stark contrast to the ICRW and remains one of its most important achievements. As noted by author Igor Karaman, "[t]he dispute settlement system under the Convention is rightly considered to be one of the most developed and sophisticated dispute resolution systems available today in international treaty-law making."[200] It is also unique to public international law in that it is "comprehensive and compulsory" and, importantly, it can be triggered by any state party.[201] It is beyond the scope of this work to provide a detailed examination of this dispute resolution process; indeed, that task has been adequately accomplished in existing works.[202] Rather, the following discussion highlights the key observations and justifications for the purposes of including UNCLOS's approach to dispute resolution in the proposed Agreement.

In essence, the new Agreement can utilize Part VIII ("Peaceful Settlement of Disputes") of the UN Fish Stocks Agreement, as it offers a template for adapting the dispute resolution approach in UNCLOS to subsequent implementing agreements. To start, states parties should be obliged to cooperate in preventing disputes wherever possible[203] and, failing this, to attempt to resolve disputes external of the formal dispute machinery wherever possible.[204] This can entail "negotiation, inquiry, mediation, conciliation, arbitration, judicial settlement, resort to [the IMMC or] regional agencies or arrangements, or other peaceful means of their own choice."[205] It is also appropriate to include the following provision in the new Agreement:

Disputes of a technical nature

Where a dispute concerns a matter of a technical nature, the States concerned may refer the dispute to an ad hoc expert panel established by them. The panel shall confer with the States concerned and shall endeavour to resolve the dispute expeditiously without recourse to binding procedures for the settlement of disputes.[206]

The regime that I propose relies heavily on scientific information and evidence as well as other technical information. Because disagreements about such matters will often turn on an interpretation of specialized knowledge rather than discrete questions of law, enabling recourse to an ad hoc panel that acts expeditiously should help prevent undue delay in the development and implementation of conservation and sustainable management measures. What qualifies as a "technical" matter should be agreed to on a case-by-case basis between states parties as the regime functions and evolves.

In the event that disputes cannot be resolved in the manner outlined above, the new Agreement can incorporate the UNCLOS's formal dispute resolution machinery by providing that the "provisions relating to the settlement of disputes set out in Part XV of the Convention apply *mutatis mutandis* to any dispute between States Parties to this Agreement concerning the interpretation or application of this Agreement, whether or not they are also Parties to the Convention."[207] In terms of issue coverage, this dispute resolution should, at a minimum, cover interpretation of this Agreement, the IMMC's activities, and the interpretation of regional agreements or regional implementation of conservation and sustainable management measures.

Turning to the actual forums that are available for dispute resolution under UNCLOS leads us to another important aspect of the UNCLOS dispute resolution process. Specifically, Article 287 ("Choice of Procedure," also known as the "cafeteria" approach) of UNCLOS enables states parties to select the form of binding dispute resolution they prefer, via declaration upon ratification or accession, which is triggered in the event that a dispute cannot be settled external to this process. States have the choice among: (1) the International Tribunal for the Law of the Sea

(ITLOS, which is a "new permanent institution dedicated to resolving law of the sea disputes [and] is rightly regarded as being at the centre of the Part XV dispute resolution system"),[208] (2) the ICJ, (3) Annex VII general arbitration, or (4) Annex VIII special arbitration. For states that previously declared a preference upon ratification of UNCLOS, that choice will govern for states parties to this Agreement, unless they indicate an alternate preference. For states parties to this Agreement, which are not also party to UNCLOS, they are free to indicate their preference at the time of ratification. Currently, the following dispute resolution preferences have been declared for UNCLOS states parties: (1) 32 nations have selected the ITLOS as their primary choice, (2) 20 nations have selected the ICJ as their primary choice, (3) 8 nations have selected Annex VII general arbitration as their primary choice, and (4) 7 nations have selected special arbitration as their primary choice.[209] In the event of a dispute between states parties that have indicated divergent preferences, the only option available to these parties is Annex VII general arbitration.[210]

Finally, the new Agreement should also articulate that provisional measures are available for disputes arising out of this new regime. Provisional measures are important to ensure that marine mammal species/population(s) are not compromised prior to final determination by the appropriate court or tribunal.

Before progressing further it is pertinent to offer a few thoughts on why it may be appropriate to be cautiously optimistic about the future treatment of scientific evidence in international dispute resolution. But first, it is pertinent to reflect on the functionality and centrality of the ITLOS to oceans law and this proposed regime. The ITLOS, created by Annex VI of UNCLOS ("Statute of the International Tribunal for the Law of the Sea"), and located in Hamburg, Germany, has become a functional, independent[211] dispute resolution body with jurisdiction over law-of-the seas issues in both a contentious and advisory capacity.[212] The ITLOS has various chambers that have been established pursuant to its Statute,[213] and continues to produce jurisprudence, especially in the areas of prompt release and provisional matters.[214] Cases of note include: (1) the *Southern Bluefin Tuna Cases (New Zealand v. Japan; Australia v. Japan)*,[215] (2) the *Case concerning the Conservation and Sustainable Exploitation of Swordfish Stocks in the South-Eastern Pacific Ocean (Chile/European Union)*,[216] and (3) *The MOX Plant Case (Ireland v. United Kingdom)*.[217] This jurisprudential record suggests that the ITLOS is an appropriate forum within which to hear substantive matters, and bolsters the decision to promote recourse to this tribunal. Most recently, the ITLOS issued an advisory opinion in response to a request from the Sub-Regional Fisheries Commission regarding legal issues surrounding flag state obligations; illegal, unreported, and unregulated fishing; and the sustainable management of shared pelagic stocks.[218] This sort of advisory assistance could be sought by regional marine mammal organizations or arrangements that require clarification or assistance in implementing the conservation and sustainable management measures produced by the IMMC.

Finally, and returning to the ICJ and more specifically its recent *Whaling in the Antarctic* decision, it is noteworthy that the approach employed toward scientific evidence was a welcome deviation from past practice. The judicial function is "to reach a decision on disputes properly brought before them,"[219] or, put another way, "to evaluate the claims of the parties before it and whether such claims are sufficiently well-founded so as to constitute evidence of a breach of a legal obligation."[220] Despite concerns that "[j]udges of international courts have an observable reluctance to engage deeply with scientific issues,"[221] scientific and technical evidence occupies an increasingly important role in international environmental dispute adjudication.[222]

Scientific evidence can come before the ICJ in different ways. The Court can arrange for an expert opinion,[223] information can be sought from specialized international organizations,[224] experts can appear as advocates/counsel before the Court,[225] an agent versed in the necessary scientific or technical information can present it in the course of oral argument,[226] or a party can call experts/witnesses as part of its case[227] in accordance with its declared list of intended witnesses/experts.[228] Although it has been common for experts to appear as counsel, in *Pulp Mills on the River Uruguay (Argentina v. Uruguay)* the Court enunciated its preference that this evidence be presented by independent experts/witnesses as this allows the evidence to be tested:[229]

> ... those persons who provide evidence before the Court based on their scientific or technical knowledge and on their personal experience should testify before the Court as experts, witnesses or in some cases in both capacities, rather than counsel, so that they may be submitted to questioning by the other party as well as by the Court.[230]

This is exactly what happened in *Whaling in the Antarctic*. Australia called two experts during the public hearings: (1) Professor Marc Mangel (Distinguished Research Professor of Mathematical Biology and Director of the Center for Stock Assessment Research, UC Santa Cruz), and (2) Nick Gales (Chief Scientist for Australia's Antarctic Programme).[231] Japan called Professor Emeritus Lars Walløe from the University of Oslo, who is also advisor to the government of Norway.[232] Each expert provided a written statement that preceded his oral testimony, was examined in chief, cross-examined, and received questions from the Court.[233]

In *Whaling in the Antarctic*, the ICJ met the criticism that it is unwilling or unable to effectively deal with highly technical matters.[234] In the portions of the judgment that investigate the terms "scientific research"[235] and "for purposes of [scientific research],"[236] and that assess "JARPA II in light of Article VIII of the Convention,"[237] the Court worked with the experts' evidence in the context of the standard of review it established.[238] By shedding its reluctance and demonstrating its ability to tackle competing opinions regarding the validity of the impugned scientific whaling, the ICJ has provided a model for the use of experts in this judicial forum moving forward, and has strengthened the case for facilitating access to judicial expertise. Further, in the event that future cases involve expert evidence that is highly ambiguous or the parties choose experts that raise concerns about bias, the Court should pursue the other options available to it in its Rules and Statute to ascertain the necessary information or alleviate these concerns to the extent practicable.[239]

4. Political Obstacles

As alluded to throughout this work, marine mammal conservation and management is complicated by its political realities; in fact, politics and legal issues are interwoven to the extent that it becomes difficult to ever distinguish between the two. As a poignantly eco-political issue, marine mammal conservation is shaped by "environmental problems, political developments, and normative considerations."[240] In his assessment of the ability to employ rationality and logic to pursue compromise with respect to the conservation of living marine resources, Professor Michael Bowman writes: "it seems clear that no truly 'rational' approach to the management of natural ecosystems can be conceived unless due account is taken of all the many internal rationalities of which they are themselves composed."[241] One way, and perhaps the most appropriate way, to understand competing foreign policies regarding marine mammal utilization, and the impact of such differences, is to consider important domestic factors of the key players.

In his article titled "Why Japan Supports Whaling," Professor Keiko Hirata argues that Japan's pro-whaling position is the product of unique domestic variables, and that contrary to popular belief materialism/economics does not rank among them.[242] He asserts that the Japanese whaling industry, including the small scale coastal whaling operations that are not subject to IWC scrutiny and the large scale scientific program contracted to Kyodo Senpaku in collaboration with the "semi-governmental not for profit organization" called the Institute of Cetacean Research that does fall within the ICRW's purview, is simply too weak to effectively influence Japanese national policy.[243] The reality being that the sale of whale meat does not cover the costs associated with running the large scale program while government subsidies and tax payer dollars have been used to keep it operational since the late 1980s.[244] Alternatively, Hirata posits that a combination of domestic cultural values and political structures explain Japan's staunchly pro-whaling foreign policy. With respect to cultural values, Hirata opines that the international anti-whaling norm has yet to be taken up in Japan because officials, scientists, and journalists have propped up nationalistic approval of whaling using three persuasive narratives: (1) that whale meat has been consumed by the Japanese for thousands of years—the so-called *gyoshoku bunka* (whale-eating culture), (2) that whales are fish rather than mammals, and (3) that Western interference and "cultural imperialism" should be resisted.[245] Although still prevalent, whale biologist Phillip Clapham, who has served as a U.S. delegate to the IWC's Scientific Committee, posits that these domestic obstacles may be slowly diminishing as "domestic demand for whale meat in Japan is low, the industry is heavily subsidized, the single factory ship is aging, and whaling is regarded by many in Japan as an international embarrassment."[246]

Even as domestic consumption wanes it is difficult to predict the consequence of this reduction. In 2005, Keirko Hirata wrote that Japan is "unlikely to change its pro-whaling stance in the near to medium term, barring any major unforeseen event."[247] This prediction was based largely on the fact that Japan's domestic political decision-making is highly centralized and dissimilar to other jurisdictions, like the United States, Australia, and many European Union countries, where environmental and animal welfare lobby groups have been successful in persuading law- and policymakers to adopt and advance the anti-whaling norm,[248] and that in Japan there is not the same proximity between NGOs and the official bureaucracy that is ultimately swayed by the pro-whaling position advanced by official agencies.[249] It is tempting to categorize the ICJ's *Whaling in the Antarctic* decision as the sort of major unforeseen event that Hirata conceded could transform Japan's official perspective on whaling, or at the very least on scientific whaling, toward the anti-whaling ethos. However, events subsequent to the decision reject this categorization and instead tend to buttress Professor Kurkpatrick Dorsey's assessment from 2013 that Japan remains unlikely to stop whaling in the near future because "[a]dmitting that whaling is no longer needed for scientific or nutritional purposes would entail a major loss of face."[250]

Japan was quick to respond to the unfavorable *Whaling in the Antarctic* decision in announcing that it would abide by the ICJ's ruling and terminate JARPA II.[251] Shortly thereafter in November 2014, Japan revealed a revamped successor Antarctic scientific research program called the New Scientific Whale Research Program in the Antarctic Ocean (NEWREP-A).[252] Japan is correct in its assessment that *Whaling in the Antarctic* is not applicable beyond JARPA II, and that it maintains the prerogative to initiate a new scientific program pursuant to Article VIII such as NEWREP-A. Moreover, NEWREP-A frequently references the Court's reasons as well as its obiter statement that "it is to be expected that Japan will take account of the reasoning and conclusions contained in this Judgment as it evaluates the possibility of granting any future [Article VIII] permits."[253] To this end, NEWREP-A seeks to justify the reasonableness and scientific validity of the decision to lethally sample 333 minke whales per year between 2015 and 2027 in light of its two main stated objectives: (1) "Improvements in the precision of biological and ecological information for the application of the RMP to the Antarctic minke whales," and (2) "Investigation of the structure and dynamics of the Antarctic marine ecosystem through building ecosystem models."[254] The main justification advanced throughout is that lethal sampling is needed to assess population dynamics and diet in light of the Revised Management Procedure and ecosystem functionality.

The IWC also had the opportunity to respond to *Whaling in the Antarctic* at its 65th meeting in 2014. Here, the Commission passed Resolution 2014-5—Resolution on Whaling under Special Permit. Although Article VIII ultimately leaves the decision regarding issuance of special permits to Contracting Governments, and despite the fact that IWC resolutions are not binding, Resolution 2014-5 is significant in that the Commission affirms and then re-scopes the Scientific Committee's[255] review and comment on proposed special permits as is required by paragraph 30 of the ICRW's Schedule, and then confirms that upon receipt and consideration of such a report it will "make such recommendations as it sees fit."[256] Specifically, it instructs the Scientific Committee to revise its review process[257] in accordance with the IWC's interpretation of *Whaling in the Antarctic* and requests that:

> ... no further special permits for the take of whales are issued under existing research programmes or any new programme of whale research until:
>
> (a) the Scientific Committee has reviewed the research programme to enable it to provide advice to the Commission in accordance with the instructions [in the resolution] above; and
> (b) the Commission has considered the report of the Scientific Committee and assessed whether the proponent of the special permit programme has acted in accordance with the review process described [in the resolution] above; and
> (c) the Commission has, in accordance with Article VI, made such recommendations on the merits or otherwise of the special permit programme as it sees fit.

As identified by Michael Johnson, Principle Legal Officer for the Office of International Law of the Australian Commonwealth Attorney-General's Department, "[e]ven though the review process does not entail legally binding outcomes for the Contracting Government proposing a program, ensuring that the scientific aspects of any new program will be scrutinized against the criteria established by the Court will go a long way to revealing whether it objectively falls within the scope of Article VIII."[258] An Expert Panel of the Scientific Committee subjected NEWREP-A to such a review at its intersession meeting in February 2015, and ultimately found that the proposed program lacked sufficient detail for a full review to be completed as required by Annex P in conjunction with Resolution 2014-5, concluding it "was not able to determine whether lethal sampling is necessary to achieve the two major objectives; therefore, the current proposal does not demonstrate the need for lethal sampling to achieve those objectives."[259] Japan has more work to do in producing the information/data to persuade these scientific experts that resuming lethal research is justified, and to do so before the IWC issues its own recommendations. In the interim, Japan may very well decide to press on with a 2015–2016 Antarctic scientific whaling campaign without the IWC's blessing, as is their right under the current scheme. Such action is likely to prompt international condemnation, and although failure to abide by the Scientific Committee's expert opinion that applies the Court's objective criteria from *Whaling in the Antarctic* is not illegal in and of itself, this is sure to be "one important element in any ultimate determination of legality" if the matter ultimately comes before an international court or tribunal.[260] On October 6, 2015, Japan formally changed its optional declaration recognizing the ICJ's compulsory jurisdiction. This new declaration excludes "any dispute arising out of, concerning, or relating to research on, or conservation, management or exploitation of, living resources of the sea," thereby likely signaling that any future dispute over scientific whaling shall have to be considered under the dispute resolution process contained in Article 287 of UNCLOS.[261]

Iceland and Norway are the other two states that maintain a commercial whale hunt. Unlike Japan's scientific whaling programs, Iceland and Norway whale on the basis of their reservations to the ICW's moratorium. Both countries base their continued pursuit of commercial whaling on rich whaling traditions that evoke cultural associations but also emphasize the goal of ecosystem-based management, and view whaling as one dimension of the sustainable use of living marine resources.[262] These whaling operations also differ from Japan's programs in that they occur within Iceland and Norway's Exclusive Economic Zones/Fisheries Protection Zones.

The states that oppose lethal utilization have also been motivated by identifiable factors. For example, the incredibly successful "Save the Whale" campaign of the 1970s ultimately culminated in the moratorium on commercial whaling.[263] It is true that it was IWC Contracting Governments that ultimately voted in favor of the moratorium, but the reality is that it was the significant efforts of emerging NGOs, especially Greenpeace, that successfully lobbied key states to adopt pro-preservationist perspectives. For example, America's consistent anti-commercial whaling foreign policy is "largely the result of the concentrated energy NGOs ... through the strength of environmental lobbyists."[264] Specifically: "US administrations, prodded by growing public pressure articulated by conservationist groups, scientists, and even labour unions, would lead the fight against the whaling both by participating in the IWC arena and by resorting to less diplomatic, or more economic, means of statecraft."[265] A key example is the use of domestic legislation, namely the Pelly Amendment to the Fisherman's Protective Act and the Packwood/Magnuson Amendment to the Fishery Conservation Management Act, to influence the practice of other states through restricting access to American markets and resources. Specifically, the Pelly Amendment afforded the president "the option of banning any or all fisheries imports from a country certified by the US secretary of commerce (who is ultimately responsible for whaling policy) as conducting fishing operations in a manner or under circumstances that diminish the effectiveness of an international fishery conservation program."[266] The Packwood/Magnuson Amendment also utilized a similar approach to "block access to US coastal waters for nations that are violating bans on killing endangered marine mammals."[267] Actual or threatened certification of Japan, the USSR, the Republic of Korea, China, Chile, Peru, and Norway effectively altered the state action.[268] The United States also collaborated with NGOs and other Save the Whale converts swayed by their own domestic environmental movements, including New Zealand, Australia, Germany, France, the Netherlands, and the United Kingdom to lobby or pressure non-whaling states to join the IWC in an effort to enhance the voting power of the anti-whaling perspective.[269] This proved to be ultimately quite a successful strategy. After a series of failures to secure the number of votes needed to pass a commercial moratorium, there was a change leading up to the 1982 meeting, as the number of Contracting Governments rose to 38, with 9 states that generally lacked any discernible whaling interest joining to "vote with the environmentalists."[270]

More recently, whaling politics witnessed the emergence of the so-called Buenos Aires Group in 2005. This anti-whaling block of 13 Latin American and Caribbean states beses their anti-whaling position on the value of the ecotourism sector.[271] The emergence of the Buenos Aires Group has been attributed to the rise of Latin NGOs promoting conservationist agendas, the emergence of small-scale local whale watching operations, and the tailing off of whaling; in fact, only the small island nation of St. Vincent and the Grenadines currently conducts a limited whaling operation.[272] In Jennifer Bailey's assessment, the Buenos Aires Group has helped pull the conservation ethos forward as it transcends the North-South divide that often threatens international environmental cooperation, and also helps rebut claims of Western cultural imperialism.[273] The Buenos Aires Group has also emphasized national sovereignty in asserting their desire to manage whale resources in a manner that most directly benefits their populations.[274] The lasting impact of this nascent preservationist group is yet to be determined, but its emergence does project the continuation of a strong conservationist voting block within the IWC and reduces the chances of the pro-utilization states reversing the commercial moratorium.

It is tempting to conclude, based upon the political positions explored above, that there is no hope of securing a rational successor to the ICRW/IWC; however, such a dire conclusion ignores some of the other lessons from the eco-political whaling drama. For example, perhaps we should be somewhat awed by the fact that the ICRW/IWC continues to exist at all and that, despite its many ups and downs, states have generally continued to participate in its regulatory processes. Even after the IWC delivered Japan's scientific whaling program a significant blow, Japan did not react by withdrawing its Contracting Government status form the IWC as it is free to do. Another reason for possible optimism is that regional regimes, such as

NAMMO, that might have initially threatened to usurp the IWC's primacy have failed to unseat it and have instead become complimentary (or at least not conflicting) cooperative initiatives.

Another reason to be cautiously optimistic is that international marine mammal controversies have not soured important existing or emerging international relationships. It is now clear post-*Whaling in the Antarctic* that Japan and Australia have effectively weathered any heightened tension that resulted from the litigation.[275] Indeed, successful visits from each head of state suggest that bilateral relations continue to be strengthened.[276] Security and defense and cultural connections remain a priority for both states, and regarding economic cooperation, the much-anticipated *Japan-Australia Economic Partnership Agreement* entered into force on January 15, 2015.[277] Although Professor Rothwell correctly observes that there is still considerable room for disagreement over the continued implementation of *Whaling in the Antarctic* and Japan's contentious decision to revamp its Antarctic whaling program,[278] there is reason to hope that compromise may yet be possible.

Strikingly similar developments in the ongoing sealing/seal-product dispute between Canada and the European Union further evince the ability for states to silo disagreements over marine mammal conservation issues to pursue stronger international relations. The European Union's ban on imported seal products that was deemed legitimate on public moral (animal welfare) grounds by the World Trade Organization's Dispute Panel (in 2013) and Appellate Body (in 2014) did not sour negotiations toward the recently completed *Comprehensive Economic and Trade Agreement*, which targets the reduction or elimination of custom duties, the establishment of new trade priorities, and the creation of jobs; it and is expected to come into force in 2016.[279] Hopefully, stronger ties will foster more effective dialogue on outstanding controversies, including marine mammal conservation, and that such dialogue will move the international community toward agreement and compromise.

It is appropriate to end this section with reference to recent developments that, even in the face of political maneuvering and wrangling, ought to be central to any discussion of marine mammal management. Although it is easy to focus on the dire situation inherited from generations gone by, we must not ignore success stories as they become available. The Northern Pacific humpback whale population has rebounded from some 1,400 individuals to a fairly robust 20,000 individuals in fairly short order.[280] Similarly, the North Pacific blue whale population off the coast of California, targeted until 1971, appears to have rebounded to some 2,200 individuals, which may represent recovery to 97 percent of this population's historic level.[281] Sea otters, extirpated along Canada's coastline as a result of a voracious fur trade, have since been reintroduced and continue to re-establish themselves.[282] The list of recoveries continues with success stories about the recovery of humpback whales around Australia, harbor porpoises in Puget Sound off the Pacific Northwest, and the northern elephant seal off Mexico and California. Obviously there are many contrasting narratives that end much less favorably for different marine mammal species, but the takeaway point is that proper management can have a discernible impact on the conservation status of some of the planet's largest and longest-lived mammals. It is imperative that we continue to press toward the production of more success stories, and that we do not let political agendas obfuscate this goal.

III. CONCLUSION

This chapter has introduced and outlined a comprehensive proposal for a new approach to the international conservation and sustainable management of marine mammals. Premised on the work contained in Chapters 1–5, this proposal embodies the compromise that I believe is necessary to achieve rational marine mammal conservation.

Objectively, the status quo is surely failing both the pro-whaling and anti-whaling states. Despite a commercial moratorium and ICJ decision, it seems almost certain that whaling will occur in the Southern Ocean Sanctuary in the near future pursuant to the controversial Scientific Permit exception. Small-type coastal whaling occurs without international oversight, marine mammals are being killed in suboptimal ways as it relates to humane killing standards, indirect threats to the long-term conservation are not being effectively addressed, Aboriginal Subsistence Whaling fails to capture the proper scope of subsistence use, the tools necessary to achieve ecosystem-based management do not exist, compliance and enforcement are elusive, and the ICRW lacks any express provision for peaceful dispute resolution.

The proposed UN Marine Mammal Agreement explored in this chapter, and presented in its entirety in Appendix 3, utilizes existing regimes and approaches as precedent, and also incorporates concepts that have been negotiated or considered in other contexts, to craft a response to these shortfalls. It envisions improved governance at the international, national, and regional levels, and strives to present a viable option that has both theoretical and practical benefits. The next chapter will address three prominent features of the proposed Agreement that require further discussion, namely the functionality of the Secretariat, the proposed use of regionalism, and the role of MPAs in achieving ecosystem-based management.

NOTES

1. Duncan Currie, *Whales, Sustainability and International Environmental Governance*, 16(1) RECIEL 45, 45 (2007).
2. 10 Dec. 1982, 21 I.L.M. 1261, 1833 U.N.T.S. 3 ["UNCLOS"].
3. 2 Dec. 1946, 62 Stat. 1716, 161 U.N.T.S. 74 ["ICRW"].
4. 4 Dec. 1995, 34 I.L.M. 1542, 2167 U.N.T.S. 3 [UN Fish Stocks Agreement].
5. 5 June 1992, 31 I.L.M. 818, 1760 U.N.T.S. 79 ["CBD"].
6. Agreement on Research, Conservation and Management of Marine Mammals in the North Atlantic. Apr. 9, 2012 ["NAMMCO Agreement"].
7. 17 Mar. 1992, 1772 U.N.T.S. 217.
8. 24 Nov. 1996, 2183 U.N.T.S. 303.
9. UN Fish Stocks Agreement, *supra* note 4, at art. 2 (recognizing that under "sustainable management" the consumptive/direct use of marine mammals is not prohibited, but also that sustainability must be understood to encompass the management of the indirect threats humans exert upon marine mammals).
10. *Id.* at art. 4.
11. *See* VED P. NANDA & GEORGE (ROCK) P   INTERNATIONAL ENVIRONMENTAL LAW AND POLICY FOR THE 21ST CE   36–37 (2d ed. 2013) ["NANDA & PRING"] (discussing the fact   internationally agreed definition of

"conservation"); *see* PATRICIA BIRNIE, ALAN BOYLE & CATHERINE REDGWELL, INTERNATIONAL LAW & THE ENVIRONMENT 655-57 (3d ed. 2009) ["BIRNIE ET AL."] (considering the use of the term "conservation" in treaty law).
12. *See* Convention on Migratory Species art. I(1)(c), 23 June 1979, 1651 U.N.T.S. 333 ["CMS"] (defining "conservation status").
13. *See* The International Union for the Conservation of Nature, *World Conservation Strategy*, 1(4)–1(7) (1980), http://data.iucn.org/dbtw-wpd/edocs/WCS-004.pdf (defining "conservation" and recognizing that for the purposes of conserving living resources one must consider ecosystem processes, genetic diversity, and sustainable utilization); RICHARD A. PRIMACK, ESSENTIALS OF CONSERVATION BIOLOGY 6 (3d ed. 2002) (describing the scope of conservation biology, noting its focus on biodiversity, human impact on species, genetic variation, and ecosystems).
14. *See* Marine Mammal Protection Act, 16 U.S.C. § 1632(2) (2007) ["MMPA"] (recognizing the goal of increasing or maintaining populations without necessarily precluding take).
15. *See* Convention for the Conservation of Antarctic Marine Living Resources art II(3)(a), 20 May 1980, 33 U.S.T. 3476, 1329 U.N.T.S. 48 ["CCAMLR"] (indicating the need to maintain certain population levels).
16. *Id.* at art II(2) (indicating that conservation "includes rational use").
17. *See* MICHAEL BOWMAN ET AL., LYSTER'S INTERNATIONAL WILDLIFE LAW 59–60 (2d ed. 2010).["LYSTER'S INTERNATIONAL WILDLIFE LAW"] (discussing the interaction between conservation and sustainable use).
18. UN Fish Stocks Agreement, *supra* note 4, at art. 1(b).
19. *See* Duncan E.J. Currie, *Ecosystem-Based Management in Multilateral Environmental Agreements: Progress towards Adopting the Ecosystem Approach in the International Management of Living Marine Resources*, WWF International 3–4 (2007); *see* ERICH HOYT, MARINE PROTECTED AREAS FOR WHALES, DOLPHINS, AND PORPOISES: A WORLD HANDBOOK FOR CETACEAN HABITAT CONSERVATION AND PLANNING 9–10 (2d ed. 2011).
20. *See* MARINE PROTECTED AREAS: A MULTIDISCIPLINARY APPROACH 2 (Joachim Claudet ed. 2011).
21. MMPA, *supra* note 14, at § 1362(11).
22. *Id.* at § 1362(2).
23. NANDA & PRING, *supra* note 11, at 29 (summarizing the principles that inform sustainable development at international law).
24. MMPA, *supra* note 14, at § 1362(2).
25. *Id.* at art 7.
26. *See* ICRW, *supra* note 3, at art. I(2) (note that in full this article reads: "This Convention applies to factory ships, land stations, and whale catchers under the jurisdiction of the Contracting Governments and to all waters in which whaling is prosecuted by such factory ships, land stations, and whale catchers").
27. UN Fish Stocks Agreement, *supra* note 4, at art. 5.
28. *Id.* at art. 6(2) (note that this is more or less reflective of the Rio Declaration on environment and Development's articulation of precaution).
29. Jorge Viñuales, *Legal Techniques for Dealing with Scientific Uncertainty in Environmental Law*, 43 VAND. J. TRANSNAT'L L. 437, 448–49 (2010).
30. *See* Jaye Ellis, *The Straddling Stocks Agreement and the Precautionary Principle as Interpretative Device and Rule of Law*, 32 OCEAN DEV. & INT'L L. 289, 295 (2001) (noting that some of the difficulties associated with conservation of straddling

stock and highly migratory species also provide "openings for reference to the precautionary principle: the best available scientific evidence, the modified conception of maximum sustainable yield, and the promotion of optimum utilization." One can set aside the optimum utilization aspect in this discussion of marine mammal conservation and still see considerable room for application of the precautionary principle in any use of the best available scientific evidence standard and the resumption and/or continuation of any limited take).

31. UN Fish Stocks Agreement, *supra* note 4, at art. 6(1).
32. *Id.* at art. 6(3)(a) (every state engaged in the new regime should be obligated by the Agreement to contribute to and pursue improving our understanding of the conservation status of marine mammal species. This is a collective responsibility that requires individual and aggregated action to be successful).
33. *Id.* at art. 6(3)(b).
34. *Id.* at art. 6(3)(c).
35. *Id.* at arts. 6(3)(d) & 6(5).
36. *Id.* at art. 6(6).
37. *Id.* at art. 6(7).
38. UNCLOS, *supra* note 2, at art. 65.
39. UN Fish Stocks Agreement, *supra* note 4, at art. 7.
40. Sheila Jasanoff, *Just Evidence: The Limits of Science in the Legal Process*, 34 J.L. Med. & Ethics 328–41, 330 (2006).
41. *See generally* A. Dan Tarlock, *Environmental Law: Ethics or Science?*, 7 Duke Environmental Law & Policy Forum 193–224 (1996) ["(Tarlock, 1996)"].
42. For a considered discussion scientific method, *see* Kristin Carden, *Bridging the Divide: The Role of Science in Species Conservation Law*, 30 Harv. Envtl. L. Rev. 165, 170–72 (2006) ["Carden"].
43. A. Dan Tarlock, *Who Owns Science?*, 10 Penn State Envtl. L. Rev. 135–54, 139 (2001–2002) ["(Tarlock, 2001–2002)"] (unfortunately, the public tends to misinterpret the truth-seeking function of science, perhaps placing too much faith in the ability of "modern science [to] support the search for *an* exclusive truth" (at 136)).
44. *Id.* at 139.
45. Cameron S.G. Jefferies, "Institutional Expertise: Reconsidering the Role of Scientific Experts in the International Conservation and Management of Cetaceans," *in* Experts, Networks and International Law (H. Cullen et al. eds., forthcoming and on file with author).
46. William Aron, *Science and the IWC*, *in* Toward a Sustainable Whaling Regime 105, 118 (Robert L Friedheim ed., 2001) (recall that Article V(2) of the ICRW provides that management decisions shall be based upon "scientific findings." This term goes undefined in the ICRW).
47. *See, e.g.,* UNCLOS, *supra* note 3, arts. 16 & 119 (asserting the "best scientific evidence available" standard. UNCLOS does not indicate what constitutes best scientific evidence, and although commentaries documenting the negotiation process indicate that it is mandatory to utilize scientific evidence, they also do not detail what evidence qualifies. *See* United Nations Convention on the Law of the Sea 1982: A Commentary Vol. II, at 594–611 (Myron H. Nordquist et al. eds., 1985); United Nations Convention on the Law of the Sea 1982: A Commentary Vol. III, at 304–13 (Myron H. Nordquist et al. eds., 1995).
48. Steiner Andresen, *The Role of Scientific Expertise in Multilateral Environmental Agreements: Influence and Effectiveness*, *in* The Role of "Experts" in

INTERNATIONAL AND EUROPEAN DECISION-MAKING PROCESSES 105, 106 (Monika Ambrus et al. eds., 2014) ["Andresen"].
49. Carden, *supra* note 42 at 125.
50. Shelia Jasanoff, *Science and Judgment in Environmental Standard Setting*, 11 APPL. MEAS. EDUC. 107–20, 112 (1998).
51. In Whaling in the Antarctic (Australia v. Japan: New Zealand Intervening), Judgment, [2014] ICJ Rep 226 ["Whaling in the Antarctic"], the Court developed an objective standard of review for assessing whether Japan's JARPA II was conducted "for purposes of scientific research," as required by Article VIII of the ICRW. Specifically, the Court articulated the following two-part test at ¶ 67:

> ... first, whether the programme under which these activities occur involves scientific research. Secondly, the Court will consider if the killing, taking and treating of whales is "for purposes of" scientific research by examining whether, in the use of lethal methods, the programme's design and implementation are reasonable in relation to achieving its stated objectives.

Australia recommended that the Court understand the use of the term "scientific research" with reference to the following requirements: "defined and achievable objectives (questions or hypotheses) that aim to contribute to knowledge important to the conservation and management of stocks; 'appropriate methods', including the use of lethal methods only where the objectives of the research cannot be achieved by any other means; peer review; and the avoidance of adverse effects on stock" (¶ 74). The Court was "not persuaded that activities must satisfy the four criteria advanced by Australia in order to constitute 'scientific research' in the context of Article VIII. As formulated by Australia, these criteria appear largely to reflect what one of the experts that Australia called regards as well-conceived scientific research, rather than serving as an interpretation of the term as used in the Convention. Nor does the Court consider it necessary to devise alternative criteria or to offer a general definition of 'scientific research'" (¶ 84). The Court concluded that "[t]aken as a whole ... JARPA II involves activities that can broadly be characterized as scientific research ... but that the evidence does not establish that the programme's design and implementation are reasonable in relation to achieving its stated objectives" (¶ 227).
52. Michael Heazle, *Scientific Uncertainty and the International Whaling Commission: An Alternative Perspective on the Use of Science in Policy Making*, 28 MAR. POL'Y 361–74, 367 (2004).
53. For consideration of competing justifications for environmental regulation, *see* Tarlock (1996), *supra* note 41.
54. William de la Mare, Nick Gales & Marc Mangel, *Applying Scientific Principles in International Law on Whaling*, 345 SCI. 1125, 1126 (2014).
55. *See* Tarlock (2001–2002), *supra* note 43, at 142 (discussing "ownership issues" associated with scientific information in the domestic United States context).
56. In addition to the ICRW/IWC, another appropriate example is the International Commission for the Conservation of Atlantic Tuna (ICCAT). Established by the International Convention for the Conservation of Atlantic Tuna, May 14, 1966, 673 UNTS 63, the ICCAT is a quota-setting body and a "controversial caretaker ... often spectacularly failing to meet its responsibilities" (Joseph Paul Heffernan, *Dealing with Mediterranean Bluefin Tuna: A Study in International*

Management 50 MAR. POL'Y 81–88, 82 (2014)). ICCAT frequently set quotas above the limits recommended by the scientists in its Standing Committee on Research and Statistics (SCRS). The ICCAT has recently reduced quotas in response to the SCRS's recommendations, suggesting that science may occupy a more legitimate role moving forward. *See also* John G. Payne et al., *Sustainability and the Atlantic Bluefin Tuna: Science, Socioeconomic Forces, and Governance*, 16 J. INT'L WILDLIFE L & POL'Y 198 (2013).

57. Andre E. Punt & Greg P. Donovan, *Developing Management Procedures That Are Robust to Uncertainty: Lessons from the International Whaling Commission*, 64 ICES J. MAR. SCI. 603, 603 (2007).
58. *See, e.g.,* Sandra Pompa, Paul R. Ehrlich & Gerardo Ceballos, *Global Distribution and Conservation of Marine Mammals*, 108 PROC. NAT'L. ACAD. SCI. 13600, 13602 (2011) ["Pompa et al."] (here "global [marine mammal] species richness, irreplaceable sites, endemism, and threatened species" is surveyed with the goal of identifying important conservation sites). *See also* Ana D Davidson et al., *Drivers and Hotspots of Extinction Risk in Marine Mammals*, 109 PROC. NAT. ACAD. SCI. 3395–400, 3395 (2012) (identifying marine mammal extinction hotspots and contributing factors, and critically observing that "hotspots of risk overlap little with current Marine Protected Areas"). *See also* Peter T. Fretwell, Iain J. Staniland & Jaume Forcada, *Whales from Space: Counting Southern Right Whales by Satellite*, 9 PLOS ONE e88655 (2014) (explaining a novel approach to estimating whale population size).
59. Andresen, *supra* note 48, at 107.
60. Pompa et al., *supra* note 58, at 13604.
61. UN Fish Stocks Agreement, *supra* note 4, at art. 24 (note that art. 24(2)(b) has been deleted because subsistence marine mammal use is addressed in draft art. 17).
62. UN Fish Stocks Agreement, *supra* note 4, at art. 25.
63. *Id.*
64. *Id.* at art. 26.
65. UNCLOS, *supra* note 3, at art. 266(1).
66. Agreement on Trade-Related Aspects of Intellectual Property Rights art. 66(2), 15 April 1994, 33 I.L.M. 1197 ["TRIPS Agreement"].
67. UNCLOS, *supra* note 3, at art. 268.
68. *Id.* at art. 269.
69. *Id.* at art. 266(2); *see generally* CBD, *supra* note 5, at art. 16.
70. TRIPS Agreement, *supra* note 66, at art. 67.
71. UN Fish Stocks Agreement, *supra* note 4, at art. 42 (similarly excluding reservations and exceptions).
72. *Id.* at art. 43.
73. UNCLOS, *supra* note 3, at art. 311 (this provision in UNCLOS indicates that UNCLOS prevails over the Geneva Conventions on the Law of the Sea of 29 April 1958).
74. UN Fish Stocks Agreement, *supra* note 4, at art. 44(1).
75. CBD, *supra* note 5, at art. 22(1).
76. UN Fish Stocks Agreement, *supra* note 4, at art. 44(2).
77. May 23, 1969, 1155 U.N.T.S. 331, 8 ILM 679.
78. *Id.* at art. 41(b).
79. *See* Jean-Jacques Macguire, *The State of World Highly Migratory, Straddling and Other High Seas Fishery Resources and Associated Species*, FOOD AND

80. NAMMCO Agreement, *supra* note 6, at art. 2 (using similar wording in establishing NAMMCO).
81. ICRW, *supra* note 3, at art. III(1).
82. NAMMCO Agreement, *supra* note 6, at art. 6(2) (formally, the IMMC would require an elected President and Vice-President, the ability to set its own procedural rules and the rules of its subsidiary bodies, as well as financial rules governing the funding of its Secretariat; *see* ICRW, *supra* note 3, at art. III(2); CBD, *supra* note 5, at art. 23(3)).
83. CBD, *supra* note 5, at art. 29(3).
84. ICRW, *supra* note 3, at art. III(2).
85. The Annex shall be construed as an integral part of the Agreement, and any reference to the Agreement shall be understood to include the Annex. Similar to the approach found in Articles 45(2) and 48 of the UN Fish Stocks Agreement, *supra* note 4.
86. The Agreement itself should stipulate that any state party can propose an amendment but that the IMMC shall make and exhaust every effort to achieve consensus before voting on a proposed amendment. With respect to Annex amendments, although it is important that the Annex be utilized as a dynamic regulatory tool, it should also be clear that it is not possible to reserve to its amendment as the proposed Agreement should not permit opt-out/objection. This is a critical feature of this Agreement and the negotiation surrounding it would truly test whether the anti-whaling and pro-whaling factions believe that the Agreement, taken as a whole, embodies rational use and the effective recognition of competing state interests. *See* Agreement on the Conservation of Small Cetaceans of the Baltic and North Seas art 6.3, 17 Mar. 1992, 1772 U.N.T.S. 217 ["ASCOBANS"]; *see* CBD, *supra* note 5, at art. 29(3); *see* ICRW, *supra* note 3, at art. III(2); *see* Agreement on the Conservation of Cetaceans of the Black Sea, Mediterranean Sea and Contiguous Atlantic Area art. 3(6); 24 Nov. 1996, 2183 U.N.T.S. 303 ["ACCOBAMS"]; *see* NAMMCO Agreement, *supra* note 6, at art. 4(3).
87. ICRW, *supra* note 3, at art. III(1); Convention on International Trade in Endangered Species of Wild Fauna and Flora, 3 Mar. 1973 art. XVII, 27 U.S.T. 1087, 993 U.N.T.S. 243 ["CITES"] (requiring a two-thirds vote for treaty amendment).
88. *See* ICRW, *supra* note 3, at art. III(2).
89. *Id.* at art. III(4).
90. The composition and functionality of these committees is discussed later in this Part.
91. NAMMCO, *supra* note 6, at art. 4(2)(c).
92. ICRW, *supra* note 3, at art. IV(2).
93. ICRW, *supra* note 3, at art. IV(1).
94. *See* International Whaling Commission, *The Revised Management Procedure*, IWC, https://iwc.int/rmp (last visited July 22, 2015); *see* Robert L. Friedheim, *Fixing the Whaling Regime: A Proposal*, in TOWARD A SUSTAINABLE WHALING REGIME 311, 321–24 (Robert L. Friedheim ed., 2001) ["Friedheim, *Fixing the Whaling Regime*"] (discussing the importance of securing a robust Revised Management Scheme and Revised Management Procedure).
95. ICRW, *supra* note 3, at art. V(1).

The Proposal: Part I   257

96. *Id.* at art. VI.
97. CBD, *supra* note 5, at art. 23(4)(h).
98. *See* CBD, *supra* note 5, at arts. 20–21 (I propose here a mechanism analogous to that employed by the CBD. Called the International Marine Mammal Conservation and Sustainable Management Fund ("Fund"), it operates under the guidance of the IMMC and is accountable to the IMMC, and shall operate with transparency and democratic decision-making. Its primary function shall be to assist developing nations in implementation of the new Agreement. It should be noted that the current IWC Financial and Administration Committee subgroup provides an analog that could be used and improved upon in establishing and implementing the Fund so long as final oversight and review is not improperly delegated by the IMMC).
99. CBD, *supra* note 5, at art. 23(2).
100. ASCOBANS, *supra* note 86, at art. 6.2.1 (ASCOBANS utilizes this approach. I propose that the following be included as eligible to send observers: CMS, ASCOBANS, ACCOBAMS, CBD, NAMMCO, CITES, the International Maritime Organization, the United Nations Framework Convention on Climate Change, the Intergovernmental Panel on Climate Change, the Antarctic Treaty, the Convention for the Prevention of Marine Pollution from Landbased Sources, the Convention on the Prevention of Marine Pollution by Dumping of Wastes and Other Matter 1972 and 1996 Protocol Thereto, the International Union for the Conservation of Nature, Regional Fisheries Management Organizations, the United Nations Environment Programme, and the United Nations Food and Agriculture Organization).
101. *Id.* at art. 6.2.2; CBD, *supra* note 5, at art. 23(5).
102. ASCOBANS, *supra* note 86, at art. 6.2.2.
103. CBD, *supra* note 5, at art 23(5).
104. *Id.*; CITES, *supra* note 87, at arts. XI(6) & (7) (stating that admitted "observers shall have the right to participate but not to vote").
105. NAMMCO Agreement, *supra* note 6, at art. 6(1).
106. *Id.* at art. 6(2); CITES, *supra* note 87, at arts. XI(6) & (7).
107. CBD, *supra* note 5, at art. 25(2)(a).
108. *Id.* at arts. 25(2)(d) & (e).
109. *See* International Whaling Commission, *The Revised Management Procedure*, IWC, https://iwc.int/rmp (last visited Dec. 8, 2015) (indicating the role that the IWC's Scientific Committee had in producing the Revised Management Procedure).
110. International Whaling Commission, *The Revised Management Procedure (RMP)*, IWC (2015), http://iwc.int/rmp2 (describing the role that science plays in the Revised Management Procedure).
111. ICRW, *supra* note 3, at art. V(2).
112. *See* CBD, *supra* note 5, at art. 25; *see* The North Atlantic Marine Mammal Commission, *About NAMMCO*, http://www.nammco.no/about-nammco/ (last visited July 28, 2015) ["*About NAMMCO*"]; *see* International Whaling Commission, *Commission Sub-Groups*, IWC (2015), https://iwc.int/commission-sub-groups ["*IWC Commission Sub-Groups*"].
113. NAMMCO Agreement, *supra* note 6, at art. 6; CITES, *supra* note 87, at arts. XI(6) & (7).

114. ALEXANDER GILLESPIE, WHALING DIPLOMACY 204 (2005) ["WHALING DIPLOMACY"].
115. Alexander Gillespie, *Aboriginal Subsistence Whaling: A Critique of the Interrelationship between International Law and the International Whaling Commission*, 12 COLO. J. INT'L ENVTL. L. & POL'Y 77, 95 (2001).
116. United Nations Permanent Forum on Indigenous Issues, *Factsheet: Who Are Indigenous Peoples?*, 2 http://www.un.org/esa/socdev/unpfii/documents/5session_factsheet1.pdf (last visited Feb. 17, 2016) ["*Factsheet*"].
117. International Whaling Commission, *Aboriginal Subsistence Whaling*, IWC (2015), http://iwc.int/aboriginal (last visited July 28, 2015) ["*Aboriginal Subsistence Whaling*"].
118. See Benedict Kingsbury, *"Indigenous Peoples" in International Law: A Constructivist Approach to the Asian Controversy*, 92 AM. J. INT'L L. 414, 455 (1998) (this portion of the definition adopts and summarizes the indicia identified by Kingsbury in a manner that remains true to the intention of his original wording. His work identifies both "Essential Requirements" and "Relevant Indicia," and this is reflected in this definition. I agree that using indicia is preferable to establishing a restricted definition that is unable to respond to changing circumstances. It also accords with the international community's inability to establish a universally agreed definition of "indigenous").
119. See WHALING DIPLOMACY, *supra* note 114, at 228–30 (discussing the idea of "culture" in the context of the IWC's ASW exemption).
120. See *id.* at 229; see Oran R. Young et al., *Subsistence, Sustainability, and Sea Mammals: Reconstructing the International Whaling Regime*, 23 OCEAN & COASTAL MGMT. 117, 120 (1994) ["Young et al."] (noting that "small-scale whaling should be regarded as permissible on grounds of sustainability and equity when it secures historically based practices of socially defined human groups that value whaling activities on a multi-dimensional basis").
121. WHALING DIPLOMACY, *supra* note 114, at 229; *see* Young et al., *supra* note 120, at 122 (discussing artisanal whaling in the context of artisanal fisheries, as follows: "Much has been written about artisanal fisheries comprised of localized, family-based activities characterized by a high degree of annual labour, and with skills and techniques based largely on traditional knowledge. Such fisheries commonly feature family-based production, household consumption, and informal trade of surplus production either within the home or nearby communities, or in local or regional markets").
122. See Young et al., *supra* note 120, at 122 (defining subsistence as "a system or mode of production in which the allocation and production in which the allocation and procurement of resources and the distribution and consumption of products is organized around family and kinship groups. There is nothing in this formulation that precludes monetized exchanges or requires that subsistence practices remain").
123. *See Aboriginal Subsistence Whaling*, *supra* note 117 (describing how states currently submit applications to the ICW on behalf of their aboriginal groups in order to secure an ASW permission).
124. Young et al., *supra* note 120, at 120–22 (providing descriptions of these criteria in the context of what is necessary to justify small-type coastal whaling for any subsistence use, and the wording found in this portion of the draft article is

125. *See* National Marine Fisheries Service, *Purchasing, Finding or Possessing Marine Mammal Skins, Muktak, Baleen, and Bones*, NOAA FISHERIES, https://alaskafisheries.noaa.gov/pr/buying-marine-mammal-products (last visited Mar. 31, 2016) (indicating the possibility of obtaining certificates for certain actions involving marine mammal parts pursuant to MMPA).
126. WHALING DIPLOMACY, *supra* note 114, at 230 (providing clearly that "indigenous needs may not drive a species towards extinction").
127. *Id.* (noting that "indigenous needs may not drive a species towards extinction—this rule has been slow to take hold at the IWC").
128. Friedheim, *Fixing the Whaling Regime, supra* note 94, at 325–27.
129. An International Study Group for Small-Type Whaling, *Similarities and Diversity in Coastal Whaling Operations: A Comparison of Small-Scale Whaling Activities in Greenland, Iceland, Japan and Norway* (1992), http://luna.pos.to/whale/gen_isgstw.html; Whale and Dolphin Conservation Society, *Small Type Whaling: A False Choice for the IWC*, WDCS (2009), http://uk.whales.org/sites/default/files/japanese-small-type-whaling.pdf; Young et al., *supra* note 120, at 122.
130. *See* Friedheim, *Fixing the Whaling Regime, supra* note 94, at 326 (endorsing Young et al., *supra* note 120, at 122).
131. *See IWC Commission Sub-Groups, supra* note 112.
132. ICRW, *supra* note 3, at art. III(4).
133. NAMMCO Agreement, *supra* note 6, at art. 5.
134. *See* CBD, *supra* note 5, at art 25; *see About NAMMCO, supra* note 112; *see IWC Commission Sub-groups, supra* note 95.
135. NAMMCO Agreement, *supra* note 6, at art. 5(1)(b).
136. United Nations Framework Convention on Climate Change, *The Secretariat*, http://unfccc.int/secretariat/items/1629.php (last visited July 28, 2015).
137. Convention on International Trade in Endangered Species of Wild Fauna and Flora, *The CITES Secretariat*, http://www.cites.org/eng/disc/sec/index.php (last visited July 28, 2015).
138. Secretariat of the Antarctic Treaty, *About Us*, http://www.ats.aq/e/about.htm (last visited July 28, 2015).
139. Convention on Biological Diversity, *Decisions on Cooperation*, http://www.cbd.int/cooperation/about/decisions.shtml (last visited July 28, 2015) (summarizing some of the CBD's key decisions on how to provide for international cooperation).
140. Bernd Siebenhuner, *Administrator of Global Biodiversity: The Secretariat of the Convention on Biological Diversity*, 16 BIODIVERSITY CONSERV. 259, 262 (2007) ["Siebenhuner"].
141. *Memorandum of Cooperation between the Secretariat of the Convention on the International Trade in Endangered Species of Wild Fauna and Flora and the Secretariat of the Convention on Biological Diversity* (Mar. 23, 1996), http://www.cbd.int/doc/agreements/agmt-cites-1996-03-23-moc-web-en.pdf; *Memorandum of Cooperation between the Secretariat of the Convention on Biological Diversity and the Secretariat of the Convention on the Conservation of Migratory Species of Wild Animals* (June 13, 1996), http://www.cbd.int/doc/agreements/agmt-cms-1996-06-13-moc-web-en.pdf.

142. *See generally, e.g.*, Secretariat of the Convention on Biological Diversity, *Report on Activities of the Secretariat on the Implementation of the Work Programme of the Convention on Biological Diversity and Its Cartagena Protocol on Biosafety*, CBD SECRETARIAT (2008), https://www.cbd.int/doc/secretariat/activities/activities-2008-report-en.pdf.
143. Siebenhuner, *supra* note 140, at 266.
144. WHALING DIPLOMACY, *supra* note 114, at 69 (in the context of urging governments to participate in the international response to climate change to reduce its impact on cetaceans).
145. CBD, *supra* note 5, at art. 24(1).
146. *See* Alexander Gillespie, *Transparency in International Environmental Law: A Case Study of the International Whaling Commission*, 14 GEO. INT'L ENVTL. L. 333 (2001); WHALING DIPLOMACY, *supra* note 114, at 409–25.
147. United Kingdom, *Proposal of Improving the Effectiveness of Operations within the International Whaling Commission*, IWC/63/F&A4, at 2 (Dec. 5, 2011), http://webarchive.nationalarchives.gov.uk/20130402151656/http://archive.defra.gov.uk/wildlife-pets/wildlife/protect/whales/documents/iwc63-improve-iwc-operations.pdf.
148. International Whaling Commission, *IWC Resolution 2014-3: Resolution on Civil Society Participation and Transparency at the IWC*, https://archive.iwc.int/pages/search.php?search=%21collection72&k= (last visited Mar. 31, 2016) (one of the main reforms included in this resolution was to afford accredited observers with speaking rights during "Plenary sessions and sessions of Commission subsidiary groups and Committees to which they are admitted to," and also the ability to "submit documents for information to the delegations and observers participating in such sessions").
149. UN Fish Stocks Agreement, *supra* note 4, at art. 12.
150. *Id.* at art. 9 (justifying the position that regional marine mammal organizations and arrangements shall be based upon a shared understanding of the marine mammal species/populations to which its adopted conservation and sustainable management measures apply, the geographic area that is covered ("taking into account the characteristics of the region, including socio-economic, geographical and environmental factors"), the relationship with existing organizations, and their intended contribution to the pursuit of enhanced scientific understanding of marine mammals).
151. *Id.* at art. 8(1).
152. *Id.* at art. 8(2).
153. *See* Erik Japp Molenaar, *The Concept of "Real Interest" and Other Aspects of Co-operation through Regional Fisheries Management Mechanisms*, 15 INT'L J. MAR. & COAST. L. 475 (2000) (offering a detailed analysis of this ambiguous term in the context of the UN Fish Stocks Agreement. At 495, Molenaar opines that those coastal states whose maritime zones overlap with a stocks distribution as well as those flag states whose vessels are presently taking from the stock must qualify as having a real interest. Then at 496, he suggests three other categories of states that should also qualify: "(1) flag states that fished in the regulatory area previously and want to resume fishing; (2) flag states without a catch history that want to fish in the future; and (3) states with no intention to fish that nevertheless want to participate . . . to further the international community's interest in sustainable management." One concern associated with the third category is

the possibility that it will be used by pro-preservationist states to overwhelm pro-utilization states, not dissimilar to how the conservationist agenda arguably overtook the IWC's voting mechanism. The corollary to this is that regional organizations may become reluctant to allow new member states if they become protectionist of existing interests).

154. UN Fish Stocks Agreement, *supra* note 4, at art. 8.
155. Article 11 of the UN Fish Stocks Agreement, *supra* note 4, offers criteria that can aid in the determination of the "nature and extent of participatory rights" for new members of regional organizations/arrangements once the "real interest" threshold has been met. These factors, which would be a useful starting point for guiding similar decisions in this proposed regime, include: membership in the Commission, the conservation status of the marine mammal species/population, any current take or other use, the interests of both new and existing members in any existing take or other use, the contribution of both new and existing members to conservation and sustainable management measures and scientific research, "the needs of coastal States who depend on" marine mammals through a take or other use, "the needs of coastal States whose economies are dependent on" a take or other use of marine mammals, and "the interests of developing States from the region in whose areas of national jurisdiction the" marine mammal species/populations inhabit or use.
156. *Id.* at art. 10.
157. *Id.* at art. 12.
158. At the outset I acknowledge that only a select number of states continue to take marine mammals in international waters in a manner that should trigger international concern, except for the by-catch issue that implicates many others.
159. UN Fish Stocks Agreement, *supra* note 4, at art. 33.
160. *Id.* at art. 17.
161. *Id.* at art. 18.
162. *Id.*
163. FAO Agreement to Promote Compliance with International Conservation and Management Measures by Fishing Vessels on the High Seas, art. IV, 29 Nov. 1993, 24 I.L.M. 968 ["FAO Compliance Agreement"].
164. UN Fish Stocks Agreement, *supra* note 4, at art. 18.
165. *Id.*
166. *Id.* at art. 18.
167. *Id.*
168. *Id.*
169. *Id.*
170. Food and Agriculture Organization of the United Nations, *Fishery Records Collection: High Seas Vessels Authorization Record*, http://fao.org/fishery/collection/hsvar/en (last visited Aug. 10, 2015). *See also* FAO Compliance Agreement, *supra* note 163, at art. VI (detailing the sort of vessel information that must be provided to the FAO for its maintenance of the HSVAR).
171. David Anderson, Modern Law of the Sea: Selected Essays 253 (Vaughan Lowe ed., 2008).
172. Rosemary Gail Rayfuse, Non-flag State Enforcement in the High Seas 511 (2004) ["Rayfuse"].
173. *Id.* at 511–12.
174. ICRW, *supra* note 3, at art. IX.

175. UN Fish Stocks Agreement, *supra* note 4, at arts. 19–23.
176. BIRNIE ET AL., *supra* note 11, at 744–55.
177. Greenpeace, *Suggested Draft High Seas Implementing Agreement for the Conservation and Management of the Marine Environment in Areas beyond National Jurisdiction,* at art. 47, GREENPEACE INTERNATIONAL (2011), http://www.greenpeace.org/international/Global/international/publications/oceans/2011/Greenpeace%20draft%20Implementing%20Agreement%2013Feb2008.pdf [*"Greenpeace Suggested Draft"*] (citing to art. III of the FAO Compliance Agreement, *supra* note 162).
178. *Id.*
179. UN Fish Stocks Agreement, *supra* note 4, at art. 19.
180. Analogous to how violations are addressed in Article 21 of the UN Fish Stocks Agreement, it is appropriate to consider a category of "serious violations" for which, failing appropriate flag state action post-notification, the inspectors "may remain on board and secure evidence and may require the master to assist in further investigation including, where appropriate, by bringing the vessel without delay to the nearest appropriate port" (Art. 21(8)). "Serious violations" include: (1) taking a marine mammal "without a license, authorization or permit"; (2) "failing to maintain accurate records of" take or take-related data, as required by the IMMC or relevant regional marine mammal organization or arrangement, or misreporting of take-related data; (3) taking marine mammals in a designated MPA or otherwise closed area, taking a marine mammal when the season is closed, taking a marine mammal beyond the take-quota established by the relevant regional marine mammal organization or arrangement in conjunction with take-limits established by the IMMC; (4) taking, or attempting to take, a marine mammal from a species/population(s) subject to a moratorium (globally or regionally) or for which taking is otherwise prohibited; (5) using prohibited technology, apparatus, or gear; (6) "falsifying or concealing the markings, identity or registration of a vessel" used for taking marine mammals; (7) "concealing, tampering with or disposing of evidence relating to an investigation"; (8) "multiple violations which together constitute a serious disregard of conservation and sustainable management measures"; or (9) "such other violations as may be specified by" the IMMC or in procedures established by the relevant regional marine mammal organization/arrangement.
181. UN Fish Stocks Agreement, *supra* note 4, at art. 22 (this article instructs both inspectors and vessel masters on appropriate conduct during the boarding and inspection process).
182. BIRNIE ET AL., *supra* note 11, at 744; *but see* Agreement on Port State Measures to Prevent, Deter and Eliminate Illegal, Unreported and Unregulated Fishing, FAO.ORG, http://www.fao.org/fileadmin/user_upload/legal/docs/2_037t-e.pdf (last visited Mar. 31, 2016) (which is not yet in force but could, in the future, alter what is understood to be customary law in this regard).
183. UN Fish Stocks Agreement, *supra* note 4, at art. 23(3).
184. Australian Government, *Compliance: Illegal, Unreported and Unregulated Fishing* (Apr. 21, 2011), http://www.daff.gov.au/fisheries/iuu/compliance.
185. Food and Agriculture Organization of the United Nations, *Stopping Illegal, Unreported and Unregulated (IUU) Fishing,* FAO http://www.fao.org/docrep/005/y3554e/y3554e01.htm#bm1.7 (last visited Aug. 7, 2015) [*"Stopping IUU"*]; RAYFUSE, *supra* note 172, at 217.

186. Food and Agriculture Organization of the United Nations, *International Plan of Action to Prevent, Deter and Eliminate IUU Fishing* (2001), http://www.fao.org/docrep/003/y1224e/y1224e00.HTM.
187. *Stopping IUU, supra* note 185.
188. Rayfuse, *supra* note 172.
189. *Id.*
190. *Id.* at 217 & 220–21.
191. Donald R. Liddick, Crimes against Nature: Illegal Industries and the Global Environment 86 (2011) (noting also that corresponding "whitelists" can also be created, indicating exactly which vessels are permitted to be fishing).
192. Northwest Atlantic Fisheries Organization, *Northwest Atlantic Fisheries Organization Conservation and Enforcement Measures*, NAFO/FC DOC 13/1, http://archive.nafo.int/open/fc/2013/fcdoc13-01.pdf (last visited Mar. 31, 2016).
193. Statute of the International Court of Justice, 59 Stat. 1031, 39 AJIL Supp. 215 (1945) ["Statute of the ICJ"] (note that 72 states have registered an optional declaration).
194. International Court of Justice, *Australia's Declaration Recognizing the Jurisdiction of the Court as Compulsory* (Mar. 22, 2002), ICJ http://www.icj-cij.org/jurisdiction/?p1=5&p2=1&p3=3&code=AU.
195. Whaling in the Antarctic, *supra* note 51, ¶ 32.
196. *Id.* ¶ 33.
197. *Id.* ¶ 34.
198. This test was articulated in *Anglo-Iranian Oil Co. (United Kingdom v. Iran), Preliminary Objection, I.C.J. Reports 1952*, ¶ 104.
199. Whaling in the Antarctic, *supra* note 51, at ¶¶ 37–41.
200. Igor V. Karaman, Dispute Resolution in the Law of the Sea 319 (2012) ["Karaman"].
201. Donald R. Rothwell & Tim Stephens, The International Law of the Sea 473 (2d ed. 2016) ["Rothwell & Stephens"].
202. *See* Helmut Turek, Reflections on the Contemporary Law of the Sea 123–58 (2012); *see* Yoshifumi Tanaka, The International Law of the Sea 390–423 (2012); *see generally* Karaman, *supra* note 200; *see* Thomas A. Mensah, Law of the Sea, Environmental Law and Settlement of Disputes (2007); Natalie Klein, Dispute Settlement in the UN Convention on the Law of the Sea (2005).
203. UN Fish Stocks Agreement, *supra* note 4, at art. 28.
204. Rothwell & Stephens, *supra* note 201, at 474.
205. UN Fish Stock Agreement, *supra* note 4, at art. 27.
206. *Id.* at art. 29.
207. *Id.* at art. 30(1).
208. Rothwell & Stephens, *supra* note 201, at 494.
209. International Tribunal for the Law of the Sea, *Declarations of States Parties Relating to Settlement of Disputes in Accordance with Article 287 (Choice of Procedure)*, http://www.itlos.org/fileadmin/itlos/documents/basic_texts/287_declarations_041111_english.pdf (last visited Feb. 17, 2016).
210. International Tribunal for the Law of the Sea, *The Tribunal*, https://www.itlos.org/the-tribunal/ (last visited Aug 10, 2015).
211. International Tribunal for the Law of the Sea, *General Information*, http://www.itlos.org/index.php?id=8 (last visited Aug. 10, 2015).

212. International Tribunal for the Law of the Sea, *Jurisdiction*, http://www.itlos.org/index.php?id=11 (last visited Aug. 10, 2015).
213. International Tribunal for the Law of the Sea, *Chambers*, http://www.itlos.org/index.php?id=19 (last visited Sept. 13, 2013).
214. International Tribunal for the Law of the Sea, *List of Cases*, http://www.itlos.org/index.php?id=35&L=0 (last visited Sept. 10, 2015); *see* ROTHWELL & STEPHENS, *supra* note 201, at 494.
215. International Tribunal for the Law of the Sea, *Case No. 3 & 4*, http://www.itlos.org/index.php?id=62&L=0 (last visited Aug. 10, 2015); *see generally* Simon Marr, *The Southern Bluefin Tuna Cases: The Precautionary Approach and Conservation and Management of Fish Resources*, 11 EJIC 815 (2000) (discussing the history of the case, including the proposed experimental Japanese fishing program that led to the challenges, and also the fact that this case is notable for applying the precautionary principle without stating its application).
216. International Tribunal for the Law of the Sea, *Case No. 7*, http://www.itlos.org/index.php?id=99&L=0 (last visited Aug. 10, 2015); *see* Press Release, Registrar of the International Tribunal for the Law of the Sea, Case on Conservation of Swordfish Stocks between Chile and the European Community in the South-Eastern Pacific Ocean before Special Chamber of the Tribunal (Dec. 21, 2000), (http://www.itlos.org/fileadmin/itlos/documents/press_releases_english/press_release_43_en.pdf) (noting that this case was directed to a Special Chamber of ITLOS established to consider issues related to swordfish exploitation in the high seas adjacent to Chile's EEZ).
217. International Tribunal for the Law of the Sea, *Case No. 10*, http://www.itlos.org/index.php?id=102&L=0 (last visited Aug. 10, 2015); *see* Press Release, International Tribunal for the Law of the Sea, Order in the Mox Plant Case (Dec. 3, 2001), (http://www.itlos.org/fileadmin/itlos/documents/press_releases_english/PR_No.62.pdf) (describing the controversial proposal to construct a nuclear waste upgrading plant and the challenge from Ireland on the basis of the United Kingdom's obligation to preserve and protect the marine environment).
218. International Tribunal for the Law of the Sea, *Case No. 21*, https://www.itlos.org/en/cases/list-of-cases/case-no-21/ (last visited Aug. 10, 2015).
219. CAROLINE E. FOSTER, SCIENCE AND THE PRECAUTIONARY PRINCIPLE IN INTERNATIONAL COURTS AND TRIBUNALS 180 (2011) ["FOSTER"].
220. Pulp Mills on the River Uruguay (Argentina v Uruguay), Joint Dissenting Opinion of Judges Al-Kashawneh and Simma, ¶ 4 ["Al-Kashawneh & Simma"].
221. Alan Boyle, *Forum Shopping for UNCLOS Disputes Relating to Marine Scientific Research*, *in* LAW, SCIENCE AND OCEAN MANAGEMENT 519, 534 (Myron Nordquist et al. eds., 2011) ["Boyle"].
222. *Id.*; FOSTER, *supra* note 219, at 4–5; *see, e.g.*, Corfu Channel case (United Kingdom of Great Britain and Northern Ireland v. Albania), [1949] ICJ Rep 4; Gabčíkovo-Nagymaros Project (Hungary/Slovakia), [1997] ICJ Rep 7; Pulp Mills on the River Uruguay (Argentina v. Uruguay), [2010] ICJ Rep 14 ["*Pulp Mills*"].
223. Rules of Court of the International Court of Justice, art 67, http://www.icj-cij.org/documents/index.php?p1=4&p2=3& (last visited Feb. 17, 2016) ["Rules of Court"].
224. *See* Statue of the ICJ, *supra* note 143; FOSTER, *supra* note 219, at 102.

225. FOSTER, *id.* at 88–89 (this is what occurred in *Gabčíkovo-Nagymaros* and *Pulp Mills*).
226. *Id.* at 93.
227. Rules of Court, *supra* note 222, art. 65.
228. *Id.* at art. 57; *See also* Al-Kashawneh & Simma, *supra* note 220, at ¶¶ 7–11 (discussing the different ways scientific evidence can come before the Court). Note that the ITLOS can select, pursuant to article 289 of UNCLOS, "no fewer than two scientific or technical experts" to "sit with" the panel in a nonvoting capacity.
229. *See* FOSTER, *supra* note 219, at 100 (noting that cross-examination plays a critical role in testing expert evidence).
230. *Pulp Mills, supra* note 222, ¶ 167; Al-Kashawneh & Simma, *supra* note 220, ¶ 2 (asserting that "the Court has not followed the path it ought to have pursued with regard to disputed scientific facts; it has omitted to resort to the possibilities provided by its Statute and thus simply has not done what would have been necessary in order to arrive at a basis for the application of the law to the facts as scientifically certain as is possible in a judicial proceeding").
231. Whaling in the Antarctic, *supra* note 51, ¶¶ 20–21.
232. *Id.*
233. *Id.*
234. Boyle, *supra* note 221; Al-Kashawneh & Simma, *supra* note 220.
235. Whaling in the Antarctic, *supra* note 51, ¶¶ 73–86.
236. *Id.* ¶¶ 87–97.
237. *Id.* ¶¶ 98–227.
238. *Id.* ¶¶ 62–68.
239. The issue of bias also raises questions about whether an expert should be required to disclose her bias to the court given that it may or may not be evident based on credentials or employment record.
240. PETER J. STOETT, THE INTERNATIONAL POLITICS OF WHALING 17 (1997) ["STOETT"].
241. Michael Bowman, *Transcending the Fisheries Paradigm*, 7 NZ YBK. INT'L L. 85, 118 (2009).
242. Keirko Hirata, *Why Japan Supports Whaling*, 8 J. INT'L WILDLIFE L. & POL'Y 129, 130 (2005) ["Hirata"].
243. *Id.* at 138–40.
244. Hiroko Tabuchi, *Japanese Subsidies Keep Industry Afloat, Report Says*, N.Y. TIMES (Feb. 7, 2013), http://www.nytimes.com/2013/02/08/business/global/japanese-subsidies-keep-whaling-industry-afloat-report-says.html?_r=0.
245. Hirata, *supra* note 242, at 141–42.
246. Phillip Clapham, *Japan's Whaling following the International Court of Justice Ruling: Brave New World—Or Business as Usual?*, 51 MAR. POL'Y 238, 238 (2015); *see also* Minuro Umemoto, *As Whale Meat Consumption Falls, Efforts Afoot to Boast Its Merits*, THE JAPAN TIMES (June 26, 2015), http://www.japantimes.co.jp/news/2015/06/26/national/whale-meat-consumption-falls-efforts-afoot-boast-merits/#.VeSyXflVhBc (observing that approximately 4,000–5,000 tons of whale meat are consumed in Japan annually, which is a fraction of the 200,000 tons consumed back in the 1960s).
247. Hirata, *supra* note 242, at 148.

248. *E.g.*, STOETT, *supra* note 240, at 86 (observing that the United States "[p]roactive wildlife policy is largely the result of the concentrated energy of NGOs, for whom the whaling issue became so important in the early 1970s," and at 91 that the presence of a strong environmental/animal rights lobby in most European Union countries has contributed to its anti-whaling and anti-sealing position).
249. Hirata, *supra* note 242, at 145–48.
250. KURKPATRICK DORSEY, WHALES & NATIONS: ENVIRONMENTAL DIPLOMACY ON THE HIGH SEAS 285 (2013) ["DORSEY"].
251. The ICJ's decision does not apply to JARPN II, Japan's scientific whaling program in the North Pacific, which continues unaffected.
252. Government of Japan, *Proposed Research Plan for New Scientific Whale Research Program in the Antarctic Ocean (NEWREP-A)* (2014), http://www.jfa.maff.go.jp/j/whale/pdf/newrep--a.pdf ["NEWREP-A"].
253. *Id.; Whaling in the Antarctic, supra* note 51, ¶ 286.
254. *NEWREP-A, supra* note 252, at 12 & 19.
255. The IWC's instructions to the Scientific Committee in this respect are binding pursuant to its power found in Article III of the ICRW. *See* Michael Johnson, *Whaling in the Antarctic—The ICJ Decision and Its Consequences for Future Special Permit Whaling*, 32 AUSTR. YB. INT'L L. 87, 92 (2015) ["Johnson"] (summarizing the current review process).
256. International Whaling Commission, (2014) *IWC Resolution 2014-5: Resolution on Whaling under Special Permit*, https://archive.iwc.int/pages/search.php?search=%21collection72&k=.
257. The review process is currently found in: International Whaling Commission, (2012) *Annex P: Process for the Review of Special Permit Proposals and Research Results from Existing and Completed Permits*.
258. Johnson, *supra* note 255, at 95.
259. International Whaling Commission, *Report of the Expert Panel to Review the Proposal by Japan for NEWREP-A, 7–10 February 2015, Tokyo, Japan* 35 (Apr. 13, 2015).
260. Johnson, *supra* note 255, at 95.
261. International Court of Justice, *Declarations Recognizing the Jurisdiction of the Court as Compulsory*, ICJ, http://www.icj-cij.org/jurisdiction/?p1=5&p2=1&p3=3&code=JP (last visited Nov. 5, 2015). Practically, this amended reservation likely precludes the ICJ from hearing a fresh challenge to the successor to JARPA II, called NEWREP-A. It is possible that fresh claims could be litigated under UNCLOS's dispute resolution machinery, but the prospects of a hypothetical challenge proceeding a hearing of the merits based on a violation of UNCLOS is murky at best (*see* Michael A. Becker, *Japan's New Optional Clause Declaration at the ICJ: A Pre-Emptive Strike*, EJIL: TALK! (Oct. 20, 2015), http://www.ejiltalk.org/japans-new-optional-clause-declaration-at-the-icj-a-pre-emptive-strike/).
262. Icelandic Ministries of Fisheries and Agriculture, "Whaling", http://www.fisheries.is/main-species/marine-mammals/whaling/ (last visited Sept. 25, 2015); The Norwegian Ministry of Trade, Industry and Fisheries, "Norwegian Whaling—Based on a Balanced Ecosystem" (Mar. 19, 2013), http://www.fisheries.no/ecosystems-and-stocks/marine_stocks/mammals/whales/whaling/#.VedTjPlVhBc.

263. NGOs have also played a significant role in advancing more recent international conservation-oriented efforts. For example, the International Fund for Animal Welfare was instrumental in initiating the preparatory work that ultimately resulted in Australia's legal action against Japan. For a summary of the work preceding Australia's application, *see* Donald R. Rothwell, *The Whaling Case: An Australian Perspective* 6–10 (2014) (unpublished conference paper on file with author).
264. STOETT, *supra* note 240, at 86.
265. *Id.*
266. *Id.*
267. *Id.* at 86–87.
268. *Id.* at 87. An interesting example of altered state action is the fact that the possibility of certification and the associated risk of losing future access to fisheries resources within the American EEZ persuaded Japan to not opt out of the commercial moratorium that the IWC ultimately passed in 1982 and made effective in 1986.
269. KELLY-KATE PEASE, INTERNATIONAL ORGANIZATIONS 256–57 (5th ed. 2016).
270. DORSEY, *supra* note 250, at 265–67 (at 267, the author notes that "Senegal, Belize, and Antigua joined the commission on the eve of the meeting, solely with the goal of voting for a moratorium"). More recently, and perhaps in response to this sort of political maneuvering, Japan has been accused by anti-whaling states of essentially vote-buying at the IWC in efforts to secure the number of votes necessary to overturn the ongoing commercial moratorium. The accusation, often founded on anecdotal evidence, being that the semi-public Japanese Overseas Fishery Cooperation Foundation works in conjunction with the fishery industry and trading companies to entice developing nation participation in the IWC by offering "cheap loans . . . and technical assistance" (P. Weber, *Protecting Oceanic Fisheries and Jobs*, in STATE OF THE WORLD 1995, at 29 (L. Brown et al. eds., 1995)). For further discussion on vote-buying, *see* Christian Dippel, *Foreign Aid and Voting in International Organizations: Evidence from the IWC*, unpublished manuscript, http://www.anderson.ucla.edu/faculty/christian.dippel/IWC_paper.pdf (Jul. 24, 2015).
271. *See* Pav Jordan, *Whaling Commission's Future to Be Tested in Chile*, REUTERS (June 21, 2008), http://www.reuters.com/article/2008/06/21/us-chile-whales-iwc-idUSN2034923120080621.
272. Jennifer L. Bailey, *Whale Watching, the Buenos Aires Group and the Politics of the International Whaling Commission*, 36 MAR. POL. 489, 492 (2012) ["Bailey"].
273. *Id.* at 491.
274. *Id.* (Bailey argues that this assertion helps counter the pro-whaling argument that the commercial moratorium violates national sovereignty by unnecessarily restricting resource use).
275. *See* Donald R. Rothwell, *The Whaling Case: Australian Perspectives*, Kokusai Mondai (International Affairs), No. 636 (2014), at 11 (writing that: "The bilateral relationship survived that disagreement and in light of Prime Minister Abe's successful visit to Australia in July 2014 there is every indication that efforts to 'silo' the disagreement over whales has been a great success").
276. Prime Minister Abbott and Prime Minister Abe Joint Statement, *Special Strategic Partnership for the 21st Century* (July 9, 2014), http://www.mofa.go.jp/a_o/ocn/page3e_000195.html.

277. Ministry of Foreign Affairs of Japan, *Joint Statement on the Entry into Force of the Agreement between Japan and Australia for an Economic Partnership* (Jan. 15, 2015), http://www.mofa.go.jp/page3e_000283.html.
278. Rothwell, *supra* note 275 (writing: "However, how Japan responds to the ICJ's 2014 judgment in the future will be a test with respect to Japan's interpretation and respect for international law which may cause further challenges for Australia/Japan relations").
279. *See* European Commission, *Comprehensive Economic and Trade Agreement* (Sept. 22, 2015), http://ec.europa.eu/trade/policy/in-focus/ceta/.
280. Mark Hume, "Humpback Whales Rebound from Near Extinction, Move Down on At-Risk Species List" (Apr. 27, 2014), http://www.theglobeandmail.com/news/national/ottawa-quietly-takes-humpback-whales-off-threatened-animals-list/article18091699/.
281. *See* Cole C. Monnahan, Trevor A. Branch & André Punt, *Do Ship Strikes Threaten the Recovery of Endangered Eastern North Pacific Blue Whales?*, 31 MAR. MAMM. SCI. 279 (2015).
282. *See* Department of Fisheries and Oceans Canada, "Resurgence of the Sea Otter" (Dec. 2013), CANADIAN GEOGRAPHIC, http://www.canadiangeographic.ca/magazine/dec13/resurgence-of-sea-otter.asp.

7

The Proposal

Part II—The Secretariat, Regionalism, and Marine Protected Areas

> "The scope and degree of the problems marine mammals face cannot be fully resolved by traditional single-species responses. Consequently, a creative and flexible regulatory response—in essence, a new ocean ethic—is necessary to restore the complex biodiversity of the oceans and ensure healthy ecosystems in which these valuable and beloved species can thrive once again."[1]

I. INTRODUCTION

In Chapter 6 I introduced the first part of the proposal for an UNCLOS implementing agreement, titled Draft Agreement for the Implementation of the Provisions of the United Nations Convention on the Law of the Sea of 10 December 1982 Relating to the Conservation of Marine Mammals ("UN Marine Mammal Agreement" or "proposed Agreement"). A full version of the proposed Agreement is available in Appendix 3. The goal in advancing this proposal is to provide a comprehensive alternative to the current insufficient, fragmented approach to marine mammal conservation and management.

It is necessary to provide more information on three aspects of the proposed Agreement: (1) the institutional structure proposed in the draft Agreement and the role contemplated for the Secretariat, (2) the emphasis on regionalism and regional implementation, and (3) the form, structure, and implementation of marine protected areas (MPAs) as contemplated as one type of conservation and sustainable management measure in the proposed Agreement.

The purpose of this chapter is to explore these important components in more detail; indeed, these areas remain the subject of considerable attention and/or ongoing advancement at the international level. Therefore, the analysis that follows focuses on key aspects of each issue as they relate to the proposed Agreement.

II. INSTITUTIONAL STRUCTURE AND THE SECRETARIAT

1. The Commission and Regional Organizations/Arrangements

The first issue raised in the proposed Agreement that requires further unpacking is its institutional structure. I argue in favor of creating a new independent intergovernmental organization whose membership is premised on ratification or accession to the Agreement itself. The decision to frame the Commission as I have is a conscious one based on organizational succession, the observation that the Commission will be performing many of the functions traditionally performed by the IWC, and the assumption that creating a new international organization dedicated wholly to marine mammals represents the optimal situation. Further, this regime places primary decision-making authority with states parties to the Agreement (the "members"), and for this reason it is inappropriate to simply piggyback on an existing international organization that may not encompass full membership.

The proposed Agreement also contemplates the use of regional organizations and/or arrangements to implement and operationalize the regulations and standards (conservation and sustainable management measures) produced by the Commission, and the creation of a Secretariat to coordinate efforts with other pertinent regimes and organizations. There is the possibility that existing regional organizations (i.e., regional fisheries management organizations or other existing regional organizations that have an interest in marine mammal conservation and management) or regional arrangements may be able to participate in this regard, but also that other new organizations or arrangements may have to be created to perform these functions. This section will now turn to discussing the Secretariat, recognizing that the functionality of the Commission and regional organizations, as well as the proposed interaction between these two aspects of the draft regime, will be considered in greater detail later in the context of regionalism.

2. The Secretariat

The proposed Agreement contemplates a Secretariat that plays an important role in coordinating the efforts of the Commission and in collaborating with existing regimes and international organizations. Secretariats generally work to "oversee the advancement of the major environmental conventions including any subsequent Protocols."[2] The Secretariat, as proposed here, will also work to help avoid or reduce duplication of effort and to ensure that the Commission's interests in marine mammal conservation and sustainable management are being properly accounted for in other fora.

Despite its importance, the proposed Agreement does not prescribe the exact identity of the Secretariat beyond prescribing that the Commission shall establish the Secretariat, on either an interim or permanent basis, at its first ordinary meeting.[3] To this end, it is worth considering whether an existing organization is properly situated to discharge the duties envisioned for the Secretariat. This section considers whether the United Nations Environment Programme (UNEP) is properly situated to participate in the creation and administration of this Agreement's

Secretariat, or alternatively if UNEP could first function as an Interim Secretariat as the regime establishes itself, and then transition into a supporting role.

The first justification for engaging UNEP in this capacity is that the proposed Agreement brings international marine mammal conservation and sustainable management under the auspices of the United Nations. Accomplishing this transition successfully and effectively requires integration, and would benefit from capitalizing upon existing infrastructure. Succinctly stated, UNEP represents the most appropriate body to accomplish this task as it stands as the only "UN body with a mandate to focus specifically on environmental issues."[4] UNEP's original mandate, "[t]o provide leadership and encourage partnership in caring for the environment by inspiring, informing, and enabling nations and peoples to improve their quality of life without compromising that of future generations,"[5] was expanded by the Nairobi Declaration on the Role and Mandate of the United Nations Environment Programme, which contemplates UNEP as "the leading environmental authority that sets the global environmental agenda, that promotes the coherent implementation of the environmental dimensions of sustainable development within the United Nations system and that serves as an authoritative advocate for the global environment."[6] Further, Chapter 38 of Agenda 21 elevated and legitimized UNEP's role in international environmental law, noting in paragraph 22(h) that it should become engaged in "[f]urther development of international environmental law, in particular conventions and guidelines, promotion of its implementation, and coordinating functions arising from an increasing number of international legal agreements, *inter alia, the functioning of the secretariats of the Conventions*, taking into account the need for the most efficient use of resources, including possible co-location of secretariats established in the future" [emphasis added].[7] UNEP has previously acted to support the creation of international environmental law, to foster the implementation of international environmental law, and to promote coordination and cooperation between existing treaty Secretariats.[8] Further, at Rio + 20 the global community agreed that it is important to continue to support and rely on UNEP, and to "strengthen and upgrade UNEP."[9]

UNEP's institutional strengths align with some of the key aspects found in the proposed Agreement. For example, UNEP is committed to ecosystem-based management and has "launched a renewed push to persuade governments, businesses and communities to consider the social and economic value of biodiversity and ecosystem services when planning and making decisions concerning the use of natural resources."[10] UNEP also occupies a leadership role in advancing integrated ecosystem-based management, evinced by the creation and maintenance of the Intergovernmental Science-Policy Platform on Biodiversity and Ecosystem Services (IPBES).[11] UNEP collaborates with other UN organizations, including the UN Development Programme, UN Food and Agriculture Organization (FAO), and the UN Educational, Scientific and Cultural Organization to cohost and support the IPBES Secretariat (for which it has served as Interim Secretariat since 2008).[12] This is significant because it exemplifies: (1) UNEP's appreciation of ecosystem-based management, which is emphasized in the draft Agreement; and (2) UNEP's collaborative capacity; the relationship between UNEP and the FAO is of particular import given the interaction between fisheries and marine mammals. In sum, UNEP's mandate, role, and integrated position within the UN indicates that it is appropriately situated to help establish and host the Secretariat contemplated by the draft Agreement.

A second justification for involving UNEP in the establishment of the Secretariat is its experience in collaboratively addressing marine mammal conservation. Although I have previously commented on UNEP's role in marine mammal conservation, certain aspects bear repeating here as they re-enforce its suitability to perform this important task. UNEP and FAO partnered between 1978 and 1983 to produce the Global Plan of Action for the Conservation and Utilisation of Marine Mammals (MMAP),[13] with the hopes of "bring[ing] governments together to agree and harmonize their policies for marine mammal conservation."[14] Although the MMAP has fallen short of this lofty goal, certain actions that have resulted from effort undertaken pursuant to MMAP demonstrate UNEP's competence to meaningfully contribute to marine mammal conservation. First, as Secretariat of the MMAP, UNEP has engaged many of the key players in marine mammal conservation, including: (1) the International Union for the Conservation of Nature, and notable nongovernmental organizations such as Greenpeace, the World Wide Fund, and the International Fund for Animal Welfare, and many others; and (2) regional and international treaty regimes including the CMS, the IWC, ASCOBANS, and ACCOBAMS.[15] Knowledge of existing, disparate regional and international approaches (and associated political undercurrents) are crucial and best understood through participation.

Further, UNEP is responsible for having created the Regional Seas Programme, which utilizes a globally oriented but regionally implemented response to ocean pollution issues and general maritime degradation.[16] Currently, there are 13 Regional Sea divisions supported by more than 143 states,[17] and efforts have been made pursuant to this program to help accomplish the goals of the MMAP.[18] A number of Regional Action Plans have been developed to address particular concerns related to marine mammal species, and "within the context of MMAP, UNEP has worked to build technical and institutional capacity in marine mammal conservation and management in several Regional Seas programmes, particularly those in Latin America and the Caribbean, Eastern Africa, the southeast Pacific, West and Central Africa, the Black Sea and South-East Asia."[19] Action Plans specific to marine mammals exist in the Mediterranean, the South-East Pacific, and the Caribbean.[20] Taken together, these initiatives indicate the UNEP has the requisite knowledge, institutional experience, and capacity to participate initially as the Interim Secretariat of the Agreement and then to transition into a support/host capacity.

A third justification for engaging UNEP as the interim Secretariat and then transitioning to UNEP's administration (i.e., hosting and supporting) of the Secretariat is UNEP's institutional experience in this exact role. This discussion has previously emphasized the role that UNEP occupies in supporting environmental agreements and, to this end, UNEP serves as the Secretariat for CITES, CMS, CBD,[21] the Global Partnership on Nutrient Management,[22] the Global Programme of Action for the Protection of the Marine Environment from Land-Based Activities,[23] and Regional Seas conventions,[24] and has been the Interim Secretariat for the Carpathian Convention since 2008,[25] and acts as the host for the Secretariat for the Vienna Convention for the Protection of the Ozone Layer and the Montreal Protocol on Substances That Deplete the Ozone Layer.[26] Additionally, UNEP supports and hosts other independent Secretariats, including the Basel Convention on the Control of Transboundary Movements of Hazardous Wastes and Their Disposal Secretariat[27] and the Stockholm Convention on Persistent Organic Pollutants Secretariat,[28] and shares responsibility with the FAO for administering the Rotterdam Convention on the Prior Informed Consent Procedure for Certain Hazardous Chemicals and Pesticides in International Trade.[29] Accordingly, UNEP has considerable experience, and it is unnecessary and inefficient to attempt to duplicate existing capabilities.

Further, UNEP currently operates a Division of Environmental Law and Conventions to foster ongoing coordination, and previously it arranged annual Meetings on Coordination of Secretariats of Environmental Conventions.[30] UNEP is also well positioned globally to assist in this role, with liaison offices in Addis Ababa, Beijing, Brasilia, Brussels, Cairo, Moscow, New York, and Vienna supporting regional efforts.[31]

The major drawbacks associated with engaging UNEP in this capacity are also readily identifiable. First and foremost, UNEP's mandate is primarily environmental, which may prevent agreement on engaging UNEP as a Secretariat, even in a temporary capacity. Throughout this book I have stressed the importance of seeking rational compromise. The key compromise necessary to achieve the rational international conservation and sustainable management of marine mammals is the return to a managed, monitored, and limited commercial take in return for expanded regulatory authority (so far as practicable) engaging the current threats to marine mammals. Second, given the unique focus of the proposed agreement, and the existence of a financial funding mechanism, it may also make sense to establish a Secretariat that is also unique in expertise and experience. One option in this regard is to engage individuals who have previous experience working with these issues at the international level with existing organizations such as the IWC or NAMMCO, or to seek the participation of individuals from different nations that have a vested interest in these areas who are committed to the compromise necessary to achieve the desired results.

A second alternative to UNEP is the Division for Ocean Affairs and the Law of the Sea of the Office of Legal Affairs (DOALOS). DOALOS has "constantly been recognized for its role in contributing to the wider acceptance and rational and consistent application of the United Nations Convention on the Law of the Sea"[32] and has the following mandate:

7.1 The Division of Ocean Affairs and the Law of the Sea is headed by a Director who is accountable to the Legal Counsel.
7.2 The core functions of the Division are as follows:
  (a) Providing advice, studies, assistance and research on the implementation of the United Nations Convention on the Law of the Sea, on issues of a general nature and on specific developments relating to the research and legal regime for the oceans;
  (b) Providing substantive servicing to the General Assembly on the law of the sea and ocean affairs, to the Meeting of States Parties to the Convention and to the Commission on the Limits of the Continental Shelf;
  (c) Providing support to the organizations of the United Nations system to facilitate consistency with the Convention of the instruments and programmes in their respective areas of competence;

(d) Discharging the responsibilities, other than depositary functions, of the Secretary-General under the Convention;
(e) Conducting monitoring and research activities and maintaining a comprehensive information system and research library on the Convention and on the law of the sea and ocean affairs;
(f) Providing training and fellowship and technical assistance in the field of the law of the sea and ocean affairs;
(g) Preparing studies on relevant Articles of the Charter for the Repertory of Practice of United Nations Organs.[33]

In discharging these responsibilities, DOALOS monitors developments in the law of the sea for the purposes of annual reporting to the United Nations General Assembly, "formulates recommendations to the Assembly and other intergovernmental forums aimed at promoting a better understanding of the Convention [UNCLOS]," "ensures that the Organization has the capacity to respond to requests for advice and assistance from States in the implementation of the Convention [UNCLOS]," and serves as secretariat for both UNCLOS and the Commission on the Limits of the Continental Shelf ("Continental Shelf Commission").[34] Taken together, these functions indicate that DOALOS is administratively capable of performing significant tasks. Still, the functions contemplated for the Secretariat created pursuant to the draft Agreement would add an additional burden and would require an amended mandate extending its capacity beyond UNCLOS proper and the Continental Shelf Commission. Nevertheless, it is well-positioned and should not be discounted as a potential candidate.

The Commission, as the decision-making body under the proposed Agreement, is responsible for establishing the Secretariat. Although the Commission can choose to establish any Secretariat that it wishes via resolution, and is free to opt for an administrative structure that exists independently of the UN, the above assessment does present a number of factors in favor of utilizing the experience and existing infrastructure offered by UNEP while also canvassing two viable alternatives. This assessment acknowledges that the Secretariat could be situated with UNEP on an indefinite interim basis or could contemplate the transition to a different arrangement, whereby the Secretariat is supported by UNEP but independently populated and/or managed by DOALOS. The latter option may be preferable for many of the participating nations who recognize the importance of capitalizing upon existing institutional experience without fully committing themselves to an overtly environmental regime that, although focused on a broad array of issues, emphasizes issues such as climate change, pollution, and toxic/harmful substances. It is not possible to predict with certainty whether the key nations involved in these discussions would be open to the possibility of engaging UNEP in this way. Still, and despite the fact that rational environmental governance should not preclude sustainable use, it is reasonably foreseeable that the current group of pro-whaling states would be highly reluctant to vest Secretarial functions with UNEP, and that an independent Secretariat should be formed. If this is the preference, it is still possible to learn from UNEP's experience and past successes in creating the new Secretariat and to focus on empowering DOALOS or the independently populated Secretariat as it administers the proposed Agreement.

III. REGIONALISM

The second point of consideration is the emphasis that is placed on regionalism and regional implementation in the proposed Agreement, a conscious decision that requires further exploration. The choice to manage international environmental issues on a regional or global scale is based on whether these are issues best addressed by decision-makers at the global or regional level of governance.[35] This portion of the analysis proceeds by first identifying what is meant by regionalism in this context, then indicating the theoretical benefits and drawbacks of employing regionalism, and finally justifying the form of regionalism advanced in the proposed regime.

1. What Is Regionalism?

The first task in this assessment of regionalism is to understand its operation. In the broadest sense of oceans management, regionalism has been described as "the management of oceans and their resources at the regional level" through "mechanisms designed to implement various types of cooperative activities among States, particularly those in a contiguous geographic area."[36] The notion of regionalism was quite important at UNCLOS III,[37] and this is reflected in the final text as regionalism and regional cooperation is contemplated, inter alia, with respect to the conservation of living marine resources, dispute settlement, in the context of enclosed and/or semi-enclosed seas, and with respect to the protection and preservation of the marine environment.[38] For example, Article 197, titled "Cooperation on a Global or Regional Basis," provides that:

> States shall cooperate on a global basis and, as appropriate, on a regional basis, directly or through competent international organizations, in formulating and elaborating international rules, standards and recommended practices and procedures consistent with this Convention, for the protection and preservation of the marine environment, taking into account characteristic regional features.

In short, UNCLOS endorses the "international practice of the two-track, global and regional (and subregional) approach and, second, that the UNCLOS Convention endorses marine regionalism...."[39] I have previously described and analyzed many approaches to oceans governance that exemplify the regional approach, including CCAMLR, NAMMCO, ACCOBAMS, ASCOBANS, the UNEP Regional Seas Programme, and the structure and function of RFMOs and, in the context of Article 65 and 120 of UNCLOS, have asserted that the plurality of "organizations" with respect to cetacean conservation in Article 65 can reasonably support the use of regional organizations and arrangements. Nonetheless, it is necessary to look beyond this working definition and superficial acknowledgment of the existence of regional arrangements to properly understand the intricacies of oceans management regionalism.

International wildlife policy analyst and advisor Margi Prideaux proffers that "[r]egionalism typically has three dimensions. Countries with defined geographical areas have historical experience in common. A developed, socio-cultural, political, or economic linkage distinguishes them from the rest of the global community.

Typically, such relations have developed to allow organizations to manage crucial aspects of their collective affairs. These three dimensions are interrelated."[40] This excerpt raises a central question that must be answered for any regional approach: What exactly constitutes an ocean region? Lewis Alexander, a leading legal expert in the area of maritime regionalism, notes that a "region is an intellectual concept, created by the selection of certain features that are relevant to an areal interest or problem"[41] and that regionalism can be conceived on either a physical basis or a functional basis.[42] According to Alexander, physical regions in the ocean include "semienclosed seas, archipelagos, oceanic areas of strong upwelling, and of course the polar regions,"[43] whereas functional regions "focus on patterns of resources, activities, and perceived policy problems that are at least analytically separable from other areas."[44]

Author Joseph Morgan provides a slightly different conception of regionalism, noting that "[t]he criteria we use to delineate the appropriate marine region should be based on the problem to be solved."[45] Morgan identifies a host of criteria that can be used to identify ocean regions, including: (1) "Physical regions," (2) "Economic regions," (3) "Cultural regions," (4) "Management regions," (5) "Political regions," and (6) "Geostrategic regions."[46] Although the first three categories are self-explanatory, "management regions" contemplates "[a]reas of the oceans in which management organizations have set up rules or procedures," "political regions" contemplates the situation "[w]here an area of the oceans is completely or almost completely under the control of a single nation," and a "geostrategic region" contemplates areas that are useful for security or tactical purposes.[47] In reality, this multifaceted categorization may simply represent the diversity of considerations encapsulated by Alexander's functional categorization, which "are characterized by common problems and/or opportunities or are covered by an international treaty or agreement,"[48] as economic considerations, cultural and political considerations, management considerations, and geostrategic considerations essentially represent a functional perspective.

Professor Alan Boyle contends that the exercise of defining regionalism "thus revolves itself largely into a question of policy: what is the most sensible geographical and political area within which to address the interrelated problems of marine and terrestrial environmental protection?"[49] Further, it is important to note that such classifications remain utilitarian insofar as they become a means to an end. Facilitating regional cooperation requires proper planning and consideration of the various ways to conceive of regional organization. For the purposes of this assessment, regionalization for the implementation of marine mammal conservation and sustainable management measures may be organized around any number of criteria. The logical starting point for defining regions in the context of marine mammal conservation and sustainable management remains the natural distribution of marine mammal species and/or populations, but this form of boundary setting can be expanded or restricted based on other important considerations, including cultural uses, political preferences, and/or the existence of particular or localized threats.

In addition to considering how regions are defined, regionalism must also be considered in the context of how the regions are organized and how they operate. Specifically, should regional arrangements exist within the auspices of the UN or exist external to its institutional structures?[50] Two related but independent inquiries ask: (1) What contribution is required from participating states (i.e., funds, personpower, and deference to regional decision-making authority); and (2) What is the scope of the regional arrangement (i.e., single issue oriented or multifaceted).[51] A final question that must be contemplated, and one that is particularly relevant for the purposes of this proposal, is the extent to which the regional arrangement operates independently, in conjunction with other regional arrangements, or as part of a regionally implemented global scheme.[52] This final query is important as it determines the extent to which decision-making authority is positioned within a particular regional organization/arrangement or remains vested elsewhere. Theoretically, this query posits consideration of whether the application of regionalism is contemplated as a "restrictive model of regionalism" or a "liberal model of regionalism."[53] As understood in the context of the interaction between UNCLOS and regional agreements, the "restrictive model of regionalism" means "the function of regional rules or treaties is relatively limited: it is to reinforce enforcement and application of the global rules"[54] whereas the "liberal model of regionalism" requires application, meaning that the production of rules and standards occurs at the regional level rather than the global level.[55] Recognizing that regionalism can take all manner of forms, the scope of regional action contemplated by this proposed Agreement will be addressed in due course.

Academic discussion of marine mammal conservation recognizes the contribution that regional arrangements have already made and the potential that they hold moving forward. For example, in her note on the emergence and functionality of NAMMCO, Brettny Hardy asserts in conclusion that a "localized approach to the management of marine mammal consumption would increase the amount of information on discrete populations, promote an ecosystem understanding of marine mammal communities, and allow for the successful operation of inspection schemes to monitor and ensure sustainable use."[56] Further, Prideaux has advanced a case for enhancing the use of regional agreements under framework agreements (i.e., ASCOBANS and ACCOBAMS, which were created pursuant to CMS), and in developing her argument for a similar agreement for cetaceans in the Indian Ocean contends that "such an agreement would be a valuable step towards the global cetacean conservation, through a network of interconnected regional agreements, but also through greater regional cooperation and domestic capacity for marine management."[57] With both this understanding of regionalism and its general applicability to marine mammal conservation in mind, this discussion now shifts to a discussion of the potential major advantages and drawbacks of emphasizing a regional approach.

2. Benefits and Drawbacks of Regionalism

This work is premised on the operative assumption that relying on national action is not a viable approach to achieving rational, global marine mammal conservation. Instead, the proposal offers a hybrid between purely global governance and regionalism. The basic justification for employing regionalism in oceans governance is that neither current threats nor ocean characteristics are equally distributed; in short, "[t]he seas ... are not homogeneous."[58] It is necessary to delve deeper and to illuminate the key advantages and disadvantages of regionalism before explaining and justifying the particular form of regionalism employed in the proposed Agreement.

Various benefits of regionalism in oceans governance have been identified. These benefits include that:

(1) It reduces the fragmentation associated with a purely national approach;[59]
(2) It has the potential to account for local variation.[60] Professor Okidi notes in the context of the protection of the marine environment that "there are different degrees and kinds of pollution in the various region; thus the strategies required for the protection of the environment would be correspondingly different";[61]
(3) It is probable that "[r]egional schemes are more likely to respond to common interests in dealing with a common problem";[62]
(4) It allows "states to agree on commitments for common action that may be more feasible to implement than under a more broadly based global scheme";[63]
(5) It recognizes that "regional cooperation may be easier to organize and may prove more effective on technical matters," including the issues of monitoring, research, and information exchange.[64] Regional arrangements also promote technology transfer and capacity, especially among developing states;[65]
(6) It "encourages maximum participation by the regional nations, especially less developed countries which might otherwise stay away from a globally organized and technologically advanced system."[66] Participation may also be cheaper as "activities are closer to home";[67]
(7) It might, in providing a "forum for consultation," help promote "habits of cooperation."[68] The very idea of the "global superagency meets with immediate objections" and "[r]egional approaches still seem the midway path acceptable for purposes of enforcement of mutually accepted standards";[69] and
(8) It might be important in "creating a synthesis between coastal communities and national governance and between global communities and global 'issue' governance."[70]

Similarly, there are drawbacks associated with regionalism that must also be acknowledged. These drawbacks include the following:

(1) If left as a completely regional approach, regionalism could produce results that counter global conservation efforts. For example, it is counterproductive to the conservation or sustainable use of marine resources if a region of like-minded states interested in utilizing resources to the point of their depletion organizes around this goal, which is detrimental to the common interest;
(2) In the context of high seas governance and marine pollution, Professor Boczek notes that "if the high seas are open to all nations, then control over any detriment to the marine environment caused by a nation, otherwise representing disregard of the interests of other members of the international community, ought to be comprehensively regulated by a

global agency authorized not only to set standards but also to carry out enforcement measures for the protection of the common enjoyment of the oceans";[71]
(3) It has been noted in the context of marine pollution control that regionalism "may fragment the possibilities for, and the effectiveness of international supervision of compliance with environmental standards";[72]
(4) It creates the potential for "conflict with third parties" in "common spaces" if states that are nonparty to a particular arrangement, and therefore not bound by it, attempt to utilize that particular region;[73] and
(5) There is the overarching concern that "[t]aken too far, regionalism may weaken the consensus on a genuinely global law of the sea."[74]

Despite having mainly been considered in the context of marine pollution governance, the advantages and disadvantages of regionalism highlighted above are applicable to marine mammal conservation. In 1978, Professor Richard Bilder opined during a discussion of how regionalism might impact treaty and customary law at UNCLOS III, that the task is "to encourage those aspects of regionalism that seem most useful, to discourage those that seem least useful, and, more generally, to ease any problems for a rational global system of ocean management that regionalism might pose."[75] The same remains true today.

3. Case Study

It is important to ensure that this assessment of regionalism and its application to marine mammal conservation and sustainable management transcends theoretical discussion and provides a practical example of how a regional organization has effectively managed an issue involving marine mammals. A suitable case study is the tuna-dolphin problem in the Eastern Tropical Pacific, where purse-seine net fishing techniques have the tendency to capture both tuna and dolphin.[76]

The RFMO responsible for the tuna fishery in this region is the Inter-American Tropical Tuna Commission (IATTC), which was initially created pursuant to the Convention for the Establishment of an Inter-American Tropical Tuna Commission[77] and subsequently bolstered and replaced in 2003 by the Convention for the Strengthening of the Inter-American Tropical Tuna Commission.[78] The IATTC has responded to the tuna-dolphin problem through the Agreement on the International Dolphin Conservation Program (AIDCP).[79] This approach adds value to this discussion of regionalism for a number of reasons: (1) it demonstrates the ability of an RFMO to respond, in a legal way, to a recognized problem; (2) it demonstrates that a functional and pragmatic response to this issue is possible; and (3) it demonstrates that this functional response can be innovative and forward-thinking. The remainder of this assessment of the AIDCP will highlight the pertinent aspects that make a suitable analog in the context of this proposal.

Regarding the legal nature of this response, the AIDCP exists pursuant to a negotiated multilateral agreement. A considerable proportion of the current development in the area of international environmental governance occurs in the form of "soft law," which is useful but not necessarily sufficient to address immediate problems. Further, this agreement is strongly grounded within the principles of UNCLOS and acknowledges in its first preambular statement that:

> in accordance with the relevant principles of international law, as reflected in the United Nations Convention on the Law of the Sea (UNCLOS) of 1982, all States have the duty to take, or to cooperate with other States in taking, such measures as may be necessary for the conservation and management of living marine resources.[80]

The preamble also states that "multilateral cooperation constitutes the most effective means for achieving the objectives of conservation and sustainable use of living marine resources."[81] Further, this legal agreement accomplishes the difficult task of balancing the future use of the tuna resource (which is noted in the preamble to represent an important "source of food and income for the populations of the Parties"[82]) with the desire to reduce dolphin mortality that is occurring as a result of a particular fishing practice. Article II then establishes the basic objectives for the program, which include: "progressively reduc[ing] dolphin mortalities in the tuna purse-seine fishery in the Agreement Area to levels approaching zero, through the setting of annual limits," "the goal of eliminating dolphin mortality in this fishery ... [and] ecologically sound means of capturing large yellowfin tunas," and to ensure "long-term sustainability" of target and non-target species in the Agreement Area.[83]

In addition to the multilateral-treaty origin of this program, other key features have contributed to the successfulness of this response. First, Article V of the AIDCP declares that "total incidental dolphin mortality" shall be limited to 5,000 individuals, and that this goal shall be achieved "through the adoption and implementation of relevant measures."[84] Article V proceeds to define the measures that will be used to achieve the stated goal, which include: promoting vessel captain action to reduce dolphin mortality, technical training and certification for captains and crews, gear improvements, equitable distribution of dolphin mortality limits (DML), tuna catch tracking and verification, data exchange, and research.[85] Although some of these represent typical compliance mechanisms, the use of a hard cap, DML, and emphasis on training and captain/vessel incentives seems innovative, and compliance is bolstered by Article XVI. Second, the AIDCP also established an "On-Board Observer Program" in Article XIII. This is an incredibly pertinent feature given the role that an analogous program could play in the resumption of limited commercial whaling or other lethal and contentious marine mammal hunts.

The AIDCP regime has given effect to these innovative measures in two ways. The first is through annexes to the agreement, and the second is through resolutions passed by the parties to the agreement. Regarding the use of annexes, Annex II establishes the details of the observer program created in Article XIII. This detailed annex notes that the observer system is to utilize a combination of national and international observers (to ensure a measure of accountability and reliability in reporting),[86] notes the duties and responsibilities owed by both the observers and the captains of the vessels on which they are performing their role,[87] and provides guidance on how the collected information shall be disseminated and used (most importantly, to ensure that vessels and nations are not exceeding their respective

DMLs).[88] Other relevant annexes include: (1) Annex III, which provides that the parties shall establish "per-stock, per-year dolphin mortality limits"; (2) Annex IV, which details the DML regime (in terms of assignment, utilization, implementation, and the use of any unused portion that remains at the end of the season); (3) Annex VIII, which sets "operational requirements for vessels"; and (4) Annex IX, which sets requirements for the tuna tracking and verification scheme.

The second mechanism through which innovative measures and features can be operationalized is resolutions. For example, Resolution A-99-01, titled "On-Board Observer Program and captain incentives," supports implementation of the observer scheme by establishing a working group to reward or further incent captains who have an exemplary record of compliance,[89] whereas Resolution A-03-02, titled "Resolution on At-Sea Reporting," requires weekly reporting from observers who are currently out at sea to ensure compliance on an ongoing basis.[90] Resolution A-04-03, titled "Resolution Regarding Dolphin Safety Gear," buttresses Annex VIII and vessel operational requirements by requiring vessel inspection assessing vessel equipment compliance to occur twice each year,[91] and Resolution A-04-07, being "Resolution to Establish a List of Vessels Presumed to Have Carried Illegal, Unreported and Unregulated Fishing Activities in the Agreement Area," contemplates the creation and maintenance of a list of vessels that are believed to be fishing using purse-seine techniques in the Agreement Area without participation or compliance with the AIDCP, and recognizes the ability of participating nations to take appropriate action to prevent or deter such action.[92] The final aspect of the AIDCP that requires evaluation is its Dolphin-Safe Certification Program (the "Dolphin-Safe Program").

The Dolphin-Safe Program is an attempt to satisfy consumers that the tuna products they are consuming were hunted sustainably and in a manner that is "dolphin-safe" (meaning "tuna caught in nets in which dolphins are not killed or seriously injured").[93] The Dolphin-Safe Program is a voluntary process with a standard procedure to be followed that parties to AIDCP can opt to implement.[94] This procedure establishes that either the state party within which the tuna is unloaded or the flag state of the fishing vessel will be responsible for issuing the certificate, which is produced in a standardized, pre-approved format.[95] Further, only vessels captained by individuals on the List of Qualified Captains, as managed by the Secretariat, can engage.[96] This procedure also contemplates addressing invalid certificates,[97] verification (through application of the AIDCP Tuna Tracking and Verification System),[98] and public education.[99] This certification system differs from the standard that is used in the United States (which requires "no tuna were caught on the trip in which such tuna were harvested using a purse seine net intentionally deployed on or to encircle dolphins, and no dolphins were killed or seriously injured during the sets in which the tuna were caught"[100]) but has been recognized by the United Nations Food and Agriculture Organization and, in 2005, was awarded the Margarita Lizarraga Medal Award[101] (which is "awarded biennially by the Conference upon the proposal of the Council to a person or organization that has served with distinction in the application of the Code of Conduct for Responsible Fisheries").[102]

In sum, AIDCP represents a regional, multilateral response to a recognized (and contentious) problem involving cetacean mortality. It has developed a series of innovative measures that seek to balance continued tuna take with dolphin protection, and is able to adapt and apply these measures through annexes and resolution. The use of on-board observers and an equitable quota-allocation mechanism is particularly relevant given the scheme that has been proposed in this work. Further, although the Dolphin-Safe Certification program may yet require improvement, it demonstrates innovation and commitment to transparency, and should be commended in this respect. As this discussion turns to a description of how regionalism is contemplated by this proposal, the AIDCP remains a potential precedent for how RFMOs and/or other regional organizations could implement the regime established by the International Marine Mammal Organization.

4. Regionalism as Contemplated in the Proposed Agreement

In the context of international action to address marine pollution, Professor Boczek asserts that "[t]he management of pollution must transcend the national boundaries. Pollution can be dealt with effectively on the international level. However, the strategy applied in marine pollution control need not be exclusively global."[103] Similarly, in the context of effective management of areas beyond national jurisdiction, "complementary action at the global and regional levels" is necessary, and "implementation of that general framework will always have an important regional component as it is simply not feasible to address this matter exhaustively at the global level."[104] The hybrid global-regional model advanced in this draft Agreement accords with these statements and also with the "restrictive model of regionalism" described above.[105]

In the course of assessing the role of regionalism in marine mammal conservation, both Hardy and Prideaux endorse aspects of the arrangement contained in the proposed Agreement. For example, Hardy suggests that in the future:

> The IWC should take steps to encourage the development of more regional marine mammal management organizations based on NAMMCO's structure. It could spend money consulting with groups of like-minded nations, who share in the consumption of discrete stocks of marine mammals, or who are located in similar geographic regions, helping them build a foundation for cooperative management. The ICW could also incorporate recommendations from regional bodies into its own decision-making process, acting more as a central authority.[106]

Hardy proceeds to envision an arrangement wherein "the IWC should act as an umbrella organization making broad regulations, while at the same time supervising the detailed management systems of more localized bodies."[107] Similarly, Prideaux considers the proliferation of regional agreements, hoping that they become "solid foundations on which to develop a set of worldwide interlocking regional agreements for the conservation of cetaceans."[108] More recently and in the wake of *Whaling in the Antarctic (Australia v. Japan: New Zealand intervening)*,[109] academic commentators have once again turned their attention to the possibility that new agreements should be created by "like-minded States" allowing them "to develop a legal framework that meets the perceived evolving needs of the international community to protect whales as keystone species in the ocean ecosystems."[110]

My proposed Agreement seeks to capture the advantages of both centralized decision-making and regional implementation and cooperation. Specifically, the draft Agreement endorses global decision-making and, to that end empowers the Commission with governance primacy. This is an important point of deviation from the UN Fish Stocks Agreement, which does not utilize a centralized global decision-making body. The Commission, rather than regional organizations or arrangements, is responsible for the promulgation of conservation and sustainable management measures (draft Article 12(f)), for creating and distributing best-practice standards and guidance (draft Article 12(g)), and for otherwise making recommendations to member states (draft Article 12(h)). This arrangement recognizes that many of the threats to marine mammals are global in nature (i.e., climate change, environmental pollution), promotes centralized decision-making, and emphasizes consensus decision-making and cooperation.

Part IV of the proposed Agreement provides the scope of action permissible for regional organizations and/or arrangements, and is based on the model of regional cooperation found in the UN Fish Stocks Agreement. Draft Articles 21 and 22 set the basic parameters for regional cooperation through regional marine mammal organizations and/or arrangements, and importantly, require an existing or proposed regional organization and/or arrangement to apply to the Commission for approval prior to it performing the functions contemplated in draft Article 23. Before elaborating on the functions that these regional organizations/arrangements can perform, it is necessary to comment on how this regime may work for existing marine mammal organizations. For example, certain existing arrangements such as NAMMCO obviously favor the sustainable management aspect for member nations interested in continuing to use marine mammals. Alternatively, ASCOBANS and ACCOBAMS represent preservation approaches that compliment IWC action by conserving small cetaceans. Each existing regional approach would be assessed independently to determine whether it is properly positioned to implement the draft Agreement and the conservation and sustainability measures created in conjunction with the Commission. If so, they can apply for approval to operate as such, and if not, the member nations involved will have to consider whether it is necessary to amend current arrangements or, alternatively, create a new or supplementary regional arrangement capable of implementing the functions required to qualify.

If we return to functionality, the key role envisioned for regional marine mammal organizations and arrangements is the adoption, application, and implementation of the Commission's conservation and sustainable management measures (draft Article 23(a)). Essentially, the proposed model leaves take-quota approval, marine protected area establishment, and other key decision-making functions with the Commission. Once the Commission has made such decisions, it falls on the appropriately situated regional organization or arrangement to give them effect. In addition to adopting, applying, and implementing conservation and sustainable management measures, these regional organizations/arrangements will implement any best-practice standards the Commission promulgates, coordinate and apply for commercial take quota approval from the Commission (which it will then administer regionally), work to bolster cooperation and coordination with national agencies, and, perhaps most important, take the lead in monitoring, control, surveillance, and enforcement.

Entrusting regional bodies with enforcement and compliance places this key aspect of regime efficacy with similarly situated nations, but it is important to emphasize that the Commission should remain involved, which minimally requires the regional organization or arrangement to report to the Commission regarding its efforts on an annual basis. Further, draft Articles 34–36 describe regionalism in the context of monitoring and enforcement, and provide the basic form of cooperation at the regional level (draft Article 34), inspection (draft Article 35), and port state control (draft Article 36). This is coupled with the possibility that the Commission could reduce, restrict, or rescind approved conservation and sustainable management measures for a particular region if said measures are not properly being implemented by the regional organization/arrangement in question.

5. Conclusion

In sum, this proposed regime advances the benefits of regionalism (i.e., aggregated self-interest, common goals, and encouraged participation) and minimizes some of its major drawbacks (i.e., fragmentation and unsupervised implementation) by positioning the decision-making Commission at the top of the hierarchy, providing the Commission with an oversight function with respect to regional organizations and arrangements, and enabling the Commission's ability to alter conservation and sustainable management measures in the event of improper regional action.

Any novel international approach to marine mammal conservation will be well-served by incorporating regionalism to the extent that it is practicable and appropriate to do so. Maximizing cooperation, engaging developing nations, encouraging compliance, and implementing enforcement are all important goals that can be furthered through regional implementation. The threats currently facing marine mammal species necessitate global action, but the variety of legitimate uses and approaches to marine mammal conservation and sustainable management justify a hybrid model of governance that engages centralized decision-making and regional implementation.

IV. MARINE PROTECTED AREAS

The third issue raised in the Agreement that requires further consideration is the use of marine protected areas (MPAs) to contribute to marine mammal conservation and to the broader overarching goals of cooperating in the conservation of high seas living resources[111] and of protecting and preserving the marine environment.[112] At this point it is useful to consider how I have accounted for MPA engagement in the proposed Agreement. The preamble expressly mentions the importance of ecosystem-based management; indeed, ecosystem-based management is subsequently defined in draft Article 1, incorporated into the definitions of "conservation" and "sustainable" also in draft Article 1, and stated as the goal that guides the work of the Scientific Committee in recommending marine protected area designations to the Commission (draft Article 16(f)(i)). "Marine Protected Area" is also a term defined in draft Article 1, and this draft Agreement charges the Commission with the responsibility of designating MPAs (in draft Article

12(1)(f)(vi)) as a conservation and sustainable management measure based on the Scientific Committee's recommendation. Like other conservation and sustainable management measures, compliance and enforcement of MPAs is covered by draft Part VII, and disputes could become subject to the dispute resolution process found in Part XI.

The scheme summarized above is premised on foundational considerations regarding long-term conservation in the twenty-first century. Ecosystem-based management that is integrated and adaptive is the successor to the failed target-species approach to conservation and management, and MPAs represent the most significant tool that can be utilized to protect ecosystems holistically in a manner that accounts for both human uses and ecological goods and services.[113]

The possibility of employing MPAs to achieve ecosystem-based management is not without problems. For example, MPAs must be well planned, monitored, enforced, and the subject of dispute resolution to be effective. Additionally, the very idea that MPAs represent a holistic approach to conservation raises the concern that their use by the Commission will negatively impact or unnecessarily impede competing uses of the ocean such as navigation or fishing. Therefore, it is essential that these competing uses be given due regard. With these concerns in mind, this assessment turns to a detailed discussion of MPAs, and considers how they can be properly utilized and then whether this tension between competing needs can be resolved satisfactorily.

1. MPAs Described

One of my stated goals for this work is to effectively account for and accommodate legitimate competing uses of the ocean. MPAs represent a definite challenge in this regard because, by their very nature, MPAs are associated with exclusive dedication of a certain portion of the ocean for a conservation purpose: an association that, although partially true, is also misleading.

It is a fact that MPAs require the dedication of some defined geographic location. MPAs have been described as "a discrete geographic area of the sea established by international, national, territorial, tribal, or local laws designated to enhance the long-term conservation of natural resources therein,"[114] and by the International Union for the Conservation of Nature (IUCN) as "a clearly defined geographical space, recognized and managed, through legal or other effective means, to achieve the long-term conservation of nature with associated ecosystem services and cultural values."[115] These important details determine the purpose and scope of any MPA. Ultimately, MPAs are probably best understood by considering the entire spectrum of possible MPA configurations. The IUCN contemplates seven "protected area" categories[116] that differ primarily on the degree and type of human use that is permitted. Domestically, MPAs within areas under American jurisdiction are broadly classified as: "no-take" MPAs, "no-access" MPAs, and "multi-use" MPAs.[117] Again, the major difference between each category is the permitted human use available within each MPA.

In theory, MPAs can occur in any area of the ocean and represent a viable mechanism through which coastal states can protect and preserve the marine environment. The more common MPA type is one that has been nationally designated and occurs within the territorial sea of a coastal state. Subject to facilitating and accommodating rights of navigation, coastal states are able to establish MPAs anywhere within their exclusive economic zones (EEZs),[118] as supported by state practice.[119] For example, the United States currently has over 1,600 designated MPAs that capture approximately 40 percent of its EEZ.[120] New Zealand's prime minister recently announced his country's intention to create a massive Kermadec ocean sanctuary that will cover 239,384 square miles or 15 percent of New Zealand's EEZ.[121] This sanctuary will be established by legislation and is predicted to ban all fishing, oil and gas exploration and development, and mineral exploration.[122] Chile also announced its intention to create a 38,000-square-mile Patagonia MPA Network, which will be designated by law and managed by a newly created Biodiversity and Protected Area's Service. Although there is some debate as to the effectiveness of large remote MPAs,[123] these types of MPAs can be monitored, managed, and enforced by the coastal state. More recently, the idea of high seas MPAs has emerged as a legitimate endeavor.

High seas MPAs are exactly as their name implies—MPAs that are established in parts of the 64 percent of the world's ocean that exist beyond the maritime zones under the influence of national regulation.[124] The legal considerations associated with high seas MPAs are similar to EEZ MPAs but are also unique. Article 87 of Part VII of UNCLOS ("High Seas") clearly established freedom of the high seas as it relates to critical issues such as fishing, navigation, and overflight. Still, the counterpoint to this is that Article 197 in Part XII ("Protection and Preservation of the Marine Environment") of UNCLOS establishes the basic obligation for global and regional cooperation toward protecting and preserving the marine environment; MPAs are a tool to accomplish this goal.[125] High sea MPA designation, monitoring, enforcement, and regulatory control all must occur at the international level of governance to be effective[126] and, according to Hoyt, "[t]he main reason why few MPAs have been proposed on the high seas is because the high seas are located outside the 200nm (370km) or more EEZ limits of the countries of the world, where no single state or authority has the ultimate power to designate MPAs, adopt management schemes or enforce compliance."[127] This assessment will return to high seas MPAs in the course of discussing current international MPA objectives and examples.

Given that MPAs can be established in both EEZs and in the high seas, another critical feature of MPA functionality, especially in the marine mammal context, is that we simply cannot consider each individual MPA in isolation. So-called "MPA networks" are "an organized collection of individual MPAs operating co-operatively and synergistically, at various spatial scales and with a range of protection levels, to fulfill ecological aims more effectively and comprehensively than individual sites could alone."[128] MPA networks can encompass MPAs that have been established nationally and/or internationally, and require collaboration to ensure that enforcement and monitoring efforts employed at one MPA in the network are not undermined by a corresponding lack of effort or infrastructure at other MPAs.[129]

Depending on MPA type and/or restricted uses, such designations have the potential to help minimize by-catch and fishing-related injuries, promote ecotourism and education, maintain ocean ecosystem structure and integrity,[130] reduce ship-strike incidences and the impact of noise, serve as control sites for scientific research, and facilitate species/population replenishment. Further, cetaceans provide intriguing possibilities for area-based management as many believe that "cetaceans have intrinsic value as species in themselves, and they have high value and play an important role in terms of conserving other species and whole ecosystems."[131] Many of the features of cetacean conservation that make them particularly useful for area-based research are based on their so-called "flagship" or "charismatic megafauna" species status, meaning they "capture public attention," "have symbolic value," and "are crucial to ecotourism," and "[their] protection automatically extends protection to other species and the community."[132] Arguably many of the same considerations apply to other marine mammal species, such as seals and sea lions, albeit at a modified scale.

Despite the potential for significant benefit, MPA designation is not a straightforward task. In addition to determining the preferred MPA type, basic requirements for establishing an MPA for cetaceans (which are likely generally appropriate for other marine mammal species as well) include:

(1) "a carefully defined purposes, with specific goals";
(2) "scientific background research into critical habitat requirements[133] of cetaceans and other species, as well as the marine ecology and an inventory of the area";
(3) "early multidisciplinary input to choose, plan, implement and review the protected area";
(4) "a good relationship with local communities and all stakeholders who participate in the protected area process because they see tangible benefits for themselves and others";
(5) "reasonable boundaries in view of the species, ecosystems and ecosystem processes that are being protected";
(6) "good protected area design, built around substantial IUCN Category I core areas, with additional zones or levels of protection, such as in the biosphere reserve model";
(7) "creation and sufficient funding for staff (management body) and operations including research, a management plan, monitoring and enforcement";
(8) "legal recognition as well as broad public acceptance";
(9) "an educational programme which is interactive, reciprocal and continuous for those who use, travel through or visit the protected area (including communities near the area, tourism operators and tourists, fishermen, mariners, shipping companies, and other commercial users of the sea within and outside the protected area)";
(10) "attention paid to the big picture: links to networks and marine planning and zoning initiatives";
(11) "management of pollution, both marine and land based"; and
(12) "reassessment and re-evaluation (both self and third party) at periodic intervals with stakeholder input."[134]

Even after the above process, or one similar to it, has been undertaken and the necessary corresponding legal and regulatory mechanisms have been established, MPA management requires ongoing commitment and support in the form of monitoring, compliance, and enforcement; in short, it is dependent upon infrastructure and financing. Although these requirements may not be too onerous for developed states committed to their use, they likely represent significant barriers for developing states. Therefore, MPAs present a useful opportunity for the developed world to help train and equip the developing world with the skills and technology necessary to make a meaningful contribution to ecosystem-based management.

Having established this basic understanding of MPAs, it is appropriate to now concentrate on scientific and legal innovations that are contributing to both the successful development and implementation of MPAs.

2. Relevance of Emerging Science

MPAs protect, at most, 3.6 percent of the world's oceans.[135] The international community has committed in Aichi Target 11 of the Convention on Biodiversity to increase this protection to 10 percent by 2020.[136] There is still time to avoid some of the defaunation events that have been documented in terrestrial ecosystems as "[f]ew marine extinctions have occurred; many subtidal marine habitats are today less developed, less polluted, and more wild than their terrestrial counterparts; global body size distributions of extant marine animal species have been mostly unchanged in the oceans; and many marine fauna have not yet experienced range contractions as severe as those observed on land."[137] Avoiding future collapse, while achieving integrated and adaptive ecosystem-based management through bolstered MPA use, depends heavily on the development and application of accurate scientific information and evidence. For example, the second step in Hoyt's list of basic requirements for establishing MPAs is predicated upon accessibility to the necessary scientific information.[138] Without such information, establishing MPAs nationally or internationally, as well as linking them into a functional network, leaves too much to chance.

Given the importance of properly balancing competing uses of the ocean, the spatial planning required to designate MPAs should be conducted with an eye to detail. Producing sound science to inform policy must be a critical goal for scientists interested in the long-term conservation of marine mammals. As observed throughout this book, increasing our understanding of marine mammals remains a work in progress. As noted by ecologist Ana D. Davidson and coauthors in 2012, "our understanding of which marine mammals are most at risk remains poor because many species are difficult to study, changes in their populations can be hard to detect, and their natural histories have not been well documented."[139] Further complicating this is the challenge "to produce timely and scientifically defensible research based on available data to address the conservation crisis now."[140] Recent studies suggest progress is being made and that the scientific information needed to properly design and establish meaningful marine mammal MPAs and networks is quickly crystalizing. This section offers two examples that I find particularly illuminating.

The first study of note, "Global Distribution of Marine Mammals," is authored by ecologists/biologists Sandra Pompa, Paul R. Ehrlich, and Gerardo Ceballos.[141] This article begins with the premise that understanding global distribution patterns is necessary to establish conservation priorities, and the observation that "such large-scale analyses are lacking for marine/freshwater mammals."[142] The goals of the study include: (1) producing descriptions of marine mammal geographic distribution, (2) determining patterns of "species richness and composition," and (3) identifying "key conservation sites as a basis for understanding global conservation needs."[143] The method employed involved compiling existing data and creating a digital grid and cell geographic database for 129 marine mammal species, which was subsequently mapped for "global species richness, irreplaceable sites, endemism, and threatened species" and analyzed to determine "key conservation sites."[144]

The study produced a number of interesting results. First, the authors note that conserving 10 percent of every marine mammal species' geographic distribution requires the dedication of approximately 45 million square kilometers of ocean, which equates to 12 percent of the entire ocean.[145] Further, the study identifies 20 "key conservation sites" that "can be the basis for identifying a comprehensive conservation strategy with MPAs representing all marine mammals, their ecological roles, and some threats."[146] Of these 20 sites, 9 were selected on the basis of species richness.[147] The remaining 11 sites were selected on the basis of being "irreplaceable because [of] the presence of endemic species."[148] The authors also examined the relationship between key conservation sites and anthropogenic forces (namely "climate disruption, ocean-based pollution, and commercial shipping," fisheries, and by-catch), noting concern for the impact that each force is likely to have on the conservation sites.[149] In conclusion, these authors recognized that an "unprecedented international effort with the development of both new attitudes and institutions" is required to tackle this problem and achieve marine mammal conservation.[150]

The second study by ecologists/biologists Ana D. Davidson et al. is titled "Drivers and Hotspots of Extinction Risk in Marine Mammals."[151] This study establishes a "predictive, spatially explicit assessment of global marine mammal extinction risk," asking: (1) "which marine mammal species are at greatest risk," (2) "why are they threatened," and (3) "where is risk greatest globally."[152] Specifically, the study analyzed 125 marine mammal species based on both life-history characteristics and the impact of external forces, compared this modeled assessment to the IUCN Red List classifications, and assessed the relative importance of known pressures.[153] Based on this assessment and IUCN Red List classifications, the authors mapped global species distribution and hot spots of extinction risk (which they map and describe) and identified the main factors contributing to current extinction risks.[154] They identified "speed of life history" as the most important factor in estimating extinction risk as it determines the ability of a species to rebound from human pressures.[155]

Importantly for the purposes of this analysis, the study notes that "risk hotspots cover only 1.7% of the global oceans, but they include at least parts of the geographic ranges of 88 (70%) marine mammal species," and that these "hotspots of risk overlap little with current Marine Protected Areas."[156] Recognizing that international efforts to increase the use of MPAs are underway, this study purports to provide the "magnitude and geographic distribution of extinction risk" necessary to assist further progress in creating the necessary MPA framework.

These articles are important both for what they contribute and what they identify as knowledge gaps. The analysis contained in each is global in scope and contributes to existing scientific efforts to inform the MPA-planning process. Pompa et al. highlight the need for science to continue to provide data to confront uncertainty in ocean trends,[157] whereas Davidson et al. recognize the need for "more and better biological data, especially on migratory routes, and the location of feeding/

pupping, and breeding grounds to protect the geographic areas and networks of critical habitats on which highly mobile marine animals and other taxa depend."[158] It is promising that this sort of research is currently being produced, and it now falls to existing or proposed governance structures to make sure that it is properly and meaningfully utilized.

3. How MPAs Are Currently Utilized by the International Community

The scientific studies considered above hint at emerging trends in international MPA progress. The purpose of this section is to succinctly indicate trends in international governance regarding MPAs.[159]

(i) The ICRW/IWC

The starting point for this discussion must be the ICRW/IWC and its Whale Sanctuaries approach. The IWC webpage describes existing sanctuaries under the heading "Whales Sanctuaries & Marine Protected Areas," but the two are not necessarily the same.[160] The IWC has established two large Whale Sanctuaries as part of its Schedule. The first is the Indian Ocean Sanctuary, established in 1979, and the second is the Southern Ocean Sanctuary, which covers Antarctic waters as established in 1994.[161] Proposals have also been advanced for a South Pacific Sanctuary and South Atlantic Sanctuary, but neither has received the requisite three-quarters majority vote necessary.[162] Most recently, at the IWC's 65th Annual Meeting in 2014 a Southern American contingent proposed a South Atlantic Whale Sanctuary.[163] Despite 40 votes being cast in favor of the proposed sanctuary and only 18 against, this did not meet the requisite three-quarters majority necessary to amend the Schedule. In addition to difficulties associated with designating Whale Sanctuaries, these sanctuaries are also controversial in that they prohibit commercial whaling but other "human activities that could have impacts on whale populations (e.g., fishing, scientific whaling) are not regulated."[164] Indeed, Japan's continued hunt for whales in the Southern Ocean Sanctuary formed the basis for *Whaling in the Antarctic (Australia v. Japan: New Zealand intervening)*.

This sanctuary process is also susceptible to many of the familiar criticisms that plague the IWC generally: (1) Schedule amendment, (2) Scientific Whaling, and (3) lack of compliance, monitoring, and enforcement.[165] Suggested improvements to the sanctuary process include: (1) increasing the role of science, (2) enhancing information sharing, (3) increasing cooperation between the IWC and other international regimes, and (4) conducting more non-lethal research in the Southern Sanctuary.[166] Despite its shortcomings, the positive aspect of IWC sanctuaries include their ability to prevent "the encroachment of pelagic whaling fleets from faraway countries, reinforce the policies of coastal States that prohibit whaling in their own jurisdictional waters and reserve whale resources for non-lethal appropriation by coastal communities," to contribute to MPA networks, and to serve as a framework.[167] I am of the opinion that the broad sanctuary designation approach ignores the scalpel in favor of the sword, in a manner that is neither scientifically nor practically justifiable.

(ii) Other International/Regional Arrangements

The IWC is certainly not the only international arrangement that is interested in or capable of establishing whale sanctuaries or other MPAs. As noted by international law lecturer Irini Papanicolopulu, "whale sanctuaries can be created under a number of different treaties, including the . . . Convention on Migratory Species (CMS), regional seas conventions (e.g., the Barcelona Protocol on Specially Protected Areas), and ad hoc agreements (e.g., the Mediterranean Marine Mammals [Pelagos] Sanctuary)."[168]

The Pelagos Sanctuary mentioned above is of considerable importance, as it demonstrated to the international community that establishing high seas protected areas is possible,[169] that they can extend to all marine mammals in the region, and that the necessary cooperation can be achieved (it was established by treaty among France, Monaco, and Italy).[170] The design of the Pelagos Sanctuary is informed by "oceanographic and ecological considerations,"[171] it covers 87,500 square kilometers,[172] it seeks to "protect marine mammals against all types of disturbances by human activity, and its objective is to reconcile the harmonious development of socio-economic activities with the necessary protection of habitats and species."[173] The Pelagos Sanctuary is also a useful model as it balances competing ocean uses by fostering information exchange among the nations, considers "marine traffic and commercial maritime transport," "fisheries and fish-farming," and improvements in scientific research.[174] This is not the only example of a high seas MPA, as one was also designated in the Southern Ocean by CCAMLR in 2009; it is called the South Orkney MPA.[175]

NOAA (National Oceanic and Atmospheric Association) has produced a useful description of different possible forms of high seas MPAs, which include the following:

(1) IMO Particularly Sensitive Sea Area designation—pursuant to the revised guidelines found in IMO Resolution A24/982 adopted in 2006, titled "Revised Guidelines for the Identification and Designation of Particularly Sensitive Sea Areas,"[176] the IMO can adopt measures that ships are to follow when using these areas;[177]
(2) MARPOL Special Area designation—pursuant to the International Convention on the Prevention of Pollution from Ships (MARPOL), and in conjunction with the guidelines contained in IMO Resolution A.927(22),[178] nations can request Special Area designation. Special Areas are meant to protect against damage associated with oil, garbage, and bulk noxious substances;[179] and
(3) IMO Areas to Be Avoided—can be designated by the IMO pursuant to regulation 10 of Chapter V of the International Convention for the Safety of Life at Sea,[180] and exists as "a ships' routing measure that comprises an area within defined limits in which either navigation is particularly hazardous or it is exceptionally important to avoid casualties and should be avoided by all ships or certain classes of ships."[181]

As important as these isolated examples are, it is also necessary to consider whether MPA networks have emerged as a viable option. Action pursuant to the Convention on the Protection of the Marine Environment of the North-East Atlantic[182] ("OPSAR Convention") is responsible for the first high seas MPA network, created pursuant to OSPAR Recommendation 2003/3.[183] MPAs in this context represent "areas for which protective, conservation, restorative or precautionary measures have been instituted for the purpose of protecting and conserving species, habitats, ecosystems or ecological processes of the marine environment."[184] This network represents the collaborative work of the 14 ratified states[185] and, as of July 2012, consisted of 283 distinct MPA sites, including 276 that are within areas of national jurisdiction and 7 that are in areas beyond national jurisdiction.[186] OSPAR has produced management guidelines but, to date "it is not possible to conduct a comprehensive analysis of the extent to which the OSPAR marine protected areas are actually 'well managed' by the concerned authorities. Generally, Contracting Parties have not submitted to OSPAR sufficiently detailed information on the management of their respective OSPAR MPAs that would allow for such an analysis."[187] Talks are also underway at CCAMLR to establish an MPA network in the Southern Ocean, but to date the parties have failed to agree to the form for a network of connected MPAs.[188]

The major drivers advancing international MPA work are the efforts produced pursuant to the Convention on Biological Diversity. First, consider the following paragraph from the Report of the United Nations Conference on Sustainable Development ("Rio + 20"):

177. We reaffirm the importance of area-based conservation measures, including marine protected areas, consistent with international law and based on best available scientific information, as a tool for conservation of biological diversity and sustainable use of its components. We note decision X/2 of the tenth Meeting of the Conference of the Parties to the Convention on Biological Diversity, that by 2020 10 per cent of coastal and marine areas, especially areas of particular importance for biodiversity and ecosystem services, are to be conserved through effectively and equitably managed, ecologically representative and well-connected systems of protected areas and other effective area-based conservation measures.[189]

The global MPA goal referenced in the paragraph above was established by the CBD in its Achivi Biodiversity Target, which seeks "effectively and equitably managed, ecologically representative and well-connected systems of protected areas."[190] It is useful in terms of its goal-setting function, but is also indicative of the work that the CBD has been instrumental in advancing for high seas MPAs and MPA networks more generally.[191] The Conference of the Parties for the CBD also produced Decision IX/20, which is notable for a variety of reasons, but most important in that it urges nations and international organizations to identify marine areas in need of protection, and crafts seven "scientific criteria for identifying ecologically or biologically significant marine areas in need of protection in open-ocean waters and deep-sea habitats" to aid in the identification process.[192] Although the CBD is responsible for establishing many umbrella targets and goals associated with the use of MPAs, it is not the only international regime/organization that is contributing important advances in this field.

(III) Innovative Work

The first innovation of note is the IUCN Global Protected Areas Programme,[193] which administers the World Commission on Protected Areas (WCPA). The WCPA is the self-proclaimed "premier network of protected area expertise ... [with] over

1,700 members in 140 countries."[194] The IUCN-WCPA has contributed to CBD efforts and most notably, has produced technical papers such as "Establishing Resilient Marine Protected Area Networks—Making It Happen"[195] and "Guidelines for Applying Protected Area Management Categories."[196]

The second area of innovation represents an extension of the emerging scientific contributions identified above. Specifically, both the Global Ocean Biodiversity Initiative (GOBI)[197] and the UNEP World Conservation Monitoring Center (UNEP-WCMC)[198] exist to collect and disseminate knowledge about ocean biodiversity and MPAs. GOBI "aims to help countries, as well as regional and global organisations, to use and develop data, tools, and methodologies to identify ecologically significant areas in the oceans, with an initial focus on areas beyond national jurisdiction," and is primarily supported by the IUCN.[199] The UNEP-WCMC exists to support national and international decision-makers,[200] and part of its established work is to aid marine assessment and enhance decision-making.

The next area of innovation, and one that is particularly relevant to this work, is the creation of the International Committee on Marine Mammal Protected Areas (ICMMPA), which is an "informal group of international experts dedicated to the conservation of marine mammals and their habitats."[201] The ICMMPA is populated by scientists, NGO representatives, and national representatives.[202] The ICMMPA held its inaugural conference in March–April 2009, a second in 2011, and a third in 2014.[203] MPAs are also likely to figure prominently at the 2014 IUCN World Parks Congress, which took place in November 2014, in Sydney, Australia.[204] Although it is early days yet for the ICMMPA, it represents an intriguing forum through which many of the ideas advanced in this discussion of MPAs could be tailored to fit the workings of the proposed Commission.

Finally, I would be remiss if I did not highlight the potential for a significant contribution that may emerge from efforts to negotiate an implementing agreement addressing the conservation and management of marine biodiversity in areas beyond national jurisdiction. UN General Assembly Resolution 99/292 formalized and affirmed the recommendations from the UN Ad Hoc Open-Ended Working Group that had been investigating the feasibility of a new treaty since 2006.[205] This Resolution formalizes the preparatory committee process that will occupy 2016 and 2017, moving toward final negotiations at an intergovernmental conference. It also decided that negotiations shall address, inter alia, "measures such as area-based management tools, including marine protected areas, environmental impact assessments and capacity building in the transfer of marine technology."[206] This work will further legitimize and clarify the role for high seas MPAs, and is an opportunity to consider implementation of some of the principles and goals of marine mammal protected areas identified here. Ultimately, I envision this implementing agreement supplementing and complementing other global efforts to advance marine mammal specific MPAs.

(IV) PROSPECTS MOVING FORWARD

At the beginning of this discussion on MPAs, I identified the framework for MPA application within the proposed new Agreement. This assessment proceeded to identify emerging trends in the development and application of MPAs, and this final portion demonstrates how the proposed framework contributes to, and utilizes, these developments.

First, this proposal establishes the new infrastructure necessary to succeed where the IWC Whale Sanctuary program has failed in that: (1) it contemplates MPAs rather than sanctuaries, meaning that the Commission can utilize the wide array of MPA types that currently exist (subject to securing agreement and properly affording other ocean uses due regard); (2) it enshrines MPAs as one form of conservation and sustainable management measure, meaning it is subject to the monitoring, compliance, and enforcement provisions contained within the Agreement; (3) it contemplates regional implementation of conservation and sustainable management measures, which is necessary to establish the requisite buy-in from affected nations (i.e., consider the regional cooperation required to establish the Pelagos Sanctuary); and (4) it prioritizes the use of science and application of the best available scientific information/evidence by emphasizing the role that the Scientific Committee plays in recommending MPA designation to the Commission.

The Commission's ability to designate high seas MPAs will be limited by the overall buy-in and support this regime receives from the international community, regional commitment to monitor and enforce associated rules and regulations, and its ability to meaningfully coordinate with existing MPA processes. Further, although the Commission may not be able to designate MPAs within areas of national jurisdiction, this remains an area where it could recommend best-practice to member states. MPAs also present a unique opportunity for cooperation between developing and developed states, and between states and nongovernmental organizations to work to produce effective infrastructure, education, and awareness programs that can enhance responsible ecotourism, domestic monitoring and enforcement capability, and technology transfer.[207] The financial mechanism contemplated by the Agreement may offer an opportunity for the Commission to invest in area-based management in the form favored by its members.

The final point of emphasis must be the enhanced role that the Agreement contemplates for the Secretariat. This brief discussion of the international use of MPAs indicates that many fora, both international and regional, are currently developing and deploying MPAs in the high seas in collaboration with MPAs established within areas of national jurisdiction. One express purpose of the Secretariat is to ensure collaboration with other international and/or regional governance regimes. In the context of MPAs, this role would enable the communication necessary to ensure that established regimes are effectively accounting for marine mammals as they design and implement MPAs. Second, and perhaps more important, this collaboration facilitates the necessary dialogue between this regime and the IMO to ensure that marine transport is given due regard, and to also allow the IMO to take the lead in evaluating transport routes and recommending the necessary restrictions or alterations to accomplish long-term marine mammal conservation.

This exploration concludes that MPAs constitute an important tool toward achieving area- and ecosystem-based management, and to accomplish the goals set by the international community regarding twenty-first century ocean conservation. The scientific evidence and information necessary to produce meaningful high seas MPAs and MPA networks is beginning to crystallize, and state practice evinces a willingness to designate EEZ MPAs and to cooperate to promote high seas conservation in this way. As more examples emerge, the requisite international collaboration necessary to realize the theoretical benefits of high seas MPAs and MPA networks also materializes. Still, I stress that the term "MPA," preferred because of its established use, remains an umbrella concept capable of supporting multiple MPA types and different uses of the ocean. Advocating in favor of extensive high sea MPAs and MPA networks that exclude all ocean uses seems superficially attractive, but in reality is not viable. Rather, the Commission should employ all manner of MPAs, collaborate with existing regional and international governance structures to ensure that their MPAs are properly accounting for marine mammals, and work with other international organizations, such as the IMO, to ensure that other users and uses of the ocean are given due regard and accommodated accordingly.

V. CONCLUSION

This chapter has investigated three key aspects of the proposed regime: the Secretariat; regionalism; and MPAs. Each aspect has unique benefits and challenges that, when taken together, represent the proposal's commitment to comprehensive and holistic marine mammal governance and to emerging ideas and trends that were not available to the parties who negotiated the International Convention for the Regulation of Whaling.

The Secretariat is a formalized mechanism for the collaboration between existing regional and international regimes and also, as drafted, provides the Commission with a legitimate lobbying tool that can be used to advocate in favor of international and regional decision-making that accounts for marine mammals in other forums, and for issues that are beyond the Commission's regulatory jurisdiction. UNEP is well-positioned to serve as either an interim Secretariat, a permanent Secretariat, or a supporting body, but its participation would be subject to agreement and its environmental mandate may render it a less than perfect organization. The logical alternative may be the creation of a new Secretariat populated by individuals with the necessary experience and expertise, or empowering DOALOS to fulfill this function. Regionalism is a feature of both UNCLOS and emerging marine mammal conservation efforts. This regime intends to capitalize on the proposed benefits of regionalism without sacrificing the utility of global, centralized decision-making. Finally, MPAs represent one tool that can be employed by the Commission to advance integrated ecosystem-based management. The scientific and legal capabilities necessary to meaningfully utilize MPAs continue to crystallize, and the Commission could coordinate with existing initiatives that are contributing to the proper application of MPAs.

NOTES

1. Randall S. Abate, *Marine Protected Areas as a Mechanism to Promote Marine Mammal Conservation: International and Comparative Law Lessons for the United States*, 88 OR. L. REV. 255, 256 (2009) ["Abate, *Marine Protected Areas*"].
2. United Nations Environment Programme, *Division of Environmental Law and Conventions*, http://www.unep.org/delc/ (last visited Mar. 31, 2016).
3. *See* Proposed Agreement, at draft Art. 19(3).
4. PATRICIA BIRNIE, ALAN BOYLE & CATHERINE REDGWELL, INTERNATIONAL LAW & THE ENVIRONMENT 65 (3d ed. 2009) ["BIRNIE ET AL."].

5. United Nations Environment Programme, *About UNEP: The Organization*, http://www.unep.org/Documents.Multilingual/Default.asp?DocumentID=43 (last visited Sept. 28, 2015).
6. *See* 1997 Nairobi Declaration on the Role and Mandate of UNEP, ¶ 2, http://www.unep.org/documents.multilingual/default.asp?DocumentID=287&ArticleID=1728&l=en.
7. United Nations Conference on Environment and Development, Rio de Janiero, Braz., June 3–14, 1992, *Agenda 21*, U.N. Doc A/CONF.151/26 (Aug. 12, 1992), at Ch. 38, ¶ 22(h) ["Agenda 21"].
8. Birnie et al., *supra* note 4.
9. United Nations Environment Programme, *2012 Annual Report*, at 46 (2012) http://www.unep.org/gc/gc27/docs/UNEP_ANNUAL_REPORT_2012.pdf ["*2012 Annual Report*"]; *see* UN General Assembly Resolution 67/213, which endorses the changes proposed in paragraph 88, sections (a)–(h) of "The Future We Want" (the Rio + 20 outcome document). "The Future We Want" was adopted by the General Assembly in UN General Resolution 66/288 where paragraph 88, sections (a)–(h) are reproduced in their entirety.
10. *2012 Annual Report*, *supra* note 9, at 64.
11. *Id.*
12. *Id.*
13. FAO/UNEP, The Global Plan of Action for the Conservation and Utilisation of Marine Mammals, *UNEP Regional Seas Reports and Studies No. 55* (1985), http://www.unep.org/regionalseas/publications/reports/RSRS/pdfs/rsrs055.pdf ["The Global Plan of Action"].
14. UNEP Regional Seas, *About UNEP and Marine Mammals*, http://www.unep.org/regionalseas/marinemammals/about/default.asp (last visited Sept. 28, 2015) ["*About UNEP and Marine Mammals*"].
15. *Id.*; UNEP Regional Seas, *Overview of UNEP's Marine Mammal Action Plan*, at 1, http://webcache.googleusercontent.com/search?q=cache:QHIyFzTl6DEJ:www.unep.org/regionalseas/marinemammals/downloads/m_m_action_plan.doc+&cd=1&hl=en&ct=clnk&gl=ca (last visited Sept. 28, 2015) ["*Overview of UNEP's Marine Mammal Action Plan*"].
16. United Nations Environment Program, *About Regional Seas*, http://www.unep.org/regionalseas/about/default.asp (last visited Sept. 28, 2015).
17. *Id.*
18. *Overview of UNEP's Marine Mammal Action Plan*, *supra* note 15, at 3.
19. *About UNEP and Marine Mammals*, *supra* note 14.
20. *Overview of UNEP's Marine Mammal Action Plan*, *supra* note 15, at 3–4.
21. *Id.* at 4–5.
22. *2012 Annual Report*, *supra* note 9, at 75.
23. United Nations Environment Programme, *Global Programme of Action for the Protection of the Marine Environment from Land-Based Activities (GPA)*, http://www.gpa.unep.org/ (last visited Sept. 28, 2015).
24. United Nations Environment Programme, *Regional Seas Programme: UNEP Administered Programmes*, http://www.unep.org/regionalseas/programmes/unpro/default.asp (last visited Sept. 28, 2015).
25. Carpathian Convention, *UNEP Vienna—Interim Secretariat of the Carpathian Convention*, http://www.carpathianconvention.org/the-interim-secretariat-iscc.html (last visited Sept. 28, 2015).

26. United Nations Environment Programme, *Ozone Secretariat*, http://ozone.unep.org/en/ (last visited Sep. 29, 2015); *2012 Annual Report, supra* note 9, at 11.
27. UNCTAD, *UNEP Secretariat of the Basel Convention*, http://new.unctad.org/Templates/OrganizationalProfile____979.aspx (last visited Sept. 30, 2015).
28. Joint Portal of the Basel, Rotterdam and Stockholm Conventions, *United Nations Environment Programme (UNEP)*, http://synergies.pops.int/Links/UNEP/tabid/2637/language/es-CO/Default.aspx (last visited Sept. 29, 2015).
29. *Id.*
30. UNITED NATIONS ENVIRONMENT PROGRAMME, UNEP HANDBOOK OF ENVIRONMENTAL LAW 46–47 (1998).
31. United Nations Environment Programme, *Offices*, http://www.unep.org/documents.multilingual/default.asp?DocumentID=296&ArticleID=3401&l=en (last visited Sept. 30, 2015).
32. Division for Ocean Affairs and Law of the Sea, *The Division for Ocean Affairs and Law of the Sea, Activities and Functions* (July 20, 2010), http://www.un.org/Depts/los/doalos_activities/about_doalos.htm ["*DOALOS*"].
33. U.N. Secretary-General's Bulletin, Organization of the Office of Legal Affairs, ST/SGB/1997/8 (Sept. 15, 1997).
34. *DOALOS, supra* note 32.
35. Boleslaw Adam Boczek, *Global and Regional Approaches to the Protection and Preservation of the Marine Environment*, 16 CASE W. RES. J. INT'L L. 39, 39 (1984) ["Boczek"].
36. *See* Lewis Alexander, *Regionalism at Sea: Concept and Reality*, *in* REGIONALISATION OF THE LAW OF THE SEA 1, 3 (D.M. Johnston ed., 1978).
37. Sophia Kopela, Regionalism and the Development of the Law of the Sea 1 (2010) (unpublished conference paper from the 4th Oceanic Conference on International Studies, June 30–July 2, 2010) (on file with author) ["Kopela"].
38. *Id.* at 4.
39. Boczek, *supra* note 35, at 68.
40. Marji Prideaux, *Discussion of a Regional Agreement for Small Cetacean Conservation in the Indian Ocean*, 32 CAL. W. INT'L L. J. 211, 232 (2001–2002) ["Prideaux"].
41. Lewis Alexander, *Regionalism at Sea: Concept and Reality*, *in* REGIONALIZATION OF THE LAW OF THE SEA 3, 5 (Douglas M. Johnston ed., 1978).
42. L.M. Alexander, *New Trends in Marine Regionalism*, 11 OCEAN YB. 1, 1 (1994) ["Alexander"].
43. *Id.*
44. *Id.* (citing to EDWARD MILES ET AL., THE MANAGEMENT OF MARINE REGIONS: THE NORTH PACIFIC 3 (1982)).
45. Joseph Morgan, *Marine Regions and Regionalism in South-East Asia*, 8(4) MAR. POL. 299, 300 (1984).
46. *Id.* at 301–02.
47. *Id.*
48. Alexander, *supra* note 42, at 3.
49. Alan Boyle, *Globalism and Regionalism in the Protection of the Marine Environment*, *in* PROTECTING THE POLAR MARINE ENVIRONMENT: LAW AND POLICY FOR POLLUTION PREVENTION 19, 27 (Davor Vidas ed., 2000) ["Boyle"].
50. Alexander, *supra* note 42, at 4.
51. *Id.* at 4–5.

52. *See* L.M. Alexander, *Regionalism and the Law of the Sea: The Case of Semi-enclosed Seas*, 2(2) Ocean Dev. & Int'l L. 151, 153 (1974) (writing, in advance of negotiations at UNCLOS III, that "if one accepted the regional concept as a necessary precondition for the adoption of a future ocean regime, there should be some internationally agreed-upon norms, both for the establishment of the geographic regions themselves, and for the particular types of rights littoral states could claim for themselves within these regions").
53. Boyle, *supra* note 49, at 23–24.
54. *Id.* at 23.
55. *Id.* at 24.
56. Brettny Hardy, *Regional Approach to Whaling: How the North Atlantic Marine Mammal Commission Is Shifting the Tides for Whale Management*, 17 Duke J. Comp. & Int'l L. 169, 198 (2006) ["Hardy"].
57. Prideaux, *supra* note 40, at 211.
58. Boleslaw A. Boczek, *International Protection of the Baltic Sea Environment against Pollution: A Study in Marine Regionalism*, 72(4) Am. J. Int'l L. 782, 782 (1978) ["*International Protection of the Baltic Sea*"].
59. Boyle, *supra* note 49, at 32.
60. Boczek, *supra* note 35, at 53.
61. C.O. Okidi, *Protection of the Marine Environment through Regional Arrangements, in* Implementation of the Law of the Sea Convention through International Institutions 474, 477 (Alfred A. Soons ed., 1990) ["Okidi"].
62. Boyle, *supra* note 49, at 32.
63. *Id.* (in the context of marine pollution).
64. *Id.*
65. Okidi, *supra* note 61, at 478.
66. Boczek, *supra* note 35, at 53 (in the context of marine pollution); Hardy, *supra* note 56, at 196 (who asserts that the regional approach can foster improved monitoring); Okidi, *supra* note 61, at 478 (noting that states are likely "compelled to put time and resources into its [regional organization] time and resources").
67. Okidi, *supra* note 61, at 478.
68. Boczek, *supra* note 35, at 53.
69. Okidi, *supra* note 61, at 479.
70. *See* Prideaux, *supra* note 40, at 233 (citing to Elizabeth Mann Borgese, Ocean Governance and the United Nations 164 (1995)).
71. Boczek, *supra* note 35, at 45.
72. Boyle, *supra* note 49, at 33.
73. *Id.*
74. *Id.* at 32.
75. Richard B. Bilder, *The Consequences of Regionalization in the Treaty and Customary Law of the Sea, in* Regionalisation of the Law of the Sea 31, 39 (D.M. Johnston ed., 1978); *see also* Kopela, *supra* note 37, at 21 (noting that "[r]egionalism poses no real threat for multilateralism and the LOSC. On the contrary, it can be a force for development and renewal and may lead, not only to effective regulation of marine affairs at the regional level, but also, as it has happened in the past, to multilateral and universal regimes, which may develop to reflect new circumstances and accommodate more effectively state interests and concerns").
76. *See supra* Chapter 2 at note 277 for a description of this problem and the role it played in domestic American marine mammal protection.

77. Convention for the Establishment of an Inter-American Tropical Tuna Commission, U.S.-C.R., May 31, 1949, 80 U.N.T.S. 3, 1 U.S.T. 230.
78. Convention for the Strengthening of the Inter-American Tropical Tuna Commission, [2005] EUTSer 2, OJ L 15.
79. Agreement on the International Dolphin Conservation Program, art. II(1), [1998] PITSE 4 ["AIDCP"].
80. *Id.* at preamble.
81. *Id.*
82. *Id.*
83. *Id.* at art. II.
84. *Id.*
85. *Id.*
86. *Id.* at Annex II para. 2.
87. *Id.* at Annex II paras. 3–6.
88. *Id.* at Annex II para. 13.
89. AIDCP, *Resolution to Support the On-Board Observer Program and Establish a Working Group to Develop Captain Incentives*, Res. A-99-01 (Oct. 11, 1999).
90. AIDCP, *Resolution on At-Sea Reporting*, Res. A-03-02 (June 25, 2003).
91. AIDCP, *Resolution regarding Dolphin Safety Gear*, Res. A-04-03 (June 9, 2004).
92. AIDCP, *Resolution to Establish a List of Vessels Presumed to Have Carried Out Illegal, Unreported and Unregulated Fishing Activities in the Agreement Area*, Res. A-04-07 (Oct. 20, 2004).
93. Inter-American Tropical Tuna Commission, *AIDCP Dolphin Safe*, http://www.iattc.org/DolphinSafeENG.htm (last visited Oct. 1, 2015) ["*AIDCP Dolphin Safe*"]. This is one example of a growing trend of so-called "green" or "sustainable" labeling initiatives that are playing an increasingly important role in educating consumers about the source and/or processes involved in the creation of the products they purchase.
94. *See* AIDCP, *Procedures for AIDCP Dolphin Safe Tuna Certification (as amended)*, 2005, http://www.iattc.org/PDFFiles2/AIDCP-Dolphin-Safe-certification-system-REV-Oct2005.pdf ["Dolphin Safe Tuna Certification"].
95. *Id.* at s.2(a) & (b).
96. *Id.* at s.2(f).
97. *Id.* at s.3.
98. *Id.* at s.4.
99. *Id.* at s.6.
100. National Oceanic and Atmospheric Administration, *Pacific Ocean Regional Fisheries Management Organizations: AIDCP*, NMFS 40, http://www.nmfs.noaa.gov/ia/agreements/regional_agreements/pacific/aidcp.pdf (last visited Oct. 1, 2015).
101. *AIDCP Dolphin Safe, supra* note 93.
102. United Nations Food and Agriculture Organization: Fisheries and Aquaculture Department, *Margarita Lizarraga Medal Award*, UNFAO (2013), http://www.fao.org/fishery/code/margarita-lizarraga/en.
103. *International Protection of the Baltic Sea, supra* note 58, at 782.
104. Erik J. Molenaar & Alex G. Oude Elferink, *Marine Protected Areas beyond National Jurisdiction: The Pioneering Efforts under the OSPAR Convention*, 5(1) UTRECHT L. REV. 5, 19 (2009) ["'Molennar & Elferink"].
105. Boyle, *supra* note 49, at 23.

106. Hardy, *supra* note 56, at 195.
107. *Id.* at 197.
108. Prideaux, *supra* note 40, at 235.
109. Whaling in the Antarctic (Australia v. Japan: New Zealand Intervening), General list No. 148, Judgment of 31 March 2014 (International Court of Justice) ["Whaling in the Antarctic"].
110. Anastasia Telesetsky, Donald K. Anton & Timo Koivurova, *ICJ's Decision in* Australia v. Japan: *Giving Up the Spear or Refining the Scientific Design?*, 45 Ocean Dev. & Int'l L. 328, 336 (2014).
111. Art. 194(5), 10 Dec. 1982, 21 I.L.M. 1261, 1833 U.N.T.S.
112. *Id.* at arts. 192 & 197.
113. Marine Protected Areas: A Multidisciplinary Approach 21–23 (Joachim Claudet ed., 2011) ["Claudet"].
114. *Id.* at 2–3.
115. International Union for the Conservation of Nature (Nigel Dudley ed.), *Guidelines for Applying Protected Area Management Categories*, at 8 (2008), http://data.iucn.org/dbtw-wpd/edocs/paps-016.pdf ["Dudley"].
116. *Id.* at 13–23; *see also* Erich Hoyt, Marine Protected Areas for Whales, Dolphins, and Porpoises: A World Handbook for Cetacean Habitat Conservation and Planning 25 (2d ed. 2011) ["Hoyt"], summarizing MPA categories as follows:

> Category Ia—strict nature reserves—are strictly protected areas set aside to protect biodiversity and also possibly geological/geomorphical features, where human visitation, use and impacts are strictly controlled and limited to ensure protection of the conservation values. Such protected areas can serve as indispensable reference areas for scientific research and monitoring.
>
> Category Ib—wilderness areas—are usually large unmodified or slightly modified areas, retaining their natural character and influence, without permanent or significant human habitation, which are protected and managed so as to preserve their natural condition.
>
> Category II—national parks—are large natural or near natural areas set aside to protect large-scale ecological processes, along with the complement of species and ecosystem characteristics of the area, which also provide a foundation for environmentally and culturally compatible spiritual, scientific, educational, recreational and visitor opportunities;
>
> Category III—national monuments or features—are set aside to protect a specific natural monument, which can be a landform, seamount, submarine cavern, geological feature such as a cave or even a living feature such as an ancient grove. They are generally quite small protected areas and often have quite high visitor value.
>
> Category IV—habitat/species management areas—aim to protect particular species or habitats and management reflects this priority. Many Category IV protected areas will need regular active interventions to address the requirements of particular species or to maintain habitats; but this is not a requirement of the category.
>
> Category V—protected landscape/seascapes—are areas where the interaction of people and nature over time has produced an area of distinct

character with significant ecological, biological, cultural and scenic value; and where safeguarding the integrity of this interaction is vital to protecting and sustaining the area and its associated nature conservation and other values.

Category VI—protected areas with sustainable use of natural resources—conserve ecosystems and habitats, together with associated cultural values and traditional natural resource management systems. They are generally large, with most of the area in a natural condition, where a proportion is under sustainable natural resource management and where low-level non-industrial use of natural resources compatible with nature conservation is seen as one of the main aims of the area.

117. *See* Abate, *Marine Protected Areas, supra* note 1, at 258–59.
118. *See* International Union for the Conservation of Nature, World Wildlife Fund & MedPAN, *Status of Marine Protected Areas in the Mediterranean Sea* 12 (2008); *see* Alison Reiser, *The Papahanaumokaukea Precedent: Ecosystem-scale Marine Protected Areas in the EEZ*, 13 ASIAN PAC. AM. L.J. 210, 215–19 (2012). Note that this discussion of EEZ MPAs must remain cognizant of the fact that Article 56(1)(a) of UNCLOS provides coastal states with "sovereign rights for the purpose of exploring and exploiting, conserving and managing the natural resources, whether living or non-living" in the EEZ rather than "sovereignty" (as exists in the territorial seas). Although they do have jurisdiction over "protection and preservation of the marine environment" pursuant to Article 56(1)(b)(iii), paragraph 2 of this Article makes it clear that the coastal states shall have "due regard to the rights and duties of other States," which includes freedom of navigation (as contemplated in Article 58, which also contemplates the user state exercising "due regard" to the rights and duties of the coastal state in paragraph 3). Therefore, it is critical that EEZs (and especially those that attempt to exclude other users of the ocean) do so in a manner that recognizes and properly balances these competing interests. For example, it is obvious that a nation designating its entire EEZ an MPA within which vessels (foreign or domestic) are not allowed is obviously improper and clearly offends the sui generis regime contemplated for the EEZ. Alternatively, an argument can be made that carefully crafted exclusionary MPAs within an EEZ, necessary for the protection of particular living marine resources is permissible so long as navigational rights are given due regard and accommodated. This is a crucial consideration that must be kept in mind so as to ensure that the exercise of jurisdiction or the regulation pursuant to "sovereign rights" does not become an impermissible attempt to assert something akin to sovereignty.
119. For a survey of state practice in this regard, *see* THOMAS DUX, SPECIALLY PROTECTED MARINE AREAS IN THE EXCLUSIVE ECONOMIC ZONE (EEZ): THE REGIME FOR THE PROTECTION OF SPECIFIC AREAS OF THE EEZ FOR ENVIRONMENTAL REASONS UNDER INTERNATIONAL LAW 423–55 (2011) (here, Dux explores various national approaches to establishing protected zones within the EEZ.)
120. National Marine Protected Areas Center, *Snaphot of United States MPAs*, at 2 (Apr., 2011) (it is also notable that 86 percent of these MPAs are designated multiple-use designations, and 8 percent are designated no-take zones, meaning their efficacy as protected zones may be questionable); *but see* Abate, *Marine Protected Areas, supra* note 1, at 266–84 (discussing how there is room for improvement in the system of MPAs employed by the United States); *see also* National Oceanic

and Atmospheric Administration, *Marine Protected Areas: What Is a Marine Protected Area* (June 9, 2015), http://oceanservice.noaa.gov/ecosystems/mpa/#1 (noting that only 3 percent of U.S. waters are "highly protected" no-take MPAs).
121. See Government of New Zealand, *Kermadec Ocean Sanctuary* (2015), http://mfe.govt.nz/sites/default/files/media/Marine/MFE7910_A4_Brochure_LR.pdf.
122. *Id.*
123. See Pierre Leenhardt et al., *The Rise of Large-Scale Marine Protected Areas: Conservation or Geopolitics?*, 85 OCEAN & COAST. MAN. 112 (2013) (discussing the geopolitical drivers that are responsible for the creation of many large MPAs); *see also* Graham J. Edgar et al., *Global Conservation Outcomes Depend on Marine Protected Areas with Five Key Features*, 506(7487) NATURE 216, 216 (2014) (identifying the following criteria as being determinative of whether an MPA will achieve a conservation goal: "no take, enforced, old, large and isolated").
124. HOYT, *supra* note 116, at 94.
125. See Molenaar & Elferink, *supra* note 104, at 7–10.
126. HOYT, *supra* note 116, at 94.
127. *Id.*
128. *Id.* at 88 (citing to IUCN–World Commission on Protected Areas (2008) *Establishing Marine Protected Area Networks: Making It Happen* (2008)).
129. *Id.* at 88–94.
130. Abate, *Marine Protected Areas, supra* note 1, at 260.
131. HOYT, *supra* note 116, at 39.
132. See RICHARD A. PRIMACK, ESSENTIALS OF CONSERVATION BIOLOGY 424 (3d ed. 2002) ["PRIMACK"].
133. See HOYT, *supra* note 116, at 7 (defining "critical habitat" as "those parts of a cetacean's range that are essential for day-to-day well-being and survival, as well as for maintaining a healthy population growth rate. Areas that are regularly used for feeding (including hunting), breeding (including all aspects of courtship), calving (including nursing), socializing, resting, as well as, sometimes migrating, are part of critical habitat. Feeding, breeding and calving areas, and activities associated with these, may be the most critical to protect; but it is also important to extend critical habitat to cetacean prey (prime fish-rearing habitat), key oceanographic processes (productive upwelling, ocean fronts) and topographic features (seamounts, canyons)").
134. HOYT, *supra* note 116, at 57 (note that this checklist is expounded upon by way of a 15-step process at pages 56–62).
135. Douglas J. McCauley et al., *Marine Defaunation: Animal Loss in the Global Ocean*, 347 SCI. 1255641, 1255641-4 (2015) ["McCauley et al."].
136. See Convention on Biological Diversity, *Aichi Biodiversity Targets*, CBD (2012), http://www.cbd.int/sp/targets/.
137. McCauley et al., *supra* note 135, at 1255641-5.
138. HOYT, *supra* note 116, at 56–57 (noting that the second step is "scientific background research into the critical habitat requirements of cetaceans and other species, as well as the marine ecology and an inventory of the area").
139. Ana D. Davidson et al., *Drivers and Hotspots of Extinction Risk in Marine Mammals*, 109 PNAS 3395, 3395 (2012) ["Davidson et al."].
140. Sandra Pompa, Paul R. Ehrlich & Gerardo Ceballos, *Global Distribution and Conservation of Marine Mammals*, 108(33) PNAS 13600, 13604 (2011) ["Pompa et al."].

141. *Id.*
142. *Id.*
143. *Id.*
144. *Id.*
145. *Id.* at 13061.
146. Pompa et al., *supra* note 140, at 13602–03.
147. *Id.* at 13603 (noting that these sites are "along the coasts of Baja California, Northeastern America Peru, Argentina, Northwestern Africa, South Africa, Japan, Australia, and New Zealand").
148. *Id.* (noting that these sites are "the Hawaiian Islands, Galapagos Islands, Amazon River, San Felix and Juan Fernandez Islands, Mediterranean Sea, Caspian Sea, Lake Baikal, Yang-Tse River, Indus River, Ganges River, and the Kerguelen Islands").
149. *Id.* at 13606.
150. *See also* Elizabeth R. Selig, *Global Priorities for Marine Biodiversity Conservation*, 9 PLOS e82898, e82898 (2014) (noting: "[w]e used modeled spatial distribution data for nearly 12,500 species to quantify global patterns of species richness and two measures of endemism. By combining these data with spatial information on cumulative human impacts, we identified priority areas where marine biodiversity is most and least impacted by human activities, both within Exclusive Economic Zones (EEZs) and Areas Beyond National Jurisdiction (ABNJ)").
151. Davidson et al., *supra* note 139.
152. *Id.*
153. *Id.* at 3395–96.
154. *Id.* at 3397–98.
155. *Id.* at 3398.
156. *Id.*; Pompa et al., *supra* note 140.
157. Pompa et al., *supra* note 140, at 13604.
158. Davidson et al., *supra* note 139, at 3398.
159. For a full survey of the international and regional instruments that are available to preserve and protect the marine environment, *see* THOMAS DUX, SPECIALLY PROTECTED MARINE AREAS IN THE EXCLUSIVE ECONOMIC ZONE (EEZ): THE REGIME FOR THE PROTECTION OF SPECIFIC AREAS OF THE EEZ FOR ENVIRONMENTAL REASONS UNDER INTERNATIONAL LAW, 229–423 (2011).
160. International Whaling Commission, *Whale Sanctuaries*, http://iwc.int/sanctuaries (last visited Oct. 2, 2015).
161. *Id.*
162. *Id.*; HOYT, *supra* note 116, at 20–22.
163. Governments of Argentina, Brazil, South Africa and Uruguay, *The South Atlantic: A Sanctuary for Whales*, IWC/65/08 (2014), https://archive.iwc.int/pages/view.php?ref=3418.
164. Doug DeMaster, *A Review of IWC Whaling Sanctuaries*, in PROCEEDINGS OF THE FIRST INTERNATIONAL CONFERENCE ON MARINE MAMMAL PROTECTED AREAS 36, 36 (2009).
165. Mike Donoghue, *How Can the IWC Better Contribute to Both IWC and Non-IWC Whale Sanctuaries*, in PROCEEDINGS OF THE FIRST INTERNATIONAL CONFERENCE ON MARINE MAMMAL PROTECTED AREAS 38, 38 (2009).
166. *Id.*

167. Jose Trudo Palazzo, Jr., *OWC Whale Sanctuaries: The Brazilian Perspective*, in Proceedings of the First International Conference on Marine Mammal Protected Areas 36, 36 (2009).
168. *See* Irini Papanicolopulu, *International Law in Relation to IWC and Other International Whale Sanctuaries*, in PROCEEDINGS OF THE FIRST INTERNATIONAL CONFERENCE ON MARINE MAMMAL PROTECTED AREAS 38, 38 (2009).
169. *See* Giuseppe Notarbartolo-Di-Sciara et al., *The Pelagos Sanctuary for Mediterranean Marine Mammals*, 18 AQUATIC CONSERV. MAR. FRESHWATER ECOSYS. 367, 375 (2008) ["Notarbartolo-Di-Sciara"].
170. International Whaling Commission, *Pelagos Sanctuary for Marine Mammals in the Mediterranean*, IWC/59/CC8 Agenda Item 5.2, 1 (2007) ["*Pelagos Sanctuary*"].
171. Notarbartolo-Di-Sciara, *supra* note 169, at 367.
172. *Pelagos Sanctuary, supra* note 170, at 1.
173. *Id.*
174. *Id.* at 2.
175. Commission for the Conservation of Antarctic Marine Living Resources, *Protection of the South Orkney Islands Southern Shelf*, Con. Mea. 93-01 (2009).
176. International Maritime Organization, *Revised Guidelines for the Identification and Designation of Particularly Sensitive Areas*, A/24/Res.982 (Feb. 6, 2006).
177. National Oceanic and Atmospheric Administration: Office of General Counsel, *Marine Protected Areas (MPAs): Particularly Sensitive Sea Areas (PSSA)*, NOAA (Aug. 12, 2013), http://www.gc.noaa.gov/gcil_mpa-pssa.html.
178. International Convention for the Prevention of Pollution from Ships, Nov. 2, 1973, 12 I.L.M. 1319, 1340 U.N.T.S. 184 ["MARPOL"]; International Maritime Organization, *Guidelines for the Designation of Special Areas under MARPOL 73/78 and Guidelines for the Identification and Designation of Particularly Sensitive Areas*, A/22/Res.927 (Jan. 15, 2002).
179. National Oceanic and Atmospheric Administration: Office of General Counsel, *Marine Protected Areas (MPAs): Special Area Designation*, NOAA (Aug. 12, 2013), http://www.gc.noaa.gov/gcil_mpa-sad.html.
180. International Convention for the Safety of Life at Sea, Nov. 1, 1974, 1184 U.N.T.S. 278, 32 U.S.T. 47.
181. National Oceanic and Atmospheric Administration: Office of General Counsel, *Marine Protected Areas (MPAs): Areas to Be Avoided*, NOAA (Aug. 12, 2013), http://www.gc.noaa.gov/gcil_mpa-aa.html.
182. Convention on the Protection of the Marine Environment of the North-East Atlantic, Sept. 22, 1992, 32 I.L.M. 1069, 2354 U.N.T.S. 67.
183. *OSPAR Recommendation 2003/3 on a Network of Marine Protected Areas (Consolidated Text)* (adopted Jan. 1, 2003 and amended by Recommendation 2010/2, Jan. 23, 2010).
184. Convention on Biological Diversity, *2012 Interim Status Report on the OSPAR Network of Marine Protected Areas*, UNEP/CBD/COP/11/INF/42, 34 (2009).
185. *Id.* at 2.
186. *Id.* at 4.
187. *Id.* at 35.
188. *Notes & News*, 14(3) MPA NEWS (Nov.–Dec., 2012), *available at* http://depts.washington.edu/mpanews/MPA129.htm#notes.

189. United Nations Conference on Sustainable Development, Rio de Janeiro, Braz., June 20–22, 2012, *Report of the United Nations Conference on Sustainable Development*, ¶ 177, U.N. Doc. A/CONF.216/16.
190. *See* Convention on Biological Diversity, *Aichi Biodiversity Targets*, CBD (2012), http://www.cbd.int/sp/targets/.
191. CBD work regarding MPAs has been ongoing since the 1995 Jakarta Mandate on Marine and Coastal Biological Diversity, and continued through the 2002 World Summit on Sustainable Development, which occurred in Johannesburg.
192. *See* Convention on Biological Diversity, *Marine and Coastal Diversity*, COP-9 Decision IX/20 (2008), http://www.cbd.int/decision/cop/?id=11663.
193. International Union for the Conservation of Nature, *Global Protected Areas Programme*, IUCN (Sept. 18, 2015), http://www.iucn.org/about/work/programmes/gpap_home/.
194. International Union for the Conservation of Nature, *IUCN World Commission on Protected Areas*, IUCN (Jan. 16, 2014), http://www.iucn.org/about/work/programmes/gpap_home/gpap_wcpa/.
195. IUCN World Commission on Protected Areas, *Establishing Resilient Marine Protected Area Networks—Making It Happen*, IUCN (2008), http://www.protectplanetocean.org/resources/docs/MPAnetworks-MakingItHappen.pdf.
196. Dudley, *supra* note 115.
197. Global Ocean Biodiversity Initiative, *Home*, GOBI, http://www.gobi.org/ (last visited Oct. 2, 2015).
198. United Nations Environment Programme, *World Conservation Monitoring Center*, UNEP, http://www.unep-wcmc.org/ (last visited Oct. 2, 2015).
199. Global Ocean Biodiversity Initiative, *About GOBI*, GOBI, http://www.gobi.org/About (last visited Oct. 2, 2015).
200. United Nations Environment Programme, *World Conservation Monitoring Center: About Us*, UNEP, http://www.unep-wcmc.org/about-us (last visited Oct. 2, 2015).
201. International Committee on Marine Mammal Protected Areas, *Welcome to ICMMPA.org*, http://icmmpa.org/ (last visited Oct. 2, 2015).
202. *Id.*
203. *See Proceedings of the First International Conference on Marine Mammal Protected Areas*, at vii (2009), http://icmmpa.org/wp-content/uploads/2014/10/FINAL_ICMMPA_PROCEEDINGS_SM.pdf; *see* International Committee on Marine Mammal Protected Areas, *Second International Conference on Marine Mammal Protected Areas*, http://second.icmmpa.org/ (last visited Oct. 2, 2015); *see Proceedings of the Third International Conference on Marine Mammal Protected Areas* (2014), http://icmmpa.org/wp-content/uploads/2014/03/FINAL-ICMMPA3-lores-4_no_binding.pdf.
204. *See* IUCN World Parks Congress, *What Is the IUCN World Parks Congress*, http://www.worldparkscongress.org/about/what_is_the_iucn_world_parks_congress.html (last visited Oct. 2, 2015) (noting the following about the conference: "The IUCN World Parks Congress 2014 is a landmark global forum on protected areas. The Congress will share knowledge and innovation, setting the agenda for protected areas conservation for the decade to come. Building on the theme '*Parks, people, planet: inspiring solutions*', it will present, discuss and create original approaches for conservation and development, helping to address the gap in the conservation and sustainable development agenda").

205. G.A. Res. 99/292, U.N. Doc. A/RES/69/292 (July 6, 2015).
206. *Id.* ¶ 2.
207. *See generally* Michael Luck, *Education on Marine Mammal Tours as Agent for Conservation—But Do Tourists Want to Be Educated?*, 46 OCEAN & COAST. MAN. 943 (2003) (suggesting that when individuals go marine mammal watching as part of a tour they would generally like to receive more information than they do).

8

Concluding Thoughts

> "UNCLOS provides a measure of hope that whalers and protectionist states will find a way to compromise."[1]

Succinctly stated, the highly publicized and politicized debate surrounding human interaction and use of marine mammals remains fixed on the continued appropriateness of hunting marine mammals. One side of the debate features organizations and states that advance a protectionist perspective, arguing in favor of eliminating a lethal, consumptive use of marine mammals. This side currently represents the majority of members in the International Whaling Commission (IWC). The other side features organizations and states that promote continued utilization of marine mammals. This perspective is currently in the minority at the IWC. There are, of course, a number of important nuances on the periphery of these positions that add context. For example, states that prefer conservation or protection (such as the United States) still allow an indigenous take of marine mammals. Second, there is an emerging push to recognize a right to life for cetaceans and the related emergence of a body of scientific inquiry that investigates the extent to which marine mammals should be recognized as unique or comparable to humans. A final example is the extent to which so-called modern threats to marine mammals, including by-catch, environmental pollution, and climate change, must inform our approach to marine mammal conservation and management in the twenty-first century.

Although these nuances have added texture to this discussion, the core issue has remained largely unchanged since the 1970s, and there are a number of unfortunate consequences of this lingering debate that cannot be ignored. First, the duration of the debate has resulted in entrenched national positions that have become comingled with national politics and policy. Second, a lack of consensus has resulted in the manipulation and misapplication of the International Convention for the Regulation of Whaling (ICRW), effectively stalling implementation of the ICRW by the IWC, and has resulted in the production of a fragmented global response to issues of common concern. The *Whaling in the Antarctic (Australia v. Japan: New Zealand intervening)* case has vaulted contentious whaling issues back to the forefront of international debate. Third, the inability to resolve this core issue has prevented the international community from responding to current threats in a holistic manner. These emerging threats arguably represent the most pressing concern given the extent to which we are degrading the Earth's marine environment. Each of these issues highlights the need to continually assess and critique the status quo—even if such an analysis concludes that the status quo is failing and in need of serious reconsideration. Breaking this deadlock remains a critical task for the international community as the current situation is unsustainable and fails to properly account for the frailties in our current relationship with marine mammals.

The proposal I have advanced here is an alternative to the status quo. It seeks compromise between those states that prefer conservation for the purposes of preservation and those states that prefer continued utilization. It is necessary to identify the risks that are averted and benefits that are gained by each side if they pursue the negotiation of a new agreement in good faith. First, and with respect to those states that prefer enhanced conservation and marine mammal preservation, the major risk that is mitigated by negotiating a new comprehensive agreement is the threat that pro-whaling/utilization states might leave the ICRW/IWC in pursuit of their own international arrangement for continued lethal utilization. This risk must be taken seriously given the closing remarks to the *Whaling in the Antarctic* case made by Japanese deputy foreign minister Koji Tsusuoka, who stated: "What would happen to stable multilateral frameworks when such assurances [of settled expectations] disappear? When one morning suddenly you find your State bound by the policy of the majority and the only way out is to leave such an organization. Japan, a country that places importance on the rule of law, trusts that the outcome of this case will uphold stable multilateralism."[2] This risk of fractured governance and of a return to commercial whaling outside the auspices of the IWC—or any successor organization—as bounded only by customary principles of international law and the obligations established in the United Nations Convention on the Law of the Sea (UNCLOS) would represent a major failure and compromise important conservation work. This risk may be averted by negotiating a successor agreement that allows for a limited commercial take so long as it is scientifically justified, conducted humanely, monitored, reported upon, and subject to compliance, enforcement, and dispute resolution.

There are also potential rewards for the contingent of preservationist states to pursue a new agreement. Specifically: (1) it both promotes and accounts for scientific information in a manner that is not possible under the existing ICRW/IWC regime, and may facilitate a shift away from continued lethal scientific research toward new innovative practices; (2) it promotes international governance with respect to all marine mammal species and in different maritime zones, so far as jurisdictional considerations can be reconciled. It also enables the production of best-practice guidelines and standards for those issues that are not the subject of conservation and sustainable management measures; (3) it promotes the cooperation and regulatory action necessary to more effectively address the modern threats facing marine mammals. Be it through the lobbying efforts of the Secretariat or the production of conservation and sustainable management measures that address by-catch, this represents a crucial step toward achieving sustainability; (4) it facilitates ecosystem-based management through the coordinated development and implementation of marine protected areas in a way that is simply not possible in the current regime; and (5) it might very well present an opportunity to create a forum for international governance within which states work with each other as opposed to against each other. In short, the risk that is avoided and the benefits that can be gained are significant and sufficient such that conservation- and preservation-oriented countries should strongly consider pursuing the negotiation of a new agreement that allows and enables a limited commercial take for those marine mammal species that can bear this use.

Second, and with respect to those states that prefer continued utilization, there are also risks associated with the possibility of leaving a cooperative regime in favor of a new pro-whaling organization. For example, it is possible that creating this sort of arrangement would impact international relations with those pro-conservationist states that have been working to transform the IWC, and it would also draw the ire of influential nongovernmental organizations that are committed to marine mammal conservation. It is essential that peace, order, governance, and the rule of law be maintained in the oceans, and this is something that the current regime cannot guarantee. Additionally, establishing a pro-utilization agreement limits the ability of the international community to collectively address the modern threats to marine mammals. Critically, these are issues of common concern that are best addressed cooperatively. The status quo demonstrates that there is room for improvement in terms of efficiency and effectiveness, and the pro-utilization states should not act to further compromise global governance given their interest in maintaining variable marine mammal species that can be used sustainably. Similarly, pro-utilization nations also face a risk in continuing to participate in the ICRW/IWC regime in that there is a strong possibility that their interests will become further marginalized by other nations in a manner that compromises national goals.

The benefits of focusing on the negotiation of a new agreement are also apparent for pro-utilization states: (1) as proposed, it enables the return to a limited commercial take for those cetacean species that can bear this take according to their conservation status; ultimately, such a hunt would likely focus on minke whales. This would help legitimize this form of commercial take and allow it to occur pursuant to a robust Management Plan that establishes quotas in an appropriate manner and subjects any take to robust conservation and sustainable management measures, and that would do away with the need to take pursuant to controversial objections/opt-out mechanisms or under the guise of science; (2) it promotes the application and utilization of modern science and would do away with the need to pursue lethal controversial scientific whaling in most instances; (3) it promotes efforts to standardize human killing methods and killing techniques and the sort of monitoring and observation necessary to assure the global community that animal welfare is appropriately being accounted for; (4) it replaces a broad whale sanctuary approach with a potentially more effective network of marine protected areas; (5) it enables technical sharing and promotes global funding in a manner that could meaningfully engage developing nations; (6) it helps promote marine mammal tourism and education; (7) it helps clarify what sort of take is permitted pursuant to a modern understanding of Indigenous and subsistence; and (8) it might entice Canada to re-engage in international governance of marine mammals.

Having indicated why an implementing agreement pursuant to UNCLOS is preferable to the status quo, my brief concluding remarks will consider the prospects for reformed marine mammal conservation and identify key issues that should inform this conversation moving forward. Although this work has employed a rational decision-making framework[3] and has identified the theoretical benefits associated with the proposed approach, I concede that states are not necessarily rational actors, and furthermore, that some organizations will simply not be satisfied by any regime that enables lethal use. Further, I recognize that considerable work is required to rebuild trust and foster understanding between states. Ideological consensus may remain elusive, but the global community must find a way forward that departs from the current lack of progress. I remain hopeful that comprise, which is the key to moving forward, can be reached given the risks associated with the current regime and the potential benefits possible within a new regime.

In crafting his "modest proposal" for reform of the IWC, Robert Friedheim cautioned that "[t]he IWC needs not be thrown out like the baby with the bathwater, and a new whaling regime or regimes need not be created."[4] A few years later, Alexander Gillespie posited that "if you want to protect whales, be aware that the debate is about ethics, politics and law. Only when all three of these over-lapping considerations are fully factored into the equation will there be a meaningful understanding of this debate."[5] My proposal is not modest, at least not in the sense described by Friedheim, as it contemplates the negotiation and conclusion of a new treaty and, further, seeks to expand the scope of the species and issues covered. Nonetheless, it remains pragmatic in its emphasis on compromise, and is alive to the ethical dimensions of marine mammal conservation and sustainable management and the highly charged political atmosphere at the IWC. The problems that have plagued the IWC for a number of decades are unlikely to be solved in this given forum. Out-dated definitions, inappropriate exceptions, and unresolved conflicts persist. Still, this proposal proceeds with cautious optimism that the failing status quo can be addressed through properly crafted legal mechanisms that account for and reconcile the competing interests that will inevitably inform the future of human-marine mammal interaction. This generation is characterized by climate change, environmental pollution, and the consequences of hyper-resource utilization; however, we also have unparalleled access to information, recognize the importance of science and critical thought, and continue to work toward appropriate solutions. Sometimes dramatic reform—a sea change—is necessary; I believe that marine mammal conservation and management is an area ready for such innovation.

The negotiating approach employed at the Third Conference of UNCLOS utilized the informal negotiating texts from the committees to produce a "single negotiating text," then a "revised single negotiating text," an "informal composite negotiating text," moving toward the informal text, and eventually the final adopted version.[6] The annotated draft agreement found in Appendix 3 does not purport to represent one distinct aspect of this negotiating process, but I include it with the hope that its core features spur future discussion. First, it embodies the comprehensive compromise that offers an alternative to the status quo in a form that has not previously been explored. Second, it employs, as a starting point and to the maximum extent practicable, language that has previously been negotiated in other contexts. Third, it incorporates and allows for the competing interests that frame the current debate surrounding marine mammal conservation. Fourth, it acknowledges and incorporates important innovations in international law and also current threats to marine mammal conservation. In sum, it is both a starting point in the exploration of the form and function of a new approach to international marine mammal governance and the draft form of a final product, so far as one can be theorized without actual negotiations.

As noted by the Center for Progressive Member Scholars in their white paper *Reclaiming Global Environmental Leadership: Why the United States Should Ratify Ten Pending Environmental Treaties*, "for more than a century, the United States has taken the lead in organizing international responses to international environmental problems," but "[i]n the last two decades, however, U.S. environmental leadership has faltered."[7] This paper identifies 10 important international agreements and advances arguments in support of American ratification, and the final convention addressed is UNCLOS. The United States led the negotiations that produced UNCLOS before encountering difficulties with Part XI, which addresses deep-seabed mining.[8] As Professor John Norton Moore observed in a *Wall Street Journal* opinion-editorial in 2012, Part XI, as originally negotiated, "contained flaws requiring renegotiation" that did constitute "treaty killers."[9] Still, these shortcomings were rectified through renegotiation prior to UNCLOS being submitted to the Senate for advice and consent.[10] The United States is currently "the only developed coastal State, the only large economy, and the only naval power that does not belong to the Convention,"[11] to the detriment of its economic, environmental, and national security interests and in the face of support from all major stakeholders—including the military.[12] Equally concerning is the fact that failure to ratify UNCLOS continues to compromise the "leadership role in global ocean affairs"[13] that the United States has traditionally enjoyed.

In addition to recommending that the United States proceed to ratify UNCLOS, this proposal represents another opportunity for the United States to re-establish itself as a leader in international oceans governance. Marine mammal conservation remains a hot-button environmental issue that attracts considerable attention in a variety of fora. The best example remains the Sea Shepherd Conservation Society's efforts to disrupt Japan's scientific whaling in the Southern Ocean Whaling Sanctuary. The Sea Shepherd sets out each year to follow and obstruct the Japanese whaling efforts, and has gained significant public support for their efforts; indeed, their work forms the substance of a television series titled *Whale Wars* that airs on Animal Planet.[14] It is difficult to predict how Sea Shepherd will respond to any renewed Japanese scientific whaling program in the Southern Ocean.

Ultimately, it may not be possible to appeal to groups such as Sea Shepherd, which are dedicated to halting the lethal use of cetaceans. This proposal represents a rational approach to the future of marine mammal conservation and sustainable management that accounts for competing legitimate interests and aims to shift the focus of this debate from public rhetoric to international negotiations where progress on the issue of international governance can be made. Given the national interest in marine mammal conservation demonstrated by the United States and its past international efforts to address this issue through UNCLOS and at the IWC, the United States remains a logical choice to lead efforts to effectively conserve marine mammals for present and future generations; however, it is not the only state capable of advancing a new approach.

Other logical candidates include the European Union or some of its member states or those South American nations that have recently taken a more active role at the IWC as part of the Buenos Aires voting bloc. Similarly, the emphasis that Norway and Iceland place on scientific-based ecosystem management suggests that they are the best positioned within the pro-utilization camp to initiate such reform. The process that is playing out at the United Nations regarding the decision to negotiate a new implementing agreement to address the conservation and management of biodiversity in areas beyond national jurisdiction will be quite informative in assessing the international community's will to promulgate new effective oceans law. Recently, a number of states articulated their opinion that this approach was "feasible from a political, legal and technical standpoint"[15] while others, including the United States, questioned whether new law was needed to address this problem or if renewed commitment to implement and administer existing law was the true problem.[16]

Our understanding of the oceans continues to change as exploration and scientific endeavors progress. As does our appreciation for marine mammal conservation and sustainable management, which is shaped by both the forces of the ocean and the people and institutions involved in its governance. I vividly remember studying marine biology at the Bamfield Marine Sciences Centre on Canada's west coast as an undergraduate student back in 2004. There, while researching sea otter extirpation and recovery along the coast of the province of British Columbia, the connection I have always felt to the ocean transformed into an academic pursuit, and my interest in the law and policy surrounding marine mammal conservation emerged. I opted to pursue legal studies and a career in the legal academy believing then, as I believe now, that despite past folly and blunder and in the face of past mismanagement and over-exploitation, the fate of marine mammals has not been determined. It is not yet too late to reform and restructure our relationship with both marine mammals and the oceans, which we simultaneously love and destroy; however, the clock continues to tick and time is running short.

NOTES

1. Joanna Matanich, *A Treaty Comes of Age for the Ancient Ones: Implications of the Law of the Sea for the Regulation of Whaling*, 8 INT'L LEGAL PERSP. 37, 71 (1996).
2. Andrew Darby, *Japan Raises Spectre of Whaling Treaty Withdrawal*, SYDNEY MORNING HERALD (July 16, 2013), http://www.smh.com.au/federal-politics/political-news/japan-raises-spectre-of-whaling-treaty-withdrawal-20130716-2q2ba.html.
3. This work has proceeded by way of a rational decision-making model. Broadly stated, and within the context of failed international governance for marine mammal conservation, past trends have been identified, alternative courses of action have been considered, and a proposal has been advanced that addresses the goals of: (1) promoting the rule of law in the oceans, (2) expanding species coverage, (3) expanding issue coverage, (4) respecting competing ocean uses, (5) enhancing cooperation and global participation, (6) incorporating current principles of international law, (7) bolstering reliance on science during decision-making and holistic management, (8) fostering regional implementation, (9) expanding the existing foundation for marine mammal conservation, and (10) advancing a rational proposal.
4. Robert L. Friedheim, *Fixing the Whaling Regime: A Proposal*, in TOWARD A SUSTAINABLE WHALING REGIME 315 (Robert L. Friedheim ed., 2001).
5. ALEXANDER GILLESPIE, WHALING DIPLOMACY 484 (2005).

6. UNITED NATIONS CONVENTION ON THE LAW OF THE SEA: A COMMENTARY VOLUME II, at 13–15 (Myron Nordquist ed., 1993).
7. Mary Jane Angelo et al., *Reclaiming Global Environmental Leadership: Why the United States Should Ratify Ten Pending Environmental Treaties*, Center for Progressive Reform White Paper 2 (2012), http://www.progressivereform.org/articles/International_Environmental_Treaties_1201.pdf ["CPR White Paper"].
8. *Id.* at 37.
9. John Norton Moore, *Conservatives and the Law of the Sea Time Warp: The Treaty Has Been Improved in Ways Regan Wanted and It's Time the U.S. Signed On*, WALL STREET J., July 8, 2012, http://online.wsj.com/article/SB10001424052702304141204577509501647789674.html ["John Norton Moore"] (noting that Part XI, as originally negotiated, was troublesome as a result of mandatory technology transfer and the permanent seat that would be given to the Soviet Union on the newly created International Sea Bed Authority).
10. *Id.*; CPR White Paper, *supra* note 7, at 38.
11. *Id.* at 37.
12. *Id.* at 37–38; John Norton Moore, *supra* note 9.
13. CPR White Paper, *supra* note 7, at 38.
14. Raffi Khatchadourian, *Whale-War Fugitive: Q. & A. with Paul Watson*, NEW YORKER, June 4, 2013, http://www.newyorker.com/online/blogs/newsdesk/2013/06/whale-war-fugitive-q-a-with-paul-watson.html.
15. Letter Dated 13 February 2015 from the Co-chairs of the Ad Hoc Open-Ended Informal Working Group to the President of the General Assembly, at 5, U.N. Doc. A/69/780 (Feb. 13, 2015).
16. *Id.* at 5–6. *See also* Dire Tladi, *The Proposed Implementing Agreement: Options for Coherence and Consistency in the Establishment of Protected Areas beyond National Jurisdiction* (Oct. 19, 2015). INTL. J. MAR. & COASTAL L. (2015), available at http://ssrn.com/abstract=2676064.

Appendix 1

Extant and Recently Extinct Marine Mammal Species

Table 1. ORDER CETACEA (WHALES, DOLPHINS, AND PORPOISES)

Scientific Name	Common Name	IUCN Status	Population Trend
Balena mysticetus	Bowhead Whale, Greenland Whale	Least Concern	Increasing
Balaenaoptera acutorostrata	Common Minke Whale	Least Concern	Stable
Balaenoptera bonaerensis	Antarctic Minke Whale	Data Deficient	Unknown
Balaenoptera borealis	Sei Whale	Endangered	Unknown
Balaenoptera edeni	Bryde's Whale	Data Deficient	Unknown
Balaenaoptera musculus	Blue Whale	Endangered	Increasing
Balaenoptera omurai	Omura's Whale	Data Deficient	Unknown, Possibly Extinct
Balaenaoptera physalus	Fin Whale	Endangered	Unknown
Berardius arnuxii	Arnoux' Beaked Whale	Data Deficient	Unknown
Berardius bairdii	Baird's Beaked Whale	Data Deficient	Unknown
Caperea marginata	Pygmy Right Whale	Data Deficient	Unknown
Cephalorhynchus commersonii	Commerson's Dolphin	Data Deficient	Unknown
Chephalorhynchus eutropia	Chilean Dolphin	Near Threatened	Decreasing
Cephalorhynchus heavisidii	Heaviside's Dolphin	Data Deficient	Unknown
Cephalorhybnchus hectori	Hector's Dolphin	Endangered	Decreasing

(*Continued*)

Table 1. (CONTINUED)

Scientific Name	Common Name	IUCN Status	Population Trend
Delphinapterus leucas	Beluga	Near Threatened	Unknown
Delphinus capensis	Long-Beaked Common Dolphin	Data Deficient	Unknown
Delphinus delphis	Short-beaked Common Dolphin	Least Concern	Unknown
Eschrichtius robustus	Gray Whale	Least Concern	Stable
Eubalena australis	Southern Right Whale	Least Concern	Increasing
Eubalaena glacialis	North Atlantic Right Whale	Endangered	Unknown
Eubalena japonica	North Pacific Right Whale	Endangered	Unknown
Feresa attenuate	Pygmy Killer Whale	Data Deficient	Unknown
Globicephala macrohynchus	Short-finned Pilot Whale	Data Deficient	Unknown
Globicephala melas	Long-finned Pilot Whale	Data Deficient	Unknown
Grampus griseus	Risso's Dolphin	Least Concern	Unknown
Hyperoodon ampullatus	North Atlantic Bottlenose Whale	Data Deficient	Unknown
Hyperdoon planifrons	Southern Bottlenose Whale	Least Concern	Unknown
Indopacetus pacificus	Longman's Beaked Whale	Data Deficient	Unknown
Inia boliviensis	Bolivian bufeo	Not Listed	Not Listed
Inia geoffrensis	Amazon River Dolphin	Data Deficient	Unknown
Kogia breviceps	Pygmy Sperm Whale	Data Deficient	Unknown
Kogia sima	Dwarf Sperm Whale	Data Deficient	Unknown
Lagenodelphis hosei	Fraser's Dolphin	Least Concern	Unknown
Lagenohynchus acutus	Atlantic White-sided Dolphin	Least Concern	Unknown
Lagenohynchus australis	Peale's Dolphin	Data Deficient	Unknown
Lagenohynchus albirostris	White-beaked Dolphin	Least Concern	Unknown
Lagenohynchus cruciger	Hourglass Dolphin	Least Concern	Unknown
Lagenohynchus obliquidens	Pacific White-Sided Dolphin	Least Concern	Unknown

Table 1. (Continued)

Scientific Name	Common Name	IUCN Status	Population Trend
Lagenohynchus obscures	Dusky Dolphin	Data Deficient	Unknown
Lipotes vexillifer	Baiji, Yangtze River Dolphin	Critically Endangered	Unknown, Possibly Extinct
Lissodelphis borealis	Northern Right-whale Dolphin	Least Concern	Unknown
Lissodelphis peronii	Southern Right-whale Dolphin	Data Deficient	Unknown
Megaptera novaeangliae	Humpback Whale	Least Concern	Increasing
Mesoplodon bidens	Sowerby's Beaked Whale	Data Deficient	Unknown
Mesoplodon bowdoini	Andrew's Beaked Whale	Data Deficient	Unknown
Mesoplodon carlhubbsi	Hubb's Beaked Whale	Data Deficient	Unknown
Mesoplodon densirostris	Blainville's Beaked Whale	Data Deficient	Unknown
Mesoplodon europaeus	Gervais' Beaked Whale	Data Deficient	Unknown
Mesoplodon ginkgodens	Ginko-toothed Beaked Whale	Data Deficient	Unknown
Mesoplodon grayi	Gray's Beaked Whale	Data Deficient	Unknown
Mesoplodon hectori	Hector's Beaked Whale	Data Deficient	Unknown
Mesoplodon layardii	Strap-toothed Beaked Whale	Data Deficient	Unknown
Mesoplodon mirus	True's Beaked Whale	Data Deficient	Unknown
Mesoplodon perrini	Perrin's Beaked Whale	Data Deficient	Unknown
Mesoplodon peruvianus	Pygym Beaked Whale	Data Deficient	Unknown
Mesoplodon stejnegeri	Stejneger's Beaked Whale	Data Deficient	Unknown
Mesoplodon traversii	Spade-toothed Whale	Data Deficient	Unknown
Monodon monoceros	Narwhal	Near Threatened	Unknown

(*Continued*)

Table 1. (CONTINUED)

Scientific Name	Common Name	IUCN Status	Population Trend
Neophocaena asiaeroientalis	Narrow-ridged Finless Porpoise	Vulnerable	Decreasing
Neophocaena phoecaenoides	Indo-Pacific Finless Porpoise	Vulnerable	Decreasing
Orcaella brevirostris	Irrawaddy Dolphin	Vulnerable	Decreasing
Orcaella heinsohni	Australian Snubfin Dolphin	Near Threatened	Unknown
Orcinus orca	Killer Whale	Data Deficient	Unknown
Peponocephala electra	Melon-headed Whale	Least Concern	Unknown
Phoeciena dalli	Dall's Porpoise	Least Concern	Unknown
Phocoena dioptrica	Spectacled Porpoise	Data Deficient	Unknown
Phocoena phocoena	Harbour Porpoise	Least Concern	Unknown
Phoecoena sinus	Vaquita	Critically Endangered	Decreasing
Phoecoena spinipinnis	Burmeister's Porpoise	Data Deficient	Unknown
Physeter macrocephalus	Sperm Whale	Vulnerable	Unknown
Platanista gangetica	South Asian River Dolphin	Endangered	Unknown
Pontoporia blanivillei	La Plata Dolphin	Vulnerable	Decreasing
Pseudorca crassideus	False Killer Whale	Data Deficient	Unknown
Sotalia fluviatilis	Tucuxi	Data Deficient	Unknown
Sotalia guianensis	Guiana Dolphin	Data Deficient	Unknown
Sousa chinensis	Indo-pacific Hump-backed Whale	Near Threatened	Decreasing
Sousa teuszii	Atlantic Humpback Dolphin	Vulnerable	Decreasing
Stenella attenuata	Pantropical Spotted Dolphin	Least Concern	Unknown
Stenella clymene	Clymene Dolphin	Data Deficient	Unknown
Stenella coeruleoalba	Striped Dolphin	Least Concern	Unknown
Stenella frontalis	Atlantic Spotted Dolphin	Data Deficient	Unknown
Stenella longirostris	Spinner Dolphin	Data Deficient	Unknown
Steno bredanensis	Rough-toothed Dolphin	Least Concern	Unknown
Tasmacetus shepherdi	Shepherd's Beaked Whale	Data Deficient	Unknown

Table 1. (Continued)

Scientific Name	Common Name	IUCN Status	Population Trend
Tursiops aduncus	Indo-Pacific Bottlenose Dolphin	Data Deficient	Unknown
Tursiops truncatus	Common Bottlenose Dolphin	Least Concern	Unknown
Ziphius Cavirostruis	Cuvier's Beaked Whale	Least Concern	Unknown

Table 2. Order Carnivora (Otters and the Polar Bear)

Scientific Name	Common Name	IUCN Status	Population Trend
Anoyx capensis	African Clawless Otter	Near Threatened	Decreasing
Enhydra lutris	Sea Otter	Endangered	Decreasing
Lontra canadensis	North American Otter	Least Concern	Stable
Lontra felina	Marine Otter	Endangered	Decreasing
Lontra provocax	Southern River Otter	Endangered	Decreasing
Lutra lutra	Eurasian Otter	Near Threatened	Decreasing
Neovision macrodon	Sea Mink	N/A	Extinct
Ursus maritimus	Polar Bear	Vulnerable	Decreasing

Table 3. Order Pinnipedia (Seals, Fur Seals, Sea Lions, and Walruses)

Scientific Name	Common Name	IUCN Status	Population Trend
Arctocephalus forsteri	New Zealand Fur Seal	Least Concern	Increasing
Arctocephalus pusillus	Cape Fur Seal, Afro-Australian Fur Seal	Least Concern	Increasing
Arctophoca gazelle	Antarctic Fur Seal	Least Concern	Increasing
Arctophoca tropicalis	Subantarctic Fur Seal	Least Concern	Increasing
Arctophoca australis	South American Fur Seal	Least Concern	Increasing
Arctophoca galapagoensis	Galapagos Fur Seal	Endangered	Decreasing
Arctophoca philippii	Juan Fernandez Fur Seal	Near Threatened	Increasing
Callorhinus ursinus	Northern Fur Seal	Vulnerable	Decreasing

(*Continued*)

Table 3. (CONTINUED)

Scientific Name	Common Name	IUCN Status	Population Trend
Cystophora cristata	Hooded Seal	Vulnerable	Decreasing
Erignathus barbatus	Bearded Seal	Least Concern	Stable
Eumetopias jubatus	Steller Sea Lion, Northern Sea Lion	Near Threatened	Increasing
Halichoerus grypus	Gray Seal	Least Concern	Increasing
Histriphoca fasciata	Ribbon Seal	Data Deficient	Unknown
Hydruga leptonyx	Leopard Seal	Least Concern	Unknown
Leptonychotes weddellii	Weddell Seal	Least Concern	Unknown
Lobodon carcinophaga	Crabeater Seal	Least Concern	Unknown
Mirounga angustirostris	Northern Elephant Seal	Least Concern	Increasing
Mirounga leonine	Southern Elephant Seal	Least Concern	Unknown
Monachus monachus	Mediterranean Monk Seal	Critically Endangered	Decreasing
Monachus schauinslandi	Hawaiian Monk Seal	Endangered	Decreasing
Monachus tropicalis	Caribbean Monk Seal	N/A	Extinct
Neophoca cinera	Australian Sea Lion	Endangered	Decreasing
Obodbenus rosmarus	Walrus	Data Deficient	Unknown
Ommatophoca rossii	Ross Seal	Least Concern	Unknown
Otaria byronia	South American Sea Lion	Least Concern	Stable
Pagophilus groenlandicus	Harp Seal	Least Concern	Increasing
Phoca largha	Spotted Seal, Largha Seal	Data Deficient	Unknown
Phoca vitulina	Harbour Seal, Common Seal	Least Concern	Stable
Phocartos cinerea	New Zealand Sea Lion	Endangered	Decreasing
Pusa caspica	Caspian Seal	Endangered	Decreasing
Pusa hispida	Ringed Seal	Least Concern	Unknown
Pusa sibirica	Baikal Seal	Least Concern	Stable
Zalophus japonicus	Japanese Sea Lion	N/A	Extinct
Zalophus californianus	California Sea Lion	Least Concern	Increasing
Zalophus wollebaeki	Galapagos Sea Lion	Endangered	Decreasing

Table 4. ORDER SIRENIA (MANATEES AND DUGONGS)

Scientific Name	Common Name	IUCN Status	Population Trend
Dugong dugon	Dugong	Vulnerable	Unknown
Hydrodamalis gigas	Steller's Sea Cow	Extinct	N/A
Trichechus inunguis	South American Manatee	Vulnerable	Decreasing
Trichechus manatus	West Indian Manatee	Vulnerable	Decreasing
Trichechus senegalensis	West African Manatee	Vulnerable	Unknown

SOURCE: Society for Marine Mammology, *Committee on Taxonomy, List of Marine Mammal Species and Subspecies*, http://www.marinemammalscience.org/index.php?option=com_content&view=article&id=645&Itemid=340 (last visited July 10, 2015); International Union for the Conservation of Nature, *IUCN Red List of Threatened Species*, IUCN RED LIST, http://www.iucnredlist.org/search (last visited July. 10, 2015) (the tables in this Appendix represent a compilation of the information from both of these sources).

Appendix 2

Ocean Zones

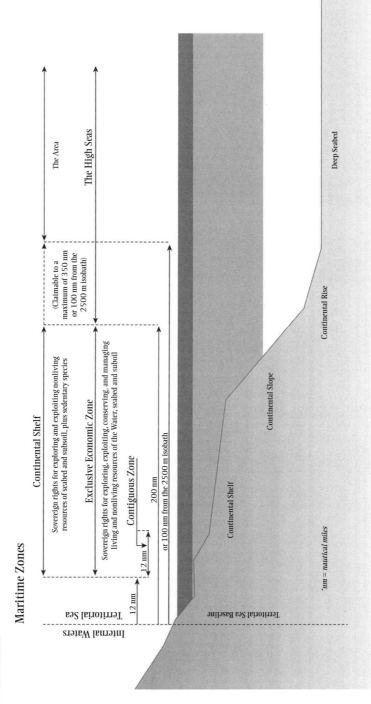

"This image was provided by the Department of Fisheries and Oceans Canada."

Appendix 3

Draft Agreement for the Implementation of the Provisions of the United Nations Convention on the Law of the Sea of 10 December 1982 Relating to the Conservation and <u>Sustainable Management of Marine Mammals</u>[1,*]

(Short form: <u>UN Marine Mammals Agreement</u>)

PREAMBLE

The States Parties to this Agreement,
  Recalling the relevant provisions of the United Nations Convention on the Law of the Sea of 10 December 1982,[2]
  Recalling that the history of whaling <u>and the targeted hunt of other marine mammal species has witnessed patterns of over-exploitation</u>,[3]
  Determined to ensure the long-term conservation and <u>sustainable</u> management of <u>marine mammals and the marine environment</u>,[4]
  Resolved to improve the cooperation between States to that end,[5]
  Calling <u>for compliance with international regulatory standards, reasonable monitoring, and</u> more effective enforcement by flag States, port States and coastal States of the conservation measures adopted for <u>marine mammals</u>,[6]
  Seeking to address in particular the problems <u>that prevent the International Whaling Commission from effectively and rationally conserving and sustainably managing cetaceans, namely, inadequate species and threat coverage; noting that there are problems with "scientific" whaling, Indigenous whaling (as currently implemented), the reservation and amendment process of the International Convention for the Regulation of Whaling, and the</u> lack of sufficient cooperation between States,[7]
  Committing themselves to <u>rational marine mammal conservation and sustainable management</u>,[8]
  Recognizing <u>the need to protect the interests of both coastal States and the international community,</u>

---

* It disrupts readability to include quotations within the draft articles, so I have underlined the portion of each proposed article that represents my contribution or modification/summation of the precedent that has otherwise been adopted, as identified in the corresponding footnote.

Recognizing the need for specific assistance, including financial, scientific, and technological assistance, in order that developing States can participate effectively in the conservation and <u>sustainable management of marine mammals,</u>[9]

Recognizing <u>that all marine mammals are susceptible to the consequences of direct and indirect sources of mortality and/or environmental change,</u>[10]

Recognizing <u>that ecosystem-based management and science-based decision-making are critical in oceans governance,</u>[11]

Recognizing that <u>there is a</u> common interest <u>in achieving rational conservation and sustainable management of all marine mammal species for present and future generations,</u>[12]

Recognizing <u>the social, cultural, and economic significance of the consumptive and non-consumptive aspects of humankinds' use of marine mammals,</u>

Convinced that an agreement for the implementation of the relevant provisions of the Convention would best serve these purposes and contribute to the maintenance of international peace and security,[13]

Convinced <u>that an agreement creating a comprehensive regime for the conservation and sustainable management of marine mammals is necessary and in the interest of humankind,</u>[14]

Affirming that matters not regulated by the Convention or by this Agreement continue to be governed by the rules and principles of general international law,[15]

Have agreed as follows:

PART I GENERAL PROVISIONS

Article 1 Use of Terms and Scope

1. For the purposes of this Agreement:
    a. "Convention" means the United Nations Convention on the Law of the Sea of 10 December 1982;[16]
    b. <u>"Conservation"</u>[17] means:
        i. <u>The maintenance of a status</u>[18] <u>for stable or increasing marine mammal species/population(s) that, at a minimum, ensures the necessary composition, genetic variability, and ecosystem integrity</u>[19] <u>required for the long-term viability of the marine mammal species/population(s).</u>[20]
        ii. <u>The recovery or rehabilitation of diminished marine mammal species/population(s) to a status that, minimally, ensures the necessary composition, genetic variability, and ecosystem integrity required for the long-term viability of the marine mammal species/population(s).</u>[21]
        iii. <u>The statuses referred to in subsections (i) and (ii) shall be informed by the best available science, including due consideration of the Red List of Threatened Species as maintained by the International Union for the Conservation of Nature.</u>
        iv. <u>The status referred to in subsection (i) for stable or increasing populations does not preclude the rational take of marine mammals, when and where appropriate, so long as this take does not compromise the status identified therein.</u>[22] <u>Populations</u>

covered by subsection (ii) shall not be taken until such time as their recovery/rehabilitation is complete.
- v. Conservation shall be achieved through sustainable management and threat mitigation.²³
- c. "Conservation and sustainable management measures" means measures to conserve and sustainably manage one or more population or species of marine mammal, as established by the International Marine Mammal Commission as part of the Annex to this Agreement, or otherwise, and adopted, applied, and/or implemented consistently with the relevant rules of international law as reflected in the Convention and this Agreement;²⁴
- d. "Ecosystem-based management" means holistic, integrated management that recognizes the uncertainty and natural variability of ecosystems but seeks to maintain ecosystem structure, function, and constituent parts;²⁵
- e. "IWC" means the International Whaling Commission;
- f. "ICRW" means the International Convention for the Regulation of Whaling;
- g. "Marine mammal" includes those species belonging to Order Cetacea, Order Sirenia, Order Pinnipedia, and the members of Order Carnivora that have adapted to the marine environment;²⁶
- h. "Marine Protected Area" means a discrete area of the ocean, established by law, designated to enhance the long-term conservation and/or sustainable management of the marine mammals therein;²⁷
- i. "Population" means a group of marine mammals of the same species or subspecies/stock in a common spatial arrangement, that interbreed when mature;²⁸
- j. "Sustainable management" means:
    - i. Management that seeks to achieve long-term human-marine mammal coexistence and encompasses the entire scope of regulatory activities necessary to conduct a modern management program, including, but not limited to research and study, the promulgation of regulations, and the production of best-practice standards and guidelines.²⁹
    - ii. Management that is guided by ecosystem-based management, intragenerational and intergenerational equity, the integration of the environment and development, and precaution in light of scientific uncertainty. It requires compliance, enforcement, and international and regional cooperation.³⁰ It does not preclude rational take of marine mammals, when and where appropriate and consistent with sound conservation science, nor the periodic or total protection of species or populations or an otherwise regulated taking.³¹
- k. "Take" means to intentionally hunt, capture, or kill; or attempt to hunt, capture, or kill any marine mammal, and to incidentally capture or kill as by-catch.³²
- l. "Vessel" means any ship or craft, or any structure capable of navigation³³ that is used for the purpose of taking, treating,

transporting, scouting, locating, towing, or otherwise engaging marine mammals.[34]
2. a. "State Party/States Parties" means the State(s) that has/have consented to be bound by this Agreement and for which the Agreement is in force.[35]
   b. This Agreement applies *mutatis mutandis* to any entity referred to in Article 305, paragraph 1 (c), (d), and (e), of the Convention which becomes a Party to this Agreement, and to that extent "States Parties" refers to those entities.[36]

Article 2 Objective

The objective of this Agreement is to ensure the long-term conservation and sustainable management of marine mammals through effective implementation of the relevant provisions of the Convention.[37]

Article 3 Application

1. This Agreement applies to the conservation and sustainable management of all marine mammals beyond national jurisdiction, and States Parties to this Agreement are members of the International Marine Mammal Commission established in Part III.[38]
2. This Agreement applies to the conservation and sustainable management of marine mammals within the Exclusive Economic Zone of coastal States to the extent that the coastal States consent to the International Marine Mammal Commission exerting regulatory governance over this maritime zone, without prejudicing the sovereign rights of coastal States for the purpose of prohibiting, limiting, or regulating marine mammal take within areas under national jurisdiction as provided for in the Convention.[39]
3. Recalling the specific obligations in Article 65 of the Convention, this agreement applies to the conservation and sustainable management of cetaceans by the International Marine Mammal Commission established in Part III within the Exclusive Economic Zone of ratified States Parties.
4. In the exercise of its sovereign rights for the purpose of conserving and sustainably managing marine mammals within areas of national jurisdiction, the coastal State shall apply mutatis mutandis the general principles enumerated in Article 6.[40]

Article 4 Relationship between this Agreement and the Convention

Nothing in this Agreement shall prejudice the rights, jurisdiction, and duties of States under the Convention. This Agreement shall be interpreted and applied in the context of and in a manner consistent with the Convention.[41]

Article 5 Amendment to Annex I of the Convention

As between those States that are States Parties to both this Agreement and the Convention, the Convention is modified as follows:

a. Paragraph 15 of Annex I of the Convention is amended to read: "15. Common dolphinfish: *Coryphaena hippurus*; *Coryphaena equiselis*."
b. Paragraph 17 of Annex I is deleted.

PART II CONSERVATION AND SUSTAINABLE MANAGEMENT OF MARINE MAMMALS

Article 6 General Principles of Conservation and Sustainable Management of Marine Mammals

In order to conserve and sustainably manage marine mammals, coastal States and States taking or otherwise using marine mammals shall, in giving effect to their duty to cooperate with a view to marine mammal conservation and to work through the appropriate international organizations in accordance with the Convention:

a. adopt measures to ensure the long-term conservation and sustainable management of marine mammal species/population(s);
b. ensure that such measures are based on the best available scientific information, evidence, and knowledge and are designed to:
   i. withstand the pressures of any limited commercial take;
   ii. take into account the interests of Indigenous and Cultural/Artisanal takes as defined in this Agreement;
   iii. account for the impact of current and emerging direct and indirect threats to marine mammals, including, inter alia, the consequences of climate change, environmental degradation, and environmental pollution (including noise pollution), by-catch, ship-strikes, and marine mammal tourism; and
   iv. account for economic factors, including the special requirements of developing States.
c. apply the precautionary approach in accordance with Article 7;
d. assess the impacts of marine mammal take, other human activities, and environmental factors on marine mammal species/population(s) belonging to the same ecosystem or associated with or dependent upon targeted prey species;
e. adopt, as appropriate, the conservation and sustainable management measures established by the International Marine Mammal Organization for marine mammal species/population(s) with a view to maintaining or restoring the species/population(s) to the appropriate conservation status;
f. work to minimize/mitigate, inter alia, the direct and/or indirect effects of climate change, by-catch, ship-strikes, habitat degradation, pollution (chemical, physical, and noise), ocean dumping, and marine mammal tourism upon marine mammal species/population(s);
g. protect biodiversity of the marine environment;

h. collect and share, in a timely manner, complete and accurate data concerning marine mammal species/population(s);
i. promote and conduct scientific research and develop appropriate technologies in support of marine mammal conservation and sustainable management; and
j. implement and enforce conservation and sustainable management measures, directly or through regional marine mammal organizations and/or arrangements, through effective monitoring, control, and surveillance.[42]

Article 7 Application of the Precautionary Principle

1. States, the International Marine Mammal Commission, and regional marine mammal organizations/arrangements shall apply the precautionary approach widely to the conservation and sustainable management of marine mammal species/population(s) in order to protect the living marine resources and preserve the marine environment.
2. States, the International Marine Mammal Commission, and regional marine mammal organizations/arrangements shall be more cautious when information is uncertain, unreliable, or inadequate. The absence of adequate scientific information shall not be used as a reason for postponing or failing to establish, adopt, apply, and/or implement conservation and sustainable management measures.
3. In implementing the precautionary approach, States, the International Marine Mammal Commission, and regional marine mammal organizations/arrangements shall:
   a. improve decision-making for marine mammal conservation and sustainable management by obtaining and sharing the best available scientific information, evidence, and knowledge and implementing improved techniques for dealing with risk and uncertainty;
   b. ensure, on the basis of the best available scientific information, evidence, and knowledge that the appropriate conservation statuses are not compromised, and determine the appropriate course of action if they are;
   c. take into account, inter alia, uncertainties relating to the size and productivity of marine mammal species/population(s), the impact of any approved commercial take, the impact of any approved Indigenous or Cultural/Artisanal subsistence take, and the impact of any other direct or indirect human impacts, as well as existing and predicted oceanic, environmental, and socioeconomic conditions; and
   d. develop data collection and research programs to assess the impact of human activity and environmental factors on marine mammal species/population(s), and adopt species specific and/or regional plans that are necessary to ensure the conservation of such species and necessary habitat protection.
4. Where the conservation status of marine mammal species/population(s) subject to any approved commercial take is of concern, States, the International Marine Mammal Commission, and regional marine mammal

organizations/arrangements shall subject such species/population(s) to enhanced monitoring to review their conservation status and the efficacy of conservation and sustainable management measures. Such measures shall be revised regularly in the light of new information.

5. For marine mammal species/population(s) previously subject to an IWC commercial moratorium, or for new or exploratory commercial take and/or Indigenous and/or Cultural/Artisanal subsistence take, States, through the International Marine Mammal Commission, shall adopt as soon as possible cautious conservation and sustainable management measures, including, inter alia, catch quota limits. Such measures shall remain in force until there are sufficient data to allow assessment of the impact of the take on the conservation status of the species/population(s), whereupon conservation and sustainable management measures based on that assessment shall be implemented. The latter measures, if appropriate, may allow for the gradual development of the take of said marine mammal species/population(s).

6. If a natural phenomenon has a significant adverse impact on the conservation status of marine mammal species/population(s), States, through the International Marine Mammal Commission, shall adopt conservation and sustainable management measures on an emergency basis to ensure that any approved take or indirect use does not exacerbate such adverse impact. States, through the International Marine Mammal Commission, shall also adopt such measures on an emergency basis where any approved commercial take presents a serious threat to the conservation status of such species/population(s). Measures taken on an emergency basis shall be temporary and shall be based on the best available scientific information, evidence, and knowledge.[43]

7. None of the foregoing prevents States, acting independently, through the International Marine Mammal Commission or through regional marine mammal organizations/arrangements, and in accordance with the Convention, from prohibiting the commercial take of marine mammals even when an assessment of a conservation status of marine mammal species/population(s) suggests that such a regulated take will not compromise the conservation status.[44]

Article 8 Compatibility of Conservation and Sustainability Measures

1. Without prejudicing the sovereign rights of coastal States for the purpose of prohibiting, limiting, or regulating marine mammal take within areas under national jurisdiction as provided for in the Convention, the ability of coastal States to consent to the competence of the International Marine Mammal Commission for the purpose of prohibiting, limiting, or regulating marine mammal take within areas of national jurisdiction as provided for in the Convention, and the competence of the International Marine Mammal Commission to prohibit, limit, or regulate marine mammal take on the high seas in accordance with the Convention:

a. the relevant coastal States and the States whose nationals take, or intend to take, marine mammals from marine mammal species/population(s) in the high seas shall seek, through the International Marine Mammal Commission established in Part III, to agree to the conservation and sustainable management measures necessary for the conservation of these species/population(s) in the high seas area;
b. the relevant consenting coastal States whose nationals take, or intend to take, marine mammals from marine mammal species/population(s) in areas of national jurisdiction shall seek, as appropriate, through the International Marine Mammal Commission established in Part III, to agree to the conservation and sustainable management measures necessary for the conservation of these species/population(s) in areas of national jurisdiction;
c. the relevant coastal States and States whose nationals take, or intend to take, marine mammal species/population(s) in a defined region shall seek, through regional marine mammal organizations/associations as established in Part IV, cooperation to adopt, apply, and/or implement the conservation and sustainability measures agreed to by the International Marine Mammal Commission.

2. Conservation and sustainable management measures established for the high seas and those established for areas under national jurisdiction, as agreed to by the International Marine Mammal Commission and adopted, applied, and/or implemented regionally, shall be compatible in order to ensure conservation and sustainable management of the marine mammal species/population(s) in their entirety. To this end, coastal States and States that take, or intend to take, marine mammal species/population(s) have a duty to cooperate through the International Marine Mammal Commission for the purpose of achieving compatible measures in respect of such marine mammal species/population(s). In determining compatible conservation and sustainable management measures, States shall:
    a. take into account existing measures established and applied in accordance with the Convention by coastal States alone or by coastal States acting in cooperation through regional and/or international agreement in areas of national jurisdiction and ensure that the effectiveness of such measures is not undermined, as appropriate;
    b. take into account existing measures established and applied in accordance with the Convention through appropriate regional and/or international agreements for the high seas;
    c. take into account the biological characteristics, including and in particular life-history characteristics, of marine mammal species/population(s) and the relationships among the species/population(s), human take or other use of them, and environmental and/or geographical particularities of each region, including the extent to which the species/population(s) occur and are taken in areas under national jurisdiction; and
    d. ensure that such measures do not result in harmful impact on the living marine resources as a whole.

Draft Implementing Agreement

3. In giving effect to their duty to cooperate, States, <u>through the Commission</u>, shall make every effort to agree on compatible conservation and <u>sustainable</u> management measures within a reasonable period of time.
4. In giving effect to their duty to cooperate, States, <u>through regional marine mammal organizations/arrangements, shall make every effort to adopt, apply, and/or implement</u> conservation and <u>sustainable management measures</u> within a reasonable period of time.
5. <u>If the duties identified in paragraphs 3 or 4 cannot be reached</u> within a reasonable period of time, any of the States concerned may invoke the procedures for the settlement of disputes provided for in Part <u>XI</u>.
6. Pending agreement on compatible conservation and <u>sustainable</u> management measures, <u>the commercial moratorium on all cetacean species regulated by the IWC shall continue in effect until such time as agreement can be reached through the International Marine Mammal Commission on the appropriate course of action. The "Scientific Permit" exception to the commercial moratorium found in Article VIII of the ICRW commercial moratorium shall no longer be available for States Parties</u>. In the event <u>that adherence to either provisional arrangement described above is contested</u>, any of the concerned States may, for the purpose of obtaining provisional measures, submit the dispute to a court or tribunal in accordance with the procedures for settlement of disputes provided for in Part <u>XI</u>.
7. Provisional arrangements or measures entered into or prescribed pursuant to paragraph <u>6</u> shall take into account the provisions of this Part, shall have due regard to the rights and obligations of all States concerned, shall not jeopardize or hamper the reaching of final agreement on compatible conservation and <u>sustainable</u> management measures, and shall be without prejudice to the final outcome of any dispute settlement procedure.
8. Coastal States, <u>directly or through the International Marine Mammal Commission or regional marine mammal organizations or arrangements</u>, shall regularly inform States <u>in the region</u> of the measures they have adopted for <u>marine mammals</u> within areas under their national jurisdiction.
9. States <u>taking marine mammals</u> on the high seas, <u>directly or through the International Marine Mammal Commission or regional marine mammal organizations or arrangements</u>, shall inform other interested States of the measures they have adopted for regulating the activities of vessels flying their flag, which <u>take or intend to take marine mammals</u> on the high seas.[45]

PART III THE INTERNATIONAL MARINE MAMMAL COMMISSION

Article 9 International Marine Mammal Commission

<u>The States Parties hereby establish</u> an international organization that shall be known as <u>the International Marine Mammal Commission, hereinafter referred to as the Commission,</u>[46] <u>which shall function in conformity with the following Articles.</u>[47]

Article 10 Objective of the Commission

The objective of the Commission shall be the pursuit of long-term conservation and sustainable management of marine mammals and effective implementation of this Agreement.[48]

Article 11 Structure of the Commission

1. The Commission is composed of one member appointed by each State Party, who may be accompanied by their advisors.[49]
2. The Commission shall be the decision-making body of this Agreement.[50]
3. The Commission may invite other experts to attend its meetings.[51]
4. The Commission shall elect from its own members a President and Vice-President, shall establish its own rules of procedure[52] and the rules for any subsidiary body it may establish, as well as financial rules governing the funding of the Secretariat.[53]
5. The States Parties shall make every effort to make decisions by consensus.[54] If consensus cannot be achieved, the Commission shall make decisions at its meetings based on a simple majority of those members[55] present and voting,[56] except that financial decisions, amendments to this Agreement, and the creation and amendment of the Annex (which includes, inter alia, the Management Plan and other conservation and sustainable management measures) shall require a two-thirds majority vote among those members present and voting.[57] Each member shall have one vote.[58]
6. For the purposes of the Article, "members present and voting" means Commission members present and casting an affirmative or negative vote.[59]

Article 12 Functions of the Commission

1. The functions of the Commission shall be:
    a. to provide a forum for the international conservation, sustainable management, and study of marine mammals;[60]
    b. to establish[61] from its own members and advisors[62] the Scientific Committee, Indigenous and Cultural/Artisanal Subsistence Take Committee, and/or other Sustainable Management Committees, as appropriate;
    c. to establish guidelines and objectives for the work of the Scientific Committee, Indigenous and Cultural/Artisanal Subsistence Take Committee, and/or other Sustainable Management Committees;[63]
    d. to approve the adequacy of existing or proposed regional marine mammal organizations and/or regional marine mammal arrangements. Once approved, the regional organization/agreement is qualified to perform regional organization/arrangement functions as provided elsewhere in this Agreement. Commission approval can be rescinded, as appropriate;

Draft Implementing Agreement

- e. to <u>independently or in conjunction with the Scientific Committee, Indigenous and Cultural/Artisanal Subsistence Take Committee, and/ or other relevant Sustainable Management Committee(s) or regional/ international organizations/agencies</u>:
    - i. encourage, recommend, and/or organize studies and investigations relating to <u>marine mammal conservation and sustainable management</u>;
    - ii. collect and analyze statistical information concerning the current condition and<u>/or</u> trend of <u>marine mammal species/ population(s) and the direct and/or indirect impacts of human activity on said species/population(s); and</u>
    - iii. study, appraise, and disseminate information regarding methods of <u>conserving and sustainably managing marine mammal populations.</u>[64]
- f. <u>to establish conservation and sustainable management measures</u> that form part of the Annex and pertain to the following matters:
    - i. <u>approval of a Management Plan, as recommended by the Scientific Committee</u>;
    - ii. <u>approval of monitoring, reporting, and compliance requirements that accompany the adoption, application, and/or implementation of the Management Plan</u>;
    - iii. <u>approval of total allowable commercial take limits for those species whose take is within the regulatory competence of the Commission, as set by the Scientific Committee through application of the Management Plan</u>;
    - iv. <u>distribution of allowable commerical take quotas to regional marine mammal organizations or arrangements, upon the request of an approved regional marine mammal organization/ arrangement</u>;
    - v. <u>approval of Indigenous and/or Cultural/Artisanal take as recommended by the Indigenous and Cultural/Artisanal Subsistence Take Committee in conjunction with the Scientific Committee</u>;
    - vi. <u>approval of individual Marine Protected Areas, or a network of Marine Protected Areas, as recommended by the Scientific Committee</u>;
    - vii. <u>designation of</u> protected and unprotected species;
    - viii. <u>designation of</u> open and closed <u>seasons for approved takes</u>;
    - ix. <u>designation of</u> open and closed waters, <u>in conjunction with</u> Marine Protected Area designation;
    - x. <u>approval of</u> gear and apparatus <u>type and specification used for marine mammal take</u>;
    - xi. <u>approval of</u> size limits for species <u>subject to an approved take</u>;
    - xii. <u>measures to combat illegal, unreported, and unregulated marine mammal take</u>;
    - xiii. <u>measures to adequately and appropriately respond to and mitigate the problem of by-catch</u>;

xiv. measures to adequately and appropriately respond to and mitigate the direct and/or indirect effects of climate change, by-catch, ship-strikes, habitat degradation, pollution (chemical, physical, and noise), ocean dumping, and marine mammal tourism, as appropriate; and

xv. approval of any other conservation and sustainable management measures the Commission deems necessary for marine mammals. This includes consideration of recommendations from the Scientific Committee, Indigenous and Cultural/Artisanal Subsistence Take Committee, and/or other Sustainable Management Committees.[65]

g. to approve and disseminate best-practice standards and guidance documents, as produced by the Scientific Committee, Indigenous and Cultural/Artisanal Subsistence Take Committee, and/or other Sustainable Management Committees, and/or otherwise;

h. to recommend to any or all States Parties, as appropriate, on any matters relating to marine mammal conservation and sustainable management and to the objective of this Agreement, including model domestic legislation;[66]

i. to contact, through the Secretariat, the executive bodies of conventions dealing with matters covered by this Agreement with a view to establishing appropriate forms of cooperation with them;[67]

j. to administer the financial mechanism established in Article 46;

k. to promote the peaceful settlement of disputes in accordance with Part XI;

l. to arrange for the publication of reports on its activities, independently or in conjunction with other organizations and/or agencies, as appropriate, as well as statistical, scientific, and other pertinent information relating to marine mammal conservation and sustainable management; and

m. to review the functioning of regional marine mammal organizations and/or arrangements and, if necessary, alter, reduce and/or rescind approved takes in the event that the regional organization and/or arrangement is failing to properly adopt, apply, and/or implement said conservation and sustainable management measures.[68]

2. Performance of the functions listed in paragraph 1 shall be guided by the best available scientific information, evidence, and knowledge.

Article 13 Meeting of the Commission

1. The Commission shall meet within one year of entry into force of this Agreement. Thereafter, ordinary meetings of the Commission shall be held not less than once every two years to consider the progress made and difficulties encountered since the last ordinary meeting, and to consider and decide upon:[69]

    a. the latest report of the Secretariat;[70]

    b. consideration of, approval of, and/or amendment to, conservation and sustainable management measures;[71]

c. consideration and/or establishment of committees as required by this Agreement or otherwise deemed necessary;[72]
d. the establishment and review of financial arrangements and the adoption of a budget for the forthcoming year;[73]
e. the time and venue for the next annual ordinary meeting;[74]
f. any other item relevant to this Agreement circulated among the members by a member or by the Secretariat not later than 90 days before the meeting, including proposals to amend the Agreement and its Annex.[75]

2. Extraordinary meetings of the Commission shall be convened by the Secretariat on the written request of at least two-thirds of the members.[76]
3. The following shall be entitled to send observers to ordinary or extraordinary meetings: the secretaries of the Convention of Migratory Species of Wild Animals; the Agreement on the Conservation of Small Cetaceans of the Baltic and North Seas; the Agreement on the Conservation of Cetaceans of the Black Sea, Mediterranean Sea and Contiguous Atlantic Area; the Convention on the International Trade in Endangered Species of Wild Fauna and Flora; the International Maritime Organization; the United Nations Framework Convention on Climate Change; the Intergovernmental Panel on Climate Change; the Antarctic Treaty; the Convention for the Prevention of Marine Pollution from Landbased Sources; the Convention on the Prevention of Marine Pollution by Dumping of Wastes and Other Matter 1972 and 1996 Protocol Thereto; the Convention on Biological Diversity; the North Atlantic Marine Mammal Commission; the International Union for the Conservation of Nature; Regional Fisheries Management Organizations; the United Nations Environment Programme; and the United Nations Food and Agriculture Organization.[77]
4. Any other body qualified in marine mammal conservation and sustainable management,[78] or nongovernmental organization qualified in the area of marine mammal conservation,[79] may apply to the Secretariat not less than 90 days in advance of the meeting to be allowed to be represented by observers,[80] in accordance with the rules of procedure established by the Secretariat.[81] The Secretariat shall communicate such applications to the members at least 60 days before the meeting, and observers shall be entitled to be present unless that is opposed not less than 30 days before the meeting by at least one-third of the members.[82]
5. Participation by any body and/or organization named in paragraph 3 or approved in accordance with paragraph 4 shall occur in accordance with the procedures established by the Secretariat, and such observers shall be entitled to active participation but not eligible to vote.[83]
6. The Secretariat shall prepare and circulate a report of the meeting to all members and observers within 90 days of the closure of the meeting.[84]

Article 14 Amendment of This Agreement

1. The Agreement and its Annex may be amended at any meeting of the members, and proposals for amendment may be made by any member.[85] The text of any proposed amendments shall be communicated to the Secretariat at least 90 days before the opening of the meeting and shall be provided by

the Secretariat to every member at least 60 days before the meeting.[86] The Commission shall make every effort to reach agreement on any proposed amendments by way of consensus, and there shall be no voting on them until all efforts at consensus have been exhausted. If all efforts at consensus have been exhausted, and no agreement reached, the amendment shall by a last resort be adopted by a two-thirds majority vote of the members present and voting at the meeting in accordance with Article 11.[87]

2. Once adopted, amendments to this Agreement shall be open for signature at the United Nations Headquarters by States Parties for twelve months from the date of adoption, unless otherwise provided in the amendment itself.[88]
3. Amendments to this Agreement shall enter into force for the States Parties ratifying or acceding to them on the thirtieth day following the deposit of instruments of ratification or accession by two-thirds of the States Parties. Thereafter, for each State Party ratifying or acceding to an amendment after the deposit of the required number of instruments, the amendment shall enter into force on the thirtieth day following the deposit of its instrument of ratification or accession.[89] An Amendment may provide that a smaller or a larger number of ratifications or accessions shall be required for its entry into force than are required by this article.[90]
4. Articles 56 [Ratification], 57 [Accession], and 65 [Authentic texts] apply to all amendments to this Agreement.[91]
5. A State that becomes a Party to this Agreement after the entry into force of amendments in accordance with paragraph 3 shall, failing an expression of a different intention by that State:
   a. be considered as a Party to this Agreement as so amended; and
   b. be considered as a Party to the unamended Agreement in relation to any State Party not bound by the amendment.[92]

Article 15 Annex of This Agreement

1. The Annex forms an integral part of this Agreement and, unless expressly provided otherwise, a reference to this Agreement or to one of its Parts includes a reference to the Annex relating thereto.[93]
2. The Annex may be revised by the Commission in accordance with Article 11.[94] The Commission should make every effort to reach agreement on Annex amendment by way of consensus and there should be no voting on proposed amendments until all efforts at consensus have been exhausted. Annex amendments that receive a two-thirds vote in favor of acceptance shall enter into force for all State Parties. It is not possible to reserve to an Annex amendment.[95]

Article 16 The Scientific Committee

1. The Scientific Committee shall consist of scientific experts appointed by the States Parties.[96]
2. Subject to Commission approval, the Scientific Committee may invite other experts to participate in the conduct of its work and observers shall be entitled to active participation.[97]

Draft Implementing Agreement   339

3. The Scientific Committee shall be responsible for:
   a. providing scientific assessments of the conservation status of marine mammal species/population(s);[98]
   b. providing scientific advice in response to requests from the:
      i. Commission;
      ii. Secretariat;
      iii. Indigenous and Cultural/Artisanal Subsistence Take Committee; and
      iv. other Sustainable Management Committees, as appropriate; utilizing the best available scientific information, evidence and knowledge;[99]
   c. designing, coordinating and recommending to the Commission a Management Plan for marine mammals subject to Commission approved catch limits, utilizing the best available scientific information, evidence, and knowledge;[100]
   d. proposing the total allowable take limits for marine mammal species regulated by the Commission, pursuant to the Management Plan, by utilizing the best available scientific information, evidence and knowledge, and in accordance with the guiding principles of this Agreement;[101]
   e. proposing, in conjunction with the Indigenous and Cultural/Artisanal Subsistence Take Committee, recommended subsistence take limits;
   f. recommending to the Commission:
      i. the establishment of a network of Marine Protected Areas to achieve ecosystem based-management. This network can include areas of the high seas and areas within national jurisdiction (with coastal State consent) and shall be designed in cooperation with other international organizations and without prejudice to other international agreements, as facilitated by the Secretariat;
      ii. protected and unprotected species; and
      iii. open and closed waters;[102]
   g. Working cooperatively with the Commission, Indigenous and Cultural/Artisanal Subsistence Take Committee and other Sustainable Management Committees, as appropriate, to produce best-practice standards and guidelines for activities that directly and/or indirectly impact the sustainable management of marine mammals, including but not limited to:
      i. marine mammal tourism and other forms of ecotourism, as appropriate;
      ii. by-catch mitigation;
      iii. mitigation of sound/noise in the marine environment;
      iv. humane killing techniques and killing technologies and associated welfare issues; and
      v. education and training programs for those who directly take or otherwise use marine mammals.[103]

Article 17 Indigenous and Cultural/Artisanal Subsistence Take Committee

1. The Indigenous and Cultural/Artisanal Subsistence Take Committee shall consist of experts appointed by States Parties.
2. Subject to Commission approval, the Indigenous and Cultural/Artisanal Subsistence Take Committee may invite other experts to participate in the conduct of its work, and observers shall be entitled to active participation.[104]
3. For the purposes of this Agreement, and in guiding the work of the Indigenous and Cultural/Artisanal Subsistence Take Committee and the Commission:
    a. "Indigenous" is used as a generic, umbrella term that encompasses other, sometimes preferred, titles including, inter alia, tribe, ethnic group, band, first nations, and first people,[105] and includes, inter alia, those peoples for which "aboriginal subsistence whaling (ASW)" is currently authorized by the IWC.[106] It also includes those peoples that, despite not being recognized pursuant to the ASW exemption at the IWC, meet and/or sufficiently fulfill, inter alia, the following criteria:
        i. the people self-identify as ethnically distinct;
        ii. the people have historically experienced significant exploitation, disruption, or dislocation;
        iii. the people have a lengthy connection with the region in question; and
        iv. the people desire to retain a distinct identity.
    This inquiry can also be assisted by the following indicia:
        i. the people are not the dominant group in the particular State;
        ii. the people identify a strong cultural association with an identified location;
        iii. the people demonstrate historical continuity of occupation, likely by descent, with previous occupants of an identified location;
        iv. the people demonstrate sociocultural and/or socioeconomic differences from the surrounding population;
        v. the people demonstrate distinctive traits, such as language, race, spiritual, or material culture; and
        vi. the people are perceived as Indigenous by the surrounding population and/or recognized as Indigenous in national/local laws/regulations/administrative processes.[107]
    b. "Cultural" means a marine mammal take that, despite not being conducted by peoples who qualify as Indigenous, is traditional in that it has a history of occurrence, has a transference of knowledge, occurs locally, represents a core aspect of community for the people concerned, and/or qualifies as an important food source.[108] The loss of this subsistence take would likely have a significant detrimental impact upon the peoples in question;[109]
    c. "Artisanal" means local, family-oriented hunting, producing, and consuming activities that are based largely on traditional knowledge that demonstrate sustainability. Artisanal use does not preclude community-scale informal trading in marine mammal products;[110]

Draft Implementing Agreement   341

   d. "Subsistence" means that the processes and procedures of marine
       mammal take, production, and distribution are locally organized
       (i.e., family- or kinship-centered), organized and/or structured in
       a manner that is separate and distinct from modern regulatory or
       market-based controls, and carried out primarily to satisfy nutritional
       demands. Subsistence take does not prevent limited, localized trade
       and/or monetized commerce, and it does not require the application
       of traditional techniques/technology to qualify as such.[111]
4. The Indigenous and Cultural/Artisanal Subsistence Take Committee shall,
   inter alia:
   a. review applications from States Parties, on behalf of groups within
       their territorial borders that identify as Indigenous, Cultural, or
       Artisanal for take-quota allocations on the basis of a proposed
       subsistence take;[112]
   b. employ the following factors in determining whether an Indigenous,
       Cultural, or Artisanal application warrants take-quota allocation:
       i.   the application supports a socially defined group that shares
            the necessary social arrangement to qualify for an Indigenous,
            Cultural, or Artisanal take as the maintenance of this social
            arrangement is significantly dependent upon a marine mammal
            take or the processing/consumption of marine mammal products.
            Non-economic benefits/purposes are required;
       ii. the application supports a geographically limited take that is
            associated with coastal and/or shore-based communities or
            aggregations. Marine mammal take beyond areas of national
            jurisdiction will not be permissible unless all other criteria
            identified in this paragraph is established;
       iii. the application supports social reproducibility in that the rules
            and knowledge directing the marine mammal take in question
            are passed intergenerationally within the same community/
            aggregation, usually in an oral manner and over an extended
            period of time;
       iv. the application supports a take that is valued multidimensionally,
            be it historically, culturally, socially, economically, and
            nutritionally (as an important aspect of the preferred diet).
            Economic significance may be important but in isolation is
            insufficient to satisfy the criteria;
       v.   the application supports historical evidence of use of the species in
            question in an attempt to avoid unnecessary species shifting; and
       vi. the application indicates that effective monitoring for
            sustainability of the take will occur and that the take will
            otherwise enable biological sustainability;[113]
   c. coordinate with the Scientific Committee to assess whether the marine
       mammal species/population(s) in question can support a subsistence
       take, in accordance with paragraph 4;
   d. recommend catch-quota allocations for Indigenous, Cultural, and/or
       Artisanal take to the Commission;

e. review and/or consider the appropriateness of other conservation and sustainable management measures as they relate to Indigenous, Cultural, and/or Artisanal take or other uses.
5. Notwithstanding the definition of "subsistence" provided in paragraph 3(d), the Indigenous and Cultural/Artisanal Subsistence Take Committee may work with the Commission and other international organizations, as appropriate, to create a subsistence certification program, which enables trade in marine mammal products beyond the local level so long as such trade otherwise complies with international law.[114]
6. Indigenous, Cultural, and/or Artisanal subsistence take shall not be permitted to endanger any marine mammal species/population(s) with extinction or to frustrate the other goals of this Agreement. The Indigenous and Cultural/Artisanal Take Committee shall not recommend to the Commission, and the Commission shall not approve, catch-quota allocations for Indigenous, Cultural, and/or Artisanal subsistence take if the species is threatened with extinction, as determined by the Scientific Committee using best available scientific evidence and knowledge and IUCN Red List criteria. If uncertainty exists, no catch-quota allocations shall be given, in accordance with Article 7 [Precautionary Principle] of this Agreement.[115]

Article 18 Sustainable Management Committees

1. The Commission may establish, from among its own members and advisors, such Sustainable Management Committees as it considers necessary to perform the functions it authorizes.[116]
2. Sustainable Management Committees shall, with respect to issues related to marine mammal species/population(s) within their respective mandates and areas of expertise:
   a. recommend to the Commission measures for the conservation and sustainable management of marine mammals;
   b. recommend to the Commission best-practice guidelines or standards for the conservation and sustainable management of marine mammals;[117]
   c. working cooperatively with the Scientific Committee and/or Indigenous and Cultural/Artisanal Subsistence Take Committee, as appropriate, to produce best-practice standards and guidelines for activities that directly and/or indirectly impact the conservation and sustainable management of marine mammals, including inter alia:
      i. marine mammal tourism and other forms of ecotourism, as appropriate;
      ii. bycatch mitigation;
      iii. mitigation of sound/noise in the marine environment;
      iv. humane killing techniques and killing technologies and associated welfare issues; and

v. education and training programs for those who take or otherwise use marine mammals.[118]
3. Recommend areas that require further study or research to the Commission.[119]

Article 19 The Secretariat

1. The Commission shall establish a Secretariat.
2. The functions of the Secretariat shall be:
   a. to arrange for and service Commission meetings as provided for in article 15;
   b. to prepare reports on the execution of its functions under this Agreement and present them to the Commission at meetings;
   c. to attend the annual meetings of other relevant international bodies and, in particular, to lobby for the adoption of regulatory mechanisms, standards, guidelines, and/or decisions that promote marine mammal conservation and sustainable management;[120]
   d. to coordinate with other relevant international bodies and, in particular to enter into such administrative and contractual arrangements as may be required for the effective discharge of its functions; and
   e. to perform such other functions as may be determined by the Commission or contemplated in the Annex to this Agreement.[121]
3. At its first ordinary meeting, the Commission shall designate, on an interim or permanent basis, the Secretariat from among those existing competent international organizations that have signified their willingness to carry out the Secretariat functions under this Agreement.[122]

Article 20 Transparency in Activities of the Commission, Scientific Committee, Indigenous and Cultural/Artisanal Subsistence Take Committee and Sustainable Management Committees

1. The Commission shall provide for transparency in its decision-making process and other activities.
2. The Commission shall provide for transparency in the decision-making process and other activities of the Scientific Committee, the Indigenous and Cultural/Artisanal Subsistence Take Committee, and other Sustainable Management Committees.
3. Representatives from regional marine mammal organizations/arrangements, representatives from intergovernmental organizations, and representatives from nongovernmental organizations concerned with marine mammal conservation and sustainable management shall have timely access to the record and reports of the Commission, the Scientific Committee, the Indigenous and Cultural/Artisanal Subsistence Take Committee, and other Sustainable Management Committees, subject to the procedural rules on access to them, which shall not be unduly restrictive.[123]

PART IV REGIONAL MARINE MAMMAL ORGANIZATIONS

Article 21 Cooperation for Application and Implementation of Conservation and Management

1. In addition to the international cooperation provided by the Commission in Part III of this Agreement, coastal States and States interested in marine mammal conservation and sustainable management shall pursue cooperation and implementation of the Agreement and its Annex either directly or through appropriate regional marine mammal organizations or arrangements, taking into account the specific characteristics of the region, to ensure effective conservation and sustainable management of marine mammals.
2. States shall enter into consultations in good faith and without delay, particularly where there is evidence that the marine mammal species/population(s) in question may be threatened by an existing take, under consideration for a proposed take, or otherwise threatened by other human action or environmental factors. To this end, regional consultation may be initiated at the request of the Commission or any interested State with a view to establishing appropriate arrangements to ensure conservation and sustainable management of marine mammals. Pending agreement on such arrangements, States Parties shall observe the provisions of this Agreement and shall act in good faith, in accordance with the directions of the Commission as the primary international organization responsible for marine mammal conservation and sustainable management, and with due regard to the rights, interests, and duties of other States.
3. Where a regional marine mammal organization or arrangement has the competence to adopt, apply, or implement the conservation and sustainable management measures established by the Commission, States taking those particular marine mammal species/population(s) on the high seas and relevant coastal States shall give further effect to their duty to cooperate by becoming members or participants in the appropriate regional marine mammal organization, or by agreeing to apply the conservation and sustainable management measures established by said organization. States having a real interest in the marine mammal species/population(s) concerned may become members of such organization or participants in such arrangements. The terms of participation in such organization shall not preclude such States from membership or participation; nor shall they be applied in a manner that discriminates against any State or group of States having a real interest in the marine mammal species/population(s).
4. Only those States that are members of such an organization or participants in such an arrangement, or that agree to apply the conservation and sustainable management measures established by such organization or arrangement, shall have access to the take of the marine mammal species/population(s) to which those measures apply. The organization shall apply to the Commission for the allocation of quotas to take said marine mammal species/population(s). Nothing in this section prevents the competence of the organization to decide to not apply for said quotas or to set zero catch quotas for said species/population(s).

5. Where there is no regional marine mammal organization or arrangement to <u>adopt, apply, or implement</u> conservation and <u>sustainable</u> management measures for a particular <u>marine mammal species/population(s)</u>, relevant coastal States and States <u>that take or intend to take from the species/population(s)</u> on the high seas in the region shall cooperate to establish such an organization or enter into other appropriate arrangements to ensure conservation and <u>sustainable</u> management of <u>such species/population(s),</u> and shall participate in the work of the organization or arrangement. <u>The appropriateness of an existing or proposed regional organization/arrangement is to be approved by the Commission.</u>[124]

Article 22 Regional Marine Mammal Organizations and Arrangements

1. In establishing <u>regional marine mammal organizations</u> or in entering into <u>regional marine mammal arrangements for marine mammal species/population(s)</u>, States shall agree, inter alia, on:
   a. the <u>marine mammal species/population(s)</u> to which <u>its adoption, application, or implementation of conservation and sustainable management measures</u> apply, taking into account the biological characteristics of the species/population(s) concerned and the nature of the <u>take and/or use</u> involved;
   b. the area of application, taking into account the characteristics of the region, including socioeconomic, geographical, and environmental factors;
   c. the relationship between the work of the new organization or arrangement and the role, objectives, and operations of any relevant existing organization or arrangement that addresses <u>marine mammal conservation and sustainable management</u>; and
   d. the mechanisms by which the organization or arrangement <u>will contribute to, apply, or utilize the scientific advice of the Scientific Committee of the Commission,</u> including, where appropriate, the establishment of a scientific advisory body.
2. States cooperating in the formation of a <u>regional marine mammal organization or arrangement</u> shall inform other States <u>that</u> they are aware have a real interest in the work of the proposed organization or arrangement of such cooperation.[125]

Article 23 Functions of Regional Marine Mammal Organizations and Arrangements

In fulfilling their obligation to cooperate <u>through regional marine mammal organizations or arrangements that have been approved by the Commission,</u> States shall:

   a. <u>adopt, apply and implement</u> conservation and <u>sustainable</u> management measures <u>as developed by the Commission</u> to ensure the long-term conservation and sustainable management of <u>marine mammals</u>;

b. agree, as appropriate, on participatory rights such as <u>preferred take quotas and apply to the Commission for approval prior to allocating said rights</u>;
c. <u>adopt, apply, and implement</u> any generally recommended international minimum <u>best-practice</u> standards <u>or guidelines</u> for the <u>take or other use of marine mammals as produced by the Commission</u>;
d. <u>contribute to the work of the Scientific Committee, as appropriate, by</u>:
   i. obtain<u>ing</u> and evaluat<u>ing</u> scientific advice, review<u>ing</u> the status of <u>marine mammal species/population(s)</u>;
   ii. agreeing on standards for collection, reporting, verification, and exchange of data on <u>marine mammal species/population(s)</u>;
   iii. compil<u>ing</u> and disseminat<u>ing</u> accurate and complete statistical data to ensure that the best scientific evidence is available, while maintaining confidentiality where appropriate; and
   iv. promoting and conducting scientific assessments of marine mammal species/population(s) and disseminating the results thereof.
e. <u>adopt, apply, and implement</u> the cooperative means for effective monitoring, control, surveillance, and enforcement <u>as produced by the Commission</u>;
f. agree on means by which the interests of new members of the organization or new participants in the arrangement will be accommodated;
g. agree on decision-making procedures <u>that</u> facilitate the adoption, <u>application, and implementation</u> of conservation and <u>sustainable</u> management measures in a timely and effective manner;
h. promote the peaceful settlement of disputes in accordance with Part <u>XI</u>;
i. ensure the full cooperation of their relevant national agencies and industries in the <u>adoption, application, or implementation of the conservation and sustainable management measures produced by the Commission</u>;
j. give due publicity to the conservation and <u>sustainable</u> management measures established by <u>the Commission as adopted, applied, and implemented by the</u> organization or arrangement; and
k. <u>report to the Commission on its functioning on an annual basis</u>.[126]

Article 24 New Members or Participants

1. In determining the nature and extent of participatory rights for new<u>/ prospective</u> members of a <u>regional marine mammal organization</u>, or for new/<u>prospective</u> participants in a <u>regional marine mammal arrangement</u>, States shall take into account, inter alia:
   a. <u>membership in the Commission</u>;
   b. the status of the <u>marine mammal species/population(s)</u> and any existing <u>take and/or other use</u>;
   c. the respective interests <u>and any existing take and/or other uses</u> of new and existing members or participants;
   d. the respective contributions of new and existing members or participants to conservation and <u>sustainable</u> management of <u>marine mammals</u>, to the collection and provision of accurate data and to scientific research on the <u>species/population(s)</u>;
   e. the needs of coastal States who depend on <u>marine mammals through a take and/or other use</u>;

f. the needs of coastal States whose economies are dependent on <u>a take and/or other use of marine mammals</u>; and
g. the interests of developing States from the region in whose areas of national jurisdiction the <u>marine mammal species/population(s)</u> also occur.[127]

2. <u>Any alteration to participatory rights that affects the substance of what has been approved by the Commission requires new approval prior to implementation.</u>

Article 25 Transparency in Activities of Regional Marine Mammal Organizations and Arrangements

1. States shall provide for transparency in the decision-making process, <u>the adoption, application, and implementation of conservation and sustainable management measures,</u> and other activities of <u>regional marine mammal organizations and arrangements</u>.
2. Representatives from <u>the Commission and from</u> other intergovernmental organizations and nongovernmental organizations <u>concerned with marine mammal conservation and sustainable management</u> shall be afforded the opportunity to take part in meetings of <u>regional marine mammal organizations and arrangements</u> as observers or otherwise, as appropriate, in accordance with the procedures of the organization or arrangement concerned. Such procedures shall not be unduly restrictive in this regard. Such intergovernmental organizations and nongovernmental organizations shall have timely access to the records and reports of such organizations and arrangements, subject to the procedural rules on access to them.[128]

Article 26 Strengthening of Existing Organizations and Arrangements

States shall cooperate to strengthen existing <u>regional marine mammal organizations and arrangements</u> in order to improve their effectiveness in <u>adopting, applying, and implementing marine mammal</u> conservation and <u>sustainable</u> management measures.[129]

Article 27 Collection and Provision of Information and Cooperation in Scientific Research

1. States shall ensure that vessels flying their flag <u>that take marine mammals</u> provide such information as may be necessary in order to fulfill the States' obligations under this Agreement. To this end, States shall:
   a. collect and exchange scientific, technical, and statistical data with respect to <u>marine mammal species/population(s)</u>;
   b. ensure that data are collected in sufficient detail to facilitate effective <u>marine mammal species/population</u> assessment and are provided in a timely manner to fulfill the requirements of the <u>Commission and/or regional marine mammal organizations or arrangements</u>; and
   c. take appropriate measures to verify the accuracy of such data.

2. States shall cooperate, through <u>the Commission and/or Scientific Committee</u> to:
    a. agree on the specifications of data and the format in which they are to be provided, taking into account the nature of the <u>marine mammal species/population(s)</u>; and
    b. to develop and share analytical techniques and <u>species/population(s)</u> assessment methodologies to improve measures for the conservation and <u>sustainable</u> management of <u>marine mammal species/population(s)</u>.
3. Consistent with Part XIII of the Convention, States shall cooperate, either directly or through the Commission, to strengthen scientific research capacity in the field of <u>marine mammals</u> and promote scientific research related to the conservation and <u>sustainable</u> management of <u>marine mammal species/population(s)</u> for the benefit of all. To this end, a State, <u>regional marine mammal organization and arrangement, or the Commission</u> shall actively promote publication and dissemination to any interested States of the results of that research and information relating to its objectives and methods and, to the extent practicable, shall facilitate the participation of scientists from those States in such research.[130]

PART V NONMEMBERS AND NONPARTICIPANTS

Article 28 Nonmembers of the Commission, or Regional Organizations and Nonparticipants in Regional Arrangements

1. A State <u>that</u> is not a member of <u>the Commission and/or a member of a regional marine mammal organization or participant in a regional marine mammal arrangement</u>, and <u>that</u> does not otherwise agree to adopt, apply, and implement the conservation and <u>sustainable</u> management measures established by the <u>Commission and as implemented by the regional marine mammal organization/arrangement</u>, is not discharged from the obligation to cooperate, in accordance with the Convention and this Agreement, in the conservation and <u>sustainable</u> management of the <u>marine mammal species/population(s)</u>.
2. Such State shall not authorize vessels flying its flag to engage in operations for <u>the take of marine mammal species/population(s) that</u> are subject to the conservation and <u>sustainable</u> management measures established by the <u>Commission and adopted, applied, and implemented by the regional organization or arrangement</u>.
3. States <u>that</u> are members <u>of the Commission and/or a member of a regional marine mammal organization or participant in a regional marine mammal arrangement</u> shall exchange information with respect to the activities of vessels flying the flags of States <u>that</u> are neither <u>members of the Commission and/or members of the organization nor participants in the arrangement</u>, and are engaged in activities that impact the relevant <u>marine mammal species/population(s)</u>. They shall take measures consistent with this Agreement and international law to deter activities of such vessels <u>that</u> undermine the effectiveness of the <u>Commission's</u> conservation and <u>sustainable</u> management measures <u>as adopted, applied, and implemented regionally</u>.[131]

PART VI DUTIES OF THE FLAG STATE

Article 29 Duties of the Flag State

1. A State <u>that has agreed to the competence of the Commission to exert regulatory control in areas of national jurisdiction</u> shall take such measures as may be necessary to ensure that vessels flying its flag comply with <u>international measures, as agreed to by the Commission and adopted, applied, and/or implemented regionally;</u> and that such vessels do not engage in activity <u>that</u> undermines the effectiveness of such measures.
2. A State whose vessels <u>take marine mammals</u> on the high seas shall take such measures as may be necessary to ensure that vessels flying its flag comply with <u>international conservation and sustainable management measures, as agreed to by the Commission and adopted, applied, and/or implemented regionally</u>, and that such vessels do not engage in any activity <u>that</u> undermines the effectiveness of such measures.
3. A State shall authorize the use of vessels flying its flag for <u>the take of marine mammals</u> on the high seas where it is able to exercise effectively its responsibilities in respect of such vessels under the Convention and this Agreement.
4. Measures to be taken by a State in respect of vessels flying its flag shall include:
   a. control of such vessels on the high seas by means of licenses, authorizations, or permits, in accordance with any applicable procedures agreed <u>at the Commission or regionally</u>;
   b. establishment of regulations:
      i. to apply terms and conditions to the license, authorization, or permit sufficient to fulfill any obligations <u>agreed at the Commission or regionally</u>;
      ii. to prohibit the <u>take of marine mammals</u> by vessels <u>that</u> are not duly licensed or authorized to use <u>marine mammals</u>, or use on the high seas by vessels otherwise than in accordance with the terms and conditions of a license, authorization, or permit;
      iii. to require vessels <u>taking marine mammals</u> on the high seas to carry the license, authorization, or permit on board at all times and to produce it on demand for inspection by a duly authorized person; and
      iv. to ensure that vessels flying its flag do not conduct unauthorized <u>marine mammal take</u> within areas under the national jurisdiction of other States;[132]
   c. establishment <u>and maintenance</u> of a national record of vessels entitled to fly its flag and authorized to be used <u>to take marine mammals</u> on the high seas[133] and shall take such measures as may be necessary to ensure that all such fishing vessels are entered in that record;[134]
   d. requirements for marking vessels and gear for identification in accordance with uniform and internationally recognizable vessel and gear-marking systems;

e. requirements for recording and timely reporting of vessel position, take of target and non-target species, and other relevant data in accordance with standards for collection of such data established or adopted at the Commission or regionally;
f. requirements for verifying the take of target and non-target species through such means as observer programs, identification schemes, unloading reports, supervision of transshipment, and monitoring of landed catches and market statistics through DNA testing or otherwise;
g. monitoring, control, and surveillance of such vessels, their marine mammal take operations and related activities by, inter alia:
    i. the implementation of national inspection schemes and regional schemes for cooperation and enforcement pursuant to Articles 33, 34, and 35 and in accordance with best-practices as agreed at the Commission, including requirements for such vessels to permit access by duly authorized inspectors from other States;
    ii. the implementation of national observer programs and regional observer programs, in accordance with best-practices as agreed at the Commission, in which the flag State is a participant, including requirements for such vessels to permit access by observers from other States to carry out the functions agreed under the programs; and
    iii. the development and implementation of vessel monitoring systems, including, as appropriate, global positioning and satellite transmitter systems, in accordance with any national programs and those that have been agreed by the Commission or regionally;
h. regulation of transshipment on the high seas to ensure that the effectiveness of conservation and sustainable management measures is not undermined; and
i. regulation of the take of marine mammals to ensure compliance with measures agreed at the Commission and adopted, applied, and/or implemented regionally.[135]

Article 30 Exchange of Information

1. Each State Party shall make readily available to the Commission the following information with respect to each vessel used to take marine mammals on the high seas, in accordance with the national record required to be established and maintained by Article 29, paragraph 4(c):
    a. name of vessel, registration number, previous names (if known), and port of registry;
    b. previous flag (if any);
    c. International Radio Call Sign (if any);
    d. name and address of owner or owners;
    e. where and when built; and
    f. type of vessel.

2. Each State Party shall, to the extent practicable, make available to the Commission the following additional information with respect to each vessel entered in the record required to be established and maintained by Article 29, paragraph 4(c):
   a. name and address of operator (manager) or operators (managers) (if any);
   b. type of take method or methods;
   c. vessel specifications including, inter alia, length, molded depth, beam, gross register tonnage, and power of main engine or engines; and
   d. any other information the Commission deems reasonably necessary.
3. Each State Party shall promptly notify the Commission and/or the regional marine mammal organization/arrangement of any modifications to the information listed in paragraphs 1 and 2 of this Article;
4. The Commission shall circulate periodically the information provided under paragraphs 1, 2, and 3 of this Article to all States Parties, and, on request, individually to any State Party. The Commission shall also, subject to any restrictions imposed by the State Party, provide such information on request individually to any regional marine mammal organization or regional marine mammal arrangement.[136]

PART VII COMPLIANCE AND ENFORCEMENT

Article 31 Duties of All States

All States Parties and regional organizations/arrangements shall ensure compliance with this Agreement and with established conservation and sustainable management measures by all nationals. To this end, all States Parties shall:

a. take legislative, administrative, or policy measures, as appropriate, with the aim of ensuring compliance by their nationals, including, where appropriate, making contravention of duties imposed by this Agreement or undermining of conservation and sustainable management measures an offense under national legislation, and taking all appropriate steps to discourage nationals from participating in activities in breach of this Agreement; and

b. ensure that sanctions applicable in respect of such contraventions shall be of sufficient gravity as to be effective in securing compliance with the requirements of this Agreement and to deprive offenders of the benefits accruing from their illegal activities.[137]

Article 32 Compliance and Enforcement by the Flag State

1. A State shall ensure compliance by vessels flying its flag with conservation and sustainable management measures for marine mammals agreed at the Commission and adopted, applied, and/or implemented regionally. To this end, that State shall:
   a. enforce such measures irrespective of where violations occur;

b. investigate immediately and fully any alleged violation of conservation and <u>sustainable</u> management measures <u>agreed at the Commission and adopted, applied, and/or implemented regionally</u>, which may include the inspection of the vessels concerned, and report promptly to the State alleging the violation and the relevant <u>regional organization/ arrangement and Commission</u> on the progress and outcome of the investigation;
c. require any vessel flying its flag to give information to the investigating authority regarding vessel position, catches, gear, operations, and related activities in the area of the alleged violation;
d. if satisfied that sufficient evidence is available in respect of an alleged violation, refer the case to its authorities with a view to instituting proceedings without delay in accordance with its laws and, where appropriate, detain the vessel concerned; and
e. ensure that, where it has been established, in accordance with its laws, a vessel has been involved in the commission of a serious violation of such measures, the vessel does not <u>engage in the take of marine mammals</u> on the high seas until such time as all outstanding sanctions imposed by the flag State in respect of the violation have been complied with.
2. All investigations and judicial proceedings shall be carried out expeditiously. Sanctions applicable in respect of violations shall be adequate in severity to be effective in securing compliance and to discourage violations wherever they occur, and shall deprive offenders of the benefits accruing from their illegal activities. Measures applicable in respect of masters and other officers of vessels <u>that take marine mammals</u> shall include provisions <u>that</u> may permit, inter alia, refusal, withdrawal, or suspension of authorizations to serve as masters or officers on such vessels.[138]

Article 33 International Cooperation in Enforcement

1. States shall cooperate, either directly, through <u>the Commission, or</u> through regional <u>marine mammal</u> organizations or arrangements, to ensure compliance with and enforcement of conservation and <u>sustainable</u> management measures <u>for marine mammals, as agreed at the Commission and adopted, applied, and/or implemented regionally</u>.
2. A flag State conducting an investigation of an alleged violation of conservation and <u>sustainable</u> management measures for <u>marine mammals</u> may request the assistance of any other State whose cooperation may be useful in the conduct of that investigation <u>through the Secretariat of the Commission</u>. All States shall endeavor to meet reasonable requests made by a flag State in connection with such investigations.
3. A flag State may undertake such investigations directly, in cooperation with other interested States, or through the <u>Commission or</u> relevant regional <u>marine mammal organization</u> or <u>arrangement</u>. Information on the progress and outcome of the investigations shall be provided to all States having an interest in, or affected by, the alleged violation <u>through the Secretariat of the Commission</u>.

4. States shall assist each other in identifying vessels reported to have engaged in activities undermining the effectiveness of <u>conservation and sustainable management measures as agreed at the Commission and adopted, applied, and/or implemented regionally</u>.
5. States shall, to the extent permitted by national laws and regulations, establish arrangements for making available to prosecuting authorities in other States, <u>through the Secretariat of the Commission</u>, evidence relating to alleged violations of such measures.
6. Where there are reasonable grounds for believing that a vessel on the high seas has been engaged in unauthorized <u>take of marine mammals</u> within an area under the jurisdiction of a coastal State, the flag State of that vessel, at the request of the coastal State concerned, shall immediately and fully investigate the matter. The flag State shall cooperate with the coastal State in taking appropriate enforcement action in such cases and may authorize the relevant authorities of the coastal State to board and inspect the vessel on the high seas. This paragraph is without prejudice to Article 111 of the Convention [Hot pursuit].
7. States Parties <u>that</u> are members of a <u>regional marine mammal organization</u> or participants in a <u>regional marine mammal arrangement</u> may take action in accordance with international law, including through recourse to <u>regional</u> procedures established for this purpose, to deter vessels <u>that</u> have engaged in activities <u>that</u> undermine the effectiveness of or otherwise violate the <u>conservation and sustainable management measures established by the Commission and adopted, applied, and/or implemented by</u> that organization or arrangement, from <u>taking marine mammals</u> on the high seas in that region until such time as appropriate action is taken by the flag State.[139]

Article 34 Regional Cooperation in Enforcement

1. In any high seas area covered by a <u>regional marine mammal organization or arrangement</u>, a State Party <u>that</u> is a member of such organization or a participant in such arrangement may, through its duly authorized inspectors, board and inspect, in accordance with paragraph 2, vessels used for <u>taking marine mammals</u> flying the flag of another State Party to this Agreement, whether or not such State Party is also a member of the organization or a participant in the arrangement, for the purpose of ensuring compliance with conservation and <u>sustainable</u> management measures for <u>marine mammals established by the Commission and adopted, applied, and/or implemented by that organization or arrangement</u>.
2. States shall establish, <u>through the Commission</u>, procedures for boarding and inspection pursuant to paragraph 1, as well as other necessary procedures. <u>Such procedures shall be implemented regionally by regional marine mammal organizations and/or arrangements</u>. Such procedures shall be consistent with this Article and the basic procedures set out in Article <u>35</u> and shall not discriminate against nonmembers of the organization or nonparticipants in the arrangement. Boarding and inspection as well as any subsequent enforcement action shall be conducted in accordance with such

procedures. States shall give, through the Commission, due publicity to procedures established pursuant to this paragraph.
3. If, within two years of the adoption of this Agreement, the <u>Commission</u> has not established such procedures, boarding and inspection pursuant to paragraph 1, as well as any subsequent enforcement action, shall, pending the establishment of such procedures, be conducted in accordance with this Article and the basic procedures set out in Article <u>35</u>.
4. Prior to taking action under this Article, inspecting States shall, either directly or through the relevant <u>regional marine mammal organization and/or arrangement</u>, inform all States whose vessels <u>take marine mammals on the high seas in the region</u> of the form of identification issued to their duly authorized inspectors. The vessels used for boarding and inspection shall be clearly marked and identifiable as being on government service. At the time of becoming a Party to this Agreement, a State shall designate an appropriate authority to receive notifications pursuant to this Article and shall give due publicity of such designations through the relevant <u>regional marine mammal organization or arrangement</u>.
5. Where, following a boarding and inspection, there are clear grounds for believing that a vessel has engaged in any activity contrary to the conservation and sustainable management measures referred to in paragraph 1, the inspecting State shall, where appropriate, secure evidence and shall promptly notify the flag State of the alleged violation.
6. The flag State shall respond to the notification referred to in paragraph 5 within three working days of its receipt, or such other period as may be prescribed in procedures established in accordance with paragraph 2, and shall either:
   a. fulfill, without delay, its obligations under Article <u>32 [Compliance and Enforcement by the Flag State]</u> to investigate and, if evidence so warrants, take enforcement action with respect to the vessel, in which case it shall promptly inform the inspecting State of the results of the investigation and of any enforcement action taken; or
   b. authorize the inspecting State to investigate.
7. Where the flag State authorizes the inspecting State to investigate an alleged violation, the inspecting State shall, without delay, communicate the results of that investigation to the flag State. The flag State shall, if evidence so warrants, fulfill its obligations to take enforcement action with respect to the vessel. Alternatively, the flag State may authorize the inspecting State to take such enforcement action as the flag State may specify with respect to the vessel, consistent with the rights and obligations of the flag State under this Agreement.
8. Where, following boarding and inspection, there are clear grounds for believing that a vessel has committed a serious violation, and the flag State has either failed to respond or failed to take action as required under paragraphs 6 or 7, the inspectors may remain on board and secure evidence, and may require the master to assist in further investigation including, where appropriate, by bringing the vessel without delay to the nearest appropriate port, or to such other port as may be specified in procedures established in accordance with paragraph 2. The inspecting State shall

Draft Implementing Agreement

immediately inform the flag State of the name of the port to which the vessel is to proceed. The inspecting State and the flag State and, as appropriate, the port State shall take all necessary steps to ensure the well-being of the crew regardless of their nationality.

9. The inspecting State shall inform the flag State and the relevant organization or the participants in the relevant arrangements of the results of any further investigation.

10. The inspecting State shall require its inspectors to observe generally accepted international regulations, procedures, and practices relating to the safety of the vessel and the crew, and minimize interference with vessel operations. The inspecting State shall ensure that boarding and inspection is not conducted in a manner that would constitute harassment of any vessel.

11. For the purposes of this Article, a serious violation means:
    a. taking a marine mammal without a valid license, authorization, or permit issued by the flag State in accordance with Article 29, paragraph 4(a) [Duties of the Flag State];
    b. failing to maintain accurate records of take or take-related data, as required by the Commission or relevant regional marine mammal organization or arrangement, or serious misreporting of take, contrary to the catch reporting requirements of the Commission, or such organization or arrangement;
    c. taking marine mammals in a designated MPA or otherwise closed area, taking a marine mammal during a closed season, or taking a marine mammal without, or after attainment of, a take-quota established by the relevant regional marine mammal organization or arrangement in conjunction with take-limits established by the Commission;
    d. taking, or attempting to take, a marine mammal from a species/population(s) that is subject to a moratorium (globally or regionally) or for which taking is otherwise prohibited;
    e. using prohibited technology, apparatus, or gear;
    f. falsifying or concealing the markings, identity, or registration of a vessel used for taking marine mammals;
    g. concealing, tampering with, or disposing of evidence relating to an investigation;
    h. multiple violations that together constitute a serious disregard of conservation and sustainable management measures; or
    i. such other violations as may be specified by the Commission or in procedures established by the relevant regional marine mammal organization or arrangement.

12. Notwithstanding the other provisions of this Article, the flag State may, at any time, take action to fulfill its obligations under Article 32 [Compliance and Enforcement by the Flag State] with respect to an alleged violation. Where the vessel is under the direction of the inspecting State, the inspecting State shall, at the request of the flag State, release the vessel to the flag State along with full information on the progress and outcome of its investigation.

13. This Article is without prejudice to the right of the flag State to take any measures, including proceedings to impose penalties, according to its laws.
14. This Article applies mutatis mutandis to boarding and inspection by a State Party that is a member of a regional marine mammal organization or participant in a regional marine mammal arrangement and that has clear grounds for believing that a vessel flying the flag of another State Party has engaged in any activity contrary to relevant conservation and sustainable management measures referred to in paragraph 1 in the high seas area covered by such organization or arrangement, and such vessel has subsequently, during the same trip, entered into an area under the national jurisdiction of the inspecting State.
15. Where a regional marine mammal organization or arrangement has established an alternative mechanism, as approved by the Commission, which effectively discharges the obligation under this Agreement of its members or participants to ensure compliance with the conservation and sustainable management measures established by the Commission, members of such organization or participants in such arrangement may agree to limit the application of paragraph 1 as between themselves in respect of the conservation and sustainable management measures that have been established in the relevant high seas area.
16. Action taken by States other than the flag State in respect of vessels having engaged in activities contrary to conservation and sustainable management measures shall be proportionate to the seriousness of the violation.
17. Where there are reasonable grounds for suspecting that a vessel that is taking, or is reasonably suspected of taking, marine mammals on the high seas is without nationality, a State may board and inspect the vessel. Where evidence so warrants, the State may take such action as may be appropriate in accordance with international law.
18. States shall be liable for damage or loss attributable to them arising from action taken pursuant to this Article when such action is unlawful or exceeds that reasonably required in light of available information to implement the provisions of this Article.[140]

Article 35 Basic Procedures for Boarding and Inspecting Pursuant to Article 34

1. The inspecting shall ensure that its duly authorized inspectors:
   a. present credentials to the master of the vessel and produce a copy of the text of the relevant conservation and sustainable management measures or rules and regulations in force in the high seas area in question pursuant to those measures;
   b. initiate notice to the flag State at the time of boarding and inspection;
   c. do not interfere with the master's ability to communicate with the authorities of the flag State during the boarding and inspection;
   d. provide a copy of a report on the boarding and inspection to the master and to the authorities of the flag State, noting therein any objection or statement that the master wishes to have included in the report;

Draft Implementing Agreement

   e. promptly leave the vessel following the completion of the inspection if they find no evidence of a serious violation; and
   f. avoid the use of force except when and to the degree necessary to ensure the safety of the inspectors and where the inspectors are obstructed in the execution of their duties. The degree of force used shall not exceed that reasonably required in the circumstances.
2. The duly authorized inspectors of an inspecting State shall have the authority to inspect the vessel, its license or authorization, gear, <u>apparatus</u>, equipment, records, facilities, <u>marine mammal take or marine mammal</u> products, and any relevant documents necessary to verify the relevant conservation and <u>sustainable</u> management measures.
3. The flag State shall ensure that vessel masters:
   a. accept and facilitate prompt and safe boarding by the inspectors;
   b. cooperate with and assist in the inspection of the vessel conducted pursuant to these procedures;
   c. do not obstruct, intimidate, or interfere with the inspectors in the performance of their duties;
   d. allow the inspectors to communicate with the authorities of the flag State and the inspecting State during the boarding and inspection;
   e. provide reasonable facilities, including, where appropriate, food and accommodation, to the inspectors; and
   f. facilitate safe disembarkation by the inspectors.
4. In the event that the master of a vessel refuses to accept boarding and inspection in accordance with this Article and Article <u>34</u>, the flag State shall, except in circumstances where, in accordance with generally accepted international regulations, procedures, and practices relating to safety at sea, it is necessary to delay the boarding and inspection, direct the master of the vessel to submit immediately to boarding and inspection and, if the master does not comply with such direction, shall suspend the vessel's authorization to <u>take marine mammals</u> and order the vessel to return immediately to port. The flag State shall advise the inspecting State of the action it has taken when the circumstances referred to in this paragraph arise.[141]

Article 36 Measures Taken by a Port State

1. A port State has the right to take measures, in accordance with international law, to promote the effectiveness of conservation and <u>sustainable</u> management measures as <u>established by the Commission and adopted, applied, and/or implemented by regional marine mammal organizations and arrangements</u>. When taking such measures a port State shall not discriminate in form or in fact against the vessels of any State.
2. A port State may, inter alia, inspect documents, gear, <u>apparatus</u>, and <u>marine mammal take</u> on board vessels, when such vessels are voluntarily in its ports or at its offshore terminals.

3. States may adopt regulations empowering the relevant national authorities to prohibit landings and transshipments where it has been established that the catch has been taken in a manner that is contrary to, or undermines the effectiveness of conservation and <u>sustainable</u> management measures <u>as established by the Commission and adopted, applied, and/or implemented regionally</u>.
4. Nothing in this Article affects the exercise by States of their sovereignty over ports in their territory in accordance with international law.[142]

Article 37 Illegal, Unreported, and Unregulated Take

<u>States shall cooperate through the Commission and/or regional marine mammal organizations and arrangements to deter, reduce, and eliminate illegal, unreported, and unregulated take of marine mammals in accordance with international law.</u>

PART VIII REQUIREMENTS OF DEVELOPING STATES

Article 38 Recognition of the Special Requirements of Developing States

1. States shall give full recognition to the special requirements of developing States in relation to conservation and <u>sustainable management of marine mammals</u>. To this end, States shall, directly, <u>through the Commission and in accordance with this Agreement, or through</u> other appropriate international and regional organizations and bodies, provide assistance to developing States.
2. In giving effect to the duty to cooperate in the establishment <u>and implementation</u> of conservation and <u>sustainable</u> management measures <u>for marine mammals</u>, States shall take into account the special requirements of developing States, in particular:
   a. the vulnerability of developing States <u>that</u> are dependent on the exploitation of living marine resources; and
   b. the need to ensure that such measures do not result in transferring, directly or indirectly, a disproportionate burden of conservation action onto developing States.[143]

Article 39 Forms of Cooperation with Developing States

1. States shall cooperate, either directly or through regional or global organizations, <u>including the Commission</u>:
   a. to enhance the ability of developing states, in particular the least-developed among them and small island developing States, to conserve and <u>sustainably manage marine mammals</u>; and
   b. to facilitate the participation of developing States in <u>the Commission and in regional marine mammal organizations/ arrangements</u>.

2. Cooperation with developing States for the purposes set out in this Article shall include <u>and</u> be directed specifically toward, inter alia:
   a. <u>technical and technological assistance, including technology transfer, as provided in Part IX</u>;
   b. financial assistance <u>as provided in Part X, including funding the development</u> of national and regional observer programs;
   c. human resources development <u>and</u> advisory and consultative assistance;
   d. improved conservation and <u>sustainable management of marine mammals</u> through collection, reporting, verification, exchange, and analysis of scientific data and related information;
   e. monitoring, control, surveillance, compliance, and enforcement, including training and capacity-building at the local level.[144]

Article 40 Special Assistance in the Implementation of This Agreement

1. States shall cooperate through <u>the Commission</u> to assist developing States in the implementation of this Agreement, including assisting developing States to meet the costs involved in any proceedings for the settlement of disputes to which they may be parties.
2. States <u>acting through the Commission</u> should assist developing States in establishing new <u>regional marine mammal</u> organizations or arrangements, or in strengthening existing organizations or arrangements, for the conservation and <u>sustainable management of marine mammals</u>.[145]

PART IX DEVELOPMENT AND TRANSFER OF MARINE TECHNOLOGY RELATED TO MARINE MAMMALS

Article 41 Promotion of the Development and Transfer of Technology Related to Marine Mammals

1. States, directly or through <u>the Commission</u>, shall cooperate in accordance with their capabilities to promote actively the development and transfer of technology relating to <u>marine mammals</u> on fair and reasonable terms and conditions.[146]
2. <u>States, directly or through the Commission</u>, shall provide incentives to enterprises and institutions in their territories for the purposes of promoting and encouraging technology transfer to developing <u>States Parties</u> in order to enable them to create a sound and viable technological base <u>relating to marine mammals</u>.[147]

Article 42 Basic Objectives

States, directly or through <u>the Commission</u>, shall promote:

a. acquisition, evaluation, and dissemination of technological knowledge related to marine mammals and facilitate access to such information and data;
b. development of appropriate technology <u>related to marine mammals</u>;

c. development of the necessary technological infrastructure to facilitate the transfer of technology <u>related to marine mammals</u>;
d. development of human resources through training and education of nationals of developing States and countries and especially the nationals of the least-developed <u>States Parties</u>;
e. international cooperation at all levels, particularly at the regional, subregional and bilateral levels.[148]

Article 43 Measures to Achieve the Basic Objectives

In order to achieve the objectives referred to in Article <u>42</u>, States, directly or through <u>the Commission</u>, shall endeavour, inter alia, to:

a. establish programs of technical cooperation for the effective transfer of all kinds of <u>marine mammal related</u> technology to States <u>Parties that</u> may need and request technical assistance in the field, particularly <u>developing States Parties that</u> have not been able to either establish or develop their own technological capacity with respect to <u>marine mammal science and/or management</u>;
b. promote favorable conditions for the conclusion of agreements, contracts, and other similar arrangements, under equitable and reasonable conditions;
c. <u>through the Commission</u>, hold conferences, seminars, and symposia on scientific and technological subjects, in particular on policies and methods for the transfer of technology <u>related to marine mammals</u>; and
d. promote the exchange of scientists and of technological and other experts required to, <u>inter alia, establish and maintain national observer programs and to achieve other conservation and sustainable management objectives</u>.[149]

Article 44 Technical Cooperation

<u>States Parties, directly or through the Commission</u>, shall provide, on request and on mutually agreed terms and conditions, technical cooperation in favor of promoting the development of <u>the technological capability of States Parties, relating to marine mammals</u>. Such cooperation shall include assistance in the preparation of laws and regulations restricting the <u>use and preventing abuse of such technologies</u>, and shall include support toward domestic implementation and <u>toward creating or improving domestic offices relevant to these matters, including training personnel</u>.[150] <u>Technical cooperation is conducted</u> with a view accelerating the social and economic development of the developing States.[151]

PART X FINANCIAL CONSIDERATIONS

Article 45 Financial Resources

1. Each <u>State Party</u> undertakes to provide, in accordance with its capabilities, financial support and incentives to support <u>national, regional, and</u>

international marine mammal conservation and sustainable management in accordance with the objective of the Agreement.
2. The developed States Parties shall provide new and additional financial resources to enable developing States Parties to support those national, regional, and global activities necessary to achieve the objective of the Agreement. These funds shall be administered in accordance with the financial mechanism provided in Article 46. Other countries, including economies in transition, may volunteer to assume the obligation of developed States Parties. The Commission shall, at its first ordinary meeting, compose a list of developed States Parties and those States Parties that voluntarily assume the obligations of developed States Parties. This list will be reviewed and revised periodically.
3. Developed States Parties may also provide to developing States Parties financial resources related to the objective of the Agreement through bilateral, regional, and other multilateral avenues.
4. States Parties shall take full regard of the specific needs and special situation of least developed countries in their actions with regard to funding.[152]

Article 46 Financial Mechanism

1. There shall be a mechanism for the provision of financial resources to developing country States Parties for the purposes of this Agreement on a grant or concessional basis, in accordance with this Article. This mechanism shall be called the International Marine Mammal Conservation and Sustainable Management Fund [hereinafter "the Fund"]. The Fund shall function under the authority and guidance of the Commission and shall be accountable to the Commission. The operations of the Fund shall be carried out by such institutional structure as may be decided by the Commission at its first ordinary meeting. The Commission shall determine the policy, strategy, program priorities, and eligibility criteria relating to the access to and utilization of Fund resources. The contributions shall be such as to take into account the need for predictability, adequacy, and timely flow of funds, in accordance with the amount of resources needed to be decided periodically by the Commission and the importance of burden-sharing among the list referred to in Article 45, paragraph 2. Voluntary contributions may also be made by the developed States Parties and by other countries and sources. The mechanism shall operate within a democratic and transparent system of governance.
2. Pursuant to the objective of this Agreement, the Commission shall at its first meeting determine the policy, strategy, and program priorities, as well as detailed criteria and guidelines for access to and utilization of the financial resources including monitoring and evaluation on a regular basis of such utilization. The Commission shall decide on the arrangements to give effect to paragraph 1 above after consultation with the institutional structure entrusted with the operation of the Fund.
3. The Commission shall review the effectiveness of the Fund, including its criteria and guidelines, not less than two years after entry into force of this

Agreement and thereafter on a regular basis. Appropriate action to improve the effectiveness of the Fund shall be based on such reviews.
4. The States Parties shall consider strengthening existing financial institutions to provide financial resources for the conservation and sustainable management of marine mammals.[153]

PART XI PEACEFUL SETTLEMENT OF DISPUTES

Article 47 Obligation to Settle Disputes by Peaceful Means

States have the obligation to settle their disputes by negotiation, inquiry, mediation, conciliation, arbitration, judicial settlement, resort to regional agencies or arrangements, the Commission, or other peaceful means of their own choice.[154]

Article 48 Prevention of Disputes

States shall cooperate in order to prevent disputes. To this end, States shall agree on efficient and expeditious decision-making procedures within the Commission and regional marine mammal organizations and arrangements, and shall strengthen existing decision-making procedures as necessary.[155]

Article 49 Disputes of a Technical Nature

Where a dispute concerns a matter of a technical nature, the States concerned may refer the dispute to an ad hoc expert panel established by them. The panel shall confer with the States concerned and shall endeavor to resolve the dispute expeditiously without recourse to binding procedures for the settlement of disputes.[156]

Article 50 Procedures for the Settlement of Disputes

1. The provisions relating to the settlement of disputes set out in Part XV of the Convention apply mutatis mutandis to any dispute between States Parties to this Agreement concerning the interpretation or application of this Agreement, whether or not they are also Parties to the Convention.
2. The provisions relating to the settlement of disputes set out in Part XV of the Convention apply mutatis mutandis to any dispute between States Parties to this Agreement concerning the activities of the Commission, including any dispute concerning the conservation and sustainable management of marine mammals, whether or not they are also Parties to the Convention.
3. The provisions relating to the settlement of disputes set out in Part XV of the Convention apply mutatis mutandis to any dispute between States Parties to this Agreement concerning the interpretation or application of a global or regional marine mammal agreement relating to the conservation and sustainable management of marine mammals, or the activities of a regional marine mammal organization or arrangement, including any

dispute concerning the conservation and <u>sustainable management of marine mammals</u>, whether or not they are also Parties to the Convention.

4. Any procedure accepted by a State Party to this Agreement and the Convention pursuant to Article 287 of the Convention shall apply to the settlement of disputes under this Part, unless that State Party, when signing, ratifying, or acceding to this Agreement, or at any time thereafter, has accepted another procedure pursuant to Article 287 for the settlement of disputes under this Part.

5. A State Party to this Agreement <u>who</u> is not a Party to the Convention, when signing, ratifying, or acceding to this Agreement, or at any time thereafter, shall be free to choose, by means of a written declaration, one or more of the means set out in Article 287, paragraph 1 of the Convention for the settlement of disputes under this Part. Article 287 shall apply to such a declaration, as well as to any dispute to which such State is a party <u>that</u> is not covered by a declaration in force. For the purposes of conciliation and arbitration in accordance with Annexes V, VII, and VIII to the Convention, such State shall be entitled to nominate conciliators, arbitrators, and experts to be included in the lists referred to in Annex V, Article 2; Annex VII, Article 2; and Annex VIII, Article 2, for the settlement of disputes under this Part.

6. Any court or tribunal to which a dispute has been submitted under this Part shall apply the relevant provisions of the Convention, of this Agreement, and of any relevant subregional, regional, or global <u>marine mammal agreement</u>, as well as generally accepted standards for the conservation and management of living marine resources and other rules of international law not incompatible with the Convention, with a view to ensuring the <u>conservation and sustainable management of the marine mammal species/population(s)</u> concerned.[157]

Article 51 Provisional Measures

1. Pending the settlement of a dispute in accordance with this Part, the parties to the dispute shall make every effort to enter into provisional arrangements of a practical nature.

2. Without prejudice to Article 290 of the Convention, the court or tribunal to which the dispute has been submitted under this Part may prescribe any provisional measures <u>that</u> it considers appropriate under the circumstances to preserve the respective rights of the parties to the dispute or to prevent damage to the <u>integrity of the marine mammal species/population(s)</u> in question, as well as in the circumstances referred to in <u>Article 8, paragraph 6 [Compatibility of conservation and sustainable management measures]</u>.

3. A State Party to this Agreement <u>who</u> is not a party to the Convention may declare that, notwithstanding Article 290, paragraph 5, of the Convention, the International Tribunal for the Law of the Sea shall not be entitled to prescribe, modify, or revoke provisional measures without the agreement of such State.[158]

PART XII NONPARTIES TO THIS AGREEMENT

Article 52 Nonparties to This Agreement

1. States Parties shall encourage nonparties to this Agreement to become parties thereto and to adopt laws and regulations consistent with its provisions.
2. States Parties shall take measures consistent with this Agreement and international law to deter the activities of vessels flying the flag of nonparties that undermine the effective implementation of this Agreement.[159]

PART XIII GOOD FAITH AND ABUSE OF RIGHTS

Article 53 Good Faith and Abuse of Rights

States Parties shall fulfill in good faith the obligations assumed under this Agreement and shall exercise the rights recognized in this Agreement in a manner that would not constitute an abuse of right.[160]

PART XIV RESPONSIBILITY AND LIABILITY

Article 54 Responsibility and Liability

States Parties are liable in accordance with international law for damage or loss attributable to them in regard to this Agreement.[161]

PART XV FINAL PROVISIONS

Article 55 Signature

This Agreement shall be open for signature by all States and the other entities referred to in Article 1, paragraph 2(b), and shall remain open for signature at the United Nations Headquarters for 12 months from the [day] of [month and year].[162]

Article 56 Ratification

This Agreement is subject to ratification by States and the other entities referred to in Article 1, paragraph 2(b). The instruments of ratification shall be deposited with the Secretary-General of the United Nations.[163]

Article 57 Accession

This Agreement shall remain open for the accession by States and the other entities referred to in Article 1, paragraph 2(b). The instruments of accession shall be deposited with the Secretary-General of the United Nations.[164]

Article 58 Entry into Force

1. This Agreement shall enter into force 30 days after the date of deposit of the thirtieth instrument [modify as appropriate] of ratification or accession.
2. For each State or entity that ratifies the Agreement or accedes thereto after the deposit of the thirtieth instrument [modify as appropriate] of ratification or accession, this Agreement shall enter into force on the thirtieth day [modify as appropriate] following the deposit of its instrument of ratification or accession.[165]

Article 59 Provisional Application

1. This Agreement shall be applied provisionally by a State or entity that consents to its provisional application by so notifying the depository in writing. Such provisional application shall become effective from the date of receipt of the notification.
2. Provisional application by a State or entity shall terminate upon the entry into force of this Agreement for that State or entity or upon notification by that State or entity to the depository in writing of its intention to terminate provisional application.[166]

Article 60 Reservations and Exceptions

No reservations or exceptions may be made to this Agreement.[167]

Article 61 Declarations and Statements

Article 60 does not preclude a State or entity, when signing, ratifying, or acceding to this Agreement, from making declarations or statements, however phrased or named, with a view, inter alia, to the harmonization of its laws and regulations with the provisions of this Agreement, provided that such declarations or statements do not purport to exclude or to modify the legal effect of the provisions of this Agreement in their application to that State or entity.[168]

Article 62 Relation to Other Agreements

1. This Agreement shall prevail, as between States Parties, over the ICRW of 2 December 1946.[169]
2. This Agreement shall not alter the rights and obligations of States Parties that arise from other agreements compatible with this Agreement and that do not affect the enjoyment by other States Parties of their rights or the performance of their obligations under this Agreement.[170] Those rights and obligations that, in their exercise, would cause a serious damage or threat to the conservation and sustainable management of marine mammals are incompatible with this Agreement.[171]
3. Two or more States Parties may conclude agreements modifying or suspending the operation of provisions of this Agreement, applicable

solely to the relations between them, provided that such agreements do not relate to a provision derogation from which is incompatible with the effective execution of the object and purpose of this Agreement, and provided further that such agreements shall not affect the application of the basic principles embodied herein, and that the provisions of such agreements do not affect the enjoyment by other States Parties of their rights or the performance of their obligations under this Agreement.[172]
4. States Parties intending to conclude an agreement referred to in paragraph 3 shall notify the other States Parties through the depository of this Agreement of their intention to conclude the agreement and of the modification or suspension for which it provides.[173]

Article 63 Annex

1. The <u>Annex forms</u> an integral part of this Agreement and, unless expressly provided otherwise, a reference to this Agreement or to one of its Parts includes a reference to the <u>Annex</u> relating thereto.
2. The <u>Annex</u> may be revised <u>in accordance with Article 12, paragraph 5</u>.[174]

Article 64 Depository

The Secretary-General of the United Nations shall be the depository of this Agreement and any amendments or revisions thereto.[175]

Article 65 Authentic Texts

The <u>[insert languages]</u> texts of this Agreement are equally authentic.

IN WITNESS THEREOF, the undersigned Plenipotentiaries, being duly authorized thereto, have signed this Agreement.

OPENED FOR SIGNATURE at <u>[insert location]</u>, this <u>[insert day]</u> of <u>[insert month]</u>, <u>[insert year]</u>, in a single original, in the [insert languages].[176]

Annex

[Management Plan and other conservation and sustainable management measures will be included in the Annex to the Agreement.]

NOTES

1. Agreement for the Implementation of the Provisions of the United Nations Convention on the Law of the Sea of 10 December 1982 Relating to the Conservation and Management of Straddling Fish Stocks and Highly Migratory Fish Stocks at title, Dec. 4, 1995, 34 I.L.M. 1542, 2167 U.N.T.S. 3 ["UN Fish Stocks Agreement"].
2. *Id.* at preamble.
3. International Convention for the Regulation of Whaling at preamble, Dec. 2, 1946, 62 Stat. 1716, 161 U.N.T.S. 74 ["ICRW"].
4. UN Fish Stocks Agreement, *supra* note 1, at preamble.

5. *Id.*
6. *Id.*
7. *Id.*
8. *Id.*
9. *Id.*
10. ICRW, *supra* note 3, at preamble.
11. Agreement on Research, Conservation and Management of Marine Mammals in the North Atlantic at preamble, Apr. 9, 2012 ["NAMMCO Agreement"].
12. ICRW, *supra* note 3, at preamble.
13. UN Fish Stocks Agreement, *supra* note 1, at preamble.
14. ICRW, *supra* note 3, at preamble.
15. UN Fish Stocks Agreement, *supra* note 1, at preamble.
16. *Id.* at art. 1(a).
17. *See* VED P. NANDA & GEORGE (ROCK) PRING, INTERNATIONAL ENVIRONMENTAL LAW AND POLICY FOR THE 21ST CENTURY 36–37 (2d ed. 2013) ["NANDA & PRING"] (discussing the fact that there is no internationally agreed definition of "conservation"); *see* MICHAEL BOWMAN ET AL., LYSTER'S INTERNATIONAL WILDLIFE LAW 59 (2d ed. 2010) ["LYSTER'S INTERNATIONAL WILDLIFE LAW"]; *see* PATRICIA BIRNIE, ALAN BOYLE & CATHERINE REDGWELL, INTERNATIONAL LAW & THE ENVIRONMENT 655–57 (3d ed. 2009) (discussing the use of the term "conservation" in treaty law).
18. *See* Convention on Migratory Species art. I(1)(c), 23 June 1979, 1651 U.N.T.S. 333 (defining the term "conservation status").
19. *See* The International Union for the Conservation of Nature, *World Conservation Strategy*, 1(4)–1(7) (1980), http://data.iucn.org/dbtw-wpd/edocs/WCS-004.pdf (defining "conservation" and recognizing that for the purposes of conserving living resources one must consider ecosystem processes, genetic diversity, and sustainable utilization); RICHARD A. PRIMACK, ESSENTIALS OF CONSERVATION BIOLOGY 6 (3d ed. 2002) (describing the scope of conservation biology, noting its focus on biodiversity, human impact on species, genetic variation, and ecosystems).
20. *See* Marine Mammal Protection Act, 16 U.S.C. § 1632(2) (2007) ["MMPA"] (setting the goal of increasing or maintaining populations without necessarily precluding take).
21. *See* Convention for the Conservation of Antarctic Marine Living Resources 20 May 1980 art. II(3)(a), 33 U.S.T. 3476, 1329 U.N.T.S. 48 (indicating the need to maintain certain population levels).
22. *Id.* at art II(2) (indicating that conservation "includes rational use").
23. *See* LYSTER'S INTERNATIONAL WILDLIFE LAW, *supra* note 17, at 59–60 (discussing the interaction between conservation and sustainable use).
24. UN Fish Stocks Agreement, *supra* note 1, at art. 1(b).
25. *See* Duncan E.J. Currie, *Ecosystem-Based Management in Multilateral Environmental Agreements: Progress towards Adopting the Ecosystem Approach in the International Management of Living Marine Resources*, WWF International, 3–4 (2007); *see* ERICH HOYT, MARINE PROTECTED AREAS FOR WHALES, DOLPHINS, AND PORPOISES: A WORLD HANDBOOK FOR CETACEAN HABITAT CONSERVATION AND PLANNING 9–10 (2d ed., 2011).
26. MMPA, *supra* note 20, § 1362(1)(6).

27. *See* MARINE PROTECTED AREAS: A MULTIDISCIPLINARY APPROACH 2 (Joachim Claudet ed., 2011).
28. MMPA, *supra* note 20, at § 1362(11).
29. *Id.* § 1362(2).
30. NANDA & PRING, *supra* note 17, at 29 (summarizing the principles informing sustainable development at international law).
31. MMPA, *supra* note 20, § 1362(2).
32. *Id.* § 1362(13).
33. International Convention on Salvage art. 1(b), 28 April 1989, 1953 U.N.T.S. 153.
34. ICRW, *supra* note 3, at arts. II(1) & (3).
35. UN Fish Stocks Agreement, *supra* note 1, at art. 2(a).
36. *Id.* at art. 2(b).
37. *Id.* at art. 2.
38. *Id.* at art. 3(1).
39. *Id.* at art 7.
40. *Id.* at art. 3(2).
41. *Id.* at art. 4.
42. *Id.* at art. 5.
43. *Id.* at art. 6.
44. United Nations Convention on the Law of the Sea art. 65, 10 Dec. 1982, 21 I.L.M. 1261, 1833 U.N.T.S. 3 ["UNCLOS"].
45. UN Fish Stocks Agreement, *supra* note 1, at art. 7.
46. NAMMCO Agreement, *supra* note 11, at art. 1.
47. ICRW, *supra* note 3, at art. III.
48. NAMMCO Agreement, *supra* note 11, at art. 2.
49. ICRW, *supra* note 3, at art. III(1).
50. Agreement on the Conservation of Cetaceans of the Black Sea, Mediterranean Sea and Contiguous Atlantic Area art III(1), 24 Nov. 1996, 2183 U.N.T.S. 303 ["ACCOBAMS"].
51. NAMMCO Agreement, *supra* note 11, at art. 6(2).
52. ICRW, *supra* note 3, at art. III(2).
53. Convention on Biological Diversity art. 23(3), 5 June 1992, 31 I.L.M. 818, 1760 U.N.T.S. 79 ["CBD"].
54. *Id.* at art. 29(3).
55. ICRW, *supra* note 3, at art. III(2).
56. CBD, *supra* note 53, at art. 29(3).
57. Agreement on the Conservation of Small Cetaceans of the Baltic and North Seas art. 6.3, 17 Mar. 1992, 1772 U.N.T.S. 217 ["ASCOBANS"]; *see* CBD, *supra* note 53, at art. 29(3); *see* ICRW, *supra* note 3, at art. III(2); *see* ACCOBAMS, *supra* note 50, at art. 3(6); *see* NAMMCO Agreement, *supra* note 11, at art. 4(3).
58. ICRW, *supra* note 3, at art. III(1); Convention on International Trade in Endangered Species of Wild Fauna and Flora art. XVII, 3 Mar. 1973, 27 U.S.T. 1087, 993 U.N.T.S. 243 ["CITES"] (requiring a two-thirds vote for treaty amendment).
59. CBD, *supra* note 53, at art. 29(5).
60. NAMMCO Agreement, *supra* note 11, at art. 4(2)(a).
61. *Id.* at art. 4(2)(b).
62. ICRW, *supra* note 3, at art. III(4).
63. NAMMCO, *supra* note 11, at art. 4(2)(c).
64. ICRW, *supra* note 3, at art. IV(1).

65. *Id.* at art. V(1).
66. *Id.* at art. VI.
67. CBD, *supra* note 53, at art. 23(4)(h).
68. ICRW, *supra* note 3, at art. IV(2).
69. ASCOBANS, *supra* note 57, at art. 6.1.
70. *Id.* at art. 6.1(a).
71. CBD, *supra* note 53, at arts. 23(4)(c)–(f).
72. *Id.* at art. 23(4)(g).
73. ASCOBANS, *supra* note 57, at art. 6.1(c).
74. *Id.* at art. 6.1(d).
75. *Id.*
76. CBD, *supra* note 53, at art. 23(2).
77. ASCOBANS, *supra* note 57, at art. 6.2.1 (this draft Article contains many of the same organizations listed in the ASCOBANS provision).
78. *Id.* at art. 6.2.2.
79. CBD, *supra* note 53, at art. 23(5).
80. ASCOBANS, *supra* note 57, at art 6.2.2.
81. CBD, *supra* note 53, at art 23(5).
82. ASCOBANS, *supra* note 57, at art. 6.
83. CBD, *supra* note 53, at art. 23(5); CITES, *supra* note 58, at art. XI(6) & (7) (stating that admitted "observers shall have the right to participate but not to vote").
84. ASCOBANS, *supra* note 57, at art. 6.4.
85. CBD, *supra* note 53, at art. 29(2).
86. *Id.* at 29(2).
87. CBD, *supra* note 53, at art. 29(3).
88. *Id.* at art. 45(3).
89. UN Fish Stocks Agreement, *supra* note 1, at art. 45(5).
90. *Id.* at art. 45(6).
91. *Id.* at art. 45(4).
92. CBD, *supra* note 53, at art. 45(7).
93. *Id.* at art. 48(1).
94. *Id.* at art. 48(2).
95. UN Fish Stocks Agreement, *supra* note 1, at arts. 45(2) & 48.
96. NAMMCO Agreement, *supra* note 11, at art. 6(1).
97. *Id.* at art. 6(2); CITES, *supra* note 58, at art. XI(6) & (7).
98. CBD, *supra* note 53, at art. 25(2)(a).
99. *Id.* at arts. 25(2)(d) & (e).
100. *See* International Whaling Commission, *The Revised Management Procedure*, IWC, https://iwc.int/rmp (last visited July 6, 2015) (describing the IWC Scientific Committee's role in producing the Revised Management Procedure).
101. *Id.*
102. ICRW, *supra* note 3, at art. V(2).
103. *See* CBD, *supra* note 53, at art. 25; *see* The North Atlantic Marine Mammal Commission, *About NAMMCO*, http://www.nammco.no/about-nammco/ / (last visited July 6, 2015) ["*About NAMMCO*"]; *see* International Whaling Commission, *Commission Sub-Groups*, IWC (2015), https://iwc.int/commission-sub-groups.
104. NAMMCO Agreement, *supra* note 11, at art. 6; CITES, *supra* note 58, at art. XI(6) & (7).

105. United Nations Permanent Forum on Indigenous Issues, *Factsheet: Who Are Indigenous Peoples?*, at 2 http://www.un.org/esa/socdev/unpfii/documents/5session_factsheet1.pdf.

106. International Whaling Commission, *Aboriginal Subsistence Whaling*, IWC (2015), http://iwc.int/aboriginal (last visited July 6, 2015) [*"Aboriginal Subsistence Whaling"*].

107. *See* Benedict Kingsbury, *"Indigenous Peoples" in International Law: A Constructivist Approach to the Asian Controversy*, 92 AM. J. INT'L L. 414, 455 (1998) (this portion of the draft Article adopts and summarizes the criteria identified by Kingsbury in a manner that remains true to the purpose of its original wording. This work identifies both "Essential Requirements" and "Relevant Indicia." I believe that using indicia is preferable to establishing a restricted definition that is unable to respond to changing circumstances).

108. *See* ALEXANDER GILLESPIE, WHALING DIPLOMACY 228–30 (2005) ["WHALING DIPLOMACY"] (discussing the idea of "culture" in the context of the IWC's ASW exemption).

109. *See id.* at 229; *see* Oran R. Young et al., *Subsistence, Sustainability, and Sea Mammals: Reconstructing the International Whaling Regime*, 23 OCEAN COASTAL MGMT. 117, 120 (1994) ["Young et al."] (noting that "small-scale whaling should be regarded as permissible on grounds of sustainability and equity when it secures historically based practices of socially defined human groups that value whaling activities on a multi-dimensional basis").

110. *See id.; see* Young et al., *supra* note 109, at 122 (discussing artisanal whaling within the context of artisanal fisheries as follows: "Much has been written about artisanal fisheries comprised of localized, family-based activities characterized by a high degree of annual labour, and with skills and techniques based largely on traditional knowledge. Such fisheries commonly feature family-based production, household consumption, and informal trade of surplus production either within the home or nearby communities, or in local or regional markets").

111. *See* Young et al., *supra* note 109, at 122 (defining subsistence as "a system or mode of production in which the allocation and production in which the allocation and procurement of resources and the distribution and consumption of products is organized around family and kinship groups. There is nothing in this formulation that precludes monetized exchanges or requires that subsistence practices remain").

112. *See Aboriginal Subsistence Whaling, supra* note 106 (describing how nations currently submit applications to the ICW on behalf of their Aboriginal groups in order to secure an ASW permission).

113. Young et al., *supra* note 109, at 120–22 (providing descriptions of these criteria in the context of what is necessary to justify small-type coastal whaling for any subsistence use, and the wording found in this portion of the draft Article is essentially a summation of these criteria. This work broadly identifies the different categories of subsistence use as accounted for in this draft Article).

114. *See* National Marine Fisheries Service, *Purchasing, Finding or Possessing Marine Mammal Skins, Muktak, Baleen, and Bones*, NOAA FISHERIES, http://www.fakr.noaa.gov/protectedresources/buying.htm (last visited Feb. 18, 2016) (indicating the possibility of obtaining certificates for certain actions involving marine mammal parts pursuant to MMPA).

115. WHALING DIPLOMACY, *supra* note 108, at 230 (noting that "indigenous needs may not drive a species towards extinction—this rule has been slow to take hold at the IWC").
116. ICRW, *supra* note 3, at art. III(4).
117. NAMMCO Agreement, *supra* note 11, at art. 5.
118. *See* CBD, *supra* note 53, at art 25; *see About NAMMCO, supra* note 103; *see* International Whaling Commission, *Commission Sub-groups*, IWC (2015), https://iwc.int/commission-sub-groups.
119. NAMMCO Agreement, *supra* note 11, at art. 5(1)(b).
120. WHALING DIPLOMACY, *supra* note 108, at 69 (in the context of urging governments to participate in the international response to climate change to reduce its impact on cetaceans).
121. CBD, *supra* note 53, at art. 24(1).
122. *Id.* at art. 24(2).
123. UN Fish Stocks Agreement, *supra* note 1, at art. 12.
124. *Id.* at art. 8.
125. *Id.* at art. 9.
126. *Id.* at art. 10.
127. *Id.* at art. 11.
128. *Id.* at art. 12.
129. *Id.* at art. 13.
130. *Id.* at art. 14.
131. *Id.* at art. 17.
132. *Id.* at art. 18.
133. *Id.*
134. FAO Agreement to Promote Compliance with International Conservation and Management Measures by Fishing Vessels on the High Seas, art. IV, 29 Nov. 1993, 24 I.L.M. 968 ["FAO Compliance Agreement"].
135. UN Fish Stocks Agreement, *supra* note 1, at art. 18.
136. FAO Compliance Agreement, *supra* note 134, at art. VI.
137. Greenpeace, *Suggested Draft High Seas Implementing Agreement for the Conservation and Management of the Marine Environment in Areas beyond National Jurisdiction*, GREENPEACE INTERNATIONAL (2011), art. 47, http://www.greenpeace.org/international/Global/international/publications/oceans/2011/Greenpeace%20draft%20Implementing%20Agreement%2013Feb2008.pdf (citing to art. III of the FAO Compliance Agreement, *supra* note 134).
138. UN Fish Stocks Agreement, *supra* note 1, at art. 19.
139. *Id.* at art. 20.
140. *Id.* at art. 21.
141. *Id.* at art. 22.
142. *Id.* at art. 23; *see also Agreement on Port State Measures to Prevent, Deter and Eliminate Illegal, Unreported and Unregulated Fishing*, FAO.ORG, http://www.fao.org/fileadmin/user_upload/legal/docs/037t-e.pdf (last visited Feb. 18, 2016) (which is not yet in force because of insufficient ratification, but requires mention because it elucidates port state measures in considerably more detail and could also be used during negotiation to bolster this draft Article).
143. UN Fish Stocks Agreement, *supra* note 1, at art. 24 (note that art. 24(2)(b) has been deleted as subsistence marine mammal use is addressed in draft art. 17).

144. *Id.* at art. 25 (note that this draft Article collapses and combines Articles 25(2) and 25(3) into one, which is appropriate given the emphasis that is provided on items contained in this draft Article in the following draft Articles).
145. *Id.* at art. 26.
146. UNCLOS, *supra* note 44, at art. 266(1).
147. Agreement on Trade-Related Aspects of Intellectual Property Rights art. 66(2), 15 April 1994, 33 I.L.M. 1197 ["TRIPS Agreement"].
148. UNCLOS, *supra* note 44, at art. 268.
149. *Id.* at art. 269.
150. TRIPS Agreement, *supra* note 147, at art. 67.
151. UNCLOS, *supra* note 44, at art. 266(2); *see generally* CBD, *supra* note 53, at art. 16.
152. CBD, *supra* note 53, at art. 20 (this application also removes subsections (4), (6), and (7)).
153. *Id.* at art. 21.
154. UN Fish Stocks Agreement, *supra* note 1, at art. 27.
155. *Id.* at art. 28.
156. *Id.* at art. 29.
157. *Id.* at art. 30.
158. *Id.* at art. 31.
159. *Id.* at art. 33.
160. *Id.* at art. 34.
161. *Id.* at art. 35.
162. *Id.* at art. 37.
163. *Id.* at art. 38.
164. *Id.* at art. 39.
165. *Id.* at art. 40.
166. *Id.* at art. 41.
167. *Id.* at art. 42.
168. *Id.* at art. 43.
169. UNCLOS, *supra* note 44, at art. 311 (this provision in UNCLOS indicates that UNCLOS prevails over the Geneva Conventions on the Law of the Sea of 29 April 1958).
170. UN Fish Stocks Agreement, *supra* note 1, at art. 44(1).
171. CBD, *supra* note 53, at art. 22(1).
172. UN Fish Stocks Agreement, *supra* note 1, at art. 44(2).
173. *Id.* at art. 44(3).
174. *Id.* at art. 48.
175. *Id.* at art. 49.
176. *Id.* at art. 50.

Appendix 4

Structure of Proposed International Regime for the Conservation of Marine Mammals

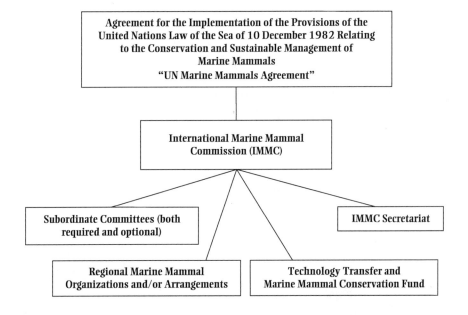

Index

Aboriginal subsistence whaling
  aboriginal whaling, defined under IWC, 104
  Alaska Eskimo Whaling Commission, weapons-enhancement project, 106
  Canada's Inuit population, 105–6
  Convention for the Regulation of Whaling, text of Article 3 (League of Nations, 1931), 104
  ethical considerations, 104–7
  great whale take, 61–62
  ICRW, Article 13, 105
  indigenous killing methods, 106
  IWC
    approach, 104–5
    lacking definition of aboriginal or aboriginal subsistence, cause of ambiguities, 106
  Japan and, 106
  lack of standardization, 106
  national regulation and, 61–62
  proposed Agreement. *See* Indigenous and Cultural/Artisanal Subsistence Take Committee of IMMC
  subsistence whaling exemption, under IWC, 104–5, 230, 232
  training and education to standardize, 106
  twentieth century indigenous whaling, changes in, 105
  Working Group on Whale Killing Methods (IWC), 106

Aborigines
  dugongs, legal hunting under Native Title Act 1993 (Australia), 60
  under proposed Agreement. *See* Indigenous and Cultural/Artisanal Subsistence Take Committee
  subsistence whaling. *See* Aboriginal subsistence whaling

adaptations, 11

Agenda 21, 165, 169, 271

Agreement on the Conservation of Cetaceans of the Black Sea, Mediterranean Sea and Contiguous Atlantic Area (ACCOBAMS), 53–54, 166

Agreement on the Conservation of Seals in the Wadden Sea ("Wadden Sea Agreement"), 54

Agreement on the Conservation of Small Cetaceans of the Baltic, North East Atlantic, Irish and North Seas (ASCOBANS), 53, 166

Agreement on the International Dolphin Conservation Program (AIDCP)
  dolphin mortality limits, 127, 280
  Dolphin Safe Certification Program, 281–82
  International Dolphin Conservation Program (IDCP), establishment of, 127
  On-Board Observer Program, 280, 281
  preamble, 280

Agreement on the International Dolphin Conservation Program (AIDCP) *(Cont.)*
  resolutions, 281
  tuna-dolphin problem, regionalism case study, 279–82
Aichi Target 11, Convention on Biodiversity, 288
Alaska Eskimo Whaling Commission, weapons-enhancement project, 106
Albania
  Corfu Channel Case (United Kingdom of Great Britain and Northern Ireland v. Albania), 264n222
Anglo Norwegian Fisheries Jurisdiction Case (United Kingdom v. Norway), 67n58
"Antarctic Seal Convention" (Convention on Conservation of Antarctic Seals, 1972), 40
archaeological evidence of utilitarian relationship
  with cetaceans, 12–13
  with pinnipeds, 15–16
Argentina v. Uruguay. See Pulp Mills on the River Uruguay
artisanal, defined
  Indigenous and Cultural/Artisanal Subsistence Take Committee, 231
Australia. *See also* Aborigines
  Aboriginal and Torres Strait Islander people, legal hunting of dugongs under Native Title Act 1993, 60
  Australian Whale Sanctuary, 60
  Australia v. Japan (Southern Bluefin Tuna Case), 244
  Environment Protection and Biodiversity Conservation Act 1999 (EPBCA), 60
  International Whaling and Marine Mammal Conservation Initiatives, 61
  Japan-Australia Economic Partnership Agreement, 250
  national regulation, 60–61
  Whaling in the Antarctic Case. *See Whaling in the Antarctic Case (Australia v. Japan: New Zealand Intervening)*
Australian Whale Sanctuary, 60

Bamfield Marine Sciences Centre (Canada), 312
Bay of Fundy Traffic Separation Scheme, 129
Bearzi, Maddalena *(Bigger, Better Brain)*, 96–97
behavior
  cetacean brain, 8
  ecotourism, changes in marine mammals due to, 138
  scientific advances, ethical considerations, 97–98
  whale watching, changes in whales due to, 138
best available scientific information, evidence, and knowledge standard, proposed Agreement, 218–19, 221–23
  regulatory approach, limitations, 222
Blue Whale Unit (BWU), 41, 44
Bowman, Michael, "The Future of the IWC" process proposal, 46, 47–48, 162–64, 167
Buenos Aires Group (Latin American and Caribbean State contingent at the IWC), 140, 249, 311
Burke, William *(The New International Law of Fisheries: UNCLOS 1982 and Beyond)*, 189
by-catch, 125–27
  current response, 126–27
  dolphin-tuna interaction, 126, 279–82
  backdown procedure, 84n283, 126, 127
  Inter-American Tropical Tuna Commission (IATTC), 57, 147n98, 187, 276
  regionalism, case study, 279–82
  gill-net fishing, 125, 126, 127
  incidental catch, 125, 184
  IWC initiatives, 126
  mortality rate, 125–26
  pingers, 127

INDEX 377

problem, 125–26
purse-seine net fishing, 57, 84n283,
    126–27, 146n86, 279–80, 281
statistical data, 125, 127
technological advances, 7, 127
types of, 125

Canada
    Bamfield Marine Sciences Centre, 312
    Fisheries Jurisdiction Case (Spain v. Canada), 67n58
    fur seals and pinniped regulation, 39, 40–41
    Inuit population, Aboriginal subsistence whaling, 105–6
    IWC commercial moratorium on whaling, withdrawal of membership in protest of, 45, 62
    North West Atlantic Seals Agreement (between Canada and Norway, 1971), 41
    pinniped take, total allowable catch (TAC limits), 62
    sealing/seal product dispute with European Union, 250
    UNCLOS Article 65, interpretation of, 184–85
carnivores (otters and polar bears)
    classification by distribution, 11
    description, generally, 10–11
    extant and recently extinct marine mammal species, Red List of Threatened Species (table), 319
        data summary and trends, 18–19
    scientific classification, 10–12
Carribean monk seal, 10, 13, 320
Case concerning the Conservation and Sustainable Exploitation of Swordfish Stocks in the South-Eastern Pacific Ocean (Chile/European Union), 244
Ceballos, Gerardo ("Global Distribution of Marine Mammals" by Sandra Pompa, Paul R. Ehrlich, and Gerardo Ceballos), 255n58, 288–89

Census of Marine Life, 9
Center for Progressive Member Scholars "Reclaiming Global Environmental Leadership: Why the United States Should Ratify Ten Pending Environmental Treaties" white paper, 311
cetacean brain
    ethical considerations, 96–97
    scientific investigation and social behavior, 8
cetaceans (whales, dolphins, and porpoises). *See also great whales; main headings for dolphins; whaling*
    classification by distribution, 11
    culture
        scientific advances, ethical considerations
            matriline social structure, 98
            objections to cetaceans utilization of culture, 99
            social learning, 98
    description, generally, 10–11
    "great whales" and other species of cetacean, distinction between, 11–12
    human-marine mammal interaction, historical background
        archaeological evidence of use, 12–13
        benefits, 12
        cultural relationship, 16–17
        utilitarian relationship, 12–15
        whaling—emergence of commercial whaling, 13–15
    Red List of Threatened Species (table), 315–19
        data summary and trends, 18–19
    scientific classification, 10–12
    small cetaceans
        common killing methods, 101–2
        take, 62
Chad
    Libyan Arab Jamahiriya/Chad (Territorial Dispute Case), 207n163
Chile
    marine protected areas (MPAs), 286

Chile/European Union (Case concerning the Conservation and Sustainable Exploitation of Swordfish Stocks in the South-Eastern Pacific Ocean), 244
Chopra, Sudhir *(Whales: Their Emerging Right to Life),* 8, 95, 96
classification of marine mammals, 10–12
 by distribution
  factors influencing, 11
  methods, 11–12
climate change, 120–25. *See also* environmental pollution
 Conservation of Antarctic Marine Living Resources (CCAMLR), 124
 current response, 123–25
 definition of, 120
 ecological scale, impact to marine mammals dependent upon, 121
 Fifth Assessment Report (IPCC), 121
 greenhouse gas emissions, 121, 123, 124
 indirect consequences, 122
 Intergovernmental Panel on Climate Change (IPCC), 120–21, 234
 International Whaling Commission (IWC), 123–24
 latitude specific and non-latitude specific effects, 121–22
 marine mammals, impact on, 121–23
 ocean acidification, 10, 122, 143*n*28
 oceans, affect on, 121
 problem, 120–23
 scientific advances, influence on conservation and management of marine resources, 7
 Standing Working Group on Environmental Concerns (SWGEC), 123
 21st Conference of the Parties (UNFCCC), 123
 United Nations Framework Convention on Climate Change (UNFCCC), 123
 World Wildlife Fund, 124
Clinton, Bill, 184, 193
common pool problem, renewable stock resources and, 34–35, 161

common property resources, 34
competing ocean uses, respect of, 91–92
conservation, 2–5
 definition
  by international instruments, 2–5
  under proposed Agreement, 216, 326
  working definition of, 4–5
 indefinite use approach to, 2, 4
 management requirement of. *See* sustainable management
 preservation approach to, 2, 19
conservation goals of proposed Agreement, 91–93
 build on the existing foundation, 93
 competing ocean uses, respect of, 91–92
 cooperation and enhance global participation, promotion of, 92
 expansion of species coverage, 91, 232
 goal setting, 90
 international law, incorporation of current principles of, 92
 rational arrangement proposal, 93
 regional implementation, promotion of, 92–93
 rule of law in the oceans, promotion of, 91
 utilizing science based decision making and conservation tools, holistic management, 92
Conservation of Antarctic Marine Living Resources (CCAMLR), 124, 292
conservation status, extant and recently extinct marine mammal species, 17–19, 315–21
 knowledge gaps, 18
 Red List of Threatened Species (IUCN), 17–18, 131, 315–21
"Constitution for the Oceans," 36, 171. *See also headings under* United Nations Convention on the Law of the Sea (UNCLOS)
Convention for the Conservation of Antarctic Marine Living Resources
 conservation, defined, 3–4
Convention for the Preservation and Protection of Fur Seals ("Fur Seal Convention" 1911), 39–40

INDEX

Convention for the Regulation of
    Whaling, text of Article 3
    (League of Nations, 1931), 104
Convention Migratory Species (CMS)
    conservation, defined, 3
Convention on Biological Diversity (CBD),
    50–51, 292
  Aichi Targets, 31n191
  Aichi Target 11, 288
  Conference of the Parties,
    Decision IX/20, 292
  conservation, defined, 3
  *Scientific Synthesis on the Impacts of
    Underwater Noise on Marine
    Biodiversity and Habitats*
    (2012), 132
Convention on Conservation of Antarctic
    Seals ("Antarctic Seal
    Convention" 1972), 40
Convention on International Trade
    in Endangered Species of
    Wild Fauna and Flora
    (CITES), 51–52
Convention on the Conservation of
    Migratory Species of Wild
    Animals (CMS), 52–54
  memorandums of understanding
    (MoU's) produced by, 54
Convention on the Prevention of Marine
    Pollution by Dumping of
    Wastes and Other Matter
    1972 (the "London
    Convention"), 135–36
Convention on the Protection of the
    Marine Environment of the
    North-East Atlantic (OSPAR
    Convention), 154n227, 291–92
  Recommendation 2003/3, 292
coral bleaching, 143n29
*Corfu Channel Case (United Kingdom of
    Great Britain and Northern
    Ireland v. Albania)*, 264n222
cruise lines
  ship-strikes, 128
cultural, defined, 231
cultural imperialism, 246, 249
cultural relationship
  human-marine mammal interaction,
    historical background, 7

culture. *See also* Aboriginal subsistence
    whaling; Indigenous
    and Cultural/Artisanal
    Subsistence Take
    Committee
  scientific advances, ethical
    considerations, 98–99
*Current and Future Patterns of Global
    Marine Mammal Biodiversity*
    (Kristin Kaschner, et al.), 123

D'Amato, Anthony *(Whales: Their
    Emerging Right to Life)*, 8,
    95, 96
Davidson et al., Ana D. "Drivers and
    Hotspots of Extinction Risk
    in Marine Mammals," 26n96,
    255n58, 288, 289
Davis, Kimberly *(International
    Management of Cetaceans
    under the New Law of the Sea
    Convention)*, 190–91
developing states
  encouraging participation in proposed
    Agreement, 223
  marine protected areas (MPAs),
    prohibitive establishment
    criteria, 287–88
  proposed Agreement, requirements of
    developing states
  forms of cooperation with, 358–59
  recognition of the special
    requirements, 358
  special assistance in implementation
    of Agreement, 359
diminishing effectiveness test. *See*
    Pelly Amendment to the
    Fisherman's Protective Act
dispute resolution
  ICRW, absence of dispute resolution
    in *Whaling in the Antarctic
    Case*, 241–42
  proposed Agreement, 241–45, 362–63
  disputes of technical nature,
    243, 362
  obligation to settle disputes by
    peaceful means, 362
  prevention of disputes, 362
  provisional measures, 244, 363

dispute resolution (*Cont.*)
   proposed Agreement (*Cont.*)
      scientific information and evidence, 243, 362
      settlement procedures, 362–63
   UNCLOS, dispute resolution approach, 242–44
      "choice of procedure" (cafeteria approach), 243–44
      International Tribunal for the Law of the Sea (ITLOS), 243–44
distinctions and variations of marine mammals, 10, 11–12
Division for Ocean Affairs and the Law of the Sea of the Office of Legal Affairs (DOALOS)
   core functions of, 273–74
   Secretariat of IMMC, engagement in creation and administration of, 273–74, 295
dolphins. *See also* cetaceans (whales, dolphins, and porpoises)
   Agreement on the International Dolphin Conservation Program (AIDCP), 127, 279–82
   by-catch
      backdown procedure, 84n283, 126, 127
      dolphin-tuna interaction, 126, 279–82
      Inter-American Tropical Tuna Commission (IATTC), 57, 147n98, 187, 276
      regionalism, case study, 279–82
   International Dolphin Conservation Program (IDCP), establishment of, 127
   mortality limits, 127, 280
   On-Board Observer Program, 280, 281
   Red List of Threatened Species (tables), 315–19
   scientific advances ethical considerations
      behavior, 97–98
   tuna-dolphin problem, regionalism case study, 279–82
Dolphin Safe Certification Program, 281–82

dolphin-tuna interaction
   backdown procedure, 84n283, 126, 127
   by-catch, 126, 279–82
   Inter-American Tropical Tuna Commission (IATTC), 57, 147n98, 187, 276
   regionalism, case study, 279–82
Draft Agreement for the Implementation of the Provisions of the UN Convention on the Law of the Sea of 10 December 1982 Relating to the Conservation and Sustainable Management of Marine Mammals. *See* United Nations Marine Mammals Agreement (proposed draft agreement)
"Drivers and Hotspots of Extinction Risk in Marine Mammals" (Ana D. Davidson et al.), 26n96, 255n58, 288, 289
dugongs. *See* sirenians (manatees and dugongs)

ecological scale, defined, 121
economic theory of international law, 34
ecosystem-based management
   defined
      generally, 6
      under proposed Agreement, 216, 327
   MPAs. *See* marine protected areas (MPAs)
   scientific advances, influence of, 8
   species and area based approaches to marine mammal management, 38–50
      fur seals and pinniped regulation, 39–41
      great whales and "sustainable" whaling, 41–50
   sustainable management under proposed Agreement. *See* sustainable management
ecosystem type classification of marine mammals, 11
ecotourism (marine mammal tourism), 137–40
   behavioral changes in marine mammals due to, 138
   current response, 138–40

INDEX

marine mammal watching, defined, 137
New Zealand, regulations, 60
ongoing compendium of guidelines and regulations, 139
problem, 137–38
scientific advances, influence of, 8
whale watching
    background and studies regarding activity of, 138
    behavioral changes in whales due to, 138
    commercial whaling's impact on, 138
    current response, 138–40
    global economics of industry, 138
    IWC whale watching initiatives, 139, 140, 165
Ehrlich, Paul R. ("Global Distribution of Marine Mammals" by Sandra Pompa, Paul R. Ehrlich, and Gerardo Ceballos), 255n58, 288–89
Elements of a Possible Implementation Agreement to UNCLOS for the Conservation and Sustainable Use of Marine Biodiversity in Areas beyond National Jurisdiction (IUCN, 2008), 176
entanglement. *See* by-catch
environmental pollution. *See also* marine pollution
    Convention on the Prevention of Marine Pollution by Dumping of Wastes and Other Matter 1972 ("London Convention"), 135–36
    current response, 132–37
    emerging concerns, 132
    greenhouse gas emissions, 121, 123, 124
    International Convention for the Prevention of Pollution from Ships (MARPOL), 136
    international responses, 135–37
    IWC initiatives, 134
    lack of single comprehensive international response, reasons for, 135
    noise pollution, 74n154, 131, 132, 136–37
    persistent organic pollutants (POPs), 131–32

problem, 130–32
Red List of Threatened Species, 131
scientific advances, influence of, 7
"stinky whale" phenomena, 131
Stockholm Convention on Persistent Organic Pollutants ("Stockholm Convention"), 135
traditional pollution problems, 131–32
UNCLOS
    Article 194 (text of), 133
    pollution, defined under Article 1(4), 131
    relevant articles, 133–34
Environment Protection and Biodiversity Conservation Act 1999 (EPBCA) (Australia), 60
"Establishing Resilient Marine Protected Area Networks-Making It Happen" (IUCN-CPA), 293
ethical considerations, 93–107
    aboriginal subsistence whaling, 104–7
    behavior, 97–98
    cetacean brain, 96–97
    culture, 98–99
    features of new response, 107
    marine mammal killing methods, 99–104
    perception of uniqueness, 94, 96
    polar bear taking, 115n133
    scientific advances, 95–99
    scope of, 94
    shift in perspective, marine mammals as object of preservation, 94
European Union
    Case concerning the Conservation and Sustainable Exploitation of Swordfish Stocks in the South-Eastern Pacific Ocean (Chile/European Union), 244
    sealing/seal product dispute with Canada, 250
expansion of species coverage, 91
    Indigenous and Cultural/Artisanal Subsistence Take Committee of IMMC, subsistence expansion, 232
extant and recently extinct marine mammal species. *See* Red List of Threatened Species (IUCN)

The Faroe Islands
    North Atlantic Marine Mammal
        Commission (NAMMCO), 54
    small cetacean take, 62
Finland
    pinniped take, 63
Fisheries Jurisdiction Case (Spain v. Canada), 67n58
Fisheries Jurisdiction Case (United Kingdom v. Iceland), 67n58, 202n63
Florida
    ship-strikes, 128, 129
free rider problem, 34, 35, 237
Friedheim, Robert, *"Towards a Sustainable Whaling Regime"* proposal, 161–62, 164, 168
    Revised Management Procedure (RMP), 46, 161
    Revised Management Scheme (RMS), 46, 161
fur seals. *See* pinnipeds (seals, fur seals, sea lions, and walruses)

General Agreement on Tariffs and Trade (GATT)
    dolphin safe response, U.S./Mexico dispute, 126
geographic range classification of marine mammals, 11
gill-net fishing, 125, 126, 127
global climate changes. *See* climate change
"Global Distribution of Marine Mammals" (Sandra Pompa, Paul R. Ehrlich, and Gerardo Ceballos), 255n58, 288–89
global ocean, 9–10
    knowledge gaps, 9–10
    modern threat assessment, difficulties of, 9–10
    risk hotspots, 289
    U.S. leadership role in global ocean affairs compromised due to failure to ratify UNCLOS, 311
Global Ocean Biodiversity Initiative (GOBI), 293
Global Plan of Action for the Conservation and Utilisation of Marine Mammals (MMAP), 55–56

great whales
    distinction between and other species of cetacean, 11–12
    "sustainable" whaling, 41–50
        commercial moratorium, 43, 44–45, 46–47, 50
            Canada, withdrawal from IWC in protest of, 45, 62
            special permit/scientific permit exemption, 45
        conservation, sanctuary designation, 45–46
        enforcement, 43
        establishment by ICRW, 42–43
        exploitation and early regulation efforts, 41–45
        fundamental reform of status quo, efforts, 47–50
        ICRW. *See* International Convention for the Regulation of Whaling (ICRW)
        IWC. *See* International Whaling Commission (IWC)
        Proposed Consensus Decision to Improve the Conservation of Whales, recommendations, 48–49
        Revised Management Procedure (RMP), 46, 161
        Revised Management Scheme (RMS), 46, 161
        schedule, 42
        scientific whaling, 43
        St. Kitts and Nevis Declaration, adoption of, 47, 145n60
        World War II, impact of, 41–42
    take, 61–62
"Greener Gun" invention, 15
greenhouse gas emissions, 121, 123, 124
Greenland
    North Atlantic Marine Mammal Commission (NAMMCO), 54
    pinniped take, 63
    small cetacean take, 62
Greenpeace
    Suggested Draft High Seas Implementing Agreement for the Conservation and Management of the Marine

INDEX 383

Environment in Areas beyond National Jurisdiction (2008), 176
"grindadrap" hunting, 62
Grotius, Hugo (*Mare Liberum* ("*The Free Sea*")), 35
"Guidelines for Applying Protected Area Management Categories" (IUCN-CPA), 293

high seas MPAs. *See* marine protected areas (MPAs)
High Seas Vessels Authorization Record (HSVAR), 238
Hirata, Keiko Hirata ("Why Japan Supports Whaling"), 246
Hogarth Initiative, 48
humane hunting
　education to ensure, 103–4
　IWC's work to improve humaneness of whaling operations, 100
　Norway, efforts to educate countries on effective whale killing, 103
human-marine mammal interaction, historical background
　cultural relationship, 7, 16–17
　　cetaceans, 16–17
　　pinnipeds, 16–17
　　significance of, trends, 17
　utilitarian relationship, 7, 12–16
　　cetaceans, 12–15
　　pinnipeds, 15–16

Iceland
　commercial whaling, 248
　Fisheries Jurisdiction Case (United Kingdom v. Iceland), 67n58, 202n63
　IWC commercial moratorium on whaling, formal objection to, 45
　North Atlantic Marine Mammal Commission (NAMMCO), 54
　pinniped take, 63
　scientific-based ecosystem management, 311–12
　violation of commercial whaling ban, sanctions waived, 59
illegal, unreported, and unregulated (IUU) take issues, 241, 358

implementing agreements
　non-UN implementing agreements, 176
　UNCLOS Implementing Agreements, 171–76
In Defense of Dolphins: The New Moral Frontier (Thomas White), 97–98
indefinite use approach to conservation, 2, 4
Indigenous and Cultural/Artisanal Subsistence Take Committee of IMMC, 226, 227, 228, 230–32, 340–42, 343. *See also* Aboriginal subsistence whaling
　artisanal, defined, 231
　authority, 232
　creation of, 226
　cultural, defined, 231
　establishment of, 229, 230–31
　functions, 231–32
　indigenous, defined, 230
　key terms, definitions, 230–32, 340–41
　management plan and, 227, 228
　recommendations by, 228
　subsistence, defined, 231
　subsistence certification program, 232
　subsistence expansion, 232
　tasks, 229–30
　transparency in activities, 343
Industrial Revolution
　commercial whaling practices, impact on, 14–15
　global ocean and, 9
Institute of Cetacean Research, Kyoda Senpaku Kaisha Ltd, Tomoyuki Ogaya and Toshiyuki Miura v. Sea Shepherd Conservation Society and Paul Watson, 50, 61
Inter-American Tropical Tuna Commission (IATTC), 57, 147n98, 187, 276
Intergovernmental Panel on Climate Change (IPCC), 120–21, 234
　climate change defined under, 120
　Fifth Assessment Report (IPCC), 121

International Agreement for the Regulation of Whaling (European whaling nations, 1937), 41, 42
International Committee on Marine Mammal Protected Areas (ICMMPA), 293
International Convention for the Prevention of Pollution from Ships (MARPOL), 136
  Special Area designation, 291
International Convention for the Regulation of Whaling (ICRW), 41. *See also* International Whaling Commission (IWC)
  Aboriginal subsistence whaling, Article 13, 105
  commercial moratorium, 43
  compliance and enforcement, text of Article IX, 238–39
  dismantling of, 193–97
    dissolution and succession of international organizations, 195–97
    treaty termination, 193–95
  enforcement, 43
  establishment of IWC, 42–43
  features of, 42–43
  fundamental reform of status quo, efforts, 47–50
  great whales and "sustainable" whaling, 41–50
  preamble, text of, 42
  schedule, 42
  scientific whaling, 43
  scope of coverage, 42
  "special permit" scientific whaling, dispute regarding. *See Whaling in the Antarctic Case*
International Court of Justice (ICJ)
  Article 38, legal foundation of international ocean governance, 35–36, 165
  text of, 36
  hearing of scientific evidence, different ways, 245
  Whaling in the Antarctic Case. See Whaling in the Antarctic Case (Australia v. Japan: New Zealand Intervening)
International Court of Justice (ICJ), Article 38
  legal foundation of international ocean governance, 35–36, 165
International Dolphin Conservation Program (IDCP), 127
international law regarding ocean governance, evolution of, 35–36
International Management of Cetaceans under the New Law of the Sea Convention (Kimberly Davis), 190–91
International Marine Mammal Commission (IMMC), 226–36, 373
  amendment of this agreement, 337–38
  annex of agreement, 338
  authority over conservation and sustainable management, 218
  best available scientific information, evidence, and knowledge standard, 228
  consensus model decision making, 226
  establishment of, 333
  functions of, 334–36
  Indigenous and Cultural/Artisanal Subsistence Take Committee, 226, 227, 228, 230–32, 340–42, 343
  main functions, 227–28
  management plan, 227–28
  meeting of the Commission, 228, 336–37
  members and advisors, 226
  non-participant state problem state empowerment, regulatory actions, 237–38, 348
  non-participant state problem—unauthorized actions, 236–38, 348
  objective of, 334
  observer participation, 228
  recommendations from Committees, 228

INDEX

regional marine mammal organizations, 235–36, 344–48, 373
regional organizations/arrangements, 270
Scientific Committee of IMMC, 226, 227, 228, 338–39, 343
Secretariat, creation and administration of, 270–74, 295, 343, 373
structure of, 334
structure of proposed regime (diagram), 373
subsidiary structures, 229–34
Sustainable Management Committees of IMMC, 226, 227, 228, 342–43
text of, 333–43
transparency in decision-making, 234–35, 343
international marine mammal conservation, legally justified options for, 160–70
ICRW/IWC, regime improvement proposals, 160–64, 310
"The Future of the IWC" process (proposal by Michael Bowman), 46, 47–48, 162–64, 167
options to normalize ICRW/IWC, 163–64
Working Group, 48, 49
"Towards a Sustainable Whaling Regime" (proposal by Robert Friedheim), 161–62, 164, 168
Revised Management Procedure (RMP), 46, 161
Revised Management Scheme (RMS), 46, 161
scheme management program, 161
national regulation, reliance upon, 167
new international regime, 167–70
benefits of being within auspices of the UN, 169–70
forms of, options, 167
proliferation of bilateral and/or regional agreements, 165–67
"soft" law approach, 164–65
status quo, continuation of, 160, 308, 309–10

International Maritime Organization (IMO)
marine protected areas (MPAs), resolutions, 291
ship-strikes, 129–30
international ocean governance, legal foundation of, 35–63
International Court of Justice (ICJ), Article 38, 35–36, 165
international law, evolution of, 35–36
jurisdictional exclusivity, 35
national regulation, 57–63
case studies, 58–61
conservation, preservation approach to, 57, 58
nations that take marine mammals, 61–63
relevant treaties and organizations, 50–57
species and area based approaches to marine mammal management, 38–50
fur seals and pinniped regulation, 39–41
great whales and "sustainable" whaling, 41–50
UNCLOS. See United Nations Convention on the Law of the Sea (UNCLOS)
International Plan of Action to Prevent, Deter and Eliminate IUU Fishing (the IPOA-IUU), 241, 358
International Tribunal for the Law of the Sea (ITLOS), 243–44
International Union for the Conservation of Nature (IUCN)
conservation, defined, 2, 3
Global Protected Areas Programme, World Commission on Protected Areas (IUCN-WCPA), 292–93
historical background, 17
implementing agreements
Elements of a Possible Implementation Agreement to UNCLOS for the Conservation and Sustainable Use of Marine Biodiversity in Areas beyond National Jurisdiction (IUCN, 2008), 176

International Union for the Conservation of Nature (IUCN) (*Cont.*)
  marine protected areas (MPAs), 285
  Red List of Threatened Species, 17–18, 131, 315–21
  World Charter for Nature (adopted by UN General Assembly), 3
  World Conservation strategy, 2
International Whaling and Marine Mammal Conservation Initiatives (Australia), 61
International Whaling Commission (IWC), 41. *See also* International Convention for the Regulation of Whaling (ICRW)
  Aboriginal subsistence whaling, ethical considerations, 104–5, 106
  Buenos Aires Group (Latin American and Caribbean State contingent at the IWC), 140, 249, 311
  by-catch, 126
  climate change, 123–24
  commercial moratorium, 44–45, 46–47, 50
    Canada, withdrawal from IWC in protest of, 45, 62
    special permit/scientific permit exemption, 45
  conservation, sanctuary designation, 45–46
  Conservation Committee, ship-strikes, 130
  environmental pollution, 134
  establishment by ICRW, 42–43
  formal management procedures, 44
  great whale take and, 61–62
  history of, phases, 43–47
  Iceland's withdrawal from, 186
  improvement proposals
    as option for international marine mammal conservation, 160–64, 310
    "The Future of the IWC" process (proposal by Michael Bowman), 46, 47–48, 162–64, 167
    options to normalize ICRW/IWC, 163–64
    "Towards a Sustainable Whaling Regime" (proposal by Robert Friedheim), 46, 161–62, 164, 168
  management issues, 44
  marine mammal killing methods
    humaneness of whaling operations, work to improve, 100
    reporting by resolutions 1999-1 and 2001-2, 101
    time to death (TTD) criteria, adoption of, 100–101
    Working Group on Whale Killing Methods, 100, 103, 106
  Normalization of the International Whaling Commission (IWC) Conference (Tokyo, February, 2007), 47, 48, 49, 164
  Proposed Consensus Decision to Improve the Conservation of Whales, recommendations, 48–49
  Resolution 2014-5 (Whaling under Special Permit), 247–48
  Revised Management Procedure (RMP), 46, 161
  Revised Management Scheme (RMS), 46, 161
  Scientific Committee
    by-catch, 126
    establishment of Standing Working Group on Environmental Concerns, (SWGEC), 123
    formalized "Environmental Concerns" as agenda item, 134
    ship-strikes, 130
    State of the Cetacean Environment Reports (SOCERs), 134
  ship-strikes, 130
  63rd Annual Meeting, United Kingdom proposal for transparency reforms, 234–35
  65th Annual Meeting, role of civil society, 235
  St. Kitts and Nevis Declaration, adoption of, 47, 145n60
  UNCLOS Articles 65, academic interpretations, 188–91

INDEX

Whale Killing Methods and Associated Welfare Issues Working Group, 100, 103, 106
whale sanctuaries approach, 290, 291, 294
  criticisms of sanctuary process, 290
  IWC, ineffectiveness of, 214
  marine protected areas (MPAs), 290
  sanctuary designation, 45–46
Working Group on Estimation of Bycatch and Other Human-induced Mortality, 126
Ireland v. United Kingdom (MOX Plant Case), 244

Japan
  fur seals and pinniped regulation, 39–40
  Southern Bluefin Tuna Cases (New Zealand v. Japan), 244
  whaling
    Australia v. Japan: New Zealand Intervening. *See Whaling in the Antarctic Case (Australia v. Japan: New Zealand Intervening)*
    Australia v. Japan (Southern Bluefin Tuna Case), 244
    domestic consumption, 246
    great whale take, regulation, 61
    IWC commercial moratorium on whaling, formal objection to, 45
    justification for, 246
    small cetacean take, 62
Japan-Australia Economic Partnership Agreement, 250
Japanese Whale Research Program under Special Permit in the Antarctic, Second Phase (JARPA II), 46, 72nn133–34, 242, 245
  New Scientific Whale Research Program in the Antarctic Ocean (NEWREP-A), as successor program to, 247–48
  program, generally, 45–46, 242

Whaling in the Antarctic Case (Australia v. Japan: New Zealand Intervening), 45–46, 72nn133–34, 242, 245, 247
Japanese Whale Research Program under Special Permit in the Antarctic (JARPA), 45
Japanese Whale Research Program under Special Permit in the North Pacific (JARPN)
  JARPN I, 72n129
  JARPN II, 72n129, 266n251
Japanese Whaling Ass'n v. American Cetacean Society, 85n299
Joint Norwegian-Russian Fisheries Commission, 40–41
jurisdiction
  exclusive jurisdiction by one party, 34, 35, 107
  international marine mammal conservation regime, limitations, 197–98
  scoping, 198
  species coverage, 197
  zones of regulation, 198

Kaschner, Kristin *(Current and Future Patterns of Global Marine Mammal Biodiversity)*, 123
killing marine mammals. *See* marine mammal killing methods
knowledge gaps
  current conservation status of marine mammals, 18
  global ocean, 9–10
  marine protected areas (MPAs), 289
krill, 122, 124

Lambert, Emily et al. *(Sustainable Whale-Watching Tourism and Climate Change: Towards a Framework of Resilience)*, 140
large cetaceans
  common killing methods, 101, 102
Latin American and Caribbean State contingent at the IWC ("Buenos Aires Group"), 140, 249, 311

latitude specific and non-latitude specific effects of climate change, 121–22
League of Nation's Convention for the Regulation of Whaling, 41, 169
   aboriginal subsistence whaling (text of Regulation), 104
Libyan Arab Jamahiriya/Chad (Territorial Dispute Case), 207*n*163
life-history characteristics of marine mammals, 11
Locke, Gary, 59
Lyster's International Wildlife Law (2nd ed.), 13

manatees. *See* sirenians (manatees and dugongs)
Mandatory Ship Reporting System, 129
Mare Liberum ("*The Free Sea*" by Hugo Grotius), 35
Margarita Lizarraga Medal Award, 281
marine ecosystem type classification of marine mammals, 11
marine mammal killing methods. *See also* take
  Aboriginal subsistence whaling, 106
  common killing methods, 101–2
  distinction from hunting terrestrial mammals or farm mammals, 102
  ethical considerations, 99–104
  "grindadrap" hunting, 62
  humane hunting, education to ensure, 103–4
  indigenous killing methods, 106
  IWC
    humaneness of whaling operations, work to improve, 100
    reporting by resolutions 1999-1 and 2001-2, 101
    time to death (TTD) criteria, adoption of, 100–101
    Working Group on Whale Killing Methods, 100, 103, 106
  large cetaceans, 101, 102
  modernization and technological advances, 14–15

  NAMMCO, 100–104
    Committee on Hunting Methods, 100, 103–4
    death criteria, 100–101
    Expert Group, 103
    humaneness, 102
    voluntary self reporting, 101
  Norway's efforts to educate countries, effective whale killing, 103, 106
  polar bears, 115*n*133
  reporting of, 101
  seals, 102
  small cetaceans, 101–2
  standards needed, 102–3
marine mammals, 10–19
  classification by distribution, 11–12
  classified groups, 11
  defined, generally, 6
  defined under proposed Agreement, 327
  description, shared characteristic, 10–11
  distinctions and variations, 10, 11–12
  killing. *See* marine mammal killing methods
  life-history characteristic, 11
  scientific classification of, 10–12
  utilization or dependence upon marine environment, 12
marine mammals tourism. *See* ecotourism (marine mammal tourism)
marine pollution
  regionalism, under proposed Agreement, 282–84, 353–58
marine protected area (MPA) networks, 290, 291–92, 294–95
  Convention on the Protection of the Marine Environment of the North-East Atlantic (OSPAR Convention), 291–92
  defined, 286
  IUCN Global Protected Areas Programme, World Commission on Protected Areas (IUCN-WCPA), 292–93
  Patagonia MPA network, 286
  terminology, 294–95

INDEX 389

marine protected areas (MPAs), 284–95
  categories of, 285
  definitions
    generally, 6
    high seas MPAs, 286
    MPA networks, 286
    under proposed Agreement, 217, 327
  description, 285–86, 291
  designation, 286–87, 294
  developing states, prohibitive
      establishment criteria, 287–88
  EEZ MPAs, 286, 294, 301n118
  establishment criteria, 287
  global goal of, 292
  high seas MPAs, defined, 286
  ICRW/IWC whale sanctuaries
      approach. See whale
      sanctuaries
  IMO Resolutions, 291
  innovative work, 292–93
  International Committee on Marine
      Mammal Protected Areas
      (ICMMPA), 293
  international/regional
      arrangements, 290–92
    Convention of Biological Diversity,
      292
      Conference of the Parties, Decision
        IX/20, 292
    Convention on the Protection of the
      Marine Environment of the
      North-East Atlantic (OSPAR
      Convention), 154n227, 291–92
      Recommendation 2003/3, 292
    Mediterranean Marine Mammals
      Sanctuary (Pelagos
      Sanctuary), 291, 294
    National Oceanic and Atmospheric
      Association (NOAA),
      descriptions of different forms
      of high seas MPAs, 291
  IUCN Global Protected Areas
      Programme, World
      Commission on Protected
      Areas (IUCN-WCPA), 292–93
  knowledge gaps, 289
  MARPOL Special Area designation, 291
  prospects moving forward, 293–95
  scientific innovations, studies, 288–90

  Secretariat of IMMC, role of, 294
  South Orkney MPA, 291
  terminology, 294–95
  trends in international
      governance, 290–95
    ICRW/IWC whale sanctuaries
      approach. See whale
      sanctuaries
    innovative work, 292–93
    international/regional
      arrangements, 290–92
    MPA networks, 286, 290,
      291–92, 294–95
    prospects moving forward, 293–95
  types of, 285–88
  UN General Assembly
      Resolution 99/292, 293
Massachusetts, ship-strikes, 129
Mediterranean Marine Mammals
    Sanctuary (Pelagos
    Sanctuary), 291, 294
Memorandums of understanding (MoU's)
    produced Convention on the
    Conservation of Migratory
    Species of Wild Animals
    (CMS), 54
Mexico
  U.S./Mexico dolphin safe response
    dispute, 126
modern threat assessment of global ocean,
    difficulties of, 9–10
MOX Plant Case (Ireland v. United
    Kingdom), 244

Namibia, pinniped take, 63
Nantucket, New England (1712)
  whaling, 14
National Marine Fisheries Service
    (NMFS), 129
National Oceanic and Atmospheric
    Association (NOAA)
  descriptions of different forms of high
    seas MPAs, 291
  ship-strikes, 129
national regulation, reliance upon
  as option for international marine
    mammal conservation, 167
navigation and vessel speed
  scientific advances, influence of, 7–8

new international regime, 167–70
  within auspices of the UN, benefits of being, 169–70
  forms of, options, 167
The New International Law of Fisheries: UNCLOS 1982 and Beyond (William Burke), 189
New Zealand
  Australia v. Japan: New Zealand Intervening. See Whaling in the Antarctic Case (Australia v. Japan: New Zealand Intervening)
  Department of Conservation Marine Mammal Action Plan 2005–2010 (Action Plan 2005–2010), 60
  ecotourism, regulations, 60
  Marine Mammal Protection Act (MMPA) (New Zealand), 59–60
  marine protected areas (MPAs), 286
  New Zealand v. Japan (Southern Bluefin Tuna Case), 244
noise pollution, 74n154, 131, 132
  regulation of, 136–37
non-contracting party schemes in regional agreements
  illegal, unreported, and unregulated (IUU) take issues, 241, 358
Noongwook, George, 106
North Atlantic Marine Mammal Commission (NAMMCO), 54–55, 166, 186
  marine mammal killing methods, 100–104
    Committee on Hunting Methods, 100, 103–4
    death criteria, 100–101
    Expert Group, 103
    humaneness, 102
    voluntary self reporting, 101
North West Atlantic Seals Agreement between Canada and Norway (1971), 41
Norway
  Anglo Norwegian Fisheries Jurisdiction Case (United Kingdom v. Norway), 67n58
  commercial whaling, 248
  effective whale killing, efforts to educate countries, 106
  fur seals and pinniped regulation, 40–41
  great whale take, regulation, 61
  IWC commercial moratorium on whaling, formal objection to, 45
  Joint Norwegian-Russian Fisheries Commission, 40–41
  North Atlantic Marine Mammal Commission (NAMMCO), 54
  North West Atlantic Seals Agreement (between Canada and Norway, 1971), 41
  pinniped take, 63
  scientific-based ecosystem management, 311–12

Obama, Barack, 59
ocean acidification, 10, 122, 143n28
oceans
  global ocean, generally, 9–10
  legal foundation of governance. *See* international ocean governance, legal foundation of
ocean zones (image), 323
On-Board Observer Program, 280, 281
optimum utilization of living marine resources, xi, 37, 176
  of highly migratory species, 37, 173
  ICNT, 180
  ICNT-Rev. 2, exemption, 180
  UNCLOS, Articles 65 & 120, 182, 186, 188, 191
  of whale resources, 43, 163, 180
otters. *See* carnivores (otters and polar bears)

Packwood-Magnuson Amendment to the Fishery Conservation and Management Act, 85n295, 249
Panama Canal traffic separation scheme, proposed, 130
Patagonia MPA network, 286
Pelagos Sanctuary (Mediterranean Marine Mammals Sanctuary), 291, 294

Pelly Amendment to the Fisherman's
    Protective Act, 59, 249
  text of, 59
persistent organic pollutants (POPs), 131–32
Peru
  IWC commercial moratorium on
    whaling, formal objection to, 45
Pew Environment Group proposal for
    incorporation of modern
    principles of international
    regional governance, 176
pinnipeds (seals, fur seals, sea lions, and
    walruses)
  bilateral agreements, 40–41
  classification by distribution, 11
  conventions, 39–40
  description, generally, 10–11
  fur seals and pinniped regulation, 39–41
  historic background, 39–40
  human-marine mammal interaction,
    historical background
    archaeological evidence of use, 15–16
    cultural relationship, 16–17
    hunting techniques, advances, 16
    recent trends in commercial take of, 16
    "sinking loss" phenomenon (wasteful
      hunt), 16, 102
    utilitarian relationship, 15–16
  Red List of Threatened Species
    (table), 319–20
  data summary and trends, 18–19
  scientific classification, 10–12
  sealing/seal product dispute, Canada
    and European Union, 250
  seals, common killing methods, 102
  "Wadden Sea Agreement" (Agreement
    on the Conservation of Seals
    in the Wadden Sea), 54
  Working Group on Seals, 40–41
pinniped take
  national regulation, 62–63
  recent trends in commercial take of, 16
polar bears. *See* carnivores (otters and
    polar bears)
pollution
  environmental, generally. *See*
    environmental pollution
  marine pollution, under proposed
    Agreement, 282–84, 353–58

noise pollution, 74n154, 131,
    132, 136–37
Pompa, Sandra ("Global Distribution of
    Marine Mammals" by Sandra
    Pompa, Paul R. Ehrlich,
    and Gerardo Ceballos),
    255n58, 288–89
population, defined, 6
  under proposed Agreement, 217, 327
porpoises. *See* cetaceans (whales,
    dolphins, and porpoises)
precautionary decision making
  defined, 6
precautionary principle
  sustainable management, proposed
    Agreement, 219, 330–31
preservation approach to
    conservation, 2, 19
proliferation of bilateral and/or regional
    agreements
  as option for international
    marine mammal
    conservation, 165–67
proposed Agreement. *See* United
    Nations Marine Mammals
    Agreement (proposed draft
    Agreement)
*Pulp Mills on the River Uruguay
    (Argentina v. Uruguay),* 245,
    264n220, 264n222, 265n225,
    265n230
purse-seine net fishing, 57, 84n283,
    126–27, 146n86, 279–80, 281

Quissac Workshop on the Legal Aspects of
    Conservation of Marine Mammals
    (organized by the United Nations
    Environment Programme), 33

rational decision-making model, 89–91
  assessment and analysis of
    alternatives, 90–91
*"Reclaiming Global Environmental
    Leadership: Why the United
    States Should Ratify Ten
    Pending Environmental
    Treaties"* (Center for
    Progressive Member Scholars,
    white paper), 311

Red List of Threatened Species
    (IUCN), 315–21
  background, generally, 17–18
  carnivores (otters and polar bears), 319
  categorization of species, 18
  cetaceans (whales, dolphins, and
    porpoises), 315–19
  environmental pollution, 131
  pinnipeds (seals, fur seals, sea lions, and
    walruses), 319–20
  sirenians (manatees and dugongs), 321
  statistics, 10
  summary of listings, 18
  tables, 315–21
  trends, 18–19
regional agreements, non-contracting
    party schemes
  illegal, unreported, and unregulated
    (IUU) take issues, 241, 358
Regional Fisheries Management
    Organizations
    (RFMO's), 56–57
  IATTC, 57, 127, 279–82
  non-contracting party schemes,
    241, 358
  shortfalls of, 56
  UN Stocks Fisheries Agreement,
    RFMO's bolstered by, 56–57,
    241, 275
Regional Fishery Bodies (RFBs), 56
regionalism, 275–84
  benefits of, 277–78
  drawbacks of, 278–79
  enclosed and/or semi-enclosed seas, 275
  marine pollution, regionalism under
    proposed Agreement,
    282–84, 353–58
  organization of regions, 276–77
  tuna-dolphin problem, case
    study, 279–82
  UNCLOS Article 197, "Cooperation on
    a Global or Regional Basis"
    (text of), 275
  UNCLOS III and, 275, 279
  varying conceptions of, 275–77
regional marine mammal organizations
    or arrangements under
    proposed Agreement,
    235–36, 344–48

  centralized and regional cooperation,
    283–84, 295
  compliance and enforcement,
    284, 353–58
  boarding and inspecting pursuant
    to Article 34, basic
    procedures, 356–57
  port state, measures taken
    by, 357–58
  regional cooperation in
    enforcement, 353–56
  text of Agreement, 353–58
  conservation and management,
    cooperation, 344–45
  establishment of, 345
  functions, 236, 345–46
  generally, 235–36
  marine pollution, 282–84, 353–58
  new members or participants, 346–47
  scientific research, collection and
    provision of information and
    cooperation, 347–48
  strengthening existing
    organizations, 347
  structure of proposed international
    regime (diagram), 373
  sustainable management measures, key
    role, 283–84
  text of proposed Agreement, 344–48
  transparency in decision making,
    236, 347
  UN Fish Stocks Agreement decision
    making and, distinctions,
    235, 283
Regional Seas Programme (UNEP), 56,
    92, 119, 134, 272
*Regional Workshop on Marine Mammal
    Watching in the Wider
    Caribbean Region* (UNEP
    Report), 137
Resolution on Preservation of the
    Habitat of Whales and
    Marine Environment (IWC,
    1981), 134
resource type and economic
    considerations, 33–35
  common pool problem, renewable stock
    resources and, 34–35, 161
  common property resources, 34

INDEX

economic theory of international
  law, 34
exclusive jurisdiction by one party, 34,
  35, 107
free rider problem, international
  regulation and, 34, 35, 237
international externalities, 34
voluntary cooperation, possible
  resource management
  solution, 34–35
Revised Management Procedure (RMP),
  46, 161
Revised Management Scheme (RMS),
  46, 161
Right Whale Ship Strike Reduction
  Rule, 129
rule of law in the oceans, promotion of, 91
Russia
  "Fur Seal Convention" (Convention
    for the Preservation and
    Protection of Fur Seals,
    1911), 39
  fur seals and pinniped
    regulation, 39–41
  great whale take, regulation, 61
  IWC commercial moratorium on
    whaling, Soviet Union's
    formal objection to, 45
  Joint Norwegian-Russian Fisheries
    Commission, 40–41

Safety Net Initiative, 48, 49
sanctuaries. *See* marine protected
  areas (MPAs)
"Save the Whale" campaign (1970's),
  30n180, 248, 249
scientific advances
  ethical considerations, 95–99
    behavior, 97–98
    culture, 98–99
  influence on conservation and
    management of marine
    resources, 7–8
scientific classification of marine
  mammals, 10–12
  adaptations, 11
  classification by distribution, 11–12
  description, shared
    characteristics, 10–11

distinctions and variations, 10, 11–12
Scientific Committee of IMMC, 226, 227,
  228, 338–39, 343
  creation of, 226
  management plan and, 227, 228
  recommendations by, 228
  transparency in activities, 343
scientific information
  best available scientific information,
    evidence, and knowledge
    standard, proposed
    Agreement, 218–19, 221–23
  conservation goals of proposed
    Agreement, 92
scientific innovations, studies
  marine protected areas (MPAs), 288–90
scientific method, generally, 221–22
scientific uncertainty, limitations,
  222–23
scientific whaling, ICRW, 43
scoping, 198
Scott, Karen *(Sound and
  Cetaceans: A Regional
  Response to Regulating
  Acoustic Marine
  Pollution),* 137
sea lions. *See* pinnipeds (seals, fur seals,
  sea lions, and walruses)
seals. *See* pinnipeds (seals, fur seals, sea
  lions, and walruses)
Sea Shepherd Conservation Society, 311
*Sea Shepherd Conservation Society and
  Paul Watson; Institute
  of Cetacean Research,
  Kyoda Senpaku Kaisha
  Ltd, Tomoyuki Ogaya and
  Toshiyuki Miura v.,* 50, 61
Secretariat of IMMC
  creation and administration of, 270–74,
    295, 343, 373
    Division for Ocean Affairs and the
      Law of the Sea of the Office
      of Legal Affairs (DOALOS),
      engagement of, 273–74, 295
  role of, 270
  structure of proposed regime
    (diagram), 373
  text of proposed agreement, 343
  transparency in activities, 343

Secretariat of IMMC (*Cont.*)
  creation and administration of (*Cont.*)
    UNEP, engagement of, 270–73, 274, 295
      drawbacks of, 273
      justifications for, 270–73
    marine protected areas (MPAs) and role of, 294
ship-strikes, 127–30
  cruise lines, 128
  current response, 128–30
  Florida, 128, 129
  International Maritime Organization (IMO), 129–30
  IWC, Scientific Committee and the Conservation Committee, 130
  problem, 127–28
  Right Whale Ship Strike Reduction Rule, 129
"sinking loss" phenomenon (wasteful hunt), 16, 102
sirenians (manatees and dugongs)
  Aboriginal and Torres Strait Islander people, legal hunting of dugongs under Native Title Act 1993, 60
  classification by distribution, 11
  description, generally, 10–11
  Red List of Threatened Species (table), 321
    data summary and trends, 18–19
  scientific classification, 10–12
small cetaceans
  common killing methods, 101–2
  take, 62
social structures, significance of, 98–99
soft law approach to international marine mammal conservation, 164–65
Sound and Cetaceans: A Regional Response to Regulating Acoustic Marine Pollution (Karen Scott), 137
Southern African Development Community Protocol on Wildlife Conservation and Law Enforcement
  conservation, defined, 4
Southern Bluefin Tuna Cases (Australia v. Japan), 244
Southern Bluefin Tuna Cases (New Zealand v. Japan), 244

South Orkney MPA, 291
Soviet Union. *See also* Russia
  IWC commercial moratorium on whaling, formal objection to, 45
Spain v. Canada (Fisheries Jurisdiction Case), 67n58
species and area based approaches to marine mammal management, 38–50
  fur seals and pinniped regulation, 39–41
  great whales and "sustainable" whaling, 41–50
species coverage
  expansion of, 91, 232
  jurisdiction, 197
St. Kitts and Nevis Declaration, 47, 145n60
St. Vincent and The Grenadines (Carribean)
  great whale take, regulation, 61–62
Standing Working Group on Environmental Concerns (SWGEC), 123
Stanford, Craig *(Bigger, Better Brain)*, 96–97
State of the Cetacean Environment Reports (SOCERs) (IWC Scientific Committee), 134
state parties
  defined under proposed Agreement, 328
  mutatis mutandis, application of, 243, 328, 356, 362
  non-participant state problem, IMMC—unauthorized actions, 236–38, 348
  regional marine mammal organizations or arrangements under proposed Agreement, new members or participants, 346–47
status quo, continuation of
  great whales and "sustainable" whaling, fundamental reform of status quo, 47–50
  of as option for international marine mammal conservation, 160, 308, 309–10
Steller's sea cow, 10, 13, 16, 321

"stinky whale" phenomena, 131
Stockholm Convention on
  Persistent Organic
  Pollutants ("Stockholm
  Convention"), 135
subsistence
  proposed Agreement. *See* Indigenous
    and Cultural/Artisanal
    Subsistence Take Committee
    of IMMC
  whaling. *See* Aboriginal subsistence
    whaling
subsistence certification program, 232
Suggested Draft High Seas
  Implementing Agreement
  for the Conservation and
  Management of the Marine
  Environment in Areas
  beyond National Jurisdiction
  (Greenpeace, 2008), 176
sustainable management, 4, 5–6
  conservation, interconnectedness
    with, 5, 6
  definition, 6, 216, 327
    difficulty of defining term, 5–6
  proposed Agreement, 329–33
    authority of IMMC, 218
    committees. *See* Sustainable
      Management Committees
      of IMMC
    compatibility of conservation and
      sustainability measures, 5,
      6, 331–33
    defined under, 216, 327
    general principles, 218–19, 329–30
    implementation efforts, focus
      of, 219–20
    precautionary principle, 219,
      330–31
    primacy of IMMC regulation, 220–21
    regional marine mammal
      organizations or
      arrangements under, 283–84
    scope of, 218–21
    UNCLOS zonal structure,
      compatibility, 220–21
    UN Fish Stock Agreement and, 219
  as requirement of conservation, 4
  working definition of, 6

Sustainable Management Committees of
  IMMC, 226, 227, 228, 342–43
  creation of, 226
  functions, 233
  management plan and, 227, 228
  recommendations by, 228
  Secretariat of the Convention on
    Biological Diversity
    (SCBD), 233–34
  transparency in activities, 343
*Sustainable Whale-Watching Tourism and
  Climate Change: Towards
  a Framework of Resilience*
  (Emily Lambert et al.), 140
sustainable whaling. *See* great whales
Sweden, pinniped take, 63

Taft, George
  U.S. position on UNCLOS III,
    Articles 65, 184
take
  definition
    generally, 6
    under proposed Agreement, 327
  great whale take, 61–62
  illegal, unreported, and unregulated
    (IUU) take issues,
    241, 358
  Indigenous and Cultural/Artisanal
    Subsistence Take Committee
    of IMMC, subsistence
    expansion, 232
  killing methods. *See* marine mammal
    killing methods
  nations that take marine
    mammals, 61–63
  pinniped take, 16, 62–63
  small cetacean take, 62
*Territorial Dispute Case (Libyan
  Arab Jamahiriya/Chad)*,
  207n163
"The Free Sea" (*Mare Liberum* by Hugo
  Grotius), 35
"The Future of the IWC" process (proposal
  by Michael Bowman), 46,
  47–48, 162–64, 167
  options to normalize ICRW/IWC,
    163–64
  Working Group, 48, 49

"The Future We Want" (UN Conference on Sustainable Development, 2012), 169
threatened species list. *See* Red List of Threatened Species (IUCN)
threats to marine mammals, 119–41
  by-catch. *See* by-catch
  climate change, 120–25
  ecotourism (marine mammal tourism), 137–40
  environmental pollution, 130–37
  features of new response, 140–41
  ship-strikes, 127–30
  time to death (TTD) criteria, adoption of, 100–101
Torres Strait Islander and Aboriginal people, legal hunting of dugongs under Native Title Act 1993 (Australia), 60
tourism. *See* ecotourism (marine mammal tourism)
"Towards a Sustainable Whaling Regime" (proposal by Robert Friedheim), 161–62, 164, 168
  Revised Management Procedure (RMP), 46, 161
  Revised Management Scheme (RMS), 46, 161
  scheme management program, 161
treaty termination and international organization succession, 193–97
  dissolution and succession of international organizations, 195–97
  treaty termination, 193–95
    ICRW, 193–94, 195
    Vienna Convention on the Law of Treaties (VCLT), 193–95
Tsusuoka, Koji (closing remarks in *Whaling in the Antarctic Case*), 308
tuna. *See* dolphin-tuna interaction
21st Conference of the Parties (UNFCCC), 123

undersea noise pollution. *See* noise pollution
United Kingdom
  "Fur Seal Convention" (Convention for the Preservation and Protection of Fur Seals, 1911), 39
  fur seals and pinniped regulation, 39–40
  Ireland v. United Kingdom (MOX Plant Case), 244
  proposal for IWC transparency reforms, 234–35
United Kingdom of Great Britain and Northern Ireland v. Albania (Corfu Channel Case), 264n222
United Kingdom v. Iceland (Fisheries Jurisdiction Case), 67n58, 202n63
United Kingdom v. Norway (Anglo Norwegian Fisheries Jurisdiction Case), 67n58
United Nations
  good faith as guiding principle for state behavior, 169
United Nations Charter, 169–70
United Nations Conference on Sustainable Development
  "The Future We Want" (2012), 169
United Nations Conference on the Human Environment (Stockholm, 1972), 44, 52
United Nations Convention on the Law of the Sea (UNCLOS), 65n35
  amending Annex I ("Highly migratory species"), 225–26
  Annexes to, 170
  Articles 65 & 120. *See* United Nations Convention on the Law of the Sea (UNCLOS), Articles 65 & 120
  Article 116, right to fish on the high seas (text of), 38
  dispute resolution approach, 242–44
    "choice of procedure" (cafeteria approach), 243–44
    International Tribunal for the Law of the Sea (ITLOS), 243–44
  environmental pollution
    Article 194 (text of), 133
    pollution, defined under UNCLOS Article 1(4), 131
    relevant articles, 133–34

INDEX 397

implementation of framework
    provisions, 38
implementing agreements. *See* United
    Nations Convention on the
    Law of the Sea (UNCLOS)
    Implementing Agreements
legal foundation of international ocean
    governance, 36–38
maritime zones, establishment of, 37
negotiation, duration of conferences, 36
optimum utilization of living marine
    resources, xi, 37, 176
parts and articles of, listing, 37–38
principles of, 37
UNCLOS II, 65n35
UNCLOS III (*See also* United Nations
    Convention on the Law of
    the Sea (UNCLOS), Articles
    65 & 120)
    consensus negotiation, 36–37, 310–11
    duration of negotiation, 65n35
    goals of, 37
    regionalism and, 275, 279
UN Fish Stocks Agreement, 38
U.S. leadership role in global ocean
    affairs compromised due to
    failure to ratify UNCLOS, 311
zonal structure, compatibility, 220–21
United Nations Convention on the Law of
    the Sea (UNCLOS), Articles
    65 & 120, 176–93
Agenda 21, 187, 190
Article 65
    ambiguities and uncertainties,
        182–83, 192
    drafting history, proposed wording/
        amendments, 177–80
    Evenson Group, 178
    Informal Composite Negotiating
        Text (ICNT), adoption of, 180
    Japan, comment/statement on, 180
    Richardson, Elliot (statement at
        time of adoption, text of), 180
    Peru, 179
    U.S., 179–80
    interpretation of, 184–88
        Agenda 21, contributions
            of, 187, 190
        Canada, 184–85
        "competent or relevant international
            organizations," 186
        interpretive guidance, UN
            Division of Ocean Affairs and
            the Law of the Sea, 186–87
        Japan, 185–86
        U.S., 184–85
    pertinent characteristics, ambiguities
        and uncertainties,
        182–83, 192
    text of, 37, 187
    UNCLOS III, U.S. position on Article
        65 (delivered by George
        Taft), 184
    U.S. position on Article 65 (delivered
        by George Taft), 184
Article 120
    drafting history, 180–81
    text of, 38
drafting history, 177–81
    Article 65, proposed wording/
        amendments, 177–80
    Article 120, 180–81
interpretation of
    academic interpretations, 188–91
    Article 65, 184–88
    competing interpretations, 181, 183
    preferred interpretation(s), 191–93
pertinent characteristics, 181–83
surrounding sections, 176–77
UNCLOS III, 177–78
    Article 65, U.S. position on Article
        65 (delivered by George
        Taft), 184
UN Oceans Division, Law of the Sea
    Bulletin No. 31, 186, 189
Vienna Convention on the Law of
    Treaties (VCLT), 181, 190
United Nations Convention on
    the Law of the Sea
    (UNCLOS) Implementing
    Agreements, 171–76
Agreement Relating to the
    Implementation of Part XI
    of UNCLOS (Implementing
    Agreement of 1994), 171–72
Article 2(1), 172
UNCLOS III, 171–72
text of, 172

United Nations Convention on the Law of the Sea (UNCLOS) Implementing Agreements (*Cont.*)
  Agreement Relating to the Implementation of Part XI of UNCLOS (Implementing Agreement of 1994) (*Cont.*)
    U.S.
      concern over Part XI, 172
      efforts and recommendations for ratification by, 172, 311
    conservation and sustainable use of marine biodiversity in areas beyond national jurisdiction, Ad Hoc Open-ended Informal Working Group, 174–75
    good faith negotiation requirement, 173
    UN Fish Stocks Agreement, 171–74, 176
United Nations Environment Programme (UNEP)
  Regional Seas Branch, 56
  Regional Seas Programme, 56, 92, 119, 134, 272
  Regional Workshop on Marine Mammal Watching in the Wider Caribbean Region (UNEP Report), 137
  Secretariat of IMMC, engagement in creation and administration of, 270–73, 274, 295
    drawbacks of, 273
    justifications for, 270–73
United Nations Fish Stocks Agreement, 171–74
  Article 63, 172–73, 174
    text of, 173
  Article 64, 172, 174
    text of, 173
  compliance and enforcement, approach, 239, 240–41
  conservation and sustainable management measures, proposed Agreement and, 219
  contributions of, 174, 176
  decision making, 235, 283
  dispute resolution, 174, 243
  distinctions from proposed Agreement, central global decision making, 235, 283
  entered into force, 174
  General Assembly Resolution 47/192, 38
  impact on UNCLOS Articles 63 & 64, 38
  implementing, 171–74, 176
  Regional Fisheries Management Organizations (RFMO's) bolstered by, 56–57, 241, 275
  RFMO's bolstered by, 56–57
  UNCLOS, amending Annex I ("Highly migratory species"), 225
United Nations Framework Convention on Climate Change (UNFCCC), 123
  21st Conference of the Parties, 123
United Nations General Assembly Resolutions
  proposed Agreement and, 213
  Resolution 47/192, 38
  Resolution 59/24, 174
  Resolution 60/30, 174
  Resolution 66/288, 296n9
  Resolution 67/213, 296n9
  Resolution 99/292, 293
United Nations Marine Mammals Agreement (proposed draft Agreement), 215–50. *See also* International Marine Mammal Commission (IMMC)
  accession, 364
  annex, 366
  authentic texts, 366
  best available scientific information, evidence, and knowledge standard, 218–19, 221–23
  compliance and enforcement, 238–41, 351–58
    cooperation through IMMC or regional organizations/arrangements, 241
    distinction between, 238
    duties of all states, 351
    by flag states, 351–52
    illegal, unreported, and unregulated (IUU) take issues, 241, 358
    international cooperation in enforcement, 352–53
    jurisdictional issues, 239–40

mechanisms, 239–40
port state actions, 240
regional mechanisms, 240
declarations and statements, 365
definitions and key terms, 216–17, 326–28
depository, 366
developing states, encouraging
    participation, 223
dispute resolution, 241–45, 362–63
    disputes of technical nature, 243, 362
    obligation to settle disputes by
        peaceful means, 362
    prevention of disputes, 362
    provisional measures, 244, 363
    scientific information and evidence,
        243, 362
    settlement procedures, 362–63
entry into force, 365
financial considerations, 360–62
flag states
    compliance and enforcement
        by, 351–52
    duties of, 349–51
    exchange of information duties
        of, 350–51
goals of proposed Agreement, 91–93
good faith and abuse of rights, 364
institutional structure. *See* International
    Marine Mammal
    Commission (IMMC)
introductory matters, 215–26
non-participant state problem, 236–38,
    348, 364
objective of, 215–16, 328
political obstacles, 245–50
    commercial whaling
        countries, 245–48
    domestic legislation, 248–49
    Japan, 245–48
    political and legal issues,
        distinction, 245–46
    reasons for optimism, 249–50
    success stories, recent
        developments, 250
    whaling, 245–50
potential rewards for pursuing new
    Agreement
    preservationist states, 308–9
    pro-utilization states, 309

preamble of, 325–26
provisional application, 365
purpose, 215–16
ratification, 364
relation to other agreements, 365–66
reservations, declarations, and
    relation to existing
    agreements, 224–25
reservations and exceptions, 365
responsibility and liability, 364
scope of new regime, 218–21
Secretariat. *See* Secretariat of IMMC
signature, 364
structure of proposed regime
    (diagram), 373
technological cooperation,
    223–24, 359–60
text of, 325–66
UNCLOS, amending Annex I ("Highly
    migratory species"), 225–26
United States
    Agreement Relating to the
        Implementation of Part XI
        of UNCLOS (Implementing
        Agreement of 1994)
    efforts and recommendations for
        ratification by, 172, 311
    U.S. concern over Part XI, 172
    "Fur Seal Convention" (Convention
        for the Preservation and
        Protection of Fur Seals,
        1911), 39–40
    fur seals and pinniped
        regulation, 39–40
    great whale take, regulation, 62
    Iceland violation of commercial
        whaling ban, sanctions
        waived, 59
    importation of products from offending
        countries, ban on, 59
    Marine Mammal Commission
        (MMC), 58
    Marine Mammal Protection Act
        (MMPA), 58
    national regulation, 58–59
    Packwood-Magnuson Amendment
        to the Fishery Conservation
        and Management Act,
        85n295, 249

United States (*Cont.*)
  Pelly Amendment to the Fisherman's Protective Act, 59, 249
  UNCLOS, leadership role in global ocean affairs compromised due to failure to ratify, 311
United States Marine Mammal Protection Act
  conservation, defined, 4
United States/Mexico dolphin safe response dispute, 126
Uruguay
  Argentina v. Uruguay. See Pulp Mills on the River Uruguay
utilitarian relationship, human-marine mammal interaction
  historical background, 7, 12–16
    cetaceans, 12–15
    pinnipeds, 15–16
utilization or dependence upon marine environment
  classification of marine mammals by, 12

vessel
  defined, 6
  defined under proposed Agreement, 327–28
vessel speed
  scientific advances, influence of, 8
Vienna Convention on the Law of Treaties (VCLT), 181, 190
  Article 41(b), treaty modification test under, 225

"Wadden Sea Agreement" (Agreement on the Conservation of Seals in the Wadden Sea), 54
walruses. *See* pinnipeds (seals, fur seals, sea lions, and walruses)
whale meat consumption
  The Faroe Islands, historical background, 62
  Japan, domestic consumption, 246
whales
  generally. *See* cetaceans (whales, dolphins, and porpoises)
  great whales. *See headings under great whales*

Whales: Their Emerging Right to Life (Anthony D'Amato and Sudhir Chopra), 8, 95, 96
whale sanctuaries, 290, 291, 294
  criticisms of sanctuary process, 290
  IWC, ineffectiveness of, 214
  marine protected areas (MPAs), 290
  sanctuary designation, 45–46
Whale Wars (Animal Planet television series), 311
whale watching, 137–40. *See also* ecotourism (marine mammal tourism)
  background and studies regarding, 138
  behavioral changes in whales due to, 138
  commercial whaling's impact on, 138
  current response, 138–40
  global economics of industry, 138
  IWC whale watching initiatives, 139, 140
    criticisms and suggestions for improvement, 140
    Whale Watching Principles, 165
  problem, 137–38
whaling
  Aboriginal whaling. *See* Aboriginal subsistence whaling
  Basque people, 13–14
  cetacean brain
    ethical considerations, 96–97
    structure and social behavior, appropriateness of continued consumptive use, 8
  commercial moratorium, 43, 44–45, 46–47, 50
    Canada, withdrwawal from IWC in protest of, 45, 62
    special permit/scientific permit exemption, 45
  dispute regarding. *See Whaling in the Antarctic Case*
  great whales and sustainable whaling. *See* great whales
  historical background, emergence of commercial whaling, 13–15

ICRW. *See* International Convention for the Regulation of Whaling (ICRW)
IWC. *See* International Whaling Commission (IWC)
Japan. *See* Japan, whaling
Lyster's International Wildlife Law (2nd ed.), 13
modernization and technological advances, 14–15
Nantucket, New England (1712), 14
"Save the Whale" campaign (1970's), 30n180, 248, 249
special permits
   dispute regarding. *See Whaling in the Antarctic Case*
   IWC Resolution 2014-5 (Whaling under Special Permit), 247–48
sustainable whaling. *See* great whales
Whaling in the Antarctic Case (Australia v. Japan: New Zealand Intervening), 7, 45, 46, 222, 244–50, 254n51, 265nn231–33, 265nn235–38, 266n253, 282, 290, 300n109
absence of dispute resolution, 241–42
closing remarks, deputy foreign minister Koji Tsusuoka, 308
ICJ decision, 242, 246
IWC's response and interpretation of ICJ ruling, 247–48
Japanese Whale Research Program under Special Permit in the Antarctic, Second Phase (JARPA II), 46, 72nn133–34, 242, 245
Japan's response to ICJ ruling, 242, 247
post-case developments between Japan and Australia, 250
presentation of scientific evidence, expert witnesses, 245
scientific evidence, expert witnesses, 244–45
scientific research, Court's objective standard of review, 254n51
White, Thomas *(In Defense of Dolphins: The New Moral Frontier)*, 97–98
"Why Japan Supports Whaling" (Keiko Hirata), 246
Working Group on Estimation of Bycatch and Other Human-induced Mortality (IWC), 126
Working Group on Seals, 40–41
Working Group on Whale Killing Methods (IWC), 100, 103, 106
World War I, 101
World War II, 41
   post-WW II, 169
   pre-WW II, 7, 41
World Wildlife Fund, 30n180, 36, 124

zero-catch quota, 72n134, 89, 94, 99–100, 107–8, 166, 214, 344